Encyclopedia of
Archival Science

Encyclopedia of Archival Science

Edited by
Luciana Duranti
Patricia C. Franks

ROWMAN & LITTLEFIELD
Lanham · Boulder · New York · London

Published by Rowman & Littlefield
A wholly owned subsidiary of The Rowman & Littlefield Publishing Group, Inc.
4501 Forbes Boulevard, Suite 200, Lanham, Maryland 20706
www.rowman.com

Unit A, Whitacre Mews, 26-34 Stannary Street, London SE11 4AB

British Library Cataloguing in Publication Information Available

Library of Congress Cataloging-in-Publication Data

Encyclopedia of archival science / edited by Luciana Duranti, Patricia C. Franks.
    pages cm
  Includes bibliographical references and index.
  ISBN 978-0-8108-8810-4 (cloth : alkaline paper) – ISBN 978-0-8108-8811-1 (ebook)
1. Archives–Encyclopedias. 2. Records–Management–Encyclopedias. I. Duranti,
Luciana. II. Franks, Patricia C., 1945–
  CD945.E53 2015
  027.003–dc23   2014049611

∞™ The paper used in this publication meets the minimum requirements of
American National Standard for Information Sciences—Permanence of Paper
for Printed Library Materials, ANSI/NISO Z39.48-1992.

Printed in the United States of America

Contents

Editorial Advisory Board

Preface

Archives can be traced to the first efforts to document and preserve traces of activities and transactions. The earliest accumulation of records resulted from commercial transactions, payment of taxes, enrollment of soldiers, and administration. They were written on wood, stone, metal, clay, and later papyrus, parchment, and paper. Over the millennia, the knowledge derived from them has formed the subsequent civilizations and shaped our cultures.

Early archives were housed in the offices of the administrations producing them, often in the treasury or secret cameras. Democratic societies kept them in public buildings (e.g., the Tabularium in ancient Rome, the Metroon in ancient Greece, the Great Library of Alexandria in Egypt) and gave the public access to them.

Archives as understood today can be traced to the French Revolution and the establishment of the *Archives Nationales* (1794) as the repository of the records of the ancient regime for which the new state took responsibility on behalf of the citizens, and the *Archives Départementales* (1796) as the repositories for current government records as well as the local archives of the prerevolutionary period. Today's archives are responsible for public and private records throughout their existence, regardless of medium and form. Archival concepts, principles, and practices as developed for more than six thousands years provide the foundation for the archival endeavor and guide professionals through the challenges presented by continuous technological as well as cultural change.

PURPOSE, SCOPE, AND TARGET AUDIENCE

The purpose of this *Encyclopedia* is to present the various and evolving interpretations and perspectives on archival concepts, principles, and practices. It is designed to aggregate the views of contemporary, well-established, and highly regarded archival scholars and professionals and those of new and aspiring scholars and professionals into one, comprehensive work describing past achievements and leading the archival field toward the future.

The *Encyclopedia of Archival Science* is a foundational reference work containing 154 articles contributed by 110 authors. The entries are presented in alphabetical order. Each entry includes keywords, related entries, and a basic bibliography. The encyclopedia is completed by an index and a brief biography of each author.

The encyclopedia was conceived as an essential resource for present and aspiring records, archival, and other information professionals and scholars, as well as allied professions, users, and the public at large, so that all those who are interested in archives will have an opportunity to understand their nature and the mission of the profession that is responsible for them.

THE DEVELOPMENT PROCESS

The encyclopedia was almost three years in the making. The process began when the co-editors, Drs. Luciana Duranti and Patricia C. Franks, identified a need for a work that would consolidate the reflections of contemporary archival professionals on fundamental archival knowledge. To aid in the preliminary work, an advisory board of distinguished scholars—including Adrian Cunningham (Australia), Fiorella Foscarini (Canada and the Netherlands), Patricia Galloway (United States), Giovanni Michetti (Italy), Shadrack Katuu (International Atomic Energy Agency), Kenneth Thibodeau (United States), and Geoffrey Yeo (United Kingdom)—was established, and its members were asked to compile a list of potential encyclopedia entries, recommend authors for each of the entries, and volunteer to complete at least one entry in their own area of expertise.

Each proposed entry was carefully considered and designated either a key term to be used as an entry, a related term that should be included in the index, or a term that should be discarded. More than 200 archival terms were identified, 154 of which were considered key terms for inclusion in the encyclopedia. The remaining terms are listed in the index and refer the reader to one of the 154 entries.

Nominations for authors were solicited from the advisory board and other authors who accepted invitations to participate. Invitations were sent to those considered to be authorities in the area about which they were asked to write, as well as emerging scholars and archival students who had distinguished themselves by receiving awards for their papers, in order to involve the next generation in this endeavor, which is intended to be continuing through regular updates and additions.

The advisory board ensured that the selected terms would provide a view of archival science as an interdisciplinary field that harmonizes a universal body of theory and a practice directed toward the development and implementation of international standards, with a practice addressing the specific, local, and unique aspects of archival material.

Authors were asked to write a clear, simple, rigorous overview of the concept, principle, or practice. They were encouraged to write on the basis of their personal expertise and/or perspective but represent common or alternate points of view on their topics, if such views existed. Each author is identified within the entry, and a complete list of authors with brief biographies is provided in the "About the Contributors" section.

The entries were reviewed and edited by the co-editors, and Mark Driskill, a recent graduate of the Master of Archives and Records Administration degree program at San José State University, was employed to check the citations and references included in the bibliography.

HOW TO USE THIS ENCYCLOPEDIA

Entries are arranged alphabetically. To locate a specific entry, refer to the index at the back of the book. To locate entries by a specific author, refer to the "About the Contributors" section.

In sum, relevant articles can be found by

1. entry title (alphabetical arrangement of articles in the encyclopedia),
2. specific topic (index at the end of the work). The index includes alternate entry titles that will refer the reader to the main entry, or
3. author name (alphabetically in "About the Contributors").

A

ACCESS/ACCESSIBILITY

A *record*'s value is realized through its use. In order to use a record, it must be accessible. A record's accessibility changes throughout its *lifecycle* and is influenced by how it is used, organizational policies around access, and applicable laws governing access and disclosure.

The Concept

The concept of access concerns whether an individual has permission or privilege to view or use a record or group of records (ISO 15498-1:2001). Users can include people, technology, and business processes that need to use records for a given purpose.

Provisions that govern access to records change over time and are also dependent on the sensitivity of the information contained in the records, including any associated *metadata*. Records are typically more highly controlled during their active and semi-active periods while fewer access restrictions exist as records pass into their inactive phase.

Organizations will take steps to protect active and semi-active records from unauthorized access and disclosure. Access controls are one part of a broader approach to securing information through an information security management system (ISO/IEC 27001:2013). The level of access controls needed to secure a record is determined by the sensitivity of the information contained in the record in conjunction with the identified security risks related to that information. Both sensitivity and risks are influenced by internal and external drivers, such as possible harm to the organization if information is inappropriately accessed or laws that require certain information is safeguarded against access by unauthorized individuals.

Most government organizations in advanced democracies are subject to Freedom of Information (FOI) laws, also known as Access to Information laws, that permit public access to records in the organization's custody or under their control (Roberts 1999). An important consideration for dealing with FOI laws is that the legal definition of record is much broader than the archival definition. A record in law is essentially any recorded information regardless of medium or format (ATI [Can]; FOIPPA [Can BC]). Therefore the scope of materials that need to be managed under the legal definition of record is much larger than what would be necessary under the archival definition.

Despite the fact that FOI laws allow for a legal mechanism to access records, they also include limited exceptions to withhold information contained in records, and sometimes even entire records, from disclosure. Even though access under FOI is defined as a legal right, there are provisions where a government organization can, or must, withhold records or information. It is also important to note that private organizations are not subject to FOI laws. As such, private organizations have no obligation or expectation to respond to a public request for records.

Another major legal consideration that governs access to records is protection-of-privacy legislation. Unlike FOI laws, which apply predominantly to government organizations, jurisdictions that have adopted privacy laws have made these laws applicable to both governmental and nongovernmental organizations.

The intent of privacy legislation is to protect the privacy of individuals through how information or data about those individuals is collected, used, managed, secured, stored, shared, or destroyed. Depending on the country and jurisdiction, there may be overarching privacy laws that apply to both the private and public sector, or many laws that apply to government and the private sectors depending on the types of information they use and the activities with which they are involved. An example of an overarching privacy regime is the European Union's Data Protection Directive (Directive 95/46/EC). Its aim is to provide one law that harmonizes how personal data is handled throughout the European Union. An example of a "many laws" approach to privacy is seen in the Unites States, where privacy rights are spread across many laws and enforcement agencies depending on sector or the types of personal information that is being protected. For example, personal health information is governed by the Health Information Portability and Protection Act that is enforced by the U.S. Department of Health and Human Services' Office for Civil Rights, whereas credit-reporting information is governed by the Fair Credit Reporting Act, which is enforced by the Federal Trade Commission.

Privacy laws may also be written either as rules or as principles. Those pertaining to more sensitive types of information or government activities tend to be more rules-based. This approach hinges on two factors. First, sensitive personal information can lead to significant harm if it is inappropriately accessed and used. Here the intent is to ensure a higher level of protection around sensitive personal information by ensuring proper management through stricter requirements. Second, governments have the power to compel or require personal information in order to provide services or protect society. Here, rules-based laws are in place to ensure there are appropriate checks on the power of government to collect, use, and provide access to personal information.

Privacy laws that resemble principles tend to be applied within the private sector and are based on the Organization of Economic Cooperation and Development's Guidelines on the Protection of Privacy and the Transborder Flows of Personal Data. Principle-based laws balance an individual's privacy with an organization's ability to carry out business that relies on personal information (OECD). These types of laws tend to rely on individual consent and reasonable actions taken given the particular circumstances governing how personal information should be managed and accessed. An example includes Canada's Personal Information Protection and Electronic Documents Act (PIPEDA). Not only do principle-based privacy laws allow the organization to use discretion when implementing reasonable measures to manage personal information, but they also include rules specifying where exercising discretion is not seen as appropriate.

Inactive records that have been donated or transferred to an archival institution become more accessible as their use primarily shifts to research purposes. This is seen in both the mandates of many public and private *archives* and the inclusion of specific provisions allowing access in many FOI, privacy, and archival laws. An example of this is the Library and Archives of Canada Act, where Library and Archives Canada is provided the mandate to "be a source of enduring knowledge accessible to all" (LAC [Can]).

Another example of where laws allow greater access over time is British Columbia's Freedom of Information and Protection of Privacy Act. This law determines that it is no longer an invasion of privacy to disclose personal information about an individual who has been dead for twenty or more years or where the record has been in existence for one hundred or more years (FOIPPA [Can BC]). Similar provisions exist in the UK FOI Act that classifies records as "historical" after thirty years from their date of creation. After thirty years several exceptions to disclosure no longer apply (FOI [Eng]).

Despite the fact that many laws have provisions allowing access to records for research purposes, there are still inconsistencies in privacy laws that make secondary use difficult. A review by Iacovino and Todd showed that privacy laws across the UK, Australia, the European Union, and North America still do not adequately address archival concerns and impose limits on using personal information for research purposes (Iacovino and Todd 2007). One recommendation they make is to streamline how personal information may be de-identified and re-identified for research purposes. This, they conclude, would help with maintaining the integrity of the records while also supporting access to records for research that complies with privacy laws.

In addition to privacy concerns, there are other considerations that affect access to records in an archival institution. These considerations become apparent when physical and intellectual control is established by the archives. At the point records are first transferred or donated and accessioned into the archives, the *archivist* determines whether there are any donor restrictions or *preservation* concerns that would limit access. Further, there may be lingering confidentiality restrictions that exist for records transferred within an organization to its archives, such as records related to state security or secrets that would only become publicly accessible after an extended period of time.

Conclusion

Access is an important consideration for both *records managers* and archivists as it impacts how records should be managed. Records managers need to take a broad view of the records in their organization based on the expansive legal definition of record and the many organizational and legal requirements that influence how records are managed. Archivists also need to be mindful of the laws governing access to records even though they may be diminished in power and applicability within an archival setting. While laws may be diminished in how they impact archives, they are still a significant consideration for accessibility and can be supplemented by additional restrictions imposed by donors and other factors such as preservation concerns. In both cases, records managers and archivists must ensure that all access restrictions are properly captured and linked to the records to which they apply.—*Greg Kozak*

Keywords: Access to Information, Freedom of Information, privacy, records, security
Related Entries: Archival Custody; Archival Legislation; Archival Reappraisal; Archives (institution); Archivist; Metadata; Records Manager

Bibliography

Access to Information Act, 1985, R.S.C., ch. A-1 (Can).
Directive 95/46/EC of the European Parliament and of the Council of 24 October 1995 on the protection of individuals with regard to the processing of personal data and on the free movement of such data [1995] OJ L281/31.
Freedom of Information Act, 2000, c. 63 (Eng.).
Freedom of Information and Protection of Privacy Act, R.S.B.C. 1996, ch. 165 (Can BC).
International Standards Organization, ISO 15489-1:2001, Information and Documentation—Records Management—Part 1: Guidelines.
International Standards Organization/International Electrotechnical Commission, ISO/IEC 27001:2013, Information Technology—Security Techniques—Information Security Management Systems—Requirements.
Library and Archives of Canada Act, 2004 S.C., ch.11 (Can).
Organization for Economic Cooperation and Development, Guidelines on the Protection of Privacy and the Transborder Flows of Personal Data, 2013.
Personal Information Protection and Electronic Documents Act, 2000 S.C. ch. 5 (Can).
Roberts, Alasdair. Retrenchment and Freedom of Information: Recent Experience under Federal, Ontario and British Columbia Law. *Canadian Public Administration* 42 (4) (1999): 422–51.

ACCOUNTABILITY

Accountability is commonly understood as a quality possessed by a physical or juridical *person*, whereby they are willing or required to furnish an explanation, to provide an account, of their actions; the 2011 *Oxford English Dictionary* defines *accountability* as "the quality of being accountable; liability to account for and answer for one's conduct, performance of duties, etc." Regarding accountability's relationship to archival materials, accountability may be supported through provision of, or access to, *records* created and maintained through the normal course of a creator's activities. With regards to accountability and archival institutions, the identification of resources (persons, facilities) responsible for *access* to and *preservation* of the materials indicates a sponsoring body's interest in preserving *evidence* of its activities; accountability may be supported by an archival institution's stated mandate, policies, and procedures, and the degree to which those principles and processes are adhered. Adherence by *archivists* to accountability as a principle flows from their custodianship, their responsibilities with respect to the practices of *appraisal*, *selection*, *arrangement*, *description*, provision of access, and preservation of archives, and their observation of professional codes of ethics. While archives' use for accountability purposes is most immediately associated with the records of government and other power institutions, accountability can be broadly considered as applying to the act of *acquisition* of *personal records* by archives with such mandates; in this regard, acquisition of these materials is understood as preserving source material with archival value for accounts that may further understanding of society.

Commentary

A trustworthy account of a matter may be supported or refuted by both the act of providing access to responsive records, and the analysis and verification of the thoroughness of any procedures and regulations applied to the records; processes and rules that, to greater or lesser degrees, have governed their use, care, and disposition. The enduring value of archives to provide explanation of actions and decisions is evidenced by the ancient origins of archival repositories, buildings dedicated to housing selected documents inscribed on durable or semi-durable media, for the purposes of consultation, be it for political, legal, administrative, or historical purposes. It is argued, therefore, that archives' purpose and the activities of the recordkeeper have always included their use as tools of accountability, regardless of the person, organization, or state with the authority to establish an archival repository and to cause the setting aside of documents. The very development of *diplomatics*, as a means to analyze documents in their procedural context and to verify *authenticity*, indicates archives' role in accountability activities.

Although accountability as a noun did not come into common use, especially in relation to archives, until the latter half of the twentieth century, various writings cited by Parkinson (1993) serve to illustrate the emerging idea that effective management by and of the early modern state was linked to efficient and systematic *recordkeeping*, and that the creation of written reports detailing the accounts of government contributed to increased expectation of state accountability. The concept of accountability

in the European archival manuals of Muller, Feith and Fruin, and Jenkinson is conveyed through their charge that the work of the archivist is to preserve the value of selected records as evidence of administrative activity, through the authority delegated to archivists by records creators (Parkinson 1993). With the expansion of modern government and advancement of society, Schellenberg's writings on archival administration illustrate what may be regarded as competing responsibilities of preserving records' *primary* and *secondary values*, the duties of *records managers* versus archivists, and the broader purposes for keeping modern archives (Schellenberg 1956). In the twentieth century the development of archival science, the development of the profession, and attendant work toward archival standards are themselves evidence of the inherent responsibility placed on archives and archivists with regards to accountability.

Discussion of the concept of accountability with regards to archival material, archival institutions, and the responsibilities of archivists in societies, democratic and otherwise, has increased along with the scrutiny of power institutions, as well as the concern over the *accessibility* and *reliability* of *digital* and *digitized* records. Kenosi (2012, 141) draws attention to a general awareness of records as "objects of accountability. . . . Records are an important cornerstone of accountability in relation to how they help to enable, enforce, limit, ignore, and deny accountability." Postmodernism's challenge to notions of universal truth, records' fixity, and the perceived objectivity of records' unassailability as evidence of facts, acts, and events, has been considered at length in the professional literature. However, as Eastwood (2010, 159) points out:

> Records themselves do not reveal either all the facts of any matter or speak its truth. We know enough about the dangers of trying to separate fact from value or interpretation to be skeptical that records can render an account of past actions in some straightforward way, but the archival faith is . . . a faith in the power of rational discourse resting on evidence of past actions.

Introduction of *archival legislation*, as well as access to information and privacy-protection laws, raises expectations concerning the rigor of processes meant to manage records throughout their *lifecycle*;

the use of records in documenting human rights violations, in identifying war crimes and acts of genocide, and in providing evidence of illegal activities reveals the role of records to assist in redress; and the analysis of perceived failures of recordkeeping to prevent harmful actions focuses attention on the workings of juridical systems and the place of archives within them.

Conclusion

Accountability as a term originates in the actions of counting and enumeration, of providing an explanation or narrative, or a statement as to the discharge of duties (*Oxford English Dictionary* 2011). Accountability is inextricably linked to the use of records to explain past actions, where the physical or juridical persons involved cannot themselves provide the required or needed account. It is understood that responsibility to provide an accounting of facts, acts, and events is a key reason for creating institutions that support preservation of the archives. Understanding a juridical system, the *context* of records creation, the *recordkeeping systems* in place to manage records use, disposition, selection, arrangement, description, access, and preservation, are critical steps in determining archives' effectiveness as tools for accountability.—*Lara Wilson*

Keywords: archives, evidence, responsibility
Related Entries: Archival Custody; Archives (Institution); Archives (Material); Documentary Evidence; Primary Value; Records; Secondary Value

Bibliography

Cox, Richard J., and David A. Wallace., eds. *Archives and the Public Good: Accountability and Records in Modern Society*. Westport, CT: Quorum Books, 2002.

Eastwood, Terry. "Archives, Democratic Accountability, and Truth." In Cheryl Avery and Mona Holmlund, eds., *Better Off Forgetting? Essays on Archives, Public Policy, and Collective Memory*. Toronto: University of Toronto Press, 2010, 143–68.

Jenkinson, Hilary. *A Manual of Archive Administration*. London: Percy Lund, Humphries & Co., 1966.

Kenosi, Lekoko. "Accountability in Archival Science since Parkinson's Thesis." *Comma* 1 (2012): 135–46. DOI: 10.3828/comma.2012.1.13.

Loewen, Candace, ed. "The Postmodern Archives." *Archivaria* 51 (Special issue, Spring 2001). http://journals.sfu.ca/archivar/index.php/archivaria/issue/view/428/showToc.

MacNeil, Heather. *Trusting Records: Legal, Historical and Diplomatic Perspectives*. Boston: Kluwer, 2000.

Nesmith, Tom. "Archivists and Public Affairs: Towards a New Archival Public Programming." In Cheryl Avery and Mona Holmlund, eds., in *Better Off Forgetting? Essays on Archives, Public Policy, and Collective Memory*. Toronto: University of Toronto Press, 2010, 169–91.

Parkinson, Jane. "Accountability in Archival Science." Master's Thesis, University of British Columbia, 1993. http://hdl.handle.net/2429/1807.

Schellenberg, T. R. *Modern Archives: Principles and Techniques*. Chicago: University of Chicago Press, 1956.

ACQUISITION

Acquisition is the process by which an archival institution obtains care and control of its documentary holdings. Acquisition typically involves the formal transfer of ownership of archival material through donation or purchase from a private person or corporate entity, or the official transfer of *records* from a *creator* that is part of the same organization, such as between a government agency and *archives*, where formal ownership does not change. Virtually all archival institutions engage in acquisition as the means of developing their holdings. As a concept, acquisition is similar to accessioning, though there are significant distinctions in usage. Accessioning also incorporates establishing basic physical and intellectual control over the records, which may include creating an accession record and other actions that are not considered processing or *archival description*.

Acquisition and Accessioning: Evolving Concepts

Broadly defined, acquisition encompasses all activity from the development of an *acquisition policy*, *appraisal*, and negotiations with creators, through to the transfer and receipt of physical custody and the accessioning of records. More narrowly, it might exclude appraisal and refer simply to the legal or physical *transfer* of records. Professional usage suggests that we more often speak of accessioning in a government-records context and acquisition in a private-archives context.

How archivists have thought about acquisition has evolved in the past century. The modern founders of the archival tradition said surprisingly little about "acquisition." The Dutch *Manual for the Arrangement and Description of Archives* (Muller 1898) referred primarily to "transfers" of records from government agencies that are "officially received" by the archives. In a similar vein, the British *Manual of Archive Administration* (Jenkinson 1922) discussed the transmission of records, stressing the importance of an unbroken chain of custody. With its emphasis on continuity, acquisition was a foreign concept. For Jenkinson, archives that acquired material from private sources risked damaging the integral "archive character" of the records. For the founders of the modern *archival theory*, steeped in the *public records tradition*, archives did not so much acquire as they received transfers of records in an orderly and official fashion. Archives were kept, not acquired.

Archivists in the postwar era conceived of institutional *records* as following a natural *lifecycle*, and later a *records continuum*: both models served to emphasize, in varying degrees, the continuity or flow of the record from creation to archives. T. R. Schellenberg scarcely mentioned acquisition in his major works, which focused on appraisal, *classification* systems, *arrangement*, *description*, and *preservation*. He did briefly define accessioning as the activity, following appraisal, that brought "records that are judged to be valuable into the physical and legal custody of the archival institution" (*Modern Archives* 1956, 118). Acquisition was implicit or assumed in the business of an archives, and unremarkable on its own except in the practice of appraisal and accessioning. *A Modern Archives Reader* (Daniels and Walch 1984, 339) preserved the distinction that only private archives were acquired, defining acquisition as "the process of identifying and acquiring, by donation or purchase, historical materials from sources outside the archival institution." In contrast, they defined the verb accession in a form

embracing all archives: "To transfer physical and legal custody of documentary materials to an archival institution."

But the concept of acquisition was broadening. The Society of American Archivists' Archival Fundamentals Series consciously expanded its meaning (Ham 1993, 2–5) to include both public and private sources by adding transfer to the definition, along with *donation* and purchase: "The process of acquiring records from any source by transfer, donation, or purchase, or the body of records so acquired." Indeed, Ham decried the traditional distinction between institutional archives and collecting repositories, "that one appraises and accessions while the other solicits and acquires," treating instead "the two types of acquisition programs . . . as part of a seamless whole—the archival selection process." In this broadened conception, acquisition encompassed appraisal and the receiving of transfers, in a manner that emphasized that a change of custody and control still occurred on receipt of records from a government agency, if not a change of ownership.

This expanded, more inclusive understanding of acquisition is reflected in more recent publications, such as the Australian manual *Keeping Archives*, which defined acquisition as "the processes associated with acquiring records that are relevant to your archives" and applicable to both in-house and collecting archives (Crush 2008, 208). Citing Ham, the SAA's *Glossary of Archival and Records Terminology* (Pearce-Moses, 2005) primarily treats acquisition as a physical noun rather than a process (e.g., the "materials received by a repository"), and links it to accessioning: "As nouns, acquisition and accession are synonymous. However, the verb accession goes far beyond the sense of acquiring, connoting the initial steps of processing by establishing rudimentary physical and intellectual control over the materials by entering brief information about those materials in a register, database, or other log of the repository's holdings." The *Glossary* well captures the more nuanced usage of accessioning as the first step of administrative control over a new accession or acquisition; the registering of documentary material in an archival system or creation of an accession notice to demonstrate that it has been acquired. For some archivists, accessioning is the first step of archival care for the records, rather than the last step of acquisition.

Variations in Practice

The broadening of acquisition to cover all archives, however, masked continuing divergence in the practices of government and in-house archives on one hand, and private and collecting archives on the other. *Keeping Archives* (Crush 2008, 207) observed:

> The simplest acquisition process is the transfer of inactive archival records from the business unit that created and maintained them to the in-house archives of that same organization. With in-house archives, ownership of the archives does not change at the time of acquisition, custody does. For the collecting archives, the acquisition process is considerably more complex. Decisions need to be made about whose records to collect, how to go about collecting them, who will own the records and how their access to researchers will be managed.

In the former case, as with a legislated relationship between a government agency and archives, much of the doubt is removed; the archives will acquire the records of that department, though perhaps not as simply as the manual suggests. The essential decision is which records will be acquired and which will be destroyed. In an era of records abundance, appraisal thus has assumed tremendous importance in the acquisition of government records and is defined in procedures and policies and carefully monitored. After archivists have made their appraisal decisions, records deemed archival are transferred to archival control while authority is granted to the creating agency to dispose of those rejected. The process, authorizations, and documentation required will vary from government to government and archives to archives, but are adhered to rigorously to ensure legal *accountability* and compliance. But when the records are in the care and control of the archives (perhaps after a stay in a *records center*), and an accession record has been created, the acquisition process is complete.

Acquisition of private archives follows its own pattern. Collecting archives develop and implement a collecting or acquisition policy that focuses acquisitions activity in the fields most relevant to its mandate. Many will adopt a form of *documentation strategy* to direct and prioritize this activity, perhaps even developing a collaborative approach with other archives. In the absence of a mandated relationship between archives and creator, archivists must identify the most relevant creators in their documentary universe, those most likely to have archival material that best fits their institution's criteria for acquisition, and contact those creators in hopes of acquiring their *fonds*, or at least provoking a response.

The creator's response may range from reluctant or hostile to indifferent or enthusiastic, and this response will determine the course of acquisition. Negotiations may stall or take many years, even generations, or proceed quite quickly. Conversely, many other prospective donors will contact the archives to offer documentary material to an institution, which may or may not fit, with varying degrees of relevance, its acquisition criteria. Archivists will have to evaluate these offers and weigh them against their acquisition policy and available resources. This latter scenario is sometimes referred to as reactive or passive acquisition, while initiating contact with priority creators is sometimes called proactive acquisition (Craig 2004). Contradictorily, proactive acquisition can involve long periods of inactivity waiting for a response while passive acquisition can invoke frantic activity. In either scenario, acquisition can only take place when both parties are in agreement.

Archival institutions have two key mechanisms to complete the legal transfer of ownership of private archives: donation and purchase. Donation is often accompanied by a tax credit based on a monetary appraisal of the material. Purchase is perhaps less common, but may be the norm for creators where there is an established market for their archives. Indeed, purchase and donation may be combined for one acquisition. Some archival material will be sold at auction. Donations will generally be formalized through the signing of a deed of gift, while some form of purchase agreement will be signed to complete purchases. In the past, many fonds changed hands simply through a handshake or an exchange of correspondence. Such arrangements may result in disputed ownership, often contested by the donor's heirs, and archivists now insist on more formal agreements. These legal instruments provide vital documentation of the terms and conditions of the donation or sale, usually including an annex with an inventory or description of the material. This transfer of physical ownership may also be accompanied by a transfer of intellectual property rights—copyright—with the fonds. Institutional policies will vary on this, for in attempting to acquire copyright, the archives might lose the acquisition. Writers and artists, for instance, will be reluctant to transfer copyright without remuneration, if at all. The terms of access to sensitive or restricted material may also be stipulated in the deed of gift, though they might also be negotiated later after the content of the donation is better known.

In some cases, however, archives may acquire material without acquiring ownership, with a deposit agreement. It acquires custody of the documents and preserves them without acquiring formal ownership. Such deposit arrangements may be dissolved by either party. Deposit is generally not an ideal means for an archives to acquire material, but it may be the only way the creator will agree to its transfer to archival custody, and it improves its long-term prospects for preservation. It is a calculated risk for an archives to invest resources without ownership, but a risk that is often later rewarded with a formal donation.

New Currents in Acquisition

The traditional waters of acquisition, which assumed the transfer of physical custody of the records, are being muddied by postcustodialism. Archivists are increasingly allowing for the possibility of distributed custody, where physical custody, particularly for *digital records*, remains with the creator after appraisal. For example, in the case of a complex database that remains on the servers of the creating agency, but that cannot be disposed of without archival authorization, the archives may be said to have acquired care and control of the record, but not custody. Postcustodialism perhaps shifts the meaning of acquisition from "custody and control" of the records to "care and control."

Archivists are rethinking custodial approaches in other ways in an era of records abundance and resource scarcity. The growing volume of records and storage costs are making archivists increasingly willing to consider *deaccessioning* or systematic *reappraisal*. Deaccessioning to other archives has long been an option, but receptiveness is increasing to returning material to its original donors or even the destruction of records formerly appraised as archival. Archivists are more accepting of the potential impermanence of acquisition.

Conclusion

Acquisition is vital to the establishment and growth of an archives. From the development and implementation of an acquisition policy through to the legal transfer and accessioning of records, the acquisition process covers a broad sweep of core archival activity. Though continuing to evolve in concept and practice, it is difficult to imagine archival practice without acquisition.—*Robert Fisher*

Keywords: acquisition, accession, transfer, custody, ownership
Related Entries: Acquisition Policy; Appraisal; Deaccessioning; Documentation Strategy

Bibliography

Boles, Frank. *Selecting and Appraising Archives and Manuscripts*, 2nd edition. Archival Fundamentals Series II. Chicago: Society of American Archivists, 2005.

Craig, Barbara. *Archival Appraisal: Theory and Practice.* Munich: K. G. Saur, editor, 2004.

Crush, Peter J. "Acquisition." In Jackie Bettington, Kim Eberhard, Rowena Loo, and Clive Smith, eds., *Keeping Archives*, 3rd edition. Canberra: Australian Society of Archivists, 2008, 207–25.

Daniels, Maygene F., and Timothy Walch, eds. *A Modern Archives Reader: Basic Readings in Archival Theory and Practice.* Washington, DC: National Archives and Records Service, 1984.

Ham, F. Gerald. *Selecting and Appraising Archives and Manuscripts.* Archival Fundamentals Series. Chicago: Society of American Archivists, 1993.

Jenkinson, Hilary. *A Manual of Archive Administration.* London: Percy Lund, Humphries & Co., 1966.

Muller, Samuel, Robert Fruin, and Johan Feith. *Manual for the Arrangement and Description of Archives.* New York: HW Wilson Co., 1898. Translated 1968.

Pearce-Moses, Richard. *A Glossary of Archival and Records Terminology.* Archival Fundamentals Series II. Chicago: Society of American Archivists, 2005.

Schellenberg, T. R. *The Management of Archives.* Washington, DC: National Archives and Records Service, 1965. Reprint, 1984.

———. *Modern Archives: Principles & Techniques.* Chicago: Society of American Archivists, 1956. Reprint, 2003.

ACQUISITION POLICY

An acquisition policy, in the United States more often referred to as a collection-development policy (Marshall 2002), but also called collection policy and documentation policy, is a written statement by a collecting *archives* of its goals for acquiring new collections (and often containing *appraisal* guidelines that apply to material within a collection). Collecting archives are also referred to as manuscripts repositories, special collections libraries, and collecting repositories—all terms for institutions that acquire material through deed of gift from private entities—distinguishing them from institutional, or internal, archives that accession only *records* generated by their parent institution. Though some writers have referred to acquisition policy as appraisal from a macro perspective, others have attempted to distinguish it from traditional appraisal altogether:

> The final decision regarding whether to acquire an individual *fonds* must be made with an eye on the larger universe that is defined by broader acquisition development policies. Stated another way, the principles of appraisal help us to answer the question, *"Why* am I saving this?" While acquisition policies force us to answer the equally important question, "Why am *I* saving this?" (Ericson 1991–1992)

Acquisition policies are necessary to ensure that collection development is planned, rational, tied to institutional needs and priorities, and realistic compared to repository resources rather than haphazard, knee-jerk, based on the interests or whims of individuals, and largely impractical. Collecting policies have been urged for *archivists* in the professional literature at least as far back as the mid-1950s and as recently as the 2000s, with different authors proposing different sets of components for a model acquisition policy. Between the mid-1980s—when several authors argued that acquisition policies should be based on full surveys of extant holdings, because it is difficult to decide what to collect if there is no information about what has been collected and why (Endelman 1987)—and the early 1990s, collect-

ing policies were a frequent topic of discussion in archival journals. Much of this writing built on the framework for collecting policies proposed by Faye Phillips, which remains the most detailed (though not necessarily the most relevant) model available in the archival literature (Phillips 1984).

Acquisitions Policy—Why?

Ham cried out in 1975 (5), "Is there any other field of information gathering that has such a broad mandate with a selection process so random, so fragmented, so uncoordinated, and even so often accidental?" Formal acquisition policies account for and therefore minimize wasteful competition among repositories and the fragmentation of material related to a particular topic or place, and are more likely to result in integrated and interrelated holdings of maximum value to students, scholars, and other researchers. Yet this call was not universally heard. Fifteen years after Ham's jeremiad, Timothy L. Ericson reflected that:

> most of our current acquisition policies are too broadly conceived to be realistic in the Information Age. . . . Just as our professional forebears began to use appraisal to help limit their intake of records at the fonds level, so must we begin to use acquisition policies to limit our intake at the repository level. (1991–1992, 72).

Around the turn of the century several significant critics continued to complain that the profession remained recalcitrant in adopting and implementing all but the most generic acquisitions policies. In 1998, surveys of over thirty-five hundred repositories in twenty-one states found that less than 40 percent of them had a collection-development policy (Sauer 2001). A survey at the beginning of the twenty-first century found that barely half of even the most elite special collections repositories in the United States had formal collection-development policies. A more recent survey of collecting policies on repository websites discovered only 38 policies out of 884 sites investigated (Marshall 2002).

"The evidence reveals . . . incredible gaps in the documentation of even traditional concerns" (Ham 1975, 6) such as a state's businesses by a state historical society. A survey conducted in the mid-1990s, for example, found that mid-nineteenth-century family-owned businesses were documented very heavily in major repositories in the United States, while twentieth-century businesses of any sort were barely documented at all (Greene and Daniels-Howell 1997). "The evidence . . . showed that many archivists waste time and space preserving random bits and pieces, as well as large accessions, of the most dubious value" (Ham 1975, 6). The appearance to an outsider, critics have noted, may be less that of a professional selecting what matters and more of a community attic.

A 2001 (limited) survey also indicates reasons for abjuring collection development policies: not enough time/staff; policy is not necessary; do not want to be limited by policy; no active collecting. It is important to note that even when collecting policies are present, they may not be functional; the 2001 survey discovered that repositories with written collecting policies were far more likely than those with informal policies to accession a collection because of a fear that the collection might otherwise be destroyed, even though the material did not fit within the policy. Ericson (1991–1992, 69) criticized this very action twenty years ago. "Our instinct is still to see ourselves in the role of a twentieth-century Horatius-at the-Bridge: the last line of defense between preservation and oblivion. This causes us to make utterly ludicrous decisions regarding acquisition by cloaking ourselves in the virtue of maintaining culture: if I don't save it, who will?" To avoid ludicrous acquisition decisions requires a sound written acquisitions policy.

Good acquisitions policies accomplish even more than improving the selection and *appraisal* of collections for a repository. First, particularly where an archives' administration and resource allocators are concerned, not only does formal policy demonstrate a clear degree of professionalism when endorsed (as it should always be) by that same administration, but it also helps ensure that the people who matter understand what the repository is doing and why. This means they are more likely to (a) back up the staff if a donor complains and (b) not sabotage the policy by making unilateral decisions to accept (or reject) collections. Second, it permits the repository to more accurately allocate resources to reasonable goals. It also permits the possibility of cooperative collecting, which is an even more efficient use of resources. Third, explaining selection and appraisal

decisions—particularly negative ones—to donors is much easier and more effective when the decisions are based on formal policy. Fourth, a policy permits curators to gauge success in documentation in a manner that is accessible to resource allocators—there is evidence of how successful an acquisition policy is or is not. Fifth, a collecting policy permits reassessment and recalibration as time passes—as resources, users, and/or competition changes. Thus a policy permits *reappraisal*, which at its simplest is merely the application of a current collecting policy to existing holdings.

Acquisition Policy—How?

"Collection analysis, the evaluation of the characteristics of a repository's holdings, is one methodology through which archivists can determine the nature and strength of a repository's holdings in specified areas and then use this knowledge to develop explicit collecting priorities" (Endelman 1987, 341). Collection analysis is the widely acknowledged first step in creating a responsible and effective acquisition policy. While the backlogs of unprocessed collections that plague many repositories hamper such analysis, it is possible to use students in a university setting (volunteers in other settings) to conduct abbreviated analysis sufficient to inform deliberations over policy. One state historical society that undertook to analyze its business collections (its largest collecting area) approached the process this way:

> Our analysis therefore divided all business collections into 20 categories by industry sector, and for every collection specified title, dates, size (in cubic feet), date first accessioned, and codes representing the predominant record types found in the collection (e.g., minutes and board packets; annual reports and financial statements; daily accounting records such as journals and ledgers; advertising material; employee records; sales or manufacturing data; sound and visual material; correspondence; government regulatory reports; legal files; research and development files). (Greene and Daniels-Howell 1997, 175–76)

"The development of collection analysis is part of a larger process of increasing systemization and standardization in all areas of the profession" (Endelman 1987, 341). After understanding extant collections, the next steps in developing an acquisition policy can be simple or complex, depending in large part on the overall holdings of the repository. An ideal approach is to involve as many members of the repository staff as possible in the collection inventory/assessment and, where possible, in the following steps as well (Collection Development Policy [a], 2008). It is important to keep the archives' director's supervisor apprised regularly of the direction and progress of the policy. True success of an acquisitions policy depends on both staff "buy-in" and approval from the administration.

Additional steps in developing an acquisitions policy are: (1) Reexamining the repository's mission statement, priority constituents, resources (for donor relations and acquisition, accessioning, processing (including supplies), storage, reference, and outreach); reference must be assessed because certain collecting areas might overreach the reference archivists' subject or language expertise, making their work extremely difficult. (2) Surveying the larger documentary universe—that is, determining which other repositories' collections or collecting activities duplicate those at the archives working on a policy—and paying close attention to the universe of secondary resources to ensure awareness of how thoroughly a topic or set of individuals might be documented therein. 3) Defining—based on the repository's particular mission, resources, and clientele—a broad set of criteria for organizing and prioritizing *records creators* into comprehensive groups (topical, geographic, chronological, function, significance, etc.); one still-useful referent is the Wisconsin State Historical Society's (now Wisconsin Historical Society) 1987 list of collection areas (with collecting priorities): an updated analysis using the same 1987 categories is located at www.wisconsinhistory.org/libraryarchives/whrab/pdfs/RecordsAssessment-FinalReport2009.pdf.

Acquisitions Policy—What?

Proponents are clear that a proper acquisition plan must focus not on the types of material collected (e.g., correspondence, minutes, diaries, email, photos), as is sometimes the case, but instead on the *record groups*/collections sought, defined by geography, subject, chronology, or creator. For example, one state historical society's "broad mandate" included documenting business, so that "any busi-

ness" that approached the acquisitions archivists offering to donate records was evaluated with the question "Are these particular series any good?" A new perspective, however, brought a new question:

> For [collecting] repositories, at least, we think this is the wrong question. Instead of analyzing record series (or functions, for that matter) first, curators need to prioritize the broad topical areas their repository seeks to document and which records creators will be solicited and accepted within each area. (Greene and Daniels-Howell 1997, 167–68)

The suggestion to prioritize the goals of an acquisition policy is a paraphrase and extrapolation of macroappraisal, a theory developed in Canada specifically for application to federal government records but ultimately applicable, too, to collecting archives.

According to two significant sources—Phillips, 1984, and Wisconsin Historical Records Advisory Board and Wisconsin Council for Local History, 1998—a model collecting policy for manuscript collections should contain the following elements: (a) mission, clientele (in priority order); (b) types of programs supported by the collection (e.g., research, exhibits, outreach, publications); (c) how collecting areas relate to existing collection strengths and weaknesses; (d) record groups/collections sought, defined by geography, subject, chronology, or creator—or types of material sought and acquired within each collecting area—and desired level of collecting to meet program needs; (e) formats sought or declined; (f) languages sought or declined; (g) statement of deaccessioning policy; (h) procedure for monitoring development and reviewing collection-development guidelines. Two sound examples of acquisition policies may be found at www.uwyo.edu/ahc/files/policies/collecting-policy.pdf (Collection Development Policy [a]) and www.library.vanderbilt.edu/speccol/policies/collectiondevelopment.shtml (Collection Development Policy [b]).

Conclusion

In a brochure for small repositories, the Wisconsin Historical Society summarizes the purposes for a collection policy as follows:

- Decisions are not personal; they are policy.
- It is easier to decline unwanted materials.

- It is easier to explain acquisitions to donors, your supervisors, and the library board.
- It provides continuity through changes in staff and administrators. (Wisconsin Historical Records Advisory Board and Wisconsin Council for Local History 1998)

There are additional benefits identified by archival authors across the decades: possibility for cooperative collecting; more focused and active collecting (e.g., underdocumented communities, modern businesses, religions beyond genealogical records) rather than random and passive acceptance of what happens to be offered; more rational disposition of existing resources—passively accepting a collection is not "free" because it requires staff time (accessioning, processing, cataloging) and space allocation; and there is much more. Acquisition policies have long since come to be recognized as an essential component of the collecting repository's strategies for thriving in the twenty-first century.—*Mark Greene*

Keywords: acquisition, collection-development policy, deeds of gift, monetary appraisal, manuscript collection

Bibliography

"Collection Development Policy [a]." University of Wyoming American Heritage Center, 2008. www.uwyo.edu/ahc/files/policies/collecting-policy.pdf (accessed June 12, 2013).

"Collection Development Policy [b]." Vanderbilt Special Collections and Archives. www.library.vanderbilt.edu/speccol/policies/collectiondevelopment.shtml (accessed June 12, 2013).

"Creating a Collection Development Policy for Historical Records." Wisconsin Historical Records Advisory Board and Wisconsin Council for Local History, 1988. www.wisconsinhistory.org/libraryarchives/whrab/wclh.pdf (accessed June 12, 2013).

Endelman, Judith E. "Looking Backward to Plan for the Future: Collection Analysis for Manuscript Repositories." *American Archivist* 50 (3) (1987): 340–55. http://archivists.metapress.com/content/m24760mh124r6u3w/fulltext.pdf.

Ericson, Timothy L. "At the 'Rim of Creative Dissatisfaction': Archivists and Acquisition Develop-

ment." *Archivaria* 33 (1991–1992): 66–77. http://journals.sfu.ca/archivar/index.php/archivaria/article/view/11799/12750.

Ham, F. Gerald. "The Archival Edge." *American Archivist* 38 (1) (1975): 5–13.

Greene, Mark A., and Todd J. Daniels-Howell. "Documentation with 'an Attitude': A Pragmatist's Guide to the Selection and Acquisition of Modern Business Records." In James M. O'Toole, ed., *Records of American Business.* Chicago: Society of American Archivists, 1997, 161–229.

Marshall, Jennifer A. "Toward Common Content: An Analysis of Online College and University Collecting Policies." *American Archivist* 65 (2) (2002): 231–56. http://archivists.metapress.com/content/d14g7x2615270j61/fulltext.pdf.

Phillips, Faye. "Developing Collecting Policies for Manuscript Collections." *American Archivist* 47 (1) (1984): 30–42. http://archivists.metapress.com/content/x07k74g7331762q2/fulltext.pdf.

Sauer, Cynthia K. "Doing the Best We Can? The Use of Collection Development Policies and Cooperative Collecting Activities at Manuscript Repositories." *American Archivist* 64 (2) (2001): 308–49. http://archivists.metapress.com/content/gj6771215231xm37/fulltext.pdf.

ADVOCACY

A description of *advocacy* by a British museum association asserts that it is "the process whereby an organization seeks to influence others in order to gain support for its mission, interests or a course of action. In order to achieve this, networks of support are developed and used to lend credibility, wield influence and offer third party endorsement." One American archivist views advocacy as "an investment we make when we intentionally and strategically educate and engage individuals and organizations so they in turn will support our work" (Hackman 2011, vii). While these perspectives are especially apt for advocacy by and for individual archives, they also apply to advocacy by *archival associations* and networks.

The Concept

Advocacy is sometimes confused or conflated with *outreach*, though advocacy differs from outreach as to purpose. The aim of advocacy ordinarily is to influence resource allocators and other decision-makers to act in ways favorable to an archives, while the main objective of outreach is to reach an existing or expanded audience, usually to better inform and serve them, often through new methods or programs. While different, advocacy and outreach are related, even complementary: effective advocacy can help secure resources that an archives needs for expanded outreach, while effective outreach can increase understanding, appreciation, and use of archives by potential advocates.

Case studies demonstrate convincingly how archives have applied advocacy to strengthen their organizational infrastructure or to obtain other dramatic results. One recent case study, for example, reviews how the first archivist of the New York Philharmonic Orchestra initially identified the internal centers of influence at the orchestra and then systematically fostered strong working relationships with these centers. As a result of this advocacy, the Philharmonic archives became fully integrated into the ongoing operations of the orchestra and viewed as a significant contributor to its success. A second case study explains how the small Butte, Montana, archives used intense customer service and imaginative community outreach to build broad interest and deep appreciation among residents of Butte. A skillful advocacy campaign then drew on this prior relationship building to convince citizens to vote overwhelmingly for a $7.5 million bond issue to rehabilitate the archives building and construct an archival vault. A third case study describes how in the 1980s the New York State Archives developed a highly ambitious statewide agenda for archival development, then addressed one key part with intense advocacy to create strong relationships with local government officials and their statewide associations and with key legislative and executive branch decision-makers. Largely as a result, the archives was able to obtain comprehensive new state laws regulating local government records and archives administration and supporting new State Archives regional offices and millions of dollars of grants for local records work each year (case studies by Haws, Crain and McCrea, and Dearstyne, in Hackman 2011). In a powerful earlier case study, *Diary of a Dream*, former archivist of the United States Robert Warner recounts the successful campaign

to obtain independence for the National Archives from the General Services Administration. Warner explains the crucial leadership, strategizing, and day-to-day personal advocacy by himself and a small staff group and how their work was linked to a coalition of archives, professional associations, and key individuals who could influence members of Congress (Warner 1985). A similar national coalition has advocated, often successfully, to rescue or to increase funding for the grant program of the National Historical Publications and Records Commission valuable to the whole archives community.

Effective advocacy for an archives ordinarily involves several closely related tasks. These have been described as deciding what you want, identifying who has what you want, and figuring out how to get them to give it to you. In the first stage it's useful to assess the archives' present condition against its vision for the future and to use the gap between as the basis for the advocacy needed. Such an advocacy agenda can identify both long-term goals and required near-term and intermediate objectives, including overcoming barriers that prevent progress toward the larger vision. Initial assessment and planning provides focus for advocacy and avoids wasted effort.

The second task is determining who can make or influence decisions that will meet the archives' needs. Usually this starts with the office or person directly above the archives, but it includes other internal advocacy targets such as members of a board of directors, senior management, and directors or key staff of core functions such as budget, personnel, legal, communications and public affairs, and technology. Part of this second task, too often ignored, is to identify external individuals and organizations who potentially can influence the internal decision-makers.

The third advocacy task is acting to convince both significant internal and external parties to support decisions desired by an archives. Gaining such decisions requires imaginative strategies and tactics to bring influence, sometimes direct pressure, to bear on those whose decisions most affect the archives. Of course, the very best basic tool to use in advocacy is a highly effective archives that produces positive benefits that are regularly communicated to targeted audiences, especially the key decision-makers. Regardless of the advocacy targets, being able to "make the case" for the archives is fundamental. Sometimes, as in a capital fund-raising or other formal campaign, it is useful to have a highly polished printed case statement capturing basic facts, arguments, evidence, examples, and endorsements in support of the archives. Every archives needs always to have the elements of this basic advocacy package at hand and in a flexible form that can be adapted for advocacy to suit particular occasions, objectives, and audiences.

With the case in mind and in hand, central to successful advocacy ordinarily is to bring "significant others," internal and external, to understand, respect, and value the archives—and to convey their interest and support to main decision-makers. This is an ongoing task, requiring a proactive approach by the archives to inform, engage, build credibility, and develop relationships with key individuals, offices, and organizations. Social media present new opportunities for an archives to expand public appreciation and understanding of the archives and for engaging some of them to become active supporters. Hard evidence of a growing audience for the archives and beneficiaries of its services usually impresses those whose decisions are critical to the archives, though by itself this may seldom be decisive. Whether through social media or other means, improved awareness of the archives is only one part, and usually the easiest part, of advocacy. Understanding and appreciation in themselves seldom produce major positive change, though they may help enable it.

In many cases influential internal and external supporters may not even need to advocate directly on a particular issue—so long as key internal decision-makers are aware of their interest and of the high regard in which they hold the archives. While having a substantial number of supporters often helps, it may take only a few prominent outsiders, and a few respected senior insiders, to sufficiently impress the key decision-makers on a particularly important archives issue—and lead them generally to react more favorably to the archives' needs on a continuing basis.

Conclusion

Experience shows that advocacy can help an archives secure many of the decisions and resources vital to success. This includes not only increases in budget and personnel but also major infrastructure changes such as increased authority, better organizational placement, and policies and procedures more favorable to the archives. To be effective in its advocacy the archives needs to be clear about its goals, to prepare and present an impressive case for the archives and for particular objectives, and to identify and then engage influential internal and external supporters.—*Larry Hackman*

Keywords: advocacy, influence, outreach, resources, support
Related Entry: Outreach

Bibliography

Hackman, Larry J., ed. *Many Happy Returns: Advocacy and the Development of Archives*. Chicago: Society of American Archivists, 2011.
Warner, Robert M. *Diary of a Dream: A History of the National Archives Independence Movement, 1980–1985*. Metuchen, NJ: Scarecrow Press, 1985.

APPRAISAL

Archival appraisal is a broad term embracing the theory, rationales, policies, and procedures for identifying, acquiring, and selecting institutional or organizational *records*, and personal or private records in all media deemed to have lasting value and worth according to criteria that are articulated and documented.

Origins of Appraisal

Appraisal for archival *acquisition* of new material and for *selection* within a body of material an institution, unit, or program was mandated to acquire or had already acquired emerged from the well-established responsibility of an archival repository to preserve the material charged to its care and keeping by *record creators*. In concert with record keepers, *archivists* have debated over time whether they should make appraisal decisions and, if so, what to keep, how to keep it, and for how long retention was either necessary or possible (Williams 2006). It could never be guaranteed that a deposit, *transfer*, or purposely chosen acquisition will be preserved permanently or remain unchanged. For example, the passage of time could affect the repository's ability to properly keep records, as the inevitable deterioration of supports and different media would require action. Abstracts could be created to summarize key information or, in some cases, copies would be prepared on new supports which may have a longer life span. Other impediments to keeping records could emerge in any repository. Changes in the repository's financial condition might have a material impact on its ability to keep the records or to deal with new and changing technical conditions. Moreover, newer accessions could alter the need for the repository to retain records from previous acquisitions. In turn, *reappraisal* undertaken on records already acquired through an appraisal process might recommend that certain records be *deaccessioned* to allow their destruction or transfer to another repository. Therefore, archivists looked for consistent criteria that would assist them in making necessary choices for the retention and destruction of records, leading in many jurisdictions to official schedules covering periods of retention (Procter 2008). For archivists, it was a short step from passively receiving transfers to looking critically at material in the light of the institution's *acquisition policy* and storage capability, and of the relationship of new acquisitions to records already held. It soon became clear to many archivists that a more comprehensive look at records well before they were acquired, and often early on in their *lifecycle* through a process of records scheduling, would better align the space and resources available for the permanent *preservation* of records with a repository mandate or mission and with the needs of administrators and of the larger user community (Procter 2008).

What Guides Appraisal?

Appraisal choices have traditionally been guided either by what can be destroyed or by what should be kept (Kolsrud 1992; Couture 2005). The conditions supporting the development of criteria for each of these lines of thought can be traced historically in various jurisdictions; nevertheless, many different criteria supporting the determination of a period of record retention were similar across repositories and countries (see Couture 2005). Though appraisal criteria differ across countries and archival repositories, they have included such considerations as the needs of law courts for records of cases and decisions; the needs of administrators for records that provided reasons for actions and promoted continuity; the needs of citizens for records at all levels of governance to empower democratic participation and to ensure protection of rights and the acknowledgment of responsibilities; and the needs of society at large to be able to know its past and to have available the building blocks of group social memory (Cook 2011; Couture 2005). While discussion often surrounds the relative merits of *evidence*, public faith, trustworthiness, and *memory* (perpetual memory) as the concepts guiding appraisal decisions, largely as a response to changing political, social, and technological conditions, generally speaking, each one of them has continued to support the achievement of the appraisal goals and mandates of archival repositories over the past century (Cook 2011; Duranti 1994).

Key Themes in Appraisal

Appraisal emerged in the nineteenth century carrying with it essential concepts intimately associated with the responsibility to keep records—that of *impartiality*, of evidence, and of continuing memory. Each has played a part in the rationales and decisions affecting new acquisitions and selection from material to be acquired by mandate or already acquired.

Once it became clear that some form of selection had to be carried out, the question soon arose as to who should rightly make the decision and what criteria should be employed to determine value. One school of thought associated with the English archivist Hilary Jenkinson emphasized that the creator, or administrator, was best suited to determining what would continue to serve his/her needs. The *objectivity* of the archivist and the impartiality of the records were bolstered by this position, because the long-term keeper or archivist remained uninvolved with making choices to serve speculative future interests (Cook 2011). This strategy implied though the existence of a strong *records management* program, to which Jenkinson in his *A Manual of Archival Administration* referred as the "administrator golden rule" (1965, 153).

Another school of thought argued that archivists, as the responsible long-term custodians of records, should be closely involved in making the decisions. Some believed that archivists should be the sole judges of what was to be kept, as they are able to balance the needs of evidence, use, memory, and research that must be satisfied by what is kept for the long term. Emphasis on the archivist as a prime actor in appraisal is associated with the American author Theodore Schellenberg, who, along with his colleagues at the National Archives, segregated the *primary value* of records to their creators from their *secondary values* to a broad spectrum of users to serve their future needs for historical evidence and information (Kolsrud 1992). Cook believes that Schellenberg's shift from passive to active records appraisal also signaled a shift from archival institutions being solely centers of evidence to their being places of memory and narrative-building (Cook 2011).

In the course of forging workable and balanced answers to the question of who should choose records for long-term preservation and through which criteria the decisions should be made, specialists in records and their uses as working tools, as sources, and as special kinds of information developed theories of value and logical procedures for recognizing types and classes of materials that are prime candidates for long-term keeping. The specific focus of appraisal on the discovery of values in each existing record was undertaken through a bottom-up, or microappraisal, method of analysis based on evidential and informational values (Williams 2006).

In the latter part of the twentieth century new ideas have emerged emphasizing a priori strategic planning as a prerequisite to building relevant and consistent documentation on persistent themes or around functions or structures that are key to a society, group, or an organization and to embrace wider groups as active participants in appraisal (Cook 2011). Discussion of appraisal has flowered along with the growth and maturity of archival repositories that serve nongovernmental organizations and loosely defined communities of shared value and need (Cook 2011). The arguments and norms that are a good fit in a large homogenous organization such as a national or municipal government with a long and stable history are not necessarily adequate guides for archival programs responsible for building a collection from the private sector, from persons, from loose or fluid communities of interest, or from multi-institutional or multijurisdictional projects.

The task of appraisal may focus in the first instance on the records themselves, as appraisers seek to understand what values they may have intrinsically, or structurally in relationship to other materials, or by virtue of their association with a group, or event. However, many appraisal theorists in the twenty-first century agree that, because such a close examination of records is a resource-intensive exercise, and predicting the future value of records based on historical interests is near impossible, appraisal is far better accomplished when it is preceded by a more abstract, strategic thinking process, as in the case of macroappraisal, which focuses on the significance of context, locates records within broader themes, and relates them to a specific mandate or an ongoing and well-defined social responsibility (Cook 2011; Cook 2005; Williams 2006).

Appraisal theories emerging in the later part of the twentieth century often began by examining the importance of the function or office or person creating the material—in the case of an institutional repository, or by defining the theme(s), movements, or persons the repository endeavors to document and employing appraisal methodologies such as a *documentation strategy* or *documentation plan*—in the case of a community-based or thematically defined repository (see Samuels 1986 and Booms 1991 for introductions to these concepts). Microappraisal of institutional records and macroappraisal defining themes, functions, or movements for which documentation is sought can be joined in a fruitful sequence.

From the critique of earlier appraisal ideas has emerged a wealth of theoretical writing and an equally rich practical experience in conducting appraisal for acquisition and for selection at the micro level and at the level of planning and strategy, or macro level. The literature discussing real projects and practical applications of appraisal theory in different countries and within different repositories adds color to the appraisal discourse since practical constraints have always played a large part in *recordskeeping* (see Craig 2008; Williams 2006). This literature helps us understand that there are factors beyond the control of any single repository that are not countenanced or discussed by appraisal theories. These factors differ greatly, but include the instability of the supports and media for records, legal norms such as freedom of information and protection of privacy, the variable levels of financial backing for an institution that is often controlled by others, a lack of inter-institutional cooperation and resource sharing, or the unpredictable effects of political or social pressures (Craig 2007). All of these factors have a material impact on appraisal, as they do on a repository's ability to preserve its holdings, or to describe them and make them fully available to users. The inherent tension between the ideal and the real is reflected in the continuing productive tension between appraisal theory and its practical and continuing manifestation. In reality, archivists often lean on their practical experience and intuition in appraisal to respond to outside impacts on a repository as much as they depend on appraisal theory to make decisions—theory and practice work together to guide the archival appraisal process (Williams 2006).

Conclusion

In seeking to express particular aims in acquiring records, the appraisal theories, processes, and procedures developed by writers and by practitioners largely revolve around a very stable battery of questions, some asked and some implied. Who should participate in making appraisal choices—the creator alone, the archivist alone, an eponymous collective of typical users, or another combination? What is the best focus for appraisal—the record itself, the function from which it arose, the place of the creator in the organizational structure, or its relevance to a group, idea, or theme? What is the proper balance among the communities of interest in the archives—the creator, the archivist, the user, and the future generations? What ways are best suited to bringing consistency to processes through procedure(s) that allows ongoing reviews? How should decisions be audited and at what intervals in order to ensure that the appraisal of records continues to meet needs and responds to new conditions and new understandings? How can the choices that were made in the past be respected and protected in order to ensure that an archival history is itself multidimensional? How should the values of the market be applied to records and who is best suited to undertaking an appraisal based on the commercial values of archival materials (monetary appraisal)?

In the course of answering these questions, the archival use of the broad term appraisal has developed many facets in its application and in the reasoning associated with it. The theoretical justifications for appraisal, the procedural and structural supports recommended for the proper implementation of appraisal, and the institutional processes are accompanied by well-defined documentation for each and, for many repositories, by well-articulated policies governing appraisal for acquisition and selection. Archives are organic, not mechanistic: the development of all facets of the broad term appraisal underscores the continuing importance of core concepts of *authenticity*, preservation, quality evidence of acts, and actions. Appraisal for acquisition and selection reflects the continuing realignment of an archival repository with the needs of its host community and/or organization for clear historical sources that are embodied in an accumulating archives of records in all media.—*Barbara Craig*

Keywords: archival value, acquisition, selection, preservation, permanence, history of appraisal

Related Entries: Acquisition; Deaccessioning; Deposit; Documentary; Evidence; Primary Value; Reappraisal; Secondary Value; Selection; Transfer

Bibliography

Booms, Hans. "Überlieferungsbildung: Keeping Archives as a Social and Political Activity." *Archivaria* 1 (33) (1991): 25–33. http://journals.sfu.ca/archivar/index.php/archivaria/article/view/11796/12747.

Cook, Terry. "Macroappraisal in Theory and Practice: Origins, Characteristics, and Implementation in Canada, 1950–2000." *Archival Science* 5 (2–4) (2005): 101–61. DOI: 10.1007/s10502-005-9010-2.

———. "'We are what we keep; we keep what we are': Archival Appraisal Past, Present and Future." *Journal of the Society of Archivists* 32 (2) (2011): 173–89. DOI:10.1080/00379816.2011.619688.

Couture, Carol. "Archival Appraisal: A Status Report." *Archivaria* 1 (59) (2005): 83–107. http://

journals.sfu.ca/archivar/index.php/archivaria/article/view/12502/13624.

Craig, Barbara L. "Doing Archival Appraisal in Canada. Results from a Postal Survey of Practitioners' Experience, Practices, and Opinions." *Archivaria* 64 (2008): 1–45. http://journals.sfu.ca/archivar/index.php/archivaria/article/view/13145/14409.

Duranti, Luciana. "The Concept of Appraisal and Archival Theory." *American Archivist* 57 (2) (1994): 328–44. http://archivists.metapress.com/content/pu548273j5j1p816/fulltext.pdf.

Kolsrud, Ole. "The Evolution of Basic Appraisal Principles: Some Comparative Observations." *American Archivist* 55 (1) (1992): 26–39. http://archivists.metapress.com/content/v05w2k-g671667v6h/fulltext.pdf.

Procter, Margaret. "Life Before Jenkinson: The Development of British Archival Theory and Thought at the Turn of the Twentieth Century." *Archives* 119 (2008): 140–61.

Samuels, Helen Willa. "Who Controls the Past?" *American Archivist* 49 (2) (1986): 109–24. http://archivists.metapress.com/content/t76m-2130txw40746/fulltext.pdf.

Williams, C. "Studying Reality: The Application of Theory in an Aspect of UK Practice." *Archivaria* 62 (2006): 77–101. http://journals.sfu.ca/archivar/index.php/archivaria/article/view/12889/14120.

ARCHITECTURAL RECORDS

The term architectural records has come to indicate most forms of design records and is often used interchangeably. Design *records*, which is a more accurate term, are fundamental to understanding society and the world around us. The places and objects they create represent values and activities both literally and symbolically. The act of designing is social, economic, and artistic, and a wide range of researchers from numerous disciplines use the records created by these processes in an infinite variety of ways.

Design Records

Design records—architecture, landscape architecture, urban planning, and industrial design in context with those generated by related processes such as engineering and construction—are those created by individual designers and by architecture, landscape architecture, engineering, urban planning, industrial, commercial, and other design fields. They may comprise a unique "collection" or be contained within larger groupings of artists' works, business and technology records, and research and development records. There are also design records created or collected by governmental agencies, institutions, and corporations. It is important, if you collect these types of records, to understand how they integrate into your collection policy. Many design archives collect the process of design and limit the records generated by construction. Institutions that have the responsibility for maintaining their buildings and grounds may choose to retain the construction records as well as design records. Government archives often only have working drawings and construction records as the designer may retain the early design records.

Architectural or design records are technically *business records* created by an individual or firm engaged in the practice of design. Given the nature of this practice, they can be separated into two distinct categories: office records and project records. Office records contain administrative and marketing materials while project records contain all types of documentation generated by the design and construction process such as reports, correspondence, drawings, technical files, photographs, models, videotapes, and electronic records. Generally project records form the bulk of the records created by a design entity. Designers create numerous types of *documents* during the process of design for a variety of participants and purposes. They produce, for example, different types of drawings, documents, and increasingly models, at different stages in the design and construction process including those for other designers, clients, builders, engineers, gardeners, public presentations, and government agencies. To best understand the creation of architectural records, it is helpful to understand architectural/design practice. It is important to remember that not all design records should be considered permanent and most require substantial *appraisal*. Architectural records should not be confused with the *personal records* of architects/designers although there may be overlap. These will be addressed later in this entry.

Figure A.1.   Proposal for a resort on Alcatraz Island. *Ernest & Esther Born Collection. Environmental Design Archives, University of California, Berkeley*

Design records created by architects, landscape architects, interior and graphic designers, and practitioners of related fields include a range of consistent document types—drawings, visual materials, and files and formats/media including trace paper, mylar, prints, digital images, video, animation, and models. Most architectural records in the twenty-first century are generated using electronic formats (Lowell and Nelb 2006; Price 2010; Kissel and Vigneau 1999).

Office Records

Design practices create financial, personnel, client, and marketing records like other businesses. These records are important for documenting both the business practices of significant firms and the administrative units that support the design process. However, unique office records generated by design practices generally include project portfolios, award submittals, and patent records. There is also some

fluidity between office and project records. For example, completed project photographs and slides are often filed in the marketing division rather than with the project records. Similarly, because publication of a project is highly desirable for professional recognition and promotion, tear sheets or reprints (published articles or images from magazines that focus on a particular project by a designer or firm) will be maintained as a file set or placed in scrapbooks by an administrative unit.

Project Records

The project *file* is the overarching intellectual documentation unit for a design project. It will include records for all phases of the project, although different formats such as photographs, *textual records*, and drawings may or may not be physically stored together. The process of design has certain consistent players. In essence, the designer serves as the formative link between the needs of the client (design) and the technology of the builder or manufacturer (construction) (Shoskes 1989). Each player creates records individually and in relation to the other players.

There are consistent phases to the design and construction process regardless of whether the final product is a structure, a garden, a city, or a perfume bottle, and each of these phases results in the production of particular types and formats of documents. Time and technology have affected the need for more, or better, or different ways of representing the documents created by the processes of design and construction, but fundamentally they all have their proscribed context once this process is understood.

Traditionally, architectural project records captured needs and ideas in two-dimensional drawings and textual format that conveyed the instructions for creating a three-dimensional object. More recently, design records are being created in electronic media that can reverse the process of *records creation* and move from three-dimensional objects or digital images to the two-dimensional representations required for construction, or from electronic records to models.

However, the types and contents of the documents being created remain the same, in that they serve the same purposes in the life of a design project (Lowell 2006). An exception to this are those designs that are rhetorical in that they are never intended to be constructed, but are created in response to a theoretical or conceptual "discussion" or idea.

Architectural records represent four main stages in the process of imagining and completing a project. The first phase—planning and programming—begins with the need for an object or place (building, landscape, chair, etc.) and generates, for example, client correspondence, consulting reports, meeting notes, site plans, and some financial and legal records. The next phase—design—results in the bulk of architectural records such as sketches, an assortment of drawn representations (traditional and electronic), models, photographs, more client correspondence, consulting reports, and meeting notes. The construction phase, which generates the bulk of the material, converts the design into a place, space, or object and requires working drawings, technical documents, change orders, submittals, transmittals, financial records, consulting reports, meeting notes,

punch-lists, and annotated field sets (as-builts or record drawings) that serve as the final record of the project as completed. For related fields such as landscape, urban planning, or industrial design unique representations may be created such as planting plans, maps of infrastructure, or patents. The final phase is post-construction, which yields photographs, final drawings, and often public responses and publication. Some of these types of records may or may not be created for nonarchitectural design projects. For example, engineers may keep studies or records for the construction phase of a building project but are unlikely to generate design sketches, while industrial designers may generate numerous sketches, but not retain manufacturing documents in their project files.

Personal and Professional Papers

This refers to types of papers created by an individual designer rather than by the business process of the design profession. It is important to remember that design is a visual profession and designers are visual people. They are trained to hone visual and creative skills, which can be reflected in their personal papers. Common to designers are the drawings and other creative works created as part of their education. In addition, many architects travel extensively and record their travels through sketches and sketchbooks as well as photography. They often paint or otherwise create unique artwork that is distinctly different than designs created for clients or professional reasons (Shepherd 2000). Many designers like other professionals may also generate papers related to their involvement or membership in professional organizations, or teaching related to their field. These professional papers, like personal records, may be important for understanding designers and their work, but they are not crucial to the design and construction process represented in architectural records.

Conclusion

In conclusion, it is best to remember that design records come from a wide range of sources in a wider range of formats and media. Nonetheless, despite that many of them are graphic in content, they are records, not art, and should be managed with a knowledge of the process of their creation and intellectual content (not their format) and preserved based on their specific media.—*Waverly Lowell*

Keywords: medium, personal records, photographic record/archives, textual records

Related Entries: Personal Records; Photographic Records; Textual Records

Bibliography

Fallon, Kristine, and associates. *Collecting, Archiving, and Exhibiting Digital Design Data.* CD-ROM. Department of Architecture, Art Institute of Chicago, 2004.

Kissel, Eléonore, and Erin Vigneau. *Architectural Photoreproductions: A Manual for Identification and Care.* New Castle, DE: Oak Knoll Press, 1999.

Lowell, W. B., and T. R. Nelb. *Architectural Records: Managing Design and Construction Records.* Chicago: Society of American Archivists, 2006.

Mattix, Carla. *Legal Issues for Architectural Records.* Architectural Records Conference Report, held May 3–5, 2000. Conservation Center for Art and Historic Artifact, Philadelphia, 2001.

Price, Lois Olcott. *Line, Shade and Shadow: The Fabrication and Preservation of Architectural Drawings.* New Castle, DE: Oak Knoll Press, 2010.

Shepherd, Kelcy, and Waverly Lowell. *Standard Series for Architecture and Landscape Design Records: A Tool for the Arrangement and Description of Archival Collections.* Berkeley: Environmental Design Archives, 2000.

Shoskes. Ellen. *The Design Process: Case Studies in Project Development.* New York: Whitney Library, 1989.

ARCHIVAL ARRANGEMENT

Records are created and maintained as a by-product of the myriad *functions* and activities that people engage in as part of everyday life. Records are a way for people to convey facts and express ideas, to communicate and maintain relationships, to take control of their environment, and to document that work has been done. Records, in turn, can be used as *evidence*, as a way of understanding human experience, and of inferring what happened in the past. Evidence can be drawn from various *contexts* internal and external to the records: from the particular place and time in which the record creator existed and the records originated, from the functions and activities in which the record creator engaged and from which the records emanated, and from the *recordkeeping* systems that were built around these activities such that people could organize records for later use. Evidence can also be drawn from what people inscribed on the records themselves (the content). We gain knowledge about the past through interrogating the records as they existed within these networks of relationships. In relocating bodies of records into the *archives*, there is a danger that records will become decontextualized, losing any value as evidence. In attempting to mitigate this loss, *archivists* use the process of archival arrangement to document the contexts in which bodies of records were created and used.

The Concept

The work of archival arrangement is "essentially a process of identifying relationships" (Eastwood 2000, 93), and this is done by dealing with records collectively (grouping records and putting them in relation to each other). In the process of archival arrangement, archivists analyze the original provenancial, structural, functional, and documentary contexts that are both internal and external to a body of records, and represent these relationships in a formal, nested, hierarchical scheme. External contexts of the records are instantiated at the *record group* and subgroup level, while internal contexts of the records are instantiated at the *series*, subseries, and *file* level. This arrangement scheme, and the knowledge gleaned by archivists in the process, is then instantiated intellectually in written format as part of the *archival description* process, and instantiated physically through the movement and storage of the records within the group to mirror the intellectual arrangement.

The principles that now guide archival arrangement were solidified in the western world in the nineteenth century. Prior to this, rules of arrangement generally conformed to Enlightenment ideals of classifying all human knowledge in anticipation of future research needs. Following library practices, pertinence-based classification involved scrutinizing the content of archives and manuscripts at the item level in order to place records in subject-based *classification* schemes that formed the basis for various finding aids. With the emergence of the modern nation state, new theories and more efficient practices were needed to manage increasing volumes of current and noncurrent government records. This work began in France in the post-revolutionary period when a new system was put in place to arrange the records of administrative divisions, known as départements. The general principle used in carrying out this scheme, *respect des fonds*, was described in a circular issued by Natalis De Wailly of the French Ministry of the Interior in 1841. In a change to French practice, and one driven by expediency, records were to be treated as a whole, with the *provenance* of records to be preserved when transferred to the archives. Records were to be "maintained in the organic units or *fonds* in which they were originally accumulated," a fonds being defined as "all records of a particular institution, such as an administrative authority, a corporation, or a family" (Schellenberg 1951, 2). However, within the fonds, records generally continued to be reorganized into subject groupings, and within the subject groupings either alphabetically, chronologically, or geographically, according to the perceived needs of researchers (see Schellenberg 1939, 1–6).

Although the principle of *respect des fonds* was not immediately adopted in all French archival institutions, the notion of arranging bodies of records according to their origin did spread to other European countries. In the 1880s, staff of the Prussian state archives made the principle of *respect des fonds* more precise, such that the provenance (*provenienzprincipz*) of records, as well as the original *registry systems* in which they were organized (*registraturprinzip*), were used as the basis for organizing records. Therefore, while French archivists rearranged the records within the fonds according to content and perceived research needs, Prussian archivists maintained the records within the fonds in accordance with the working of the administration and the recordkeeping officials' original filing system (see Schellenberg 1939, 6–8).

In 1898, Dutch archivists Samuel Muller, Johan Feith, and Robert Fruin gave theoretical and practical justifications for the principles of provenance and original order in their manual of rules for archival arrangement and description, *Handleiding voor Het Ordenen en Beschrijven van Archieven* (*Manual for the Arrangement and Description of Archives*). From the authors' perspective, keeping the organic body of records and its underlying structure (the fixed series and dossiers around which the documents were originally organized) intact ensured that the purposes and activities of the administrative body could be fully understood and, from a practical standpoint, was seen as the one system that could be consistently applied. The translation of the Dutch manual into German (1905), Italian (1908), and French (1910) helped to cement these new ideas as part of European archival practice. In 1910, at the International Congress of Archivists and Librarians in Brussels, delegates from France, Netherlands, Germany, Russia, Austria-Hungary, Italy, Spain, Great Britain, Portugal, and the United States endorsed the principle of provenance as the best system for the arrangement and description of archives, "not only from the point of view of a logical classification of pieces but also in the best interest of historical study" (Wosh 2011, 145).

Archival Arrangement in the United States

At the turn of the twentieth century, the American archival profession was still in its infancy. Manuscript curators, historians, and archivists typically arranged records (both private manuscripts and public records) chronologically and grouped them into series, with large holdings often classified according to predetermined subject, chronologic-geographic, administrative, or historical schemes (see Schellenberg 1988, 36–41). However, the new European principles were discussed at meetings of the Public Archives Commission and at the American Historical Association's Annual Conference of Archivists. Through these fora, and in print, calls were made (including by archivists Arnold J. F. Van Laer and Waldo G. Leland, both of whom had been representatives at the international congress in 1910) to adopt the European principles as the basis for American classification work. Recognition of the European archival principles was further aided by the translation of the Dutch manual into English in 1940 by Arthur H. Leavitt, a staff member of the newly formed National Archives and Records Service (NARS).

By the early 1940s, the NARS had adopted the principle of provenance for the management of federal records, and the term arrangement replaced the term classification, to denote the work that archivists carried out to organize records. The National Archives also determined that the American equivalent of the fonds was the record group, a group that usually equated to the administrative unit at the bureau level of the federal government. Over the next several decades, Theodore Schellenberg further cemented these ideas about archival arrangement in a number of staff information circulars, and through publication of books on archival principles and techniques. In his later writings, he also helped contribute to the idea that the same principles used to manage large volumes of public records could also be applied to private papers and manuscripts (see Schellenberg 1988, 172–88).

The notion that archival arrangement involves "a breakdown of a whole into its parts" (Schellenberg 1988, 88) was most clearly delineated in a model put forth by National Archives staff member Oliver Wendell Holmes (1964). His model reinforced the notion that the principles of provenance and original order could be implemented through standardized levels of control, and in the creation of an order in and among these levels. These levels were articulated as a nested hierarchical model of depository, record group, subgroup, series, filing unit, and document. Arrangement at the record group and subgroup level was seen as the practical instantiation of the principle of *respect des fonds*, while arrangement at the series level and below was tied to the principle of original order. To Holmes, the process of grouping records in direct relation to each other, and storing these holdings in defined locations in an archive stack area, gave these levels a clear physical manifestation.

Conclusion

While the model that Holmes put forth is still in use today, our understanding of archival arrangement continues to evolve, as archivists refine the activities and principles on which arrangement is based. Particular aspects of arrangement that continue to be the subject of debate include (1) whether or not the principle of original order is applicable in all contexts, and (2) whether the principles of provenance and original order should continue to be implemented through hierarchical and standardized levels of control.

Schellenberg himself was something of a skeptic when it came to original order, warning archivists that "no archival principles should be 'ridden to death,' literally to become fetishes which will prevent a common-sense arrangement of records designed to promote the research needs of scholars and government officials" (1939, 18). Schellenberg's comments reflect an ever-present tension about the proper role of the archivist. The notion that the primary role of the archivist is to preserve the story of the creator has become the dominant paradigm over the last one hundred years. In this scenario, it is the duty of the archivist to preserve the evidentiary capacity of records, restoring the original filing system in order to reflect the records' original use. An ancillary viewpoint suggests that the job of the archivist may also involve actively shaping a body of records in order to meet the needs of the researcher. In this scenario, original order is no longer used, or is at least weakened, as archivists seek to reorganize records based on anticipated use of the materials, and where the informational value of records is privileged over their ability to serve as evidence.

The utility of original order as an organizing method for public records has also been questioned. Such skepticism arises from a belief that even well-organized recordkeeping systems may be illogical or fail to adequately serve official purposes (see Schellenberg 1996, 188–93). On the other hand, skepticism about the value of original order arises from the fact that government records and recordkeeping systems are said to be "infinitely more complex and disorganized" in some jurisdictions compared to others (Schellenberg 1939, 18). There has also been strong resistance to the application of the principle in managing *personal records*. In this scenario, archivists, including the writers of the Dutch manual, have questioned whether people are methodical in their personal recordkeeping and thus whether personal records have the same level of internal cohesion as public records. Lastly, the question has arisen as to whether the idea of original order is still valid when dealing with born digital material. Even locating where that order might reside is problematic when *digital records* exist as physical (things that are inscribed), logical (objects that can be recognized and processed by programs and software), and conceptual objects (objects as they are presented and viewed by the user) (Thibodeau 2002).

The final area of major contention centers on whether hierarchical and standardized levels of control do an adequate job of representing the complex network of provenancial and recordkeeping relationships. Fredric Miller is among those archivists who have criticized Holmes's mono-hierarchical model of arrangement, rejecting, for example, the notion that a body of records can have one and only one *creator*, or that record series naturally exist in a hierarchical relationship to each other. Miller's view of arrangement as two independent but interrelated systems—a duality of "arrangement by provenance/records creator and arrangement by filing structure" (Miller 1990, 61)—has now been implemented in access systems that draw upon archival authority control and context control in the form of the series system.

—*Ciaran Trace*

Keywords: provenance, original order, context, interrelatedness
Related Entries: Archival Bond; Archival Fond; Archival Theory; Archives; File; Principle of Pertinence; Principle of Provenance; Record Group; Respect des Fonds; Respect for Original Order; Series; Series System

Bibliography

Eastwood, Terry. "Putting the Parts of the Whole Together: Systematic Arrangement of Archives." *Archivaria* 50 (2000): 93–116. http://journals.sfu.ca/archivar/index.php/archivaria/article/view/12767/13959.

Holmes, Oliver Wendell. "Archival Arrangement—Five Different Operations at Five Different Levels." *American Archivist* (1964): 21–41. http://archivists.metapress.com/content/l721857l17617w15/fulltext.pdf.

Miller, Fredric M. *Arranging and Describing Archives and Manuscripts*. Chicago: Society of American Archivists, 1990.

Muller, Samuel, Johan Adriaan Feith, and R. Fruin. *Manual for the Arrangement and Description of Archives*, 2nd ed. trans. Arthur Leavitt. New York: H. W. Wilson, 1940.

Schellenberg, T. R. *European Archival Practices in Arranging Records*. Office of the Executive Officer, Staff Information Circulars, no. 5. Washington, DC: National Archives, July 1939.

———. *The Management of Archives*. Washington, DC: National Archives and Records Administration, 1988.

———. *Modern Archives: Principles and Techniques*. Chicago: Society of American Archivists, 1996.

———. *Principles of Arrangement*. Staff Information Papers, no. 18. Washington, DC: National Archives, June 1951.

Thibodeau, Kenneth. "Overview of Technological Approaches to Digital Preservation and Challenges in Coming Years." In Council on Library and Information Resources, *The State of Digital Preservation: An International Perspective*, pub. 107, 2002.

Wosh, Peter J. *Waldo Gifford Leland and the Origins of the American Archival Profession*. Chicago: Society of American Archivists, 2011.

ARCHIVAL ASSOCIATIONS

Archival Associations have been key players in the development of the archives and information management profession. For over 120 years, they have worked to grow the numbers and develop the professionalism of those engaged in the creation, identification, preservation and making available the *records* of the human experience. These associations have promoted the goals of the archival and information-management profession. They have been instrumental in developing standards and guidelines of professional practice, encouraging the development of archival education programs, providing educational and training activities and opportunities for those engaged in the archival enterprise, providing opportunities for students and newly hired, mentoring by experienced practitioners, advocating on behalf of professional issues and practices, engaging in public awareness activities, providing communication avenues for professional discussion and debate and providing means for scholarly and scientific publication, and others.

The Concept

Among the first archival association was Verenigang van Archivarissen in Nederland established in the Netherlands in 1891. This was followed in 1904 by the Association des Archivistes Français and in 1907 by the Association des Archivistes et Bibliothécaires Belges. The British Records Association was created in 1932 and the Society of American Archivists in 1934. There appear to be over 1,300 associations in 69 countries with approximately 1,000 in China alone. With so many associations it is impossible with any degree of certainty to determine the exact size of membership, let alone common patterns of structure, mandate, and scope. This is further complicated by the number of persons and institutions who hold memberships in more than one association. For example, a person could hold a membership in local, national, and international organizations as well as in related associations that combine several professional groupings such as records managers, librarians, and museum groups. For example, of 6,084 members of the Society of American Archivists, 231 have non–United States addresses with 101 of these having Canadian addresses. And there are media or institutional organizations such as those of audiovisual archivists, map archivists and librarians, municipal archivists, religious archivists, business archivists, labor archivists, and others. Many local (provincial and state) and regional (groupings of provincial or state) archival associations grew out of national associations in an effort to make services available in a more geographically cohesive and cost-effective manner, allowing them to embrace potential members with minimal professional archival qualifications.

Archival organizations have many origins. Some developed out of historical societies. Some developed out of library associations. Some came out of museum associations. Some came about as a consequence of the amalgamation of archival institutions and archivists or of allied professional groups bringing librarians, records managers, or museum curators together. This often came about as a consequence of geographical distances and relatively

small numbers making individual professional associations impractical and unsustainable from a financial or voluntary staffing perspective.

Most archival associations have some form of legal status. Many are incorporated under the laws of a nation, state, or province. This gives some level of financial security to executive members and enhances the fiduciary responsibility of the association. Some associations such as in South Korea are legally approved by their national archives and may be seen as an arm of that institution.

Membership categories in archival associations can often be complicated. However, there is typically a certain similarity. Memberships often combine individuals and institutions. The individual category is often subdivided into professionals or waged persons, students, retirees, and associates (usually including volunteers or others who are interested in supporting the objectives of the association). Institutional membership, if it exists, is often for those institutions with recognized formal archival programs or for those institutions that are in the process of establishing such programs.

Association income varies considerably. Income usually comes from membership dues, conference and educational and training opportunity fees, sponsorships, sales of publications, bequests, and grants. Membership fees vary from association to association with individual fees contributing much if not most of the revenues. Some associations charge a flat fee. Others have a graduated rate based on salary. For institutions, membership rates either are a flat sum or are based on the number of employees or size of their operating budgets. Many organizations derive the bulk of their income from conference and educational and training opportunity fees. Many encourage attendance by offering early registration, student, and retiree discounts. In addition, significant income is often derived from conference trade shows and sponsorships. While potential sales of professional monographs and other publications are often limited to individual professionals and libraries, associations that publish try to ensure that revenues from sales at least equal production and distribution costs. Many associations receive bequests from individuals or grants organizations, governments, or foundations to further the work of the association. These usually relate to specific association programs or the activities of a specific operating priority. Some associations have established foundations of their own, usually to provide student scholarships and bursaries.

Benefits of membership also vary considerably. Voting rights are often limited to professional members who pay full membership dues or, if institutionally based, such as the International Council on Archives, to their institutional membership. Members can participate in and, if qualified, can vote at the general membership meeting, which is usually held annually consequent to association bylaws and the requirements of legal incorporation. Members are entitled to receive the associations' publications such as professional journals and newsletters. They may receive reduced prices for association-published monograms, guides, and other publications. They may pay reduced or receive complimentary rates for conference fees and charges for association workshops, seminars, and similar education or training opportunities. Association websites often offer free advertising for employment opportunities. Associations offer members the opportunity to participate in an executive capacity on association governance, on professional committees, and in other capacities such as serving on publication editorial boards. Association conferences offer members opportunities to engage in professional and social networking, professional discussions, and debates as well as to provide input into association governance and budgeting.

Over time, archival associations have developed from a voluntary staffing model to a model that combines paid staff supported by volunteers. Volunteers are certainly involved in executive positions, typically including presidents, vice presidents, secretaries, and treasurers. Often volunteers run the publications process except the final stages of production. Volunteers also provide committee and other structural memberships and take leadership roles where associations have sections concerning professional practices (e.g., preservation and training), organizations (e.g., municipal and business archives), specific records (e.g., maps and audiovisual), and issues (e.g., human rights and freedom of information). With the growth of membership and increased income, more and more associations have one or more paid staff. Typically, such staff manage day-to-day operations, membership services, and conferences logistics and

coordinate specific initiatives in the areas of advocacy and public awareness, and relations with other organizations or associations.

Organizational structures are varied. While most are nationally based, some associations such as the International Council of Archives and the Association of Records Managers and Administrators International have branch or regional structures. Most associations are structured with an executive board (e.g., president, vice president, secretary, and treasurer), several governance committees (e.g., advocacy, public awareness, education, awards, publications, communications, finance, and bylaws), and groupings of members with common professional interests usually called sections (e.g., labor archives, media archives, human rights, and freedom of information). Some associations have a broader-based executive structure with an elected council (the Society of American Archivists) or a broadly representative executive board. For example, the International Council on Archives has an executive board composed of elected officers, the head of each section, and the head of each of its geographical branches. Presidents typically have significant roles as the chief spokesperson for the association. However, in some associations they are the first among equals with other members of the executive, council, or board. In others, presidents are seen as chief executive officers with hired staff playing the role of chief operating officer. The personalities of the incumbents often define the role of the office, especially where organizational constitutions or bylaws are less than specific.

Archival associations have goals and objectives common with most professional associations. Typically they are concerned with the development of professional standards or guidelines and best practices or with the endorsement of such standards and guidelines and their promotion of their membership to the general public. Archival education and training have always been a concern of professional associations, especially with the growth of the profession, the increased body of archival knowledge, and the explosion in the number of university and college-level archival studies programs. Response to this concern has varied from developing standards and guidelines to providing quality conference sessions, workshops, seminars (the latter often targeted for new hires or for upgrading existing qualifications), and institutes, to offering webinars and on-line discussions, and to developing mentorship programs that seek to bring together students and newly employed archivists with experienced practitioners for their mutual benefit.

Archivists have long been concerned with their role in society and society's appreciation of that role. While not trade unions or guilds, many associations have assumed an important role in advocacy. They have developed advocacy initiatives in the larger public arena (e.g., the encouragement of freedom-of-information and protection-of-privacy legislation and human rights records protection) and within specific institutions (e.g., the unauthorized and inappropriate destruction of records such as census records and the establishment of or increase in user fees in public archival institutions).

Archival associations are often engaged in what many believe is the partner of advocacy—public awareness. Initiatives are designed to increase public awareness of the essential roles archivists play in civil society. Such initiatives have ranged from the observance of local, national, and international archives days or weeks (such as the International Audio-Visual Archives Day); printed or web-based compendiums of information on archival institutions or archival functions; statements of archival ethics and codes of conduct; statements of such as the Universal Declaration on Archives (initially developed by the Association des archivistes du Québec, refined and promoted by the International Council on Archives and adopted by UNESCO); and the production of individual consumer products such as the publication and distribution of calendars using photographs from various archival institutions and the distribution of association luggage tags.

Archival associations offer a variety of member services. They promote member communication and networking. They hold conferences as legally required by the rules of incorporation. Occasionally, some archival associations hold their conferences concurrently or in conjunction with other archival, library, museum, or records management associations. They may publish newsletters in paper or electronic form with various degrees of regularity; manage list serves and websites for timely discussions, announcements, and job advertisements; manage social media accounts; publish peer-reviewed professional journals of archival theory, issues, and practice,

often with book reviews; and publish monographs and guides to archival theory and practice. These services help develop a professional community of interest. They enhance the value of the organization to its members. Member services ensure the ongoing relevancy of the association.

Conclusion

Archival associations have been instrumental in the historical development of the archival and information-management profession. They have provided the means through which archival educators and practitioners can interact. They have promoted the development of archival theory and practice. They have provided the milieu and the structure for professional and social networking among the diverse group of persons who consider themselves archivists. They have taken a leading role, sometimes on their own and sometimes with others, in advocacy and public awareness initiatives. While as local or national associations they are under no obligation to work with other archival associations, many have found that working under the umbrella of the Section of Professional Associations of the International Council on Archives has been beneficial. From the establishment of the first archival association in 1891 until today, the profession has grown in number and sophistication. So has the number and sophistication of archival associations. —*Bryan Eldon Corbett*

Keywords: professional associations, advocacy, education, public awareness, training
Related Entries: Advocacy; Outreach

Bibliography

There are no published references but conversations with various contacts. Sources of information for this entry are fourfold: the author's own experience at the local, national, and international levels with the Archives Society of Alberta, the Edmonton Chapter of the Association of Records Managers and Administrators (ARMA) International, the Association of Canadian Archivists, and the International Council of Archives; a survey of associations and councils (conducted by the author); the results of a survey of members of the Section of

Professional Associations (SPA) of the International Council on Archives; and an unpublished presentation "Au bonheur de la diversité: une introduction aux associations professionelles dans le monde" by Mr. Didier Grange, archiviste de la ville de Genève, presented to the annual conference of l'Association des archivistes du Québec in 2013 (soon to be published in the revue ARCHIVES. The later sources are available through SPA and from Mr. Grange. The author wishes to especially thank Mr. Fred Van Kan of SPA and Mr. Grange for making their information available and to thank Nancy Beaumont, Society of American Archivists, John Chambers of the Archives and Records Association, and Duncan Grant, Association of Canadian Archivists, and all others who participated in the survey.

ARCHIVAL BOND

An *archives* (or *archival fonds*) is constituted of two components: the *records* and their interrelationships (Lodolini 1998). The interrelationships among the records come into being when *documents* are first associated with other records of the same creator, that is, when each is added to an accumulation of records, filed, saved to a folder, classified, or all of the above. The arising of this connection, called "archival bond," transforms a document into a record, is determined by the nature, mandate, *function(s)*, and activities of their creator, and is represented by the physical or intellectual order (i.e., *classification*) of the records themselves.

The Concept

The term *archival bond* is a translation of the Italian term "vincolo archivistico," coined by Giorgio Cencetti (1939) to express the *interrelatedness* that characterizes all records (Jenkinson 1937) and elevate it to the status of key archival concept and foundation of the concept of archives. The archival bond is the network of relationships that each record has with the records belonging in the same aggregation. It is "originary," because it comes into existence when a record is created (i.e., made or received, and kept in connection with other records), "necessary" because it must exist for every record (i.e., a document unrelated to others is not a record),

and "determined," being qualified by the aggregation in which it belongs.

The archival bond first arises when a document is saved and linked to another in the course of activity, but it is incremental, in continuing formation and growth, until the aggregation in which the record belongs is no longer subject to expansion or change, that is, until the activity in which the aggregation of records participates is complete (Duranti 1997). Thus, the archival bond determines the identity of each record, because the relationships that a record has with other records contribute to its meaning as much as its content and form do: as a consequence, two identical documents existing in different records aggregations are two different records. In a paper system this may happen when multiple originals are sent to different offices or when several copies are kept in different files or cross-referenced (Duranti, Eastwood, and Mac-Neil 2002). In a digital recordkeeping system, one document may have several classification or identification codes associated with it as *metadata*: this means that such a document is as many different records as are the codes linked to it (Duranti and Thibodeau 2006).

As the archival bond expresses the development of the activity in which each record participates, because it contains within itself the direction of the cause-effect relationship of one record with another, it determines the structure of an archives, that is, its order. However, the archival bond is also very fragile. This is the reason why the arrangement of the records needs to be identified at the time of acquisition by an archival institution or program and frozen by archival description as soon as possible. Describing the records in their documentary context, that is, making explicit the archival bond, reveals, perpetuates, and authenticates the meaning of the records. In the digital environment, archival description constitutes the only possible collective authentication of an archives.

In addition to providing identity to the records in an archives, the archival bond is also evidence of the integrity of the archives itself, or lack thereof. This is why appraisal requires accurate documentation. The archival bond makes each record equally important to the existence of the whole, and the elimination of any record hurts the integrity of the archives. Any form of selection, at any level (e.g., *file*), alters the meaning of the remaining records, and thus it is best conducted at the highest levels of aggregation, where the archival bond is expressed in the classification schema or in a folder directory, and the relationships between aggregations would not be lost (e.g., *series*) (Duranti 1997). Although a gap in content would be inevitable, the meaning in context of the remaining records would remain intact.

Conclusion

The concept of archival bond was theorized in the twentieth century, but it has been implicitly respected since the beginning of the archival profession, when Baldassarre Bonifacio in 1632 first spoke about the meaning of the order of the records (Born 1941). While its importance was clear in traditional environments (from clay tablets to paper), it has become fundamental in the digital environment, because the relationship among records participating in the same activity is no longer self-evident from their physical position with respect to each other. Thus, the archival bond must be made explicit in digital recordkeeping and records preservation systems through records metadata identifying the aggregation(s) in which each record belongs and its cause-effect relationship to other records. This is the only way of establishing the authenticity (i.e., identity and integrity) of digital records and perpetuating their meaning (InterPARES 2005).—*Luciana Duranti*

Keywords: archives (material), records, documents, interrelatedness, documentary context
Related Entries: Archival Fonds; Archives (Material); Authenticity; Interrelatedness (Record); Record(s)

Bibliography

Born, Lester K. "Baldassarre Bonifacio and His Essay 'De Archivis.'" *The American Archivist* 4 (1941): 221–37. http://archivists.metapress.com/content/36u35457n6g45825/fulltext.pdf.

Cencetti, Giorgio. "Il fondamento teorico della dottrina archivistica." *Archivi II* 6 (1939): 7–13. Reprint in Giorgio Cencetti, *Scritti archivistici*. Roma: Il Centro di Ricerca editore, 1970, 38–46.

Duranti, Luciana. "The Archival Bond." *Archives and Museum Informatics* 11 (1997): 213–18. DOI: 10.1023/A:1009025127463.

Duranti, Luciana, and Kenneth Thibodeau. "The Concept of Record in Interactive, Experiential and Dynamic Environments: The View of InterPARES." *Archival Science* 6 (1) (2006): 13–68. DOI: 10.1007/s10502-006-9021-7.

Duranti, Luciana, Terry Eastwood, and Heather MacNeil. *Preservation of the Integrity of Electronic Records*. Dordrecht; Boston: Kluwer Academic, 2002, 11.

InterPARES, Authenticity Task Force. "Requirements for Assessing and Maintaining the Authenticity of Electronic Records." In Luciana Duranti, ed., *The Long-Term Preservation of Authentic Electronic Records: Findings of the InterPARES Project*. San Miniato, Italy: Archilab. www.interpares.org/book/interparesbookkapp02.pdf.

Jenkinson, Hilary. *A Manual of Archival Administration*. London: Percy, Lund, Humphries, & Co., 1937, 37–38.

Lodolini, Elio. *Archivistica. Principi e Problemi,* 8th edition. Milano, Italy: Franco Angeli, 1998, 186.

ARCHIVAL BUILDINGS AND FACILITIES

Archives, also referred to as archival buildings or archival facilities, house archives and special *collections*. These facilities provide the proper environment for storing and processing *records* and materials that require permanent protection and lifetime storage and *preservation*. Their first priority is to preserve the unique collections. Archival buildings also serve as the public face of the collections and offer spaces for staff and researchers to safely access the materials. They store a wide variety of media, including paper-based materials, maps, photographs, films, multimedia materials, and electronically formatted records. Archival materials require buildings to be constructed with specific building materials, environments, lighting, fire protection, security, and equipment. The appropriate site, structure, building systems, environmental and system controls, materials and finishes, equipment, and storage and functional spaces of an archival facility serve to protect the archival collections from deterioration, natural disasters, and theft. Ideally buildings should be planned for future collection and program growth.

Building Site

The proper building location can mitigate many of the dangers that threaten an archival facility, including flooding, natural disasters, fire, hazardous materials, and pollution. Strategic placement can be critical to the safety of the facility, its contents, staff, and visitors. A thoughtfully situated building also can aid in reduced energy consumption. Site selection for an archival facility must include careful review of its location, size, security, and access.

Building Construction

Archival construction, whether for new or renovated buildings, must balance the need to protect the archival collections with the requirements of the life safety codes. Archival construction must protect people but also must provide for a higher level of protection for the archival collections. Archival facilities must be constructed with noncombustible materials and incorporate fire protection systems and structural systems that avoid catastrophic failure due to uncontrolled fire, natural disaster, or industrial disaster. All major systems must be designed with long operating life expectancies. The construction must implement as many methods as possible to guard against water intrusions. All archival facilities must be fully accessible and comply with laws that apply to accessibility.

Archival Environments

The most important preservation measure for archival materials is to provide the best possible storage conditions. All archival records are subject to deterioration over time and are threatened by chemical, biological, and physical damage. Proper environmental conditions and controlled access to storage areas are necessary for the long-term care and protection of the collections. Environmental control systems minimize deterioration by controlling temperature, relative humidity, airborne particles, and gaseous contaminants in areas where records are stored.

Fire Protection

Fire is one of the most significant threats to archives. Facilities must provide protection against damage or loss from fire, combustion products, and fire-suppression actions. Critical fire-safety aspects of the facility must include: water supply to the building; fire detection, suppression, and alarm systems; properly rated construction, roof materials, and doors; compartmentalized building spaces to prevent migration of fire and smoke; appropriate furniture and finishes that have low flame-spread ratings. Records storage areas must have the highest fire-safety levels. All archives should be designated as smoke-free facilities.

Security

Archives must be rigorously protected against theft, burglary, vandalism, terrorism, unauthorized alteration, other criminal acts, and casual damage from inexpert or careless handling. Layers of security should start at the site's perimeter and include the building envelope, the building interior, and the collections. Security systems may include alarms, manual locks, electronic access controls, lighting, motion detectors, and surveillance equipment. In addition, security steps must be incorporated into basic archival functions and staff and researcher procedures.

Lighting

Most archival materials are highly sensitive to light exposure and can be quickly damaged through improper lighting. *Archivists* must take measures to protect the collections from the damage caused by excessive light levels, ultraviolet (UV) light, and infrared (IR) light. Archival lighting must strike a balance between three essential goals: economy, safety, and function. Minimum light exposure, lower lighting levels, less damaging lighting sources, and adequate ventilation and cooling will aid in minimizing light damage to archival collections. Other steps include curtailing exterior windows, avoiding skylights, and using UV protective filters on windows and lighting fixtures.

Materials and Finishes

In addition to the proper climate and filtration conditions, archival collections require storage environments that are constructed with materials and finishes that minimize the off-gassing of volatile organic compounds (VOC) and chemicals that can contaminate the air and degrade the records. Materials that contain biological contaminants or might invite mold must also be avoided in archives. Certain materials must be prohibited from archival storage areas because of their deleterious properties that are known to rapidly damage records. Prohibited materials include asbestos, cellulose nitrate, lacquers and adhesives, sulfur-containing materials, unstable chlorine polymers (PVC), and formaldehyde (for a complete list, see Pacifico and Wilsted 2009). All materials and finishes must meet the building life safety and fire codes and should be of the highest quality and durability. Off-gassing of harmful substances should be minimized in the areas where records are used, including processing areas, exhibit areas, laboratories, and research rooms. As much as possible, paints, sealants, caulks, wood products, foams, and other materials selected for archival facilities should have low or no VOC emissions.

Storage Equipment

A major challenge in archival facilities is the storage and protection of collections while still making them accessible to staff and researchers. A key component in this strategy is the records storage equipment, which includes shelving, cases, cabinets, racks, and other furniture. Storage equipment is a long-term investment, and care and planning are crucial in selecting appropriate products.

The choice of a shelving system depends on a number of factors, including space, budget, technical considerations, and the size and quantity of the collections. Archival shelving, most commonly steel, can be either static or mobile, with the latter having manual or electrically operated carriage systems. Materials and finishes, construction, performance, and configuration must all be considered when determining the specific equipment requirements of the archival facility.

Functional Spaces

Archival facilities balance collection preservation with the needs of staff and researcher access and use. This begins from the time the records arrive at the building through processing, *conservation* treatments, researcher use, and public display. The movement of records into and through the archival facility involves many different functional spaces; all must be considered in the overall plan to protect the collections. In addition to the storage areas, archival facility spaces may include a loading dock, conservation laboratories, reproduction and reformatting spaces, processing rooms, offices, and staff spaces such as lunchrooms and locker rooms. Public spaces may include a lobby, research rooms, classrooms, exhibit galleries, and food service areas. Some of these spaces, like loading docks, processing rooms, and labs, address the records directly. Others, such as the lunchroom and restrooms, support the staff and visitors. Careful planning will divide the archives between spaces open to the public and those solely accessible to staff to ensure good collection security and increased functionality.

Conclusion

All archival buildings should meet the same basic requirements: preserve the collections with safe and secure storage; protect them against fire, water, excessive environmental conditions, insects, burglars, and other threats; provide appropriate work spaces for staff to process and conserve the collections; and offer public areas for patrons to review and learn about the collections.—*Michele F. Pacifico*

Keywords: preservation, storage, systems, environment
Related Entries: Archives; Conservation

Bibliography

Pacifico, M., and T. Wilsted. *Archival and Special Collection Facilities.* Chicago: Society of American Archivists Press, 2009.
Wilsted, Thomas P. *Planning New and Remodeled Archival Facilities*. Chicago: Society of American Archivists Press, 2006.

ARCHIVAL COLLECTION
(INCLUDES THE VERB *TO COLLECT*)

An archival collection has several synonyms: manuscript collection, *personal records* or papers, organizational records, private *fonds* (Canada), and mixed collection (primarily Canada). The term usually refers to an organic set of *documents* (that is, with a unified *provenance*) and/or *records* created by a private entity—whether individual, family, organization, or business—and acquired (collected) by a repository not legally conjoined to the *creator*:

> If, however, the curator has developed a plan of collecting with a sound historical basis, his richest material consists of bodies of organic papers of persons or families, organizations, or institutions, in their original order of arrangement, as the hypothetical archivist of any one of them would have preserved them. If they are transferred to a research library in what is obviously their original state, the curator's first guiding principle dictates that they be preserved in that system. Whatever modification he imposes after careful examination should not in substance violate this archival dictum. (Cappon 1956, 103)

That is, archivists are foresworn to respect the twin principles of *respect des fonds* (or provenance) and *original order*, just as they would if working with a *record group* within an institutional *archives*.

More recently, however, the postmodern view of archives offers a different, perhaps more nuanced, way of apprehending the traditional *collection*:

> Archivists need to acknowledge the fact that the archives left in front of us . . . are only fragments of a larger story, part of a journey. Our job is to tell as much of that story as possible. To that end . . . we draw on the archaeological and artistic interpretations of provenance to expand our own definition, so that the concept encompasses not just the creation of the records but also their history over time and our role in their management. The question we need to ask is not "how did the records come to be?" The question, rather, is "how did *these* records come to be *here*?" (Millar 2002, 12)

How these records came to be here is, at the simplest, the result of the act of collecting.

To collect by a repository is a verb encompassing several discreet actions: selection, fieldwork, *appraisal*, *donation*, accession. Selection and appraisal are often considered synonyms, but can instead be considered as, the former, the act of identifying *creators* whose collections a repository might wish to acquire and, the latter, the act of determining which portions of each total collection should be preserved by the repository. Canadian appraisal theorist Terry Cook distinguished the two functions by specifying that appraisal of records is the last step, after assessing the importance and functions of records creators (Cook 1992).

Fieldwork, or donor relations, is the sometimes-quite-extended and -extensive process of establishing connections with prospective donors, introducing one's repository (including its mission and collections already in hand that are relevant to the prospective donor), answering questions, often meeting with the prospective donor, preparing and discussing a deed of gift, ensuring signature of the deed, appraisal, and *transfer* of the records. It may take as long as fifty years from the time a prospective donor is first contacted to the date he/she/it agrees to donate material. Sometimes meetings with donors are to appraise the records—it can be beneficial to have the donor's insight into the provenance and significance of material, though sometimes donors merely wish to reminisce about every item's importance (Lee 2011). It is important to note here that *archivists* and curators must often be both delicate and highly ethical in approaching and working with grieving spouses or children about papers of the deceased.

Donation is the documented process of the creator or owner of a collection transferring legal *custody* of the physical material (and sometimes also the copyrights to those materials in the collection that are owned by the creator) to the repository. Donation is documented by a deed of gift.

> In legal terms, a gift means that title to the property passes from the giver to the recipient, i.e., from the donor to the archives. . . . All transfers of personal property to an archives should be documented in a clear, unambiguous fashion. As archival materials have both a physical and an intellectual component (i.e., a medium and a message), it is important that the transfer document record the disposition of both the physical and the intellectual property. (Huskamp Peterson 1979, 61–62)

Accessioning is the process by which the repository internally documents the acquisition of a collection. In recent years, as an extension of so-called "minimal processing," accessioning has taken on new importance. "Accessioning as processing is now the goal. . . . During the accessioning process, whenever possible, we arrange and describe the materials, including the creation of the finding aid, so that they are ready for research use and never enter our backlog." (Weideman 2006, 276)

Archival Collection

Note that an archival collection is not to be confused with an artificial collection, which is a set of individual items with separate provenance brought together by a collector around a theme. A repository may collect or even create artificial collections, but they are generally a very small part of what an archives is concerned with.

The concept of an organic collection has been relatively unexplored in the archival literature, which has been heavily dominated by authors from institutional archives rather than collecting repositories. Many of the references are of this sort: "The . . . level . . . of the collection, is the level on which *respect des fonds* applies. The collection level for personal papers is the same as the record group level for archival records." On the other hand, "the sanctity of original order" may not be applicable to a manuscript collection because "not all original order is rational, nor are all people who create or collect papers orderly" (Desnoyers 1991, 87).

Though pragmatically acceptable, such definitions are missing more thoughtful distinctions between collections and record groups, the complex discussions of *series*—not record groups—as potential normative organizing levels of both groups and collections, the influence of the postmodern turn on the conception of provenance, and the perspective of a growing multiplicity of "community archives." In addition there remains debate about whether the digital age imposes particular shifts in the perception of collections as well as the process of collecting.

For example, postmodern conceptions affect "the basis of the principle of provenance which changes it from being 'defined by stable offices and roles to one of dynamic process-bound information.' By broadening the notion of provenance so that it en-

compasses a society dimension the complex identities and multifaceted interactions which go towards its formation are highlighted." Similarly "rather than working on the idea that when an archive comes into a repository its order represents its original state 'we should speak of the received order of the records'" (Hill 2011, 12).

This reconfiguring of centuries-old principles gains further momentum because they are directly reflective of our users' apprehension of archival collections: "The user may well have no interest in the context of a document except as it relates to the subject of their own research, their focus being simply the meaning which it has for them in relation to other sources they have found" (Hill 2011). This potential tension between users' decontextualization and archivists' commitment to provenance and original order can be mitigated with searchable online finding aids, though not necessarily with the traditional construction and representation of those finding aids.

There is an interesting parallel between the undermining of organic collections by users interested in isolated items and the activities and values of so-called "community archives." These are often very small agencies engaged in rescuing the traces of marginalized groups: "When seeking to record grassroots organization . . . the only surviving material traces of these activities may be slight and ephemeral. . . . The fact that something may be isolated and not part of a larger surviving documentary accumulation should not undermine its archival significance" (Hill 2011, 158). In such repositories a collection may have little or no organic interrelationships and still be prized by the archivists and researchers.

To Collect

Collecting should be defined and driven by an *acquisition policy* rather than occurring haphazardly or serendipitously. It follows logically that "to collect" should be viewed as an active rather than passive verb; that is, collecting should take place by soliciting donations rather than simply receiving what might be offered. The process by which the goals of an acquisition policy are translated into actual collections, the actual incarnation of the verb to collect, is the process of fieldwork or donor relations.

"A well-organized solicitation of potential donors enables repositories to acquire collections whose contents support their collecting focus" (Bradsher 1991).

An archivist, having identified a possible donor based on the priorities and delimiters of a collecting mandate, must then make contact with the individual or organization (and if an organization it is important to choose which administrator or leader to contact). Despite the variety of introduction media available today, the use of surface mail and repository letterhead may still be the medium of choice for a first contact, conveying as it does the substantiality and professionalism of the institution. Follow-ups using other methods then may make good sense.

The continuation of fieldwork entails what fundraisers term cultivation: to engage and maintain the interest and involvement of a donor or prospective donor with an organization's people, programs, and plans. It may take months, years, or decades of cultivation before a donor is ready to part with his/her/its papers. This may be for several reasons; e.g., too close to the time of a loved-one's passing or feeling overwhelmed by the quantity of materials. Cultivation is meant to mitigate these concerns and bring donation to fruition.

After a deed of gift is signed, the next step is often physical transfer of the collection to the repository. During this activity field archivists may truly get their hands dirty—for example, retrieving partially rotted wooden record crates from a collapsing barn, hauling sixty boxes up a narrow winding staircase in a church, or tipping over a thousand boxes down off high shelves only to dislodge a century's worth of coal dust and dirt. Or this work may take place in a pleasant living room, with time for lemon bars and tea, where the donor may or may not recount the entire history of his/her family or the sentimental value of every item; more fortunately the donor may restrict his/her remarks to providing provenance and significance for major files.

Then follows "stewardship," or maintaining the relationship with the donor beyond the point of transferring materials. Sometimes stewardship will last only through sending the donor a copy of the finding aid, but in other situations, particularly where the repository hopes for continuing accretions of records from the individual or organization, stewardship may

endure decades. Such long-term relationships are difficult for most repositories to successfully implement, because the immediacy of responding to newer donors often takes precedence over continued work with existing—usually more passive—donors.

This predilection to address the donor knocking at the door, rather than the several whose earlier papers are already in the repository, often results in holdings of partial documentation, such as where there is now a gap of three decades between the first donation and the present. Those three decades of records are at risk of being destroyed (because no one in the organization remembers that "old" records were of interest to anyone) or even donated to another repository (out of forgetfulness that the earlier records were somewhere else).

Conclusion

The definition of a collection may be changing as a result of the digital and postmodern ages, though the principles of provenance and received (perhaps not original) order seem largely to remain important (though not inviolable). One inescapable characteristic of a collection is that it is collected—acquired by a repository not legally mandated to preserve it and make it accessible. The steps of selection, cultivation, fieldwork, appraisal, deed of gift, transfer, accessioning, and stewardship are themselves resilient in the face of born-digital collections, though the methods of some steps are changing.

For example, some archivists argue that it is essential to cultivate prospective donors even earlier in their careers so that curators can advise them on how to preserve and organize/identify their born-digital collections. As of yet, however, there has been little written about how a repository can gracefully renege on a solicitation of personal papers if the prospective donation evolves to being less or different than imagined when the selection was made. Saying "no" when approached by a willing donor has been difficult enough for most archivists to do; explaining no after already saying yes will be that much harder!

—*Mark Greene*

Keywords: papers, manuscript collection, mixed collection, accessioning, deeds of gift

Related Entries: Acquisition Policy; Appraisal; Archival Fonds; Donation; Manuscript Tradition;

Personal Records; Private Archives; Selection; Series; Total Archives

Bibliography

Cappon, Lester J. "Historical Manuscripts as Archives: Some Definitions and Their Application." *American Archivist* 19 (1956): 101–10. http://archivists.metapress.com/content/4402r63w3t257gv8/fulltext.pdf.

Cook, Terry. "Mind over Matter: Towards a New Theory of Archival Appraisal." In Barbara L. Craig, ed., *The Archival Imagination: Essays in Honour of Hugh A. Taylor*. Ottawa: Association of Canadian Archivists, 1992, 38–70.

Desnoyers, Megan Floyd. "Personal Papers." In James Gregory Bradsher, ed., *Managing Archives and Archival Institutions*. Chicago: University of Chicago Press, 1991, 78–91.

Hill, Jennie, ed. *The Future of Archives and Recordkeeping: A Reader.* London: Facet Publishing, 2011.

Huskamp Peterson, Trudy. "The Gift and the Deed." *American Archivist* 42 (1) (1979): 61–66. http://archivists.metapress.com/content/w564608441652jun/fulltext.pdf.

Lee, Christopher, ed. *I, Digital: Personal Collections in the Digital Era.* Chicago: Society of American Archivists, 2011.

Millar, Laura. "The Death of the Fonds and the Resurrection of Provenance: Archival Context in Space and Time." *Archivaria* 53 (2002): 1–15. http://journals.sfu.ca/archivar/index.php/archivaria/article/view/12833/14048.

Weideman, Christine. "Accessioning as Processing." *American Archivist* 69 (2) (2006): 274–83. http://archivists.metapress.com/content/g270566u745j3815/fulltext.pdf.

ARCHIVAL CUSTODY

Archival custody is the safe keeping by an *archives* of the *records* entrusted to its care. Archival custody has a physical dimension, which requires physical possession, ownership, and control of records in order that they might be protected against alteration, destruction, or theft. Archival custody also has a legal dimension, in the sense of archives being the legitimate and legally appointed guardians of records. The *preservation* of records in archival custody is essential in terms of ensuring and maintaining the *integrity* and *authenticity* of archival records.

Origins of the Custodial Function

The earliest reference to records being in archival custody is from *Against Ctesiphon* (330 BCE). The idea that records were afforded protection in the public archives of ancient Greece was well established by this point. It can be traced back to earlier practice in the ancient world of storing records in temples so that they might receive divine protection. The Metroön, the central archives of the city-state of Athens, was, not coincidentally, the temple to the "Mother of the Gods." Storing the public records of the state, as well as the private records of its citizens, in religious sites made sense simply for reasons of their physical safe keeping. But by the Classical period, the protection afforded by archival custody was understood to imply more than merely preservation against destruction; it was also preferred so that documents would remain unaltered. That is, a record's integrity came to be associated with its preservation in the public archives. This is evident in the legislation of the period. In 330 BCE, Lycurgus recommended the death penalty for anyone who altered a record in the Metroön, while another law was issued that forbade the bringing of false documents into the Metroön. This suggests that the place of preservation had already come to be associated with the perceived authenticity of a record. That is, a false record produced from the Metroön was more likely to be believed than one produced privately— its evidential value as a record had been increased.

This function of public archives—of attesting to the authenticity of the records they held—became more prominent during the Hellenistic period. Public archives began increasingly to accept, register, and validate records of private transactions, including those pertaining to business, property, status, and other acquired rights. While registration of certain types of private records appears to have been compulsory, for others voluntary registration within the public domain acted to increase the record's validity. Being valid meant that the record was considered effective; a registered record was more likely to be able to produce the desired result.

It had greater weight than an unregistered record. A registered record was better able to stand for the facts to which it attested; its *reliability* as a record had been increased. Hellenistic Greek archives thus took on a new role, becoming not just repositories of official records but bodies that could officially validate records of private transactions.

Roman archival practice borrowed heavily from Greece and, as with Greek practice, Roman archives fulfilled a similar authenticating role. The Justinian Code defines archives as "the public place where deeds are deposited so that they remain uncorrupted, provide trustworthy evidence, and be continuing memory of that to which they attest." Records were consulted by Romans because of their ability to perpetuate the memory of past acts—their ability to function as "perpetual memory." They were able to do this because filing and preserving records in the public archives was considered to grant the records "public faith." Once records had been deposited in an archives—once they had crossed "the archival threshold"—and were physically preserved among the other records of the state, the records were afforded an authentic character. It was literally this act of deposition within the archives that endowed the record with "public faith," and it was this that enabled records to function as legal proof. While filing was a procedural requirement for all acts in order to make them effective, Roman officials were not above making false documents for a price. In Plutarch's *Life of Cato the Younger*, the author recounts a story of how Cato had been reluctant to file a decree that some claimed to have passed the Senate. Cato insisted that the consuls swear an oath as to its validity before he would agree to send it for preservation in the *Aerarium*. The insistence was presumably made because Cato was aware that once the record was accepted into the repository, its authenticity would no longer be in doubt. In this, Cato understands that transferring the record to its place of custody is not merely a movement from one place to another; it is an action that allows the record to function as evidence and continuing memory of action.

Custody and the Authenticating Function

In both ancient Greece and Rome, it is, therefore, evident that authenticity was not a characteristic of *documents* themselves but was afforded to them by virtue of their preservation within archival custody. That this practice left archives open to abuse is also obvious. Private persons could deposit false records in the public archives in order to lend these records greater reliability. The solution to the problem lay in the elaboration of strict procedures of documentary form; measures that could ensure the authenticity of the document itself.

Despite this new emphasis on documentary form, archives did not lose their former role. The Roman law, which was inherited by much of Western society, continued to define archives as physical places of deposit, under a public authority, where records are provided with authenticity and trustworthiness so that they may act as evidence and continuing memory of action. This remained the case, even when public archival repositories began to disappear in the fifth and sixth centuries CE. During this period, the custodial function of public archives came to be replaced with the preservation of records by discrete bodies: the Church, the palace chapel, the city, the university. In each of these cases, establishing the authenticity of a record certainly relied on interrogating elements of its documentary form, or even of elements extrinsic to the document—such as the remembrances of witnesses to the event recorded. But the ability to confer authority to documents, to endow them with authenticity—what is termed the "archival right"—was in time also acquired by these various administrative institutions. The palace chapel and the iron chest continued to carry on the core custodial functions of safeguarding records against loss, alteration, or destruction.

As written records began to be created and relied on with greater frequency from the twelfth and thirteenth centuries onward, so too they began to accumulate again in some numbers. During the early modern period, the emerging nation states began to establish new archives of concentration. Their purposes were twofold: to protect records in secure locations and to concentrate together in one place the key records required in order to administer the state. Jurists of the period also understood the authenticating function that archival custody continued to provide. In the seventeenth century, Ahasver Fritsch enumerated the following requirements necessary for an archives to maintain authentic records: the archives had to belong to a public sovereign authority, its records had to be deposited by a public official, those records had to be physically and intellectually ordered with other like records, and this placement was to be permanent. Like other writers of the time, Fritsch understood that the central purpose of the archives was to keep and protect the documentary residue of actions so that they could continue to function as trustworthy evidence.

Custody in the Modern Era: Lost and Found

This view of archives was overturned as a result of the French Revolution. The notion that records functioned as *evidence* of the past was certainly well understood; hence the creation of a new national repository to house the records of the former regime. Though these records had lost their legal validity, their continued *preservation* for purposes of historical instruction was quickly recognized. What changed with the Revolutionary period, however, was the differentiation that arose between records of the old regime and those of the new. While "old" records were transferred to the National Archives, those of the new order remained largely with their creating agencies. It was these agencies, rather than a central state archives, that assumed responsibility for the management of their records. Only when time had transformed the records into historical source material would the question of their transfer to the archives arise. This new differentiation, between "archives" (i.e., old records) and "administrative archives" (i.e., active and semi-active records), obscured the authenticating function that archives had once performed.

As a result of this historical repurposing of archives, the authenticating function of archival custody had to be rediscovered, largely through the elaboration of archival theory. In England, which had escaped the administrative effects of the Revolution, this connection was not lost, and the authenticating function of archival custody remained fundamental to archival management. Jenkinson argued that the preservation of an impartial record was the main reason why material passed into archival custody and the primary role of the archivist was to ensure the integrity of the record—through their physical and moral defense. This role could not be filled by the original *creators* of the record once the record no longer served the purposes for

which it had been created. At this point, the record is at risk of alteration; the creator no longer relies on the record, yet they continue to remain accountable through the record. Such records must be transferred to the *archivist*—Jenkinson's *trusted custodian*—where they can be preserved disinterestedly and for more general purposes. This is also why Jenkinson insisted on an uninterrupted chain of custody from creator to archives as an essential element in ensuring a record's authenticity.

Given the orphaned status of many of the records that came to the National Archives in the United States, T. R. Schellenberg rejected Jenkinson's notion that continuous custody was an essential element in determining records' evidentiary value. However, Schellenberg agreed that taking physical custody over records was essential if archives were to preserve their integrity. The ability to safeguard the integrity of a record remained dependent on records first crossing the archival threshold.

The Post-Custodial Challenge

By the mid-twentieth century there was widespread theoretical agreement on the role that archival custody played not only in terms of the physical preservation of records but also in terms of maintaining the integrity of records and in enabling attestations of authenticity to be made with respect to records in archival custody. This view, however, would come to be challenged as archivists began to consider the implications of digital recordkeeping. Influenced by the ideas of David Bearman, archival theorists began to argue for a new post-custodial paradigm for archives, one in which archivists no longer physically acquired and maintained records but rather provided oversight for records that remained with their creators. Rather than managing a single, centralized repository, archivists would engage with multiple creators in order to influence the records' creation process and guide their management. Surrendering physical custody, archivists would allow the records' creators themselves to manage the records that they had created and used.

Conclusion

Despite the post-custodial challenge, accepting records into archival custody remains a core function of archives. More than taking physical control over records, custody is also an act that attests to records' authenticity. Furthermore, it is the moment at which the archives accepts the responsibility for preserving records' authenticity into the future. Records cannot be secured from alteration—intentional or otherwise—if they remain with their creator. It is not in the creator's interests to preserve unaltered records that have outgrown their administrative usefulness. Indeed, there may be pressures to distort records through which creators can be held to account. By taking custody over records, the archives fulfills its role of providing physical security and for ensuring the integrity and authenticity of archival records.

—*Reto Tschan*

Keywords: custody, authenticity, preservation
Related Entries: Archival Preservation; Authenticity; Chain of Preservation; Trusted Custodian

Bibliography

Clanchy, M. T. *From Memory to Written Record: England 1066–1307*, 3rd edition. Hoboken, NJ: Wiley-Blackwell, 2013.

Cook, Terry. "Electronic Records, Paper Minds: The Revolution in Information Management and Archives in the Post/Custodial and Post/Modernist Era." *Archives and Manuscripts* 22 (2) (1994): 300-328. http://search.informit.com.au/document Summary;dn=950302854;res=IELAPA.

Culham, Phyllis. "Archives and Alternatives in Republican Rome." *Classical Philology* 84 (2) (1989): 100–115. www.jstor.org/stable/270265.

Duranti, Luciana. "Archives as a Place." *Archives and Manuscripts* 24 (2) (1995). http://search.informit.com.au/documentSummary;dn=97050540 4;res=IELAPA.

Henry, Linda J. "Schellenberg in Cyberspace." *American Archivist* 61 (2) (1998): 309–27. http://archivists.metapress.com/content/f493110467x38701/fulltext.pdf.

Jenkinson, Hilary. *Manual of Archive Administration*, 2nd edition. Oxford: Clarendon Press, 1937.

Schellenberg, Theodore R. *Modern Archives: Principles and Techniques*. Chicago: University of Chicago Press, 1956.

Sickinger, James P. *Public Records and Archives in Classical Athens*. Chapel Hill: University of North Carolina, 1999.

ARCHIVAL DEPOSIT

A deposit agreement is a statement of intent to transfer title to the materials at some (usually unspecified) date. In the meantime, the donor deposits the physical property with the *archives* for safekeeping. Most archives try to avoid deposit arrangements unless the *collection* has great value and there is no other way to guarantee its *preservation*.

The Concept

The National Archives in its 1984 *A Modern Archives Reader: Basic Readings on Archival Theory and Practice* emphasizes the fact the legal title to the materials is retained by the donor. A similar definition is provided in the Internal Records Management Trust's Glossary of Terms published in 2009, where the focus is on *records* and in additional notes that the term "deposit" also refers to the records included in any one such placement.

A disadvantage of deposits is that the chance always exists that the *archives* will use its resources to process the collection, only to have the *creator* change his/her mind and demand the return of the items. There are some indications that fewer institutions are using deposits because of the possibility that the materials might be removed and given to another institution. In his article that appeared in the *American Archivist* spring issue in 1993, Ronald Becker describes the perils that Rutgers University encountered when it accepted the archives of the *Partisan Review* as a deposit, performed archival processing on these materials, and then, when the relationship between the literary journal and the state university changed, had to send the archives to Boston University.

A new form of deposit is actively encouraged by the National Archives and Records Administration (NARA) with electronic files. Called pre-accessioning, the NARA encourages federal agencies to transfer to the NARA a copy of permanently valuable records while retaining legal *custody* and control over *access* to the records. The NARA will process and preserve these records and maintain physical custody until the time at which the records are scheduled to be transferred into the NARA's legal custody. Agencies will keep their duplicate copy of the records and retain responsibility for responding to discovery efforts, Freedom of Information Act requests, or reference inquiries until legal custody of the records is transferred to the NARA.

Conclusion

Deposits are often reviewed as a means to begin a relationship with a donor that will hopefully lead to formal *transfers*. This is often used when archival repositories are beginning to move in new directions with their collections. Deposits are beginning to reappear with digital materials as more institutions recognize the need to acquire digital collections.

—*Fynnette Eaton*

Keywords: deposit, deposit agreement, transfer, pre-accessioning
Related Entries: Acquisition; Donation

Bibliography

Becker, Ronald L. "On Deposit: A Handshake and a Lawsuit." *American Archivist* 56 (1993): 320–28. http://archivists.metapress.com/content/f3v10656540j3060/fulltext.pdf.

Daniels, Maygene. *A Modern Archives Reader: Basic Readings on Archival Theory and Practice.* Washington, DC: National Archives and Records Service, 1984.

Hunter, Gregory S. *Developing and Maintaining Practical Archives. A How-To-Do-It Manual,* 2nd edition. New York: Neal-Schuman, 2003.

Millar, Laura; Ed. *Training in Electronic Records Management. Glossary of Terms.* London: International Records Management Trust, 2009. www.archives.gov/records-mgmt/initiatives/pre-accessioning.html.

ARCHIVAL DESCRIPTION

Definitions of *archival description* are as numerous as discussions of archival practice in general, for the one is an integral part of the other. In their classic 1898 discussion of practice, Muller, Feith, and Fruin simply equated description with the preparation of a summary overview of (or guide to) a well-arranged body of *records*. Archival experience during the following century has led to a much fuller understanding of the concept. An Ad Hoc Commission on Descriptive Standards, sponsored by the International Council on Archives, captured this broader sense in a 1994 definition that serves well to introduce this entry: "Archival description. The creation of an accurate representation of a unit of description and its component parts, if any, by the process of capturing, collating, analyzing, and organizing any information that serves to identify archival material and explain the context and records systems which produced it." In the minds of some, the power of web searching and browsing calls into question the need for and value of archival description. But as long as the record (as opposed to mere information) has a role to play in human activity, the collection and *preservation* of data that establishes its identity and *integrity* (and the clear presentation of this data) remains an essential part of archival responsibility.

Description Defined

In Muller, Feith, and Fruin's day, the work of description began after archival material had settled comfortably in an institution devoted to its protection. Good archival practice called for examination of a cohesive body of records, an archival *series*, to discover the reason for its accumulation and the nature of its composition. This focus on the whole of a body of records rather than each component *document*—emphasis on collectivity rather than individuality—was then and remains now the fundamental characteristic of archival description. When they describe, *archivists* are capturing, collating, analyzing, and organizing information about a whole *recordkeeping system*.

In today's world, the best descriptive work begins long before the records of interest enter archival *custody*. Critical information about modern *recordkeeping* processes, particularly when these processes involve electronic devices, may only be available while the *records* are still active. Ideally, archivists (or their designees) capture and preserve useful contextual and technical information at the moment the permanent value of a system of records has been recognized.

Capture and preservation of information about the why and how of recordkeeping is important because this information enables uninvolved but interested parties to rely on and benefit from the kept records. Indeed, it is these uninvolved, but interested, parties who form the expected audience for the description associated with archival records. Much of the discussion of description in the archival literature over the years has focused on the means of reaching this audience. What do they need to know? What do they want to know? How do they want to know it?

Authors responding to these questions a century ago advocated production of booklike, published guides to the holdings of an archival repository. Such guides, it was thought, should clearly distinguish the individual recordkeeping systems in the archives and convey basic identifying information about each system. For records of an organization, basic information consisted of:

- the name of the entity responsible for establishing and using the recordkeeping system;
- the name of the recordkeeping system;
- the dates of accumulation of the records in the system;
- the form of the documents constituting the system; and
- a brief account of the transactions documented by the system.

Archivists early recognized that the size or importance of the accumulated records of an organization might warrant descriptive attention beyond entry in a general repository guide. This recognition led to recommendations for the preparation of what has become the descriptive product most associated with archival practice: the *inventory*. This product has played such an important role in archival work—for both archivists and users of archives—that it is the focus of a separate encyclopedia entry. Suffice it to say generally here that the exemplary inventory:

- presents information about a single *fonds*, that is, a set of records in an archives that share a common *provenance*;
- organizes the information in a manner that reflects (to the extent possible) the organization of the recordkeeping entity responsible for accumulating the fonds;

- provides the recordkeeping context for each recordkeeping system (or series) and, in discussing each system, emphasizes the whole rather than individual documents; and
- proceeds from the general to the specific, avoiding repetition of descriptive information.

While continuing to rely on the inventory as the primary means of delivering descriptive information, archivists have developed other descriptive tools (or finding aids) intended to meet the needs of researchers. In their published paper form, the two most familiar of these tools are known as calendars and subject guides. In the archival context, a calendar lists individual documents, usually in chronological order, and provides brief descriptive information about each listed document. The subject guide directs users to records relevant to a specific topic by identifying these relevant records and providing information sufficient to enable their delivery to a user. Although welcomed by users of archives, the level of descriptive detail presented in these publications takes time to prepare and update, time not available to the staff of most repositories.

Description Transformed

Paper-based descriptive products provided entry to otherwise-obscure archival resources through much of the twentieth century, until two developments changed the history of this practice for everyone involved and affected. These developments—which influenced and continue to influence archival practice on an international scale—were the advent of networked computing and a recognition of common interests among archivists, librarians, and scholars. Initially, networked computing enabled archivists within a repository to collaborate in the capture and timely updating of descriptive information and, more importantly, to readily share current information with researchers. Later, the expansion of local area networks to Internet proportions greatly increased opportunities for comparison of approaches to description of research materials, regardless of the nature of these materials.

Experience with automated searching led to an understanding that success in this activity improves with standardization within the scope of the search. Librarians had long recognized that searches for books benefitted from a highly standardized approach to description. The extensive rules they applied to the production of library catalog cards facilitated transition to automated systems, international exchange of cataloging data, and scholarly discovery of relevant resources. Archivists took note, and by the 1980s they began to collaborate in strengthening the general guidelines that had informed archival descriptive practice since the nineteenth century.

In North America, working groups that included participants familiar with library practice surveyed the products of archival description. To the surprise of many, these groups identified important consistencies in the specific elements of information captured about archival materials across repositories. This finding led to support for adoption of increasingly precise rules for the delivery of the captured, collated, analyzed, and organized descriptive data conveyed via these elements. The resulting rules, readily referenced as "APPM" (Hensen 1979) and later "DACS" (Society of American Archivists 2013) in the United States and "RAD" (Bureau of Canadian Archivists 2008) in Canada, drew considerably on the experience of librarians.

At about this time archivists in Great Britain and Europe also began to review descriptive practice and to propose strengthened guidance. The attention of the International Council on Archives (ICA) was drawn to what appeared to be growing enthusiasm for standardization in this area and in 1988 convened an Invitational Meeting of Experts on Descriptive Standards that advocated establishment of a working group to "develop international standards for the description of archives." Such a group was established as an Ad Hoc ICA Commission in 1990 and continues standards work today under the designation Experts Group on Archival Description. The initial product of the ICA-sponsored work, titled General International Standard Archival Description or ISAD(G), was published in 1994 with general rules for the use of twenty-six elements of description. Revised in 1999 to include examples of application of the rules, ISAD(G) has been translated into more than a dozen languages. Building on this foundation, ICA-sponsored working groups have developed rules for increasingly precise presentation of information about the *context* of creation of archival material. The multiple translations of these

additional rules—International Standard Archival Authority Records for Corporate Bodies, Persons and Families (ISAAR[CPF], first issued in 1995 and revised in 2004) and International Standard for Describing Functions (ISDF issued in 2007)—evidence growing worldwide interest in these initiatives.

The availability of international descriptive *standards* does not guarantee their successful application, particularly when a clear understanding of their relationship to one another is lacking. In an effort to fill this apparent gap, the ICA has tasked its Experts Group on Archival Description with developing a conceptual model for archival description that explains how standards can work together to achieve best results not only for the benefit of the archival record but also for the benefit of users who rely on this record. The work of the group in this area has begun with a review of British Commonwealth, Finnish, and Spanish modeling research that is reaching agreement on the entities that form a complete description and thus must play a role in modeling it. Early results identify such candidate modeling entities as: agent, business or *function*, event, mandate, place, record, relationship, and subject. The Experts Group has set a goal of completing its modeling work by 2016.

Growth of professional recognition of the value of descriptive standards owes much to collaborative efforts to improve researcher access to archival materials. The Research Libraries Group, a consortium of research libraries in the United States, influenced the direction of many such activities by inviting archivists in 1984 to contribute descriptions of their materials to its online catalog, the Research Libraries Information Network (RLIN). Participation in the RLIN demonstrated that delivery of standardized descriptive information via networked computers can greatly improve the discoverability of archival materials. This recognition, combined with development of the World Wide Web, has prompted increasing conversion of analog descriptive products into digital finding aids made available through "portals" such as ArchiveGrid (a successor to RLIN), Archives Canada, and Archives Portal Europe.

Exposure to new audiences via the Internet has enabled new measures of researcher interaction with descriptive information through the use of web analytics. These, in turn, are suggesting improvements to the display of this information, particularly when it is linked to the increasing web presence of digitized and electronic records. A second impact of web delivery of descriptive information has been growing interest on the part of users to contribute to this information. In 2005 a Finding Aids Next Generation Research Group at the University of Michigan launched a project that illustrates the extent to which these developments can affect the future of archival description. The group collaborated with the Bently Historical Library to examine user interaction with its Polar Bear Expedition Digital Collections, to apply results of this examination to improve the clarity of presentation of archivist-created description, and to invite users to collaborate with archivists to enrich this description. The experiment has encouraged further analysis of user interaction with digital description and expanded opportunities for user contributions. For example, the National Archives and Records Administration in the United States recently has added a Citizen Archivist Dashboard to its website with, among other options, an invitation to add descriptive data to its online finding aid.

Conclusion

While archivists have welcomed new approaches to the capture, collation, analysis, and organization of information that serves to identify and explain archival material, they have not lost sight of their obligation to ensure that the resulting description is an accurate representation of this material. The standards they have developed, the networks they have created, and the research they continue to conduct combine to support this primary goal. For more information about the standards affecting archival description, see *Archival Standards*. For more information about the classic archival finding aid, see *Archival Inventory.—Sharon Thibodeau*

Keywords: calendar, catalog, finding aid, guide
Related Entry: User Behavior

Bibliography

"Citizen Archivist Dashboard." National Archives and Records Administration (Web portal). www.archives.gov/citizen-archivist.

Describing Archives, A Content Standard. Society of American Archivists, 2013. http://files.archivists.org/pubs/DACS2E-2013.pdf.

"The Expert Group on Archival Description." International Council on Archives, 2009. www.ica.org/13799/the-experts-group-on-archival-description/about-the-egad.html (accessed December 2013).

Gueguen, G., V. M. Marques de Fonseca, D. Pitti, and S. de Grimouard. "Toward an International Conceptual Model for Archival Description: A Preliminary Report from the International Council on Archives' Experts Group on Archival Description." *The American Archivist* 76 (2) (2013): 299–301. http://archivists.metapress.com/content/p071x02401282qx2/fulltext.pdf.

Hensen, S. L. *Archives, Personal Papers, and Manuscripts: A Cataloguing Manual for Archival Repositories, Historical Societies, and Manuscript Libraries.* Chicago: Society of American Archivists, 1989.

Krause, M. G., and E. Yakel. "Interaction in Virtual Archives: The Polar Bear Expedition Digital Collections Next Generation Finding Aid." *The American Archivist* 70 (2) (2007): 282–314. http://archivists.metapress.com/content/lpq61247881t10kv/fulltext.pdf.

Muller, S., J. A. Feith, and R. Fruin. *Manual for the Arrangement and Description of Archives*, 2nd edition. Translated by Arthur H. Leavitt with new introductions by Peter Horsman, Eric Ketelaar, Theo Thomassen, and Marjorie Rabe Barritt. Chicago: Society of American Archivists, 2003.

"Rules for Archival Description." Canadian Committee on Descriptive Standards, Canadian Council on Archives, 2008. www.cdncouncilarchives.ca/archdesrules.html.

ARCHIVAL EDUCATION

Developing programs for archival education is a balancing act for educators, standing firmly in the present digital age while drawing on established principles developed in the document-focused paper world of the past and, at the same time, preparing students to work and research in the ever-changing future. There are many models for archival education, which vary for reasons of history and to meet national legislative structures and requirements.

The Academic Establishment of Formal Archival Education Programs

In many countries, national and state *archives* have played a role in training *archivists* and fostering and supporting the development of university-based archival education. The École Nationale des Chartes, part of the University of Paris, was founded in 1821 to educate archivists, historians, and librarians. Italy has a long tradition of schools of archival studies connected to state archives in the states existing prior to Italian national unification in the 1860s (Tamblé 1984).

Ernst Posner started the first formal archival education in the United States in 1940 at American University (Bastian and Yakel 2006). The Archivschule Marburg, founded in 1949, educates archivists, who must have a master's degree or PhD and employment in either the German Federal government or one of the states of the federation to be accepted into their program. The Diploma in Archives Studies at University College London was the first archival education program in the United Kingdom, inaugurated in 1947 with a lecture by Sir Hilary Jenkinson, then deputy keeper at the Public Records Office.

In China, the Central Committee of the Communist Party commissioned an Archival Studies Specialization at Renmin University of China in Beijing in 1952, which began to enroll undergraduate students in 1955 and teaching at the Master's degree level in 1979. The first University-based archival education program in Japan was inaugurated in 2007 at the Gakushuin University; there is also a program at Hankuk University of Foreign Studies in South Korea.

In 1966 at a meeting in Washington, DC, the ICA resolved to work for the development of two regional archival training centers in Africa to overcome challenges presented by the continent's diversity and complex colonial history: one in Dakar, Senegal, to serve Francophone countries, and the other in Accra, Ghana, to serve Anglophone countries (Katuu 2009). By 2009 there were twenty-seven universities offering archival education programs (Katuu 2013).

The appropriate placement of archival studies programs in university faculty structures and the best academic background for students in archival science has been debated. Duranti (2007) explores four approaches to archival education: historical, philological, managerial, and scholarly, noting that all have their advantages, depending on national cultural approaches and legal frameworks. Ketelaar (2000, 322–40) notes that education must be comparative and multidisciplinary because professionals must understand "the organizational culture and the people in the organizations who create records; and all this in their social, religious, cultural, political contexts."

Many university-based archival education programs in Europe were associated with history programs, while in the United States many programs were established in association with library education programs (Bastian and Yakel 2006). As professional focus turned to *digital records*, some programs have been placed within schools of information technology or computer science, with examples in Australia and Sweden. In Sweden both Uppsala and Lund universities have programs that blend archives, library, and museum education to educate a professional capable of working in all types of cultural-heritage institutions. In 2005 the iSchool organization (http://ischools.org) was founded in North America based on a shared fundamental interest in the relationships between information, people, and technology focusing on both digital and physical information management and communities. The iSchool organization is growing internationally and a number of its members include archival programs.

In a special issue of *Archival Science*, Jeannette Bastian remarked that it was "abundantly clear that the archives profession faces similar educational concerns no matter where the education is happening. The complex issues surrounding technology, electronic records, the curriculum, and career choices are shared by all" (Bastian 2006, 131–32).

Curriculum Guidelines and Collaboration

Archival educators and professional associations have worked together to document, share, and set standards for archival education curricula. In 1996 the International Council on Archives Section for Archival Education and Training published the first edition of *What Students in Archival Science Learn:*

A Bibliography for Teachers, followed by a revised and updated second edition covering literature in more than nineteen languages (see www.ica-sae.org/bibliography/bibliography.html).

The Association of Canadian Archivists first developed guidelines in 1976, which by 1992 evolved into the *ACA's Education Programme and Plan*. In 1997 the Society of American Archivists (SAA) published its first guidelines for education programs. The latest iteration is the 2002 *Guidelines for a Graduate Program in Archival Studies*. In 2006 the SAA also adopted *Guidelines for Archival Continuing Education*, revised from the 1996 *Guidelines for the Development of Post-Appointment and Continuing Education and Training Programs* (see www2.archivists.org/prof-education/ace-guidelines).

Jeannette Bastian and Beth Yakel (2006) conducted an investigation of archival studies courses offered by sixty-two North American universities to identify what constitutes core archival curriculum. They found that many institutions offered only one introductory course on archives, although the average number of core courses was 3.5, which they note was "very close to the standard three-course sequence that was considered state of the art in the 1970s and early 1980s" (141). Another finding was that the number of full-time faculty across the universities surveyed increased from five in the late 1970s to thirty by 2005. Whether an international "core" curriculum can be defined to develop internationally shared courses was discussed in 2013 at the third Asia Pacific Conference on Archival Education. Further research is planned. An important project to identify the scope and development of archival education on the Pacific Rim was led by Gilliland and McKemmish, *Pluralizing the Archival Paradigm through Education (2005–2008)*. One outcome of the project was an "Agenda for Action," which included a call to "reconfigure educational programs to be more inclusive, culturally sensitive and diverse" (Gilliland, Lau, Yang, McKemmish, Rele, and White 2007, 10).

In the United States, five university programs in archives, information and library science, or public history—Auburn University, Indiana University, Louisiana State University, Middle Tennessee State University, and University of Wisconsin Milwaukee—form the Archives Education Collaborative

(AEC), sharing faculty and students specializing in archives management. Other groups are collaboratively developing virtual labs for teaching, providing students with the opportunity to use digital systems and tools for managing records and archives. Simmons College in Boston began to develop a Digital Curriculum Laboratory (DCL) in 2010 with funding from grants from the National Historical Publications and Records Commission and the Institute of Museum and Library Services (IMLS). It was first shared with Mid Sweden University and then with University College London and is open to new members. PAVEL—Preservation and Access Virtual Education Lab—made public in 2013, is a two-year project hosted at the University of Michigan School of Information and funded by the National Endowment for the Humanities' Preservation and Access Education and Training Program to develop and implement a virtual education laboratory featuring digital *access* and *preservation* tools.

Aware of the urgent need to share expertise and provide curriculum resources on managing and preserving digital records for educators and trainers around the world, the ICA-SAE embarked on a collaborative project in 2009 jointly funded by the ICA Programme Commission and the InterPARES Project at the University of British Columbia. Eight fully developed modules were published online in 2012 as *Digital Preservation Pathways*, together with an introductory video.

Quality Evaluation and Accreditation Strategies

Professional associations in both the United Kingdom and Australia recognize or accredit archives and records management programs. In some other countries quality evaluation is undertaken by the country's higher-education authority. In Sweden, for example, all programs in a particular discipline are evaluated across all universities at the same time on a five-year cycle.

In the 1980s the Society of Archivists (UK), now the Archives and Records Association (ARA), established both a post-qualification registration system for professional members and a recognition process for university programs that continues to the present day (Shepherd 2009, 151).

The Australian Society of Archivists (ASA) and RIM Professionals Australasia (RIMPA) collaboratively developed a *Statement of Professional Knowledge* and use this as the basis for evaluation in the course-recognition process. The latest version of the *Statement* as of 2015 is a 2012 Exposure Draft published by the ASA.

Although they have developed guidelines for graduate programs, neither the ACA nor the SAA evaluates programs or courses. The SAA has published a *Directory of Archival Education* since 2001. In 2002 the ICA-SAE published a second edition of their international *Directory of Schools and Courses of Professional Training for Archivists*. These are important and useful initiatives, but both directories rely on education providers to voluntarily submit entries and keep them updated.

Educators' Networks

In October 1977 the ICA set up a Committee for Professional Training and Education. Amadou M. Boussou from Dakar, Senegal, was the first president of the committee. In 1990 the committee was transformed into the Section for Archival Educators and Trainers and held its first meeting as ICA-SAE in The Hague, Netherlands. It aims to promote cooperation between archival educators and trainers in order to assist in the development of research and qualifications for recordkeeping around the world.

Archival educators in the United States have met regularly since 1994 at SAA's Annual Meeting. A significant development in the United States is the *Building the Future of Archival Education and Research Initiative*, which gained funding through two four-year grants from the Institute of Museum and Library Services. It is the first collaborative initiative to focus on doctoral students in archival science and provided for two cohorts in 2009 and 2010 of competitive four-year fellowships for doctoral students at one of the eight participating colleges or universities.

The Forum for Archives and Records Management Education and Research for the UK and Ireland (FARMER) was formed in 1999 for teaching and research. The membership includes representatives of the five postgraduate programs formally recognized by the Archives and Records Association (UK) (formerly the Society of Archivists) and for institutions seeking such accreditation. The FARMER also runs conferences for national and international educators.

In 2005 a subgroup of ICA-SAE members, the North West European Network of Archival Educators and Trainers (NAET), met in Amsterdam with the purpose of developing a collaborative summer school for archival students at master level. In 2011 the group obtained funding from the European Union Erasmus Intensive Program and ran three annual two-week residential intensive programs: *Archival Challenges in the Digital Information Society* (ARCHIDIS) focusing on *appraisal* theory and strategy. Teachers and students from fourteen universities and archives schools participated over the three years, gathering in Marburg, Germany, in 2011; Härnösand, Sweden, in 2012; and Dundee (UK) in 2013. Initially planned to focus on Master's students, the program also accepted advanced undergraduate students and doctoral students. The NAET plans a joint summer school for doctoral students commencing in 2015.

Doctoral Programs and Archival Research

The number of doctoral programs has increased markedly since the last decade of the twentieth century. "What has resulted is an unparalleled diversity of what is being studied and how" (Gilliland and McKemmish 2004, 3–4). In their article "Research in Archival Science: A Status Report," Carol Couture and Daniel Ducharme (2005) develop a typology of research in the field of *archival science* analyzing archival literature published in the ten years prior to 1999 (see http://journals.sfu.ca/archivar/index.php/ archivaria/article/view/12500/13620). Looking at archival research less than ten years later, Gilliland and McKemmish demonstrate both a broadening of the range of research topics and greater granularity. Contributing factors include, among others, the increasing number of doctoral programs; increased support for research by archival institutions, professionals, and user communities; and willingness to explore and use research designs and methodologies that are new to the archival discipline. Archival educators have also been active in broadening opportunities for scholarly publication.

Conclusion

Increasing interest in and willingness to experiment with cooperative ventures is evident in both archival education and research. Educators are finding more ways to network and to collaboratively develop and share courses and teaching resources.—*Karen Anderson*

Keywords: archival education, archival educators, archival research, records management education

Bibliography

Bastian, Jeannette Allis. "Introduction," *Archival Science* 6 (2006): 131–32. DOI: 10.1007/s10502-006-9023-5.

Bastian, Jeannette A., and Elizabeth Yakel. "Towards the Development of an Archival Core Curriculum: The United States and Canada." *Archival Science* 6 (2) (2006): 133–50. DOI: 10.1007/s10502-006-9024-4.

Couture, Carol. "Education and Research in Archival Science: General Tendencies." *Archival Science* 1 (2) (2001): 157–82. The full report, titled "La formation et recherche en archivstique dans le monde: une étude comparative," is available at http://mapageweb.umontreal.ca/couturec/recher.htm.

Duranti, Luciana. "Models of Archival Education: Four, Two, One, or a Thousand?" *Archives and Social Studies: A Journal of Interdisciplinary Research* 1 (2007). http://archivo.cartagena.es/files/36-162-DOCFICHERO1/04-durantimodels.pdf.

Gilliland, Anne, Andrew Lau, Yang Lu, Sue McKemmish, Shilpa Rele, and Kelvin White. "Pluralizing the Archival Paradigm through Education: Critical Discussions around the Pacific Rim." *Archives and Manuscripts* 35 (2) (2007): 10. www.infotech.monash.edu.au/research/about/centres/cosi/projects/pacrim/am-pacific-rim-pre-publication.pdf (accessed April 6, 2014).

Gilliland, Anne, and Sue McKemmish. "Building an Infrastructure for Archival Research." *Archival Science* 4 (3–4) (2004): 149–97. DOI: 10.1007/s10502-006-6742-6.

Katuu, Shadrack. "Archives and Records Management Education and Training: What Can Africa Learn from Europe and North America?" *Information Development* 25 (2) (2009): 133–45. DOI: 10.1177/0266666909104714.

Ketelaar, Eric. "Archivistics Research Saving the Profession." *American Archivist* 63 (2) (2000): 322–40. http://archivists.metapress.com/content/0238574511vmv576/fulltext.pdf.

Shepherd, Elizabeth. *Archives and Archivists in 20th Century England*. Farnham: Ashgate, 2009.

Tamblé, Donato. "The Teaching of Archival Science in Italy and the Role of the Schools of the State Archives." *Archivaria* 19 (1984): 247–48. http://journals.sfu.ca/archivar/index.php/archivaria/article/viewFile/11165/12102.

ARCHIVAL ETHICS

The field of ethics is concerned with the relative morality of human behavior. Professional ethics is a type of applied ethics that deals with the standards of conduct in different professions. *Archivists* have developed standards for ethical practice that are warranted by the responsibilities required of their positions as caretakers of essential *records*. Many professions, including the archival profession, have developed codes of ethics to set *standards* for conduct within the profession and to help clarify the issues underlying ethical conflicts. Having a code of ethics has often been acknowledged as one of the hallmarks of a true profession. Such codes also serve as a kind of compact between the profession and the public it serves. For the archival profession, they affirm the archivist's obligation to conduct business in ways that will build and sustain trust among the users of *archives*. Archives serve many different constituencies with competing interests and demands. Archivists must make decisions on selection, *appraisal*, *preservation*, and *access* that protect the rights of individuals, deal fairly with users, and protect records for use by future generations. Conflicting claims can create ethical dilemmas. Codes of ethics are designed to help professionals make ethically informed decisions.

Codes of Ethics

Ethical codes can be based on two radically different ethical theories. Deontological ethics consider actions strictly in terms of their rightness or wrongness. By contrast, a teleological approach bases its recommendations on the consequences of particular actions. Codes of archival ethics have tended to take a more prescriptive, deontological approach, with specific pronouncements or requirements on how archivists should behave. Explanations of ethical principles, however, often rely on the practical implications of various actions by archivists (Dingwall 2004).

The first code of ethics for archivists was developed at the U.S. National Archives in the mid-1950s for use in the archives' in-service training program. "The Archivist's Code," as it was called, was a decidedly prescriptive document, full of "musts" and "shoulds." Its opening statement clearly shows a connection to Sir Hilary Jenkinson's concept of the moral defense of archives: "The archivist has a moral obligation to society to preserve evidence on how things actually happened and to take every measure for the physical preservation of valuable records" (Glover 1955, 307). Other points touched on in this early code include the archivist's obligation to the future, the requirement to both promote access and respect restrictions, the requirement not to personally profit from the use of knowledge of records, and the need freely to share knowledge of records with professional colleagues.

Spurred in part by charges made in 1969 by Professor Francis Loewenheim that the Franklin D. Roosevelt Presidential Library had improperly withheld from him *documents* that library staff were using for their own publication project, the Society of American Archivists created a committee on ethics in 1977, which led ultimately to SAA's first "Code of Ethics for Archivists," approved in 1980. The language of this code was more prescriptive, but cast in an affirmative tone, spelling out archival tasks and responsibilities in terms that archivists might aspire to emulate. The code was accompanied by an extended commentary to explain the thinking underlying the code and to foster further discussion of the ethical issues addressed in the code.

The Society of American Archivists approved a revised code of ethics in 1992, and the code was revised again in 2005. A significant change in the 2005 revision was the omission of the commentary, which had been seen as a useful interpretive tool for thinking about the application of the code's pronouncements, but that legal counsel recommended be removed. In 2011, however, the SAA issued a "Statement on Core Values for Archivists" in order "both to remind archivists why they engage in their professional responsibilities and to inform others

of the basis for archivists' contributions to society" (*SAA Core Values Statement and Code of Ethics*). This document fulfilled some of the purposes of the earlier commentary on the code of ethics. The SAA Code of Ethics was then revised in 2012, with the idea that the code and the core values statement should be read together.

During the 1990s other professional *archival associations* began issuing codes of ethics, including the Association of Canadian Archivists, the Australian Society of Archivists, and the International Council on Archives. The Society of Archivists in the United Kingdom, now the Archives & Records Association (UK and Ireland), called its statement a "Code of Conduct." The ARA is distinctive in its requirement that applicants for membership must assent to abide by its Code of Conduct. The ARA also has a mechanism in place to take disciplinary actions against members who violate the code.

There is considerable commonality in the topics covered in these different ethical codes. Protection of the *integrity* of records is a central tenet as well as general injunctions to conduct business in a professional manner. Collegial relations between archival repositories are encouraged. Promotion of the use of archives is stressed, though respect for the privacy of individuals, particularly those who "have no voice or role in collections' creation, retention, or public use" is encouraged ("SAA Core Values Statement and Code of Ethics"). Respecting the privacy of researchers is another important aspect of privacy.

Closely related to questions of privacy are those of equal access. It was once not uncommon for some researchers to be given privileged access to records, but this practice is now officially discouraged unless explicitly required by a donor's deed of gift or by institutional policy. In the interests of promoting access, however, archival ethics discourages extended restrictions on records donated to archives.

Questions have arisen also about the ethical dilemmas that may emerge when archivists conduct research in their own collections. Archivists are encouraged to remember that their first duty is to serve their researchers and that they should not receive any personal advantages because of their privileged access to records.

Archivists are also expected to abide by the law in all of their actions, but there is a difference between an action being legal and an action being ethical.

48 Archival Ethics

Law and ethics can intersect, most notably in the areas of privacy and confidentiality. Clearly the ethical archivist needs to be familiar with the laws governing his or her jurisdiction, but there will still be gray areas left to ethical interpretation.

Applying Codes of Ethics

Ideally the various archival codes of ethics can serve as reference documents assisting archivists when confronted with moral dilemmas or conflicts of interest in the workplace. The codes are generally written in terms of broad principles, however, and are therefore rather inadequate as guides to decision-making in particular instances. Furthermore, few of the organizations issuing codes of ethics for archives have any mechanisms whereby those who violate the code are in any way sanctioned. Some archivists undoubtedly view this as a real defect in ensuring that all archivists adhere to high ethical standards. But the impracticality and the legal risks of trying to enforce an archival code of ethics suggest that these codes will remain largely aspirational documents. The colleagues of archivists in both the library and historical professions have similarly shied away from any direct enforcement of their ethical codes.

One of the difficulties in applying ethics in archival work is the institutional setting in which ethical quandaries may occur. Issues of access to records may be different in a public records repository, where access to everybody should be the normal and legal expectation, compared to a private repository, such as a corporate archives. Archival ethics exist within the context of the particular mission of any given archives. Archivists need to be even-handed, however, within the constraints under which they work. Ethical codes have been written for individual archivists, though the possibility that they could also be applied to institutions has been raised (Cook 2006).

Archivists rightly like to think of themselves as guardians of a documentary heritage for future generations. Ethical issues can arise when the demands of an employer seem at odds with the claims of society for an accurate and complete record of events. Ethics codes will ultimately be of little help in such a dilemma, and the archivist will have to rely on his or her own conscience. While the default position of the profession as a whole would probably be to lean toward supporting fuller access to records, different interpretations can support different outcomes without violating accepted standards of archival ethics.

Conclusion

The recognition that there is such a thing as archival ethics is testimony to the maturation of the archival profession. Codes of ethics issued by professional associations proclaim to the world the commitment of archivists to be good stewards of the world's documentary heritage and to ensure equitable and open access to records by current and future generations. Ethical issues involving records in business and government are a regular feature of the news. The nature of ethical dilemmas is that there are often no clear-cut answers. Vigorous debate and discussion of these issues within the archival community will continue to be informed by well-articulated standards for ethical conduct by archivists.—*Philip Eppard*

Keywords: ethics, professionalism, privacy, access
Related Entries: Access/Accessibility; Accountability, Archival Associations; Archives (Institution); Public Service

Bibliography

Benedict, Karen. *Ethics and the Archival Profession: Introduction and Case Studies*. Chicago: Society of American Archivists, 2003.
Cook, Michael. "Professional Ethics and Practice in Archives and Records Management in a Human Rights Context." *Journal of the Society of Archivists* 27 (1) (2006): 1–15. DOI:10.1080/00039810600691205.
Danielson, Elena S. *The Ethical Archivist*. Chicago: Society of American Archivists, 2010.
———. "The Ethics of Access." *American Archivist* 52 (1) (1989): 52–62. http://archivists.metapress.com/content/6m2m41171612j058/fulltext.pdf.
Dingwall, Glenn. "Trusting Archivists: The Role of Archival Ethics Codes in Establishing Public Faith." *American Archivist* 67 (1) (2004): 11–30. http://archivists.metapress.com/content/mw0914r2p52xx2t4/fulltext.pdf.
Glover, Wayne C. "Prepared for the National Archive in Service Training Program; The Archi-

vist's Code." *American Archivist* 18 (4) (1955): 307–8. http://archivists.metapress.com/content/g027u80688293012/fulltext.pdf.

Horn, David E. "The Development of Ethics in Archival Practice." *American Archivist* 52 (1) (1989): 64–71. http://archivists.metapress.com/content/nk661527341j0610/fulltext.pdf.

MacNeil, Heather. *Without Consent: The Ethics of Disclosing Personal Information in Public Archives*. Metuchen, NJ: Society of American Archivists and Scarecrow Press, 1992.

"SAA Core Values Statement and Code of Ethics." www2.archivists.org/statements/saa-core-values-statement-and-code-of-ethics (accessed December 2013).

ARCHIVAL EXHIBIT

An archival exhibit is a display of archival material, primarily for educational purposes, that respects the nature of archival *records* and the principles of *archival theory*. It does not rely on thematic interpretation, but instead offers information promoting the understanding of the nature of archival material and the archival profession. It protects that material's *impartiality*, makes all its administrative and documentary interrelationships intelligible, and authenticates its meaning by showing, with the material items, their immaterial *context*.

Types of Archival Exhibitions

In mounting any exhibit, an *archivist* will first establish the purpose of the project and select a particular type of exhibit to create, bearing in mind their institution's mandate and the exhibition's target audience. Ideally, they also consider the body of archival theory that guides the work of archivists. That theory demands that archival material be treated in a different manner from the material in the custody of libraries, museums, or any other organization that may create exhibits. Thus, the nature of an archival exhibit is defined, in large part, by the fundamental concepts of archival theory. The theoretical limitations imposed by the nature of archival material affect the way in which that material is used. Respecting these limitations helps ensure that the exhibits mounted by archival institutions send the most appropriate and valuable messages to their intended audience.

There are four basic types of exhibits usually mounted in an archival environment: thematic, celebratory, institutional, and functional. The thematic exhibit is an outcome of the popular perception that *archives* only deal with the *preservation* of history. To this end, it uses archival material to document an historical subject, much as museums use discrete artifacts to illustrate historical themes. In this case, the development of the exhibit theme and the interpretation of the records to tell a story take precedence over the principles governing the nature and treatment of the records.

The celebratory exhibit draws attention to a person, place, or thing that warrants special recognition at a specific time. As the anniversary of a significant historical event approaches, an exhibit exploring some aspect of that event also provides some often needed publicity for the archives: in those cases where the occasion is well known, the archives would appear to be doing its part to aid in the celebrations; if instead the targeted audience is largely unaware of the occasion, the archives can use the celebratory exhibit to generate some awareness and understanding of the event in question. As with thematic exhibits, they can violate various archival principles by presenting the material as discrete items, isolated from their documentary context.

Less frequently mounted, but more reflective of archival theory and the profession, are institutional and functional exhibits. The role of the institutional exhibit is to make potential users aware of the sources available in archives. In some cases, the institutional exhibit serves to show wider audiences that archival institutions and their holdings actually exist. Functional exhibits, on the other hand, are mounted in order to educate viewers about archival theory, methodology, and practice. These exhibits clarify the often-misunderstood differences between professions in the cultural field. Either can promote holdings but also illustrate the nature of archival material and of its many interrelationships. As a result, potential users become knowledgeable about the infinite ways in which archival documents can be sources of information and better understand the rules and regulations they encounter in archives: why they cannot change the order of the material given to them in consultation, why they cannot always have the original of a document, and so on.

Conclusion

All exhibits should make the public aware and appreciative of archival institutions, encourage the use of archives, inform about holdings, encourage donations, and encourage further or new research. An archival exhibit does all these things, but also educates users about archival functions and services and the nature of archival material.—*Heather Gordon*

Keywords: archival exhibit, archival environment, archival material, archival theory
Related Entries: Archival Theory; Archives (Material)

Bibliography

Gordon, Heather Marie. *Archival Exhibitions: Purposes and Principles*. Vancouver: The University of British Columbia, 1994.

ARCHIVAL FONDS

The Society of American Archivists' *A Glossary of Archival and Records Terminology* defines *fonds* as "the entire body of records of an organization, family, or individual that have been created and accumulated as the result of an organic process reflecting the functions of the creator" (see www2.archivists. org/glossary/terms/f/fonds). A fonds is clearly distinguished from a *collection,* which is an artificial accumulation of *documents* of any *provenance.*

The Concept

According to the *archival theory*, the archival fonds is the whole of the *records* that every administrative body, every physical or corporate entity (the *creator*), automatically and organically accumulates by reason of its *function* or of its activity, and keeps for administrative, legal, evidential, or informational reasons.

The records sediment throughout the life of the creator form many strata reflecting its activities in their diversity, complexity, and evolution. The archival fonds is a living organism that is formed and

transformed by the development of its creator. If the creator's functions change, the accumulation of its records also changes. It is in the normal functioning of persons and organizations that a fonds is constituted.

The organic nature of the fonds gives it its *authenticity*; the fonds is not an artificial creation, but the raw residue and testimony of existing or passed activities. Each archival document, or record, is an integral part of a whole; it cannot be appreciated outside the *context* of its creation and transmission. All records belonging to the archival fonds have an evidentiary capacity that enhances their ability to provide information. The records that are maintained within an archival fonds can be attributed, used, and produced in court as legal evidence.

This legal approach has long dominated archival theory and is found in many writings: "To qualify as records, documents must have been created during the performance of what we could call, broadly, an administrative or management activity, whether public or private. . . . An archival fonds forms spontaneously as a result of a documentary sedimentation and consists of records related to each other by structural links, due to their origin" (Lodolini 1984, 13–14).

The evidentiary capacity of an archival fonds is even greater if the *archivist* respects the principle of provenance and the original order of the records in the fonds.

The order of the records in the archival fonds derives from the internal organization and activities of the creating body and is organic, as argued in 1898 by Muller, Feith, and Fruin, in 1922 by Jenkinson, in 1956 by Schellenberg, and in 1977 by Duchein. In 1994, ISAD (G)—*The General International Standard for Archival Description*—published by the International Council on Archives (ICA/CIA)—affirmed the validity of the concept of fonds, defined it as "the whole of the records, regardless of form or medium, organically created and/or accumulated and used by a particular person, family, or corporate body in the course of that creator's activities or functions," and identified inside the fonds a hierarchy of levels of *arrangements* and *description*: subfonds, *series, file*, item.

The Use of the Term *Archival Fonds*

The term archival fonds has a French origin. In 1841, the concept of *fonds* and its corollary principle *respect des fonds* appeared in the writings of French *archivist* and historian Natalis de Wailly, and were used in the April 24, 1841 ministerial instructions on the arrangement of the Archives Départementales. By recommending "gathering the various documents by fonds, that is, making a collection of all the documents accumulated by an organization, institution, family or individual" without mixing them with others, de Wailly made a sharp break with the tradition of arrangement by subject, which was the methodological arrangement framework instituted for the Archives Nationales (1808) in accordance with the scientific classification systems used in the eighteenth century.

Clearly stated in 1841, the principle of *respect des fonds* was not developed on a theoretical level until very recently in France. The Italians, Germans, and Dutch must take the credit for analyzing its nature and consequences. In 1867, the Toscan archivist Francisco Bonaini laid down the foundations of the historical method ("metodo storico")—extended by legislation to the whole of Italy in 1875 —which states that a document must remain in the fonds it came from and in its original place within that fonds, because the fact of belonging to a fonds and the place occupied in it are by no means arbitrary but derive from the organic nature of the fonds.

The principle of *respect des fonds* was adopted by Prussian archivists with the name of *Strukturprinzip* about 1880, and was illustrated in their manuals by Muller, Feith, and Fruin in 1898, and by Jenkinson in 1922.

The organic nature of the fonds has since been articulated in all the glossaries of archival terminology and archival manuals, and the principle of *respect des fonds* has become the main principle of archives administration. The Anglo-Saxon terminology favored until recently the terms "archive group" and "record group" over *archival fonds* to express the same concept. The development of descriptive standards, first in Canada, then internationally through the ICA, promoted the French term *fonds*, purposely chosen "in order to avoid certain terminological confusion which has grown around the terms 'record group,' 'manuscript group,' 'collections,' and so on, in North American Practice" (Hayworth 1993, 56).

If the concept of fonds is easy to state, it is much more difficult to identify the body generating it within a hierarchy of creating agencies. Jenkinson in England and Duchein in France agreed to define the fonds as "the Archives resulting from the work of an Administration which was an organic whole, complete in itself, capable of dealing independently, without any added or external authority, with every side of any business which could normally be presented to it" (Jenkinson 1966, 101; Duchein 1977). Consequently a creator with no power of decision could create only a sub-fonds. However, these two authors differed on whether the archives of a private creator is an archival fonds. Jenkinson, like Muller, Feith, and Fruin before him, did not believe that a private archives has organic nature, while Duchein did, consistently with the French tradition inaugurated by Charles-Victor Langlois and Henri Stein (1891).

Evolving Ideas about Archival Fonds

Even though the term *fonds* is generally used in the archival literature, the application of the concept is challenged by increasingly fast institutional, administrative, and technological changes. The growing complexity of creating agencies—with their endless ramifications and changing functions—and the use of digital technology to create records that are modified and used simultaneously by several agencies, call into question the validity of the concept of fonds. In this context, the archival fonds is considered a theoretical idea rather than a material reality:

> The fonds, therefore, should be viewed primarily as "an intellectual construct." The fonds is not so much a physical entity in archives as it is the conceptual summary of descriptions of physical entities at the series level or lower, and descriptions of the administrative, historical and functional character of the records creator(s)—as well as descriptions of the records-creating processes (metadata). The fonds is thus the conceptual "whole" that reflects an organic process in which a records creator produces or accumulates series of records which themselves exhibit a natural unity based on shared function, activity, form or use. It is at the heart of this process or relationship linking the creator to the records that the essence of *respect des fonds* can be found and must be protected. (Cook 1993, 33)

In the case of records produced by multiple record creators, new approaches are developing that focus on function as the aggregating entity rather than on organizational unit. The Society of Americans Archivists' *Glossary of Archival and Records Terminology* notes:

> Functional provenance allows for intellectual control of multi-provenance series that result from administrative or political change. The concept ensures that, with a transfer of functions from one authority to another, relevant records or copies thereof are transferred to ensure administrative continuity. (See the note for "Functional Provenance" at www2.archivists.org/glossary/terms/f/functional-provenance)

Thus, the question can be raised of whether this type of aggregation is still a fonds or whether the concept of archival fonds is not applicable to records created using digital applications and systems.

Into the Future

The large-scale computerization of business processes and the increasing "dematerialization" (i.e., digitization of paper records) of their documentary residue have caused a major disruption in the way that records are managed throughout their *lifecycle*. Indeed, we move from a compartmentalized vision of silo structures to data stream production and transmission among interoperable information systems that contribute to shared data repositories.

The form of the records is evolving, and we are moving from the concept of a static "document" to evolving data that in various ways are integrated in files defined as "single" *via* connections and interfaces between business applications (e.g., single medical file, single criminal case file, single personal file) of different organizations. It follows that the notion of *fonds* based on the idea of one identifiable creator is lost and replaced by the notion of "aggregation of records" resulting from the same function, often performed by several entities. We can see this change in the 2012 "reform of information system of the French State," which classifies the major functions performed by the state and removes from the resulting records the names of the ministries producing them as one business application documents a function performed by several departments. This trend gives rise to a reconsideration of the concept of records creator.

The consequences are noteworthy for *archival description* as static descriptive models are being replaced by flexible multifaceted models. The same records are linked by metadata to one or more files and series produced by several functions and administrative bodies. In this context, the principle of provenance can no longer be based on the concept of creator and, thus, of archival fonds.

Conclusion

In 2012, Anne J. Gilliland-Swetland wrote:

> In archival appraisal, more sophisticated conceptions of provenance, such as functional provenance and multi-provenance, have been developed for electronic records that apply business process analysis and functional decomposition. Functional provenance views the business function through which a record came into being as that record's provenance rather than the office or individual creating the record. This view is based on the rationale that recordkeeping functions are likely to remain more or less constant whereas bureaucratic hierarchies and technologies shift over time. Multi-provenance recognizes that a record may be simultaneously created through the interaction of multiple offices or jurisdictions. (13)

Does this mean that the concept of archival fonds is outdated or even dead? Perhaps, at least as it regards archives in the making and future archives. However, for the understanding, control, and research use of now-closed fonds or even series, and in those cases or places where technological progress has not changed the way organizations and individuals create records, the concept of archival fonds is still a pillar on which our understanding of archives rests.—*Francoise Banat-Bergere and Christine Nougaret*

Keywords: creator, arrangement, description, *respect des fonds*
Related Entries: Archives (Material); Principal of Provenance; *Respect des Fonds*

Bibliography

Banat-Berger, Françoise. "Les fonctions de l'archivistique à l'ère du numérique." In *Les chantiers du numérique. Dématérialisation des archives et métiers de l'archiviste*. Louvain-la-Neuve: Publications des archives de l'université catholique de Louvain, 2012, 39–59.

Cook, Terry. "The Concept of Archival Fonds and the Post-Custodial Era: Theory, Problems and Solutions." *Archivaria* 35 (Spring 1993): 24–37. http://journals.sfu.ca/archivar/index.php/archivaria/article/view/11882/12835.

Duchein, Michel. "Le respect des fonds en archivistique: Principes théoriques et problèmes pratiques." *La Gazette des Archives* 97 (1977): 71–96;

———. "Theoretical Principles and Practical Problems of Respect des fonds in Archival Science." *Archivaria* 1 (16) (1983): 63–82. http://journals.sfu.ca/archivar/index.php/archivaria/article/view/12648/13813.

Gilliland-Swetland, Anne J. *Enduring Paradigm, New Opportunities*: *The Value of the Archival Perspective in the Digital Environment*. Washington, DC: Council on Library and Information Resources, February 2012, 13. www.clir.org/pubs/reports/pub89/pub89.pdf.

Hayworth, Kent M. "The Voyage of RAD: From the Old World to the New." *Archivaria* 35 (Spring 1993): 55–63. http://journals.sfu.ca/archivar/index.php/archivaria/article/view/11885/12838.

Jenkinson, Hilary. *A Manual of Archive Administration*. London: Percy Lund, Humphries, 1966.

Lodolini, Elio. *Archivistica: Principi e problem*. Edited by Franco Angeli, Franco. Milano, 1984.

Muller, Samuel, Johan Feith, and Robert Fruin. *Manual for the Arrangement and Description of Archives Drawn Up by Direction of the Netherlands Association of Archivists*. Groningue, 1898. Translated by Arthur Leavitt. New York: H. H. W. Wilson, 1968.

Schellenberg, Theodore R. *The Management of Archives*. New York: Columbia University Press, 1965.

———. *Modern Archives: Principles and Techniques*. Chicago: University of Chicago Press, 1956.

ARCHIVAL HISTORY

Archival history is more than describing the development of *archival programs*, *archives*, and *archivists*; archival history should also strive at understanding (Cox 2000) why *records* and *record-keeping systems* have been created; what uses they had; how they were influenced by power, politics, gender, social and cultural constraints, and what we call "archival consciousness."

Why Archival History?

Historians, anthropologists, and other scholars have discovered archival history in a wider context, as shown at international conferences like "Toward a Cultural History of Archives" (2006) (Blair and Milligan 2007). As early as 1979 Michael Clanchy made the archival *documents* themselves the object of study, instead of viewing them merely as "quarries of information" (Clanchy 2013). His approach was followed by researchers on orality and literacy, in particular "pragmatic literacy," that is, literacy and the culture of writing for pragmatic purposes (Clanchy 2013, 336–43; Britnell 1997; O'Toole 2004). For the practicing *archivist* the argument in favor of knowing archival history is that, as Richard Cox wrote in 1988, "a better-developed archival history can both enrich and strengthen the archival profession in its quest to accomplish its mission" (Cox 1988, 147; 1990, 200; 1983). Moreover, archival history is a field of study that could bring historians and *archivists* together (again) (Blouin and Rosenberg 2011; Cook 2011; Jeurgens 2005). In 1992 Barbara Craig warned archivists that, if they left archival history to others, their future would be at stake. She mentioned a number of reasons for researching, writing, and learning about archival history. First, the history of *archives* and *records creation* offers the archivist a perspective to answer current and future challenges: to solve a problem without knowledge of the past—she writes—is like carrying out a surgical operation without anatomical knowledge. Second, archival history can bridge the gap between archival scholars and practitioners: insights into the history of archives, for example, help to cope with the uncertainties of the digital era. Finally, archival history is essential for the professional identity of the archivist in the modern age, because it is an aid in understanding "the contextual place of records in the world of affairs, of thought, and of information. In short we would benefit greatly from a historical sociology of the record and a diplomatic of the document" (Craig 1992, 121).

Barbara Craig, Philip Eppard, and Heather Mac-Neil hosted the first International Conference on the History of Records and Archives (I-CHORA) in 2003. They stressed that archival history is important because it "holds the promise of providing a better understanding of human experience and human needs" (Horsman, Eppard, and MacNeil 2006, 7–8). Subsequent I-CHORA conferences were held in Amsterdam (2005), Boston (2007), Perth (2008), London (2010), and Austin, Texas (2012). Selections of the presented papers were published in *Archivaria*, *Archival Science*, and *Libraries & the Cultural Record*.

Research Models

As a framework for research in archival history, Peter Horsman developed a conceptual model, based on a business-management model by Blumenthal (Horsman 2011), shown in figure A.2. It identifies the relationships between the organization (structure, culture), the business process, the information (records), the controls, and the environment. The same model can also be viewed as dividing the area of research into four domains: organization, acting (functions and processes), documenting (making and using documents), and recordkeeping.

Documenting and *recordkeeping* are not just natural processes, but the result of the conscious and unconscious decisions made by *persons* to create archival documents or records (hereinafter simply document[s]), and eventually to preserve them. Documenting starts with the decision to use documents for a business process. As German archival thinker Papritz explained, not every act results in a document, and not every document will necessarily be kept. Content and structure of the archives are for a great part defined by the *recordkeeping system*. We define a recordkeeping system as the whole of documents, metadata, processes, procedures, knowledge, rules, means, and people with which a physical or juridical person provides itself with reliable and enduring information for administration, memory, and *accountability*. Recordkeeping systems are not static, but have a behavior. This behavior is conditioned by *context*, such as the legal system, technology, ideas and capacity of people, organizational changes, and organizational structure. Because the behavior of the recordkeeping system determines the composition of the archives, the structure of the

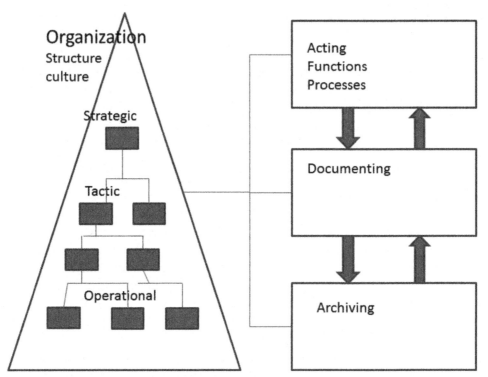

Figure A.2.   Conceptual model to be used as a framework for research in archival history. *Peter Horsman*

archives changes over time. For a meaningful interpretation of an archives, the reconstruction of the original order and the analysis of the relationships between the component parts are not sufficient. Above all the behavior of the recordkeeping system must be known and understood.

The usage of modern terminology in research models must not result in projecting modern concepts into the past. Often archivists have "been inventing archival tradition by retroactively identifying and confirming certain conceptions of modern public archivy in the record-keeping and records destruction practices of the Renaissance and earlier," Richard Brown warns (Brown 1997, 24).

Charles Jeurgens introduced the concept of historical archival science in order to discover, by looking at records creation, how the recorded information was born (Jeurgens 2005). A fine example of this approach is JoAnne Yates's *Control through Communication: The Rise of System in American Management* (Yates 1989).

Reading the Archives

The challenge for research into the behavior of an historical recordkeeping system is that the system itself cannot be observed and that no living memory of the system is available. The most important source of knowledge is the archives that have been formed by the recordkeeping system and maintained. Inspiration for such a method of collecting data about the recordkeeping system can be found in the concept of "reading the archives," the idea that the texts in archives rarely speak for themselves, but always have to be read in their context. Reading the archives has different aspects: indirect reading, contextual reading, physical reading, structural reading, direct reading, and close reading.

In her work on Dutch colonial archives Ann Stoler stressed the need to use contextual knowledge to understand records from the past. This particular way of reading the archives is called "contextual reading." The four domains model presented above is one possible conceptual framework for contextual reading.

Contextual reading implies reading the documents, but it needs to be preceded by indirect reading, the use of finding aids. Finding aids are prepared by archivists, through the processes of arrangement and description. Current archival discourse recognizes the fact that the archivist can never achieve the ideal of being impartial in his or her interpretation of the records, and that, although following archival principles, harmonized archival methods, and the international standards, she or he makes choices that influence the way in which the user will understand the archives. The reader of the archives who starts with the finding aid, therefore, has to be acquainted with the relevant systems, practices, and policies.

Another type of reading focuses on the physical aspects of the documents, such as the support, the ink, the script, seals, and special signs. Diplomatists, usually focusing on individual documents, pay attention to physical characteristics more than archivists. The fact that a document is written on parchment, for instance, indicates that it was supposed to be preserved over time, as did binding loose documents. A well-formed paper file suggests a well-organized administration. Physical reading involves also looking at damages, water stains, and so on, and at location and distribution: the buildings, rooms, chests, and other furniture used for recordkeeping.

Structural reading has a *diplomatics* component as well: the manner in which the content of the document has been formatted, its formulation, intellectual form. The language can be more or less formal, but it is intended to meet the requirements of the audience and the legal system, and changes over time. Structural reading refers also to the interrelationships among the records, as defined by the recordkeeping system: the *series*, *files*, indexes, or any other entity chosen for aggregating and organizing documents. The structure is contemporary to the original system, but it may have been modified one or more times.

Direct reading is analyzing administrative instructions and rules, how activities had to be recorded, what documents should be set aside in the recordkeeping system, what rules existed about structure of the documents and the system, which *classification* schemas were in place. Instructions are always about the ideal situation, which does not always correspond to reality. People are essential components of the recordkeeping system, and they do not always work following rules or guidelines.

Finally, close reading is finding in a document direct or indirect references to other documents. By doing so, not only hidden structures are revealed, but also documents that have disappeared by purposeful destruction or accidental loss without leaving other traces. Close reading often requires a thorough knowledge of the administration and its procedures. Reconstruction of financial systems, for example, requires a thorough close reading of the entries to understand how, for example, various types of ledgers interrelate.

Social and Cultural Archival Science

As early as 1981 Frank Burke called for research on questions such as:

> What is it within the nature of society that makes it create the records that it does? Is the impulse a purely practical one, or is there something in the human psyche that dictates the keeping of a record, and what is the motivation for that act? (Burke 1981, 42)

In the opinion of Burke, the benefit of asking and answering this type of question was the enhancement of not only the theoretical basis of the archival endeavor, but also possible practical outcomes. He suggested that, by determining the motivation for *record creation* and researching its sociological aspects, one might be able to "devise practices that will satisfy a basic human need" (Burke 1981, 42). This is the mission of what Eric Ketelaar has named social and cultural *archival science*: studying the characteristics of documents in their social and cultural contexts and the way in which they are created, used, selected, and transferred through time. Social and cultural archival science focuses on socially and culturally situated *archival practices*. These practices experience and sustain changes in society, causing changes as well as continuity in recordkeeping.

The relation between sociocultural context and archives has also another dimension. According to Brien Brothman, in the hands of people archival systems have power, "a kind of communicative power that can effect change in our lives" (Brothman 2008, 154). But he also sounds a warning in saying that archives function not only as agents of political continuity and social solidarity, but also as powers of political denial, upheaval, and discontinuity. These aspects now begin to be researched in archival history. Examples are the studies of archives of

totalitarian regimes, their secret services and police, and the archivists and the archival institutions under these regimes (Kretzschmar 2007). But also in "normal" conditions, record formation is subject to power and, at the same time, exerts power (Ketelaar 2005).

Posner wrote in 1972 that archival history should not be limited to the reconstruction of the techniques for archives management, but must provide a view of the cultural context:

> Archives administration is so intimately connected with the governance of secular and religious affairs and with the individual's conduct of business that it must be viewed within the context of the cultures in which the archives originated and which now they help to bring back to life. (Posner 1972, vii)

For Tom Nesmith this implies that the history of society should be the starting point for historical research by the archivist. The archivist's scholarship, Nesmith argues, is "grounded in the study of the nature and purposes of archival records and institutions" (Nesmith 1982, 6; 1993, 161). Creation and use of records are integral aspects of the history of a society. Archival history should treat society's influence on practices of recordkeeping and vice versa: recordkeeping conditioning or facilitating societal practices. Such a social history of archives is important for the user of archives, the archivist, and the archival policy maker (Ketelaar 2014, 55).

Conclusion: Archivists, Archives, and archives

Naturally, the history of the profession and professionals is part of archival history. In fact, this is the genre of archival history which thus far has occupied the primary place in the literature written by practicing archivists.

Archives may refer to *archives (institution)* or to *archival programs*. Histories of these archives abound. Many of these studies, however, would be a prey to Richard Cox's criticism:

> Archivists who have written about the history of specific archival institutions have tended to treat them in virtual isolation, ignoring how they compare to repositories in other states or how they function in their own cultural milieu. There has also been little effort to use sociological or other organizational models to understand how or why these programs

come to be, flourish, change, or die. (Cox 1988, 140; 1990, 190–91)

Indeed, archival history should take into account the wider social, cultural, and political context of recordkeeping. This entails looking up after having read the archives, and looking beyond, and questioning its boundaries. Documenting, recordkeeping, and archival preservation are embedded in society's "archival consciousness" (Brothman 2010, 155) or "archival mentality" (O'Toole 2004, 170–71, 173). Such archival consciousness that precedes the appearance of formal archives manifests itself in oral tradition, rituals, social practices, monuments, and art. In that archival consciousness we may find at least some of the answers to fundamental questions like:

Over the course of history, what kinds of purposes have animated individuals and societies to keep and preserve documentation in its many forms, and what kinds of social consequences have induced them to continue to do so, to stop doing so, or to change how they do so? (Brothman 2010, 143)

—*Peter Horsman and Eric Ketelaar*

Keywords: history, archives, archival consciousness, social and cultural archival science

Related Entries: Archival Science; Archives (Institution); Functional Analysis; Recordkeeping System(s)

Bibliography

Blair, A., and J. Milligan. "Introduction." *Archival Science* 7 (4) (2007): 289–96. DOI: 10.1007/s10502-008-9069-7.

Blouin, F. X., and W. Rosenberg. *Processing the Past: Contesting Authority in History and the Archives.* Oxford: Oxford University Press, 2011.

Britnell, R. *Pragmatic Literacy, East and West 1200–1330.* Woodbridge, Suffolk, UK: Boydell Press, 1997.

Brothman, B. "Perfect Present, Perfect Gift: Finding a Place for Archival Consciousness in Social Theory." *Archival Science* 10 (2010): 141–89. DOI: 10.1007/s10502-010-9118-x.

Brothman, Brien. "Pekka Henttonen: Records, Rules and Speech Acts." *Archival Science* 8 (2) (2008): 149–56. DOI 10.1007/s10502-009-9080-7.

Brown, R. "Death of a Renaissance Record-Keeper: The Murder of Tomasso da Tortona in Ferrara, 1385." *Archivaria* 44 (1997): 1–43. http://journals.sfu.ca/archivar/index.php/archivaria/article/view/12195/13208.

Burke, F. G. "The Future Course of Archival Theory in the United States." *American Archivist* 44 (1) (1981): 40–46. http://archivists.metapress.com/content/485380l307551286/fulltext.pdf.

Clanchy, M. T. *From Memory to Written Record: England, 1066–1307,* 3rd edition. Chichester, West Sussex, UK: Wiley-Blackwell, 2013.

Cox, R. J. "American Archival History: Its Development, Needs, and Opportunities." *American Archivist* 46 (1) (1983): 31–41. http://archivists.metapress.com/content/n43kl32721m250g1/fulltext.pdf.

———. "The Failure or Future of American Archival History: A Somewhat Unorthodox View." *Libraries & Culture* (2000): 141–54. www.jstor.org/stable/25548803.

———. "On the Value of Archival History in the United States." *Libraries & Culture* (1988): 135–51. www.jstor.org/stable/25542039. Reprinted in R. J. Cox. *American Archival Analysis. The Recent Development of the Archival Profession in the United States.* Metuchen, NJ, and London: Scarecrow Press, 1990, 182–200.

Cook, T. "The Archive(s) Is a Foreign Country: Historians, Archivists, and the Changing Archival Landscape." *American Archivist* 74 (2) (2011): 600–632. http://archivists.metapress.com/content/xm04573740262424/fulltext.pdf.

Craig, B. L. "Outward Visions, Inward Glance: Archives History and Professional Identity." *Archival Issues* 17 (1992): 113–24. www.jstor.org/stable/41101829.

Craig, B. L., P. B. Eppard, and H. MacNeil. "Exploring Perspectives and Themes for Histories of Records and Archives. The First International Conference on the History of Records and Archives (I-CHORA)." *Archivaria* 60 (2006): 1–9.

Horsman, P. *Abuysen ende desordiën. Archiefvorming en archivering in Dordrecht 1200–1920.* The Hague: Stichting archiefpublicaties, 2011.

Jeurgens, K. J. P. F. M. *Een brug tussen twee werelden.* Leiden, the Netherlands: Universiteit Leiden, 2005. https://openaccess.leidenuniv.nl/handle/1887/2722 (accessed November 21, 2014).

Ketelaar, E. "Prolegomena to a Social History of Dutch Archives." In A. Aad Blok, J. Lucassen, and H. Sanders, eds., *A Usable Collection. Essays in Honour of Jaap Kloosterman on Collecting Social History*. Amsterdam: Amsterdam University Press, 2014, 40–55. www.oapen.org/search?identifier=496214 (accessed November 21, 2014).

————. "Recordkeeping and Societal Power." In S. McKemmish, M. Piggott, B. Reed, and F. Upward, eds., *Archives: Recordkeeping in Society*. Wagga-Wagga, New South Wales, Australia: Charles Sturt University, 2005, 277–98.

Nesmith, T. "Archives from the Bottom Up: Social History and Archival Scholarship." *Archivaria* 14 (1982): 5–26. http://journals.sfu.ca/archivar/index.php/archivaria/article/view/10937/11869. Reprinted in T. Nesmith, ed. *Canadian Archival Studies and the Rediscovery of Provenance*. London: Metuchen, 1993, 159–84.

O'Toole, J. M. "Back to the Future: Ernst Posner's Archives in the Ancient World." *American Archivist* 67 (2) (2004): 161–75. http://archivists.metapress.com/content/h124276213041315/fulltext.pdf.

Posner, E. *Archives in the Ancient World*. Cambridge: Harvard University Press, 1972.

Yates, J. *Control through Communication: The Rise of System in American Management*. Baltimore and London: Johns Hopkins University Press, 1989.

ARCHIVAL INVENTORY

In the context of archival work, the concept of inventory has evolved from the general notion of a listing for administrative purposes of the contents of an archival repository to a very particular form of *description* of *archives* intended to assist researchers. This entry focuses on the latter understanding of the term, emphasizing the lasting impact of this approach to delivery of information about archival materials. In their seminal work, *Manual for the Arrangement and Description of Archives*, Dutch archivists Muller, Feith, and Fruin present a blueprint for the archival inventory that repositories around the world continue to build on. Until recently, the normal first step for potential users of archives has been consultation of a paper inventory in a repository's reading room. Now, thanks to development of encoding standards, many of these paper inventories have been digitized and opened to online research. Internet availability presents opportunities for continuing assessment of the usability and usefulness of this venerable descriptive product.

The Inventory Tradition

The inventory that is the subject of chapter 4 of Muller, Feith, and Fruin's Manual is a description of a body of archival material deriving from a single administrative entity and organized (or arranged) according to the filing practices of that entity. Nineteenth-century Dutch archivists referred to this inventoried set as an archival *collection*, but other traditions use the terms *fonds*, *record group*, or *class* to identify the focus of their inventory. The manual recommends that the information presented in an inventory be divided into sections that reflect the activities that led to the production or accumulation of the *records* being described. Each section should be headed by a brief discussion of the history and functions of the entity that created the records dealt with in the section. According to the manual, descriptions of the records, grouped into filing systems (or series), should follow these introductory notes in an order consistent with their administrative relationships (a *file* of letters received described before the corresponding file of letters sent, for example). The recommended representation of each filing system consists of an identifying number; a title (preferably the one used by the creator when referring to the system); a "general description" of the contents of the file; the dates "over which the documents [in the file] extend"; and an indication of the form or genre of the materials constituting the filing system (volumes, files, *documents*).

Muller, Feith, and Fruin emphasize that the "general description" of the contents of a given inventory entry is what "matters most." They explain at length the importance of capturing in this element the essence of the nature of the filing system or *series*, presented in such a way that "the user of the inventory may perceive immediately what documents he will find in it." This description is not about individual documents; it is about the whole—the attributes common to all the records constituting the collective set.

Soon after its establishment in the mid-twentieth century, the National Archives of the United States adopted the inventory as the basic source of information about each of the major subdivisions of its holdings. A subdivision, called a record group, encompassed the records of a major component of government—usually a department or independent agency. A staff information circular (no. 14, first issued in 1950 and revised in 1982) provided rules for the preparation of the adopted form of record group description. The circular recommended that the inventory information be organized into the following sections: an introduction to the record group (its provenance, general composition, research strengths, and accessibility); a listing of the filing systems or series constituting the records along with a description of each series; and appendices presenting folder listings or other filing information for particularly important series. Large groups of records might be divided into subgroups consistent with administrative subdivisions; in these cases each subgroup would be introduced with contextual information similar to that provided in the general introduction to the inventory.

An important characteristic of the inventory is its hierarchically nested, multilevel nature. The descriptive information presented proceeds from the general to the specific. Contextual information provided in the general introduction applies to all of the subgroups and series included in the inventory. Any contextual information provided at the subgroup level supplements the general introduction and applies only to the series included in that subgroup. Lists of file folders inherit important *recordkeeping* information from the description of the series of which they are a part. In order to benefit fully from all that an inventory is intended to offer, the potential user of the archives it covers must understand how to navigate this nested approach. Wide adoption of the inventory as the finding aid of choice within the archival community over the last half-century presents researchers with many opportunities for development of this understanding.

With minor adjustments, the inventory approach also met the descriptive needs of manuscript repositories. Adopted initially at the Library of Congress in the 1950s, preparers there called this hierarchically structured finding aid a register. When describing personal papers, as it most often does, the register opens with a biographical note and continues with a discussion of the scope of the papers followed by descriptions of component series usually accompanied by container lists.

The Inventory and the Internet

When, in the 1980s, archivists began to explore the potential for electronic delivery of descriptive information, they looked upon the paper-based inventories and registers they had been preparing as chief sources of information to be shared in this way. Some, particularly archivists in the United States, welcomed the adaptation of the library world's Machine Readable Cataloging (MARC) format to enable capture of inventory-held information about archives, and they began to contribute this information to national networks popular with researchers. The intricacies of MARC cataloguing and (despite adaptation) the limitations of its ability to accommodate multilevel descriptive practice prompted mid-1990s investigation of the feasibility of digitizing whole inventories and encoding them for appropriate Internet searching and display. The investigation, directed by Daniel Pitti, then at the University of California, led to development of encoding standards that archivists around the world are now using to make their inventories accessible to Internet users.

The encoding standard resulting from Pitti's initial collaborative research effort is called Encoded Archival Description (EAD). Its application involves using Standard Generalized Markup Language (SGML) to assign codes (called tags) to text in an order that conforms to a document type definition (DTD). The document type that is the basis of EAD is the archival inventory with all of its information elements and hierarchical relationships; the DTD tags preserve these elements and relationships. The Society of American Archivists partners with the Library of Congress to maintain EAD, assisted by an internationally representative technical subcommittee.

The use of EAD to encode archival inventories creates one-stop searching opportunities for those who visit websites such as ArchiveGrid, Archives Canada, and Archives Portal Europe. These sites provide access to EAD-tagged inventories (and other descriptive resources) from multiple repositories.

They exploit EAD tags both to increase the accuracy and precision of searching and to facilitate consistent web display of results.

Conclusion

Muller, Feith, and Fruin's modern counterparts still identify the inventory (or the register) as "the core archival finding aid" (Roe 2005). But absent the development of EAD, this descriptive product might easily have become an artifact of archival history, rarely produced de novo and seldom consulted by researchers increasingly unfamiliar with paper. Internet availability gives this staple of archival description a new lease on life. It is, however, a life threatened by information seekers unwilling or unable to navigate within the hierarchy of an inventory in order to benefit from its guidance. This reality and questions now being raised about the role of an archival inventory in delivering information about digitized and electronic records are challenging today's archivists to re-imagine the descriptive tool that has been most closely associated with archival research for more than a century. For more information about the development of EAD, see *Archival Standards.—Sharon Thibodeau*

Keywords: Encoded Archival Description, finding aid, hierarchy, multilevel description register
Related Entries: Archival Description; Archival Arrangement; Archival Standards

Bibliography

"Encoded Archival Description." Library of Congress. www.loc.gov/ead (accessed December 2013).

Hill, E. "The Preparation of Inventories." Staff Information Paper 14, National Archives and Records Service, Washington, DC, 1982.

Muller, S., J. A. Feith, and R. Fruin. *Manual for the Arrangement and Description of Archives*, 2nd edition. Translated by Arthur H. Leavitt. New introductions by Peter Horsman, Eric Ketelaar, Theo Thomassen, and Marjorie Rabe Barritt. Chicago: Society of American Archivists, 2003.

Roe, K. *Arranging and Describing Archives & Manuscripts*. Chicago: Society of American Archivists, 2005.

ARCHIVAL LEGISLATION

According to Luciana Duranti in her entry on *archival science* in the 1996 edition of the *Encyclopedia of Library and Information Studies* (New York: Marcel Dekker), early *archival theory* on the nature of *archives* was based on the archival legislation of ancient Rome. These concepts subsequently spread to other countries in Europe and other parts of the world as the common law. Archival concepts such as the principle of *provenance* and the principle of *original order* were based on nineteenth-century laws issued in Naples, Holland, Prussia, and France, and these "juridical norms" subsequently became the "historical core of archival science" (Duranti 1996, 4).

Historical Development of Modern Archival Legislation

The outbreak of the French Revolution and the decree of June 25, 1794, was a landmark event in the history of modern archives administration (Posner 1984). One of the major outcomes of the decree was the establishment of a central Archives Nationales in France as a central agency for the *custody* and *preservation* of *archives*. Countries such as Holland and Belgium, which were influenced by the French Revolution, established their National Archives as newly established institutions. However, countries like the UK and Sweden, whose administrative structures were not dismantled, were able to develop their archival institution "in a more organic way" and the national archives from these countries evolved from one of their existing government departments, like the chancery (Posner 1984, 6).

Definition of Archival Legislation

The term *archival legislation* or *archives-enabling legislation*, as defined by the International Research on Permanent Authentic Records in Electronic Systems (InterPARES) Project, is "legislation that enables (brings into existence and assigns responsibilities) an archival institution or repository" (Suderman, Foscarini, and Coulter 2005, 4). Unlike records-related legislation, which "deals with records or information generally," archival legislation is an "enabling statute, because it establishes the overall mandate and functions of an archival institution and specifies the powers of the National Archivist" (Suderman, Foscarini, and Coulter 2005, 4).

Overall Mission and Functions of the Archival Institution

Both the International Council on Archives (ICA) Committee on Archival Legal Matters (Choy 2006) and the United Nations Educational, Scientific and Cultural Organization (UNESCO) studies (Ketelaar 1985) recommend that the archival legislation should specify the mission and functions of an archival institution. There are, however, a number of pieces of archival legislation that do not articulate the overall mission of the archival institution, which tends to be articulated in the annual reports or websites of the archival institution. Nevertheless, most pieces of archival legislation focus on what an archival institution does. As Victoria Lemieux (1993) states in her article "Archival Solitudes: The Impact on Appraisal and Acquisition of Legislative Concepts of Records and Archives" in *Archivaria*, "Archival institution, as policy sanctioned by an elected body, establishes a framework within which archival institutions carry out the functions of appraisal and selection, acquisition, arrangement and description, and making archival materials accessible" (153).

Creation and Maintenance of Public Records

Although the archival institution is the authority for archival *preservation* of public *records* in the government, the archival legislation in itself may not necessarily address the wide spectrum of issues relating to the *creation* and capturing of *records*. There is a network of other related legislation, directives, codes of practice, and policies. For example, the Library and Archives Canada (LAC) Act (SC 2004, c11) by itself does not specify the responsibility of the department to create reliable and accurate records. The act operates in tandem with other related directives and policies. The Directive on Recordkeeping (2009) states that the department needs to document records that "align with business activities, and that address accountability, stewardship, performance measurement, reporting and legal requirements" (section 6.1.4). Similarly in the UK,

the archival legislation is notably silent on the roles and responsibilities of the department in creating and capturing records. However, the Lord Chancellor's Code of Practice (2009) on the management of records issued under section 46 of the Freedom of Information Act 2000 states that departments should establish governance structure and lines of responsibility for records and information management. Departments should also ensure that records are authentic, are reliable, have *integrity*, and are usable (para. 8.3).

Unlike Canada and the UK, there are some examples of archival legislation that specifies the responsibilities of the creating agency. In the United States, the Records Management by Federal Agencies Statute (44 U.S.C. c. 31, §3101) states that the head of the federal agency is responsible in ensuring that there is "adequate and proper documentation of the organization, functions, policies, decisions, procedures, and essential transactions of the agency." In addition, the Managing Government Records Directive (2012, para 2.1) also states that all agencies should appoint a senior agency officer, who is responsible for ensuring that their agency "complies with all applicable records management statutes, regulations, and [National Archives and Records Administration] NARA policy," and the directive.

Appraisal and Transfer of Public Records

Despite *appraisal* being one of the core archival activities, many pieces of archival legislation do not define the term nor have specific legislative provisions relating to appraisal. Instead, the legislation often focuses on the *disposition* and destruction of records and accords the archival institution the power to authorize the destruction of public records. In reality, a number of the archives laws lack teeth, as they have no penalties even if the department destroys public records without seeking prior approval from the National Archives.

The archival institutions in Canada can potentially rely on other records-related legislation, such as the Access to Information Act (1985 s. 67.1), which imposes a fine and/or imprisonment to individuals who "destroy, mutilate or alter a record," "falsify a record or make a false record," or "conceal a record." However, such legislative provisions in the Access to Information Act (1985, s. 67.1) are geared toward cases of "obstructing right of access" and are thus difficult to apply to incidents where there is no request for access to information. There are usually no built-in penalties within the archival legislation, such as the LAC Act in Canada (2004), in the event that departments destroy public records without seeking the approval from the archives. At the most, what the LAC Act (2004, s. 13) can do is to ensure that the departments transfer records that "are in the opinion of the Librarian and Archivist at risk of serious damage or destruction." Such a legislative provision in the act requires the development of a policy in order to specify conditions for records that are at risk.

There are a number of archives laws that specify a time frame of several decades before the records are transferred to *archival custody*. In the UK, the Constitutional Reform and Governance Act (c25 2010, s. 45) reduces the time span for the "transfer to Public Record Office or to other appointed place of deposit of public records selected for permanent preservation" from thirty years to twenty years. Despite the reduction in time frame for the transfer of public records, the archival legislation still operates on a paper-based environment, and there is an assumption that records are adequately protected and that they remain reliable, authentic, and accessible after twenty years, despite changes in technology. Similarly, the Managing Government Records Directive (2012) in the United States stipulates that permanent records that are kept in government agencies more than thirty years should be "identified for transfer and reported to NARA." Since preservation requirements need to be incorporated during the early stages of the record's *lifecycle* in order to maintain the *authenticity* of records over space and through time, it is preferable that the transfer of records to archival custody be incorporated as part of the appraisal decision rather than by imposing a time frame. The "time-based" requirement for the transfer of records reflects the segregation between *records management* and the archives sphere of activities (Foscarini 2007, 126).

Preservation of Records

As *trusted custodians*, archival institutions have traditionally assumed the responsibility of maintaining the authenticity of records over time and have the

authority to certify copies of records within their custody. Unlike in an analogue environment, where the authenticity of a record is assumed, the authenticity of records in a digital environment is at risk when records are transmitted over space and through time. Moreover, it is possible to have multiple copies of records even after the creating or transferring agency hands over the custodianship of the records to the archives since *digital records* can be easily duplicated, modified, and reformatted. Questions potentially arise on which copy of the digital records would be the authentic copy. There are also risks when agencies bypass traditional chain of custody by outsourcing records to service providers in the cloud. However, the term authenticity is notably absent from many archival laws, even though maintaining and preserving the identity and integrity of records is of concern to archival institutions. Since maintaining the authenticity of records, such as instituting controls for the *transfer*, maintenance, and reproduction process, is a joint responsibility between the creating agency and the archival institution, the archival legislation should delineate the lines of responsibilities between both parties.

Conclusion

As an enabling act, the archival legislation facilitates the work of archival institutions by defining their mandate and objectives and by conferring powers to the institution and to the national archivist. However, the identification of a specific institution—the national archives—and the linkage of this institution with the archival legislation also constrain the institution, as there are limits on how the national archives operates in terms of exercising its authority within the government bureaucracy. These limits are especially telling in the operation of the archival institution when it cannot exercise oversight on records management in the government. Given the general "piecemeal treatment of the lifecycle in legislation," it is timely for archivists to consider how *archival theory* and archival concepts, such as authenticity requirements, can better inform the development of new legislative provisions and policy framework for the management and preservation of records (Suderman, Foscarini, and Coulter 2005, 22). At the same time, it must be acknowledged that the government may have other priorities, and that making changes to the archival legislation may not necessarily align with these priorities. As such, archivists have to examine the overall policy objectives and what they wish to achieve in terms of management and preservation of records.—*Elaine Goh*

Keywords: legislation, archives-enabling legislation, enabling act, statute

Related Entries: Appraisal; Archival Preservation; Archival Theory; Archives (Institution); Authenticity; Digital Record; Principle of Provenance; Record Creation

Bibliography

Access to Information Act, Revised Statutes of Canada 1985, c. A-1. http://laws-lois.justice.gc.ca/eng/acts/A-1.

Choy, Sarah. "Principles for Archives and Records Legislation." *International Council on Archives Committee on Archival Legal Matters* 19 (2006): 11–24. http://archivesactiongroup.org/main/wp-content/uploads/2012/05/Sarahs-article-in-ICA-Study.pdf.

Constitutional Reform and Governance Act 2010, United Kingdom, c. 25. www.legislation.gov.uk/ukpga/2010/25/contents (accessed April 6, 2014).

Foscarini, F. "InterPARES 2 and the Records-Related Legislation of the European Union." *Archivaria* 63 (Spring 2007): 121–36. http://journals.sfu.ca/archivar/index.php/archivaria/article/viewFile/13131/14375 (accessed April 6, 2014).

Ketelaar, Eric. "Archival and Records Management Legislation and Regulations: A RAMP Study with Guidelines." Paris, 1985. http://unesdoc.unesco.org/images/0006/000649/064948eo.pdf.

Library and Archives of Canada Act, Statutes of Canada 2004, c. 11. http://laws-lois.justice.gc.ca/eng/acts/L-7.7.

Lord Chancellor's Code of Practice on the Management of Records Issued under Section 46 of the Freedom of Information Act 2000. *The National Archives*, 2009. www.justice.gov.uk/downloads/information-access-rights/foi/foi-section-46-code-of-practice.pdf (accessed April 6, 2014).

Posner, Ernst. "Some Aspects of Archival Development Since the French Revolution." In Daniel Maygene and Timothy Walch, eds., *A Modern Archives Reader: Basic Readings on Archival Theory and Practice*. Washington, DC: National Archives Trust Fund Board, 1984, 3–14.

"Records Management by Federal Agencies." *About the National Archives, United States of America, 44 U.S.C. c. 31.* n.d. www.archives.gov/about/laws/fed-agencies.html.

Secretariat, Treasury Board of Canada. Directive on Recordkeeping, 2009. www.tbs-sct.gc.ca/pol/doc-eng.aspx?id=16552&section=text (accessed April 6, 2014).

Suderman, Jim, Fiorella Foscarini, and Erin Coulter. *Archives Legislation Study Report.* InterPARES 2 Project, 2005. www.interpares.org/displayfile.cfm?doc=ip2(policy)archivallegislationstudyreport.pdf (accessed April 6, 2014).

U.S. Executive Office of the President, Office of Management and Budget and National Archives and Records Administration. *Managing Government Records Directive.* From Jeffrey D. Zients and David S. Ferriero. Washington, DC, August 2012. www.whitehouse.gov/sites/default/files/omb/memoranda/2012/m-12-18.pdf.

ARCHIVAL MANAGEMENT SYSTEM(S)

While the ever-increasing penetration of information technology (IT) in all areas of activity has created substantial challenges for *archives* in the management and *preservation* of electronic *records* and in responding to customers' desires for online *access*, it has also produced opportunities for using the technology to improve *archival practice*. Options range from automated tools for specific tasks, such as conversion from obsolete *formats* of electronic records or production of *descriptions* in Encoded Archival Description format, to systems that support a range of archival *functions*. Among the applications available to archives is a class commonly called *archival management systems* (AMS), although other terms, such as "archival information management systems" and "archival content management systems," have also been used. There is no standard definition of the term, but contrasted to tools that automate or facilitate the performance of a specific type of work, an AMS should support the management of archival processes and the data used or produced in those processes, as well as data about the records processed.

There is considerable variation in the functions supported by AMS both in actual products and in the literature; however, both largely exclude generic management functions, such as financial and human resources management, concentrating on requirements that are specifically archival. A report published by the Society of American Archivists identified the following basic components of an AMS: *appraisal*, processing, space management, *preservation* management, disposal management, and reference (Hickerson 1990, 26–27). But many products do not support all of these areas. A report published by the Council on Library and Information Resources in 2009 stressed the importance of workflow automation and concentrated on systems that contribute to the production and online publication of descriptions and finding aids (Spiro). An AMS may support management of both hard copy and electronic records. A significant difference between the application of AMS to the two types of records is that data about hard-copy records and work done on them must be entered manually, while a system can automatically produce or capture data about electronic records.

The potential benefits of using an AMS include increased speed and efficiency and improved control over archival work, more consistent, complete, and accessible data about holdings and processing, and facilitation of the production, publication, and maintenance of descriptions and finding aids. Improved efficiency is an obvious result of the automatic extraction of *metadata* from electronic records and automatic production of data about actions performed in the system. Improved efficiency specifically for hard-copy records can occur when an AMS enables the input of data about the *arrangement* and links this information to data about the location of the records, eliminating the need to reorganize the records physically to conform to the arrangement. An AMS can also enhance the implementation of management policies, such as conformance to *standards* and enforcement of quality requirements for data. An AMS that spans multiple areas of practice can improve overall management by ensuring consistency and improving data sharing across archival processes.

Given that much of the data about archival records and processes performed on them should be preserved as long as the records themselves, an AMS qualifies as an Archival Information System (AIS) as defined in the ISO standard, *Open Archival Information System (OAIS)—Reference Model* (ISO 14721:2012). While this standard is commonly held to describe requirements for repository management, it defines an archival information system as a system used to manage any information for a time long enough for technological change to be significant. Thus, the design of AMS would benefit from taking into consideration both the functional requirements and the information model articulated in the OAIS standard.

State of the Art

Current offerings of AMS can be divided into two subclasses. The first might be characterized as "archival management" systems and the second as archival "management systems." The first subclass provides institutions with possibilities for automating the execution of archival work, typically spanning several areas of practice and potentially the entire gamut from appraisal to reference. The automation of archival management is enabled by a workflow engine, with which an organization can define a sequence of steps involved in completing a process, the persons or roles involved in human actions along the way, the data that are either needed, produced, or modified in each step, and the criteria for completion of both individual steps and the entire process. The AMS then manages the execution of each instance of this defined pattern, notifying the persons involved of the need for action at the appropriate points, prompting data entry where needed, and executing or triggering the execution of automated actions. One example is ArchivesSpace, a system produced by the fusion of two earlier efforts, Archon and the Archivists' Toolkit. Developed by collaboration among academic archives in the United States, it supports end-to-end archival management, including accessioning and deaccessioning, arrangement and description, location management, authority control, metadata management, and access to descriptions and digital objects.

Some AMS have strengths in particular areas of archival practice, such as description, repository management, or *digital preservation*. For example, the International Council on Archives' Access to Memory application (ICA-AtoM) is an open-source, web-based archival description application compliant with ICA descriptive standards. ICA-AtoM is web-based and supports collections that span several repositories. Developed by a for-profit company, Archivematica is a free and open-source suite of tools supporting workflow for processing electronic records from ingest to access, including digital preservation.

The integrated Rules Oriented Data System (iRODS) is in a class by itself. iRODS is open-source middleware that enables the definition and management of collections of data, including data objects such as electronic records or descriptions of, or proxies for, hard-copy records. At the core of iRODS is a rule engine that enables the articulation and implementation of policies, such as disposition instructions, conditions on use, and triggers for preservation actions. Policies are implemented as micro services that can be executed across a variety of IT platforms. iRODS also includes a metadata catalog that can be used to store information about records. iRODS can be linked to various front-end applications, including workflow management, digital preservation tools, and discovery and access systems. For archives, iRODS has a special advantage in that its rule engine can serve as a record of changing policies and the records to which particular policies were applied.

There is considerable variation in the genesis of AMS. Some AMS have been developed in single institutions and are specifically customized for the legal, policy, and business needs of the sponsor. Some AMS have been developed by individual organizations but with a view to satisfying the needs of similar institutions. Other AMS have been sponsored by professional organizations or by ad hoc collaborations. Still other applications were originally developed for libraries but have been extended or adapted for archives. Some are produced and supported by commercial companies.

The origination of an AMS gives some indication of the likelihood that the system will be supported over time and enables an initial assessment whether that system responds to the needs of an organization considering acquiring one. There is, for example, a risk that an AMS developed under a grant may not survive over the long term unless the developer finds some other, more durable source of funding. An AMS developed for a specific institution may

not be suitable even for other similar institutions because it is fine-tuned to the requirements of the original sponsor. Archives considering the acquisition of applications developed for libraries should consider how well they address archival needs and how far and how easily they could be adapted to those needs.

AMS also differ in the IT infrastructure required to run them. Some run within Web browsers. Some run on Unix or Linux platforms; others require Windows or Apple systems. Some can only be installed locally, while others can be hosted remotely. Some are designed essentially to operate in stand-alone mode, while others are better suited for distributed implementation.

Selection and Implementation

The differences in features of various AMS products provide archival institutions with significant choices; however, as with the introduction of any new technology, the most important criteria that should drive the selection of an AMS are not technological. An institution should base its choice on a determination of its business requirements articulated on the basis of its mission, responsibilities, and organizational environment, and assessed against its resources, accomplishments, shortcomings and challenges. Development of this assessment can be strengthened by involving all categories of stakeholders, including the archives management and staff, higher authorities, researchers, those responsible for technical support, and representatives of other entities, such as records creators or peer institutions that interact with the archives in areas covered by the AMS. Once the business needs are determined, the organization should consider alternative ways of satisfying them, including nontechnical options, such as revising policies, modifying procedures, reassigning responsibilities, as well as opportunities for applying IT.

Several different types of criteria should be brought to bear in selecting an AMS. They include business requirements, technology, acquisition and support, and finance.

- Business Requirements
  - Range of archival practice: does the applicability of an AMS correspond to the areas of

greatest need? While a comprehensive AMS that spans all archival functions theoretically offers the greatest benefits, if the needs of the organization are concentrated in one or two areas, it might be preferable to select specialized applications for those areas.

- Functional needs: Do the strengths and potential benefits of a particular AMS correspond to the activities targeted in the organizational assessment?
- Records: Is the AMS applicable to the genres and types (analog or digital) of records that need to be processed?
- Data: How well does the AMS provide for the generation, collection, and use of data the institution needs for management of archival work and for other purposes, such as preservation, discovery, and assessment of authenticity?
- Standards: Does the AMS support the implementation of archival and other relevant standards adopted by the archives?
- Adaptability: Can the AMS be fine-tuned to local policies and practices?
- Technology
  - Infrastructure: Is the AMS compatible with existing or planned IT infrastructure?
  - Quality: Is the system robust, secure, and sustainable?
  - Usage: Is the system easy to install, adapt, maintain, and use?
  - Compatibility: Can the AMS interoperate with other relevant applications across the entire relevant range of its functions?
- Acquisition and Support
  - Source: Is the AMS free and open source or proprietary? Does the owner or provider appear to be stable?
  - Implementation Options: Does the AMS satisfy local implementation options? Can it be installed on the existing IT infrastructure? Can it be installed by current staff? Can it be configured to support staff who work in different locations, such as at the sites of records creators or donors?
  - Support: Does the provider offer sufficient technical and user support at an affordable rate? How much support is needed within the

institution itself? Can current staff provide this support?
- Finance
  - Initial costs: How much will it cost to acquire and install the system?
  - Ongoing costs: How much will it cost to operate the system?
  - Savings and offsets: Do the benefits offered by the AMS yield actual savings? Will the AMS produce cost avoidances, such as reducing the need for additional staff?

Conclusion

Archival management systems can benefit archives by improving efficiency, consistency, and access to holdings. Current possibilities span a range from specific archival functions, such as digital preservation, to the entire process from accessions to access. Institutions considering the adoption of such applications should articulate their needs in terms of their business requirements and organizational environment. This will enable assessment of whether and how they can be best served by the technology.

—_Kenneth Thibodeau_

Keywords: information technology, archival practice, management

Related Entries: Archival Description; Archival Preservation; Archival Standards; Digital Preservation

Bibliography

Archivematica. www.archivematica.org/wiki/Main-Page (accessed December 2012).

Hickerson, H. Thomas. "Standards for Archival Information Management Systems." _American Archivist_ 53 (1) (1990): 24–28. http://archivists.metapress.com/content/51073745867024r0/fulltext.pdf (accessed December 2013).

ICA-AtoM. www.ica-atom.org (accessed November 2013).

IRODS: Data Grids, Digital Libraries, Persistent Archives, and Real-Time Data Systems. www.irods.org (accessed December 2013).

International Organization for Standardization. _Space Data and Information Transfer Systems—Open Archival Information System (OAIS)—Ref-_

erence Model. ISO 14721:2012. Geneva: International Organization for Standardization, 2012.

Matienzo, Mark, and Katherine Kott. "ArchivesSpace: A Next-Generation Archives Management System." MW2013: Museums and the Web 2013. The annual conference of Museums and the Web, April 17–20, 2013. http://mw2013.museumsandtheweb.com/paper/archivesspace-a-next-generation-archives-management-system (accessed October 2013).

Moore, Reagan, Arcot Rajasekar, Paul Watry, Favio Corubolo, John Harrison, and Jerome Fuselier. "Evolving Persistent Archives and Digital Library Systems: Integrating iRods, Cheshire3 and Multivalent." *The International Journal of Digital Curation* 8 (2) (2013): 47–67. www.ijdc.net/index.php/ijdc/article/view/8.2.47/334 (accessed December 2013).

Spiro, Lisa. *Archival Management Software. A Report for the Council on Library and Information Resources*. Washington, DC: Council on Library and Information Resources, 2009.

ARCHIVAL METHOD

Every area of knowledge creates its own theories, models, methods, and practices to investigate its research object. The archival method is the distinguishing method of the discipline *archival science*. It was developed in the course of the nineteenth century and soon regarded as the pillar of archival scholarship. It is not a theory, a principle, or a practical technique. It is rather the application of principles developed from *archival theory*, within a coherent framework where theory guides methodology.

A discipline is "a systematic and ordered study based upon clearly defined models and rules of procedure" (Clarke 1968, xiii). This means that a discipline "encompasses both a way of gaining knowledge—rules of procedure that discipline the scholar's search—and the resulting knowledge itself" (Livelton 1996, 44). In practice, a discipline usually has:

- an object of research which may be not peculiar to the discipline and may be shared with other disciplines;

- a body of knowledge related to the object of research that is generally not shared with other disciplines;
- specific theories, concepts, and paradigms according to which its body of knowledge is structured;
- a language embedding its technical terminology and characteristic idiom;
- specific research methods; and
- some institutional manifestation, usually "in the form of subjects taught at universities or colleges, respective academic departments and professional associations connected to it" (Krishnan 2009, 9).

Archival science has identified *records* and their aggregations as the primary objects of its investigation: in order to understand their nature, meaning, and functions, and control them throughout their life, archival science has developed through the centuries methods, models, and techniques aimed at both investigating archival issues and managing record processes. Duranti and Michetti (2015) in their chapter in *Research in the Archival Multiverse* state:

> It did so by borrowing from different fields: the debate between historians and archivists led to the affirmation of the historical method of analysis; the strong relationship with library science affected retrieval practices and theories; the first attempts to introduce mechanization in public administration changed documentation processes; information science changed the relationship of archives with technology; social sciences questioned archival behaviour, processes, and policies; and post-modernism spurred a debate about archival identity and purposes.

The Origin of the Archival Method

The body of archival knowledge is based on a very small core that has been continuously expanded through concepts, methods, theories, and practices taken from other disciplines, in a very peculiar process of assimilation: whenever possible, knowledge borrowed from outside and applied to the archival domain has been integrated consistently into the theoretical and methodological archival framework already in place, in such a way that becomes impossible to distinguish between native and imported archival knowledge. What really makes the difference is the goal: if theories and methods external to archival science are used to understand or manage archival entities, they may augment archival knowledge and become part of the archival framework. "In other words, 'external' knowledge borrowed to work on or to analyse 'internal' entities produces 'internal' knowledge" (Duranti and Michetti, 2015). This is the reason why *archivists* cannot rest on their consolidated body of knowledge: their discipline is intrinsically grounded upon and propelled by theories, methods, and practices taken from other fields of study. A discipline may well be a melting pot of principles and methods: "What is essential to maintaining its integrity is that those entities coming from outside are gathered into a cohesive system. A discipline must have its own methodology—even if resulting from a variety of processes taken and adapted from other disciplines . . . —which constitutes, and is assessed and recognised as, an integral part of its body of knowledge" (Duranti and Michetti, 2015).

The origins of the archival method as the method of archival science may be traced back to the nineteenth century, when Francesco Bonaini, the first director and superintendent of the Tuscan Archives, wrote: "The evidence of facts and the sequence of events is recorded into documents. These, more or less, had an arrangement and a title. Therefore, first rule: respect the fact; second: re-establish it, if it were altered" (Bonaini 1867, 174). This statement is considered to have given origin to what Bonaini called the "historical method" because its roots were in history, not because it was meant to serve history (Panella 1957, 187). Bonaini's words must be framed in a wider context. In the mid-nineteenth century, a new approach to *archives* had spread throughout Europe, taking different names and meanings in different countries: *Respect des fonds* in France, *Provenienzprinzip* in Germany, *Herkomstbeginsel* in Holland, *Metodo storico* in Italy. This approach came from the same cultural environment and affirmed the need for a new understanding of documentary phenomena, based no longer on an erudite study of single *documents* but rather grounded on the analysis of documents in their *context* of *creation* and sedimentation, hence moving toward the study of documentation processes and *creators'* activities.

However, the historical method was born as a procedure, a technique: "Pragmatism gave birth

to the notion—not pure theory. . . . The method was spontaneously born as a practical solution for problems in archival arrangement" (Horsman 2002, 6–7). It took almost a century before another Italian scholar, Giorgio Cencetti, stated that the historical method, although born as a method of *arrangement*, "should rather be considered something more and all encompassing, a fundamental *principle* of archival doctrine, and the necessary condition for using an archives" (Cencetti 1970, 63). This was the crucial step forward: "Moving from practice to theory, [Cencetti] recognized how the historical method could serve as a fundamental instrument for developing new theory and methods, thus making of it the pillar on which all archival knowledge rests" (Duranti and Michetti, in press). Cencetti also changed the name of the method, from historical to archival method, to highlight the fact that such method is grounded upon the nature of the archival materials that are the object of its study. As a matter of fact, "Cencetti not only changed a name, he changed the entire archival worldview" (Duranti and Michetti, 2015).

What Is the Archival Method?

Records are the primary objects of archival investigation. In order to understand their nature and meaning, and to determine how to control them, the archival method assumes that archivists must focus on *records creators* as the main sources of information about records. "More precisely, archival researchers are interested in the documentary manifestation of records creators: the life and history of creators, be they persons or organizations, interest them only inasmuch as these help defining the context of the records and gaining knowledge about each creator's interaction with its fonds" (Duranti and Michetti, 2015). As Cencetti put it, the archival questions are indeed always the same, as they aim "to determine the records creator's functions, to study how they were fulfilled, and to ascertain the way they were documented" (Cencetti 1970, 65). The archival perspective is not an ahistorical one, though. Archivists cast their research questions in a historical framework, and they may even consider further dimensions in order to get a deeper knowledge of context: the societal environment determines the role and nature of both archives and archivists; the technological context affects documents and related processes; the economic profile is usually a relevant constraint in any archival action; and the juridical framework is key to understanding the nature and meaning of documents, along with the actions to which they are related. However, any additional dimension contributing to define a larger and richer picture is valuable only as long as it helps in getting a deeper knowledge of the documentary phenomena.

The archival method is rooted in archival theory and is the result of a coherent system in which theory guides methodology: "Theoretical ideas about the nature of a fonds, for example—generally or in the abstract—dictate the archival methodology by which a particular fonds is examined by the archivist, which in turn determines the resulting scholarly product" (Livelton 1996, 45). Due to such an approach, the archivist's activity is nonevaluative in nature, because it is not based on some external criteria, but on principles and methods belonging to the discipline itself. This is the reason why the outcomes of archival research—for example, the acquisition of a specific body of records, the arrangement given to the records in a fonds, the attribution of previously unidentified documents, the selection conducted on a fonds, the determination of what social media products have a record nature, the development of a preservation policy—can provide support to any kind of research, historical or otherwise, subsequently carried out by the users of the archives, who can trust the outcomes of research undertaken by archivists in the course of their work (Cassese 1955).

The archival method and the historical method are not in opposition: they may be used in relation to different objectives, as noted by Adolf Brenneke in his *Archivkunde* (1953). The archival method is the fundamental and primary tool to understand the history of an *archival fonds*, while the historical method is meant to reveal the history of its creator. Unfortunately, the two dimensions, archival and historical, do not always coincide: the fonds is the result of the natural accumulation of materials, which may not be perfectly aligned with the creator's activities. Brenneke proposed to bridge the gap by allowing archivists to reorganize the archival fonds so that it reflects the activities of the creator, while Angelika Menne-Haritz highlighted the different purposes of archival and historical research

and strongly objected to such method of arrangement on the grounds that it would involve the loss of the records' evidentiary capacity (Menne-Haritz 1994, 532).

The archival method does not evaluate its object of study: all records in a fonds "are equally important because they are equally necessary to the existence of the whole, and all archival fonds are equally important because they are equally necessary to the formation of the global documentary heritage" (Duranti and Michetti, 2015). Rather, the archival method tries to understand its object of study and uses archival theory as an interpretative framework. This means that the meaning associated with objects, aggregations and relationships can be understood in the light of concepts and models provided by the theory: a record is not its content, and its content is not just what it talks about. There are patterns of processes, aims and mandates, procedures and results, signs and signals, not only words (Menne-Haritz 1994, 537). In other words, the archival method seeks to reconstruct the relationships among internal and external elements of the records, their structure, and their context. To this aim archivists may need to employ tools drawn from the philological disciplines, especially when they need not only to understand their object of investigation, but also to make decisions, "either as part of an archival function (e.g., arrangement or selection), or in order to produce a conceptual, methodological, or policy finding (e.g., a new definition of record, a new metadata application profile for authenticity, or a policy for the use of social media)" (Duranti and Michetti, 2015).

Conclusion

Every discipline creates its own theories, models, methods, and practices to investigate its objects of research. The archival method is the distinguishing method of archival science, the result of an unceasing action of assimilation from outside and reconfiguration from inside, the pillar that supports the complex architecture of archival scholarship, and the tool that validates the consistency of any change in such architecture with its existing structural components. However, a discipline is a collective and historical endeavor, developed through ongoing additions and stratifications. Not only do concepts and theories change, thereby allowing asking new questions and discovering new data, but also methods vary in time. The archival method is not immune from such cultural and historical influences; it is not an ahistorical, aseptic tool through which we can develop archival knowledge. Therefore, archivists in the future may need to alter "the interpretative framework of both archival theory (*what* archivists work with) and methodology (*how* they work) in conjunction with the tools of philological disciplines" (Duranti and Michetti, 2015). Nonetheless, the archival method will continue to hold its full validity as a coherent system in which theory guides methodology. It is very likely that in the future the archival questions will still be the same—Who is the creator? What are the functions? What is the nature of records?—but a totally different meaning will be attached to the terms creator, function, and nature. In other words, the archival method has a key feature: it involves change, because it is grounded upon theory, which is continuously refined and reshaped. "Everything needs to change, so everything can stay the same," said the prince in the famous novel by Tomasi di Lampedusa. *Au contraire, au contraire....*

—*Giovanni Michetti*

Keywords: archival discipline, historical method, archival research, archival science

Related Entries: Archival History; Archival Science; Archival Theory; Context

Bibliography

Bonaini, F. *Relazione al Ministero dell'Istruzione pubblica*, 1867. As cited in E. Lodolini. *Storia dell'archivistica italiana*, 3rd edition. Milano: Franco Angeli, 2004.

Cassese, L. "Del metodo storico in archivistica." *Società* 11 (5) (1955): 878–85.

Cencetti, G. "Inventario bibliografico e inventario archivistico." In *Scritti Archivistici*. Rome: Il Centro di ricerca Editore, 1970, 56–69.

Clarke, D. L. *Analytical Archaeology*. London: Methuen, 1968.

Duranti, L., and G. Michetti. "The Archival Method: Rediscovering a Research Tradition." In A. Gilliland, A. Lau, and S. McKemmish, eds., *Research in the Archival Multiverse*. Clayton, Victoria, Australia: Monash University Publishing, 2015.

Horsman, P. "The Last Dance of the Phoenix, or the Re-discovery of the Archival Fonds." *Archivaria* 54 (2002): 1–23. http://journals.sfu.ca/archivar/index.php/archivaria/article/view/12853/14076.

Krishnan, A. *What Are Academic Disciplines? Some Observation on the Disciplinarity vs. Interdisciplinarity Debate*. Southampton: University of Southampton, National Centre for Research Methods, January 2009.

Livelton, T. *Archival Theory, Records, and the Public*. Lanham, MD: Scarecrow Press; and London: The Society of American Archivists, 1996.

Menne-Haritz, A. "Appraisal or Documentation: Can We Appraise Archives by Selecting Content?" *The American Archivist* 57 (3) (1994): 528–42. http://archivists.metapress.com/content/g114464381p11324/fulltext.pdf.

Panella, A. "Francesco Bonaini." *Rassegna degli Archivi di Stato* 17 (2) (1957): 181–202.

ARCHIVAL POLICY

The broad term *archival policy* is a collection of rules and procedures archival organizations use to manage overall organization operations. The key here is management. The third clause at *BusinessDictionary.com*'s definition lists *policy* as: "The set of basic principles and associated guidelines, formulated and enforced by the governing body of an organization, to direct and limit its actions in pursuit of long-term goals." A foundation of any archival policy is a mission statement. Relying on a mission statement, archival management policies are collections of principles and guidelines tailor-fit to an individual archives. These include: *selection* and *appraisal*, accessioning, *arrangement* and *description*, security, and *disaster planning*.

What Is a Mission Statement?

Brinkley wrote in 1939 that "the public should learn to expect in the *archives* of its own community the same kind of reference service that its public library gives" (163). Brinkley's article looks at archival policy as a "strategic objective." The mission statement, therefore, should reflect the strategic objective of the archives and be approved in writing by upper management. It should be as concise as possible and reflect in narrative form the foundational archival management policies. Hunter (2003) refers to a mission statement as an "Authorizing Policy Statement" (43). Additionally, many archival mission statements include clauses that reflect the goals of the archives, which often include "history" and "enduring value" for the public. The strategic objective of a mission statement is an intellectual bond between patrons that access the information and the *archives*.

Selection and Appraisal

Because there is a huge volume of material that has potential archival value, institutions must prioritize and decide which items to house in their *collections*. Whereas a mission statement is a public starting point, selection and appraisal policies specifically tell an *archivist* what types of *records* belong in their care. State and federal archives reflect often complicated regulatory environments. The strategic objectives for these types of institutions support government *accountability*. For the United States, the National Archives and Records Administration (NARA) follows mandates set down by the Federal Records Act and other pertinent laws. The UK and their National Archives rely on the Public Records Act and the Grigg Committee.

For cultural, corporate, and other private archives, selection and appraisal are subjectively based on factors such as enduring value, records retention policies, and/or specific historical reflections. These factors in themselves reflect strategic values. For cultural and other private archives donor agreements and/or deeds of gifts specifically reflect which type of items will be part of the archives. Corporate archives selection policies reflect a specific corporate vision. In all cases the specific instructions for obtaining items become selection policy where appraisal is an intrinsic element of choosing items—sometimes archivists decide, and sometimes the decision is made for them.

Accessioning Policy

The American Alliance of Museums defines *accessioning* as "the formal act of legally accepting an object or objects" (4). In other words, if selection and appraisal policies outline what items belong in an archives, accessioning policies begin a formal

process that an archivist uses to insert the items in a legal capacity into the archives. This legal process begins with an official form such as the one used by the City College of New York's CUNY Dominican Studies Institute. A review of the CUNY document and some examples at the Library of Congress identifies text fields that report information about the item(s) that:

- establishes preliminary physical control;
- establishes preliminary intellectual control; and
- documents holdings to facilitate planning, budgeting, and prioritization. (Carnell 2004, 1)

Accession policies are crucial parts of overarching archival management policies because they provide a legal starting point for processing archivists who arrange and describe items in their care. They support archival objectives from a legal perspective.

Arrangement and Description Policies

Once archivists take possession of items, a specific process, arrangement and description, must be undertaken. This illuminates items and their placement in the physical *archives*. This process involves several steps that are outlined in an internal policy document. The outcome of this process is the availability of the item(s) for researchers and other users. Although over the past century much has been written about this process and the development of guidelines for standardization, the process can vary from country to country and even from local region to local region. That said, archives can rely on specific guidelines and standards. In the United States, the Society of American Archives maintains *Describing Archives, a Content Standard (DACS)*. For an international guideline, archivists look to the International Council on Archives, which published *General International Standard Archival Description ISAD(G)*. This is by no means an exhaustive listing. The point is that using a specific standard should be identified in a policy that standardizes *arrangement* and *description*.

Security and Public Access

Although the public is well informed on how to use libraries, archives are a different matter. Brinkley stated in 1939 that "a fully developed archives may have to go much further than the library in teaching people to use it" (163). Whether it is a researcher "borrowing" an item for convenience or a thief wanting to sell a rare manuscript on the black market, theft of archival material is a real problem for those charged with protecting archives (see Mason 1975 for historical examples of thefts). Broadly speaking, most security-policy documents cover access to their collections, through both requirements (e.g., use of designated research areas, gloves worn to handle items, signatures verifying rules have been read and are understood) and prohibitions (e.g., personal bags or backpacks, other folders or books [to guard against placing items inside], and ink pens [this protects marking up the items]. This list is not exhaustive. Depending on the requirements of the particular archive, security policies can vary from institution to institution. Fortunately there are guidelines to provide protection for these items. The *Northeast Document Conservation Center* publishes detailed guidelines for security. Any issue or rule should ultimately be part of a written security policy. Such policy documents protect staff and patrons alike. According to Totka (1993), "A written policy, with clearly defined limits, should promote consistency and provide some legal protection for the repository and its staff" (671).

Disaster Planning and Preservation Policy

Unfortunately disasters do occasionally occur. It is essential then that archival institutions have in place a policy document that instructs staff on safety procedures, protection of the collections, and disaster recovery. According to Lyall (2009), "A comprehensive disaster plan consists of several independent but interrelated smaller plans" (para. 3). These smaller parts address three phases of disasters: before, during, and after. Put in writing, the plans are instructions in the form of policy that reflect back in some way to the mission statement.

Disaster prevention typically involves preserving archival collections. For instance:

- Disaster prevention plans instruct archivists on housing vital records in water- and fire-proof containers.

- Disaster plans also instruct staff on procedures to undertake during a disaster. Such a document should focus first on staff safety.
- Disaster recovery plans provide disaster staff and other recovery professionals with instructions to reopen the institution and recover the collections. For instance, in the case of water damage to records, the disaster recovery plan instructs professionals on the steps needed to preserve the damaged records.

Training is a necessary part of any disaster plan because it prepares staff to react in an automatic nature. Lyall explains that a disaster plan helps staff "cope better with the reality than they would have been able to without any disaster preparedness training" (para. 42). Disasters are events that cause substantial emotional distress. Following a disaster plan as institutional policy is a means of getting control of the situation and combating the chaos a disaster can cause.

Conclusion

Archival policy is not one specific policy but, rather, a collection of interrelated policies and instructions that connect together to manage the institution. The mission statement is a broadly defined authorizing policy that gives patrons and staff a starting point for understanding the goals and purpose of the institution. Selection and appraisal policies instruct staff on which items reflect the mission statement. Because we live in a complex world of interconnected archives with similar mission statements, accessioning policies offer a chance for standardization and universal access. Security policies protect the collections, staff, and patrons from theft or other damaging actions. Finally, disaster preparedness and recovery policies guide staff in the event of a large or small disaster and protect records that are vital to the core values laid out by the mission statement. Brinkley closes with this statement: "The objective of archival policy . . . must be nothing less than the enriching of the complete historical consciousness of the people as a whole" (168).—*Mark Driskill*

Keywords: accession policy, arrangement and description policy, disaster preparedness, mission statement.

Related Entries: Acquisition Policy; Archival Policy; Collection Management Policy; Information Policy

Bibliography

American Alliance of Museums. "Developing a Collections Management Policy." Alliance Reference Guide, 2012. www.aam-us.org/docs/continuum/developing-a-cmp-final.pdf?sfvrsn=2 (accessed November 23, 2014).

Binkley, Robert C. "Strategic Objectives in Archival Policy." *American Archivist* 2 (3) (1939): 162–68. http://archivists.metapress.com/content/j5263704635335lu/fulltext.pdf (accessed November 22, 2014).

Carnell, B. "Accession Forms: Representative Samples." Washington, DC: Library of Congress, Prints & Photographs Division, 2004. www.loc.gov/rr/print/tp/Accession%20Form%20Samples.pdf (accessed November 23, 2014).

CUNY Dominican Studies Institute. "Accession Policy." City College of New York, 2011. www.ccny.cuny.edu/dsi/upload/ARCHIVES-ACCESSION-FORM.pdf (accessed November 23, 2014).

Hunter, Gregory S. *Developing and Maintaining Practical Archives. A How-to-Do-It Manual,* 2nd edition. New York: Neal-Schuman, 2003.

Lyall, Jan. "Disaster Planning for Libraries and Archives: Understanding the Essential Issues." *National Library of Australia Staff Papers*, 2009. www.nla.gov.au/openpublish/index.php/nlasp/article/viewArticle/979/1249.

Mason, Philip P. "Archival Security: New Solutions to an Old Problem. *American Archivist* 38 (4) (1975): 477–92. http://archivists.metapress.com/content/0w3j718102253120/fulltext.pdf.

Northeast Document Conservation Center. "Emergency Management, Section 3.11-Collections Security: Planning and Prevention for Libraries and Archives." www.nedcc.org/free-resources/preservation-leaflets/3.-emergency-management/3.11-collections-security-planning-and-prevention-for-libraries-and-archives (accessed November 24, 2014).

"Strategic Directions: Appraisal Policy." National Archives and Records Administration, 2007. www.archives.gov/records-mgmt/initiatives/appraisal.html (accessed November 22, 2014).

Totka, Vincent A. "Preventing Patron Theft in the Archives: Legal Perspectives and Problems." *American Archivist* 56 (4) (1993): 664–72.

ARCHIVAL PRACTICE

In his *Archives in the Ancient World*, Ernst Posner describes evidence of archival practice among Mesopotamian ruins. The evidence takes the form of rooms set aside for the specific purpose of storage of *records* and lists of the contents therein. This evidence indicates that these basics of archival responsibility—segregation and protection of documentation of human transactions—have a very long history. Further elaboration of the character of archival practice has, of course, occurred in the centuries following the Mesopotamian era, but nothing has usurped the fundamental nature of the segregate and protect actions. Writing in the twentieth century, Sir Hilary Jenkinson identifies the primary duties of an *archivist* as (1) the "physical defense of *archives*" and (2) the "moral defense of archives." The first of these duties entails provision of appropriate storage (setting aside or segregation), the second, insurance against loss or alteration (protection). This entry considers Jenkinson's "defenses" in light of current understanding of the archival profession.

Defending the Record

Until the advent of electronic *recordkeeping*, the physical defending of archives was generally understood to occur within a "brick-and-mortar" repository, well designed (over time, increasingly so) to minimize risks presented by fire, weather, and vermin. Research on the effects of temperature and humidity on recording media led to installation in these repositories of mechanisms to control such variables. The individuals staffing these repositories engaged in archival practice when they housed the records in their charge in environments, usually called stack areas, intended to prolong the life of the media on which the records had been recorded. As electronic records took on archival status, the archivists who accepted responsibility for their physical defense found they needed to think differently about appropriate *preservation* environments, developing as they did the concept of trusted *digital repositories*.

The moral defense aspect of archival practice entails a broad range of activities intended to ensure that archived records (whether analog or digital) retain the identity and *integrity* (*reliability* and *authenticity*) intended by their *creators*. Accomplishment of this paramount goal requires capture and maintenance of information about the origins of the records; their form, genre, and physical characteristics; relationships that exist among them; and actions taken on the records by successive custodians. These are labor-intensive processing actions (*arrangement*, *description*, and *preservation*) that demand a significant portion of the resources available for investment in archives. Additional important moral defensive actions include implementation of procedures and systems designed to manage archival holdings and monitor their use.

Defense Systems

The ideal holdings management system for analog records stores information about the "at rest" stack locations of these records and tracks any changes to this location, whether temporary or permanent. The most effective system tracks all movements of records, in particular delivery to a research room for consultation. Techniques available for achieving this level of analog records tracking include barcoding of containers or attachment of radio frequency identification (RFID) tags to file folders. Holdings management information to be collected and stored systematically also includes data about *conservation* or reformatting actions taken on records.

The ideal monitoring system deters any attempt to alter, destroy, or remove archived records regardless of media. Such a system limits and controls access to the storage locations for records and, to the extent possible, tracks all *access* events. In addition, the ideal monitoring system provides for close oversight of researcher review of original records and implementation of "clean research room" rules that circumscribe researcher behavior. The "Regulations for NARA Researchers" section of the website of the National Archives and Records Administration includes an example of such rules. Other protective actions include requiring researchers to review copies of particularly vulnerable or valuable originals.

Conclusion

While the Jenkinsonian understanding of archival practice is an essential one, it by no means encompasses the full range of activities associated with the profession in the twenty-first century. One need only consult any recently published manual for archivists to discover that practice today frequently entails much more than segregation and protection of the record. It may begin with consultation with records creators and continue with *appraisal* and *selection* as a prelude to *acquisition* and *custody* and to the arrangement, description, preservation, and holdings security activities that form Jenkinson's core. Today's archivists take a much more proactive view of access than did their nineteenth-century counterparts, reaching out to potential users via onsite lectures, training, and *exhibits* and expanding the content of virtual reading rooms on the World Wide Web.—*Sharon Thibodeau*

Keywords: holdings management, holdings protection, processing

Related Entries: Acquisition; Advocacy; Appraisal; Archival Arrangement; Archival Buildings and Facilities; Archival Custody; Archival Description; Archival Management System(s); Archival Preservation; Environmental Systems

Bibliography

Carucci, P., and M. Guercio. *Manuale di Archivistica*. Rome: Carocci editore, 2008.

Direction des Archives de France. *La Practique Archivistique Francaise*. Paris: Archives Nationales, 1993.

Hunter, G. S. *Developing and Maintaining Practical Archives: A How-to-Do-It Manual*. Chicago: Neal-Schuman, 2003.

Jenkinson, H. *A Manual of Archive Administration*. Oxford; London: Clarendon Press, 1922.

Muller, S., J. A. Feith, and R. Fruin. *Manual for the Arrangement and Description of Archives*, 2nd edition. Translated by Arthur H. Leavitt with new introductions by Peter Horsman, Eric Ketelaar, Theo Thomassen, and Marjorie Rabe Barritt. Chicago: Society of American Archivists, 2003.

"National Archives and Records Administration Regulations for NARA Researchers." www.archives.gov/research/start/nara-regulations.html (accessed December 2013).

Nesmith, T., ed. *Canadian Archival Studies and the Rediscovery of Provenance.* Metuchen, NJ: Scarecrow Press, 1993.

Pederson, A., ed. *Keeping Archives.* Sydney: Australian Society of Archivists, 1987.

Posner, E. *Archives in the Ancient World.* Cambridge: Harvard University Press, 1972.

"Trends in Archives Practice Series." *Society of American Archivists.* www2.archivists.org/sites/all/files/TAP-2013-V4.pdf (accessed December 2013).

ARCHIVAL PRESERVATION

Preservation has three distinct meanings. "In the early years of modern archival agencies—prior to World War II—preservation simply meant collecting. The sheer act of pulling a *collection* of manuscripts from a barn, a basement, or a parking garage and placing it intact in a dry building with locks on the door fulfilled the fundamental preservation mandate of the institution" (Conway 2000, 26). This use of preservation is exemplified in many statutory definitions of record, such as that in the U.S. Code:

Records includes all books, papers, maps, photographs, machine readable materials, or other documentary materials, regardless of physical form or characteristics, made or received by an agency of the United States Government under Federal law or in connection with the transaction of public business and preserved or appropriate for preservation by that agency or its legitimate successor. (44 USC 3301)

More recently, preservation has been used in a narrower context to encompass "those activities and functions designed to provide a suitable and safe administrative *context* and environment that enhances the usable life of collections" (Ritzenthaler 2010, 3). It includes storage, use and handling, collections maintenance, reformatting, *conservation* treatment, and disaster planning. Preservation often includes conservation, which protects and stabilizes materials in their original format. Traditional preservation practice, already focused on a wide range of materials, has expanded to include electronic records, treated separately under *digital preservation.*

Finally, preservation or litigation hold is used within a legal context to prevent *records* from routine destruction based on a retention schedule when there is reasonable anticipation those records may be potentially relevant to litigation, audit, or investigation. This broader interpretation of preserving materials where there is a "reasonable anticipation," rather than formal notice, gained momentum as the result of Judge Shira Scheindlin's opinion in *Zubulake v. UBS Wahrburg* (Sedona Conference WG1 2010, 267).

History

Much of early preservation focused on the restoration of items, "concerned with cosmetic improvement [rather] than stabilization" (Ritzenthaler 2010, 3). Restoration ranged from

the repair of a torn leaf, or removal of a simple stain, to the complete rehabilitation of the material, including, at times, deacidification, alkaline buffering, resizing, filling in missing parts, resewing, replacement of endpapers and/or boards, recovering or restoration of the original covering material, and refinishing in a manner sympathetic to the time of the original binding of the publication. (Roberts and Etherington 1982)

The introduction of paper made from wood pulp, rather than rags, created problems of long-term stability due to materials in the pulp and chemicals used in the manufacturing process. Deacidification to stabilize acidic paper using basic metal compounds in an aqueous solution was patented by Otto J. Schierholtz in 1936, although a similar technique was promoted by and commonly associated with William J. Barrow (Roggia 2001, 31). Although modern papermaking techniques incorporate these ideas to significantly lengthen the life of paper, many publications from the late nineteenth through the late twentieth century are fragile and were the focus of mass deacidification projects, as well as the National Endowment for the Humanities' Brittle Book Project and the National Newspaper Project efforts to preserve them using microfilm.

The 1966 flood of the Arno River in Florence, Italy, caused significant damage to numerous artworks and manuscripts collections. Teams of conservators, known as "mud angels," from around the world came together to care for the materials. Where conservators had often learned their craft and worked in isolation, this mass effort provided an opportunity to share knowledge and experience, and was in many ways the start of modern conservation practice (Hooper 2006).

A last item in this abbreviated list of key events includes the shift from conservation of individual objects to preservation of collections. Conservation, largely growing out of care for valuable materials in museum, rare book, and manuscript collections, needed to find ways to address problems of individual records in massive, archival collections that were important but that did not justify the costs of individualized treatment. In the late twentieth century, preservation management (sometimes called preservation administration) evolved as an approach to address factors that affect the long-term care and stability of collections, throughout the archival process, starting with *appraisal* and *acquisition*, through processing, storage, and use. A key aspect of preservation management is phased preservation, a "technique that emphasizes actions that have the greatest impact on the preservation of collections as a whole, rather than concentrating on treating individual items . . . and includes surveys to establish priorities, disaster planning, environmental controls, and holdings maintenance" (Pearce-Moses 2005, s.v. "phased preservation").

Challenges

Virtually all materials used to create records deteriorate over time. Many of the problems are the result of inherent vice, "the tendency of material to deteriorate due to the essential instability of the components or interaction among components" (Pearce-Moses 2005, s.v. "inherent vice"). Records are complex physical and chemical objects, and they may be made from different materials that age differently, making preservation even more complicated. For example, bound records may have, in addition to paper pages, a leather cover over board, as well as glue, metal, and string used in the binding. Magnetic recordings often have a plastic base and a binder holding a film of magnetic particles that carries the audio or video signal.

High temperature accelerates aging and deterioration. High humidity can trigger mold and metal corrosion, while low humidity can make documents

brittle. Changes in humidity and temperature cause records to shrink and expand, a particular problem that can result in delamination of records made from different types of materials. Accelerated aging tests, based on the Arrhenius function, can predict the longevity of materials based on temperature and humidity (Pearce-Moses 2005, s.v. "Arrhenius function").

Ironically, many older records are made using materials that are, by comparison to modern records, relatively stable. As noted above, rag papers used before the mid-nineteenth century are often in better condition than more recent paper made from wood pulp. Manuscripts written using iron gall ink may deteriorate as the acidic ink attacks the paper. Copies made using technologies to reproduce or transmit records are often particularly short lived. For example, letterpress copybooks become brittle and the text fades. In some instances, the copy was not intended to be kept permanently, so the process was inherently unstable and the image becomes unreadable in a few years.

Starting in the late nineteenth century, black-and-white photograph negatives and movies were made from nitrocellulose film (often called nitrate), which is inherently unstable and highly flammable. Much of the history of early cinema has been lost due to deterioration and fire. Nitrate film began to be replaced by cellulose diacetate in the early twentieth century, but it poses its own problem of the image-bearing gelatin pellicle becoming detached from the base. Color photography suffers from unstable dyes, resulting in color shift.

Records in all formats are also at risk from biological agents. Mold can weaken and stain paper. Pests and vermin feed off cellulose and gelatin used to make the records, and urine and feces can create a significant—even life-threatening—health condition for those working with the records.

Ultimately, the greatest risk to records may be humans. Well-intentioned individuals may make inappropriate repairs, such as using adhesive tape to mend a tear. They mishandle records, unfolding—and breaking—brittle records or tearing pages when removing staples. Directives to carefully unfold and remove staples from records while transferring them to archival folders and boxes have been standard in many archival preservation books and processing guides. More recently, Mark Greene and Dennis Meissner challenged that notion, especially for large, modern collections. "We will (or should) find that we have larger, more urgent tasks in front of us—first and foremost converting our massive backlogs into usable resources for our patrons" (Greene and Meissner 2005, 221).

Theft or malicious damage, by staff or patrons, presents a graver concern. Stacks and reading rooms should be secured. In general, personal items—briefcases, purses, heavy coats—should not be allowed in these areas. A "buddy system" that disallows individuals from working alone in storage areas helps prevent internal threats. An *archivist* should have clear sight of researchers in reading rooms, both to avoid potential theft, as well as mishandling. Ironically, archivists should take care to prevent deposit of false documents into the archives that distort the archival records (Hirtle 2000).

Lastly, natural and human disasters are major risks to preservation. Many such disasters are small and localized; a broken water pipe or a fire quickly suppressed by sprinklers. At the other extreme, Hurricane Katrina and the 9/11 attacks on New York resulted in the wholesale destruction of entire archives. See *Disaster Plan*.

Protecting Records

In spite of the numerous challenges of natural aging and threats, archivists can take action to significantly extend the longevity of documents in their care by factoring preservation into every phase of archival work. In the field, archivists should make an initial assessment of the condition of the records and factor the need for potential treatment into a decision to select the records for acquisition. Records selected should be packed with care, not only to minimize physical damage but also to protect the intellectual integrity of original order.

Accessioning is the first step in protecting the intellectual and physical *integrity* of the collection, making note of what has been received, its source, and where it is stored in the archives. Records should be inspected when received at the *archives*, preferably in a room that is isolated from the rest of the archives, to prevent spread of undiscovered mold, pests, or vermin. Infested records may require fumigation or, in some instances, may be destroyed.

Processing typically includes inventorying the records and transferring them to archival quality fold-

ers and boxes. Particularly fragile documents may be encapsulated in polyester or copied onto acid-neutral paper. Ultimately, as Greene and Meissner point out, the level of processing should be driven by the nature of the records; those of greater value merit greater care and description during processing. They should also consider the value and likelihood of use of those records against the time that would delay access to a backlog of inaccessible collections. Because archivists are not trained conservators, they should make cautious decisions on how to stabilize records for long-term storage. They should avoid treatments they have not been trained to perform and know when to call in a professional conservator.

To preserve exceptionally important collections, archives may invest in large-scale duplication projects. Originally done using microfilm, and now generally by *digitization*, these approaches can minimize handling of the originals and place a copy offsite in case of disaster. Digitization can also make the collection widely available via the web, within the limits of copyright.

Storing records in a stable environment with reasonable temperature and humidity adds significantly to their longevity. Records generally last longer in cooler, drier conditions. For example, the useful life of paper is estimated to be halved for every 10°F rise in temperature (Ritzenthaler 2010, 96). At the same time, achieving this goal can be difficult and expensive. Archives in modern office buildings may have reasonable, if not ideal, climates with temperatures between 68° and 72°F and relative humidity below 40 percent. However, adjusting the temperature (up in the summer, down in the winter) to save money when the building is unoccupied causes physical stress on the materials and ultimately shortens the life of the materials.

Ideally, storage spaces should be designed to minimize risk from building hazards, such as overhead plumbing, and have a fire-suppression system. Storage space should be regularly inspected for pests and vermin, and to ensure that all records are in boxes and off the floor.

Conclusion

Many archivists consider preservation to be the cornerstone of archives. If the records are not acquired and if the records are not protected from deterioration and damage, they cannot be used in the future. Archivists must understand the material nature of the records to know how best to preserve them as artifacts, and they must take appropriate measures to protect their *authenticity* and *integrity*. Many records are relatively stable and deteriorate slowly if kept in reasonable conditions. Others require immediate attention, not only for their own preservation but also to avoid their damaging other records. Contemporary approaches to the preservation of archival materials focuses on efforts that have the greatest impact to stabilize the most materials, rather than focusing on protection or restoration of individual items.—*Richard Pearce-Moses*

Keywords: preservation management, conservation, reformatting, records

Related Entries: Conservation; Digital Preservation; Disaster Plan; Records Center

Bibliography

Conway, Paul. "Overview: Rationale for Digitization and Preservation." In Maxine K. Sitts, ed., *Handbook for Digital Projects: A Management Tool for Preservation and Access*, 1st edition. Northeast Document Conservation Center, 2000. www.nedcc.org/assets/media/documents/dman. pdf (accessed November 27, 2014).

Greene, Mark A., and Dennis Meissner. "More Product, Less Process: Revamping Traditional Archival Processing." *American Archivist* 68 (2) (2005): 208–63. http://archivists.metapress.com/content/c741823776k65863/fulltext.pdf.

Hirtle, Peter B. "Archival Authenticity in a Digital Age." In *Authenticity in a Digital Environment*. Council on Library and Information Resources, 2000, 8–23.

Hooper, John. "Remembering the 'Mud Angels' of the 1966 Floods." *The Guardian*, November 10, 2006. www.theguardian.com/artanddesign/artblog/2006/nov/10/rememberingthemudangelsof.

Pearce-Moses, Richard. *A Glossary of Archival and Records Terminology*. Chicago: Society of American Archivists, 2005. www2.archivists.org/glossary.

Ritzenthaler, Mary Lynn. *Preserving Archives and Manuscripts*, 2nd edition. Chicago: Society of American Archivists, 2010.

Ritzenthaler, Mary Lynn, and Diane Vogt-O'Connor, with Helena Zinkham, Brett Carnell, and Kit A. Petersen. *Photographs: Archival Care and Management*. Chicago: Society of American Archivists, 2006.

Roberts, Matt T., and Don Etherington. *Bookbinding and the Conservation of Books: A Dictionary of Descriptive Terminology*. S.v. "restoration." Washington, DC: U.S. Government Printing Office, 1982. (Citation taken from an on online edition originally prepared by Walter Henry at Conservation Online in 1994.) http://cool.conservation-us.org/don/ (accessed November 2014).

Roggia, Sally Cruz. "The Great Promoter: William J. Barrow and His Role in the History of Conservation." *The Book and Paper Group Annual* 20 (2001): 31–34.

Sedona Conference Working Group 1. "The Sedona Conference Commentary on Legal Holds: The Trigger and the Process." *The Sedona Conference Journal* 11 (2010). https://thesedonaconference. org/system/files/sites/sedona.civicactions.net/ files/private/drupal/filesys/publications/legalhold-ssept2010.pdf (accessed November 2014).

"Title 44: Definition of Record." U.S. Code (44 USC 3301). In *Public Printing and Documents*, chapter 33, "Disposal of Records." www.law. cornell.edu/uscode/text/44/chapter-33 (accessed November 2014).

ARCHIVAL PROGRAMS

An *archival program* is an established, organized, continuing, institutionally based administrative structure for activities to systematically acquire, manage, preserve, and make available archival *records*. The definition of archival program is necessarily broad and encompasses two general categories. The first is institutional and organizational archival programs that appraise, acquire, and care for the archival records created by their own institutions. The U.S. National Archives, state archives, and university archives would be examples. The second category includes collecting programs in libraries, historical societies, museums and other settings that acquire archival records from beyond their own institution. Sometimes, the two are combined or exist side-by-side in the same administrative setting. A university, for instance, may have a university archives and a library that collects records of enduring value from individuals and institutions beyond the archives for *preservation* and research.

The Concept

Formal definitions or standards for what constitutes an archival program have not been established, though there are canons of best practice for programs in the areas of college and university archives, state archives, and a few other areas. But all responsible archival programs adhere to and follow the professional concepts, principles, and practices described in this encyclopedia. Whatever their size or setting, archival programs need several traits and capacities to responsibly carry out their work:

- Statement of legal authority and authorization to operate, often in the form of a law, charter, or directive from the governing board or chief executive officer of the sponsoring institution.
- Statement of purpose, mission, and administrative setting within the sponsoring institution.
- Work of the program is continuing and ongoing rather than one-time or intermittent.
- Systematic planning processes to regularly evaluate the program, update its mission, goals, objectives, and services, and keep it responsive to the evolving expectations of its parent agency, the changing needs and expectations of its customers, and the impact of shifting technologies.
- Financial resources dependably and continually available that are adequate to carry out the program's stated purpose.
- Sufficient number of staff who possess, through training and/or experience, professional competence in archives management.
- Adequate, suitable, secure facilities for storing and preserving archival records and making them available for research use.
- Acquisitions policy that describes areas of collecting and *appraisal* and other criteria that are applied when evaluating particular records to determine if they merit archival preservation.
- Provision for managing archival records regardless of format, including those in electronic form.

- Preservation facilities and practices to ensure the continuing survival and availability of archival records.
- Processes for *arrangement* and *description* that meet *archival standards* including preservation of original order whenever possible.
- *Access* policies and reference services that make the archival records held by the program available for research on a regular basis, sometimes with appropriate restrictions on their use.

In addition, many programs feature newsletters and other information-sharing formats, often online, exhibits of selected holdings, public events such as lectures related to the issues or topics documented in the records, presentations by staff members on their work, and outreach to schools, often in the form of document packets. Some, such as state archives, provide advice and support to other archival programs in their areas.

Conclusion

Archival programs are in effect the essential infrastructure for archival work. Strengthening existing programs, and establishing new ones as needs arise, will constitute major challenges and opportunities for the archival profession in the future.—*Bruce Dearstyne*

Keywords: programs, organization, management
Related Entries: Archives (institution); Archival Practice; Archival Preservation

Bibliography

"Core Values Statement." Society of American Archivists, 2011. www2.archivists.org/statements/saa-core-values-statement-and-code-of-ethics.

Dearstyne, Bruce W., ed. *Leading and Managing Archives and Records Programs: Strategies for Success*. New York: Neal-Schuman, 2008.

"Guidelines for Evaluation of Archival Institutions." Society of American Archivists, 1982; approved as a standard, 1994. www2.archivists.org/groups/standards-committee/guidelines-for-evaluation-of-archival-institutions.

Kurtz, Michael J., *Managing Archival and Manuscript Repositories*. Chicago: Society of American Archivists, 2004.

Purcell, Aaron D. *Managing the Next Generation of College and University Archives, Records and Special Collections*. New York: Neal-Schuman, 2012.

"The State of State Records." Council of State Archivists, 2013. www.statearchivists.org/reports/2012CoSAARMSurveyReport07-30-2013Narrativefinaldraft.pdf.

ARCHIVAL REAPPRAISAL

Reappraisal is the process of revisiting past *appraisal* decisions to identify archival materials that are no longer suitable for permanent *preservation*. Reappraisal decision-making processes identify the scope and rationale for reappraisal; systematically inspect the contents and *contexts* of materials; and examine *provenance*, *donation*, and accessioning documentation. The reappraisal process is concluded by a determination to retain or permanently remove materials from an *archives* by *deaccessioning*. Though reappraisal and deaccessioning are now considered aspects of responsible *collections* management, debate on the topic occurred during the 1980s and 1990s, leading to case studies, articles, and papers on its theoretical, ethical, and practical implications. In 2012, the Society of American Archivists approved *Guidelines for Reappraisal and Deaccessioning* to clarify processes and encourage transparency and *accountability* for archives conducting reappraisal.

Context

The concept of reappraisal was formally introduced to the archival literature by Leonard Rapport's seminal 1981 article "No Grandfather Clause: Reappraising Accessioned Records." Though library literature had addressed deaccessioning beginning in the 1950s, reappraisal constitutes a unique development of the concept as it emerges from a long legacy of theory on archival appraisal. Literature on appraisal tends to assume that once appraised and accessioned, archival materials will be preserved permanently. However, a 1974 glossary of terms compiled by Frank B. Evans et al. in the *American Archivist* includes the term "permanent withdrawal," defined as "the permanent transfer of records from the physical and legal *custody* of a repository," which suggests that the practice of removing materials from holdings was a recognized practice (427). Rapport formally addressed these practices in his argument for reappraisal as a function of archival management. Focusing his attention on the legacy of large volumes of *records* stored in public archives following World War II, Rapport states that the primary reason for preserving records is to serve citizens. If the cost of keeping records outweighs the benefit to citizens, Rapport writes, public archives cannot justify the continued expense of permanent preservation. Rapport identifies faulty appraisal decisions or the neglect of proper appraisal as the cause of records that "if offered today, we would not accept" (143). As a solution, Rapport suggests that records be reappraised at regular intervals of twenty to thirty-five years. During this time, archivists should advertise the records' availability to potential users, analyze what potential uses may be made of them, and as a final preventative measure before deaccessioning, a review panel should approve or reject reappraisal decisions.

In response to Rapport, Karen Benedict published "Invitation to a Bonfire: Reappraisal and Deaccessioning of Records as Collection Management Tools in an Archives—A Reply to Leonard Rapport" in 1984. Benedict challenges Rapport by arguing that reappraisal and deaccessioning fundamentally undermine basic archival principles. Benedict states that reappraisal and deaccessioning activities are too risky except as a last resort during a financial or storage space-related crisis: once records are destroyed, they cannot be retrieved. Due to the shifting nature of appraisal criteria, Benedict argues present appraisal standards cannot be prioritized over past ones. Finally, in response to Rapport's emphasis on use as criteria for reappraisal, Benedict counters that a lack of past use is not an accurate predictor of future use in order to accurately preserve the historical record.

The same issue of the *American Archivist* containing Benedict's counterpoint included a favorable case study by Richard L. Haas and commentary on the subject by F. Gerald Ham. These have been followed by many other case studies and examinations of the theory, praxis, and *archival ethics* of reappraisal, the majority of which have been positive toward the concept (Crowder 2011). *Archivists* have come to recognize reappraisal as a useful tool to re-evaluate past appraisal decisions when clear benefits may result. As Sheila Powell writes in a 1992 case study, reappraisal can support "the highest-quality historical record possible" by creating and introducing new information to refine and strengthen holdings (104). Recognizing the diversity of professional opinion on the subject, the Society of American Archivists approved *Guidelines for Reappraisal and Deaccessioning* in 2012 to assist archives in making responsible and transparent choices around reappraisal.

Reappraisal Process

Reappraisal is a decision-making process that, like appraisal, artfully combines theory and practice to identify value. Prior to beginning, reappraisal should be defined in the policies and procedures of an archives and built into donor agreements in relation to deaccessioning. Reappraisal decisions and outcomes should be fully documented for consistency and transparency. Archives conducting reappraisal must anticipate and manage the ethical, legal, and donor- or user-community-related issues that surround the practice. The ownership of collections must be established, including applicable legal statutes for government records and previous donor agreements, especially if these agreements did not include clauses allowing for deaccessioning. Finally, an archives must ensure open communication with donors where necessary by explaining the process and possible outcomes sympathetically and honestly.

Reappraisal begins by defining the rationale and the scope of the reappraisal. Reasons for reappraisal include improving overall access to materials, assessing and prioritizing backlogs, correcting faulty appraisal decisions, refining collections focus, and balancing institutional resources for preservation and storage against collection use. Defining scope determines the extent of the holdings to be reappraised. It may include the entire holdings of the archives, individual items, or be limited to such areas as subject, creator, format, and time period. Individual *fonds* or *series* may also be subject to reappraisal as required. In all situations, the reappraiser should examine the whole fonds, series, and/or collection rather than its constituent parts to understand the contexts of the materials and past reasons for their acquisition.

Once the rationale and the scope has been defined and documented, the reappraiser should review existing appraisal or collections management policies, and any legal obligations an archives may have in keeping the materials. The reappraiser then proceeds to systematically inspect the materials in scope by noting characteristics that may make them candidates for deaccessioning. An institution should have a list of defined appraisal criteria available during this process, which may include records that do not fit the institution's current appraisal or *acquisition policies*; have no accessioning records or known *provenance*; are not unique materials; have never been accessed; contain highly restricted or private information; do not appear to provide long-term research value; consist of formats not collected by the institution; are permanently inaccessible due to format obsolescence; or are physically degraded to the point where information cannot be retrieved from the materials. In many cases, new information about materials is added during this process, which should be documented by updating finding aids and collections documentation.

Prior to making a final decision, the reappraiser should take into account any additional information about the materials under consideration that may explain why the records were accepted initially, including donor information, correspondence, and agreements; usage statistics; contents of the materials; physical condition assessments; retention schedules; and superseded acquisition and appraisal policies. Ownership should be conclusively determined. If no deed of gift exists, the institution should make best efforts to contact original donors or claim ownership under applicable legislation. The final reappraisal decision can be made by committee, in consultation with users, or by other means depending on the institution. The outcome of reappraisal may be the retention of materials, partial or sampled retention of materials, deferral of reappraisal until more information becomes available, or deaccessioning.

Conclusion

Despite past controversy, reappraisal is a useful concept for archivists to manage collections responsibly. However, reappraisal decisions should not be made lightly. As F. Gerald Ham writes, it is "a creative and sophisticated act" that permits holdings to be refined and strengthened when scope and rationale is defined and decisions are applied systematically and well documented (17). Once reappraisal decisions have been made, materials may proceed to deaccessioning.—*Grant Hurley*

Keywords: appraisal; deaccessioning; disposition; collections management; withdrawal

Related Entries: Acquisition; Acquisition Policy; Appraisal; Archival Collection; Collecting Archives; Collection Management Policy; Deaccessioning; Documentation Strategy; Permanence

Bibliography

Benedict, Karen. "Invitation to a Bonfire: Reappraisal and Deaccessioning of Records as Collection Management Tools in Archives—a Reply to Leonard Rapport." *American Archivist* 47 (1) (1984): 43–49. http://archivists.metapress.com/content/gt26318774q20241/fulltext.pdf.

Crowder, Ashby. "Reappraising Leonard Rapport's 'No Grandfather Clause' at Thirty." *Provenance, Journal of the Society of Georgia Archivists* 29 (1) (2011): 49–66. http://digitalcommons.kennesaw.edu/provenance/vol29/iss1/5.

Evans, Frank B., Donald F. Harrison, Edwin A. Thompson, and William L. Rofes. "A Basic Glossary for Archivists, Manuscript Curators, and Records Managers." *American Archivist* 37 (3) (1974): 415–33. www.jstor.org/stable/40291669.

Haas, Richard. "Collection Reappraisal: The Experience at the University of Cincinnati." *American Archivist* 47 (1) (1984): 51–54. http://archivists.metapress.com/content/t1476206695m7170/fulltext.pdf.

Ham, F. Gerald. "Archival Choices: Managing the Historical Record in an Age of Abundance." *American Archivist* 47 (1) (1984): 11–22. http://archivists.metapress.com/content/v382727652114521/fulltext.pdf.

Powell, Sheila. "Archival Reappraisal: The Immigration Case Files." *Archivaria* 33 (1) (1991): 104–16. http://journals.sfu.ca/archivar/index.php/archivaria/article/view/11802/12753.

Rapport, Leonard. "No Grandfather Clause: Reappraising Accessioned Records." *American Archivist* 44 (2) (1981): 143–50. http://archivists.metapress.com/content/b274w3126t430h52/fulltext.pdf.

Society of American Archivists. "Guidelines for Reappraisal and Deaccessioning." Chicago: Society of American Archivists, 2012. www2.archivists.org/sites/all/files/GuidelinesForReappraisalAndDeaccessioning-May2012.pdf (accessed November 2014).

ARCHIVAL RETRIEVAL

Archival retrieval or production is the process of removing *archives* from storage. Archives may be retrieved for *archivists*, researchers, and other users to consult, or for use in *outreach* programs such as *exhibitions*. Retrieval may seem a straightforward process, but its proper management is essential to maintain the physical and intellectual *integrity* of archival materials. Sir Hilary Jenkinson, in his *A Manual of Archive Administration*, argued for "the strictest rules" to be put in place: "The efficient administration of Archives involves a system for their 'production'" (Jenkinson 1965, 64–66).

Retrieval in Practice

Unlike library stock, archival material is not usually available in the search room or reading room for users to browse. In order to consult items, it is necessary for users to request that material be retrieved from the storage area. In some archives this request may be made using a computerized system, perhaps a *collection* management system, in which the item requested can be automatically linked to its location and to details of the user requesting it. In others the user may be required to complete a consultation slip or request form, which is often in duplicate or triplicate. One part of the slip or form will be put in the place of the item that is removed from the shelf or box in the storage area so there is a record of what has been removed. One part will accompany the item, and, depending on the repository's system, a third part may be filed as a record of the retrieval. Repositories that use barcoding can record information about location and removal automatically.

Whatever system is in place, it should enable the archivist to keep track of what has been removed from the store, when, by whom, and why. It should also demonstrate that the item has been successfully replaced and can then be used to identify any items that have not been returned, either because they have been misfiled or because they have been moved elsewhere, perhaps for reproduction. If the user wants a part of the retrieved material to be copied, systems should be in place to accommodate and track this. The system protects the integrity and security of the material, and the information recorded on the slips or forms (or in the automated system) should be carefully thought out. Many repositories ask users to sign the request forms "to acknowledge in writing the receipt of archives delivered to them in order to insure an accountability for them" (Schellenberg 2003, 231–33). For Jenkinson it was important to have a record of everyone involved in the process of retrieval: "No Archive passes from its place on the shelves without a signature being given for every hand which touches it on the way" (Jenkinson 1965, 31), and you could add "on the way back."

Other information recorded will include the reference number of the item, a brief description, and perhaps a location and further user details. Records of what has been retrieved should be kept as they can be used in statistical analysis to demonstrate the number of items retrieved, popular collections, types of *records* consulted by particular user groups, and so on. Again attention should be paid to the information recorded on any retrieval records, and links to information about researchers, to ensure that useful statistical information can be extracted. However, it is also important to remember practicalities; a user does not want to complete pages of forms every time they request that an item be retrieved.

Different archive repositories will have different systems and policies in place with regard to retrieval. Some may restrict the members of staff who perform retrieval for reasons of security and preservation: "Retrieval and return of material should be limited to one or, at most, a few authorised and trained staff members" (Jeremy, Woodley, and Kupke 2008, 357), while others may have a more flexible approach and even use volunteers (if properly trained) for the task. Retrieval is closely tied to the wider *access* policy of an archives. Repositories may or may not allow the retrieval of items from uncatalogued *collections* but, if they do, it must be clear where they have come from. It must be clear to the researcher, the archivist, and the person retrieving the material if access to any items is restricted for whatever reason.

Other differences between repositories may include the number of items that can be requested on one retrieval form or slip, the number of items that can be retrieved at any one time, and the number of items that can be consulted at once. According to Jeremy, Woodley, and Kupke, "Users should be limited to three containers, or equivalent in unboxed materials, at any one time" (2008, 360). If a policy of limiting the number of items that can be retrieved is applied, it can be frustrating for users wishing to consult large amounts of material. If such a policy is in place, it should be clearly publicized and explained. This is particularly true for archives where the retrieval process may be limited to certain times of the day, or in repositories that require advanced notice either because of limitations on staff time or because material is stored off-site.

Effective retrieval requires a robust preservation policy to be in place. Material should be stored in an environment that prevents damage from taking place if items are retrieved, so correct packaging, boxing, and shelving is important. Ideally archival material, particularly photographs and other items that are stored in cool or cold conditions, should be gradually acclimatized before moving to a warmer reading room or exhibition area. Retrieval staff should be trained in handling archival material and in spotting signs of damage or deterioration. It is also important that staff are aware of the health and safety issues involved in lifting boxes, using kick stools and ladders to reach items, or handling heavy or oversized material.

Conclusion

As has been seen, archival retrieval is closely linked to a number of core archival functions and policies including *public service*, *access*, *archival preservation*, *archival arrangement*, and *archival description*. It is a key process, and it is essential to have effective procedures in place both to protect archival materials and to provide an efficient service to users.—*Caroline Brown*

Keywords: production of archives, removal of archives, replacing archives
Related Entries: Access; Public Service

Bibliography

Jenkinson, H. *A Manual of Archival Administration*. London: Percy Lund, Humphies, 1965.

Jeremy, E., E. Woodley, and L. Kupke. "Access and Reference Services." In J. Bettington, K. Eberhard, R. Loo, and C. Smith, eds., *Keeping Archives*. Canberra: Australian Society of Archivists, 2008, 351–78.

Schellenberg, S. *Modern Archives Principles and Techniques*, 3rd edition. Chicago: Society of American Archivists, 2003.

Williams, C. *Managing Archives Foundations Principles and Practice*. Oxford: Chandos Publishing, 2006, 145.

ARCHIVAL SCIENCE

Archival science is an academic and applied discipline that involves the scientific study of process-bound information, both as product and as agent of human thoughts, emotions, and activities, in its various *contexts*. Its field of study encompasses personal documents, *records*, and *archives* of communities, government agencies, and other formal organizations, and archival materials in general, whether or not kept by archival institutions, units, or programs. It covers both the records themselves and their contexts of creation, management, and use, and their sociocultural context. Its central questions are why, how, and under what circumstances human beings create, keep, change, preserve, or destroy records, and what meanings they may individually or jointly attribute to records and to their *recordkeeping* and archival operations.

In most universities archival science programs are situated in the faculty of humanities/arts. The main focus is on human beings in their capacity of *records creators*, managers, users, preservers, and destroyers of records. The discipline has an interface with informatics and communication science, but it does not belong to the natural sciences, though the word *science* in the name may suggest otherwise.

What Is Archival Science?

Archival science is both a pure and an applied science. Archival science as a scholarly discipline deals with records and archives as traces of *memory*, information objects, documentary evidence, sources of history, symbols of past events, and cultural heritage objects. It analyzes the relative value of records and archives and the meanings attributed to them. It investigates the reasons and motives of people, acting as private persons or as members of formal organizations, for creating, managing, using, preserving, or destroying records and archives, the strategies and instruments they choose in order to document their lives, their work, and their operations, and the ways in which their records- and archives-related behavior is determined by the social and historical environment in which they display it.

Archival science as an applied discipline provides a scientific basis for *records management* and archival administration. It provides the theoretical and methodological framework for designing, managing, and using sustainable information processes and formal and informal *recordkeeping systems*, for preserving and—if necessary—remediating archives from different times and cultures, for safeguarding and evaluating the short- and long-term value of records and archives as *evidence* or information, and for acquiring, storing, arranging and describing, searching, and interpreting archival materials kept by archival institutions, units, or programs, and by public archives in particular.

Archival science has a longer tradition as an applied than as a scholarly discipline. Pragmatic literature on archives administration and records management, on archival functions and professional practices, on how to make archives accessible, and how to exercise other professional duties is abundant and fed by a tradition of centuries. More recent archival literature, however, reflects rapidly growing scientific research activities and a flourishing scholarly debate on academic issues. Increasingly, the archival discourse is not predominantly a professional discourse but also an academic discourse, one that is not primarily debated within associations of archivists but within an international academic environment. Without losing its close ties with the archival field in general and the operations of archival services in particular, archival scholars have successfully demonstrated that archival science can flourish independently of the interests and missions of professional stakeholders.

In the academic discourse of the last decades, the classic concepts, theories, and methods of archival science have been called into question. The discipline appears to be going through a paradigm shift, a shift from a custodial to a postcustodial paradigm. The points of departure of the classic paradigm— paper archives kept in archival repositories and controlled by *archivists* acting as custodians—maintain their validity in a traditional archival environment. It cannot, however, provide archival scholars with an integrated model of analysis for both electronic and nonelectronic records, for more or less stable records physically kept in one place and records behaving like processes and kept in distributed custody, for archives under the control of archivists and archival institutions, and for archives simply mediated by archivists or out of their control in social media and other online platforms. The more recent postcustodial paradigm is a label for a coherent set of concepts, models, theories, and methods providing such an integrated approach. This paradigm has moved archival thinking and archival analysis to a higher level of abstraction and allows archival scholars to ask new questions, give new answers, and enter new fields of research and application.

From the beginning of the twenty-first century, the archival discourse is also penetrated by postmodern views and approaches. Postmodern thinkers are moving away from paradigms of *archival theory* as far as these can be considered to be metanarratives claiming universal validity. They have made the community of archival scholars more sensible to the context of *recordkeeping* practices and principles, to the intentionality of records *creation*, to the gender and power relationships shaping the records, the recordkeeping habits, the archival system, and the collective memory as such, and to the illusion of the archivists' classic claim to *objectivity* and neutrality.

The academic skepticism of postmodernism and the growing awareness of curatorial power have not only penetrated the archival academic discourse but also generated scholarly interest in archives from other disciplines, usually labelled as "archival turns." Scholars of history, art history, linguistics, media studies, sociology, political science, and other humanistic disciplines demonstrate a growing inter-

est in the fingerprints left by records creators, recordkeepers, and archivists on records and archives, and consequently on human memory and history.

Changing views on the sciences and their interrelationships, and the blurring of boundaries between scholars of allied fields, are subtracting from all scientific disciplines, including archival science, their alleged universal applicability and their exclusiveness. This does not prevent archival science from being described as a distinct and autonomous scientific discipline, with a consistent approach, comprising a coherent system of concepts, theories, and methods, providing scholars of records and archives with an analytic framework that allows them to exchange their research results and views.

The main characteristic of archival science is its contextual approach. This approach turns the scientific background of a domain that seems to study a large variety of objects (records and archives, records *creation*, management, *preservation* and use, and creators, managers, and users of records and archives) into one integrated body of knowledge. Archival science has been described so far in terms of the academic and pragmatic scientific problems archival scholars deal with, but as a distinct and autonomous scientific discipline it can also be described in terms of its epistemological characteristics, particularly in terms of its object, its theory, and its methodology.

Records and archives, the physical objects archivists traditionally deal with, are without any doubt material objects of study of the archival discipline, but they are not to be identified as its central objects of knowledge. The central object of knowledge of archival science is constituted of records in their contexts, records as part of processes of attribution and communication of meanings. As already stated, archival research centers on context, the context of the data within a record and the contexts of creation, management, and use, as well as the sociopolitical, cultural, and economic contexts underlying these contexts. In so doing, archival research provides an integrated view of records and the processes by which they are generated, structured, and controlled and in which they play an active part.

The core of archival theory is about the continuous processes of creation, recreation, and remediation of records and archives, about the subsequent and parallel functions in which records can be used in the course of these processes and the interaction among creators, curators, and users and their consequences on the stability, meaning, effects, and value of the records.

Also *archival methodology* is contextual and process oriented. Based on "the *principle of provenance*," it aims at analyzing the records in terms of the relationship between records and the processes by which they are created, mediated, and recreated. Archival methodology enables the development of strategies for appraising records for preservation and for continuously maintaining, strengthening, extending, or—if necessary—reconstructing this relationship over time through *archival arrangement*.

Conclusion

An international community of archival researchers is a prerequisite for the scientific development of archival science. From the 1980s, archival thinking and research has grown to the point of establishing in academia its own educational infrastructure consisting of bachelor's, master's, and doctoral degree programs, placing archival research firmly among university research programs. Archival researchers communicate with each other in peer-reviewed journals and disseminate archival knowledge through presentations and publications. As a consequence, archival science has developed into a distinct scientific discipline, with a growing community of archival researchers achieving scientifically justified consensus on questions that can be asked and types of answers that may be given on the basis of shared archival concepts, theories, methods, and (other) presuppositions. Scholars in archival science have broadened the scope of the discipline by replacing the traditional object orientation with a process orientation. Challenged by archival turns in other fields of scholarship, they are widening the discipline's perspectives and enhancing its analytic potential by exploring the metaphorical power of the concept of the archive(s) and by adding research methods from these disciplines to their own methodological repertoire.

The number of archival scholars is still relatively small, and the call for more pragmatism by the archival community to which it is closely linked is relatively strong. But the future of archival science is promising in light of the centrality of archives to contemporary scholarship on the one hand and the ubiquity and increasing value of information as an asset on the other.—*Theo Thomassen*

Keywords: archival discipline, archival program, post-custodial paradigm
Related Entries: Archival Method; Archival Practice; Archival Theory

Bibliography

Eastwood, Terry, and Heather MacNeil, eds. *Currents in Archival Thinking*. Santa Barbara, CA: Libraries Unlimited, 2010.

Ketelaar, Eric. "Archival Turns." In Anne J. Gilliland, Sue McKemmish, and Andrew Lau, eds., *Research in the Archival Multiverse*. Clayton, Victoria, Australia: Monash University Press, in press.

McKemmish, Sue, and Anne Gilliland. "Archival and Recordkeeping Research: Past, Present and Future." In Kirsty Williamson and Graeme Johansen, eds., *Research Methods: Information Systems and Contexts*. Prahran, Victoria, Australia: Tilde, 2013, 79–112.

Shepherd, Elizabeth. "Archival Science." In Marcia J. Bates and Nary Niles Maack, eds., *Encyclopedia of Library and Information Sciences*, 3rd edition. Boca Raton, FL: CRC Press, 2009, 179–91.

Thomassen, Theo. "A First Introduction to Archival Science." *Archival Science* 1 (2001): 373–85.

ARCHIVAL STANDARDS

Archival standards are standards developed and used in the domain of *archives*. A proper definition of this compound term does not exist. However, there are definitions for each of the components:

- archival: "of or pertaining to archives" (SAA, *A Glossary of Archival and Records Terminology*)
- standard: "something used as a measure, norm, or model in comparative evaluations" (Oxford Dictionary).

Work on developing standards for archival purposes started in the late 1980s. The main reason was an increasing need to establish consistency in the way records were described due to the emergence of the computer. Information technology made it possible to exchange information about records more easily and to share finding aids in order to improve *access* to *archives*. If the descriptions of archival *records* were not harmonized within or among repositories, it would be difficult, if not impossible, to achieve that. The initiative for more standardization came from the ICA Automation Committee.

Context

Archival standards focus on archival records (the holdings of archives) and especially in paper *format*. Records still under control of record-creating organizations and not transferred to an archival institution do not fall within their scope. They have their own standards (see *Records Standards*). This distinction was based on the fact that transferred, paper-based archives often lacked sufficient *context* information and needed additional description to make them accessible to the public. With the emergence of *digital records*, however, it has become questionable whether this distinction is still useful. The very nature of digital records makes it difficult to describe them in hindsight. Descriptive, process, and technical information (in general, *metadata*) needs to be added right from the point of creation and use.

Currently, the explicit distinction between *records standards* and *archival standards* is blurring, and there is a tendency to develop integrated standards that regard records during their entire existence, from their *creation* through use, retention, and *preservation*, to their final *disposition*.

International *archival standards* are developed by different (international and national) organizations, such as the International Council on Archives (ICA), through its Committee for Descriptive Standards (CDS), W3C for web-based standards, and the International Standardization Organization (ISO). At the national level professional organizations such as the Society of American Archivists (SAA), national standardization bodies (ANSI, Standards Australia, AFNOR), and recordkeeping institutions, such as the Public Records Office of Victoria (PROV, Australia), are active in developing standards.

This overview describes the archival standards that are of greatest significance. It is not easy to define the boundaries of this field, because there are many standards that are closely related or cover more than just archival records. The limited space here does not allow for a discussion of all of them.

Generally speaking there are two main clusters of archival standards: "archival description standards" and "digital preservation standards." The background, objective/purpose, scope, and impact of each of these clusters are described in the following paragraphs.

Archival Description

In the area of *archival description* the first standard to be developed addressed the description of records and their aggregates. An Ad Hoc Commission on Descriptive Standards (ICA/DDS) was established by the ICA in 1991 (for a comprehensive history see www.icacds.org.uk/eng/history.htm). After wide consultation with the international archival community and an initial "statement of principles" on which the standard would be based, the first edition of the new *General International Standard on Archival Description* (International Council of Archives) was published in 1994 (second edition released in 2000).

The purpose of the standard is "to identify and explain the context and content of *archival material* in order to promote its *accessibility*" (ICA 2000, 7). It consists of twenty-six elements, divided over seven areas of descriptive information that may be combined to construct a description. Apart from descriptive information about records, the standard also includes structural relationships between records and their aggregates. Six of the elements are mandatory. As an international standard that provides general rules it may be adapted to support the development of national rules of description.

It soon became clear that it was not sufficient to describe the records. Their *creators* also had to be described in so-called "authority records" that could control the "access points" to records. As a result, a separate standard was developed, called *International Standard Archival Authority Records for Corporate Bodies, Persons and Families* (ISAAR [CPF]), which was published in 1996 (second edition in 2004). A similar, but more specific standard is the *International Standard for Describing Institutions with Archival Holdings* (ISDIAH), published in 2007.

ISAAR (CPF) provides "guidance for preparing archival authority records which provide descriptions of entities (corporate bodies, persons and families) associated with the creation and maintenance of archives." By creating an authorized description it is possible to control the creation and use of access points in archival descriptions (ISAAR/CPF 2004, 8).

After the development of ISAD(G) and ISAAR the next and logical step was to develop a standard on "activities" and "functions": the *International Standard for Describing Functions* (ISDF), published in 2007. Based on these three standards, encoding schemes in XML were developed:

- Encoded Archival Description (EAD) for ISAD/G
- Encoded Archival Context (EAC) for ISAAR

Currently, an encoding scheme is being developed for ISDF (EAF).

The purpose of these standards is to provide encoding schemes for finding aids on archival material in a networked environment. The schemes are maintained by the Library of Congress (United States). A good example of a cross-organizational attempt to provide an access portal to archival material using this standard is the European APEnet project (part of the larger Europeana network that also includes libraries and other cultural-heritage institutions).

Archival standards are widely used in the archival community and thus stimulated the development of guides and other tools. In the United States a guide titled *Describing Archives: A Content Standard*, second edition, 2013 (DACS), has been developed by the Society of American Archives standards committee (and the general archival community), based on the ISAD/G and ISAAR standards.

Similarly, ICA-AtoM (Access to Memory) is an open-source software developed by Artefactual Systems (Canada) and sponsored by the ICA, and compliant with both standards. It supports the description of archival collections both within and across archival institutions.

Although not an archival standard, the *Dublin Core Metadata Element Set* (DCMES) is an important standard that is often referenced by the archival community. The objective of the DCMES is to increase the accessibility of information on the web and to facilitate publication on the web. This standard was used as the basis for the *Open Archives Initiative Protocol for Metadata Harvesting* (OAI-PMH), which provides a means for gathering metadata from different sources in different communities and bringing them together in a central database designed to support access. It serves as an independent interoperability framework.

Digital Preservation

The second cluster of archival standards is that of *digital preservation*. It is broader than archival records and relates to the "archiving" of all digital information objects. The term *archiving* is used here in the sense of IT, that is, storing digital information when it is no longer needed for immediate use.

The standards developed in this cluster are many. They range from standards on management and preservation requirements, to audit and certification, to descriptive information and other metadata, to preservation processes, to technical aspects such as formats. They were also developed by different organizations. One of them is the Consultative Committee for Space Data Systems (CCSDS), which developed a reference model for the preservation of digital information in general. It is called the "Open Archival Information System" (ISO 14721:2003 OAIS), and it has been accepted around the world as a reference model for the processes involved in digital preservation:

> An OAIS is an Archive, consisting of an organization, which may be part of a larger organization, of people and systems that has accepted the responsibility to preserve information and make it available for a *Designated Community*.

A free version of the standard is available as CCSDS 650.0-B-1 (2002). However, this has been superseded by a newer 2012 version. This reference model is widely used by organizations responsible for preserving digital information for the long term, especially in the development of digital repositories. Based on the model other instruments have been developed, such as an auditing tool to assess the reliability, commitment, and readiness of institutions with respect to the long-term preservation of digital information. This assessment tool has since become a standard (see ISO 16363:2012, "Audit and Certification of Trustworthy Digital Repositories). At another level a standard for preservation metadata was developed, called *Preservation Metadata Implementation Strategies* (PREMIS). It consists of a data dictionary and an XML encoding scheme, identifying five categories of data elements: intellectual entities, objects, events, agents, and rights.

Another important standard in this context is the "Metadata Encoding and Transmission Standard" (METS), which is a type of wrapper in XML format. It is intended to bring together digital files and their descriptive and technical metadata in a structure that is easier to manage. For instance, it helps to ensure the integrity of a compound digital object. METS also includes, for instance, the abovementioned EAD and EAC.

A similar kind of standard used at the regional level is the "Victoria Electronic Records Strategy" (VERS). This also is an XML structure for wrapping digital records in their metadata in order to ease their future use and management.

On the process level a standard for conversion and migration exists: ISO 13008:2012—"Digital Records Conversion and Migration Process." This standard provides guidance "for the planning issues, requirements, and procedures for the conversion and/or migration of digital records (which includes digital objects plus metadata) so as to preserve the authenticity, reliability, integrity, and usability of such records as evidence of business transactions."

At a more technical level, the ISO 19005 series (PDF/A) intends to provide open archivable document formats based on each of the different versions of PDF (see www.pdfa.org/2013/02/the-most-important-reasons-to-use-pdfa).

A smaller area of standardization is that of *digitization*, which focuses on the conversion of paper records (and other paper documents) into digital versions through the use of scanning technologies and techniques. The ISO TC46/SC11 has recently published a set of guidelines to support digitization initiatives. It is called ISO 13028:2010—"Implementation Guidelines for Digitization of Records." Apart from the digitization process, there are many other types of more technical standards, such as file formats for images (e.g., TIFF, PNG, JPEG).

Conclusion

As stated in the beginning, the field of archival standards is quite broad (see *A Guide to Archival Standards* for an overview of different types of standards: www.archives.org.uk/si-dsg/guide-to-standards.html). In this overview two main clusters of standards are discussed: descriptive and digital preservation standards. They do not necessarily relate exclusively to archival material but could also cover other objects, especially when it regards digital material. EAD for instance is also used in libraries. The impact of information technologies on information and, more specifically, records is changing the landscape of the standards supporting the management and use of archival records.—*Hans Hoffman*

Keywords: standard, archives, archival standard, records, digital preservation
Related Entries: Archival Description; Digital Preservation; Metadata; Records Management Standards

Bibliography

Ballegooie, Marlene van, and Wendy Duff. "Archival Metadata." In *DCC, Digital Curation Manual*, 2006. www.era.lib.ed.ac.uk/bitstream/1842/3347/1/Duff%20archival-metadata.pdf.

International Council on Archives. *General International Standard Archival Description*, 2nd edition, 2000. ISAD(G). www.icacds.org.uk/eng/ISAD%28G%29.pdf (accessed November 27, 2014).

———. "International Standard Archival Authority Record for Corporate Bodies, Persons and Families," 2nd edition, 2003. www.icacds.org.uk/eng/ISAAR%28CPF%292ed.pdf.

———. "ISDF: International Standard for Describing Functions." 2011. www.ica.org/10208/standards/isdf-international-standard-for-describing-functions.html.

International Organization for Standardization. "Audit and Certification of Trustworthy Digital Repositories." ISO 16363:2012—Space Data and Information Transfer Systems. http://public.ccsds.org/publications/archive/652x0m1.pdf.

———. "Digital Records Conversion and Migration Process." ISO 13008:2012—Information and

Documentation. www.iso.org/iso/cataloguedetail. htm?csnumber=52326.

———. "Implementation Guidelines for Digitization of Records." ISO 13028:2010—Information and Documentation. www.iso.org/iso/cataloguedetail. htm?csnumber=52391.

"Metadata Encoding and Transmission Standard." Library of Congress. Last modified November 7, 2014. www.loc.gov/standards/mets.

"PREMIS Data Dictionary for Preservation Metadata." Version 2.2, 2012. Library of Congress. www.loc.gov/standards/premis/v2/premis-2-2.pdf.

"Reference Model for an Open Archival Information System (OAIS), Recommended Practice, Issue 2." http://public.ccsds.org/publications/archive/650x0m2.pdf.

"Victoria Electronic Records Strategy (VERS)." Public Record Office Victoria (Australia). http://prov.vic.gov.au/government/vers.

Weber, Lisa B. "Archival Description Standards: Concepts, Principles, and Methodologies." *American Archivist* 52 (4) (1989): 504–13. http://archivists.metapress.com/content/hj02171620727331/fulltext.pdf (accessed December, 2013).

ARCHIVAL THEORY

Archival theory may be ubiquitous, or virtually nonexistent. It depends on what you mean by *theory*.

In common English usage, theory has had various meanings over the years, two of which predominate. Most commonly, theory is used in the sense typically associated with natural science; we have theories of relativity, gravitation, and the big bang—among many others. This sense of the term can also apply to human nature and action. We can speak, for example, of Jung's theory of archetypes or Freud's theory of dreams. This is theory in the sense of description or explanation. It covers a lot of ground, encompassing the natural world and humanity as part of it.

The other prominent sense of theory is somewhat narrower. It has less to do with description than prescription, being more about guiding, rather than explaining, human action. This is theory from the actor's, rather than the observer's, perspective. Examples would include Rousseau's social contract theory and Thoreau's theory of civil disobedience.

In both senses—as an explanation of things and as a guide to action—theory is a product of thought, inseparable from ideas or concepts. When sufficiently developed, it can be viewed as organized conceptual knowledge (Livelton 1996, 9–58).

What Is Archival Theory?

Among *archivists*, theory has been viewed in a number of ways. The term has on occasion been used in the explanatory, scientific sense. It has also been used a number of times to refer to the meaning or purpose of archival work in the grand scheme of things. But by far the most common view of archival theory considers it archival thinking as a whole. There are of course variations. In the loosest sense, theory comes to mean anything written in the professional journals. At the other end of the spectrum, theory takes on a practical, normative cast in the work of archivists like Jenkinson and Schellenberg, who view it as the principles that guide everyday work.

On reflection, it becomes clear that both these senses of theory—archival thinking and principles guiding the work—are based on a simple distinction between theory and practice. This distinction is both understandable and problematic. It is understandable to contrast archivists' thinking about their work from the work itself, simply because it reflects reality; archivists, as practitioners of an applied field of work, both think and do. However, if theory is considered the whole of archivists' thinking, then the term becomes a synonym for "thought." This invites no end of potential confusion, since it means that all different types of thought would inevitably have to be viewed as species of theory. Thinking is hard enough in itself without referring, for instance, to empirical studies as a kind of theory and methodology as another kind of theory. It becomes even worse when one realizes that such usage leaves precious little room for speaking about theory itself as a distinct kind of thought.

One way to avoid this potential (and, at times, actual) confusion, would be to employ the existing, respectable, and eminently useful definition embedded in standard English, as mentioned above: theory as organized conceptual knowledge. This usage is helpful in a variety of ways. Not only does it give archivists a way to speak of theory as distinct from other forms of knowledge, but it can give a new twist to the common distinction between theory and practice.

Theory as thought distinct from practice, if taken as fundamental, tends to dichotomize thinking and doing. This has at times led to acrimonious, and largely unprofitable, debate among archivists—on the questionable assumption that thinkers are not doers, and vice versa. From the conceptual knowledge view of theory, by contrast, the difference between theory and practice is essentially the difference between ideas and their practical application. Archivists have, and use, ideas; they do their work the way they do because of the ideas they hold about the nature of that work and the material they're working with. An archivist's beliefs about the nature of *records*, for example, will result in treating them one way rather than another.

As well as reframing the relations between theory and practice, theory as conceptual knowledge also clearly distinguishes itself from scholarship. And it does so while illuminating the relations between them as complementary kinds of knowledge— broadly speaking, the rational and the empirical. The archivist as scholar explores the world around him or her, looking for patterns among relevant facts— whether studying a body of records, an organization's structure, or even the history of *recordkeeping systems*. In doing so, the archival scholar employs concepts of various sorts—strands of theory, assumptions about the nature of things that allow him or her to discern patterns—or, indeed, sift the relevant from the irrelevant facts. Theory underlies and supports scholarly inquiry.

Looked at through the lens of theory as conceptual knowledge, theory can be seen to support scholarship by enabling, and empowering, a layer of methodology between the two. Methodology itself certainly has a conceptual dimension, but that conceptual aspect consists largely of borrowing from theoretical ideas. The archival scholar employs one or another methodology, as appropriate, to guide and discipline investigation; one of the components of that discipline is a set of assumptions about the nature of records, or structures, or *functions*—depending on the nature of the investigation.

On this view of theory, methodology also acts as intermediary between theory and practice. This is in fact what Jenkinson and Schellenberg are referring to when speaking about theory as principles that serve as guides to practice. Methodology is a set of normative tools, because it presents itself as a guide to action for both scholarship and practice. The conceptual knowledge view of theory, by enabling access to the notion of methodology, opens up fresh ways of articulating the structure and content of archival work as both a knowledge-seeking discipline and a practical activity.

As noted, archival theory in the broad sense of archival thinking (or, practically speaking, writing) exists in relative abundance. Archival theory as organized conceptual knowledge, on the other hand, takes up rather less space on the bookshelf. But this is neither surprising nor regrettable. Archivists are busy people, with important work to do. So, it should come as no surprise that the vast majority of the thinking they've shared with one another over the years has had considerably more to do with methodology and practice than with theory in the narrower sense.

Since the early 1990s, however, their presence has increased significantly in North American universities. Before this growth in university programs, Frank Burke had argued that archival theory could only thrive when archivists were admitted into the university. He envisioned them seeking "the discovery of transcendent concepts, a body of literature and counter-literature that will ultimately support challenges, analyses of counter-trends, heuristic exercises, taxonomic systems, paradigmatic explications, and unimpeachable antitheses leading to further Hegelian progressions" (Burke 1981, 45).

Burke's exuberant vision has not yet come to pass. But with the imminent arrival of a third generation of archival academics, there may be hope, especially given a new trend. In recent years, the universities have provided leadership for a number of multidisciplinary, transnational teams of academics and nonacademics working in concert to explore broad issues of archival importance such as the preservation of electronic records. While eminently urgent and practical, these ventures have engendered considerable scholarship and fresh conceptual thinking, all of which bodes well for the further development of archival theory (Duranti and Preston 2008). The shelf of books on that theory may yet be small, but some seeds have been planted.

Conclusion

The common understanding of theory among archivists is both limited and limiting. By adapting a broader notion of theory embedded in common English usage, archivists can take a fresh—and meaningful—look at themselves, the work they do, and the ideas they hold.—*Trevor Livelton*

Keywords: theory, scholarship, practice
Related Entries: Archival Method; Archival Practice; Archival Science

Bibliography

Burke, Frank G. "The Future Course of Archival Theory in the United States." *American Archivist* 44 (1) (1981): 40–46. http://archivists.metapress.com/content/485380l307551286/fulltext.pdf.

Duranti, Luciana, and Randy Preston, eds. *Inter-PARES 2: Interactive, Dynamic and Experiential Records*. Padua, Italy: CREUP, 2008.

Eastwood, Terry. "What Is Archival Theory and Why Is It Important?" *Archivaria* 1 (37) (1994): 122–30. http://journals.sfu.ca/archivar/index.php/archivaria/article/view/11991/12954.

Livelton, Trevor. *Archival Theory, Records, and the Public*. Lanham, MD: Scarecrow Press, 1996.

ARCHIVES (INSTITUTION)

Types of Archives

From time immemorial people have used various means of communication to recall their thoughts and activities. They have designated one or more places to keep them—in memories and on bodies, in nature, rituals, a location at home or work, or an entire building or other shelter specifically dedicated to that purpose. They have undertaken this task themselves or assigned all or some of it to one or more individuals or groups. We might call those who undertake it archival institutions of one kind or another because at heart any archival institution is people doing archival work. No definition of an archival institution accounts for all of the many ways in which *archives* have been conceived or created. We might explore this by saying that archival institutions are people engaged in identifying, preserving

indefinitely, and making available representations of human actions and perceptions. This broad definition will mean different things to different people. There will be debate about what these terms mean, whether others are necessary, and how close to a particular vision of them we must come in order to identify some entity or even someone as an archival institution.

These visions of archival institutions can embrace the most general conceptions, such as the Foucaldian archive, or what a society (as an ultimate institution, archiver, or repository) makes possible to think or say at a given historical moment. Archives can be created by formal organizations or in personal life, as oral communications, objects (including those in nature), publications, and unpublished records in all media, and we can call archives where many are held: historic sites, libraries, museums, particular places in nature, and institutions such as the National Archives and Records Administration of the United States. Any communication is eligible to be archival material, and the entities engaged in identifying, preserving indefinitely, and making them available do so as types of archival institution. More conventional definitions of archival institutions, as only actual formal organizations and repositories of certain types of representations that have certain prescribed evidential qualities that make them *records*, can exclude one or more of the others on grounds that are difficult to justify. In some cases, this has done grievous harm, especially to indigenous and many other non-Western people, as well as the less literate and less powerful everywhere, whose *archival practices* and records have not seemed to measure up to that allegedly higher standard, or to an ideal record and institution that have not really existed.

Although a more hospitable view of archival institutions is needed in order to avoid segregation of the overall human record into a hierarchy of largely unrelated parts, distinctions between types of archival institutions need to be respected. The challenge is to find ways to reduce the segregation while respecting the distinctions—primarily by fostering greater collaboration between the various types of archives, as digital connection in particular now makes possible. Lack of understanding of these distinctions can result from the institutional landscape of archives itself. The terms archives, libraries, and museums, for example, are often used interchangeably. That is understandable since an institution that is formally called an archives may contain a library unit or museum, and those that are formally called libraries and museums may have archival units within them. Sometimes all three can be found in the same facility under the same overall administration and a very different name, such as "The Rooms" in Newfoundland and Labrador, which brings together the state-sponsored provincial archives, museum, and art gallery. Minnesota goes even further and houses in the Minnesota History Center the state archives, a museum, library, art gallery, and management of archaeological and historic sites in the state. Similar configurations of one or more of these entities can be found in many places, often under the banner of a heritage center at a local community or municipal level, including increasingly among indigenous communities, such as the Stó:lo Nation "Resource Centre" in British Columbia. And some archives are formally associated with libraries in particular, such as Library and Archives Canada and Bibliothèque et Archives nationales du Québec. Perhaps compounding the confusion is the fact that not only do some archives have library or museum units or formal affiliations with them, but also many hold some published materials, artifacts, or artworks actually embedded in or related to otherwise typical documentary *recordkeeping systems*.

Although this varied landscape makes blurring of distinctions between its components understandable, important differences remain. Distinct entities called archives, rather than libraries, museums, or history or heritage centers, exist for a reason within this mixture of institutional configurations. They are descendants of a long tradition of archival thought and work that has produced an extraordinary number and variety of such institutions. They are a response to the particular substantive challenges of identifying, preserving, and making available a certain type of the overall human record—the largely unpublished record—rather than the largely published record concentrated in libraries, and other types of artifacts found for the most part in museums. They have nurtured the creation of the archival profession because the chief characteristics of the documentary record require for its care the *archivist's* specialized approach rooted in extensive knowledge of the records' complex *provenance*, or multiple *contexts*

of *creation*, or histories. The distinguishing features of these records are: they originate in and are typically very rare *evidence* of a myriad of often ongoing institutional or personal actions and processes; they are expanding and thus generally massive bodies of records of multiple provenance; they have a constitutive *interrelatedness*, whether in a highly organized or less formal recordkeeping system; they come in highly varied media types (such as paper, still and moving film images, sound, and now digital materials) and in even more varied individual documentary forms (ranging from letters, memoranda, diaries, scrapbooks, census forms, passports, and wills to photographs, maps, videos, and more recently born-digital counterparts of these documents, as well as new digital multimedia documents); their complex institutional and personal origins, systems, media, and forms are constantly evolving over time; and they are unrelentingly aging.

The Concept of Archives as Institutions

These distinct records require institutions that can meet the particular challenges their care presents with the archivists' specialized knowledge. The antecedents of this institutional archival work reach back into recordkeeping activities carried out in the ancient world, which produced such early specialized institutions for their maintenance as the Metroon in classical Athens and Tabularium in republican Rome. These and similar ancient institutions are forerunners of state archives, institutions around the world that have been established primarily to preserve records created by governments. Archives for government records have grown in number and prominence since the eighteenth century, although there are major earlier examples such as the Spanish royal archives at Simancas that was established in the late sixteenth century, and is now part of the National Archives of Spain. Most countries today have a national archives for national government records and separate provincial, state, regional, and municipal archives for government records in those jurisdictions. These archives are among the largest individual archival institutions. The National Archives of the United Kingdom, for example, which was established in 1838 as the Public Record Office, holds government records as old as a thousand years, which in total occupy about 185 kilometers of shelf space.

Archives have also been long established by other institutions as well, as exemplified by religious institutions of all kinds, whether international, national, or local. Long-term institutional record-keeping has also been done by businesses such as the Hudson's Bay Company, which was created in 1670 under an English royal charter. It established a company archives unit in the 1920s at its London head office, then transferred its approximately three thousand linear meters of archives to the Archives of Manitoba in 1974. The business sector more generally, however, has not established nearly as many notable archives as the government sector, and most business archives are not as accessible. Educational institutions such as universities, colleges, and some schools have established a great number of archives for their records. Although not all institutions have archival units, they can also be found in international organizations such as the United Nations and NATO, as well as in hospitals, professional associations, unions, organizations sponsored by cultural or social minorities such as lesbian, gay, bisexual, transgender, and questioning (LGBTQ) communities, and in other communities ranging from social clubs to neighborhood groups.

Archival institutions of this type have particular mandates, often arising in the state sector from specific archival legislation. The mandates of state-sponsored and other archives may also be subject to other laws such as those governing access to information and protection of privacy. Although these laws may also shape the work of nonpublic archives, the latter work mainly under formal bylaws or policies set by their own sponsors. The regulations relevant to a given archives spell out its mandate within the applicable jurisdiction of the regulations. In addition to giving them responsibility for the long-term *preservation* of the records of their sponsor, these regulations may also authorize the *acquisition* of records created by others and the development of thematic programs for the records of certain organizations, families, and individuals that serve their sponsors and other users. The legal and *policy* framework governing an archives will also usually specify its place in an administrative reporting structure. Many state archives, for example, report to cultural ministries. Others report to a wide variety of agencies, including departments of education and the offices of presidents or prime ministers

(for a comprehensive list of archives throughout the world, see http://en.wikipedia.org/wiki/Listofarchives).

Archival institutions do various things within their differing mandates. They may also have different degrees of authority to perform functions they may be given, and the priorities for activities within a function may vary and change over time. In general, archives engage in identifying records of lasting value by assessing the records' provenance or their creators' functions and impact, more than the records' information content; they represent records in accordance with knowledge of the records' particular origins and the interrelationships of bodies of records with a common provenance; they make them available through reference services on the basis of that knowledge; and they employ it to preserve records indefinitely.

In recent years, *archivists* and many others have come to understand that this work involves far more than mere accumulation of records about the past. Rather, the decisions by archivists and others to identify, make available, and preserve the documentary heritage shape profoundly the understanding of current and future generations. Since this vast body of records in the world's many archives documents an incalculable array of human experiences, it is being used today in an extraordinary variety of ways—from academic historical to literary, artistic, economic, scientific, medical, environmental, and human rights and other social justice purposes. Archival institutions have long quietly engaged in such powerful acts of knowledge creation far from public view. Emerging awareness of this role has spurred much new interest in the history and current activities of archives among archivists and many others. This work shows that archives have always shaped and been shaped by their particular societal-political circumstances.

This insight sheds light on the most pressing contemporary challenge this type of archival institution faces—archiving the now-pervasive born-digital documentary record such as e-mail and digital photographs. Archival budgets, which are much lower than those of most libraries and museums, are pitifully inadequate for this task, regardless of mandates that give archives that responsibility. Very few such archives have made even modest headway in this respect because there is scant political and societal understanding or support of archival roles. Thus, most older *digital records* either no longer exist or are irretrievable. The future of this long-standing form of archival institution is thus at stake, and especially for those archives sponsored by the state and other public institutions, which have a vital responsibility to serve society's need for the unpublished public record in all its forms.

Conclusion

Will public archival institutions be eclipsed by allocation to the highest corporate or private high-tech bidder of control over born-digital records in order to "solve" quickly the long-neglected digital archives problem? Or will renewed understanding of the power of these archives to address society's central concerns reveal their importance and result in granting them the necessary authority and other means to fulfill the public trust invested in them? Will society's profound stake in the fate of all archives—state-sponsored or not, digital or analog—also be recognized by creation of much needed additional archives across the government, corporate, and non-governmental sectors and better access to all such archives? And will new forms of collaboration among all the various types of archival institution discussed above—that digital means now allow—enable unpublished documentary archives to play their distinct role in even more fruitful ways? Or will lack of understanding and financial support render them unable to acquire, preserve, and make available the born-digital record and thus be marginalized among the much more numerous and better known and resourced cultural heritage or bureaucratic recordkeeping entities? Or may a new type of interconnected collaborative even "global" publicly accessible "archival institution" emerge instead to serve both analog and digital needs—one built on the distinctive contributions of the various custodians of the overall human archive?—*Tom Nesmith*

Keywords: digital records, historic sites, indigenous, libraries, museums
Related Entries: Archives (Material); Community Archives; Digital Archives

Bibliography

Bastian, J. A., and B. F. Alexander, eds. *Community Archives: The Shaping of Memory*. London: Facet, 2009.

Blouin, F. X., and W. G. Rosenberg, eds. *Archives, Documentation, and Institutions of Social Memory: Essays from the Sawyer Seminar*. Ann Arbor: University of Michigan Press, 2007.

Brosius, M., ed. *Ancient Archives and Archival Traditions: Concepts of Record-Keeping in the Ancient World*. Oxford: Oxford University Press, 2003.

Cunningham, A. "Archival Institutions." In S. Mc-Kemmish, M. Piggott, B. Reed, and F. Upward, eds. *Archives: Recordkeeping in Society*. Wagga Wagga, New South Wales: Charles Sturt University, Centre for Information Studies, 2004, 21–50.

Gilliland, A. J. *Conceptualizing 21st-Century Archives*. Chicago: Society of American Archivists, 2014.

Hamilton, C., V. Harris, J. Taylor, M. Pickover, G. Reid, and R. Saleh, eds. *Refiguring the Archive*. Cape Town: David Philip Publishers, 2002.

Jimerson, R. C. *Archives Power: Memory, Accountability, and Social Justice*. Chicago: Society of American Archivists, 2009.

Nesmith, T. "Seeing Archives: Postmodernism and the Changing Intellectual Place of Archives." *The American Archivist* 65 (1) (2002): 24–41. http://archivists.metapress.com/content/rr48450509r0712u/fulltext.pdf.

Schwartz, J. M., and T. Cook. "Archives, Records, and Power: The Making of Modern Memory." *Archival Science* 2 (1–2) (2002): 1–19. DOI: 10.1007/BF02435628.

United Nations Educational, Scientific and Cultural Organization (UNESCO). *Memory of the World: The Treasures That Record Our History from 1700 BC to the Present Day*. Paris and Glasgow: UNESCO and HarperCollins, 2012. See also www.unesco.org/new/en/communication-and-information/flagship-project-activities/memory-of-the-world/register (last accessed July 2014).

ARCHIVES (MATERIAL)

An archives is the whole of the *documents* made or received by a physical or juridical *person* in the course of activity and kept for further action or reference by this person or a legitimate successor. The documents by means of which a practical activity has been carried out are reciprocally linked by a relationship determined by the nature, mandate, and *function(s)* of their creator, called the *archival bond*. Such a bond is originary, because it comes into being when a document is made or received and kept (i.e., created); necessary, because all archival documents have it; and determined, because it is qualified by the activity in which the document participates. This complex of documents spontaneously and organically created is maintained by their creator for its memory in its own interest and in order to reach its purposes. It can also be maintained out of a legal or social duty, or for *accountability* purposes.

Evolution of the Concept

Archival writers have agreed on the concept of archives as outlined above since the seventeenth century, albeit using different phraseology, level of detail, and emphasis in their definitions (for example, see Muller, Feith, and Fruin 1898; Jenkinson 1922; Casanova 1928; Favier 1959; Bautier 1970; Papritz 1983). The two notable exceptions are the German author Adolf Brenneke and the American author Theodore Schellenberg. In his lectures, published in 1953 by one of his students, Wolfgang Leesch, Brenneke redefined the term *archiv* (i.e., archives) on the basis of its use, by stating that the documents of a *registry* become archives when they are permanently preserved to serve as sources and evidence of the past (Brenneke 1953, 97). Following his lead, in 1956, Schellenberg theorized a clear distinction between the documents that are *records* and those that constitute archives on the basis of where they are preserved, by whom they are preserved, and why they are preserved. Records are preserved in the creating office, by their creator, because of their value to their creator, while archives are preserved in an archival institution, by the *archivist*, because of their research value to persons other than the creator (Schellenberg 1956, 16). The determination of what records are to be preserved as archives is made by the archivist exercising the *appraisal* function. Brenneke's and Schellenberg's reformulation of the concept of archives has had an enduring impact in Germany and the United States—where the term *archives* since then refers to the records of one creator that are selected for continuing preservation in an archival institution, unit, or program, as well as to the holdings of such entity, interchangeably

with *archival collection*—and a moderate impact in Canada. The latter, in the late 1980s, adopted the term *archival fonds* to refer to the all-inclusive concept of archives, using the term *records* to refer to its components and, in general, to all documents created (i.e., made or received and kept) as by-products of activities, and limiting the term *archives* to refer to the holdings of archival institutions, units, or programs.

Sir Hilary Jenkinson—who never defined the term *archives*, considering the concept equivalent to that embodied in the term *archival document* (Jenkinson 1922, 11)—commenting on the definition of archives provided by Schellenberg, stated:

> Potential value for Research is no doubt the reason why we continue to spend time and money on preserving Archives and making them available, but the fact that a thing may be used for a purpose for which it was not intended—a hat, for instance, for the production of a rabbit—is not part of its nature and should not, I submit, be made an element of its definition, though it may reasonably affect its treatment. (Jenkinson 1956)

Irrespective of whether archives should be defined according to their nature or not, it is essential to examine such nature, which—as is the case for all things—is determined by the circumstances of creation.

The Nature of Archival Material

Archives are the by-product of activity and as such derive their meaning from their context. Italian author Elio Lodolini writes that archives are composed of documents made or received in the course of activity and of the relationships established among them when set aside for further action or reference; these two components make up also the archival *document* or *record*, and embody two types of information, that provided by the documents and that revealed by their order and relationships (Lodolini 1998). The consequent *interrelatedness* of archival documents or records—their archival bond, that is—is expression of the process of development of the activity from which the records result (Cencetti 1970). The archival bond is also the reason for the *uniqueness* of records, as identical documents with different relationships to other documents in the same archives or in different archives are different archival documents or records. Because the records composing an archives are not the intended outcome of the activity producing them, but a means to a purpose, an archives is characterized by *naturalness* and has been compared to the bed of a river (Lodolini 1998), a geological sediment (Bautier 1970), and the roots of a tree (Jenkinson 1922). As the records are not created to serve the purposes for which they will later be used by persons other than their creator, archives are also characterized by *impartiality* with respect to such purposes, and, as they are relied on by their creator in the usual and ordinary course of activity, they also have the characteristic of *authenticity* with respect to such activity (Jenkinson 1922, 12; Eastwood 1994).

Archival Material versus Library Material

The distinction between archival and library material is not always clear. The general statement that an archives (or an archival fonds, or an archival collection) is made up of documents and a library (or a library collection) of books is often inaccurate and always insufficient. Both an archives and a library are universalities of separate things (Ulpianus, *Corpus juris civilis*, D. 48, 19, 9: *universitates ex distantibus*)—that is, the single, individual components of the corpus subordinate their individuality to the bond of their common destination, and constitute a collective unit (Cencetti 1970). But the analogy stops here. The individual components of the universality library have each their own purpose, which they reach with their means—that is, they have a primary autonomy. They can be connected to one another analogically (e.g., on the basis of the subject matter, the identity of the author, the similarity of external characteristics, like the format, the binder, the publisher, etc.) but not organically, like archival documents. The fact that, after their creation as autonomous entities, the will of their owner (e.g., an institution, an organization, or a private person, family, or group) associates these entities in a major unit by giving them a common destination (i.e., the library collection), or creating with them a corpus, is not an essential attribute of their nature but something that may or may not happen.

The components of an archives not only are all created (i.e., made or received and kept) by the same physical or juridical person, but, being one of the means used by that person to realize its purposes, mandate, functions and/or activities, carry with themselves, since their origin, the bond of the common destination. The universality archives is therefore necessary while the universality library, like a museum or a gallery, is voluntary. This means that a library collection can be divided; this may reduce its practical usefulness or its value, but it will not change its nature or the meaning of its components. Dividing an archives (for example, by distributing parts of a family archives among the heirs of the patriarch) would break the archival bond among the records, destroy it as an archives, and transform it into a collection of meaningless documents.

The fact that a library collection is a voluntary universality also means that the items within it can be arranged according to a system external to them, and dependent on the scientific, practical, or personal choice of the owner of the collection. The fact that an archives is a necessary universality means that its units have embedded in them an original order determined by the archival bond they have acquired when associated with other units in a *file* or a *series*, at the time when they were kept rather than discarded. It is this order that gives meaning to the archival documents and reveals the development of the activity in which they participate while supporting its further development.

Related to such genetic differences between an archives and a library are the differences between their respective constitutive units. Each archival unit (e.g., a document, a file) is authentic with respect to its creator if used in the ordinary course of its activity, even when, as an item, it is false, because it is the actual instrument of the creator's activity. For example, if an individual applies to a university program submitting a forged transcript, which is included in the applicant's file within the series of that year's application files for the program of the department to which the individual applied, such transcript is an authentic archival document (or record) of the department, which received it, filed it, processed it, and made a decision upon it. If in the course of the department's admission activity the transcript is suspected to be a forgery, a procedure is initiated to establish its *authenticity*, and the transcript, with the file to which it belongs, will be transmitted to a special office in charge of authentication and will become an authentic archival document (or record) also of that office, albeit a different one, as the application file will exist in a different context, and will have an archival bond with different records. This characteristic of authenticity with respect to the creator does not exist for the items of a library collection, because even an original manuscript would be authentic with respect to its author, but not with respect to the body that has accumulated the items of the library collection. As a consequence, the individual items of a library can be substituted without changing the meaning of the whole, while those of an archives cannot (single exceptions which can be met in practice, such as the unique book, or the double original of a document in the same documentary context, are accidental).

Part of the nature of library material is the idea of publication and dissemination, while archival material is only created for those involved in the activity of which they constitute the natural instrument, by-product and residue. The fact that, after their creation, some of them may be accessible to the public because, for example, they are submitted as evidence in a lawsuit, or, after they are no longer needed for the purposes producing them, they may be preserved to be used as sources for research is not part of the reason why they were created and does not define their nature. One of the consequences of this difference between the items of a library and those of an archives is that the former are commercial entities, while the latter are not. There is indeed commerce of archival documents or even of entire archives, but in such cases the commercial value of the material is not part of their nature, but derives from external factors, like illuminations, autographs, and interest of the content.

The equivocation between the two types of material is often a consequence of the names of the institutions holding them, especially in the United States, where the establishment of the national archives only occurred in 1934 and, until 1952, it was the Manuscripts Division of the Library of Congress that preserved the archives of the nation, including the Declaration of Independence and the Constitution. Still today, the Presidential Libraries, part of the U.S. National Archives, preserve mixed materials, including archival documents, books, and artifacts.

Conclusion

An archives is an integrated organic whole of documents and relationships produced as instrument and by-products of activity and accumulated by a person or an organization in order to fulfill its purposes, and kept for further action or reference by the same person or organization or a legitimate successor. Archival material is characterized by *naturalness, interrelatedness, uniqueness,* authenticity, and *impartiality.* Because of its nature, archival material is considered the most reliable source for understanding the past.—*Luciana Duranti*

Keywords: record, document, archival bond, archival nature, creator
Related Entries: Archival Bond; Authenticity; Document; Impartiality; Interrelatedness; Naturalness; Record(s); Record Creation; Uniqueness

Bibliography

Bautier, R. H. "Les archives." In Ministere des Affaires culturelles, Direction des Archives de France, *Manuel d'Archivistique.* Paris, 1970.
Brenneke, A. *Archivkunde.* Leipzig: Koehler & Amelang, 1953.
Casanova, E. *Archivistica.* Siena: Lazzeri, 1928.
Cencetti, G. Il fondamento teorico della dottrina archivistica. In G. Cencetti, *Scritti archivistici.* Rome: Il Centro di ricerca editore, 1970, 7–13.
Eastwood, T. "What Is Archival Theory and Why Is It Important?" *Archivaria* 37 (1994): 122–30. http://journals.sfu.ca/archivar/index.php/archivaria/article/view/11991/12954.
Favier, J. *Les archives.* Paris: Presses Universitaires de France, 1959.
Jenkinson, H. *A Manual of Archive Administration.* London: Percy Lund, Humphries and Co., 1922.
Jenkinson, H. "Modern Archives. Some Reflections on T.R. Schellenberg: Modern Archives: Principles and Techniques." *Journal of the Society of Archivists* (1959): 147–49.
Lodolini, E. *Archivistica. Principi e problemi,* 8th edition. Milano: Franco Angeli s.r.l., 1998.
Muller, S., J. A. Feith, and R. Fruin. *Handleiding voor het ordenen en bescrijven van Archiven.* Groningen, 1898. (The English translation is titled *Manual for the Arrangement and Description of Archives.* New York, 1940).

Papritz, J. *Archivwissenschaft*, 2nd edition. Marburg, 1983.

Schellenberg, T. R. *Modern Archives. Principles and Techniques.* Chicago: University of Chicago Press, 1956.

ARCHIVES AND MEMORY

Memory is a concept closely associated with *archives* and the role of *archivists*, although there is no clear consensus on the nature of that relationship. Archival repositories are sometimes referred to as institutions of memory, houses of memory, or places of remembrance. Archival *documents* seem to embody or preserve personal (individual) memory or to represent collective (or social) memory. Yet as a fixed representation of past events, ideas, and transactions, archival documents also serve as a corrective for personal or collective memory. Whereas memory changes according to present needs and new perspectives, documents remain stable (unless altered). Archival documents may also serve as surrogates for memory, preserving *evidence* of events and ideas for future reference. Although archives may represent part of the memory of society, they thus also serve as a corrective or oppositional force for both individual and collective memory.

Concepts of Memory

The human need for accurate remembrance of important events, decisions, and actions led to the first creation of writing and *records*. From early clay tablets to papyrus, paper, and electronic *recordkeeping*, such archival documents have represented a form of information storage (for *accessibility*), dissemination (across distances), and *preservation* (over time). The archival profession grew out of these needs for preservation and access to documents, as a form of "archival memory."

To conceptualize the relationship between archives and memory, it is useful to distinguish four separate but often intersecting planes of memory: personal, collective, historical, and archival.

Memory is most properly understood as a cognitive and physiological function of individuals. Personal memory includes both short-term and long-term memory. Long-term memory includes episodic memory (recollection of direct personal experience), semantic memory (of facts and concepts), and procedural memory (of skills, habits, and performance) (Jimerson 2009, 197–98; Hedstrom 2010, 164–65).

The concept of collective memory posits that groups of people, such as members of an ethnic group or a nation, share some common perceptions of the past, such as "shared origins, values, and experiences" (Hedstrom 2010, 166; Jimerson 2009, 201–2). When archivists engage in documenting specific social groups they may contribute to this sense of identity formation and validation. Although collective memory provides a convenient metaphor for self-consciousness among a societal group, only an individual can truly form and access actual memory (Le Goff 1992, 111).

There is a complex relationship between history, as the study of the past, and memory. Historical memory comes from interpretation of earlier events based on evidence and analysis. Historians may either assist in shaping collective memory—and the related concepts of tradition, heritage, and folklore—or to challenge such societal constructs. In constructing "historical memory" of the past, historians often rely on primary sources created at the time the events they depict took place or soon after. Rules of evidence, *authenticity*, and *reliability* require the historian to use only trusted sources of information.

History thus often stands as a corrective for personal or collective memory. As Jacques Le Goff states, "History must illuminate memory and help it rectify its errors" (1992, 111). Although they profess to seek *objectivity*, historians are inevitably subjective in how they frame their analytical questions, select evidence, and interpret its meanings. "History is interpretation, and as such it is subject to exactly those same societal biases that are supposedly the weakness of 'memory,'" Mark Greene argues (2003/2004, 97). The acknowledged biases of personal and collective memory thus also emerge in historical interpretation, or historical memory.

Memory in an Archival Context

Because memory is fragile and malleable, since ancient times people have created artifacts, written documents, and other surrogates for memory. Such fixed media do not change with new circumstances of time or place. All archival documents serve the purpose of transmitting and preserving information over time. As Kenneth Foote notes, "Unlike verbal and nonverbal action, which is ephemeral and disappears as it occurs, the physical durability of objects, artifacts, and documents allows them to be passed from person to person and place to place over long periods of time" (1990, 379). Archives materials thus provide a form of remembrance, although they do not constitute memory itself.

The choice of placing documents in an *archives institution* represents an act of archival memory construction. As carriers of information about the past, *archives materials* represent a surrogate for personal and collective memory, which enables people to access information. Such *access* requires assistance from archivists, who serve a role as "mediators between records creators and records repositories, between archives and users, between conceptions of the past and extant documentation" (Blouin 1999, 111). Archivists select what materials will become part of the archives and thereby determine, usually in consultation with others, what aspects of society will be remembered in the future.

Archives represent one portion of human documentation serving the need for memory of the past. As Joan Schwartz and Terry Cook state, "Memory, like history, is rooted in archives. Without archives, memory falters, knowledge of accomplishments fades, pride in a shared experience dissipates" (2002, 18). However, archives do not constitute memory. As Margaret Hedstrom argues, in relation to archives the concept of memory is "more than a metaphor, less than an analogy"; archives are valuable especially when used as "sources for the potential discovery or recovery of memories that have been lost" (2010, 163, 176).

The profound impact of electronic media on *archival practices* made understanding the impact of new technologies for external memory essential for archivists. Memory studies relating to ancient, medieval, and modern forms of *recordkeeping* provide needed *context* for evaluating the impact of electronic records, particularly in relation to concerns about "parallels between previous changes in recording technology and the contemporary problems of authenticity, integrity, and persistence" (Hedstrom 2010, 171).

Although archives have traditionally been regarded as neutral and unbiased repositories of reliable information, recent scholarship challenge this assumption. Because archival sources can be used to establish or strengthen a group's sense of collective memory, the archives may help to create a sense of group identity. Art, literature, museums, libraries, and archives share this role. According to Elisabeth Kaplan, "The archival record doesn't just happen; it is created by individuals and organizations, and used, in turn, to support their values and missions" (2000, 147). This places the archive in a political and cultural context.

This engagement in memory construction and perpetuation is not neutral. Throughout much of human history written records and archives supported the interests and power of those with wealth, political power, and intellectual influence in society. As an alternative to the hierarchical and bureaucratic framework for understanding *provenance*, Jeannette Bastian posits the concept of a "community of records" in which a marginalized community is both "a record-creating entity and a memory frame for the records it creates" (Bastian 2003, 3–4).

As previously marginalized groups seek a claim to power and recognition, they have often sought to secure a presence in the archives. When they could not have their voices heard in mainstream archives, they have sometimes created their own repositories (Kaplan 2000, 145–50).

Archives thus become institutions fully engaged, whether knowingly or not, in the business of constructing memory and identity. As Brien Brothman states, "The making of memory involves the active construction of present knowledge out of continually evolving informational materials" (Brothman 2001, 71). Terry Cook contends that every record is shaped by its *creator* and presented or signified by an archivist. "No text is an innocent by-product of administrative or personal action, but rather a constructed product," he writes (2001, 25). Each decision to create a record, or to preserve it, or to place it in an archival repository becomes an act of memory construction.

Remembering and Forgetting

Memory cannot be fully understood without considering its opposite: amnesia. Each act of remembering entails an element of forgetting. As Foote states,

"A society's need to remember is balanced against its desire to forget, to leave the memory behind and put the event out of mind" (Foote 1990, 385).

Ruling powers often seek to maintain control by effacing memory. For example during the Protestant Reformation church leaders destroyed offending books and documents. At other times *records*—and the archival memory they represent—have been destroyed by those seeking to eliminate vestiges of the old order. During the French Revolution, for example, bonfires consumed records of the feudal past as the revolutionaries sought to remove evidence of prior oppression.

Beyond such willful destruction of archival records, the simple act of retaining some documents and not others entails an effacement of archival memory. As Socrates warned, writing weakens memory by encouraging reliance on written records and diminishing personal powers of remembering.

Preserving records in archives requires a *selection* of certain documents and the destruction of others. "There is no remembering without forgetting. They open out of each other, light becoming darkness, darkness becoming light" (Harris 2007, 47). In South Africa Harris witnessed the deliberate destruction of records to exclude oppositional voices from official memory. Although there is no simple formula for calculating the relationship between memory and amnesia, the daily acts of archival selection and *appraisal* constitute decisions to remember and to forget.

Some aspects of a society's history may be so painful or controversial that people seek to efface them from public memory. Examples include destruction of buildings in Berlin associated with Nazi rule, the site of Salem witches' executions, or the former home of a mass murderer (Foote 1990). Similar deletions have occurred many times with written records and archival documents. In the silences of postcolonial archives, for example, social and political power shapes the future of the past. Whose history will be preserved? Whose records? Whose memory? Whose stories? These are ongoing challenges in determining the relationship between memory and archives.

Conclusion

The relationship between archives and memory is more complicated than a simple equation stating that archives are houses of memory or that archival documents constitute part of the memory of society. Recorded information is a surrogate for memory, which can be used to carry aspects of personal or collective memory across time and distance. Because they are less susceptible to alteration and change, archival documents can be used as a corrective for human memory. Thus, archives serve as a form of remembrance, a vehicle for preserving information about past events, activities, and interactions. Since not all events can be documented, and not all documents are preserved indefinitely, archives also entail forgetfulness. The information embedded in documents may thus obscure information not accorded this form of longevity. Archives thus serve as sites of memory preservation and also of forgetfulness or amnesia. This gives special importance to the functions of archival selection, appraisal, and preservation.—*Randall C. Jimerson*

Keywords: appraisal, archival history, archival theory, evidence, provenance

Related Entries: Accountability; Appraisal; Archival Theory; Community Archives

Bibliography

Bastian, J. *Owning Memory: How a Caribbean Community Lost Its Archives and Found Its History*. Westport, CT: Libraries Unlimited, 2003.

Blouin, F. X. "Archivists, Mediation, and Constructs of Social Memory." *Archival Issues* 24 (1999): 100–112. www.jstor.org/stable/41102013.

Blouin, F. X., and W. Rosenberg, eds. *Archives, Documentation, and Institutions of Social Memory*. Ann Arbor: University of Michigan Press, 2006.

Brothman, B. "The Past That Archives Keep: Memory, History, and the Preservation of Archival Records." *Archivaria* 1 (51) (2001): 50–80. http://journals.sfu.ca/archivar/index.php/archivaria/article/view/12794/13993.

Cook, T. "Fashionable Nonsense or Professional Rebirth: Postmodernism and the Practice of Archives." *Archivaria* 1 (51) (2001): 14–35. http://journals.sfu.ca/archivar/index.php/archivaria/article/view/12792/13989.

Foote, K. E. "To Remember and Forget: Archives, Memory, and Culture." *American Archivist* 53 (3)

(1990): 378–92. http://archivists.metapress.com/
index/d87u013444j3g6r2.pdf.

Greene, M. A. "The Messy Business of Remembering: History, Memory, and Archives." *Archival
Issues* 28 (2) (2003/2004): 95–104. www.jstor.
org/stable/41102082.

Harris, Vern. *Archives and Justice: A South African
Perspective*. Chicago: Society of American Archivists, 2007, 47.

Hedstrom, M. "Archives and Collective Memory:
More Than a Metaphor, Less Than an Analogy."
In T. Eastwood and H. MacNeil, eds., *Currents of
Archival Thinking*. Santa Barbara, CA: ABC-Clio,
2010, 163–79.

Jimerson, R. C. *Archives Power: Memory, Accountability, and Social Justice*. Chicago: Society of
American Archivists, 2009.

Kaplan, E. "We Are What We Collect, We Collect
What We Are: Archives and the Construction
of Identity." *American Archivist* 63 (1) (2000):
126–51. http://archivists.metapress.com/index/
h554377531233l05.pdf.

Le Goff, J. *History and Memory*. New York: Columbia University Press, 1992.

Schwartz, J., and T. Cook. "Archives, Records,
and Power: The Making of Modern Memory."
Archival Science 2 (2002): 1–19. DOI: 10.1007/
BF02435628.

ARCHIVES AND THE WEB

Archives today are increasingly using the Web to
their advantage and to the advantage of their users. The Web is no longer a place where traditional
practices, tools, and objects are simply replicated
using new technologies. The Web today is rather
a framework demanding for a change of attitude in
order to explore how such a widespread, participatory environment may provide new meaning to the
traditional archival functions.

Before the Web

"In the pre-digital world, archival work processes
were largely invisible to the general public. . . . Until
the collection was fully processed . . . information
about the collection was generally not made available to potential users" (Gerencser 2011, 167). Such

an approach was perfectly consistent with the traditional role held by *archivists* as *trusted custodians*.
The fundamental duty of archivists has always been
to preserve and protect records, and such a physical
defense has resulted for a long time in a physical
and intellectual limitation to access. It needed the
French Revolution to define access as a guaranteed
right. However, the need to maintain control and
authoritative power over archives has been a major
limitation to a full exploitation of this principle: before the Web, *access* has never been considered as
an absolute value or a key archival function. Users
and their needs were hardly on the archivists' ra-
dar—the creation of finding aids, for example, was
a philological exercise, a descriptive action aimed
at providing a correct representation of an archives,
rather than an activity intended to produce a usable
tool for patrons. The focus was on the materials.

The Web 1.0

The situation started changing when computers and
machine-readable catalogues appeared on the scene
and made evident the benefits coming from union
catalogs in terms of data interoperability and search-
ability. For the first time, archivists had to cope with
the issue of standardizing *archival description* practices on a large scale. As a result, collection-level
catalog records started populating distributed databases, providing the users with a first-level access to
archival and manuscripts holdings. However, it was
only the creation and consolidation of the Web that
changed the scene, since it provided an environment
where archivists could disseminate their finding
aids, distribute digital surrogates of original archival
materials, and increase awareness and understanding of archives. "The archival profession successfully established itself on Web 1.0: archives have
websites, online exhibits, and databases of online
images; they post finding aids . . . and they communicate with their researchers via individual e-mails
and via e-mail groups and listservs" (Theimer 2011,
xi). The focus started shifting from materials to users, rather, users became an integral and relevant
part of the picture, and archivists discovered and
enhanced their role as cultural intermediaries. The
development of national and international archival
description standards as well as the creation of
national networks of archival institutions and cata-

logues were strategic steps toward enhanced online access. Issues about interface design, usability, and users' needs emerged in the archival discourse.

The Web 2.0

"With the advent of new social technologies, which are low-cost and easy to implement or participate in, attention is now more focused on direct engagement and active interaction with users in online spaces. Through these approaches, archives ideally become collaborative spaces when mediated through online spaces" (Palmer and Stevenson 2011, 6). Web 2.0 is an environment based on technologies "intrinsically participatory and focused on sharing, collaboration, and mutual meaning-making" (Palmer and Stevenson 2011, 1). The Web at its origins is a collaborative space; Web 2.0 is the deployment of its potential as a social tool. Web 1.0 is mainly about publishing and retrieving information; Web 2.0 is characterized by interaction. The former considers the network as a medium; the latter views the network as a platform. These features make the Web 2.0 a stimulating environment for archivists to reach out to users, engage in a discourse with them, involve them in traditional archival activities—in short, interact with them. Web 2.0 has become the space for archival *outreach*. "Tools such as YouTube, Second Life, Facebook, and Twitter are all potential mechanisms for unobtrusively inviting new users to engage with the archive and to view items, or even collections, online" (Palmer and Stevenson 2011, 1).

Facebook & Co.

Facebook is the most famous social networking service. Many archival institutions have chosen it as "a relatively easy way to create a Web presence . . . in a 'place' with millions of potential visitors" (Theimer 2010, 159). "Most archives seem to be using Facebook groups and pages more to promote their current activities than to share information about their historical collections" (Theimer 2010, 169). However, some of them are experimenting with more innovative solutions: the "featured image of the week"; the "just accessioned" section with pictures of the latest acquisitions; the "just found" section providing information and/or images of any interesting materials retrieved from the holdings; the

"today on history" section highlighting every day a historical event and possibly linking to some related archival materials; a "gift application" to allow users to send each other "gifts" from the archival collection. These are all examples of an effective exploitation of new media and tools.

Twitter too has attracted many archival institutions and professionals, due to its simplicity of use. This social networking tool has a strong characterization: communication is fast and short, with no frills. Therefore, images from the holdings and links to online resources are posted on Twitter, but archivists are using it mainly to gather users around a theme and create communities, whether permanent (as in the case of an archival institution's account) or temporary (as in the case of an exhibition), and to give announcements about events and activities. Tips to patrons can be provided effectively and timely with a tweet; a campaign to save materials from destruction can be launched and supported through tweets. "One way to create a different voice for your Twitter account is to literally give it a different voice—that of an inanimate object" (Theimer 2010, 127), for example, writing the post from the point of view of the building hosting the repository.

YouTube, Vimeo, and similar video-sharing websites are increasingly used by archives to reach both new and existing users, even if with limited interaction. These platforms are mostly used to upload videos and audios retrieved from the archival holdings, and recordings of educational or scientific events. Some archives have gone further on the road to innovation, uploading video tours of their repositories, exhibitions, and collections, to help users orientating in the archives or provide a virtual experience for those unable to visit it. Interviews to staff members, short clips illustrating back-office archival activities, instructional videos to educate patrons: these are all examples of how audiovisuals can be used to enhance archivists' outreach endeavors.

Flickr, Pinterest, and other image-sharing websites are often preferred to video-sharing websites, because the skills and efforts needed to digitize a document or take a decent picture are less sophisticated than those needed to create a presentable video. Secondly, photos and images are easier to manage than videos: they can be uploaded in a systematic and massive way, as a result of a digitization processes; or they can be selected, aggregated, and put in a specific context in order to create an online exhibition. Thirdly, they allow for a stronger interaction with users: online followers may comment on and establish links among pictures, suggesting different paths to their understanding; they may link pictures from their websites, establishing a connection with the archival institution and enhancing its outreach action; they may identify people and places, hence helping archivists to provide better descriptions; in the most advanced cases, users are given the possibility to contribute archival description by providing metadata in the context of a crowdsourcing initiative.

Blogs, wikis, podcasts, widgets, and chats are other social tools that have been progressively adopted by those archives wishing to explore the potential of the Web. Second Life is a peculiar environment, but it requires "a considerable investment of time and resources for a somewhat limited return" (Theimer 2010, 194). This may be the reason why there is nearly no archival presence on this virtual world, although it does have a potential value for archives. Probably, the most promising tools on the Web 2.0 are mashups, that is, web applications that use content from more than one source to create a single new service displayed in a single graphical interface. Maps, photos, videos, documents, audio recordings—they all contribute to the creation of integrated systems that are undermining consolidated archival principles and practices. Some groundbreaking work has already been done in this area, and many archives are now using geotagged data, historic overlays, timelines, and similar features.

Conclusion

"The concept of the archive online is still a relatively new one, and as a community we are still exploring the implications of these evolving spaces for understanding. In the last decade, certain online activities have become common place in our outreach practices" (Palmer and Stevenson 2011, 5), but we still need to investigate how they affect archival objects, functions, and actors. "Archives are imbued with authority" (Yakel 2011, 75). Engaging with users with an approach "that emphasizes openness, sharing, and collaboration . . . 'de-privileges' archival authority" (Palmer 2009), so the question is: "How much power and control do we want users to enjoy? How much power do we, as archivists,

wish to share?" (Hedstrom 2002, 42). Are we ready to negotiate authority in exchange of more participation from users? What happens to *authenticity* when we start playing with mashups based on remixing? To what extent does intrinsically biased technology affect our role of neutral mediators? "As awareness and understanding of archives has increased in recent years, other users and uses of them have appeared" (Baxter 2011, 292). Reaching out to new users makes archives more "popular": What is the new targeted audience of the archives? What are the cultural mashups that we are going to cope with?

Many questions, more still on the way, no easy answers. The Web has become a space that "drives work, research, education, entertainment and social activities—essentially everything that people can do" (Storey 2006, 7). Therefore, "Archives and the Web" is going to be an area of permanent investigation. In this environment, being proactive and experimental is not an option for archivists—it is their mission.—*Giovanni Michetti*

Keywords: outreach, social media, Web
Related Entries: Outreach; Public Service

Bibliography

Baxter, T. D. "Going to See the Elephant; Archives, Diversity, and the Social Web." In K. Theimer, ed., *A Different Kind of Web: New Connections between Archives and Our Users*. Chicago: Society of American Archivists, 2011, 274–303.

Gerencser, J. "New Tools Equal New Opportunities: Using Social Media to Achieve Archival Management Goals." In K. Theimer, ed., *A Different Kind of Web: New Connections between Archives and Our Users*. Chicago: Society of American Archivists, 2011, 159–79.

Hedstrom, M. "Archives, Memory, and Interfaces with the Past." *Archival Science* 2 (2002): 21–43. DOI: 10.1023/A:1020800828257.

Palmer, J. "Archives 2.0: If We Build It, Will They Come?" *Ariadne* 60 (July) (2009), as cited in J. Palmer and J. Stevenson. "Something Worth Sitting Still For? Some Implications of Web 2.0 for Outreach." In K. Theimer, ed., *A Different Kind of Web: New Connections between Archives and Our Users*. Chicago: Society of American Archivists, 2011, 1–21.

Palmer, J., and J. Stevenson. "Something Worth Sitting Still For? Some Implications of Web 2.0 for Outreach." In K. Theimer, ed., *A Different Kind of Web: New Connections between Archives and Our Users*. Chicago: Society of American Archivists, 2011, 1–21.

Storey, T. "Web 2.0: Where Will the Next Generation Web Take Libraries?" *OCLC Nextspace* 2 (2006): 6–7. https://oclc.org/content/dam/oclc/publications/newsletters/nextspace/nextspace002.pdf.

Theimer, K. *Web 2.0 Tools and Strategies for Archives and Local History Collections*. New York: Neal-Schuman, 2010.

Theimer, K. "Preface." In K. Theimer, ed., *A Different Kind of Web: New Connections between Archives and Our Users*. Chicago: Society of American Archivists, 2011, xii–xvii.

Yakel, E. "Balancing Archival Authority with Encouraging Authentic Voices to Engage with Records." In K. Theimer, ed., *A Different Kind of Web: New Connections between Archives and Our Users*. Chicago: Society of American Archivists, 2011, 75–101.

ARCHIVIST

An archivist is an individual who keeps *records* of enduring value so that they may function as reliable *evidence* of past actions. To "keep" records requires the archivist perform the routine archival tasks of *acquisition, appraisal, arrangement* and *description*, and *preservation*. The archivist is also responsible for managing *access* to the records in their care. These tasks are carried out in accordance with the theory and practice of *archival science* in order to ensure the *preservation* of authentic records within rich *context*.

The archivist generally exercises their oversight for records within an *archives*, or another repository in which records have been deposited. In North America, archivists typically have responsibility for inactive, or "historic," records, while active records remain the responsibility of *records managers*. In the European tradition, however, archivists may also have responsibility for active and semi-active records. Depending on the institutional arrangements, therefore, the term records manager may be analogous to that of archivist. In the United States, there is a distinct tradition of referring to archivists with responsibility for private or personal archives as manuscript curators.

Historical Evolution

In its modern articulation, the role of the archivist was elaborated in the nineteenth and twentieth centuries. The roots of archiving, however, reach into antiquity. Evidence of the *creation* and preservation of records dates from the emergence of the earliest literate societies in the late fourth millennium BCE. With some notable exceptions, however, the long-term preservation of inactive records was not the main function of *archives* in antiquity. Rather, most record aggregations appear to have been maintained for reasons of their immediate administrative utility. Apart from a few rare exceptions—notably the Papacy—it was not until the eleventh and twelfth centuries CE that administrations began again to accumulate and preserve records. Borrowing directly from late Roman Imperial practice, records during the early medieval period would typically have been kept by a *scrinarius*—meaning one who had *custody* over records and books, and who worked in the administrative writing offices—the *scrinia*. By the fourteenth and fifteenth centuries, a similar, secretarial-like, position might also be referred to as *archivus*. The term *archiviste*—to describe a keeper of records—was in use in France by at least the early seventeenth century, while archivist is first attested in English in 1753.

By the fifteenth and sixteenth centuries, records began to be amassed and concentrated together in some numbers. In response, theoretical approaches around the methods of their preservation began to be written about and archival principles, like methods of arrangement, began to be discussed. Von Rammingen's *Von der Registratur* (1571), Bonifacio's *De Archivis* (1632), and Giussani's *Methodus archiviorum* (1684) represent the origins of this professional literature. It was a literature that addressed how to best handle, make use of, and maintain large and relatively recent aggregations of records. As such, these treatises emphasized practical concerns: how to create, file, arrange, and describe records, all with a view toward facilitating the rapid retrieval of information. The tasks of the archivist included accepting records into custody, providing for their orderly preservation, as well as preparing transcriptions and finding aids. Treating, as they do, the active records of administrations, we would today consider these treatises to be directed primarily toward records managers. At the time, however, this division of labor was unknown; there was no distinction between active and inactive, or "historical," records. The authors understood archives to refer to all of the records of the creator, and the responsibility for keeping that entire body of records fell to the archivist. The early modern archivist differed from their modern counterpart in another fundamental respect. The archives they administered were administrative records' repositories, assembled and maintained by their creators in order to function as "arsenals of law and administration." Records were preserved as documentary proof: to substantiate legal claims, rights, and other privileges. There was little or no ability for those external to the administration to consult records—their value often lay precisely in their being kept secret. Records' greater utility—beyond their function in the exercise of civil power—were not generally emphasized. In his defense of archives for their ability to "instruct and teach," and for their usefulness in understanding the past, Bonifacio provides a rare suggestion that records possess these broader values.

Emergence of the Profession

The transformative event that fundamentally altered the functions of archivists was the French Revolution. In France, and elsewhere, the disjuncture of revolution caused legal and administrative discontinuity, which, in turn, resulted in many of the records preserved in archives losing their administrative utility. Rendered effectively invalid, many of the records of past regimes were destroyed—for both practical administrative reasons, as well as for symbolic and political ones. Those that were preserved were concentrated together in newly established national archives as monuments of the past and made available to researchers. Those who made most use of the newly available archival resources were historians—schooled in the new methodology of scientific historiography, with its insistence on authentic, primary source material. This repurposing of archives as historical laboratories would profoundly

influence the developing archival profession. Previously archivists had carried out functions that were more akin to the duties of records managers. But the new historical repositories, which brought together numerous separately created bodies of records, required a different methodological approach, presented a different set of problems, and required specific skills. Eventually the old approaches, based on administering the records maintained by a single creator, were recognized as unsuitable in a situation where multiple creators' records were concentrated together. The predominance of the historical role of these new archives also attracted historical scholars to work in them, and these factors combined to provide the impetus for the creation of a specialized education for the new archival professionals. The earliest schools offering an education in archives were the *Scuola del Grande Archivio* in Naples (1811) the *Archivalische Unterrichtsinstitut* in Münich (1821), and the École de Chartes in Paris (1821). Students were taught *diplomatics*, along with its closely related fields of paleography, sigillography, and philology, along with legal and institutional history. As such, it was, essentially, an education for historians interested in the medieval period, steeped in the scientific historiography of the period. As a result of this education, and the historical role that archives were seen to play, archives were increasingly staffed by historians, displacing the clerks formerly trained in governmental administration and law. The context of their professional origins meant that the overriding purpose of the archivist became that of providing the historian with the raw material to support the historical project. As the interests of historians lay with older material, the transfer of newer material to the archives was not routinely sought or, in some cases, only reluctantly accepted. Furthermore, recognition of records' research value began to become definitive in terms of making the distinction between records of everyday, as opposed to those of long-term, importance. As a result, the conception of archives as the whole of the creators' records was broken. This is the origin of the distinction, made in many jurisdictions, between records (i.e., active records) and archives (i.e., inactive/historical records).

In this new milieu, a methodology particular to what is today termed *archival science* was gradually developed. While archival science traces its roots to the emergence of a critical historical methodology, and to the related development of diplomatics during the early modern period, there was very little in what constituted the archivist's professional knowledge that was not also shared by the historian. The distinct body of knowledge referred to as archival science is a product of developments in the mid- to late nineteenth century. Its central tenants include the *principle of provenance*, or *respect des fonds*, and *respect for original order*. These ideas were at the heart of the new professional literature, written in the late nineteenth and early twentieth centuries by Müller, Feith, and Fruin, Jenkinson, Casanova, Schellenberg, and others. However, it would be some time before the practicing archivist emerged as a distinct profession. In North America, in the absence of professional archivists, amateur historians and private antiquaries, local history societies, and librarians largely assumed the role of keeping historic records. The twentieth century would see the establishment of professional *archival associations* and, somewhat later, graduate-level degrees offered in archival science.

At the same time that the archival profession was being professionalized, the *recordkeeping* environment was being profoundly altered. The increased volume of records being produced by the modern technological bureaucracies of the late nineteen and early twentieth centuries required archivists to abandon the notion that they merely kept records and forced them to become active participants in selecting the records that would be kept. That is, appraisal came to be seen as a core function of the archivist. The shift toward digital recordkeeping in the later twentieth century added further impetus to the changing role of the archivist: the inherent fragility and complexity of *digital records* require early archival intervention if they are to be preserved.

Conclusion

Both the necessity to appraise records and the early intervention required to preserve digital records have resulted in a greater awareness of the archivists' role in shaping, or indeed creating, the historical narrative. Influenced by postmodernist thought, archivists came to be seen not simply as unbiased custodians passively accepting records, but as active agents, creating societal memory. As "society's professional agents appointed by law to form its collective memory," the task facing the archivist was how best to ensure an accurate representation of society. Part of the reinterpretation of the role of the archivist has been to emphasize the importance of provenance and context. By focusing on the *function* of records within organizations, archivists seek to understand records in context: both in terms of their creation in specific administrative, technological, and legal contexts, and in broader cultural and societal ones.—*Reto Tschan*

Keywords: archivist, records manager, history, profession
Related Entries: Archival History; Recordkeeping; Records Manager

Bibliography

Cook, Terry. "An Archival Revolution: W. Kaye Lamb and the Transformation of the Archival Profession." *Archivaria* 60 (Fall 2005): 185–234. http://journals.sfu.ca/archivar/index.php/archivaria/article/view/12521/13656.

———. "The Archive(s) Is a Foreign Country: Historians, Archivists, and the Changing Archival Landscape." *The Canadian Historical Review* 90 (3) (2009): 497–534. DOI: 10.1353/can.0.0194.

Duchein, Michel. "The History of European Archives and the Development of the Archival Profession in Europe." *The American Archivist* 55 (1992): 14–25. http://archivists.metapress.com/content/k17n44g856577888/fulltext.pdf.

Duranti, Luciana. "The Odyssey of Records Managers." In *Canadian Archival Studies and the Rediscovery of Provenance*. Metuchen, NJ: Scarecrow Press, 1993, 29–60.

ARTISTIC RECORDS

Neither of the great classic texts about *archives*, Hilary Jenkinson's *A Manual of Archival Administration* (1937) nor T. R. Schellenberg's *Modern Archives: Principles and Techniques* (1956), specifically mention artistic records or archives. Schellenberg noted that archives can exist in "various physical forms, such as books, papers, maps and photographs" (113), while Jenkinson concluded that "collections made by private or semi-private bodies or persons, acting in their official or business capacities" should be considered as "archives" (Vaknin, Stuckey, and Lane 2013, 8). As postmodern theorists Jacques Derrida, Michaeal Foucault, Gilles Deleuze, and others have focused on the nature and meaning of archives, approaches to the existence of artistic *records* and art archives have become increasingly complex. Both the nature of what constitutes an "artistic record" and what an "art archives" actually includes have become the subject of intense debate in the past few decades.

Artistic Records

Artistic Records can be defined as the physical *evidence* produced in the course of creating works of art in any medium, whether two dimensional (paintings, watercolors, drawings, prints, and other media) or three dimensional (sculpture, relief, ceramics, pottery). Artistic records demonstrate the act of creativity up to and including the final product of an artist's imagination or efforts and, as such, can take form as both textual and graphic materials, and in more contemporary situations, film, audio, and other broadcast media. The art involved may be the product of either a commission, for commercial sale, or created in the course of professional employment, but such art may also be the product of amateur artists documenting their personal experiences.

Art archives are entities specifically charged with the goal of appraising, acquiring, selecting and arranging, and making available the archives of individuals and organizations involved in the process of creating works of art. They may exist as independent bodies but are usually a component of a larger organization, such as an art gallery, museum, or library.

Artistic records can include materials that document the career of the artist or the history of the artistic organization. This could include resumes and artists' statements or biographies; samples of work, contracts and agreements, invoices and receipts, and other working documents; bills of sale or appraisals, correspondence, financial records (accounting and payroll), tax records (property, income, sales), inventory lists, and other legal documents; lists of suppliers, vendors, and shippers; lists of contacts,

including collectors, customers, agents, gallery owners, art dealers, and show producers; visual documentation of worksites or offices and installations; notes relating to the creative process; information about grant applications and awards; personal correspondence; flyers, postcards, catalogs, chapbooks, one-of-a-kind or last-of items, and other ephemera; portfolios; and press releases. Former Tate Gallery archivist Anna McNally notes:

> Most artists' personal papers consist of a combination of letters (received), photographs (of their work, themselves, of unidentified people), sketches, any writings they might have drafted or published (autobiographies, articles, dubious poetry), printed materials about themselves or their interests. There might also be papers related to projects they've been involved with . . . or their wider interests and influences (Vaknin, Stuckey, and Lane 2013, 99–100).

Tate director Penelope Curtis has also noted that "archives tend to be seen as two dimensional, which is a great problem for artists who try out their ideas in the round. Rather few places keep much in the way of three-dimensional artistic archives, though architectural archives are an obvious exception" (Vaknin, Stuckey, and Lane 2013, 7).

History

Although the lives and experiences of individual artists have been recorded since classical times, artists as a whole were considered to be craftsmen rather than creative individuals well into the early Renaissance in Europe. Not until the Italian Giorgio Vasari published the first edition of *Le Vite de' più eccellenti pittori, scultori, ed architettori* (English translation: Lives of the Most Eminent Painters, Sculptors, and Architects) in 1550 did there develop an interest in learning more about the background, upbringing, and creative processes of most artistic practitioners, who were seen more as craftsmen and guild members than individuals. Our current knowledge of many late Gothic and Renaissance artists, for example, usually derives not from individual archives, but from church or state records, including birth and death registers and contracts for ecclesiastic or lay commissions or decorative schemes, and from brief mentions in such records as letters or diaries. What we now consider to be artistic records, for example, the notebooks, sketchbooks, and journals of Leonardo Da Vinci, survived only because the artist may have been in the service of a monarch or pope, an ecclesiastic patron, or an aristocratic family.

Following the publication of Vasari's *Le Vite*, the Accademia di San Luca (Academy of Saint Luke) was founded in Rome in 1577 as an association of artists with the purpose of elevating the work of "artists," which included painters, sculptors, and architects, above that of mere craftsmen. Other countries followed suit—for example, the Académie royale de peinture et de sculpture (Royal Academy of Painting and Sculpture) was founded in Paris, France, in 1648; the Royal Academy of Arts was founded in London, Great Britain, in 1768, both of which sought to bring the artistic profession into higher repute. In the same period, more serious efforts to document the lives of individuals, including artists, began to emerge in Western European life (Jimerson 2009, 24–75). By the early nineteenth century, most countries had established national libraries and art galleries, and within these entities began the practice of documenting artistic endeavor.

In 1954, the Archives of American Art was established in Detroit by the Detroit Institute of Arts in cooperation with a private collector, becoming one of the first dedicated repositories for documenting artistic endeavor as its mission (Smithsonian Institution, ix). Initially the goal of the archives was to serve as a microfilm repository of papers housed in other institutions, but the organization quickly moved to collect and preserve original material itself. In 1970, the archives joined the Smithsonian Institution, sharing the institution's mandate—the increase and diffusion of knowledge. It is now the preeminent and most widely used research center dedicated to collecting, preserving, and providing access to primary sources that document the history of the visual arts in America. (See *Government and Art: A Guide to Sources in the Archives of American Art*. Washington, DC: Smithsonian Institution, 1995.) This interest in documenting artistic endeavor has been reflected in other countries as well, although no single institution exists on the same scale as the *Archives of American Art*. In Great Britain, the Association of Art Historians proposed the creation of *The Artists' Papers Register* in 1985, which

coordinates knowledge about holdings throughout the country (see www.aah.org.uk/resources/artists-paper-register#sthash.OTmMsq8u.dpuf), while in Canada, the National Gallery of Canada created *Artists in Canada* in 1988, a guide to documentation and holdings of Canadian art and artists. This now-electronic resource continues to be updated on a regular basis (see www.rcip-chin.gc.ca/application/aac-aic/description-about.app?lang=en).

Although national organizations of art librarians were founded in both France and Canada in 1967, a major step in the development of the concepts of *Artistic Records* and *Art Archives* took place with the foundation in Great Britain in 1969 of the Art Libraries Society. The society, currently an educational charity with over seven hundred members worldwide, including librarians, archivists, libraries, publishers, and specialist library suppliers, includes both people and organizations with an interest in the documentation of art and design and the provision of library and information services to artists, designers, and architects. In 1972, an ARLIS North America branch was organized, and various other groups subsequently appeared around the world. As the original ARLIS began to subdivide into subspecializations, an Art Archives Committee was founded in 1995, where specific issues relating to *art archives* became the focus of participants.

The International Council of Archives also includes the professional Section for Archives of Literature and Art (SLA). This section was originally founded in the mid-twentieth century and played an important role within the ICA for some years before it fell into inactivity. Reborn in 2009, the SLA now plays an important role in debates on the nature and approach to such archives. The Society of American Archivists also includes a Visual Materials Section, which since its foundation in the mid-1980s, now plays an important role in the discussion of issues surrounding *art archives*.

Anna McNally has noted that the reality faced by all art archivists in acquiring, appraising, selecting and arranging, and describing such archives is a difficult one, as much *archival theory* comes from dealing with business or institutional records, which is not much help in dealing with personal papers where a sketch might be done on the back of a piece of paper two decades old and where the contents might have arrived in fruit baskets, with no order whatsoever (Vaknin, Stuckey, and Lane 2013, 103). Art archives can also create major concerns for archivists relating to fiscal and space limitations in dealing with bulky, unusual, or three-dimensional objects, questions about the appropriateness of long-term storage, questions of copyright, access, and use, the cost of description, the maintenance of digital records, and the demand for "creative archiving," for example. Art Gallery of Ontario art archivist Amy Furness's University of Toronto PhD thesis, *Towards a Definition of Visual Artists' Archives: Vera Frenkel's Archives as a Case Study*, provides one example of the problems relating to the acquisition of an artist's archives.

The description of art collections have generally followed *Anglo-American Cataloguing Rules* (AACR), a national cataloging code first published in 1967, and its successor, the *Anglo-American Cataloguing Rules, Second Edition* (AACR2), first published in 1978 and subsequently revised several times. In addition to AACR2, the Library of Congress's Prints and Photographs Division has created the *Thesaurus for Graphic Materials*, "a tool for indexing visual materials by subject and genre/format, which includes more than 7,000 subject terms to index topics shown or reflected in pictures and 650 genre/format terms to index types of photographs, prints, design drawings, ephemera and other categories" (Library of Congress 1995). Since 2010, *Resource Description and Access (RDA)* has succeeded AACR2 as the cataloguing standard for use by libraries and other cultural organizations such as museums and archives. RDA provides instructions and guidelines on formulating data for resource description and discovery and has been adopted by many major organizations worldwide.

Conclusion

Issues relating to artistic records and art archives, especially in relation to the original creators, have become increasingly of interest to a wider community over the past decade. As Charles Merewether (2006) wrote in his introduction to *The Archive*, "It is in the spheres of art and cultural production that some of the most searching questions have been asked concerning what constitutes an archive and what authority it holds in relation to its subject" (10). Artists/creators and users of art archives have been challenging the archival status quo, looking to theo-

reticians such as Jacques Derrida, Michel Foucault, and Gilles Deleuze as sources for the overthrow of traditional, and conservative, approaches to archival practice. Issues surrounding such archival concepts as creation, curation, and consumption, as well as the constituencies involved, including archivists, artists, and researchers, have made the area of art archives a major intellectual concern for archivists worldwide. There seems to be no singular approach to acquiring, appraising, selecting and arranging, and describing art archives, nor is there a singular definition of what constitutes an art archive. In the past decade alone, there have been symposia held at the Vancouver Art Gallery (2005), the Tate Gallery, London (November 2007 and June 2009), the Art Gallery of Ontario (March 2011), the New York Public Library (October 2011), the Getty Institute (November 2011), and the National Archives of the UK (Kew 2013). However, as the example of RDA demonstrates, there is an increasing awareness of the necessity of sharing and codifying best practices within every organization.—*Jim Burant*

Keywords: art archives, artistic records, collecting archives

Related Entries: Archives; Archival History; Audio-Visual Records

Bibliography

Archivists Round Table of Metropolitan New York. *Artists' Records in the Archives: A Two Day Symposium Oct. 11–12, 2011.* www.scribd.com/doc/122514235/Artists-Records-in-the-Archives-Symposium-Proceedings.

Art Libraries Society of North America—Ontario Chapter. *Research and Intersections Within Practice: Artists & Librarians, March 16, 2011.* (Information about this symposium is summarized in an article by Effie Patelos of Concordia University, available online at www.arlisna.org/news/conferences/2012/sescolouring-patelos.pdf.)

"Artists & Archives: A Pacific Standard Time Symposium." Getty Institute, 2011, video presentation. www.getty.edu/research/exhibitionsevents/events/artistsarchives.

"Artists in the Archives." National Archives of Great Britain, September 2013. www.nationalarchives.gov.uk/events/artists-in-the-archive-conference.htm.

Jenkinson, Hilary. *A Manual of Archival Administration* London: Percy Lund, Humphries & Co., 1937.

Jimerson, Randall C. *Archives Power: Memory, Accountability, and Social Justice.* Chicago: Society of American Archivists, 2009.

Merewether, Charles. *The Archive.* London: Whitechapel; Cambridge, MA: MIT Press, 2006, 10.

"RDA: Resource Description and Access." Joint Steering Committee for Development of RDA, last modified May 15, 2014. www.rda-jsc.org/rda.html.

Schellenberg, T. R. *Modern Archives: Principles and Techniques.* Chicago: University of Chicago Press, 1956.

"Thesaurus of Graphic Terms." Library of Congress, Prints and Services Division, last revised 1995. www.loc.gov/rr/print/tgm1.

Vaknin, Judy, Karyn Stuckey, and Victoria Lane. *All This Stuff: Archiving the Artist.* Faringdon, Oxfordshire: Libri Publishing, 2013.

Weihs, Jean, ed. *The Principles and Future of AACR: Proceedings of the International Conference on the Principles and Future Development of AACR, Toronto, Ontario, Canada, October 23–25, 1997.* Ottawa: Canadian Library Association, 1998.

AUDIO-VISUAL RECORDS

Many definitions are available of just what constitutes audio-visual *archives*, but here we focus on what is most practical for the intellectual organization of holdings, namely photographs, moving images, and sound. These types of documents are relatively recent, all dating from the nineteenth century. Other types of holdings, not considered here, and usually subject to different rules for their organization and storage, include ancient drawings and paintings, prints of all types, drawings, maps, and plans. Although text is not strictly speaking a component, a great deal of text, usually in the form of *metadata*, is associated with the management of audio-visual archives. Like many other kinds of archives, analog *formats* prevailed but are now moving to digital formats. In the case of audio-visual archives, digitization of content held in analog formats is a necessity for long-term *preservation* as

supports become unviable or the format technology obsolete. For this reason, the present article concentrates on audio-visual archives in digital form. The supports used for storing audio-visual *documents* have never been stable for the long term, and this remains true when they are in digital format. Audio-visual archives have long been the poor cousin of textual archives, suffering neglect in *acquisition*, organization, and use. However, in the twenty-first century, the volume of production engendered by technological advances makes audio-visual archives much more important than before. Formats evolve rapidly, and all existing supports and formats for audio-visual archives must be considered as temporary. Happily, standards are emerging, and although they too evolve over time, they already offer a reassuring degree of stability in this volatile technological environment.

Formats

Like most other types of archives, audio-visual documents were originally all created in analog format, using physical supports as a container to store the content. In digital format, a file container stores the content as data in encoded bitstreams. The content data is commonly referred to as data or essence. Unlike many other kinds of archives, audio-visual archives, whether analog or digital, typically require technology in the form of playback devices to provide access to holdings. All format types evolved through a series of technological advances and processes, with commerce always being the driver. As a result, audio-visual *archivists* have always needed to have strong technical skills, replacing company technicians for care and maintenance of the machinery needed to consult the documents long after the manufacturer has ceased to offer parts and technical support for its discontinued models. In the digital age, technical skills include strong computer skills. Photography preceded moving images and sound by more than half a century, and long lists can be made of the types and models of cameras used to record images, film stock, chemicals and processes used in the darkroom, papers available for printing, and additional special processes such as coloring, toning, and trickery of all sorts. Sound came next, the oldest known recorded sounds dating from 1860. Techniques and supports for recording evolved from paper to cylinders to wire to discs, each with a number of types and technologies. Moving images on film date from the end of the nineteenth century. These are preceded by a number of technologies not considered in our definition, involving animated drawings and various apparati for viewing, including flipbooks, thaumatropes, stereoscopes, phenakistoscopes, and zoetropes. Moving images on video date from the 1950s. Moving images on both film and video also involve long lists of equipment, cameras, supports, and formats. We see now with hindsight that the rapid development and evolution of all audio-visual archives share this spectacular characteristic with other aspects of the twentieth century. Typically, all audio-visual types were quickly adopted by the public, and their use to communicate news, art, and entertainment content spread rapidly over the entire planet.

Digital Audio-Visual Archives

In this second decade of the twenty-first century, the legacy holdings of audio-visual archives are still largely in analog formats, but many analog-to-digital conversion projects are taking place, including massive conversion projects in support of *preservation* efforts. In addition, audio-visual materials are now captured and produced in digital formats almost entirely. From their beginnings, audio-visual documents have been recorded on supports that are physically fragile and chemically unstable, and this characteristic continues in the digital world. No support is available for long-term preservation of digital information, and nothing is on the horizon of the scale of adoption that the nearly ubiquitous 35mm film format achieved worldwide in the twentieth century. Even 35mm black and white polyester film is threatened because projectors for screening it are becoming scarce, as are laboratories, equipment, and tools for handling it, along with the necessary expertise.

Although unstable supports are a serious problem, the primary problem, as several authors have indicated, is rather technological obsolescence accompanied by the volatility of file formats. Thus even if it were possible to freeze data permanently on long-term storage supports, this would not suffice, since hardware and software technology continue to evolve. Ultimately, the trick is to maintain meta-

data regarding holdings in such a way that newer and future technologies can still read the metadata and *access* the data correctly. This activity is in the domain of *digital preservation*. Of interest in our context here is that digital preservation has become a necessity for audio-visual documents of all kinds. When they are preserved in digital formats, they require scheduled verification, refreshing, and migration programs to ensure continuing viability. Unlike audio-visual documents held in analog formats, which after only a few generations of copies suffer loss of quality that is unacceptable, there is no loss of quality with digital holdings because digital technologies make an exact copy of the documents, including as part of the process a checksum verification of the exactitude of the copy, and thus of the *authenticity* if it has already been established.

Other issues are also of primary importance for the digital audio-visual *archivist*. As materials are transferred from one situation to another, there is a need to verify the content. In digital transfers, a checksum provides proof of the exactitude of the *transfer* (i.e., that the data has not been corrupted en route), but this is not enough. Just as in the analog world the film archivist, for example, needs to check that all the reels received are there and marked in correct sequence, that the sprocket holes are in good repair, that color correction has taken place on the copies received, and so on, in the digital world the archivist needs to verify that the materials are well formed, for example that there is no spurious noise, that no pixels have changed color, that everything is in place so that the correct sound accompanies the correct image and is synchronized to it, that the elements meet the appropriate technical standards, and so on.

In addition, the preservation metadata needs to be well formed, conforming to agreed specifications, so that it and the corresponding essence can be migrated forward over time. The documentation of metadata and procedures needs to be such that preservation strategies like migration and emulation can be applied to the materials, that in the event of a disaster recovery can occur, that the multiplicity of versions are distinguished one from another, to mention some of the concerns.

Another key issue related to digital audio-visual archives is rights management. This area has always been exceptionally complex as regards audio-visual production of all kinds, and in the digital world this complexity becomes even more acute. This situation is also present in the conversion of audio-visual documents from analog to digital formats. For example, an archives may own or have had long-term custody of the object in hand but no rights to the content, nor to a digital representation of the object. In addition, technological change drives the evolution of rights management itself. Existing models are crumbling, and worldwide efforts are required to protect the rights of the multiple parties that are necessarily involved in the creation of audio-visual materials.

Intellectual Organization

Since the turn of the twenty-first century, methods for accessing the intellectual content of audio-visual documents have evolved very significantly, because of the possibility of networking information using the web, and because of the involvement of user communities in producing and offering audiovisual documents on the web. Thus many of the new methods have been developed by communities other than the professional community. At one extreme, systems still exist that record minimal information on cards, such as *creator*, title, date of creation, and so on. At the other extreme, technologies are in place that can propagate user-created indexing terms automatically to other photos or moving images that are similar. Work on automatic translation has indicated that such indexing can also be attached automatically to images and sound in other languages, with a great degree of accuracy. In between are user tags attached to photographs, shot-by-shot user descriptions of moving images, including for the blind, song lyrics and scores posted by users to the web, reviews and descriptions of recordings, and a great deal of work in the computer science community to identify automatically objects and calculate their relationships, with a view to generating indexing terms automatically. In general, cataloging and indexing of completed works is systematized by the library community, and more in-depth analysis of audio-visual records, when it takes place at all, is assured by the archives community. However, most systems at this level of analysis use in-house methods, and there is little uniformity from one institution to another, and often a lack of uniformity internally as well. The challenge now is to build

bridges of all kinds to allow diverse systems to communicate with one another.

Standards

Audio-visual archives, especially those in production facilities, have almost always been managed using ad hoc systems, a situation no longer acceptable in the networked world. As production methods have evolved to take advantage of new technological possibilities, standards for recording, processing, storing, transmitting, receiving, and distributing digital audio-visual productions have become an absolute necessity, if only to ensure the interoperability of the digital objects involved. Development has been rapid in recent years, and happily some stability has been achieved. Although standards will continue to evolve, those in place now allow a degree of control that permits archiving and some hope of achieving digital preservation.

Standards-making bodies primarily work by consensus and concern themselves with particular areas of interest to its members. The Society of Motion Picture and Television Engineers (SMPTE) has a long history of publishing technical standards created by engineers in the motion picture and television industry. The International Organization for Standardization (ISO) publishes a wide range of standards, in a number of fields, including many related to audio-visual archives. Other organizations may publish standards as an outcome of research that may also be applicable to audio-visual archives. The Online Computer Library Center (OCLC) and the Research Libraries Group (RLG) jointly formed a working group concerned with digital preservation, which resulted in the publication of Preservation Metadata Implementation Strategies (PREMIS). Some technologies introduced into the marketplace, such as Linear Tape-Open (LTO), are adopted so readily that they become ubiquitous, with publication of a standard to follow.

Conclusion

Audio-visual archives are challenged by the transition from analog formats to digital formats. More than ever, archivists must acquire and hone a wide variety of technical skills in order to effectively acquire, manage, and preserve collections. Legacy analog collections are by necessity being digitized in great numbers in order to provide access to content held on endangered and obsolete analog formats. Digital formats are not a panacea, however, as they evolve quickly, and rapidly become obsolete. Rights management remains an unresolved issue, and is the subject of ongoing work. Finally, audio-visual archives benefit greatly from the stabilizing effect provided by the adoption of standards.—*James Turner and Randal Luckow*

Keywords: audio-visual, still images, photographs, moving images, sound

Related Entries: Digital Preservation; Digital Records; Metadata; Photographic Records; Preservation; Record Format

Bibliography

Frick, Caroline. *Saving Cinema: The Politics of Preservation.* New York: Oxford University Press, 2011.

Jörgensen, Corinne. *Image Retrieval: Theory and Research.* Lanham, MD: Scarecrow Press, 2003.

Shefter, Milt, and Andy Maltz. *The Digital Dilemma: Strategic Issues in Archiving and Accessing Digital Motion Picture Materials.* Beverly Hills: The Science and Technology Council of the Academy of Motion Picture Arts and Sciences, 2007.

———. *The Digital Dilemma II: Perspectives from Independent Filmmakers, Documentarians and Nonprofit Audiovisual Archives.* Beverly Hills: The Science and Technology Council of the Academy of Motion Picture Arts and Sciences, 2012.

Wells, Nick, Bruce Devlin, Jim Wilkinson, Matt Beard, and Phil Tudor. *The MXF Book: An Introduction to the Material eXchange Format.* Amsterdam and Boston: Focal Press, 2013.

AUDIT AND CERTIFICATION (TRUSTED DIGITAL REPOSITORIES)

The exponential rise in the production of *digital records* throughout the 1990s necessitated repositories capable of preserving those *records* over the long-term. The subsequent claims from repositories that they could be trusted to provide *access* to those records for as long as needed were easy to make,

but without an agreed upon framework for assessing these claims, they were difficult to substantiate. To increase the overall climate of trust in *digital preservation* activities, repository self-declarations needed to be replaced with a set of criteria against which the trustworthiness of a repository could be evaluated. Developing such a mechanism was a decades-long, multidisciplinary, international effort that addressed three challenges: defining what it means to be a trusted digital repository; creating a set of measurable criteria based on that definition; and finally, a process by which repositories could provide evidence of conformance to the criteria. The result of this effort was adopted by ISO as an audit and certification process through which custodians of *digital records* can assess and document their ability to provide long-term *preservation* against a defined set of criteria in order to be considered a trusted digital repository.

Defining a Trustworthy Digital Repository

Determining what constitutes a trustworthy digital repository (TDR) had its genesis in a 2002 report issued by Research Library Group-Online Computer Library Center (RLG-OCLC) that laid out the foundation for defining a TDR by describing those attributes and responsibilities that the repository must possess (RLG, 2002). While useful in solidifying the concept of a TDR, the report provides little in the way of offering existing repositories measurable requirements for assessment. Building upon this report, the RLG and National Archives and Records Administration (NARA) formed a joint task force to develop specific, verifiable criteria that could be used to assess a repository's ability to reliably store, migrate, and provide access to digital records over the long-term. To bridge the various disciplines engaging in digital preservation, the task force chose to frame the wording of its criteria around the definitions and conceptual repository framework provided by the Consultative Committee for Space Data Systems' (CCSDS) Open Archival Information Systems (OAIS) Reference Model (ISO, 2003).

A public draft of the audit checklist for certifying digital repositories was released in 2005 and after nearly two years of comments, revision, and test bed evaluation, the task force released its final report, commonly referred to as TRAC (OCLC, 2007). TRAC contained a set of criteria detailing those attributes, policies, procedures and qualities that must be present to be considered a TDR. Organized as a checklist, TRAC provided the first comprehensive tool for objective evaluation and audit of a repository's ability to provide long-term preservation. CCSDS submitted a further revised version of TRAC to ISO for ratification as an international standard, which was adopted and approved in 2012 as ISO 16363 (ISO, 2012).

Audit and Certification Criteria of Trusted Digital Repositories

Preservation does not happen in an isolated environment. Technology alone is insufficient to achieve long-term preservation; rather it requires the integration and interaction of policies, procedures, technology, and *organizational culture*. A breakdown in any one area can irreparably harm a repository's ability to preserve digital records over the long-term. Employing a comprehensive view of digital preservation, the audit and certification criteria require that a repository possess the mandate, resources, policies, procedures, ability, and support necessary to ensure the ongoing maintenance of the digital records into the foreseeable future. Reflecting the breadth of these requirements, the metrics used in the audit and certification process are grouped into three functional categories:

- organization infrastructure contains twenty-five metrics in five subcategories that evaluate a repository's staffing, planning, organizational support, financial sustainability, and readiness for long-term preservation;
- digital object management contains fifty-eight metrics in six subcategories that evaluate a repository's ability to perform the functions described in the OAIS Reference model from ingestion through access, including preservation planning and *information management*; and
- infrastructure and security *risk management* contains twenty-three metrics in the two subcategories of technical infrastructure risk management and security risk management that evaluate a repository's system monitoring, security, and incident response.

As not all metrics factor equally into a repository's ability to preserve digital records, the word-

ing of the criteria follow a common convention that emphasize the relative importance of each criterion by using:

- *shall* and *must* for binding and verifiable specifications;
- *should* for those specifications that are optional, but recommended;
- *may* for optional specifications; and
- *is*, *are*, and *will* for statements of facts.

To assist repositories in understanding the criterion being measured, a majority of the 106 metrics provide one or more of the following: supporting text that provides additional detail about the metric and why it is important; examples of ways that a repository can demonstrate that it is satisfying the criterion, such as the types of documentation or other evidence that can be examined; and a discussion of the intent of the metric.

Conducting an Audit and Certification

Audit and certification, as the name implies, is generally conducted as a two-step process. The first step is performing an internal audit as an exercise to gain a better understanding of both the scope and the depth of the evaluation metrics, as well as the documentation necessary to provide evidence of conformance. A by-product of this exercise is an assessment of those areas where a repository falls short of the criteria, either in execution or ability to provide evidence of such. As the criteria contained within the standard are not worded in a way as to be quantifiable, determining whether the evidence gathered by a repository is sufficient to prove that a criterion is satisfied becomes a judgment call on the part of the auditor. The aim of an internal audit is to create a process of continuous improvement by addressing those areas of weakness as they are discovered. Once a repository is satisfied that it meets all the criteria, it can either self-certify as a TDR knowing that it possesses the necessary evidence to back up the claim, or continue to the next step to obtain formal certification.

The second, and more rigorous, step of the process is the more generally accepted method of certification through the use of an external auditor. The documentation gathered by the repository during the internal audit is provided to the external auditor for examination and report. If, in the opinion of the auditor, the repository has conformed to all the requirements laid out in the standard, then the auditor body can provide the repository with certification as a TDR. The validity of this external certification, however, is based largely on the competency and reputation of the auditing body. The audit and certification standard does not address what knowledge, experience, and competencies an auditor must possess in order to be qualified to perform an audit, evaluate the evidence, and determine whether a repository can be certified as trustworthy. Recognizing this, the CCSDS has submitted another specification to ISO for evaluation that details the specific requirements for accrediting those auditors seeking to audit and certify a repository as a TDR conforming to ISO 16363. At the time of this publication, the requirements for auditing bodies, provisionally ISO 16919, is currently listed "in development" and at "approval stage."

Conclusion

To be considered trustworthy, a repository must understand and mitigate the threats to and the risks within its system while providing evidence of its ability to store, migrate, and provide access to digital records over the long-term. This process of preservation is not one of simple accumulation; rather it is a resource-intensive process that requires constant and proactive monitoring, maintenance, planning, and migration involving not only the repository but also the record donors, designated community, executive management, and various other stakeholders. Conducting an audit, either internal or through the use of an external auditor, allows a repository to take measure of its ability to preserve digital records over the long-term. Achieving conformance with the audit and certification criteria ensures that a repository has sufficient documentation of its organizational infrastructure, digital object management, and infrastructure and security risk management to attain status as a trusted digital repository. This status, however, is not a permanent honor. As technology, institutions, and designated communities evolve, so must the repository. To retain its status, a trusted digital repository must perform periodic evaluations and updates of its policies, procedures, resources, infrastructure, and documentation so that it can continue to provide evidence of conformance through an ongoing cycle of audit and certification.—*Adam Jansen*

Keywords: trust, digital preservation, audit, risk management
Related Entries: Digital Preservation; Digital Records; Preservation; Archival Standards

Bibliography

International Organization for Standardization. *ISO 14721:2003 Space Data and Information Transfer Systems—Open Archival Information System—Reference Model*. Geneva: ISO, 2003.

———. *ISO 16363:2012 Space Data and Information Transfer Systems—Audit and Certification of Trusted Digital Repositories*. Geneva: ISO, 2012.

Online Computer Library Center. *Trusted Repositories Audit and Certification: Criteria and Checklists*. Dublin, OH: OCLC, 2007.

Research Library Group. *Trusted Digital Repositories: Attributes and Responsibilities*. Mountain View, CA: Research Library Group, 2002.

AUTHENTICATION

For most people the word *authentication* might raise images of art historians determining whether a painting is genuine or a forgery, or perhaps it suggests the process of user identification and verification required to access a computer system using a password or some other technique. Archival glossaries generally define authentication using some variation of: the process by which we verify that a thing is what it is purported to be; the process of assuring *authenticity*. For archivists, authentication includes the concept of verification, but sidesteps the assertion of truth implicit in colloquial use. This entry will distinguish archival authentication from the everyday understanding of the concept, discussing both the traditional and digital environments, including electronic signatures, digital signatures, and public key infrastructures (PKI).

Traditional Authentication

There are two senses in which the term authentication is used in *archival practice*. In the more colloquial sense of the term it is a process of establishing that a *record* is what it is purported to be. In the second, legal and diplomatic, sense an authentication is a specific "declaration of authenticity made by a competent officer, and consists of a statement or an element, such as a seal, a stamp, or a symbol, added to the record after its completion." In this context a declaration of authenticity "only guarantees that a record is authentic at one specific moment in time, when the declaration is made or the authenticating element or entity is affixed" (Duranti 2009, 53).

The authentication of archival *documents* in a traditional paper-based context uses both internal and external evidence to make an assertion that a record was created authentic and has not been modified since its *creation* or that the record is an authentic copy of such a record. The analysis of internal evidence is one of the functions of *diplomatics* and is based on careful analysis of the intrinsic and extrinsic properties of the record in order to verify that it has the features that documents of that type are most likely to have and is lacking elements that it should not have (Duranti 1998). The external evidence is primarily that of *provenance*, the chain of custody, and the record's place in aggregation, the preservation and elucidation of which is the *archivist*'s responsibility.

The level of confidence one can have in an authentication is related to the strength of the evidence, and should not be considered absolute. In a strong case, the authenticity of a record is established (authenticated) at its creation through the testimony (e.g., via seal, stamp, or symbol) of a juridical *person* competent to attest to the fact. The record is used by the creator in the regular course of business and maintained in the creator's *recordkeeping system*, then transferred to the *archives* when no longer needed. The initial authentication and subsequent reliance on the record by the creator attests to the record's *authenticity*, and the chain of custody ensures that the record has been protected from alteration between the time the record was received and when the authentication is required.

There are many records for which this ideal process will not be entirely followed; it is impractical to authenticate every single business record, and *personal records* are unlikely to be maintained in a formal recordkeeping system. In those cases all of the factors, both internal and external, will need to be evaluated insofar as those features are present and available for analysis. Diplomatic analysis of the document, paleographic analysis of the handwriting, application of historical knowledge, or other more extreme methods (e.g., laboratory analysis of the paper and ink) may all be required for the authentication of an out-of-context record or a record of otherwise dubious authenticity (Cullen, Hirtle, Levy, Lynch, and Rothenberg 2000). An out-of-context record is self-authenticating if it is notarized or certified by a third party who is competent to do so (e.g., certified copies of public records), while an old record might fall into the ancient documents exception, legally, and can be presumed authentic if it is found where it is reasonably expected to be found and shows no evidence of tampering.

The archivist, as the custodian of the records, can only attest, or formally certify, if required, that a record in their care is the record received from the creator and that it is as authentic as it was when it was received. Further analysis, if necessary, is generally the responsibility of the user.

Digital Authentication

In the digital domain the traditional physical tools (i.e., seal, stamp, symbol, or notary signature) used in the authentication of paper records cannot be directly applied to a *digital record*, and therefore new tools are required to fulfill this function. The two concepts "electronic signature" and "digital signature" are closely related, and it is important to understand the distinction. An "electronic signature" is a general class of signatures transmitted in an electronic format that perform the attestation function of traditional signatures. These may be as simple as signing an email with one's name typed at the bottom, or as complex as digitized biometric signatures; the essential element is the signer's intention to apply a signature; the specific technology is secondary (see E-Sign and UETA in the United States). A digital signature is a cryptographic function that serves to authenticate both the signer and the specific bitstream of the signed document. In addition to the function of attestation, a digital signature is also "characterized as an electronic seal because, like the traditional seal, it allows the recipient to verify the origin of the record and check that it has not been altered during its transmission" (MacNeil 2000, 62). While all kinds of electronic signatures play some role in digital record authentication, it is the more specific cryptographic digital signature that is discussed below. To understand how a digital signature works, it is important to understand the basics of encryption and hash functions.

There are many types of encryption and many uses for it, but the kind of encryption involved in digital signatures is asymmetric, or public-key, cryptography. Cryptographic algorithms begin with a long random number and generate two related numbers, called "keys." The security of the encryption is related to the algorithm used and the key length, measured in bits (e.g., 128 bit, 256 bit, 1024 bit, and so forth). Generally speaking, the longer the key, the more secure, but longer keys are slower to use, so there is a practical upper bound on key length in a given technological context. In asymmetric cryptography, one key is used to encrypt the target text and the other key to decrypt it. In public-key cryptography one key is kept private, and the other key is made public. A message for an individual then can be encoded using the public key and transmitted; only someone knowing the private key would be able to decode it. When Alice wants to send an encrypted message to Bob, she can use his public key, knowing that only Bob has the private key needed to unencrypt it. Similarly, when Bob encrypts a message using his private key and sends it to Alice, she can unencrypt it with Bob's public key; while anyone can unencrypt Bob's message, Alice knows that only he could have encrypted it, so she can be certain it came from him.

A hash function is an algorithm that takes an input (e.g., a message) and generates a string of fixed size, called a hash, which is relatively unique to that input. If the message changes by even one bit, the output hash will be different. A digital signature is created by generating a hash of the record and encrypting that hash with the private key of the signer. The document remains in plain text and the encrypted hash is the signature. The public key of the signer can be used to decrypt the signature, and the hash can verify that the record is unchanged. The use of the private key ties the signature to the individual whose key it is, and the hash ties the signature to the specific record in question. The signature authenticates the record when all three elements (record, signature, and public key) are bit-perfect,

but if any element is corrupted or altered in any way, or the wrong key is used, the authentication will fail.

One problem with this method is ensuring the association between the public key and the signer. It is not practical to expect users to personally verify the key/person association of everyone whose digital signature they want to authenticate. The solution to this problem is a public-key infrastructure (PKI). A PKI is a set of trusted systems whose responsibility it is to certify the association between a person and a public key. The certificate authority (CA) is an entity in the system which issues documents known as certificates. These certificates contain information about the identity of the person to whom it is granted, the public key associated with that identity, and the digital signature of the CA. Thus within the PKI, trust in the key/person association is ensured by the CA, who has a business interest in ensuring these associations and is disinterested in the matter to which the exchange between users pertains.

Due to the relationship between the person signing the document, the strong sense in which the signature verifies the identity of the record, and the third-party authority maintaining the PKI, digital signatures are substantially more volatile over time than their traditional parallels. Where a paper record might sustain substantial damage and still allow authentication, a digital signature is a binary pass/fail. If even a single bit is changed, perhaps as a result of bit rot or a glitch in copying, the cryptographic functions will return a failure, regardless of the impact that change has on the record. Responsible *digital preservation* often necessitates document migration in order to combat issues of *format*, hardware, or software obsolescence, and while a digital signature will theoretically always be able to verify the original unmodified document, its strong verification will not migrate with the record. Since the strength of a digital signature is related to the computational difficulties of attacking it, the ability to confidently use the signature on the original bitstream for authentication diminishes as computing power and the technology for cryptographic attacks improve over time. Digital signatures have another type of obsolescence to worry about: infrastructure obsolescence. If the third-party authority that maintains keys ceases to perform this function (e.g., bankruptcy, hardware failure, or human error), then the digital signature will not be able to verify the signer.

These issues might not be problematic during the active life of the record, but on the archival timescale they can pose significant challenges that require attention. As in the traditional context, the preservation of electronic records, in both the "physical" sense and the "moral" (provenancial) sense, is carried out by a *trusted custodian* in a preservation environment that maintains the digital files, manages required migration, and records archivally relevant *metadata*. The digital signature (electronic seal) is one of those pieces of metadata; it authenticates the record upon its introduction to the preservation environment, but thereafter that environment itself takes over the authentication role, the nonauthentication functions of the signature are recorded, the process is documented, and the digital signature becomes redundant.

Conclusion

Authentication is not only a one-time certification but also a continuous process throughout the life of the record, since the process of maintaining or preserving authenticity is a prerequisite to future authentication. Specific elements of authentication such as signs, seals, or symbols, digital signatures, or a later assessment or certification of authenticity by a person competent to make it, make the assertion that the document was authentic at that specific point in time. The authentication function performed by them is, therefore, temporally limited. This single, bounded act of authentication is carried forward by the custodian of the record, be it the creator or a record custodian such as an archives or electronic document and records management system.—*Will Suvak*

Keywords: authentication, signature, signs, digital signature, public key infrastructure

Related Entries: Accountability; Archives (Institution); Archives (Material); Authenticity; Digital Records Forensics; Diplomatics; Electronic Document and Records Management Systems (EDRMS); Provenance

Bibliography

Blanchette, Jean-François. *Burdens of Proof: Cryptographic Culture and Evidence Law in the Age of Electronic Documents*. Cambridge, MA: MIT Press, 2012.

Cornell University Law School. "Rule 902. Evidence That Is Self-Authenticating." Legal Information Institute, 2011. www.law.cornell.edu/rules/fre/rule902.

Cullen, Charles T., Peter B. Hirtle, David Levy, Clifford A. Lynch, and Jeff Rothenberg. *Authenticity in a Digital Environment*. Washington, DC: Council on Library and Information Resources, 2000.

Duranti, Luciana. *Diplomatics: New Uses for an Old Science*. Lanham, MD: Scarecrow Press, 1998.

———. "From Digital Diplomatics to Digital Records Forensics." *Archivaria* 68 (2009): 39–66. http://journals.sfu.ca/archivar/index.php/archivaria/article/view/13229/14548.

Jenkinson, Hilary. *A Manual of Archive Administration Including the Problems of War Archives and Archive Making*. Economic and Social History of the World War (British Series). London: Clarendon Press, 1922.

MacNeil, Heather. "Providing Grounds for Trust: Developing Conceptual Requirements for the Long-Term Preservation of Authentic Electronic Records." *Archivaria* 1 (50) (2000): 52–78. http://journals.sfu.ca/archivar/index.php/archivaria/article/viewArticle/12765.

"National Conference of Commissioners on Uniform State Laws." Uniform Electronic Transactions Act, 1999. www.uniformlaws.org/shared/docs/electronic%20transactions/uetafinal99.pdf.

Public Law 106–229, 106th Congress. "Electronic Signatures in Global and National Commerce Act." U.S. Code, Title 1—Electronic Records and Signatures in Commerce, 2000; 464–73. www.gpo.gov/fdsys/pkg/PLAW-106publ229/pdf/PLAW-106publ229.pdf.

United Nations Commission on International Trade Law. *Uncitral Model Law on Electronic Signatures with Guide to Enactment, 2001*. New York: United Nations, 2002.

AUTHENTICITY

The predominant notion of authenticity in *archival science* is derived from the field of *diplomatics*, the critical analysis of *records*. In diplomatics, authenticity speaks to the status of a record, and is therefore relevant to *archivists*, who seek to identify and describe the materials in their *custody*, and historians, who seek to build narratives on them.

Diplomatic authenticity is assessed through a comparison of the forms, formulae, and *format* of a particular *document* with those of other instruments issued by the same source and produced under similar circumstances. Special attention is paid to the internal and external elements of a document, for instance, the style, vocabulary, signatures, or seals, as well as textual layout and orientation, which may betray idiosyncrasies of an era or office. If a document shares adequate similarities with its peers, it may be deemed authentic from a diplomatic point of view. As the result of an informed judgment, the assessment of authenticity cannot be absolute. Indeed, "the designation of being diplomatically authentic indicates only that a particular record "appears" to meet a measure of consistency with other similar documents of the same origin" (Mak 2012, 5). Furthermore, the adjudication of documentary authenticity relies on the ability of the scholar to understand the record in the *context* of comparable instruments. At the same time that early diplomatists were cultivating their notion of authenticity around the material aspects of documents in the seventeenth and eighteenth centuries, a competing school proposed that institutional custody should instead be the principal criterion for determining trustworthiness. Emerging from the practices of the imperial courts, the *ius archivi* capitalized on the Roman tradition of public faith. This view understood the public archives to be the only reliable guarantor of authenticity, and thus marked a developing bifurcation in the work of historians and jurists with respect to the constitution of reliable evidence. As Randolph C. Head characterizes it, "Whereas the diplomatists eagerly catalogued seals, subscriptions, and hands, the *ius archivi* actively denied that such material details necessarily mattered for the authority of a document from a sovereign archive" (2013, 929). According to the *ius archivi*, archival *provenance*— that is, the institutional context of the records—supersedes all other considerations in the assessment of authenticity.

The Concept

The adoption of digital technologies for activities related to the *creation* and *preservation* of records

has prompted a resurgence of interest in the notion of authenticity. Heather MacNeil, reporting on her work with the Authenticity Task Force of the International Research in Permanent Authentic Records in Electronic Systems (InterPARES) Project, explains that despite technological differences between paper and electronic records, authenticity can nevertheless be adjudicated through the identity of the record, or its particular characteristics and attributes—"i.e., was it written by the person who purports to have written it?"—as well as its integrity, namely, soundness and completeness inferred through the appearance of the record and an unbroken chain of custody—"i.e., has it been altered in any way since it was first created and, if so, has such alteration changed its essential character?" (2000b, 53, 69). The notion of continuous custody was further developed by the Preservation Task Force of the InterPARES Project in relation to electronic records to entail an unbroken *chain of preservation*, which recognized that digital entities might demand an active and intentional program of refreshing, migrating, and copying to remain accessible and legible (Duranti 2005, appendix 6). Because these practices are frequently undertaken by agents who may not be invested with public trust, supporting documentation of each transformation is required to aid the determination of the authenticity of the records in their care. Furthermore, the comprehensiveness of such documentation may be subject to scrutiny. As MacNeil writes, "Verification of the authenticity of electronic copies of authentic electronic records depends on the accuracy of the documentation of the reproduction process, and on the preservation of the documentary and administrative context of the records themselves" (2000b, 72). This approach to authenticity in contemporary archival science thus blends the perspective of early modern diplomatists and historians, in which material form, formulae, and format were paramount, with that of the *ius archivi* ramified through Hilary Jenkinson's emphasis on continuous custody.

The recent participation of computer scientists in discussions related to the preservation of *digital records* has brought forward yet another understanding of authenticity. This specialized notion of authenticity concerns itself with information security, and often with data integrity in particular. The authenticity of data, in this view, may be assessed by the deployment of communication protocols, for example, checksum algorithms that attach a code to the data that are later used as a control with which to detect modifications or errors. The checksum value itself may furthermore be verified with regards to when that assertion was made, and the identity of the person who made it, for instance, with a digital signature (Blanchette 2012, 68ff). Like diplomatic analysis, such tools offer a measure of consistency, and their results are subject to interpretation. For instance, checksum mismatches may occur for a variety of reasons, ranging from disk error or the poor implementation of the algorithm to more serious interventions, such as intentional tampering. Meanwhile, other changes may not be flagged at all. Luciana Duranti observes that the notion of authenticity in fields with a computational orientation, such as digital forensics, seems to focus on "the data or content in the record rather than on its formal aspects" (2009, 57), and thus can be distinguished from the conventional uses of the same term in diplomatics and archival science that refer to not only the content, but also the form, material instantiation, social context, history, and provenance of a document.

Also relevant to the present discussion are the notions of legal and historical authenticity, neither of which should be conflated with diplomatic authenticity or data integrity. Legal authenticity is a status conferred by the legal system, and relates to the admissibility and weight of a document as evidence in a particular case (MacNeil 2000, 32ff; MacNeil and Mak 2007, 38ff). The admissibility of a document as *evidence* is a matter of discretion on the part of the judge, and the weight accorded to it is negotiated through the adversarial process and ultimately determined by a judge or jury. Thus, even after a record has been admitted for consideration in the common law system, its *reliability* may be cross-examined and its authoritativeness destabilized by a competing narrative. Because the field of digital forensics was developed chiefly to assist in establishing the admissibility of digital evidence, its particular notion of authenticity continues to evolve in response to the rules governing digital evidence and the expectations of the courts with regards to demonstrating chain of evidence in the service of litigation. Despite the controls of digital forensics that support attestations of data integrity and an unbroken chain of evidence, the admissibility and reliability of the testimony is still evaluated in each individual instance by the courts. For this reason, what may be deemed authentic by the field of digital forensics cannot be assumed to be legally authentic, nor does data integrity guarantee legal authenticity. Likewise, establishing the legal authenticity of a record may rely in part on diplomatic or documentary authenticity, but it need not; furthermore, diplomatic authenticity operates separately from the status of the document in the eyes of the law, and has independent and nonjuridical applications in historical and archival research.

Meanwhile, historical authenticity may indicate faithfulness to an object, image, text, event, or attitude. It is often employed to indicate the ability of a source to stand as witness to a historical moment or experience, and may be used in reference to archival as well as nonarchival materials, including images, artwork, performances, and cuisine. Although historical authenticity is sometimes used to refer to the reliability or truth-value of the information relayed in a document's message, it can also refer more narrowly to the circumstances in which the record was produced. For this reason, a forgery from the twelfth century may still be called historically authentic insofar as it is a relic of the twelfth century and is a reliable witness of its time. Such a forgery can be exploited by the historian in an examination of the ways in which contemporaries conceived and communicated information, or in a broader discussion of the symbolic function of such instruments within a community. Likewise, the recreation of an obsolete video game from the early twentieth century might be called authentic even if it violates the computational notion of authenticity, for instance, relying on a different platform, operating system, hardware, and arrangement of data; nevertheless, its performance in an updated and modified context could prove critical for investigations of storytelling, aesthetics, or game-play. The foregoing examples illustrate that competing notions of authenticity can operate simultaneously, and that a document may be valuable and trustworthy for certain kinds of analyses despite being considered inauthentic by some measures. As Alfred Hiatt observes, most scholars "have been sensitive to the ambiguous status of many documents that are neither 'pure and simple' forgeries, nor completely authentic" (2004, 6).

Conclusion

The purpose of establishing the authenticity of a record is to position it as trustworthy for a particular purpose, and authoritative within a particular framework. As such, the determination of authenticity is specific to and delimited by the needs of a community, and therefore should not be taken as a characteristic that is universally recognized, or one that inheres in the document itself. Rather, what constitutes authenticity in any given context is negotiable, and will change over time.—*Bonnie Mak*

Keywords: trustworthiness
Related Entries: Archival Custody; Authentication; Diplomatics; Principle of Provenance; Reliability

Bibliography

Blanchette, J.-F. *Burdens of Proof: Cryptographic Culture and Evidence Law in the Age of Electronic Documents.* Cambridge, MA: MIT Press, 2012.

Duranti, L. *Diplomatics: New Uses for an Old Science.* Lanham, MD: Scarecrow Press, 1998.

———. "From Digital Diplomatics to Digital Records Forensics." *Archivaria* 68 (Fall 2009): 39–66.

———, ed. *The Long-Term Preservation of Authentic Electronic Records: Findings of the InterPARES Project.* San Miniato: Archilab, 2005, appendix 6.

Duranti, L., T. Eastwood, and H. MacNeil. *Preservation of the Integrity of Electronic Records.* Dordrecht and Boston: Kluwer Academic, 2002.

Head, R. C. "Documents, Archives, and Proof around 1700." *The Historical Journal* 56 (4) (2013): 909–30. http://dx.doi.org/10.1017/S0018246X12000477.

Hiatt, A. *The Making of Medieval Forgeries. False Documents in Fifteenth-Century England.* Toronto: University of Toronto Press, 2004.

MacNeil, H. "Providing Grounds for Trust: Developing Conceptual Requirements for the Long-Term Preservation of Authentic Electronic Records." *Archivaria* 50 (Fall 2000): 52–78. http://journals.sfu.ca/archivar/index.php/archivaria/article/view/12765/13955.

———. *Trusting Records: Legal, Historical, and Diplomatic Perspectives.* Dordrecht and Boston: Kluwer Academic, 2000.

MacNeil, H., and B. Mak. "Constructions of Authenticity." *Library Trends* 56 (1) (Summer 2007): 26–52. DOI: 10.1353/lib.2007.0054.

Mak, B. "On the Uses of Authenticity." *Archivaria* 1 (73) (2012): 1–17. http://journals.sfu.ca/archivar/index.php/archivaria/article/view/13381.

AUTHORITY CONTROL

Until the mid-1980s few *archivists* were familiar with "authority control," although the phrase had long been part of the basic vocabulary of librarians. In introducing the concept to archivists, writers in North America explained that authority control is the process of ensuring the consistency of certain terms used to describe entities. For librarians the controls applied to headings or access points (names and subjects) incorporated in book catalog entries in order to increase both the accuracy and the precision of searches (particularly automated searches) conducted against these entries. By the mid-1990s archivists worldwide were embracing the idea that searches of *archival descriptions* might also benefit from the incorporation of controlled access points. In 1996 the Ad Hoc Commission on Descriptive Standards, sponsored by the International Council on Archives, gave substance to this thinking by formalizing the concept of archival authority control and issuing a standard for undertaking it.

Traditional Authority Control

The "control" in traditional authority control is provided by a list of terms approved for use in a given descriptive element. The descriptive element might be the name of the author of a book (or the *creator* of archival *records*) or another element that serves as an access point, such as a book's subject (or the function that led to *records creation*). In a fully functional authority control system, each of the approved terms in the controlling list is itself the subject of a descriptive record, called an authority record. The organized set of such records constitutes an authority file. Authority work consists of establishing, through research and/or collegial consultation, a preferred term (or name) and associating with this term information that serves to disambiguate it from similar terms. The term and associated disambiguating information form the authority record available to a cataloger or an archivist engaged in selecting the most appropriate term to be used in completing a controlled descriptive element.

Enhanced Authority Control

In 1985 a path-breaking article (Bearman and Lytle 1985) reminded archivists that their long-maintained practice of preserving contextual information about *records* can serve as much to enable discovery of these records as it does to establish their identity. The two authors made a strong case for capturing and presenting this contextual information in a way that would increase its usefulness to researchers, particularly researchers interacting with an automated information system. They proposed that the information be considered as a candidate for authority control and introduced the concept of a "provenance authority record." They suggested that such a record might include both data elements and index terms (or access points) with a typical record including the controlled term (e.g., a corporate name), the source of its authority, variant terms, and information about its active dates, mission, functions, and relationships. A file of such authority records used to control entry of creator names in linked files of information about archives would ensure discovery of records by the same creator regardless of their location. Moreover, a well-crafted provenance authority file might itself be a starting point for research, enabling discovery of relationships among records creators and consequent potential for pursuing documentary connections.

Publication of the article about provenance authority drew the attention of the archival profession in North America to the topic of authority control and prompted exploration of the potential value of separate but linked files of administrative history and archival records information in automated systems. In 1993 the Bentley Library's Research Fellowship Program supported the work of a small team that conducted a systematic study of issues relating to archival authority information. The team saw potential for development of standards for the form and content of authoritative descriptions of persons and organizations and shared their findings informally within the profession. In particular, they provided a report of their work to the Ad Hoc Commission on Descriptive Standards sponsored by the International Council on Archives. The commission, which had itself begun to explore the potential for standardizing description of contextual information linked to archival records, adopted the Bently project team's results as the basis for development of ISAAR(CPF) International Standard Archival Authority Record for Corporate Bodies, Persons and Families, issued in 1996 and revised in 2011.

Archival Authority Control

ISAAR(CPF) provides general rules for the de novo creation of authority records that serve not only to establish canonical authority control of names but also to enable sharing and searching of information essential to understanding and appreciating the circumstances of records creation. The standard organizes twenty-seven potentially applicable elements of description into four information areas: an identity area, a description area, a relationships area, and a control area. The six elements in the identity area establish the authorized form of name of a corporate body, family, or person and enable capture of other forms of this name. Eight elements in the description area parse administrative or biographical background information such as dates of existence, history, places, legal status, and functions or activities. Four elements in the relationships area support links among authority records by enabling capture of information about the nature and dates of these links. The nine elements in the control area assign a unique identifier to the authority record and capture information about its creation and maintenance.

A separate section of the ISAAR standard (section 6) provides important guidance on how a file of archival authority records should be linked to descriptions of records and other resources in order to realize its potential to facilitate the virtual unification of divided fonds and the recognition of otherwise-obscure recordkeeping dependencies and generally to enrich research in history and cultural heritage. Successful achievement of these desired results depends on cross-repository exchange of ISAAR-compliant archival authority information. This dependency has inspired development of a related standard intended to support exchange via the World Wide Web. The standard, Encoded Archival Context (EAC), is an XML-Schema that specifies tags for the elements included in all four areas of the authority record defined by ISAAR. The Society of American Archivists endorsed EAC as a professional standard in 2011 and cooperates with the Berlin State Library in its maintenance. The availability of EAC has prompted efforts to realize its potential for building a shared contextual resource. In the United States these efforts proceed as part of the Building a National Archival Authorities Infrastructure project and the Social Networks and Archival Context Project (SNAC). In Europe work toward this goal is being undertaken by supporters of the Archives Portal Europe.

Conclusion

As ongoing research projects bear fruit, the role of authority control in improving access to archival material will become increasingly clear. It is already apparent from the literature and from professional discussion that archivists now fully understand the once-foreign concept of authority control and value the descriptive consistency that it entails. For more information about the role of standards in archival work, see *Archival Standards.—Sharon Thibodeau*

Keywords: archival authority record, authority file, authority work, encoded archival description

Related Entries: Archival Description; Archival Standards

Bibliography

Bearman, D. A., and R. H. Lytle. "The Power of the Principle of Provenance." *Archivaria* 1 (21) (1985): 14–27. http://journals.sfu.ca/archivar/index.php/archivaria/article/view/11231/12170.

Dooley, J. M. "An Introduction to Authority Control for Archivists." *Archival Informatics Technical Report* 2 (2) (1988): 5–18. www.archimuse.com/publishing/archauth/archauthDooley.pdf.

Durance, C. "Authority Control: Beyond a Bowl of Alphabet Soup." *Archivaria* 35 (1993): 38–46. http://journals.sfu.ca/archivar/index.php/archivaria/article/view/11883/12836.

Gagnon-Arguin, L. *An Introduction to Authority Control for Archivists*. Ottawa: Bureau of Canadian Archivists, 1989.

ISAAR (CPF). *International Standard Archival Authority Record for Corporate Bodies, Persons and Families*, 2nd ed. International Council on Archives, 2011. www.ica.org/10203/standards/isaar-cpf-international-standard-archival-authority-record-for-corporate-bodies-persons-and-families-2nd-edition.html (accessed December 2013).

"One Dream Many People." Archives Portal Europe, 2013. www.archivesportaleurope.net/about-us (accessed December 2013).

Social Networks and Archival Context. "Institute for Advanced Technology in the Humanities." University of Virginia, 2013. http://socialarchive.iath.virginia.edu/NAACindex.html (accessed December 2013).

Szary, R. "Encoded Archival Context (EAC) and Archival Description: Rationale and Background." *Journal of Archival Organization* 3 (2–3) (2006): 217–27. DOI: 10.1300/J201v03n0216.

Thibodeau, S. "Archival Context as Archival Authority Record: The ISAAR (CPF)." *Archivaria* 1 (40) (1995): 75–85. http://journals.sfu.ca/archivar/index.php/archivaria/article/view/12097/13084.

AUXILIARY SCIENCES (CODICOLOGY, CHRONOLOGY, DIPLOMATICS, DIGITAL FORENSICS, HERALDRY, HISTORIOGRAPHY, INFORMATION SCIENCE, PALAEOGRAPHY, SIGILLOGRAPHY, TOPONOMY)

It is first of all necessary to define and limit the area of interest and analysis to avoid risks of vagueness. The expression *auxiliary sciences* will be here considered from the point of view of its historical evolution in relation to the autonomous nature of the sciences herein listed and with reference to their role for supporting historical research and the critical study of documentary sources dynamically created by individuals and corporate bodies in the course of their practical and intellectual activities (i.e., archival *documents* or *records*). Documentary sources can be identified on the basis of their form, nature, and *function*, and auxiliary sciences are intended to support such identification.

The Concept

The concept of auxiliary sciences was first used at the end of the eighteenth century, when history became an autonomous scientific discipline thanks to the studies first developed in German universities. It includes a variable set of specialized disciplines according to their systematic capacity of critically analyzing and assessing the validity of historical sources using scientific methods and consolidated tools.

Leopoldo Cassese (1980), one of last century's most careful scholars in archival and documentary disciplines, developed a systematic approach to the analysis of documentary sources by broadening Marc Bloch's discussion on the dichotomy theory/ practice or technique/philosophy. He believed that auxiliary sciences are necessary to support historical investigation (as defined in the mature age of historicism) because of their mature methodologies aimed at recognizing and reconstructing human actions and facts through the study of the extrinsic and intrinsic characters of the documentary sources, regarding them as a complex "system of signs." Their scientific nature is linked to their rigorous criteria and a wide range of interpretative tools for assessment and control, and methods based on robust principles and concepts.

The need of comparing different documentary sources on the basis of rigorous methods developed by other scientific disciplines has a long tradition and was at the center of Marc Bloch's investigation on *The Historian's Craft* (Bloch 1954, 67): "It would be sheer fantasy to imagine that for each historical problem there is a unique type of document with a specific sort of use. On the contrary, the deeper the research, the more the light of the evidence must converge from sources of many different kinds." All the disciplines identified below have a direct connection with the chronological and geographical analysis of specific types and production of records, but each of them has its own genesis, goal, objectives, context, and scientific identity: palaeography, for instance, focuses on the history of writing and specific scripts, while diplomatics focuses on formal elements of records. Chronology studies the temporal sequence of past events, and sigillography analyzes seals and their forms. Each discipline has its own theory, principles, and methods, but their use requires contact, interference, and relationship with the scientific dimension of historical analysis.

The multicenter nature of the historical disciplines as a whole is a key concept, which is needed to de-velop a comprehensive but not generic definition of auxiliary sciences; they form a constellation of specialized interests, similar but not identical. As a consequence, auxiliary sciences, because of their individual scientific goal, must be (and are) aware of their origin and objectives and need have (and have) a clear sense of their specific domain in relation to other disciplines and to the historical processes in which they are involved. This is the reason why they have developed a robust terminology, rigorous definitions, a logical framework, a specific methodology, and clear criteria for assessing and verifying their findings. In conclusion, they are sciences in their own right and, at the same time, they provide a set of tools for the historical study of human facts and, more specifically, for their *documentary evidence*. In the context of this entry, the auxiliary sciences identified and described are those useful and relevant to the analysis of archival documents, or records. For each of them the description includes a brief contextual definition, which is more detailed for the sciences which play a significant role in archival studies and in the formation of records professions. In effect, the class of auxiliary sciences is a dynamic one with regard to both the list of disciplines included in it and the nature of the disciplines themselves.

- Chronology: the study, classification, and determination of temporal sequence of past events to locate them historically. The discipline has its origin at the end of the sixth century BC but the first scientific approach was developed by Erodoto (fifth century BC).
- Codicology: the study of manuscripts as cultural artifacts from the point of view of their manufacture.
- Digital forensics: a component of forensic science focusing on the application of proven scientific methods and techniques in order to recover and authenticate data from electronic/ digital media.
- *Diplomatics*: the critical study of concepts, techniques, and processes for assessing the *authenticity* of records and evaluating their authority as evidence. It has been defined as the theory of records forms, and it is applied today to any writing created for juridical or practical purposes, compiled according to forms and rules able to be compared to models or paradigms.

- Heraldry: the study of armorial devices or coats of arms aimed at recognizing, describing, and cataloguing the graphic elements used to identify a person, a family, a group of individuals, or an institution. Its origin dates back to the twelfth century.
- Historiography: the study of the discipline of history aimed at supporting the critical interpretation of the historical analysis based on scientific investigations and methodological principles.
- Information science: a large interdisciplinary area of study related to the analysis, collection, organization, management, maintenance, access, and preservation of information.
- Palaeography: the study of the history of writing, scripts, and inscriptions with the aim of reading, interpreting, and critically analyzing ancient texts, establishing their authenticity, and contextualizing their use. The graphic signs are evaluated not on their own but according to their social use and on the basis of genre (notarial, librarian, or *cancelleresca*) and types (such as Uncial, Beneventan, or Gothic scripts).
- Sigillography: the critical study of seals as a relevant and sometimes essential tool for records validation, for personal recognition, for legal imputation, for symbol and expression of the authority, and for juridical component for public and, even more, private transactions. A scientific disciplinary approach was developed in the course of the seventeenth century and focused on the diplomatic, juridical, and historical study of the seals.
- Toponomy: the study of names for places and their origins.

Conclusion

Auxiliary sciences are scientific disciplines that use rigorous and verifiable methods and robust and consistent principles to identify, analyze, and assess documentary sources from multiple perspectives. These disciplines—such as palaeography, diplomatics, sigillography, chronology, and codicology—had and have subsidiary relations with history as "science of men in time" (Bloch 1954,

67) for the integration and comparison of data. Their role was defined subsidiary or auxiliary not per se, but because each of these disciplines conducts investigations where the historical method is used itself to play an auxiliary function. As many scholars have emphasized, each historical discipline is subsidiary or auxiliary to the others. At the same time, the complexity of human actions implies the cooperation among disciplines, as well as the specialization provided by unique disciplinary principles and tools.—*Maria Guercio*

Keywords: allied disciplines, archival science, archival studies, archivist
Related Entries: Archival Science; Digital Records Forensics; Diplomatics

Bibliography

Bascapé, G. C. *Sigillografia. Il sigillo nella diplomatica, nel diritto, nella storia, nell'arte.* Milano: Giuffré, 1969–1978. www.icar.beniculturali.it/biblio/viewvolume.asp?IDVOLUME=63.

Bloch, M. *The Historian's Craft.* Translated by Alfred A. Knopf. Manchester: Manchester University Press, 1954.

Boyle, L. E. *Medieval Latin Palaeography: A Bibliographical Introduction.* Toronto: University of Toronto Press, 1954.

Cappelli, A. *Lexicon abbreviaturarum*, 5th edition. Milan: Hoepli, 1954.

Cassese, Leopoldo. *Teorica e metodologia. Scritti editi e inediti di paleografia, diplomatica, archivistica e biblioteconomia, a cura di Attilio Mauro Caproni.* Salerno: Pietro Laveglia editore, 1980.

Duranti, Luciana. *Diplomatics: New Uses for an Old Science.* Lanham, MD: Scarecrow Press, 1998.

Duranti, Luciana, and Barbara Endicott-Popovsky. "Digital Record Forensics: A New Science and Academic Program for Forensic Readiness." *The Journal of Digital Forensics, Security and Law* 5 (2010). http://oaji.net/articles/1095-1407797239.pdf.

Filby, P. W. *American and British Genealogy and Heraldry: A Selected List of Books*, 3rd edition. Boston: New England Historic Genealogical Society, 1983.

C

CAPTURED RECORDS

The term *captured records* refers to the seizure of public enemy analog and digital materials by foreign or internal dissident forces for intelligence and strategic advantage during armed hostilities. Following the 9/11 al-Qaeda terrorist attacks in the United States and the advent of stateless terrorist groups, national security imperatives have broadened this definition to include not only materials captured in combat operations from enemy States, but also *records* seized from current and previously hostile organizations and individuals. Despite the appearance of wartime pillage, the capture of public enemy records for strategic advantage and occupation is permissible under the laws of war. Article 53 of the 1907 Hague Convention Respecting the Laws and Customs of War on Land and its annexed regulations allows the seizure of movable government property for military operations and necessity. Under this convention, captured movable government property can be freely requisitioned by the occupying power and becomes its property without compensation. In other words, it becomes spoils of war (Hague 1907).

Similarly, article 52 (2) of Protocol I Additional to the Geneva Conventions (1949) permits attacks on or seizures of "objects which by their nature, location, purpose or use make an effective contribution to military action and whose total or partial destruction, capture, or neutralization, in circumstances ruling at the time, offers a definitive military advantage" (Protocol 1977). Further, just as foreign invading and occupying armies can lawfully capture public enemy records, so can internal dissident forces that are engaged in "noninternational" conflicts against the state. To meet the definition of a noninternational conflict, internal dissident forces must have formed a military command, control part of the territory of the state, and possess the ability to implement the provisions of Geneva Additional Protocol II (1978). The 1956 U.S. Army field manual also considers personal documents of private property validly captured on the battlefield to be war booty.

Cultural Property Protections

The lawful capture of public enemy records in war and occupation does not conflict with the cultural property protections under the laws of armed conflict that aim to safeguard cultural property in war and occupation. The conventions and protocols of warfare include the 1907 Hague Convention, the 1949 Fourth Geneva Conventions and its two protocols of 1977, and the 1954 Hague Convention and its two protocols of 1954 and 1999. These treaties prohibit pillage, destruction, theft, or misappropriation of cultural heritage by attacking or occupying forces. The laws of war aim to immunize the property of municipalities and cultural institutions devoted to religion, charity, education, and the arts and sciences from seizure, attack, or willful damage. The 1954 Hague Convention expressly lists repositories of cultural objects and materials, including those found in museums, libraries, and *archives*, as examples of cultural patrimony that must be protected during times of armed hostilities (Convention for the Protection 1954).

Nonetheless, the 1954 Hague Convention's cultural property protections can be waived or ignored in cases where military necessity requires, although there is no clear definition of what constitutes military necessity (article 17). In other words, this ambiguous provision allows attacking or occupying forces great latitude to seize almost anything, including archival records, in the name of military necessity. The current *Manual of the Law of Armed Conflict of the United Kingdom's Ministry of Defense*, for example, illustrates this right to seize official enemy archives for military operations: "Official documents and papers connected with the armed conflict may be seized, even if they are part of official archives, because they will be of military significance. However, other types of archival documents, as well as crown jewels, pictures, and art collections, may not be seized" (UK Ministry 2004, 11.89.1).

In other words, the laws of war provide little protection from the capture of archival or current enemy government records if they are deemed imperative for military operations or occupation, even though they may reside as cultural property in libraries, archives, or other institutions dedicated to the arts and sciences. These laws favor capturing forces in determining what records hold strategic intelligence for military operations. In World War II, for example, the American military ordered its officers to consider all archives important for intelligence, "whether located in ancient archives, large depositories, the most modern archives, or in current office papers" (Pomrenze 1957, 57). Indeed, in a foreign land where invading or occupying forces may not know the language and culture, almost anything may be swept up in the hunt for enemy intelligence. Further, nothing in international law regulates the capture or exploitation of enemy records.

Captured Enemy Documents

In modern warfare, invading armies may employ mobile collection teams to seize enemy records with potential intelligence value. The U.S. military defines captured enemy *documents* as including any piece of recorded information—written, printed, engraved, and photographic material, as well as data on weather and terrain conditions. This might comprise printed personal and identity materials taken from enemy combatants, including letters, notes, diaries, photographs, passports, driver's licenses, or

military police or civil ID cards. Other high-value materials might involve anything from field orders, maps, codes, field manuals, and reports, to all manner of flash drives, hard drives, computer peripherals, and digital devices, to cell and satellite phones. The effort to extract actionable intelligence about the enemy from this vast range of data requires a highly technical and sophisticated operation.

As part of this documents exploitation operation, analysts use a variety of methods to extract and assess intelligence from captured enemy records. In the digital age, the forensic tools used to harvest and analyze seized records and data have been evolving rapidly and broadening the scope of what can be gleaned from captured materials. The seizure and exploitation of this information comprises only part of a greater effort to establish information supremacy on the battlefield and other operational environments to understand enemy forces. Gleaning intelligence from captured records has always been imperative in warfare. Military commanders use this intelligence to anticipate, visualize, and understand the full range of the operational environment, as well as influence the outcome of operations. In war, this typically involves providing armed forces with timely and accurate assessments of an adversary's dispositions, strategy, tactics, intent, objectives, strengths, weaknesses, values, capabilities, and critical vulnerabilities. In addition to military data, intelligence gleaned from captured records may be important for assessing political, economic, social, information, and infrastructure factors in hostile operational environments (Joint Publication 2012).

The seizure of wartime adversary records, however, comprises only one critical element in the overall effort to capture data and assess enemy capabilities and intentions. In war, advanced intelligence operations will often use an array of methods aimed at capturing human, signal, geo-spatial, biometric, overhead reconnaissance, and other intelligence data. Innovative technologies also may be employed to harvest actionable data, including artificial intelligence or psyche-assessing algorithms that have proven more accurate than human analysts in sifting through reams and bits of data to predict the behavior of capricious regimes.

The extraction of time-sensitive intelligence from captured materials requires a rapid process of triage, translation, and promulgation. The 2003 Iraq War illustrates how modern intelligence operations may exploit captured enemy analog and digital materials. Following the capture of vast amounts of Iraqi materials in the invasion, the U.S. military built a large media processing and exploitation center in Qatar, where thousands of Arab linguists and analysts sifted through, prioritized, and processed thousands of boxes of captured analog and digital materials. Media-processing linguists identified analog materials including print, video and audiotapes, photographs, and other materials of high exploitation priority. Forensic investigators and Arab translators also assessed and performed in-depth analyses of the content of such digital media as hard drives, cell or smart phones, and computer peripherals. This process involved producing English and Arabic keyword search, file signature, email address search, graphic-file finder search, and JPEG picture search. Analysts also used special filters to extract text, Internet, graphics, e-mail, as well as audio and video files for use. The most significant step included triage, enabling translators and analysts to prioritize data of highest intelligence value. Translations teams summarized the contents of the materials as well as produced keyword indexing of organizations, personalities, equipment, and other key data named in the files. Finally, scanned documents and media were uploaded daily to a shared intelligence database to maximize their exposure for analysis by the American intelligence community (Combined Media 2005).

Since the laws of war consider captured records spoils of war, the victorious state may use, exploit, or dispose of them according to its own discretion. There is no obligation to repatriate them after the end of armed hostilities. Nonetheless, countries may return captured records to former adversaries as a gesture of normalizing relations. The most notable example occurred after World War II when the Western Allies engaged in a prolonged diplomatic process of repatriating captured Nazi records to the Federal Republic of Germany after it had become a prosperous constitutional democracy and a Cold War ally. Records glorifying the Nazi regime, relating to German occupation of other countries, or posing national security risks were initially withheld by the Americans, but later returned through diplomatic agreements. Other captured records involving personnel and Nazi Party membership were withheld under U.S. control at the Berlin Documents Center

for use in war crimes and de-Nazification trials until they were repatriated to a reunited Germany in 1994. If nothing else, this example illustrates that the victorious state owns the position of determining when the exploitation of captured records has been exhausted, when this strategic intelligence may be considered the cultural property of its former adversary, and when, if at all, some or all of these materials can be returned.

Conclusion

As a final note, in the digital age, the nature and restitution of captured materials has perhaps become more complicated. It is not clear to what extent email and digital objects extracted from captured hard drives and computer peripherals, as well as captured cell phone communications and geo-spatial, biometric, and overhead reconnaissance data, will be considered the cultural patrimony of former adversary countries for purposes of return at the end of hostilities. The laws of war allow captured records to be treated as spoils of war, but the diplomatic process concerning restitution may be more difficult than ever as former adversaries sift through these complicated issues.—*Bruce P. Montgomery*

Keywords: captured, seizure, exploitation, restitution, repatriation
Related Entries: Archives and Memory

Bibliography

Combined Media Processing Center, Qatar. *Standard Operating Procedures*. Section 2.2.2. U.S. Department of Defense, February 4, 2005. www.dcoxfiles.com/cmpcsop2.pdf (accessed August 12, 2013).

Convention (IV) Respecting the Laws and Customs of War on Land and Its Annex: Regulations Concerning the Laws and Customs of War on Land. The Hague, Comite International Geneva, Treaties and States Parties to Such Treaties, October 18, 1907. www.icrc.org/ihl/INTRO/195 (accessed September 24, 2013).

Convention for the Protection of Cultural Property in the Event of Armed Conflict. The Hague, Comite International Geneva, Treaties and States Parties to Such Treaties, May 14, 1954. www.

icrc.org/ihl.nsf/INTRO/400?OpenDocument (accessed September 24, 2013).

Cox, Douglas. "Archives and Records in Armed Conflict: International Law and the Current Debate over Iraqi Records and Archives." *Catholic Law Review* 59 (4) (2010): 1002–44. www.dcoxfiles.com/iraqarchives.pdf.

Fleck, Dieter, ed. *The Handbook of International Humanitarian Law*, 2nd edition. Oxford: Oxford University Press, 2008.

Green, Leslie C. *The Contemporary Law of Armed Conflict*, 3rd edition. Manchester, UK: Manchester University Press, 2008.

"Joint Publication 2-01, Joint National Intelligence Support to Military Operations." January 5, 2012, xi–xvi, I-4. www.dtic.mil/doctrine/new_pubs/jp2_01.pdf (accessed July 2, 2013).

Pomrenze, Seymour J. "Policies and Procedures for the Protection, Use, and Return of Captured German Records." In Robert Wolfe, ed., *Captured German and Related Records*. Athens: University of Ohio Press, 1974, 57.

Protocol Additional to the Geneva Conventions of 12 August 1949, and Relating to the Protection of Victims of International Armed Conflicts (Protocol I). Comite International Geneva, Treaties and States Parties to Such Treaties, June 8, 1977. www.icrc.org/ihl/INTRO/470 (accessed September 24, 2013).

Protocol Additional to the Geneva Conventions of August 12, 1949, and Relating to the Protection of Victims of International and Non-international Armed Conflicts (Protocol II). Comite International Geneva, Treaties and States Parties to Such Treaties, December 7, 1978. www.icrc.org/applic/ihl/ihl.nsf/INTRO/475?OpenDocument (accessed September 24, 2013).

UK Ministry of Defense. *The Manual of the Law of Armed Conflict*. Oxford: Oxford University Press, 2004.

CASE FILE

Within archival and information-management literature, a case *file* has generally been described as a folder or file containing an aggregation of standardized *documents* that relate to a specific (trans)action, event, person, place, project, or subject. Case files are also sometimes referred to as "transactional" or "project" files, and can be further subdivided into two categories: "particular instance" papers or files that relate to a single event or transaction, or "continuing event" files that relate to one individual or project, but include many events or transactions over time. Because of the huge extent of *records* involved, case files are a recognized problem for which all modern *archives* need to find appropriate and transparent solutions. Over the years, however, clear definitions of exactly what comprises a case file have been slow to be recognized; this imprecision in terminology may have been a complicating factor in the development of strategies for handling such records. In recent years, as *archivists* and *records managers* began to recognize the many challenges presented by case files, more precise definitions and strategic approaches have emerged in order to establish a framework to solve the identified problems.

Emergence of Case Files

Case files began to emerge within *recordkeeping systems* toward the end of the nineteenth century as modern offices and large bureaucracies, especially those supporting governments, developed and expanded. Governments began to focus on more direct interaction with citizens, especially by creating various social programs. To support this shift in activity, recordkeeping systems, which had often been based on separate dockets, letter books, and *registers* for incoming and outgoing correspondence, expanded and shifted to file systems that could more easily organize information related to specific cases in one file.

As Terry Cook has observed, "Paper (or textual) records . . . usually aggregated into series of case files, form the most voluminous records of twentieth century governments" (Cook 1991a). Others have estimated that as much as 95 percent of records created during this period were case files. The existence of such an information mass, particularly in the current era of additional overabundance of digital information, means that government records must be appraised and selected to identify records that are of archival value to society. Ironically, the anticipated benefits of the introduction of the desktop computer (speed and ease of information creation and dissemination) have instead posed some of the most significant challenges for modern *recordkeeping*. The "paperless office" is still a rarity; more common are situations where the volume of paper records is actually increasing due to the ease of their creation using computer technology. Institutions and their archives are now faced with mountains of paper files and an ocean of electronic data that used to form the heart of a traditional case file.

While case files have long been recognized as a potentially rich source for social historians because they document the interaction between the state and its citizens, particularly those from marginalized groups, increasingly such files present archivists with a variety of challenges that are common across jurisdictions. A central issue facing archivists is how to identify and select case files, particularly at a time when archives users' increasing interest in these types of records conflicts with the increasing pressure on archives from shrinking financial resources and lack of physical storage space (Iacovetta and Mitchinson 1998).

Appraisal and Selection of Case Files

Within a developing theoretical framework for archival *appraisal*, postwar archivists began to turn their attention more specifically to developing conceptually based yet practical strategies to address the growing need to select only a subset of the vast amounts of available textual paper case files for permanent preservation.

In the United Kingdom, recommendations of the Royal Commission on Departmental Records chaired by Sir James Grigg (1954) led to the UK's *Public Records Act* (1958) and the establishment of a review and selection framework for UK government records, known as the "Grigg system." The commission, while recommending that case files not be a part of this review system, proposed establishing a Public Records Office–led committee to conduct a census of case files in departments and determine what and how much to preserve; however, when The National Archives (TNA) reviewed the Grigg system in 2004, it was noted that this process remained to be implemented (TNA 2004).

In the early 1980s the National Archives of the United States outlined a strategy for the appraisal of case files in *Disposition of Federal Records: A Records Management Handbook* (NARS 1981, updated 1997), which identified specific categories of case files to be preserved. The National Archives' subsequent appraisal of the Federal Bureau of Investigation (FBI) records (Bradsher 1988) resulted in the creation of a checklist of archival criteria for selecting case files.

In the early 1990s the National Archives of Canada developed a new strategic appraisal methodology that encompassed case files. "Macroappraisal" was developed contemporaneously with guidelines for *sampling* or selecting case files containing personal information. In his RAMP study, Cook (1991a) outlined a comprehensive "macro" approach to appraising case files that began with a high-level assessment of the citizen-state interaction based on three factors (program, agency, and citizen). Put simply, the approach begins with an assessment of the *context* of an entire series of case file records to determine if the series possesses any archival value at all. Once that high-level decision is made, the archivist must then determine whether the entire *series* should be preserved, or whether a subset of the records should be chosen. Finally, if a subset of records is to be preserved, the archivist chooses the appropriate method (sampling, selection, or exceptional *selection*) to identify that subset (Cook 1991b). As Cook summarized,

> In this comprehensive approach, therefore, actually looking at the records containing personal information is, ironically, the last rather than the first step in appraising such records. To look at personal information case files in isolation from these other factors and these other records is a prescription for poor archival appraisal. (1991a, 51)

Solutions for Case Files

Archival jurisdictions around the world have developed and shared high-level strategic solutions to manage the challenges posed by case files, with varying success. For example, the Netherlands PIVOT project (1991–2003) aimed to address the backlog in appraisal and transfer of Dutch government records based on macrolevel research into institutions and their functions. PIVOT asserted that only 5 percent of post-1945 government records should be permanently preserved, as most modern records were transactional in nature and did not offer any knowledge of government policy and activity; unfortunately, PIVOT did not succeed in its goal of conquering the backlog (Dixon 2005). At Archives New Zealand (ANZ), case files are identified as archival only where it is evident that government activity has had significant impact on the lives of individuals or the community.

Canada: Library and Archives Canada (LAC)

In 2005, to provide clarity and precision to government archivists and records managers seeking legal authority to dispose of case files, LAC provided the entire government of Canada with the required legal authorization to dispose of operational case files.

In the *Multi Institutional Disposition Authority for Operational Case File Records*, LAC refined the case file definition established by Cook in 1991 to a multipart definition with three basic characteristics. Case files:

1. are transactional in nature;
2. consist primarily of replicated documentation in standardized formats and structures; and
3. have a definite beginning and end.

If a case file series meets this definition, authority is given to the creating department to dispose of the majority of the files, excluding some exceptional files that may fall under one or more of seven archival criteria based on the type of records. LAC identified for archival *preservation*: files crucial for the protection of individual or collective rights or obligations of citizens; some judicial and quasi-judicial decisions; some decisions authorized by senior bureaucrats or government ministers; documentation of fiduciary obligations; treaty obligations; documentation of some investigative activities; and some research activities (Dixon 2005).

United States: National Archives and Records Administration (NARA)

NARA developed a strategic approach to appraisal without specifically targeting case files. *Strategic Directions: Appraisal Policy* (2007) does not specifically refer to case files; however, under "General Appraisal Guidelines," it allows for appraisal decisions calling for sampling "to be made only after careful analysis of all other options and the costs and benefits of implementing a sampling decision. A sampling disposition will not be used where this option merely defers problems" (NARA 2007). Appendix 2 further outlines special considerations for types of records, many of which are often associated with case files, such as personal data; observational data; environmental health and safety; and research and development. The NARA disposition handbook addresses the selection of case files, by providing specific criteria. These criteria can be summarized as those records that are precedent setting; involved in extensive litigation; receive widespread media attention; widely recognized as unique; files reported in the Annual Report; "fat files"; and files that document agency procedures (NARA 2007).

United Kingdom: The National Archives (TNA)

In its 2004 review of the Grigg System, which reaffirmed its use, TNA addressed three broad issues: the timing of Grigg reviews; file by file review; and case files, which had not originally been included in the system. In the resulting *Appraisal Policy* (TNA 2004), TNA announced its intention to strengthen the system by "implementing Grigg recommendations for a government-wide approach to case files and datasets, to ensure rational archival selection" (TNA 2004). *Operational Selection Policy (OSP) 48: Case Files*, which followed in 2009, applies selection criteria to the case files of individual departments and agencies not already covered by an existing OSP. The process outlined for selecting operational case files directs that the series first be appraised as a whole, followed by a determination of what if anything is to be selected for preservation, with the caveat that "specimens of case files will not be selected simply to preserve examples of departmental work" (TNA 2009). Selection can involve consultation with temporary advisory panels comprised of external researchers, and the OSP concludes by providing additional guidance on selecting case files, making a distinction between "simple" ("generally returns on a printed form or to a standard questionnaire . . . the type of information now commonly entered into a dataset") and "complex" case files (those "characterised by a low degree of document similarity and a high degree of variation between files") (TNA 2009).

Further Implications for Case Files: The Digital World

In some jurisdictions, datasets are now identified as the "approximate digital equivalent of case files," and their appraisal is treated in a similar fashion (TNA 2004). This begs the question: Can—or should—the appraisal and selection methods and decisions be the same for both paper and digital case files? In terms of the storage challenge posed by the volume of case files/datasets, perhaps one implication is that case files in digital form, which have tremendous potential for future aggregation and manipulability, need no longer be subjected to detailed selection. Instead, all such files could be preserved in an archives and then retrieved for secondary use through a variety of sophisticated search engines that rely on embedded metadata. Such an approach can, however, create significant technological and practical problems for the archives at a later date (Dixon 2005).

Conclusion

For more than a century, governments and other large bureaucracies have produced many types of case files, which are often of interest to social historians and other secondary users interested in the citizen-state interaction. While the voluminous nature of these files has increasingly presented archives with challenges, especially in appraisal and selection, many of these challenges are now being addressed in a variety of ways, typically on a strategic level.—*Catherine A. Bailey and Tina Lloyd*

Keywords: case file, personal information, appraisal, selection, macroappraisal, sampling

Related Entries: Appraisal; Document; File; Recordkeeping; Sampling; Secondary Value, Selection; Subject Files; Vital Records

Bibliography

Bradsher, James Gregory. "The FBI Appraisal." *The Midwestern Archivist* 13 (2) (1988): 51–66. http://minds.wisconsin.edu/bitstream/handle/1793/45526/MA13_2_2.pdf?sequence=3.

Cook, Terry. *The Archival Appraisal of Records Containing Personal Information: A RAMP Study with Guidelines*. Paris: UNESCO, 1991a.

———. "'Many Are Called but Few Are Chosen': Appraisal Guidelines for Sampling and Selecting Case Files." *Archivaria* 32 (Summer 1991b): 25–50. http://journals.sfu.ca/archivar/index.php/archivaria/article/view/11759/12709.

Dixon, Margaret J. "Beyond Sampling: Returning to Macroappraisal for the Appraisal and Selection of Case Files." *Archival Science* 5 (2–4) (2005): 285–313. DOI: 10.1007/s10502-005-9017-8.

Iacovetta, Franca, and Wendy Mitchinson. "Introduction: Social History and Case File Research." In Franca Iacovetta and Wendy Mitchinson, eds., *On the Case: Explorations in Social History*. Toronto: University of Toronto Press, 1998.

The National Archives. *Appraisal Policy*. London: The National Archives, 2004.

———. *Operational Selection Policy (OSP) 48: Case Files*. London: The National Archives, 2009.

National Archives and Records Administration. *Strategic Directions: Appraisal Policy*. Washington, DC: NARA, 2007. www.archives.gov/records-mgmt/initiatives/appraisal.html (accessed February 2014).

National Archives and Records Service. *Disposition of Federal Records*. Washington, DC: NARS, 1981. Current version: *Disposition of Federal Records: A Records Management Handbook 2000 Web Edition* (of 1997 printed publication). www.archives.gov/records-mgmt/pdf/dfr-2000.pdf (accessed February 2014).

Rapport, Leonard. "In the Valley of Decision: What to Do about the Multitude of Files of Quasi Cases." *The American Archivist* 48 (2) (1985): 173–89. http://archivists.metapress.com/content/jm56229574506134/fulltext.pdf.

CHAIN OF PRESERVATION

The Chain of Preservation (CoP) is a series of managed *records*-centric activities identified by the InterPARES2 project that contribute to the *authenticity* and *preservation* of *digital records*. It employs a records *lifecycle* approach toward modeling those activities involved in records making, *recordkeeping*, and records preservation within a *digital repository*. Through extensive interdisciplinary case study research, InterPARES2 developed a functional model that employs a record-centric approach by focusing specifically on those activities that influence a record's preservation and authenticity over the long term. The CoP model is both prescriptive, in that it provides criteria for determining if a record can be presumed authentic, and descriptive, by detailing those activities that influence the presumption of authenticity and long-term preservation of digital records.

Chain of Preservation (CoP) Model

The Chain of Preservation is one of two models, along with the *records-continuum*-based Business-Driven Recordkeeping, developed as part of the InterPARES2 research project that focus on records-related activities that support the authenticity and preservation of digital records over time. It incorporates and expands on three earlier record activities models: the *creator*-centric preservation model developed by the UBC-MAS project (Duranti, Eastwood, and MacNeil 2002), and the two preserver-centric models detailing the *selection* function and the preservation function developed as part of the InterPARES1 research (Duranti 2005). The record-centric approach of the CoP model demonstrates that preserving authentic digital records must take into account all the activities that a record participates in throughout its entire life; a lack of understanding or control in any single activity compromises a *trusted custodian*'s ability to ensure that the record will be accessible, readable, usable, and authentic over time.

This concept of a continuous chain of activities all participating in the preservation of authentic digital records is reflected in the name chosen for the model—Chain of Preservation. As with a real chain, all activities that a record participates in are linked together and act on one another. Any weakness, omission, or compromise in any single link can deteriorate that chain's ability to perform its ultimate function—in this case, preserving trustworthy digital records. This interrelationship between records activities modeled by the Chain of Preservation validates one of the findings of InterPARES1: since the activities that a record participates in over its lifetime influence an organization's ability to maintain that record as authentic, the preservation of authentic digital records begins at *creation*.

Modeling the Records-Related Activities

To conceptually represent the extent and diversity of the activities involved in the creation, maintenance and preservation of digital records from a *diplomatics* and an *archival science* perspective, the InterPARES project modeled the record activities involved in the Chain of Preservation using the Integrate Definition (IDEF) modeling language (Eastwood, Ballaux, and MacNeil 2008). Specifically, IDEF was used to provide a structured, visual representation of the functions, activities, and processes represented in the model. One of the strengths of IDEF modeling is that in addition to depicting the flow of one activity to another, it also focuses on those resources—in the form of inputs, outputs, mechanisms, and constraints—that are involved in each activity. By identifying the resources involved in a given activity, a greater understanding of the interrelated nature of the activities and how they influence, and are affected by, other activities can be achieved. As represented by the model's workflows diagrams:

- Inputs enter an activity from the left and represent those pieces of information or objects that are involved in the process but originate from outside the activity being defined. These inputs can come from other activities, or from external sources not involved in the process prior to the activity.
- Outputs exit an activity on the right and are the result of the activity, typically in the form of the records themselves or additional information about the records that were discovered/created as a result of the activity. These outputs can stand on their own, and as such much can be preserved along with the records for the entirety of the lifecycle, or are inputs that provide needed information for activities that are further down the process chain.
- Mechanisms are pulled into an activity from below and are resources that help to create, manage, control, and preserve the digital records. These resources can take the form of any technology, equipment, and/or personnel that are necessary to complete a given activity.
- Constraints on the records influence the activity from above and vary by the *context* of the creation and maintenance of the record, as well as

the particular phase of the lifecycle that the record is in at the time. These constraints vary on a case-by-case basis and are influenced by such factors as the juridical system within which an organization operates, laws and regulations, technology employed within an organization, and national and international standards of operation.

The Chain of Preservation deconstructs a record's lifecycle into four primary activities (see figure C.1): manage framework for chain of preservation, manage records in a record-making system, manage records in a recordkeeping system, and manage records in a permanent preservation system. "Manage framework for chain of preservation" contains those activities involved in the design, implementation, and maintenance of a framework to control records throughout its lifecycle. "Manage records in a record-making system" contains those activities involved in the creation and setting aside of records, as well as monitoring the performance of record-making systems themselves. "Manage records in a recordkeeping system" contains those activities involved in the maintenance, storage, retrieval, *access*, and *disposition* of records in a recordkeeping system, as well as monitoring of the performance of any recordkeeping systems. Lastly, "manage records in a permanent preservation system" contains those activities involved in the *appraisal*, *selection*, *acquisition*, *description*, storage, and access of permanent records.

Each of these primary activities is then decomposed further into those subactivities that are necessary to accomplish the task, with each subactivity being further decomposed until a base activity is reached. By decomposing the activities and documenting the resources involved, the CoP details the interrelationship that exists between the records activities through the inputs, outputs, mechanisms, and constraints that span activities. This visual representation of the workflow is supported by narratives describing each activity and resource, as well as a glossary of terms used within the model.

Conclusion

The CoP model incorporates extensive case-study research and previous records activities models into an ideal functional model that contains all the

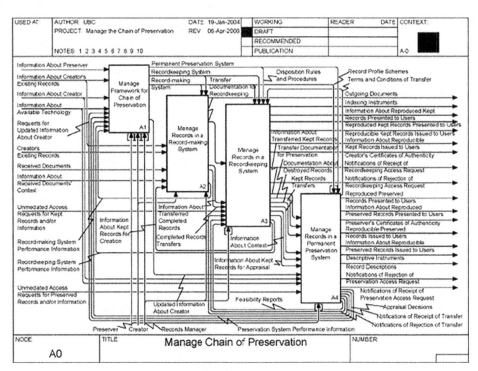

Figure C.1. Chain of Preservation Model showing the four primary records activities. *Inter-PARES*

record-related activities that contribute to a record's authenticity and preservation over time. The purpose of the CoP model is to provide a baseline for organizations to compare their existing creation, maintenance, and preservation activities against those contained with the model. Through analyzing the comparison, an organization can assess their readiness to preserve authentic digital records. Any deviation noted between the CoP model and an organization's existing practices would suggest areas where additional resources—in the form of additional inputs, outputs, mechanisms, constraints, or procedures—might be warranted. The findings of such an assessment provide an effective framework for guiding *archival policy* decisions and implementing appropriate activities that have been identified by InterPARES research as necessary to support the authenticity and preservation of digital records over the long term.—*Adam Jansen*

Keywords: digital preservation, InterPARES, authenticity, chain of custody

Related Entries: Archival Management System(s); Archival Policy; Archival Standards; Audit and Certification (digital trust repositories); Digital Preservation; Digital Repository

Bibliography

Duranti, L. *The InterPARES Project: The Long-Term Preservation of Authentic Electronic Records: The Findings of the InterPARES Project.* San Miniato (PI), Italy: Archilab, 2005.

Duranti, L., T. Eastwood, and H, MacNeil. *Preservation of the Integrity of Electronic Records.* Dordrecht, Netherlands: Kluwer Academic, 2002.

Eastwood, T., B. Ballaux, R. Mills, and R. Preston. "Appendix 14: Chain of Preservation Model Diagrams and Definitions." In L. Duranti and R. Preston, eds., *International Research on Permanent Authentic Records in Electronic Systems (InterPARES) 2: Experiential, Interactive and Dynamic Records.* Padova, Italy: Associazione Nazionale Archivistica Italiana, 2008.

CLOUD ARCHIVES

A cloud archives is a cloud storage service that specializes in long-term data retention for electronic *archives*. Instead of the traditional private or in-house archival storage infrastructure, archives are hosted virtually by an external cloud provider. Data search and retrieval (i.e., *accessibility*), data security, and the application of data management policies (e.g., retention and *disposition*) are determined and regulated by the provider, the type of cloud (public, private, hybrid, community), and the cloud service (SaaS, PaaS, IaaS) chosen to host the archives.

What Is the Cloud?

In order to properly understand the components that make up a cloud archives, we must begin by understanding the cloud itself. "Cloud computing" can be defined as a style of ubiquitous or pervasive computing, where IT-enabled capabilities, such as applications, platforms, and infrastructures, are delivered as services to external customers using Web 2.0 technologies. The cloud is an on-demand self-service that enables rapid elasticity, scalability, and pay-as-you-go or pay-per-use resource billing for clients. As a virtual computing infrastructure, the consumers' need to purchase additional hardware and/or software, datacenter space, or network equipment is eliminated. Rather, the needs are outsourced to third-party cloud providers. With broad network access and multi-tenancy capabilities, the cloud promotes widespread collaboration across various networks.

The cloud can be delivered to users in one of three models: Software as a Service (SaaS); Platform as a Service (PaaS); or Infrastructure as a Service (IaaS). Each is subsequently built onto the next: platform services build onto software services, as infrastructure services build onto platform services. SaaS is the most basic model of software deployment and offers its users little to no control over the cloud's infrastructure, network, server, operating system, storage limitations, or individual applications that enable the delivery of the service; popular examples include Google Drive, Microsoft OneDrive, and iCloud. A PaaS cloud model allows users the ability to build and deliver their own applications and services onto a predetermined cloud software and hardware, or infrastructure. Lastly, the IaaS model extends to users the most control, giving them access to the cloud's resources, networks, and underlying infrastructure.

Each of these services can be deployed onto one of four variable types of clouds. First, the public cloud is among the most popular and commonly used type of cloud model. This model does not extend to users any measure of control with the cloud's physical infrastructure (i.e., the location of your data) or allow for any control over security features. Secondly, the community cloud is established within the realm of one specific cloud provider, often as a result of various organizations sharing similar service requirements (e.g., security control; tenancy specifications; and location of data). Next, the private cloud is the most secure of the four models of deployment since the actual physical infrastructure of the cloud is often a single-tenant environment (i.e., one user, one cloud infrastructure), owned by and/or physically located in a client's data center. Lastly, the hybrid cloud is an infrastructure that integrates components from both the public and private cloud, allowing for the possibility of application compatibility and portability, as well as some extension of management and security measures to the user. A cloud archives can therefore be deployed onto either model and delivered through any of the four services; accessibility, security, and overall control over the archives will thus vary accordingly.

The benefits of cloud computing vary within each of these models and levels of services. The cloud's elasticity, storage capabilities, scalability, and security will likely be greater in a private cloud deployed on an IaaS model than in a public cloud built on a SaaS model, for example. However, greater control and therefore greater security in the former scenario is ultimately substituted for the benefit of the supposed "reduced cost" that is most likely found in the latter. While the benefits of one model may be presented as the solution for risks found within another, they are inevitably accompanied by a series of other important issues in need of consideration. These "chained benefits" are important to consider when assessing the possible deployment of one's archives to the cloud. Failing to do so can be to the detriment of the *user*, their data, and the identity and integrity of the organization as a whole.

Key Components of a Cloud Archives

Risks posed to archives when deploying to the cloud are varied and each an individual cause for concern. The location of the archives, general access, the application of retention and *disposition* schedules, as well as *classification* systems, legal holds, data privacy, questions of general ownership over the *metadata* that guarantees the integrity of the *records*, as well as the records themselves, are all points of concern and consideration for an organization choosing to entrust its archives to the cloud.

The current landscape of archival institutions is ever-changing; archives are now accepting electronic record transfers as opposed to traditional paper files and Bankers boxes. The current landscape is one where archival institutions are opting for the use of the cloud as an alternative storage model to the traditional in-house model (i.e., localized server or network). Archives are then faced with the challenge of dealing with these records once they have reached the end of their *lifecycle* and are assessed for permanent *preservation*. Should the records be transferred from the cloud *to* a trusted *digital repository*, or to another digital preservation platform located within an archives? Or should the records be transferred onto an "archival" cloud platform? The latter has become a more viable, cost-effective option for organizations dealing with mass volumes of electronic archives, especially those previously maintained within a cloud environment. Cloud providers have thus begun to conceive and introduce cloud archives or "storage-as-a-service" infrastructures in an effort to consolidate these *information management* efforts. However, in order for a cloud archives to be considered a reliable and trustworthy archival repository, as a "housing place" for archival material, it must extend beyond the characterization of the cloud as a simple space for storage.

A trustworthy cloud archives must account for the transfer of records, from their active and semi-active states, to a state of permanent preservation. While the systems that maintain these records in their various states must be technologically interoperable, each individual system must also be independently interoperable within itself; for example, a cloud archives suggests the long-term preservation of records, which would require regular system updates in order to avoid data obsoletion. The values that are unique to that record must also not be altered in any way when the record inherits a status of permanent preservation. Archives that are held within the cloud must be as trustworthy as those that are held within a physical archival building. *Access* and security of the archival material must also be regulated to the level of that of in-house archives; while there is a need for privacy, there is also a certain level of openness that is expected of an archives.

In addition, the cloud, or "virtual" nature of the archives, cannot affect or alter the *archival bond* that exists between aggregations of records and *archival fonds*; properly assigned and preserved *metadata*, which speaks to the records' *creation*, use, and technological context, is key in this regard. Similarly to active or semi-active records held within the cloud, questions and concerns over custody, control, and privacy of the cloud archives, as well as *authenticity*, integrity, and *reliability* of the archives contained within must be addressed to a satisfactory level, ideally through the provider's terms of service and contractual Service Level Agreements between vendor and user. In order to properly address the requirements of trustworthy cloud archives, a dependable cloud framework or certification system would be required (e.g., an OAIS model for cloud archives), where consumers could feel confident that the system to which they have entrusted their records is one which will guarantee not only the security of their archives but also their reliability and integrity as authentic records.

Conclusion

Since its introduction, the cloud has become one of the fastest-growing business models for pervasive computing. As a result of its unique capabilities and overall cost effectiveness, some organizations have begun to rely on it for their recordkeeping and preservation needs. Until recently, *cloud archives* was an expression seldom used within the written context of information management research. Nevertheless, the cloud has become an increasingly viable storage option for archives that are unable to afford or maintain an in-house, private electronic infrastructure suitable for the long-term preservation of their electronic holdings. However, a reliable cloud archives that meets the requirements and expectations of a trustworthy, virtual repository still remains within the early stages of conception.

—*Valerie Léveillé*

Keywords: archives, cloud, preservation, storage
Related Entries: Digital Preservation; Digital Repository; Disposition, Records

Bibliography

Askhoj, J., S. Sugimoto, and M. Nagamori. "Preserving Records in the Cloud." *Records Management Journal* 21 (3) (2011): 175–87. DOI: 10.5120/6369-8736 (accessed March 2013).

Consultative Committee for Space Data Systems. "Reference Model for an Open Archival Information System (OAIS): Recommended Practice CCSDS 650.0-M-2." Magenta Books, June 2012. http://public.ccsds.org/publications/archive/650x0m2.pdf (accessed February 2013).

———. "Requirements for Bodies Providing Audit and Certification of Candidate Trustworthy Digital Repositories: Recommended Practice CCSDS 652.1-M-1." Magenta Books, November 2011. http://public.ccsds.org/publications/archive/652x1m1.pdf (accessed February 2013).

Duranti, L., and C. Rogers. "Trust in Digital Records: An Increasingly Cloudy Legal Area." *Computer Law & Security Review* 28 (5) (2012): 522–31. http://dx.doi.org/10.1016/j.clsr.2012.07.009 (accessed March 2013).

Gellman, R. "Privacy in the Clouds: Risks to Privacy and Confidentiality from Cloud Computing." World Privacy Forum, last modified February 23, 2009. www.worldprivacyforum.org/pdf/WPF_Cloud_Privacy_Report.pdf (accessed March 2013).

Hogane, M., F. Liu, A. W. Sokol, and T. Jin. "NIST Cloud Computing Standards Roadmap." National Institute of Standards and Technology (NIST), Special Publication 500-291: Gaithersburg, Maryland, 2011. www.nist.gov/manuscript-publication-search.cfm?pub_id=909024 (accessed March 2013).

MacNeil, Heather. "Providing Grounds for Trust: Developing Conceptual Requirements for the Long-Term Preservation of Authentic Electronic Records." *Archivaria* 50 (2000): 52–78.

Prince, J. D. "Introduction to Cloud Computing." *Journal of Electronic Resources in Medical Libraries* 8 (4) (2011): 449–58. DOI: 10.1080/15424065.2011.626360 (accessed March 2013).

Singh, A., and M. Shrivastava. "Overview of Security Issues in Cloud Computing." *International Journal of Advanced Computer Research* 2 (1) (2012): 41–45. www.theaccents.org/ijacr/papers/current_march_2012/8.pdf (accessed March 2013).

Subashini, S., and V. Kavitha. "A Survey on Security Issues in Service Delivery Models of Cloud Computing." *Journal of Network and Computer Applications* 34 (2010): 1–11. http://dx.doi.org/10.1016/j.jnca.2010.07.006 (accessed March 2013).

"Top Threats to Cloud Computing, Version 1." Cloud Security Alliance (CSA), March 2010, 1–14. www.cloudsecurityalliance.org/topthreats/csathreats.v1.0.pdf (accessed February 2013).

COLLECTING ARCHIVES

Introduction to the Range of Acquisition Models

There are, broadly, three organizational models in place for the acquisition of *archives* by archives services: in-house, collecting (sometimes known as "delegated"), and a combination of the two—the combined model. While each has defining characteristics, all are part of a spectrum that allows such characteristics or elements to be present in different degrees in each model (Williams 2006, 29).

A specific model does not derive from the nature of the organization: governments, states, local authorities, universities, business, and specialist archives (public or private) may follow any one of the three, depending on their specific business remit. The category into which a particular archival organization falls depends on a range of factors and influences (Williams 2006, 28). These may include:

- Source of authority: From where does the archival organization receive its remit to act?
- Legislative and regulatory environment: What kinds of legislation and industry regulations are applicable in this environment?
- Source of funding: Where does the capital and revenue income come from?
- Goal or mission: What is the strategic aim of this body?
- Stakeholders: Who has an active or passive interest in the performance of this organization?
- Acquisitions remit: What is the archival collection policy of this organization?
- Access remit: Who is eligible to access the archives of this body?

A description of the attributes of each model, together with some examples, follows.

In-House Archives

The in-house archives is dedicated to the management of *records* and archives of its parent-body. The archives are thus derived from a single creating organization and its predecessors, and its purpose is to '"document the functions, development, history and contributions of the parent body" (Ellis 1993, 139). While organizations create records primarily to enable the conduct of business and to support *accountability*, an in-house archive allows them to be used for cultural purposes too, for research and to promote awareness and understanding of corporate or organizational history. In this model there is no external collecting function. Ellis (1993, 463) defines an in-house archive as:

> that part of an institution or organization maintained for the purpose of keeping the archives of that institution or organization. An in-house archive usually restricts its acquisition to records generated by its parent institution or organization or by other closely associated bodies or people. It is also referred to as corporate archives, dedicated archives or institutional archives.

Commercial businesses, for example, banks and retail, are likely to follow this model: they find that their "old" records have great reuse potential. Coca Cola, Rothschild, Unilever, and HSBC are examples. HSBC's global archives contain historical records of HSBC bank plc (formerly Midland Bank) as well as of banks acquired and of their predecessors: HSBC Bank Middle East (formerly the British Bank of the Middle East), the Mercantile Bank of India, and of the Hongkong and Shanghai Banking Corporation up to 1993.

Some governmental archives follow the in-house model: The UK National Archives only acquires records created by the UK government, and so it is the exclusive repository for the records of government departments, central courts, and tribunals. Similarly nearly all the records at the National Archives of Australia are received, created, or kept by government agencies.

Universities may maintain an "in-house" acquisition policy too: Oxford University Archives holds only the administrative records of the university itself, which date from 1214, and constituent legislative and executive bodies.

The provenance and sources of the archives derived by this acquisition model remain closely linked to the organizational archive that acquires them.

Collecting Archives

A collecting archives is primarily dedicated to collecting archival material generated by bodies external to their parent-body in line with an *acquisition policy*, for purposes of research. While provision may be made for the management of the records of the collecting archives itself, this is not its prime focus. A collecting archives may step in where an organization does not run its own archives service, thus rescuing its noncurrent records. Ellis (1993, 463) defines a collecting archives as "an organization or part of an organization that has as its principal function the collection of the records of a variety of organizations, families and individuals. Collecting archives are often referred to as manuscript libraries or manuscript repositories."

The last sentence of the above quotation is particularly pertinent in the United States. Here the term *public records tradition* related to bodies whose main function was to service the archives generated by their employing bodies, and their records belonged in state archives—the in-house model. The *historical manuscripts tradition* referred to institutions whose remit was to collect materials from outside and to foster research: such records went to the state libraries.

Collecting archives are not restricted to a specific type of organization; rather they are defined by their mission to document specific subjects, themes, individuals, and formats. They operate typically within national institutions, universities, and specialist repositories, in independent bodies and community archives.

National archives may have an external collecting function, but since they are also responsible for acquiring the records of respective governments, they fall more appropriately into the combined model described below. National libraries and museums may accumulate archives of relevance to their wider collections: the national Australian War Memorial acquires solely archives that commemorate Australians who have died in war. The British Library's Western Manuscripts section is devoted to modern historical, medieval, and earlier manuscripts and modern literary manuscripts. Universities tend to acquire material that will support the research of their academics. The University of Glasgow takes in archives of shipping industry in Scotland, and the University of Manitoba the archives of early Arctic exploration, early Native language syllabics, spiritualism, and philosophy, among others.

Specialist collecting archives may focus on a specific media type (e.g., film or sound), for example, the British Film Institute National Archives and the BBC Sound Archive, or on a particular subject, theme, or individual: the Wordsworth Trust collections relate to the poet William Wordsworth, while the Labour History Archive & Study Centre (LHASC) in Manchester, UK, is the main specialist repository for the political wing of the UK labor movement, holding the archives of working-class political organizations. The Museum of English Rural Life is a national collecting repository for archives of agriculture and rural life and collects records of agricultural manufacturing firms, organizations and cooperatives, and *personal records* and journals of farm workers.

In the United States some state historical societies focus on a collecting remit. The Massachusetts Historical Society established in Boston in 1791 specializes in early American, Massachusetts, and New England history. UK local authority record offices also tend to operate a geographical acquisition policy, taking in historical material from individuals and organizations within the boundaries of the authority concerned: however, since they are also responsible for records of their parent authority, they fall more readily into the combined model.

The development of local community archives, which do not usually depend on established archival organizations for support, means that new *collections* are developing at a local level. In the UK the Belfast Indian Community Centre archives in Northern Ireland supports an organization that focuses on fostering an understanding of and good relations with the local and wider Indian Community. The Butetown History and Arts Centre (BHAC) in Cardiff Bay, South Wales, researches and promotes people's histories of the area and collects, preserves, copies, and uses oral histories, old photographs, and other documents.

Ellis (1993, 139–40) notes that collecting archives acquire records relating to a particular specialization regardless of their *provenance*. This can lead to problems of definition as to what to include and what to exclude, and where to draw the line. It is therefore important for collecting institutions to establish clear acquisitions policies that set out the collecting mandate in order to avoid problems of overlap with other archives. Problems may develop where one archives' acquisition policy, based on a geographical area, conflicts with that of another where the basis is a subject or theme. "The wider the collecting ambit, the greater the task and the greater the possibility that it may overlap with the acquisition interest of other institutions" (Ellis 1993, 40).

Combined Archives

The third organizational model of acquisition is the combined model. Here the focus is balanced between the management of the parent body's in-house records and archives and those created by external bodies and individuals and collected in line with an acquisition or collection policy. The relationship and interdependence of the respective records management and archives services varies, and each may be managed in different parts of the organization, but the assumption is that records created by the parent organization and assigned for permanent retention will be transferred to the archives.

"Combined archives are responsible for acquiring the records their host or parent organization and for collecting within a particular specialisation" (Ellis 1993, 140).

Once again, types of organization adopting this model come from across the spectrum. As noted, national archives that include an external collecting function alongside the management of governmental records comply with this model. The *total archives* remit of predecessors of Library and Archives Canada meant that this publicly funded institution would acquire, preserve, and make available for public use both government and private-sector archives in all media. Similarly the National Records of Scotland acquires both the records of government and those of private individuals, families, and businesses.

Some U.S. state historical societies operate a combined function. The Idaho State Historical Society is required to maintain a unified state archives in order to preserve both official state, county, and city archives as well as to collect others of historical significance. In the UK local authority sector combined services are offered although each function may be separately operated. In Derbyshire the "long-term management and preservation of the records of Derbyshire County Council is part of the remit of Derbyshire Record Office which is managed by the County Archivist." Universities too may adopt the combined remit. At Harvard University the Records Management Services "provide guidance and resources for all stages in the records and information lifecycle, from creating records through destruction of non-permanent records or transfer of permanent records to other staff at the Harvard University Archives." Both Derbyshire County Council and Harvard University also have external collection remits: Derbyshire's is for material relating to its geographical remit, while Harvard University archives collects records that reflect life at Harvard over the centuries, from seventeenth- and eighteenth-century diaries and scientific observations to twenty-first-century websites, student and alumni memorabilia and papers, and records of Harvard-affiliated organizations.

Conclusion

Collecting archives are one of three recognized models of *acquisition* to collections. As with the in-house and combined models, it may be adopted in a range of organizational and institutional environments. Since "collecting" can imply the acquisition of archives in terms of subjects, themes, and individuals, material "about" a topic is as relevant as that "created by" an organization, institution, or individual. As such, issues of provenance need to be considered, and a clear acquisition or collections policy maintained in the public domain. —*Caroline Williams*

Keywords: archives, records, collecting archives, in-house archives, combined archives
Related Entries: Acquisition; Acquisition Policy; Archival Collection; Archives (Institution); Collection-Management Policy; Records Management

Bibliography

"Derbyshire County Council Corporate Records Management Policy." Section 2.4.4. www.derbyshire.gov.uk/images/Corporate%20Records%20Management%20Policy%20(PDF%2C%20165kb)_tcm44-16973.pdf (accessed July 2014).

Ellis, J., ed. *Keeping Archives*, 2nd edition. Port Melbourne: Australian Society of Archivists, 1993.

"Managing University Records: Overview." Harvard University Archives, Harvard Library. http://library.harvard.edu/university-archives/managing-university-records/homepage (accessed July 2014).

Williams, C. *Managing Archives: Foundations, Principles and Practice*. Oxford: Chandos Publishing, 2006.

COLLECTION-MANAGEMENT POLICY

Collection-management policy is used to designate a variety of documents used in U.S. repositories, both institutional *archives* and collecting institutions. There is virtually no reference to such policies—even to the components of such policies—in archival literature. One minor exception notes:

> In the 1980s the concept of library collection development was placed into the broader discussions of collection management, focusing on the systematic, efficient, and economic stewardship of library resources. Library collections have been developed and maintained through policies that articulate relatively well-defined priorities. These priorities vary according to the type of library and its objectives, the clientele, the extent and condition of materials already in a collection, and preferred format types (based on the ability of the library to support access to these formats). (Kaczmarek 2007, 216)

The main references to collection-management policy are extant policies posted to the web, where it is easy to notice that many repositories either conflate or confuse collection-management policies with collection-development policies. While the latter guides what will be acquired, the former explains how the repository will control what is acquired.

Fortunately, the museology and library professions have focused more, and more precise, attention to collection-development policies ("Developing a

Collections Management Policy," 2012; "Collection Development Training for Arizona Public Libraries," 2008). Between museum and library recommendations and a concatenation of select archival institutions' policies on the web, the outlines of a policy can be discerned. The minimum content for a collection-management document is still far from clear, as no two of these examples closely mirrors another; however, it may be for the best that each repository select those sections of most relevance to their particular need. A critical consideration, however, is how much of the archives' philosophy and purpose should be encompassed by the policy—it is certainly possible for the document to become so extensive as to be unwieldy and therefore ignored. The sections gleaned from six examples (see the bibliography) follow, with a brief explication of the purpose or importance of each. They are listed in very rough order of their logical appearance in a policy.

Mission Statement—A reference to the repository's purpose, goals, and objectives, and how these are reflected in or advanced by the collection-management policy.

Statement of Authority—Lists who has the authority to create the policy, adopt the policy, and enforce the policy.

Link to *Collection* Development Policy—This can be as brief as a link to the collecting policy or as lengthy as an interweaving of the collecting policy with the "scope and categories of collections," which follows. Moreover, "Recognizing the implications of collection development for other library operations is an important aspect of being able to actually 'do' collection development well in your library" ("Collection Development Training for Arizona Public Libraries," 2008).

Scope and Categories of Collections—As explained by one document, formulated specifically for libraries:

> The policy statement should define the boundaries for the collection. Such boundaries may be geographic, topical, chronological, linguistic, or consist of any number of other types of boundaries. For example, if the library is going to collect fiction by state authors, one must define what constitutes a state author:
>
> • Does one have to have been born and raised in the state but one can write about anything?

- Does one have to write about the state but it does not matter where the author was born and raised or where one lives at present? ("Collection Development Training for Arizona Public Libraries," 2008)

Pursuit of New Acquisitions—On the assumption that the repository actively solicits collections as well as passively accepts them, some reference should be made to which staff members are authorized to identify prospective donors, establish relationships, conduct *appraisal*, and make "the ask."

Accepting New *Acquisitions*—Very simply, lays out authorities and processes for legally accepting new collections. In some institutions this requires approval of a committee and the counter signature (on a deed of gift) of the director ("Collection Management Policy," Center for Sacramento History 2009a); in other institutions it may require only the counter signature of an acquisition archivist. This section also usually specifies the types and lengths of restrictions acceptable to the repository, and whether there is a different approval process necessary for accepting deeds with restrictions.

Conditions for Material to Be Acquired—This section normally includes such criteria as the donor having clear title, the material being in sound condition, there being no requirements to exhibit or display the material, and no unreasonable restrictions.

Collections Care—"All staff members should understand their role in preserving and protecting the collections as well as the standards CSH has established for the preservation of the materials it owns or manages" (Center for Sacramento History 2009a). These sections usually include institutional standards, policies, and procedures for enclosures, storage conditions, security protocols, and the like.

Access and Use Policy—Usually such sections include discussions of access to unprocessed and/or fragile collections, policies on use of cameras and other technology in the reading room, qualifications (if any) for researchers, researcher registration, repository-made reproductions (procedures rather than prices, which change too frequently to be included in a major policy document).

Digitization Workflow—It is difficult to find such a section in current collection-management policies, but it should be essential. Workflows vary so significantly from repository to repository, have the possibility of impacting researcher access to collections, may involve collections care, and otherwise fit easily into collection-management policies.

Loan Policy (Incoming and Outgoing)—As one would expect, this section outlines the procedures, policies, and required documentation for incoming and outgoing loans. This will normally include the requirements that a receiving institution must meet in order to qualify to borrow an item(s) including such details as credits, insurance riders, and the like. Some archives include in this section their protocols for loaning collections (or boxes or *series*) to other archives for the use of researchers, though this is still very much a minority activity.

Reappraisal and *Deaccession* Policy—While not long ago it was necessary to borrow such policies from museums and libraries, archival repositories now need look no further than "Guidelines for Reappraisal and Deaccessioning" (2012). The guidelines establish "a step-by-step approach to reappraisal and deaccessioning in archival repositories and outlines general steps, problems, and solutions yielding responsible and ethical reappraisal and deaccessioning decisions."

Records—Often overlooked in both policy and practice, it is essential that a well-conceived and rigorously executed program of documentation accompany collection-management work. This documentation can include such things as donor communications, appraisal notes, *exhibition* agreements, deeds of gift, processing reports, use statistics, shelving records, and the like.

Performance Indicators—Though there are those in the archival profession who abjure the very idea of metrics (arguing that each repository is unique and cannot be compared to another), it is becoming more and more accepted that benchmarks and other performance indicators are necessary.

Key performance indicators provide valuable information which enables the Library to evaluate the quality, competitiveness and value for money of its services. . . . We will select [performance] indicators that will provide transparent and regular comparisons for our internal processes and disseminate these regularly to our customers to show our contribution to the Library's strategic objectives.

- We will identify Key Performance Indicators to benchmark our performance against other research libraries.
- We will gather qualitative and quantitative statistics through consultation with our customers, including focus groups and feedback on the quality of our services. . . .
- We will provide regularly updated Key Performance Indicators to assist library management decisions relating to resource allocation, evaluation of services, cost effectiveness and collection relevance.

These figures will be appropriate to the type and format of material acquired. ("Collection Management Policy," 2009c)

Insurance—How are the collections to be evaluated for insurance purposes? Who (usually, which unit within the parent organization) is responsible for purchasing and maintaining insurance coverage for the collections? While it is considered, by many, a truism that archival collections, being irreplaceable, are literally priceless and thus uninsurable, this is certainly not so. Some material, such as rare books, can be replaced. Archival collections, though indeed irreplaceable, may not be destroyed during a disaster, but may require extensive conservation treatment. The cost of that treatment, of replacement containers and folders, of repairs to shelving, all can be insured against. This section of the policy often includes reference to the repository's emergency-response plan.

Policy Review *Schedule*—Merely, though importantly, a commitment to review the collection-management policy on a regular schedule (for example, every five years).

Ethics Statement—Generally an explication of certain prohibitions on actions by repository employees. One example:

A possibility for conflict of interest exists whenever an employee of the AHC collects items of a type collected by the AHC. . . . An employee considering the acquisition of historically significant material that may be within the AHC's collecting goals . . . should bring the intended acquisition to the attention of the Acquisitions Committee in a timely manner to determine whether or not the AHC is interested in acquiring the material for the collections.

AHC employees may not use their institutional affiliation to promote their own or their family members' personal collecting or business activities. . . . Information of a sensitive and/or confidential nature that an employee might acquire in the course of performing his/her duties must be treated as proprietary to the AHC. ("Collection Management Policy," American Heritage Center 2004)

Creating the Policy

The process of developing a collection-management policy is important. As a guide for collection policies in museums argues, one size does not fit all, and process is as important as product:

The process of creating and implementing a policy is far more important and beneficial to the museum than the actual policy itself. The policy may seem like the end result, but in actuality, the end result is a broad understanding of ethics and procedures, which influences how the museum operates. *There are many different ways to create policies.* Each museum has its own set of challenges, which requires thoughtfulness in policy-making. Museums are encouraged to take time to explore their circumstances and articulate them accurately in their policies. *Policy-making should be integrated in order to be effective.* Each of the museum's official documents should speak to one another consistently and comprehensively to support the museum's mission. ("Collection Management Policy," 2004, emphasis in original)

The last point is particularly important because it is so easy, as policies and their accompanying forms change over time, that they become out of sync, such that the collection-management policy may specify that researchers may not use personal scanners, cameras, or photocopiers in the reading room while reference policies now permit cameras.

That said, the initial iteration of a collection-management policy should not simply be an exercise in assembling current policies and forms and codifying summaries in a new document. It is an opportunity to discuss and, if sensible, revise existing practice, as part of a broad view of repository operations.

Conclusion

Collection management, while much less visible in the archival literature than collection development, is equally important and more visible on repository websites. Encompassing everything from acquisition procedures to reappraisal and deaccessioning, management concerns embrace much of the daily operations of an archival institution, including such vital areas as access and use, collection care, and the documentation of repository procedures. It is an essential tool for administering a professional archival program.—*Mark Greene*

Keywords: papers, organizational records, manuscript collection, mixed collection, artificial collection

Related Entries: Appraisal; Archival Collection; Deaccessioning; Donation; Personal Records; Private Archives; Selection; Series; Total Archives

Bibliography

"Collection Development Training for Arizona Public Libraries." Arizona State Libraries, Archives, and Public Records, 2008. www.azlibrary.gov/cdt.
"Collection Management Policy." American Heritage Center, University of Wyoming, 2004. www.uwyo.edu/ahc/_files/policies/collection-mgmt-policy.pdf.
"Collection Management Policy." Center for Sacramento History, 2009a. www.cityofsacramento.org/ccl/history/pdf/about/Collection-Management-Policy.pdf.
"Collection Management Policy." Greater Southwest Historical Museum (OK), 2009b. http://gshm.org/pdf/collections_mgt_policy.pdf.
"Collection Management Policy." John Rylands University Library, University of Manchester (UK), 2009c. www.library.manchester.ac.uk/aboutus/policies/_files/Collection-management-policy.pdf.
"Developing a Collections Management Policy." American Alliance of Museums, 2012. http://aam-us.org/docs/continuum/developing-a-cmp-final.pdf.
Kaczmarek, Joanne. "The Complexities of Digital Resources: Collection Boundaries and Management Responsibilities." *Journal of Archival Organization* 4 (1–2) (2007): 215–27.
Society of American Archivists. "Guidelines for Reappraisal and Deaccessioning." Chicago: Society of American Archivists, 2012. www2.archivists.org/sites/all/files/GuidelinesForReappraisalAndDeaccessioning-May2012.pdf.

COMMUNITY ARCHIVES

Despite growing international usage, the term community archives has not been precisely defined or even deemed capable of precise definition. In some countries the term is used mainly to describe local, geographically located communities and *archives*, elsewhere instead of or in addition to place, the term refers to communities self-identifying by race, ethnicity, faith, nationality, gender, sexuality, disability, class, occupation, shared interest, or a combination of the above.

The Concept

In practice while community archives are often fluid, boundary spanning, and often self-defining, they also frequently exhibit some common traits (relating to collections, motivation, usage, and relationship to their community/ies). In acknowledging this diversity, many professional and academic studies describe community archives by concentrating on these common attributes in as an inclusive fashion as possible. For some it is not sufficient that the *collections* are about the community, the community must also be fully involved, maintaining that community archives are "grassroots activities of documenting, recording and exploring community heritage in which community participation, control and ownership of the project is essential. This activity might be wholly independent or might involve formal heritage organizations but the direction should come from within the community itself" (Flinn 2007, 153).

Community archives do not sit easily inside professional silos. The activities frequently described as community-based or community-led archiving shares many attributes with other related endeavors such as community history, oral history, community-based museums and heritage groups, radical archiving, resource centers, and autonomous archives. Crooke's (2007) portrayal of the "interesting, passionate and relevant exhibitions or collections" of community museums as "sometimes transient, often personality led, and frequently only best used and known amongst the community from which they emerged" perfectly describes many community archives. These various terms often indicate differences of origin and orientation but can also mask significant similarities, so the compound term community archives has been commonly employed in the UK and elsewhere to encompass many of these different activities. Although the term is not unproblematic (the appropriateness of both community and archives has been questioned), it has now acquired significant levels of professional and public recognition.

Prior to this more recent understanding of community archives as a broad term, we can identify a number of earlier (and still current) interpretations that stressed either community or archives. In many cases it is the local or other identity-based community that takes precedence (such as the Budapest Jewish Community Archive or local community archives in Canada and Germany). Here the archives is dependent on community; they are the community's archives without any implications regarding independence from professional bodies or a political agenda. The *community archives* that were created in the UK in the 1980s such as the Totnes Community Archive and the Brighton Community Fishing Archive describe a local grassroots approach embracing oral history (semi-)independent of the mainstream heritage sector. Developments in the 1990s facilitating the storing and sharing of digital heritage by online communities also had a significant impact on the spread of community archival practice and further popularized the term community archives to describe their mainly web-based activities.

Finally, from the 1970s onward and drawing inspiration from earlier activist and identity-related libraries, archives, and museums, there was a persistent usage that described not only an archive, documenting a defined community and an independence from mainstream heritage bodies but also the collection and use of archives by social movements to challenge existing historical and political narratives. For instance, a 1998 South African workshop of *archivists* and activists organized by the Gay and Lesbian Archive (GALA) (a "repository of community histories and cultural artifacts" that "in keeping with the concept of a community archive" encouraged its community "to participate in determining what should be preserved in the archives") to discuss community archives noted that "a key premise of community archiving is to give substance to a community's right to own its own memories" including collecting materials otherwise neglected by main-

stream heritage bodies and highlighted "community participation [as] a core principle of community archives" (Eales 1998).

From the late 1990s one can identify the increasingly frequent use of community archives as a compound term incorporating community participation and ownership, some degree of autonomy from mainstream institutions, and in some cases an explicit challenge to the perceived misrepresentations in mainstream historical narratives. In the UK the term was widely used to describe archival *collections* developed and shared within a specific community, often without the support of professional archivists and held beyond the walls (and virtual spaces, for many new community archives shared their collections online) of any formal archive. By the late 2000s the UK had a community archives movement with its own organization, the Community Archives and Heritage Group (CAHG) and an annual conference.

However, it is significant to acknowledge that the use of the component parts, community and archives, has been critiqued by some archivists and activists. Dislike of community relates to its slipperiness and lack of definition, and its exploitation by government and the media as a device for "othering" and marginalizing, conveying an impression of a "separateness" of a group from society at large (as in the "black community" or the "gay community") (Waterton and Smith 2010). Qualifications such as community-based or community-led at least indicate that control and agency is located within the group.

Criticism of the use of *archives* is less common but has been articulated by professional archivists arguing for a more traditional understanding of archives than most community archives support. Community archives are often the result of active collection and *creation* rather than accumulation, and include documentary materials, material culture, published works and duplicates, oral histories and audio-visual material, ephemera, clothes, and works of art. Community archivists are rarely troubled by professional boundaries or in accord with conventional notions of archival value, reliability, and "recordness." The existence of many local and identity-focused community archives is rooted in dissatisfaction with existing archival provision and constitute a critical, historically located, and contestatory intervention into mainstream heritage narratives (Hall 2001), and professional definitions are not a priority. However, by employing the term archives, groups utilize the symbolic power of word to represent meaning, memory, and evidence with which activists engage in the process of making and remaking history.

The activity of community archiving was demonstrably not a new practice in the 1990s and 2000s, even in the politically engaged form described here. However, interest in the practice in the UK and elsewhere did signify greater visibility of community archives resulting from technological advances; funding availability; and social, economic, and demographic changes such as migration, deindustrialization, and gentrification, which impacted on communities and their sense of identity. In the UK this visibility resulted in various professional and governmental initiatives to support community archives and to encourage their social policy impacts (e.g., neighborhood renewal and community cohesion [Jura 2009]), including the Community Access to Archives project (2003–2004), the Archives Task Force report (which noted that "archives in the community are as important to society as those in public collections") the "Impact of Community Archives" research (2007) and the *Community Archives and the Sustainable Communities Agenda* report (Jura 2009). One result was the formation of CAHG as a membership body to represent, advocate for, and provide services to the community-archive movement (Mander, 2009).

Incorporated in these various public-policy and research activities were a number of descriptions or definitions of community archives. Broad-based, these definitions sought to include as much community-based heritage activity as possible as long as it involved grassroots participation. The Jura report argued that community archiving could encompass both projects initiated and driven by the community as well as projects initiated by statutory organizations "which encourage involvement and deposit of information from communities" (Jura 2009). Definitions developed by CAHG followed a similar pattern. The key elements of its description of *community archives* emphasized self-definition but stated that there should be actual collections (physical or digital), the subject matter of the collection should be about a particular community, and the community should be involved in the activity. More recently CAHG has attempted to further refine its definition, offering the following description of community archives:

- a project initiated and maintained by a community group, that is a "not-for-profit" voluntary group operating with and for the benefit of their community, either solely or in collaboration with other bodies and individuals including archive and heritage professionals,
- in which archival and other historical materials are collected, preserved and shared to tell the stories of that same community,
- such communities often define themselves in relationship to place and locality but also by other single or often multiple intersecting identities including ethnicity, sexuality, gender, faith, language, nationality, social class, disability, and occupation.

Similarly the CAHG vision recognized that community archive activity might be conducted in collaboration with heritage or other professionals or entirely independently without formal, professional participation. Other observers such as Flinn (2007) have put forward a narrower, research-derived description of grassroots community activity in which "community participation, control and ownership" are essential and any association with formal heritage organizations should be directed by the community itself. But by not defining community archives too prescriptively, CAHG has been able to represent both those who are primarily motivated by local history and work closely with local heritage professionals, and also those social movements with a stronger alignment toward social justice or civil rights agendas and a commitment to independence and community ownership.

Taking account of the inclusiveness of existing community archives definitions, researchers have also tried to identify some common characteristics that might offer the possibility of more nuanced understandings. For instance Anne Gilliland's (2012) community-centric "Voice Identity Activism" (VIA) framework for approaching archives and *record-keeping* identifies examples of grassroots, identity-based, and social-justice-oriented community groups engaged in community-archives activity, some of the motivations for engaging in such activity, the manifestations and impacts of these engagements, the types of materials and knowledge held within community-archive collections, and the implications for recordkeeping thinking and practice.

Other studies (e.g., Gilliland and Flinn 2013) similarly emphasize the variety of materials held by community archives and the emotional value vested in those materials by the community; note both the long history of community-based archives activity and its development and responsiveness to technological changes; observe the connection between community-based archives and other D-I-Y, participatory knowledge creation practices; suggest a closer relationship between the collector/donor, the curator, and the user in community archives than might often be found in more traditional archives; identify the collection of material for making critical interventions into otherwise exclusionary narratives with the aim of refiguring those narratives, engendering a strategic essentialism for the purposes of building unity, and acting as a shared community space to debate complex identifications and aspire to different reimagined futures (Caswell 2014); and finally operate as space (symbolic and actual, physical and virtual) that acts to articulate belonging, community and self-confidence, a place of safety, and a locus for organization and action.

Conclusion

Like all organizations, community archives do not remain fixed but develop through time; perhaps evolving from being the passion of one or two individuals to something closer to a mainstream local archive, or from social-movement resource center to an archives of historically focused materials contributing knowledge of a "useful past" to contemporary social-justice campaigns. However, these changes may represent significant challenges in terms of ensuring the sustainability of the archives and the *preservation* of the collections over time. How are the collections and the infrastructure that surrounds them to be sustained if the prime motivators are no longer present, or if the community changes? While some fear that the long-term instability of independently minded community archives threatens the future survival of the very collections that the community archives values, others, while not dismissing possible future custodial roles, also identify the potential for fruitful and mutually beneficial relationships between community archivists and their professional collaborators, which results in collections

being sustained within their community context and a rethinking and reorientating of recordkeeping practice in a more community-centric framework (Stevens, Flinn, and Shepherd 2010).

—*Andrew Flinn*

Keywords: community-based, independence, identities, collecting, do-it-yourself, social movements
Related Entries: Archival Programs; Archives and Memory; Private Archives

Bibliography

Caswell, M. "Inventing New Archival Imaginaries: Theoretical Foundations for Identity-Based Community Archives." IdentityPalimpsests. Sacramento, CA: Litwin Books, 2014.

Crooke, E. *Museums and Community: Ideas, Issues and Challenges*. Abingdon: Routledge, 2007.

Eales, K. "Community Archives: Introduction." *South African Archives Journal* 40 (1998).

Flinn, A. "Community Histories, Community Archives: Some Opportunities and Challenges." *Journal of the Society of Archivists* 28 (2) (2007): 151–76.

Gilliland, A. *Voice, Identity, Activism (VIA): A Community-centric Framework for Approaching Archives and Recordkeeping*. Los Angeles: Center for Information as Evidence, University of California Los Angeles, 2012.

Gilliland, A., and A. Flinn. "Community Archives: What Are We Really Talking About?" In L. Stillman, A. Sabiescu, and N. Memarovic, eds., *Nexus, Confluence, and Difference: Community Archives Meets Community Informatics: Prato CIRN Conference Oct 28–30 2013*. Prato, Italy: Centre for Community Networking Research, Centre for Social Informatics, Monash University, 2013.

Hall, S. "Constituting an Archive." *Third Text* 54 (2001): 89–92.

Jura Consultants. *Community Archives and the Sustainable Communities Agenda*. London: Museums, Libraries and Archives Council, 2009.

Mander, D. "Special, Local and About Us: The Development of Community Archives in Britain." In J. Bastian and B. Alexander, eds., *Community Archives. The Shaping of Memory*. London: Facet, 2009, 29–46.

Stevens, M., A. Flinn, and E. Shepherd. "New Frameworks for Community Engagement in the

Archive Sector: From Handing Over to Handing On." *International Journal of Heritage Studies* 16 (1–2) (2010): 59–76.

Waterton, E., and L. Smith. "The Recognition and Misrecognition of Community Heritage." *International Journal of Heritage Studies* 16 (1–2) (2010): 4–15.

CONSERVATION

Conservation refers to both a profession and an activity. The goal of the profession is to preserve cultural property over time. In the archival context, it is undertaken as part of a preservation-management program. Conservation as an activity involves a chemical and/or mechanical act of intervention to an archival record resulting in the stabilization of the record and an increase in its life expectancy.

The Concept

In archives, "preservation management" is an umbrella term for all activities undertaken to minimize the chemical and physical deterioration of archival objects. Conservation is one element in a *preservation*-management program, which is based on scientific principles and professional practice.

The contemporary practice of science-based conservation began in the late 1800s with publications such as the Russell and Abney (1888) report on the *Action of Light on Water Colours*. In the United States, conservation was introduced at the Fogg Art Museum. Edward Waldo Forbes, director of the Fogg Art Museum (1909–1944), supported technical investigation into materials, treatments, and publications such as *Technical Studies*. In the mid-twentieth century, research by William J. Barrow on paper deacidification helped to define this new science-based approach (Barrow 1972).

Conservation further evolved, in part, from lessons learned in the aftermath of the Arno flood in Florence in 1966. Peter Waters, Library of Congress, and many others became known as "mud angels" for their work in Florence. Prior to the Florence flood, most conservation training was apprenticeship based and reflected more of a restoration approach rather than a conservation stabilization approach.

The 1970s saw the introduction of academic, science-based training programs in North America. These training programs adhere to the American Institute of Conservation Code of Ethics and Guidelines for Practice (AIC 1994). An ethical approach to conservation is based on minimal intervention and the premise of reversibility. Elements of conservation treatment may include object examination, condition and treatment documentation, treatment leading to stabilization, and reformatting and rehousing when necessary. Given the scale of archival holdings, conservation treatment can include both individual object treatment and mass treatments. Mass treatments, such as mass deacidification, are also designed to meet the code of ethics and best practice.

Conservation should not be confused with restoration. The goal of restoration is to return the object to its original appearance and may not lead to an increase in life expectancy or stabilization of the object.

Conclusion

Conservation is a science-based discipline that leads to the stabilization and increase in the life expectancy of archival records, through the use of minimal intervention. All conservation treatments are designed to be reversible. Traditionally, archival conservation has focused on analog specializations such as book and paper, photograph, film, and audio conservation. Currently, as archives collect born-digital records and digitize holdings, new areas of conservation are being developed.—*Rosaleen Hill*

Keywords: conservation, preservation, restoration
Related Entries: Digital Preservation; Preservation

Bibliography

"AIC Code of Ethics and Guidelines for Practice." American Institute for Conservation. www.conservation-us.org/about-us/core-documents/code-of-ethics#.UsGJJHmExuY (accessed December 1, 2013).

Barrow, William, J. *Manuscripts and Documents: Their Deterioration and Restoration*, 2nd edition. Virginia: University of Virginia Press, 1972.

James, Carlo. *Old Master Prints and Drawings: A Guide to Preservation and Conservation.* Amsterdam: Amsterdam University Press, 1997.

Muños-Viñas, Salvador. *Contemporary Theory of Conservation.* Oxford: Elsevier Butterworth Heinemann, 2005.

Pearce-Moses, Richard. *A Glossary of Archival and Records Terminology.* Chicago: Society of American Archivists, 2005.

Ritzenthaler, Mary Lynn. *Preserving Archives and Manuscripts*, 2nd edition. Chicago: Society of American Archivists, 2010.

Russell, William James, and William Abney. *Report to the Science and Art Department of the Committee of Council on Education on the Action of Light on Water Colours: Presented to Both Houses of Parliament by Command of Her Majesty.* Printed for H.M.S.O by Eyre and Spottiswoode, 1888.

Spande, Helen. *Conservation Legacies of the Florence Flood of 1966.* London: Archetype Publications, 2009.

CONTEXT

Context is the set of elements that influence the *creation* of *records* and that are essential to endow records with meaning, to sustain records' evidential value, and to establish the disciplinary identity of *archival science*. Though the boundary of context is a matter of debate, it is universally accepted that the key elements in defining the context of records include the records' creator, its organizational structure, and its *functions* and activities.

Context and the Evidential Nature of Records

The significance of context to the evidential nature of records is grounded in the archival concept of *evidence*, which in turn is based on the legal understanding of evidence. Duranti (1997) states that "in jurisprudence, and consequently in evidence laws, evidence is not an entity, but a relationship. It is a relationship shown to the judge of a fact between the fact to be proven and the fact that proves it" (214). Based on such understanding, an archival concept of evidence is proposed as a relation between a record and an event (Meehan 2006). Yet, unlike the legal understanding, where the establishment of this evi-

dential relationship entails inference from the fact that proves to the fact to be proven, the archival understanding sees the evidential relationship between record and event as determined and "found in a written document." Duranti (1997) writes that "the facts to be proven were clear; the facts proving them had to be the records in the name of which the facts existed and which embedded the relationship necessary to consider them evidence" (214). However, this does not mean that records cannot be regarded as "evidential facts" (facts that prove) for "principal facts" (facts to be proven) that researchers might conceive, which are different from the facts that gave rise to the records.

The relation between a fact and a record arises in the course of activity and comes into existence at the moment the record is created; it can take different forms depending on the function of the record in the performance of the activity. Moreover, this relation exists at two different levels, the individual level and the collective level, with the former referring to the relation between a record and the act or fact in which it participates, and the latter referring to the relationship between the whole of the records and the set of activities of a creator that create them.

The archival understanding of context is essential to this evidential relationship. This significance is embodied in the two types of contextual information and their contribution to the evidential relationship. One type is circumstantial context—that is, the context that is not directly related to the content of the record but is crucial to guarantee that the purpose of the record be successfully discerned and achieved (e.g., technical, juridical, social, organizational requirements on the form of and the procedure generating the records). The other type is direct context, which is directly related to the content of the record and describes the fact that gives rise to the record, the preceding and following record, and so on (e.g., a creator's organizational mandate, functions, structure).

Hence, the identification, documentation, and communication of the context of records, which protects the evidential relationship between records and the activities that gave rise to them, is the primary concern of archival science; as Gilliland-Swetland (2000) writes, "The archival perspective brings an evidence-based approach to the management of recorded knowledge. It is fundamentally concerned with the organizational and personal processes and contexts through which records and knowledge are created as well as the ways in which records individually and collectively reflect those processes" (2).

Context and the Meaning of Records

Not only is context essential to the evidential nature of records, but also it is crucial to the understanding of the meaning of records; as Yeo (2013) points out, the content of records is rarely explicable without at least some knowledge of their context. Both circumstantial context and direct context are needed for the interpretation of the meaning of records, although their function is different in such interpretation. The circumstantial context allows to situate the record back in the technical, social, juridical environment, and so on, in which it was created thereby facilitating the understanding of its intended effect; the direct context allows to situate the record back in the organizational function, business process, and so on, that produced it, thereby revealing its intended meaning. Concern over the latter is at the heart of *archival description*, a core area of *archival science*.

A great many national and international *standards* have been developed to facilitate archival description (e.g., *RAD, DACS, ISAD[G]*, etc.). Among them, there is one standard specifically focusing on context control: *International Standard Archival Authority Record (Corporate Bodies, Persons, Families) (ISAAR [CPF])*. Though most studies on archival description are focused on the *principle of provenance*, more and more researchers are starting to recognize that the fundamental concept for conveying the meaning of records is context. For instance, in her essay discussing the conceptual foundation of *RAD*, MacNeil (1992) argues that external and internal structure of a *fonds* correspond to the organizational context, functional context, and documentary context. Moreover, while the traditional understanding of context is mainly confined to the context of creation, this is increasingly expanded to the context of use and management.

Context and Diplomatics for the Protection of the Authenticity of Records

In addition to the evidential nature and meaning of records, context is also the conceptual foundation for ascertaining and guaranteeing the *authenticity* of records, as demonstrated in *diplomatics*. Duranti (1997) notes that "the essential assumption of diplomatics is that the context of a document's creation is made manifest in its form, and that this form can be separated from, and examined independently of, its content" (215).

As a discipline developed to ascertain the authenticity of ancient *documents*, diplomatics is "the study of the *Wesen* [being] and *Werden* [becoming] of documentation, the analysis of genesis, inner constitution and transmission of documents, and of their relationship with the facts represented in them and with their creators" (Duranti 1998). More specifically, diplomatics dissected the form of *documents* into its constituent elements to understand how these elements communicate contextual information and how they together help achieve the purpose of the document. With such knowledge, the main criterion for determining the authenticity of documents is the consistency of the form of the document with the documentation practices of the time and place where the document was prepared.

With the advancement and diffusion of information technology, the relationship between context and records becomes increasingly complicated. According to MacNeil (2004),

> The problem of context as it affects the authenticity of electronic records is twofold: firstly, electronic records are deeply embedded within multiple and overlapping contexts that are complex and subject to rapid change; nevertheless, these contexts must be understood and described in order to both establish and protect the records' authenticity (meaning their identity and integrity) over time. Secondly, the boundary between records and their surrounding context tends to blur in electronic record-keeping environments, further exacerbating the difficulty of establishing and preserving their authenticity. (200–201)

Yet the significance of context for establishing and maintaining the authenticity of records remains unchallenged, as shown by several case studies carried out by the InterPARES project: "Elements relating to context and, in particular, procedural and technological context, were most relevant to an understanding of the electronic record-keeping environment and appeared to provide the main grounds on which record creators based their presumption of the records' authenticity" (MacNeil 2002, 34). To make explicit the relationship between context and records, it is important to examine the role of contextual information for the identity and *integrity* (i.e., the authenticity) of records. The InterPARES project has divided context of records into five categories ranging from the general to the specific: juridical-administrative context, provenancial context, procedural context, documentary context, and technical context. However, additional research is needed to decompose the five types of context into their parts to understand their role for the authenticity of records.

Context and the Principle of Provenance

The exact relationship between context and provenance is a matter of debate (Yeo 2013). To safeguard the evidential nature of records and to facilitate their interpretation, it is essential that *archivists* "describe the context of archival records accurately and . . . make this context available and obvious to anyone who wants to use the records, either as evidence or as a source of information" (Diamond 1994, 140). The principle of provenance is the *archival method* archivists use to fulfill such responsibility. As the fundamental principle of archival science, the assumption of the principle of provenance is that, by keeping together, without mixing them with others, the records of the same creator, the context of records will be identified, fixed, and communicated. Thus, to a certain extent, traditionally, provenance is perceived as equal to records creator.

Yet its interpretation in the Australian *series system* and in the writings of Terry Cook ("conceptual provenance") and others has developed the concept from referring merely to the records creator to including business functions, administrative and documentation processes, and *recordkeeping systems*. Hence, Horsman (2011, 2) asserts that "more conceptually, provenance is now rather defined as context."

Conclusion

As a central concept of archival science, context is essential to the evidential nature of records, their interpretation of records, and the protection of their

authenticity. Though context and the principle of provenance are often seen as the same thing, it becomes increasingly clear that what underlies the principle of provenance is the intention to protect the context of records. Accordingly, the principle of provenance can be regarded as the methodology that guides *archival practice* in the identification, documentation, and communication of context.

The challenges posed by information technology to the trustworthiness of records make it vital that the context of records be identified and transmitted with the records across time and space so that when users are presented with the records, they can evaluate their trustworthiness.—*Weimei Pan*

Keywords: evidence, archival description, appraisal, diplomatics, authenticity, provenance
Related entries: Archival Description; Archival Science; Authenticity; Diplomatics; Principle of Provenance; Principle of *Respect des Fonds*; Principle of Respect for Original Order

Bibliography

Diamond, Elizabeth. "The Archivist as Forensic Scientist: Seeing Ourselves in a Different Way. *Archivaria* 1 (38) (1994): 139–54. http://journals.sfu.ca/archivar/index.php/archivaria/article/view/12031/13002.

Duranti, Luciana. "The Archival Bond." *Archives and Museum Informatics* 11 (3) (1997): 213–18.

———. *Diplomatics: New Uses for an Old Science.* Lanham, MD: Scarecrow Press, 1998.

Gilliland-Swetland, Anne J. *Enduring Paradigm, New Opportunities: The Value of the Archival Perspective in the Digital Environment.* Washington, DC: Council on Library and Information Resources, 2000.

Horsman, P. "Wrapping Records in Narratives: Representing Context through Archival Description." Presented at the Usability of the Archives of the International Tracing Service Workshop at the ITS, October 10–11, 2011. www.its-arolsen.org/fileadmin/user_upload/Dateien/Archivtagung/Horsman_text.pdf (accessed October 2014).

MacNeil, Heather. "Contemporary Archival Diplomatics as a Method of Inquiry: Lessons Learned from Two Research Projects." *Archival Science* 4

(3) (2004): 199–232. DOI: 10.1007/s10502-005-2592-x.

———. "The Context Is All, Describing a Fonds and Its Parts in Accordance with the Rules for Archival Description." In T. Eastwood, ed., *The Archival Fonds: From Theory to Practice*. Ottawa: Bureau of Canadian Archivists, Planning Committee on Descriptive Standards, 1992, 198–224.

———. "Providing Grounds for Trust II: The Findings of the Authenticity Task Force of InterPARES." *Archivaria* 54 (2002): 24–58. http://journals.sfu.ca/archivar/index.php/archivaria/article/view/12854/14078.

Meehan, Jennifer. "Towards an Archival Concept of Evidence." *Archivaria* 61 (2006): 127–46. http://journals.sfu.ca/archivar/index.php/archivaria/article/view/12538/13681.

Yeo, Geoffrey. "Trust and Context in Cyberspace." *Archives and Records—The Journal of the Archives and Records Association* 34 (2) (2013): 214–34. DOI:10.1080/23257962.2013.825207.

D

DEACCESSIONING

Deaccessioning is a *collections management* practice of permanently removing previously accessioned material. Best practice asserts that a thorough *reappraisal* be conducted before material is deaccessioned. Deaccessioning involves various considerations including ownership status, content and type of material, and disposal options. Deaccessioning typically, or at least eventually, requires the physical removal of collection material from a repository's holdings, but it can also include the removal or deletion of the collection record from catalogs and databases. Several disposal options exist for deaccessioned material. While the practice of deaccessioning was once quite controversial, it has become an increasingly accepted practice in *archives* because of the reported benefits and advantages.

History

Removing previously accessioned material as a collections management practice originated in the library field around the middle of the twentieth century. In the archives field, deaccessioning has a shorter history and has been inextricably linked to reappraisal, with articles and conference sessions on reappraisal appearing in the beginning of the 1980s. The first seminal article on reappraisal and deaccessioning was published in 1981 by Leonard Rapport, who argued that because archives have limited resources, regular reappraisal of holdings is necessary to determine what material is and is not worth keeping. In 1984 Karen Benedict countered

Rapport's article by arguing that reappraisal and deaccessioning would undermine the basic mission of an archives and should only be used in the midst of a crisis. These two articles began a discourse on the ethics and methods of deaccessioning in archives. In the following decades, archivists examined the causes, advantages, pitfalls, and risks of deaccessioning as a collections management practice and published numerous case studies and articles touting the advantages of deaccessioning (and its related practice, reappraisal). Ashby Crowder (2011) stated that few actual opponents of reappraisal are found in the literature (50). In 2012, the Society of American Archivists endorsed a standard guideline for reappraising and deaccessioning material.

What It Is

Deaccessioning is a collections management tool enabling the removal of unwanted material to subsequently make resources available for wanted material and create more focused collection holdings. Deaccessioning is not the same as weeding materials from a collection during accessioning or processing, although the two processes have similar causes and disposal methods. Rather, the practice of deaccessioning is most applicable (and beneficial) as a collections management tool when applied to entire series, collections, or related groups of collections.

Deaccessioning occurs after reappraising a collection or series leads to the decision to remove it. Archival material may be deaccessioned for several reasons including but not limited to: the content of the material does not fall within the strictures of the repository's collecting policy; the types of materials are inaccessible due to format or decay; the donor wants the material returned or removed and the act of a gift cannot be definitively documented; to make split collections whole; and to correct faulty appraisal at the time of acquisition.

While many of the reasons to deaccession equate with the benefits gained from deaccessioning, there are a number of beneficial outcomes that must be distinct from the primary reason or cause to deaccession. For example, increased shelf space is a natural result of deaccessioning but should not be the main impetus to deaccession. In addition, money can be realized from the sale of deaccessioned material but should not be the primary reason why the material was deaccessioned. For deaccessioning to be an ethical practice, there must be sound appraisal reasons that the collection should not be maintained in the repository that acquired it. Deaccessioning is an especially beneficial tool for repositories that have a large backlog because the practice allows for entire collections to be removed before processing; however, selecting collections to be removed ought to be based on collecting policy, condition, or other determining factor. Deaccessioning can also establish more refined collection holdings.

There are five main options to physically removing deaccessioned material from the repository. It can be: transferred to another repository; transferred elsewhere within the repository's parent institution; returned to the donor or donor's heirs; sold; or destroyed. The outcome will generally depend on the ownership status of the material. Transfer to another archives or organization is perhaps the ideal option as it will probably keep the material available to the public, may mitigate or eliminate donor backlash, and can build collecting collaboration among repositories. Returning material to the donor is typically only done under two circumstances: (1) the repository does not definitively own the collection and the donor wants it returned; or (2) there is no alternative and the repository and the donor both prefer return to destruction. Sale is a legitimate option but can lead to controversy. Best practice is to only sell materials such as publications and ephemera that are unlikely to be unique and that hold minimal research value, or to sell material (possibly at a discount from fair market value) to another repository if it was originally purchased. Moreover, the Association of Art Museum Directors' (AAMD) policy

on deaccessioning states that funds realized from such sale must be used for acquisitions, not for operating expenses, supplies, or equipment. Although the archives profession lacks a formal statement about proceeds from deaccessioned material, this directive is typically followed among archivists and often expanded to include collection preservation. Material that has no value and cannot be transferred, returned, or sold can be destroyed. Although this is the least favorable option, it is feasible for materials that do not have any research value, that are not unique records, or for which all other options have been exhausted.

Controversy and Arguments Against

The practice of deaccessioning is increasing among archival institutions but is still not as common as, for example, processing and reference. Some institutions may never need to deaccession, but others avoid the practice for fear of public controversy and negative attention. Most public controversies about deaccessioning occur in museum settings rather than archival repositories, although there are exceptions. In most cases of negative media attention and public outcry in response to archives deaccessioning, a significant percentage of the repository's holdings or a high-profile collection was sold for the purpose of making a profit, to meet budget shortfalls, or to sustain endowment or foundational funding. Repositories deaccessioning miniscule portions of total holdings for the purpose of sound collections management—whether sold or not—have not experienced intense media attention.

In addition, the sale of material can fuel controversy because, unless sold to another archives, library, or museum, material once available to the public is no longer accessible. This is a general argument against deaccessioning and applicable to every disposal option except transfer to another repository. This problem is compounded when the material has been cited in publication. Although disconcerting to researchers, the problem will occur rarely because records of actual research value ought to be transferred to another public repository.

Perhaps one of the most common reasons, and misperceptions, why archivists avoid deaccessioning is a fear of donor backlash. Donors (or their heirs) may expect the archives to keep their material forever and become upset when they learn it is no longer of value to the repository. While this can indeed occur, in the multiple case studies about deaccessioning, none reports damage in donor relations and at least one asserts that most donors understand why the decision was made and are glad to see the material transferred to a better-suited repository or have it returned (Jackson and Thompson 2010, 680).

One of the only published arguments against deaccessioning is that it undermines a repository's mission and purpose to preserve and care for the materials that it acquires (Benedict 1984, 44). When intended for the wrong purposes, deaccessioning can have this consequence. Conversely, when used to improve *access* and funnel limited resources toward retained collections, then consequences of deaccessioning can align with the repository's mission and goals.

Conclusion

To avoid controversy and backlash, deaccessioning is a practice best done for the purpose of good collections management—that is, to focus collection holdings and enhance access. Most of the options and factors that are part of the decision to deaccession can be achieved through reappraisal. After the decision is made to deaccession, the material can be removed both physically and intellectually. Although there is a perceived risk of harming relationships with donors and experiencing negative media attention, the benefits of deaccessioning as a collections management tool are multifold and generally outweigh the risks. Benefits include better access to existing collections, more focused collecting areas, more space on the shelf, and a decreased backlog.

—*Laura Uglean Jackson*

Keywords: appraisal, reappraisal, disposal, collections management
Related Entries: Appraisal; Disposition, Records; Reappraisal

Bibliography

Benedict, Karen. "Invitation to a Bonfire: Reappraisal and Deaccessioning of Records as Collection Management Tools in Archives—a Reply to Leonard Rapport." *American Archivist* 47 (1) (1984): 43–49. http://archivists.metapress.com/content/gt26318774q20241/fulltext.pdf.

Crowder, Ashby. "Reappraising Leonard Rapport's 'No Grandfather Clause' at Thirty." *Provenance* 29 (2011): 49–66.

Greene, Mark. "What Were We Thinking? A Call to Embrace Reappraisal and Deaccessioning." *Provenance* 20 (2002): 33–49.

"Guidelines for Reappraisal and Deaccessioning." Society of American Archivists, 2012, 1–33. www2.archivists.org/sites/all/files/Guidelines-ForReappraisalAndDeaccessioning-May2012.pdf (accessed December 2013).

Jackson, Laura, and D. Claudia Thompson. "But You Promised: A Case Study of Deaccessioning at the American Heritage Center, University of Wyoming." *American Archivist* 73 (2) (2010): 669–85. http://archivists.metapress.com/content/297691q50gkk84j4/fulltext.pdf.

Rapport, Leonard. "No Grandfather Clause: Reappraising Accessioned Records." *American Archivist* 44 (2) (1981): 143–50. http://archivists.metapress.com/content/b274w3126t430h52/fulltext.pdf.

DIGITAL ARCHIVES

While some might prefer the term digital archives be used only to describe archival *collections* of born-digital materials, in practice it is used to refer to collections of both born-digital as well as digitized materials. In addition it is used to refer to collections of materials that come from the same source as well as to collections created from assembling digitized materials from many disparate sources. For the general public as well as scholars and some information professionals, any website offering representations of material with historic significance is a digital archives. Many archives also refer to the website through which they provide *access* to their digitized collections, or their digitized collections in addition to those from other sources, as their digital archives. In fact, it is this usage, rather than an archives or collections of born-digital materials, that currently appears to be the most prevalent.

The Challenge of Defining *Digital Archives*

Frederick Stielow wrote in 2003:

What is a digital archive? The definition of "digital archive" continues to evolve. The original concept was the preservation of institutional records that originated in the computer—i.e., were "born digital"—but now the definition also encompasses computerized images of two- and three-dimensional objects, electronic publications, online displays, policies, and a variety of location pointers and professional descriptions. (Stielow 2003, x)

The broad use of the term noted by Stielow more than a decade ago has continued and expanded. Today there are four primary ways in which the term digital archives is commonly used: for collections of born-digital *records*, for websites that provide access to collections of digitized materials, for websites featuring different types of digitized information around one topic, and for web-based participatory collections.

Collections of Born-Digital Records

In discussing their digital archives specialist continuing education program, the Society of American Archivists specifies that for the purposes of that program, digital archives "are permanent digital records that require a computer to create and use them. The term *archives* may refer to both materials and the repositories that house them; similarly 'digital archives' may refer to an archival institution focused on the management of permanent *digital records* or a cache or collection of such materials" ("What Is the Difference," para. 3). This usage, for archives both as bodies of records and as repositories, is consistent with the concept defined by the Open Archival Information System (OAIS) Reference Model (CCSDS 2012) and later by the *Trusted Repositories Audit & Certification: Criteria and Checklist*, which provides this definition for "digital repository/digital archive":

These two terms are often used interchangeably. OAIS uses *archive* when referring to an organization that intends to preserve information for access and use by a designated community(ies). *Trusted Digital Repositories: Attributes and Responsibilities* prefers the term digital repository. Digital archives and digital repositories should not be confused with either *digital libraries*, which collect and provide access to digital information, but may not commit to its long-term preservation, or *data archives,* which do commit to long-term preservation but limit their

collections to statistical datasets. (Online Computer and Library Center 2007, 75)

In keeping with their goals, both these documents use digital archives (or digital repository) to refer to an organization rather than a body of permanent digital records. However, in practice and in usage within the profession, specific collections of born-digital materials, such as the Richard Rorty born-digital files at the University of California Irvine (http://ucispace.lib.uci.edu/handle/10575/7) or the born-digital materials in the Salman Rushdie Papers at Emory University (http://findingaids.library.emory.edu/documents/rushdie1000), are referred to as digital archives. The term "digital archiving" is also used to describe the *preservation* of electronic information, although the same diversity of meaning that surrounds digital archives also applies to digital archiving. However, within the professional literature of the archival profession, digital archives appears to apply most frequently to bodies of born-digital records and to the repositories that preserve them.

Websites That Provide Access to Collections of Digitized Materials

Outside of the professional literature, a more common usage of digital archives is as an umbrella term for a website that serves as a portal through which digitized collections can be accessed. In one model, the digital archives provides access to digitized collections from a specific geographic region. This can be seen, for example, in the Washington State Archives' digital archives (www.digitalarchives.wa.gov) and the Connecticut Digital Archive (http://ctdigitalarchive.org). However, in both of these cases digital archives also describes an organization that provides preservation and management services for the digital holdings as well as providing a unified access portal. In other cases, such as the Alaska's Digital Archives (http://vilda.alaska.edu) and the West Texas Digital Archive (http://wtda.alc.org), only a common portal is provided for digitized content from state or regional project partners.

Another model is for the digital archives to provide access to the digitized collections of only one organization, as is done in the Delaware Public Archives' digital archives (http://archives.delaware.gov/exhibits/exhibits-toc.shtml), the New York Philharmonic Digital Archives (http://archives.nyphil. org), and the Hagley Digital Archives (http://digital. hagley.org). In other cases, the digital archives feature only a specific subset of holdings from a repository, such as the Turing Digital Archive (www. turingarchive.org).

Variations on this type of digital archives are *collections* that bring together digitized copies of materials from different repositories into one virtual digital archives, usually around a specific person or topic. Examples of this type are the Marcel Breuer Digital Archive (http://breuer.syr.edu/page-about. php), the Wilson Center's Digital Archive (http:// digitalarchive.wilsoncenter.org), and the Avestan Digital Archive (www.avesta-archive.com). These topical digital archives are often indistinguishable from other web-based projects that simply label themselves as "archives" (without the "digital") as seen in the Shelley-Godwin Archive (http://shelley-godwinarchive.org) among others.

Websites Featuring Different Types of Digitized Information around One Topic

Similar to the previous kind of digital archives, but slightly different, are websites that contain both digitized copies of materials from archival sources as well as digitized versions of texts and other related materials. These sites provide a broader range of materials around their subject, such as bibliographies and electronic versions of key texts in addition to scanned archival materials. The Walter Scott Digital Archive (www.walterscott.lib.ed.ac.uk) and the First World War Poetry Digital Archive (www.oucs. ox.ac.uk/ww1lit) demonstrate this kind of usage. Again, there are also sites such as the Walt Whitman Archive (www.whitmanarchive.org), which are essentially the same in nature, but which omit the "digital" from their title.

Web-Based Participatory Collections

A usage that is growing more common is digital archives as collections that actively solicit online contributions. Such collections may be comprised entirely or in part of user-contributed material. These kinds of digital archives may arise to document a specific event or series of events, such as the September 11 Digital Archive (http://911digitalarchive.

org), the Digital Archive of Japan's 2011 Disasters (http://beta.jdarchive.org/en/home), or Our Marathon: The Boston Bombing Digital Archive (http:// marathon.neu.edu). They may also seek to capture individual stories, as does the Digital Archive of Literacy Narratives (http://daln.osu.edu). This type of digital archives is also an example of a *participatory archives.*

Conclusion

In 2008 Adrian Cunningham wrote, "From a recordkeeping perspective, the phrase digital archive has been misused, even hijacked," and that is probably even more true today (Cunningham 2008, 530). While in professional archival literature, the phrase will perhaps continue to refer primarily to collections of born-digital materials, in common usage both inside and outside the profession, the application of the term to collections of digitized materials from one or many sources, as well as to participatory collections of born-digital collections and to topical websites with digitized content from archival collections, will no doubt continue and expand.—*Kate Theimer*

Keywords: virtual archives, digital collections, born-digital
Related Entries: Digital Repository; Digitization; Participatory Archives

Bibliography

Cunningham, A. "Digital Curation/Digital Archiving: A View from the National Archives of Australia." *The American Archivist* 71 (2) (2008): 530–43. http://archivists.metapress.com/content/p0h0t68547385507/fulltext.pdf.

"Digital Archiving in the 21st Century." Council of Australasian Archives and Records Authorities, 2006. www.caara.org.au/wp-content/uploads/2010/03/DigitalArchiving21C.pdf (accessed March 21, 2014).

Online Computer and Library Center. "Trusted Repositories Audit & Certification: Criteria and Checklist." Online Computer and Library Center and the Center for Research Libraries, 2007. www.crl.edu/sites/default/files/attachments/pages/trac_0.pdf (accessed March 21, 2014).

"Reference Model for an Open Archival Information System (OAIS)." Consultative Committee for Space Data, June 2012. http://public.ccsds.org/publications/archive/650x0m2.pdf (accessed March 21, 2014).

Stielow, F. *Building Digital Archives, Descriptions, and Displays*. New York: Neal-Schuman, 2003.

"What Is the Difference/Relationship between 'Digital Archives' and 'Electronic Records'?" Society of American Archivists, 2014. www2.archivists.org/prof-education/das/FAQs/2 (accessed March 21, 2014).

DIGITAL PRESERVATION

Digital preservation encompasses the processes and controls that enable digital information objects to survive over time. Besides satisfying the requirements for preserving any type of *records* (see *Archival Preservation*), digital preservation must address the special challenges of digital data. Electronic records are subject to both intentional and accidental corruption or loss throughout their existence, requiring that they be controlled under an unbroken *chain of preservation* that extends over their life span from the instant of *creation* (Duranti 2005).

Challenges of Digital Preservation

Digital preservation involves four basic types of challenges. One concerns the physical media on which digital data are recorded. Two, format obsolescence and technical opportunities, relate to the tools necessary to retrieve and use preserved information resources. The fourth relates to ways information is encoded digitally. Preserving records entails the additional challenge of preserving archival aggregates.

Digital Storage Media

Digital storage media have been developed using durable materials, such as tempered glass and indestructible metal alloys; however, no such products have proven economically viable because increasing data densities and data transfer rates, along with decreasing costs, have made optical, magnetic, and more recently solid-state media more attractive. These media tend to be fragile and short lived.

Moreover, the life expectancy of most digital media is uncertain because they are composed of several layers. There is no scientific method for calculating how different materials in contact with each other will interact over time. Further, the viability of any type of storage media may be less than its life expectancy because the continuing introduction of new storage technologies makes maintaining the equipment necessary to read older media increasingly difficult and costly.

Format Obsolescence and Technical Opportunities

Digital information becomes inaccessible when the hardware or software needed to retrieve and render older formats is no longer available and current products do not support either the media on which the data are stored or the formats in which they are encoded. Obsolescence will remain a problem as long as new information technology products continue to be introduced. Even if the obsolescence of digital *formats* were solved, there would still be a significant challenge because, for most purposes, people want to use the best technology to find, retrieve, and exploit digital information. What is best will often depend on users' particular intentions and their familiarity with available tools. They are likely to be more familiar with current technology rather than that used to create preserved records. Thus, *archives* face the dual challenge of capitalizing on new opportunities offered by technology, while maintaining *authenticity* in the face of changes that newer technology can introduce in the characteristics of electronic records.

Encoding of Digital Information

Preservation techniques must address the specific format in which data is encoded; however, the content of even a single record, such as a letter or graphic, may include multiple data formats. For example, a word processing file may contain digital photographs and spreadsheets, or an email message may embed a HTML page. The relationship between a record and data in storage is not necessarily one-to-one. It may be one-to-many, many-to-one, or many-to-many. Rendering a record from stored data may require complex processing.

Archival Aggregates

Preserving records entails preserving the aggregates in which records are grouped and organized. Techniques for digital preservation have been developed largely to solve specific technical challenges, such as the preservation of data in a given format, and often without consideration of scale. Archival aggregates may contain numerous records in many different formats, requiring either broad solutions that can span the range of formats or sets of specific techniques that can be implemented together in a coherent fashion. Moreover, the techniques used to aggregate and arrange electronic records are also subject to obsolescence, independently from the obsolescence of individual records.

Managing Digital Preservation

Digital preservation requires a comprehensive management approach that addresses considerations such as the volume of data, the numbers of records, data objects, genres, and data formats, the organization of records, their relationships to analog holdings, the means and frequency of *transfer* from producers, as well as conditions and expectations for access. The Open Archival Information System reference model provides a conceptual framework suitable for articulating a comprehensive management strategy (International Standards Organization 2012).

Given the explosive growth of digital information, and the complex challenges and substantial costs of preserving it, the management strategy should look for opportunities for collaboration and cooperation. Possibilities include collaboration among institutions with similar requirements, broad alliances along disciplinary or national lines, adoption of formal *standards*, and use of open-source software.

Techniques

Techniques for preserving digital information include those for ensuring physical survival and others for overcoming format obsolescence and benefiting from opportunities.

Physical Survival

At least two copies of electronic records should be preserved in separate locations. Storing at least one set of these copies offline in a preservation facility reduces overall risk. Magnetic tape offers advantages over other media for offline storage, including greater durability, lower costs, better security, and lower power requirements.

Fragility and obsolescence of storage media and equipment require copying data to new media periodically. With offline storage this requirement can be labor intensive and costly. If one set of the records is preserved online or near-line in a data center, it may be more economical to produce new copies for offline storage from that set. Periodic refreshment of storage media and subsystems is part of normal data-center operations, but is not necessarily done in a way that preserves records. Agreements that entrust electronic records to data centers should include provisions to maintain the records intact and uncorrupted and to report on, and recover from, errors.

Preservation of Electronic Records

Responses to format obsolescence have taken three main paths: migration, normalization, and emulation. Under migration, the data are converted to new formats compatible with current technology. Under normalization, electronic records are converted to standard formats. Under emulation, the data are left in original formats but special software is introduced that enables the obsolete software necessary for those formats to run on current computers. Two other noteworthy techniques focus on the presentation or rendering of preserved records on current platforms.

Migration

Conversion of records to newer versions of the formats in which they were created can be relatively simple to implement. In many cases the conversion capability is included in newer versions of a software product. However, there are two basic problems with this approach. The first is that the conversion is target driven: old *documents* are changed to conform to the specifications of newer formats. This can introduce changes in the documents and, given that the old formats are no longer accessible, it may not be possible to determine what those changes are. The second problem is that the newer formats will themselves become obsolete. Migrations will have to be performed repeatedly. Over time, it will not be possible to perform conversions from the original formats because software producers generally limit the range of backward compatibility. Migrating from prior migrations opens the door to accumulating changes in the records.

Normalization

Normalization may be seen as a subtype of migration, but conversion to standard formats has two obvious advantages: reducing the range of formats that need to be managed and adopting formats that are likely to be viable longer than proprietary format. The disadvantage of normalization is that it too can introduce changes that affect the interpretation and authenticity of the records.

Emulation

Emulation has the advantage of keeping electronic records in their original formats; however, there are major difficulties in implementing emulation at scale. One lies in the user experience. The greater the lapse of time between the creation of the records and their use, the greater the likelihood that the original software will be unfamiliar to *users* and that users will have to learn to use it. This would constitute a substantial burden on users whose interest spans a variety of formats or a considerable period of time; moreover, the need to use different software and different versions of software to access the records would impede opportunities for exploiting them. The other difficulty is in requirements for technical support. Proponents of emulation have suggested reducing these requirements by emulating the operating systems rather than each of the multiple applications that ran on those systems. Even so, as records accumulate over decades, the number of versions of operating systems and of combinations of operating systems and versions of applications that would have to be installed and supported would be formidable. Furthermore, providing support for end users to learn and use hundreds of varieties of software products would be both economically and technically challenging.

Presentation of Preserved Records

A narrower approach than emulation restricts the functional requirements for accessing preserved records to simply presenting them on current platforms. This is advantageous because the software originally used to create records enables modifying them, which must be prohibited for preserved records. While appropriate for electronic records that are counterparts of traditional records printed on paper, this approach does not enable full access to electronic records with interactive capabilities, such as viewing formulas behind the numbers in spreadsheets.

A broader technique, the Multivalent Document Model, retains digital data in its original formats, but avoids the complexities of emulation by limiting the technical requirement to that of creating runtime versions of the preserved objects. For each such object, this approach defines a graph that captures the semantics and layout, and identifies the data type encoded by each format. The runtime version then enables use of any software appropriate for a data type (Moore, Rajasekar, Watry, Corubolo, Harrison, and Fuselier 2013).

Future Prospects

Over the last few decades, increasing attention, expertise, and resources have been devoted to digital preservation. Interest has grown not only among archivists and other professions that focus on information with a relatively long-term perspective, but also from other areas, including the natural sciences, health care, architecture, and civil and mechanical engineering. These fields face complex digital-preservation challenges even in maintaining current records. Their interest and the resources they can commit provide a basis for optimism.

Conclusion

Digital preservation entails special challenges due to technological obsolescence, digital-media fragility, the complexity of digital encoding and the need to take advantage of technological progress. Considerable progress in addressing these challenges has been made in the last two decades, but digital preservation will remain challenging as long as information technology and user expectations continue to change.—*Ken Thibodeau*

Keywords: preservation, electronic records, digital information

Related Entries: Archival Preservation; Archival Standards; Audit and Certification (digital trusted repository); Chain of Preservation; Digital Repository

Bibliography

Duranti, Luciana, ed. *The Long-Term Preservation of Authentic Electronic Records: Findings of the InterPARES Project*. San Miniato (PI), Italy: Archilab, 2005. www.interpares.org/book/index.cfm (accessed November 2013).

Giaretta, David. *Advanced Digital Preservation.* Heidelberg: Springer, 2011.

International Standards Organization. *ISO 14721:2012: Space Data and Information Transfer Systems—Open Archival Information System (OAIS)—Reference Model*. Geneva, Switzerland: International Standards Organization, 2012.

McGovern, Nancy Y., and Katherine Skinner, eds. *Aligning National Approaches to Digital Preservation*. Atlanta, GA: Educopia Institute, 2012. www.educopia.org/sites/educopia.org/files/ANADP_Educopia_2012.pdf (accessed October 2013).

Moore, Reagan, Arcot Rajasekar, Paul Watry, Fabio Corubolo, John Harrison, and Jerome Fuselier. "Evolving Persistent Archives and Digital Library Systems: Integrating iRods, Cheshire3 and Multivalent." *The International Journal of Digital Curation* 8 (2013): 47–67. www.ijdc.net/index.php/ijdc/article/view/8.2.47/334 (accessed December 2013).

Thibodeau, Kenneth. "Overview of Technological Approaches to Digital Preservation and Challenges in Coming Years." Council on Library and Information Science, conference proceedings, The State of Digital Preservation: An International Perspective, April 24–25, 2002, publication 107, 4–31. www.clir.org/PUBS/reports/pub107/thibodeau.html (accessed November 2013).

———. "Wrestling with Shape-Shifters: Perspectives on Preserving Memory in the Digital Age." Conference proceedings, The Memory of the World in the Digital Age: Digitization and Preservation, an International Conference on Permanent Access to Digital Documentary Heritage. Edited by Luciana Duranti and Elizabeth Shaffer. UNESCO, 2013, 15–23. www.ciscra.org/docs/UNESCO_MOW2012_Proceedings_FINAL_ENG.zip (accessed July 2013).

DIGITAL RECORD

Archives New Zealand defines digital record in a simple, elegant, and straightforward way: "A digital record is a record that has been created in digital form" (Archives New Zealand n.d.). Although this is a good starting point, it is important to explore more fully the concepts that lay behind individual terms such as "digital" and "record." In the case of the word "digital," for instance, the *Oxford Dictionary* (2013) defines it as "(of signals or data) expressed as series of the digits 0 and 1, typically represented by values of a physical quantity such as voltage or magnetic polarization." In other words, a digital record is an entity that presents all of the attributes of a record but is recorded as a series of the digits 0 and 1 that requires a combination of computer hardware and software to render the record readable and understandable to a human. The Archives New Zealand definition includes "records that are born digital or have undergone conversion from a non-digital format" (National Archives of Australia n.d.).

The Concept

The expression "digital record" is relatively recent. In the early 1970s the term used by archivists and other records professionals to refer to what is today called a digital record was "machine-readable record," that is, record that can only be read by a machine. At the time, and decades before PCs and memory sticks, the definition conjured images of tapes and large disk packs. While the term was applied to what was stored on the tapes and disks, the focus was on the media. In fact some of the early approaches to retention and *disposition* of machine-readable records focused on scheduling tapes, the assumption being that there was a one-to-one correlation between a tape and its content. The media orientation is reflected in the definition developed by the Society of American Archivists (SAA), where a machine-readable record is "in a medium or format that requires a mechanical device to make it intelligible to humans" (Pearce-Moses 2005). Similarly, the definition developed by the International Council on Archives (ICA) states that machine-readable records are "records/archives, usually in code, recorded on a medium such as a magnetic disc, magnetic tape, or punched card/tape, whose contents are accessible only by machine" (International Council on Archives n.d.).

While the ICA definition seems to focus on recording *formats* requiring computer hardware and software to render, read, and understand, the SAA definition is broader because it embraces analogue recordings such as microfilm, videotapes, cassettes, and presumably the punch cards used in nonelectronic devices (e.g., weaving machines, tabulating equipment). This broader perspective is reflected implicitly in the definitions that were used in the Canadian access to information law and national archives legislation where it was embedded in the definition of record: "includes any correspondence, memorandum, book, plan map, drawing, pictorial or graphic work, photograph, film microform, sound recording, video tape, machine readable record, and any other documentary material, regardless of physical form or characteristics, and any copy thereof" (National Archives of Canada Act, section 2). An example of the broader perspective where machine-readable records can include records created through nonelectronic as well as electronic means is the definition developed by the British Columbia Ministry of Technology, Innovation and Citizen's Services, according to which a machine-readable record "means anything upon which information is stored or recorded such that a computer or other mechanical device can render the information intelligible" (British Columbia Ministry of Technology, Innovation and Citizen's Services 2008).

This broad interpretation of the expression *machine-readable record* became a concern to those who were looking for a term that referred specifically to records that could only be read by computer hardware and software. In the late 1970s there was a short-lived effort in the Canadian federal government to refer to such records as electronic data-processing (EDP) records. Within a short time, however, it was found that IT specialists and others thought the term referred to records documenting what was then called EDP systems rather than to the records generated as a result of the work processes supported by these systems.

The shift away from machine-readable record and EDP record occurred in the 1980s as networked personal computers were introduced and organizations began creating records that were being kept in electronic form on a variety of media, from floppy disks to hard disks in personal computers to hard disks supported on servers. The need to be more precise about what was being managed in this environment from a *recordkeeping* perspective increased with the volume and significance of records recorded in electronic form. Several organizations responded to this need by developing definitions of what became known as electronic records. Some of these definitions were somewhat stark, such as the ICA definition ("records on electronic storage media" [ICA 2005]) and the definition developed for the Model Requirements for records systems (MOREQ) by the European Commission ("a record which is in electronic form" [European Commission 2008]). In other cases, however, efforts were made to bring some precision to the definition in order to enable the term "electronic record" to be applied specifically to records that could only be read using a combination of computer hardware and software. One example of this is the definition developed by the Bureau of Canadian Archivists, "Electronic records are records that are encoded for manipulation by a computer" (2008). Another is that of the National Archives of Australia, which states that an electronic record is "a record created, communicated and/or maintained by means of electronic equipment. Although this term can refer to analogue materials (e.g., videotapes), it generally refers to records held in digital form on magnetic or optical computer storage media" (n.d.). Others, however, recognized that, even though the concept of electronic record was more specific than machine-readable record, the term could still be applied broadly to encompass a wide variety of analogue and digital recording formats and storage technologies from video tape and microfilm to hard disks and flash drives—in effect any device that was powered by electronic means.

At some point in the 1990s the term digital record began to appear. It arrived at an exciting time when new innovative thinking from research endeavors such as the Pittsburgh project, the UBC project, and Australian initiatives that shaped *continuum* theory provided records professionals with deeper insight into the nature of those records that could only be read by computer hardware and software. It put to rest the simplistic view that it was enough to say that such records were bits and bytes stored on a tape. Certainly the recording medium was viewed as part of the digital record, but it was also recognized that many other components of a record also come into play. Duranti and MacNeil explained that

> an electronic record, just like every traditional record, is comprised of medium (the physical carrier of the message), *form* (the rules of representation that allow for the communication of the message), *persons* (the entities acting by means of the record), action (the exercise of will that originates the record as a means of creating, maintaining, changing, or extinguishing situations), *context* (the juridical-administrative framework in which the action takes place), *archival bond* (the relationship that links each record to the previous and subsequent one and to all those which participate in the same activity), and content (the message that the record is intended to convey). However, with electronic records, those components are not inextricably joined one to the other, as in traditional records: they, and their parts, exist separately, and can be managed separately, unless they are consciously tied together for the purpose of ensuring the creation of reliable records and the preservation of authentic records. Strictly speaking, it is not possible to preserve an electronic record. It is always necessary to retrieve from storage the binary digits that make up the record and process them through some software for delivery or presentation. (Duranti and MacNeil 1996, 41)

While electronic record was used in the quote above, it is clear that the intent was to focus not on electronic analogue records but on those records that were recorded in the 0s and 1s that require a combination of hardware and software to access, render, understand, and use—in other words, digital records. Today there are several organizations that have developed definitions that capture not only the recording mode of the record but also the sophisticated and complex nature of the various components of the record that reside in its digital form. For instance, the InterPARES glossary states that a digital record is "a digital document that is treated and managed as a record" (n.d.). As mentioned at the beginning of this entry, Archives New Zealand

got right to the point by stating that a digital record is a "record that has been created in digital form" (n.d.). The State Records Authority of New South Wales elaborated on this definition by explaining that "a digital record is digital information, captured at a specific point in time, that is kept as evidence of business activity. Digital records means 'born digital' records such as emails, web pages, digital photographs, digital audio files, GIS files or database records, as well as scanned versions of paper records that have been digitized in business processes" (standard 10, sec. 1.6).

Conclusion

In stepping back and reviewing the terminological evolution that has taken place since the 1970s, one could argue that the path followed has been relatively linear with one term being superseded by another. The seemingly archaic term machine readable gave way to electronic, which in turn has been supplanted gradually by the term digital. While in some respects this evolutionary path has some validity and is being reflected in the migration many are making from electronic record to digital record, in actual fact the terms are highly related to one another and, collectively, provide the context within which terms such as digital record can be positioned and understood. The interrelationships can be best represented through a Boolean chart where the universe or the "whole" are machine-readable records. These are analogue and digital records that can only be read by machines that are powered through either electronic or nonelectronic means. Within this whole there is a subset of records called "electronic records." These are analogue and digital records that can only be read by machines that are powered through electronic means. Digital records are a subset of electronic records recorded in digital form by a certain class of electronically powered machines—namely computer hardware running software that enables the records to be accessed, rendered, and used. This interrelationship among the key terms is not new. For instance, the definition of digital record adopted by the National Archives of Australia makes it clear that digital records are a subset of electronic records: "A digital record is a record created and/or maintained by means of digital computer technology. Includes records that are 'born digital' or have undergone conversion from a non-digital format. Digital records are a subset of electronic records" (n.d.).

The term digital record is increasingly being adopted by a wide range of communities involved in various activities pertaining to the lifecycle management of records in a form and format requiring a combination of computer hardware and software to access, understand, and use. How long this term will remain in vogue before another term emerges to dominate the vocabulary is an open question. If a new term does emerge, it will be interesting to see how it will relate to the terms that have come before.—*John McDonald*

Keywords: electronic record, machine readable record, format, media

Related Entries: Digital Archives; Digital Records Forensics; Record(s)

Bibliography

Archives New Zealand. "Glossary." http://archives.govt.nz/advice/continuum-resource-kit/glossary/definitions-full-list#D.

British Columbia Ministry of Technology, Innovation and Citizen's Services. "FOIPP Act Policy and Procedures Manual." 2008. www.cio.gov.bc.ca/cio/priv_leg/manual/definitions/def.page#M.

Bureau of Canadian Archivists, Planning Committee on Descriptive Standards. "Appendix D: Glossary." In *Rules for Archival Description*. Ottawa: Bureau of Canadian Archivists, 1990; revised edition, July 2008.

Duranti, Luciana, and Heather MacNeil. "The Protection of the Integrity of Electronic Records: An Overview of the UBC-MAS Research Project." *Archivaria* 1 (42) (1996): 46–67. http://journals.sfu.ca/archivar/index.php/archivaria/article/view/12153/13158.

European Commission. "Model Requirements for the Management of Electronic Records." 2008. http://ec.europa.eu/archival-policy/moreq/doc/moreq2_spec.pdf.

International Council on Archives. "Multilingual Archival Terminology." www.ciscra.org/mat/termdb/term/230, www.ciscra.org/mat/termdb/term/165.

International Research on Permanent Authentic Records in Electronic Systems (Interpares) "Terminology Database." N.d. www.interpares.org/ip3/ip3_terminology_db.cfm?letter=d&term=222.

Kirschenbaum, M. G., R. Ovenden, and G. Redwine, with research assistance from R. Donahue. *Digital Forensics and Born-Digital Content in Cultural Heritage Collections*. Washington, DC: Council on Library and Information Resources, 2010.

National Archives of Australia. "Glossary." N.d. www.naa.gov.au/records-management/publications/glossary.aspx#d.

Pearce-Moses, Richard. *A Glossary of Archival and Records Terminology*. Chicago: Society of American Archivists, 2005. www.archivists.org/glossary/index.asp.

"Standard 10—Standard on Digital Recordkeeping." State Records Authority of New South Wales, 2008. www.records.nsw.gov.au/recordkeeping/rules/standards/digital-recordkeeping/resolveuid/4ff40081ee934d2ea78be5fa0b2ff664.

DIGITAL RECORDS FORENSICS

Two of the most challenging issues presented by digital technology to the law enforcement, *records management*, archival and legal professions, researchers, business, government, and the public are the identification of *records* in digital systems, and the determination of their *authenticity* (Duranti 2009). These issues may be addressed from the archival perspective, backed by *archival theory* and methodology, and specifically by digital *diplomatics*. They are also addressed from a technological perspective, by the methods and tools of digital forensics. At a basic level, both digital *archivists* and digital forensics practitioners are concerned with discovering, understanding, describing, and presenting information inscribed on digital media. In recent years, tools and methods developed by digital forensics specialists have been adopted and adapted by cultural heritage institutions for *digital preservation* and curation (John 2012).

A convergence of perspectives and methods of the digital forensic investigator and the digital archivist is gaining momentum, and may be referred to as digital records forensics, or archival forensics. Shared theoretical perspectives include: (1) authorship and identity (authenticity of origin and forgery), (2) informational pattern and change over time (reconstruction and relationships among extant traces and objects), (3) evidential *reliability* (provenance and *integrity*), and (4) digital materiality and ornament (contextual detail and interpretation). There are also common pressing challenges in finding, processing, and sustaining digital information: (1) the volume of a person's life information spread across myriad devices, and the exacerbating complexity of diverse applications and locations—local devices, network servers, and remote cloud services; (2) the necessary versatility of tools, techniques, and models required to capture and investigate digital information, including *metadata* and *description*; (3) the forward-looking process and activity required to ensure sustainability and long-term digital preservation; and (4) the intensifying role of *information assurance*, data security planning, and protection of privacy and other digital rights (Rogers and John 2013).

The Archival Functions

The core archival functions "upon which archivists build their scientific, professional and educational profiles" are identified as *appraisal* and *acquisition*, *arrangement* and *description*, retention and *preservation*, management and administration, and reference and *access*. Furthermore, research is the foundation of each archival activity, "a professional function if not the core of all functions" (Duranti and Michetti 2012, 2).

Archival research has focused historically on records, defined as *documents* made or received in the course of practical activity, and set aside for further action or reference (Duranti and Thibodeau 2006), as the primary objects of investigation. *Archivists* are concerned with establishing the evidentiary capacity of documents, and analyzing their evidential value, whether they are preserved primarily as records (as with a public organization) or for their informational value as personal memory or legacy (as with a personal archives). According to Menne-Haritz, "Evidence . . . consists of signs, of signals, not primarily of words. . . . All those are nonverbal signs that must be interpreted in context to disclose their meaning. To one who understands them, they will tell how processes worked and who was responsible for which decision" (Menne-Haritz 1994, 537).

The science of diplomatics originated in the seventeenth century to establish the authenticity, and indirectly, the reliability, of archival documents, in order to determine rights and to identify and eliminate forgeries. It studies the genesis, forms, and transmission of archival documents, the relationships of the documents with associated actions, *persons*, and legal consequences (Duranti 1998). Digital diplomatics has developed and refined the theory and methodology of traditional diplomatics and the principles of archival knowledge to provide a framework for assessing the authenticity in digital systems, and offers archivists a powerful methodology for analyzing *digital records*. However, digital diplomatics alone may not be sufficient to understand the challenges posed to information inscribed by increasingly complex digital systems (Duranti 2009).

The Digital Forensic Functions

Digital forensics developed for the purposes of law enforcement in order to investigate computer crime and bring digital *evidence* to trial. It applies scientific principles and methodologies in reconstructing past events and artifacts, and forensic tools have developed apace with technological advancements. It is defined as "the use of scientifically derived and proven methods toward the preservation, collection, validation, identification, analysis, interpretation, documentation, and presentation of digital evidence derived from digital sources for the purpose of facilitation or furthering the reconstruction of events found to be criminal, or helping to anticipate unauthorized actions shown to be disruptive to planned operations" (Palmer 2001, 16).

Drawing on computer science theory and the physical forensics disciplines, digital-forensics practitioners and researchers are actively developing models to help standardize digital-forensics investigations and form the basis of new theory. These models identify core digital-forensics activities, from which we can draw parallels with archival functions. Beebe and Clark (2005) have proposed a general process model that isolates preparation and incident response, data collection, data analysis, presentation of findings, and incident closure. The first three may be compared with archival functions of appraisal and acquisition; data analysis parallels arrangement and description elements of presentation of findings (also evident in arrangement and description) may be seen in reference and access; and elements of incident closure may be compared with archival retention and preservation.

Convergent Utility of Evidence

Digital forensics thus offers archivists another way of conceptualizing digital objects and assessing their integrity and authenticity (Duranti 2009). Digital forensic tools and techniques are increasingly being tested in trusted *digital repositories* to assist acquisition, *selection*, appraisal, description, and preservation of cultural and scientific heritage materials (Kirschenbaum, Ovenden, and Redwine 2010).

Both digital-forensic scientists and practitioners and digital archivists are faced with a diversity of digital media, a huge and increasing volume of digital material, and the complexity of the problems of capture and analysis of digital objects and media that come from almost anywhere. To address this diversity, it is necessary to have a variety of tools and not to rely on any single technology or methodology. Workflows and procedures need to be receptive to change, designed for flexibility and adaptability so that new *functions* can be quickly embraced and integrated.

This novelty, diversity, and complexity of tools and digital objects in turn calls for a careful and extensive marshalling of *metadata* and documentation. This is a requirement that may draw on the rapidly increasing experience and expertise of the digital *archives* and data curation communities.

Historically, much of the analysis software used by digital forensics practitioners has been proprietary and commercial or custom-built for local use. Increasingly, open source solutions are being sought and developed, particularly open-source formats for storing disk images. This benefits forensics analysts, supports admissibility requirements of digital evidence at trial, and enhances capacity for archival processing and long-term preservation in digital repositories (Altheide and Carvey 2011).

Long-Term and Lifecycle Considerations for Digital Preservation

The long-term sustainability of digital objects and their continuing accessibility and usability over time have been primary drivers for the digital-preservation community, and are increasingly a concern for the digital-forensic community as well. Although the time frames of legal and archival activities are different, with archives generally holding material indefinitely if not "forever," also in the legal context it is often necessary to care for artifacts for periods longer than digital media and objects can be expected to survive without due care and attention.

Security, Privacy, and Digital Rights

The ease with which digital material can be altered, intentionally or accidentally, and disseminated, shared, combined, and repurposed has driven security, privacy, and rights concerns across domains and disciplines. Information and network security, measured in various types of integrity analysis and control, is foundational to digital forensics, while protection of privacy and management of digital rights are at the forefront of archival concerns. While digital forensics addresses privacy and security in the context of intrusion detection and incidence response, digital archivists and curators must be aware of privacy and rights requirements in order to manage description of and access to material entrusted to their care.

Shared Theoretical Perspectives— Authorship and Identity

Traditional concepts of *provenance* and identity are severely undermined by the default of anonymity on the Internet. The identity of creator, author, writer, or originator may be obscured and separated from the inscribed message by virtue of the layers of technology that mediate between physical person and transmitted document. Just as archival principles have been combined with diplomatic concepts to provide a methodology to analyze traditional digital objects, new knowledge from digital forensics is extending digital diplomatics to address issues of provenance, identity, and integrity in increasingly complex digital environments.

Integrity and Change over Time

Integrity, once presumed from the controls on the procedures dictated by records' creators, now may be assessed in the absence of or further to provenance and explicit identity, at both the physical (bits) and logical (meaning) layers of the record. Digital forensics offers a way of conceptualizing digital objects and assessing their integrity that complements and is complemented by digital diplomatics in understanding and assessing the authenticity of digital objects (Duranti 2009).

Procedures for Establishing Authenticity and Reliability of Evidence

Preservation and forensics share a concern with provenance and the application of tested and certifiably reliable protocols and tools: the collection of a set of digital objects, the evidence (legal or historical), and its subsequent demonstrable authentication, once it is in the care of the responsible custodian.

Three central requirements of digital forensics match those of archivists: capturing the information without changing it, demonstrating that the information has not been changed or that the changes can be identified, and analyzing and auditing the information, again without changing it.

Some of the functionality of forensic software can be found in assorted tools that exist independently of the forensic community, some freely available on the internet. An important distinction is that forensic software is subject to the scrutiny of the courts as well as rigorous formal testing conducted according to specified protocols and overseen by independent bodies such as the National Institute of Justice and the National Institute of Standards and Technology in the United States.

Because digital evidence is extracted from digital media, its reliability and integrity depends in part on the means of its extraction, which must be conducted and accounted for according to scientific principles. The assessment of reliability and integrity is based on procedures that are repeatable, verifiable, objective, and transparent. Digital forensics tools are subject to a demonstration that they have been tested, that the error rate is known and within acceptable limits, that the tool or procedure has been published and subjected to peer review, and that it is generally accepted in the relevant scientific community.

Digital Materiality, Virtualization, and the Importance of Ornament

Just as curators and scholars attach significance to the materiality of objects, to their look and feel and

behavior, in the fullest detail, so forensic examiners have come to realize the importance of these qualities. Virtual forensic computing, involving the use of virtual machines, emulators, and 3-D virtual reality, allows material to be presented in a manner that matches (to varying degrees) the original computer environment as well as the real landscape setting itself (Schofield 2009).

Conclusion

Descriptive process models for digital forensics, however generalized, are necessarily limited. At the most basic level, abstracted models of digital forensics activities are based on three major functions: acquisition, analysis, and presentation. The theoretical concepts to be embedded and realized in any abstract model are revealed in principles of practice that protect the authenticity, integrity, and reliability of digital material for the immediate purpose: presentation of digital evidence at trial or investigation of intrusion. Increasingly, long-term preservation is also required.

Compare this with key archival functions, articulated in a wealth of scholarly archival literature, and central to the work of digital-heritage preservation: appraisal and acquisition, arrangement and description, retention and preservation. Preservation of digital heritage depends on tools and methodologies that protect the authenticity, integrity, and reliability of digital material, and ensure its accessibility and usability over time and across technological change. The affordances of digital technologies are driving a synergy between archival practice and digital forensics to create an emerging discipline of digital records forensics.—*Corinne Rogers*

Keywords: digital diplomatics, digital forensics, digital records
Related Entries: Authenticity; Digital Preservation; Digital Records; Diplomatics

Bibliography

Altheide, C., and H. Carvey. *Digital Forensics with Open Source Tools*, 1st edition. New York: Syngress, 2011.

Beebe, N. L., and J. G. Clark. "A Hierarchical, Objectives-Based Framework for the Digital Investigations Process." *Digital Investigation* 2 (2) (2005): 147–67. DOI: 10.1016/j.diin.2005.04.002.

Carrier, B. "Defining Digital Forensic Examination and Analysis Tools Using Abstraction Layers." *International Journal of Digital Evidence* 1 (4) (2003): 1–12.

Duranti, L. *Diplomatics: New Uses for an Old Science*. Lanham, MD: Scarecrow Press, 1998.

———. "From Digital Diplomatics to Digital Records Forensics." *Archivaria* 68 (Fall 2009): 39–66.

Duranti, L., and G. Michetti. *Archival Method*. Unpublished manuscript. Vancouver, BC, 2012, 1–14.

Duranti, L., and K. Thibodeau. "The Concept of Record in Interactive, Experiential and Dynamic Environments: The View of InterPARES." *Archival Science* 6 (1) (2006): 13–68.

John, J. L. "Digital Forensics and Preservation." *Digital Preservation Coalition*, 2012. DOI: http://dx.doi.org/10.7207/twr12-03.

Menne-Haritz, A. "Appraisal or Documentation: Can We Appraise Archives by Selecting Content?" *The American Archivist* 57 (3) (1994): 528–42.

Palmer, G. "A Road Map for Digital Forensic Research." DFRWS Technical Report, 2001. www.dfrws.org/2001/dfrws-rm-final.pdf.

Rogers, C., and J. John. "Shared Perspectives, Common Challenges: A History of Digital Forensics & Ancestral Computing for Digital Heritage." In *The Memory of the World in the Digital Age: Digitization and Preservation*. Vancouver, BC: UNESCO, 2013, 314–36.

Schofield, D. "Graphical Evidence: Forensic Examinations and Virtual Reconstructions." *Australian Journal of Forensic Sciences* 41 (2009): 131–45.

DIGITAL REPOSITORY

A repository, traditionally, has been a place of protected storage. Contemporary digital repositories, however, are defined by the communities that they serve and the services that are offered through them rather than the mere act of storage. Services offered through digital repositories may include long-term *preservation* and storage, but they are just as likely to include implementing *access* protocols, serving up convenience copies of materials preserved elsewhere, enabling collaboration, or promoting the review or reuse of data. The services provided through digital repositories are as numerous as the communities they serve or the types of data that they store. Digital repositories may offer open or restricted access to materials, and may offer free or paid access to content.

A digital repository is neither a thing nor a location. Layered system architectures and distributed computing environments make it likely that a digital repository will consist of various software layers performing discrete functions while running on distributed hardware components. Major components or functions that make up digital repositories include: *metadata* management systems; storage locations; content-management systems to regulate access; search systems; *authentication* systems to determine roles and responsibilities for human and machine agents; validation systems to ensure the *authenticity* and *reliability* of digital materials; *format* and media management for *accessibility* and digital *preservation*; and systems to control redundancy to protect against errors, disasters, and routine bit decay.

The characteristics and qualities of a digital repository are determined by the composition and objectives of a given designated community, the resources, computing constraints, and regulatory/policy environment of the hosting organization and the capacities of the individuals who manage and run the various hardware and software implementations that make up the system. There is no standard digital repository, only countless unique digital repositories. The remainder of this article will discuss three types of digital repositories that are often identified in the literature: trusted digital repositories, institutional and community repositories, and data repositories.

Trusted Digital Repository (TDR)

In 2002 the Online Computer Library Center's (OCLC) Research Library Group (RLG) issued *Trusted Digital Repositories: Attributes and Responsibilities: An RLG-OCLC Report*. Explicitly indebted to the emerging *Reference Model for an Open Archival Information System* (OAIS), the trust digital repository (TDR) report helped to establish the concept that a digital repository consists of more than just hardware and software. Stressing the inclusion of administrative responsibility, organizational viability, and financial sustainability among the attributes of a TDR, the RLG report helped to move the conversation beyond the technical capacities of a particular system. The TDR report recognized that technology is not enough to create trust: organizations create trust through responsible stewardship, itself demonstrated by transparent and accountable management of the repository, and by demonstrating long-term financial stability.

The report also acknowledged that moving forward on *digital preservation* would require that institutions work together. To enable this common effort, the first attribute of a TDR is identified as compliance with OAIS, thus ensuring that different projects could discuss their efforts with reference to a common terminology and conceptual library.

The RLG report included a list of recommendations, the first of which was to develop a process for the certification of digital repositories. In 2003 RLG, with the U.S. National Archives and Records Administration, launched a task force to create a certification process for TDRs. The result is the Trusted Repositories Audit and Certification (TRAC) criteria and checklist. In keeping with the principles articulated in the RLG TDR report, the TRAC criteria address organizational infrastructure (including governance, procedural accountability, and financial sustainability), digital object management (including preservation planning, information management, and access management), as well as technical infrastructure and security risk management. The International Standards Organization subsequently issued standards based on OAIS (ISO 14721) and TRAC (ISO 16363). ISO 16919 establishes requirements for bodies providing audit and certification of candidate trustworthy digital repositories.

The Centre for Research Libraries (CRL) uses the TRAC criteria to perform formal audits of digital repositories that aim to become certified TDRs. As of 2013 only four repositories have been certified by CRL as TRAC-compliant, despite the proliferation of institutional repositories, community repositories, and data repositories on the Internet. This suggests that the TRAC certification process serves a limited, though important, niche. Paucity of certifications notwithstanding, the TRAC criteria remain important for self-audit and establishing community standards, as are other auditing criteria such as the

Digital Repository Audit Method Based on Risk Assessment (DRAMBORA).

Institutional Repositories and Community Repositories

In the early 2000s the apparent consensus was that institutional repositories were for capturing and providing access to the intellectual output of research institutions such as universities. Since then institutional repositories have come to serve a multiplicity of communities and objectives and have been completely redefined. Institutional repositories today fulfill a number of roles, including but not limited to capturing and providing access to intellectual outputs. Other services include the creation of temporary aggregations for use in teaching, publishing services for journals, monographs or conference proceedings, and space to enable intra- and inter-institutional collaborations. As increasingly diverse institutions and communities have deployed digital repositories, they have been used to assert and protect intellectual property and create cultural and social cohesion.

The shifting mandate for institutional repositories reflects the fundamental logic of the OAIS reference model: that repositories exist not to serve institutions but to serve communities. Institutions host repositories, but they do so on behalf of communities that only occasionally exist within institutional boundaries. The initial justification for institutional repositories—to capture the intellectual output of a research institution—did not always work because the diversity contained within a modern research university does not result in a cohesive community in terms of research interests or outputs. Hosting temporary aggregations for use in teaching is one example of a genuine community—a course—that exists within the bounds of a research university. Hosting a journal or conference proceedings is an example of an institutional repository serving a community that exists only partly within its institutional boundaries.

The emergence of open-source and specialized tools or components for digital repositories, designed to meet the needs of specific communities, has enabled the spread of digital repositories beyond research institutions. Indigenous digital repositories offer one example of how digital repositories serve the needs of diverse communities.

Ngata et al. (2012) describe the use of a digital repository put in place by the Maori tribal organization Toi Hauiti. This repository enables the restoration, consolidation, and expansion of traditional knowledge through the digital repatriation of objects and documents dispersed by colonialism, and by making the resulting digital collections available to tribal members themselves scattered throughout the world. Christen 2011 describes the development of Mukurtu, a content-management system designed to implement indigenous access protocols while working with a variety of back-end data-management tools. Ara Irititja KMS (Ormond-Parker and Sloggett 2012) is a knowledge-management system developed to meet the specific needs of the Anangu people of Central Australia, but that may be adaptable to meet the needs of other indigenous communities. Like the digital repository described by Ngata et al. (2012), tools such as Mukurtu CMS and Ara Irititja KMS allow indigenous communities to reclaim and control digital representations of objects and documents to advance the objectives of indigenous communities themselves.

Data Repositories

Research data repositories offer a clear example of how digital repositories are evolving to fit into ever-changing digital information ecologies. Data archiving provides a necessary counterpart to the journal publication of research findings, allowing other researchers to verify, extend, and reapply the analysis and conclusions of their peers. This is remixing for researchers: data repositories allow researchers to verify, repeat, sample, and mash-up the work of others in their field.

Uploading data into a data repository provides a surrogate measure of the trustworthiness of a particular study, as well as the ability to test that trustworthiness as necessary, by re-running experiments or by sampling data. Data repositories, then, exist as part of an information ecology that remains focused on peer-reviewed publication as its gold standard. Researcher requirements to have data structured according to domain-specific metadata standards reduce the likelihood that interdisciplinary data repositories can meet their needs. This conforms to expectations set in the OAIS reference model that a

digital archives requires an identifiable and specified designated community.

Digital repositories have developed to meet the needs of specific designated communities. Archives are increasingly turning to linked and open data as a means of making their holdings discoverable and usable by their users. It is possible that semantic structuring and markup will enable *digital archives* to serve multiple designated communities from within a common digital infrastructure.

Conclusion

Digital repositories defy generalization, both in their architectures, which are often heterogeneous, layered, and distributed, and in their uses, which may include information preservation, promoting open access to information, promoting collaboration within a community, or supporting the nondigital knowledge base of a community. Shifting mandates for institutional repositories reflect the fundamental logic of the OAIS reference model: that repositories exist to serve communities.—*Greg Bak*

Keywords: digital repository, trusted digital repository, OAIS reference model

Related Entries: Archival Standards; Audit and Certification (Trusted Digital Repositories); Chain of Preservation; Digital Preservation

Bibliography

Canadian Association of Research Libraries. *Research Data: Unseen Opportunities*. Ottawa: CARL, 2009.

Christen, Kimberly. "Opening Archives: Respectful Repatriation." *American Archivist* 74 (2011): 185–210. http://archivists.metapress.com/content/4233nv6nv6428521/fulltext.pdf.

Consultative Committee for Space Data Systems. *Audit and Certification of Trustworthy Digital Repositories*. Magenta Book. Washington, DC: CCSDS Secretariat, September 2011.

———. *Reference Model for an Open Archival Information System (OAIS)*. Magenta Book. Washington, DC: CCSDS Secretariat, June 2012.

Digital Curation Centre and Digital Preservation Europe. "DRAMBORA: About." Last modified February 1, 2008. www.repositoryaudit.eu/about.

Fear, Kathleen, and Devan Donaldson. "Provenance and Credibility in Scientific Data Repositories." *Archival Science* 12 (3) (2012): 319–39. DOI: 10.1007/s10502-012-9172-7.

Furlough, Mike. "What We Talk about When We Talk about Repositories." *Reference and User Services Quarterly* 49 (2009): 118–23, 132. DOI: 10.5860/rusq.49n1.18.

International Standards Organization. *ISO 14721:2012: Space Data and Information Transfer Systems—Open Archival Information System (OAIS)—Reference Model.* Geneva, Switzerland: International Standards Organization, 2012.

———. *ISO 16363:2012: Space Data and Information Transfer Systems—Audit and Certification of Trustworthy Digital Repositories.* Geneva, Switzerland: International Standards Organization, 2012.

———. *ISO 16919:2014: Space Data and Information Transfer Systems—Requirements for Bodies Providing Audit and Certification of Candidate Trustworthy Digital Repositories.* Geneva, Switzerland: International Standards Organization, 2012.

Ngata, Wayne, Hera Ngata-Gibson, and Amiria Salmond. "Te Ataakura: Digital Taonga and Cultural Innovation." *Journal of Material Culture* 17 (3) (2012): 229–44. DOI: 10.1177/1359183512453807.

Ormond-Parker, Lyndon, and Robyn Sloggett. "Local Archives and Community Collecting in the Digital Age." *Archival Science* 12 (2) (2012): 191–212. DOI: 10.1007/s10502-011-9154-1.

DIGITIZATION

Digitization involves the transfer of analog material to binary code through the use of a scanner or digital camera. According to the Digital Library Toolkit (2003), the creation and management of digital information incorporates a two-stage process. The first stage is the process of digitization, which converts the physical medium into a digital (or binary) representation of the analog material (Noerr 2003, 11). Digitization is dependent on the use of a scanner or digital camera to create a computer-readable image of a scanned object. Most scanning devices consist of a platen made of glass, a series of mirrors and lenses, as well as a light-sensing integrated circuit known as a charged coupled device (CCD). "Light-sensitive photosites arrayed along the CCD convert levels of brightness into electronic signals that are then processed into a digital image" ("Moving Theory into Practice," para. 1).

The second stage involves the extraction of information from the digital object. The extraction process utilizes optical character recognition (OCR) software, which identifies the shapes of the letters of the alphabet (Noerr 2003, 11). Yet, not every scanned object requires the use of OCR software. In fact, certain objects such as photographs require manual, text-based indexing methods. The digital image technician must understand how to manage the available technology in order to appropriately capture and catalog the information.

Digital imaging technology has changed the way many organizations collect, store, and disseminate information. Digital imaging technology has also changed the way users understand information by enhancing their perception of the scanned material. Many *collections* are selected for digitization to enhance the user's knowledge of the physical object. With the help of image-editing software such as Adobe Photoshop, information contained within a *document* or photograph that was once imperceptible to the unaided eye could be enhanced, viewed, and experienced for the first time (Darnton 2009, 57).

Selecting for Digitization

To build a trusted repository of digital objects, successful digitization programs require extensive planning and collaboration on the part of staff and volunteers. The materials selected for digitization should reflect not only the mission and goals of the organization but also the needs of its users. According to the Northeast Document Conservation Center (NEDCC) (2000), successful digitization projects are dependent on the relationship between three factors: how the objects will be used, the status of the analog material, and technological requirements during the conversion process (15). According to the NEDCC (2000) the methods for evaluation are based on three factors: use, value, and risk. Value is best determined by informational, administrative, artifactual, associational, evidential, and monetary issues (55). Risk is most often associated with *preservation* needs, but other forms include legal and social issues (56). Use is determined by the amount of times an item or a collection is requested.

Stewards of cultural heritage should consider the costs and risks before starting a digitization project. One area of risk relates to the copyright status of items found in the collection. Works published in the United States prior to 1923 (or before 1964 and not renewed) are in public domain and available for digitization. An institution does not have the right to digitize and virtually reproduce copyrighted material. For more information, refer to the U.S. Code, title 17, section 108, "Limitations on Exclusive Rights: Reproduction by Libraries and Archives" and Stanford University's *Copyright and Fair Use Overview*.

Planning for Digitization

The focus of any digitization project should be on the creation and long-term management of high-resolution digital surrogates. Digitization involves the transfer of analog material into binary code. The size of the digital object varies depending on the scanning software's resolution and bit depth. It is important to note that digitization does not ensure long-term *preservation*. An institution is responsible for managing digital objects through curation procedures such as monitoring an object's *lifecycle* process (i.e., *creation*, retention, transformation, or *disposition*). *Digital preservation* requires a long-term investment in terms of funding, resources, and a knowledgeable staff to maintain the collection. The financial commitment alone is often too great for an organization to take lightly. The planning phase of a digitization project will explore whether an organization has the finances, resources, and staff capable of creating and maintaining the *integrity* of hundreds, possibly thousands of digital objects, through multiple hardware and software migrations, indefinitely.

The more material selected for digitization, the longer and more costly a digitization project becomes. Prior to starting a digitization project, it is helpful to conduct benchmarking evaluations in order to determine the most appropriate technological requirements. Benchmarking is an essential activity for determining conversion requirements and image quality. Benchmarking also helps an institution determine the time it will take to perform scanning and image-editing tasks. During a benchmarking evaluation, the organization establishes guidelines on quality measures such as resolution, threshold, bit depth, color management, compression, and file format type.

Scanning Workflows

Developing a workflow for specific portions of a digitization project improves scanning time while also keeping the process consistent. During a digitization project, there are different workflows to develop. For instance, the preset workflow for a printed image prescribes the color, resolution, and type of file desired for the resulting digital surrogate. The presets for large format prints, glass negatives, film negatives, and slides are all different. Workflows also describe the process of preparing analog material for scanning, including best practices in handling and processing. By developing a workflow, an organization can become more proficient at scanning and processing hundreds of images in a single session.

Scanning Software

Creating a quality scan is dependent on many factors including the knowledge of the individual and the capability of the hardware and software. The most important aspect of a digitization project is to determine long- and short-term goals. What is the purpose of scanning the images? For cultural-heritage institutions, the inspiration might be to improve access, limit handling, and ensure long-term retrieval. All of these factors play a role in determining the type of scan created.

Adjusting the scanning software's input and output options affect the quality of the scan as well as the files in the collection. The interface of most scanning software features options such as input, output, crop, filter, color, and preferences. It is important to use the options panel to adjust the software's scanning settings. The input options, or image-adjustment options, use keywords such as source, mode, media, bits per pixel, or resolution. Input and output options vary depending on the software, but aspects such as media, bits per pixel, and resolution are consistent with most programs.

The "mode" option is automatically sensed for most scanners; yet in some cases, this option is set manually. The "mode" option for most Epson photo-scanning software specifies the type of scan and whether the scanned data came from reflective (paper-based) or transmissive (cellulose) media. There are many different types of reflective media to choose from such as continuous tone (photographic prints) halftone (magazine or newspaper) or bi-level (line art or text). Two of the most important input options are "bits per pixel" and "resolution." The method in which these options are set depends on how much detail or the level of image quality the organization wants, as well as how much storage space (i.e., local or network storage) is available. The number of bits assigned per pixel determines the number of colors displayed; the higher the bits per pixel, the greater the quality and file size. For higher-quality scans, most organizations set their options to sixteen bits per pixel or higher.

Output options enable an organization to specify the types of files written while scanning, as well as the file names and their pathways. It is important to specify a default folder for file operation. The file name also indicates a path to a subfolder of the default folder through a relative path. Determining which file format to select for scanning depends on various factors such as the type of material in the collection, costs and budget, and capacity of the local and/or networked storage. For photographic images, master files are typically scanned as TIFF (Tagged Image File Format) to create higher-quality, lossless files. Lossless compression ensures that the original data from a file can be reconstructed after it is compressed. However, lossless compression also leads to large file sizes. The organization must determine the level of commitment and investment in local and/or networked storage options prior to scanning large quantities of TIFF images.

Digitization Concepts

- Bit Depth: Determines the number of bits used to indicate the color of a single pixel in a bitmapped image. The precision to which a pixel could specify color is considered its bit depth, or color depth.
- DPI (Dots per Inch): A measurement of printer resolution defined by how many dots of ink are placed on the page when the image is printed.

- Dynamic Range: Involves the tonal ratio between the maximum and minimum light intensities, or the lightest light and the darkest dark. Dynamic range could also be used to describe a scanner's ability to reproduce the tonal information of an image.
- Grayscale: Range of shades of gray varying from the darkest possible shade (black) to the lightest possible shade (white).
- PPI (Pixels per Inch): The amount of pixels on a computer monitor. Pixels per inch describe the creation and display of images for onscreen use. DPI is often mistaken for PPI.
- Resolution: Measured by the numbers of pixels per inch, resolution enables the viewer to distinguish fine spatial detail. Resolution affects the level of detail contained within an image; the higher the resolution, the more pixels captured.
- RGB: A color model where red, green, and blue are added to produce a broad array of other colors.

Conclusion

An organization has much to consider before, during, and after a digitization project. Such a project involves not only an understanding of the mission, goals, and needs of an organization and its assets but also technical knowledge of imaging hardware and software, operating systems, file management, as well as local and network storage. Collaboration during a digitization project is essential. Most organizations consult with individuals who have knowledge and experience with digital-imaging technology. As always, it is important to seek advice from organizations such as the National Archives and Records Administration, the Society of American Archivists, the North East Document Conservation Center (NEDCC), and the Association for Information Science and Technology.—*Matt Carmichael*

Keywords: digitization, scanning, resolution, dynamic range, bit depth, DPI
Related Entries: Digital Archives; Digital Records; Digital Repository

Bibliography

Besser, H., and J. Trant. *Introduction to Imaging: Issues in Constructing an Image Database.*

Santa Monica, CA: Getty Art History Information Program, 1995. www.getty.edu/research/publications/electronic_publications/introimages/index.html (accessed November 11, 2012).

"Copyright and Fair Use Overview." Stanford University, 2010. http://fairuse.stanford.edu/Copyright_and_Fair_Use_Overview/index.html.

"Copyright Law of the United States and Related Laws Contained in Title 17 of the United States Code." U.S. Copyright Office, 2012. www.copyright.gov/title17/circ92.pdf.

Darnton, R. *The Case for Books: Past, Present, and Future*. Public Affairs: New York, 2009.

"Moving Theory into Practice. Digital Imaging Tutorial. How Scanning Works 2000–2003." Cornell University. www.library.cornell.edu/preservation/tutorial/technical/technicalB-02.html.

NISO Framework Advisory Group. *A Framework of Guidance for Building Good Digital Collections*, 2nd edition. Bethesda, MD: National Information Standards Organization, 2004. http://framework.niso.org (accessed November 11, 2012).

Noerr, P. *The Digital Library Tool Kit*, 3rd edition. Santa Clara, CA: Sun Microsystems, 2003. www.ncsi.iisc.ernet.in/raja/is214/is214-2005-01-04/digital_library_toolkit-ed3.pdf (accessed November 11, 2012).

Sitts, M., ed. *Handbook for Digital Projects: A Management Tool for Preservation and Access*, 1st edition. Andover, MA: Northeast Document Conservation Center, 2000. www.ncsi.iisc.ernet.in/raja/is214/is214-2006-01-04/dman.pdf (accessed November 11, 2012).

DIPLOMATICS

Diplomatics (diplomatic—British; *diplomatique*—French) is defined as the analysis of the *creation*, form, and *status of transmission* of archival documents or *records*, and their relationship with the facts represented in them and with their creator, in order to identify, evaluate, and communicate their true nature (Duranti 1998). Its focus of inquiry is the *document*, specifically the archival document, defined as "the written evidence, compiled according to a determined form—that is variable depending on place, period, person, transaction—of facts having a juridical nature" (Von Sickel 1867, quoted in Duranti 1998, 43). Diplomatics provides a systematic method to analyze the external and internal elements of documentary form, the circumstances of the writing, and the juridical nature of the fact communicated.

Diplomatics developed in Europe in the seventeenth century in order to establish the *authenticity* of medieval deeds and charters whose origins were unknown or suspect. Following publication of Dom Jean Mabillon's foundational text on the subject, *De Re Diplomatica Libre VI* (1681), diplomatics came to be taught in faculties of law across Europe, and formed the foundation of modern *archival science* and of textual criticism of historical sources. While diplomatic criticism continues to be used today in the study of ancient documents, the science of diplomatics has been extended to aid analysis of contemporary legal, governmental, and bureaucratic documents, and its theory and methods are finding particular relevance in the study of born-digital material.

History of Diplomatics

The term *diplomatic* derives from the Greek *diploo* (to double), and Latin *diploma* (doubled), exemplified by the Roman diptych formed from two plates hinged together and conferring various rights and privileges. The use of the term *diploma* to refer to formal documents was resurrected by Renaissance humanists and still today describes legal records characterized by solemnity, such as those conferring academic degrees.

The need for a rigorous analysis of ancient diplomas arose from the proliferation of forgeries in the early Middle Ages, due to war, dislocation, and the increasing requirement to document transactions previously validated by oral traditions. Until the sixth century, however, there were no formal criteria for identifying these documentary forgeries. Authenticity—the quality of an archival document or *record* that it is what it purports to be—was understood as deriving from the circumstances of documents' *creation*—if known, or from the place of *preservation*. As historical documents of questionable *provenance* were increasingly presented as *evidence* of rights, the need for alternative ways of establishing authenticity increased, and techniques of documentary criticism began to be developed and formalized.

Sophisticated methods of analysis developed in the seventeenth century in response to legal conflicts resulting from the Thirty Years' War in Germany and struggles to assert ancient privileges in France (known as the *bella diplomatica* or diplomatic wars). One specific conflict led to the articulation of the fundamental principles and methods of the science of diplomatics. Dom Jean Mabillon, of the Benedictine order, wrote the seminal work on diplomatics, *De Re Diplomatica* (1681), to systematically refute claims of forgery of Merovingian documents (most of them from Benedictine monasteries) made by the Jesuit Daniel van Papenbroeck. Papenbroeck subsequently acknowledged the validity of Mabillon's work, which became the foundation of subsequent treatises on diplomatics in Germany, Spain, England, Italy, and France. One of the most comprehensive was the book produced by Dom René-Prosper Tassin and Dom Charles-François Toustain, the *Nouveau traité de diplomatique* (1750–1765), which introduced "special diplomatics," that is, the application of the concepts and methods of diplomatics to the criticism of documents produced by specific chanceries (Duranti 1998). Subsequently, diplomatics began to be taught in faculties of law across Europe and, from the nineteenth century onward, studies in diplomatics and paleography became part of the medieval history curriculum. Publication of collections of medieval documents promoted diplomatic knowledge. When in 1821 the École des Chartres was founded in Paris to train French *archivists*, diplomatics was further developed to support the study of documents for both historical and legal research.

General Diplomatics

General diplomatics is the body of concepts and methods that guide diplomatic criticism. At its core is the concept that all records can be analyzed, understood, and evaluated in terms of a system of formal elements that are universal in their application and decontextualized in nature. The *context* of a record's *creation* is revealed in elements of its form, which can be separated from, and analyzed independently of its content. Regardless of where and when a record is created, it can be conceived as a system comprising the act that causes the record's creation, the *persons* who concur in its formation, the procedures by which the act is realized, and the rules of representation determining its form.

Diplomatic Criticism and Special Diplomatics

Diplomatic criticism is the use of diplomatic concepts and methods to assess the authenticity and authority of a given record. A decontextualized analysis based solely on general diplomatics can only take a scholar to a basic understanding of the record, in terms of time period, *function*, documentary type, purpose, and so on, but cannot proceed to a complete *authentication* without the use of special diplomatics, based on the knowledge of documentary traditions and procedures of the alleged author's specific environment.

Diplomatic criticism starts from the record form, comprising extrinsic elements that constitute the physical make-up of the document, and intrinsic elements that represent its internal logical structure.

Extrinsic elements of form can be examined without reading the content of the record, and will only be fully visible in the original, defined as the first complete and effective version of a record. They are: medium, script, language, special signs identifying the persons who participated in the making of the record, seals, and annotations. While the detailed analysis of the first three elements is the subject of paleography, diplomatics analyzes them for their capacity to illuminate administrative processes and activities.

The medium and its preparation are critical to helping establish date and provenance and test authenticity. Mass production of paper lessened the relevance of medium in analysis of modern documents, although there have been some notable examples of its value in identifying forgeries (e.g., the Hitler Diaries). With the advent of digital document production, medium has lost its status as an extrinsic element of form and has become part of the technological context.

An analysis of script may include description of the layout of the document, the presence of different hands or typefaces, correspondence between paragraphs and conceptual sections of text, punctuation, abbreviations and initials, inks, and erasures or corrections. In modern type-written documents some of these elements lose their influence, and in *digital records* or archival documents the software can be considered as part of the script, where it may give clues to procedure, function, purpose, provenance, modes of transmission, and so on. Language reveals rhetorical or genre conventions.

Special signs identify persons involved in document production. They may be the signs of writers and subscribers (e.g., symbols of notaries or crosses or other signs used by subscribers in place of names) or the signs of chancery or record offices (including the *rota* and *bene valete* of the papal chancery, the *manu propria*—"signed with one's own hand," sometimes used at the end of typewritten or printed documents or official notices when there is no handwritten signature, monograms of a sovereign's name, and various office stamps). Seals, the subject of the discipline of sigillography, are of great importance to medieval documents but are of lesser relevance in modern document analysis, although they are still the primary clue to the forgery of official diplomas, especially the embossed seals. Seals reveal the degree of formality, provenance, function, and authority of a document.

Annotations most clearly reveal the formative process of the document and may be added in the process of execution, as a means of authentication or registration, in the process of handling a complete and effective document while carrying out subsequent steps in the transaction in which the document participates, or in the process of managing the document in a records office or *archives* for purposes of *classification* and retrieval.

Intrinsic elements of form are the integral components of the document's intellectual articulation manifested through the presentation of the document's content. These elements tend to be arranged in groups according to their purpose, regardless of the provenance or date of the document. Every document can be divided into three sections: the protocol, which presents the administrative context of the action; the text, which articulates the object or purpose of the document; and the eschatocol, which presents the documentation context of the action. The protocol and eschatocol can display great variety depending on the practice of the chancery or record office in any given time period.

The protocol may identify all or some of the persons involved in authoring or issuing the document (through entitling or superscription—the modern letterhead) and the person to whom the document is directed (general or nominal inscription—the modern addressee), the date (including time and place), title, subject, invocation (symbolic or textual, lending a character of solemnity to the document), and initial *formulae*, the most common of which is the salutation (also the *formula perpetuitas*, typical of documents conferring privileges and rights that are not circumscribed by time: *in perpetuum, ad perpetuam rei memorian, p.p.*), and the appreciation, a short prayer for the realization of the content of the document (*feliciter, amen*).

The text consists of preamble, notification, exposition, disposition, and final clauses. Of these parts, the disposition, which states the action or purpose of the record, must be present. The other parts may be present. The preamble is an introduction expressing the ideal motivation guiding the issuing of the record, but no concrete or immediate reason as to why the document is generated. It may cite ethical or juridical principles, general considerations not directly linked to the subject, moral or pious expressions, administrative policies, political conceptions, legal principles, expressions of friendship or admiration, cooperation, interest, sympathy, and so on. The notification, when present, is a publication of the purport of the document, introduced by a phrase such as "be it known" or "know ye." The exposition sets out the real motives determining the issuing of the document. It is a narration of the concrete and immediate circumstances generating the act and the document and may include history, or the names of participants in the action. The core of the text is the disposition, the expression of the will or judgment of the author. Any final clauses may impart instructions to the addressee, ensure the fulfillment of the disposition, or guarantee the validity of the document.

The eschatocol presents the documentary context of the action and may enunciate the means of validation (the corroboration). It may begin with a complimentary clause, followed by the core of the section, which is the attestation, or subscriptions through signature(s) or special sign(s), and by the qualifications of the persons involved in issuing and witnessing the document. If not already expressed respectively in the text and in the protocol, the eschatocol may include an appreciation (a wish for the realization of the disposition), and the date (time and/or place).

Diplomatic criticism results in the determination of the authenticity of the record and of its authority, based on the identification of its *status of transmission*, or degree of perfection (i.e., on whether it is found to be a draft, an original, or a copy).

Conclusion

In the digital age the science of diplomatics continues to be relevant and is developing in two directions. The first direction involves the use of digital tools and techniques to support the diplomatic criticism of digitized medieval and early modern charters and legal documents or compare their extrinsic elements (in modern terms, *metadata*). These include tools for analyzing and interpreting historical sources such as optical character recognition (OCR), the production of critical editions, and the use of analytics and visualization to assist in the comparisons of large numbers of items.

The second direction involves the application of diplomatic concepts, principles, and methods to the analysis of born-digital records, documents, and data. Diplomatics is helping to identify digital records in information systems and applications, and to understand their characteristics and behavior in relation to their use, management, and preservation. At the University of British Columbia, Canada, the InterPARES Project has applied traditional diplomatics, integrated with archival knowledge (hence, archival diplomatics), to various digital objects in a variety of digital environments, and extended the knowledge of classic diplomatics to a diplomatics of *digital records*. Digital diplomatics defines a digital record as a digital component, or group of digital components, that is saved, treated, and managed as a record. The classic diplomatists were concerned with legal records, and categorized them according to their relationship to the actions in which they participated, acknowledging records that put the action into effect (dispositive records) or documented a juridical action undertaken before the issuing of the record (probative records). As diplomatics developed to encompass a wider range of documentary forms through the nineteenth and twentieth centuries, new categories of discretionary records were recognized (narrative records and supporting records), whose existence was not required by the juridical system in which they were created.

Digital diplomatics identifies two more categories of records: instructive records, which indicate the way in which data, documents, or records are to be presented, and enabling records, which allow for automations of such things as the performance of digital artworks, business workflows, the conduct of experiments, or analysis of observational data. The salient characteristic of instructive records is that the record as it is stored differs from the record as it is manifested on the computer screen, while the salient characteristic of enabling records is that they usually do not have a corresponding manifested record. Research will continue to make advances in this field.—*Corinne Rogers*

Keywords: diplomatic criticism, document analysis, digital diplomatics
Related Entries: Auxiliary Sciences; Document; Record(s); Record Functions; Status of Transmission (Records)

Bibliography

Duranti, Luciana. *Diplomatics: New Uses for an Old Science*. Lanham, MD: Scarecrow Press, 1998.

———. "Diplomatics." In Mary Bates, Niles Maack, and Miriam Drake, eds., *Encyclopedia of Library and Information Science*. New York: Marcel Dekker, 2009.

———. "From Digital Diplomatics to Digital Records Forensics." *Archivaria* 68 (Fall 2009): 39–66. http://journals.sfu.ca/archivar/index.php/archivaria/article/view/13229/14548.

———. *The Long-Term Preservation of Authentic Electronic Records: Findings of the InterPARES Project*. San Miniato: Archilab, 2005.

Duranti, Luciana, and Randy Preston. *Research on Permanent Authentic Records in Electronic Systems (InterPARES) 2: Experiential. Interactive and Dynamic Records*. Padova, Italy: Associazione Nazionale Archivistica Italiana, 2008.

Duranti, Luciana, and Kenneth Thibodeau. "The Concept of Record in Interactive, Experiential and Dynamic Environments: The View of InterPARES." *Archival Science* 6 (1) (2006): 13–68. DOI: 10.1007/s10502-006-9021-7.

Herde, Peter. 1975 *The New Encyclopedia Britannica*. 15th ed., Volume 5. S.v. 'diplomatics.'

Mabillon, Dom Jean. *De Re Diplomatica*. Paris, 1681.

MacNeil, Heather. *Trusting Records: Legal, Historical, and Diplomatic Perspectives*. Dordrecht: Kluwer Academic, 2000.

Tessier, Georges. "Diplomatique." In Charles Samarin, ed., *L'Histoire et ses methods*. Paris: Librarie Gallimard, 1961, 633–76.

DISASTER PLAN

A disaster plan is an essential tool employed by organizations to ensure they can continue operations after an earthquake, flood, terrorist incident, pandemic, power outage, or other serious disruption. The loss of life as a result of a natural or man-made disaster is tragic, and the damage to the local infrastructure can be significant. These sudden and unexpected events can also result in a "records disaster," the loss of *records* and information essential to an organization's continued operations.

A disaster plan is also referred to as a business-continuity plan, a disaster preparedness and recovery plan, or an emergency preparedness plan. However, each of these plans strives to achieve different goals; therefore, the overall disaster plan should address three elements: preparedness, recovery, and continuity. *Recordkeeping* professionals can lend their expertise to the development of a disaster plan for their organization that protects the organization's valuable business assets, its *vital* (essential) *records*.

Disaster Preparedness and Recovery

While many disasters cannot be prevented, steps can be taken to lessen the impact of records loss or damage by many of those hazards. Disaster preparedness and recovery should be addressed in a single document. "The disaster preparedness and recovery plan should identify procedures to be implemented to prevent disasters from occurring in the first place, and steps that can be taken to mitigate the effect of those disasters that cannot be prevented" (Franks 2013, 210).

Pre-Disaster Preparedness

"Pre-disaster preparedness involves identifying the types of risks most likely to impact an organization, including natural hazards, human-caused events, and technologically caused events" (Franks 2013, 211).

The first step in preparing for a records disaster is to prioritize your data—identify those records containing information necessary to the operations of the organization during the emergency created by a disaster and those records containing information necessary to protect the rights and interests of *persons* or to establish and affirm the powers and duties of governments in the resumption of operations after a disaster (Sturgeon, Gray, and Lucente-Kirkpatrick 2014, 11, 35). Refer to the "Vital Records" entry in this encyclopedia for additional information.

All physical installations face risk from natural disasters and, therefore, to records retained at those locations. Preparedness can take the form of planning to store copies of records in a geographic location not affected by similar natural threats; for example, companies located in earthquake-prone areas could protect physical and digital assets by locating disaster-recovery sites in a region not likely to be affected by earthquakes.

"In spite of the attention devoted to loss of information due to major disasters, records damage most often comes from preventable conditions such as equipment failures, arson, terrorism, vandalism, and carelessness" (Franks 2013, 211–12). Pre-disaster preparedness efforts can take the form of more thorough pre-employment screening, frequent equipment safety checks, improved security systems, and initial and ongoing employee training.

Technology-related events affect computer systems located within the enterprise, records and information stored in third-party systems, and support systems (e.g., telecommunications and utilities). Pre-disaster planning can include care taken in negotiating terms of service agreements with service providers and implementing cyber-security *risk-management* programs.

Disaster Recovery

Disaster-recovery plans should include steps to recover essential records, regardless of the medium used to store the records. As soon as possible after a disaster, a records damage assessment site survey should be conducted to determine the type of damage incurred. Physical records should be treated based on priorities set previously and the severity of the damage (Franks 2013, 214). Electronic records can be recovered from off-site disaster recovery centers hosted by the organization or a third-party provider. Cloud-based disaster recovery services began to appear toward the end of 2009 and are growing in popularity in order to increase efficiency, security, and scalability while reducing cost (Packer 2011).

Lessons learned from disasters that destroyed paper records underscore the benefits of storing information electronically. For example, within hours of Hurricane Katrina hitting New Orleans, Louisiana, in 2005, millions of medical records stored on paper were reduced to pulp due to flooding. Healthcare providers were unable to access medical records required to provide medical services to the public. A very different result was seen after Hurricane Sandy brought destruction to New York State in 2012. The disaster response was a success from a healthcare perspective due to the Statewide Health Information Network of New York (SHIN-NY) (Rontal n.d.).

The tactical decisions made to recover from a record disaster must be performed within an overall disaster-recovery policy framework that includes a risk assessment to determine requirements for the disaster-recovery plan, as well as the plan itself.

Business Continuity

Business continuity is the strategic and tactical capability of the organization to plan for and respond to incidents and business disruptions in order to continue business operations at an acceptable pre-defined level (Bird 2012).

Business-continuity activities can be placed into four categories: (1) planning for the impact of the unexpected or catastrophic event on the business—for example, understanding which processes are mission-critical to the survival of the business; (2) assessing data and technology needs in the event of an operations failure—for example, setting clear recovery time objectives for each of the organization's business/technology areas; (3) communicating the plan to employees and vendor partners—for example, determining the need for a designated recovery site for employees to resume work, including communications, data connectivity, desktops, and workspace at the site; (4) coordinating with external organizations and helping the community—for example, collaborating with the local government

agency to share plans and understand their capabilities in the event of a business-impacting catastrophe (AT&T 2006).

Business-Continuity Standards

Various standards provide guidance related to business continuity. The British Standards Institution (BSI) produced a two-part standard, BS 25999-1:2006, *Business Continuity Management: Code of Practice*, and BS 25999-2:2007, *Business Continuity Management: Specification.* In 2010, the American National Standards Institute (ANSI) approved the ASIS/BSI BCM.01-2010: *Business Continuity Management Systems: Requirements with Guidance for Use* standard. The U.S. standard shares the core of BS 25999, and the two standards are interchangeable in many areas while reflecting the differences between the infrastructures, systems, and terminology of the United Kingdom and the United States. The common elements used in BCM.01 and BS 25999 can be used by international organizations to build business-continuity programs (Franks 2013, 220).

Catastrophic Events and Technology Considerations

The terrorist attacks on September 11, 2001, had a devastating impact on American lives and livelihoods. In addition to the tragic loss of life and physical property was the impact the events had on normal business operations in the heart of New York's financial district. The attacks exposed one area of vulnerability to business continuity: almost no paper records survived the attacks on the World Trade Center (Franks 2013, 216). 9/11 changed the way business continuity professionals plan for catastrophic events.

Lessons learned from the events of that day reveal specific technology-related actions that should be contemplated, including: (1) considering an off-site real-time mirrored failover location on a separate power grid so that operations can continue in the event of a power outage localized to the immediate area; (2) planning for all possible communication issues, including the use of satellite phones, hotlines, and web alerts; (3) planning for extended recoveries, in case business is displaced longer than expected;

(4) providing an alternative method of accessing your data and documents; and (5) ensuring all vendor contracts are complete and up to date, including those with providers of media storage, insurance, and fuel (Laserfiche 2011).

Conclusion

Records and information managers have a key role to play in the development of a disaster plan, which includes not only disaster preparedness and recovery but also business continuity. A well-devised disaster plan cannot prevent a disaster but can mitigate loss of records and information through both protection and recovery efforts. Business continuity is essential to continue business operations in spite of interruptions in order to meet legal, regulatory, and contractual obligations in the face of any disruption to the business.—*Patricia C. Franks*

Keywords: business continuity plan, disaster preparedness, recovery plan

Related Entries: Archival Buildings and Facilities; Preservation; Recordkeeping; Records Center; Records Management; Records Management (RIM) Standards; Risk Management (Records); Vital Records

Bibliography

Bird, Lyndon. "Business Continuity." In *Dictionary of Business Continuity Management Terms*, version 2. January 2012, 10–11. www.thebci.org/glossary.pdf.

Franks, Patricia. *Records and Information Management*. Chicago: Neal-Schuman, 2013.

Laserfiche. "Streamline Business Continuity Planning with Enterprise Content Management." 2011. White paper. www.laserfiche.com/PDF/Document/1914804/Streamline-Business-Continuity-Planning-with-Enterprise-Content-Management.

Packer, Rack. "Blue Cloud Thinking—Why Cloud Computing Must Be Included in Disaster Recovery Planning." Rack Pack Blog, January 25, 2011. http://rackpack.iomarthosting.com/?p=596.

Rontal, Robyn. "Health Information Exchange: The Vision, the Reality, and Pathways to Success." ABA Health Law Section, Physician Issues Interest Group Webinar. www.americanbar.org/content/dam/aba/administrative/healthlaw/hie_physician_issues_2014.authcheckdam.pdf.

DISPOSITION, RECORDS

Disposition is the set of policies and procedures concerning a record's retention and final destiny (i.e., destruction or long-term *preservation*) following its active use within its records-generating system. Considered broadly, disposition activities represent the final phase in the archival function of *selection*. Selection attends to the *appraisal* of records—the assignation of value—and implements the consequences of appraisal in the disposition activities (Duranti 1994). An important component of a modern records management system, disposition combines with *creation*, receipt, maintenance, and use to ensure the archival *records* of an organization are authentic and reliable *evidence* of its transactions and activities (ISO 15489:2001; Shepherd and Yeo 2003). A document known as a record's disposition authority, also commonly known as a *schedule*, formally and legally articulates a record's disposition. It is the central tool in the disposition process. Creators and preservers of records will combine, at a level decided within the operational model of the organization, to compose a disposition schedule. The document is built on a foundation of research that will combine the needs and requirements of the appraisal with the administrative procedures and organizational resources capable of addressing the requisite *transfer*, storage, disposal, and/or preservation of the records. Properly managed, the disposition should apply clearly defined procedures for destruction of particular records appropriate to the sensitivity of the information the records contain. It will also include the formalities for the transfer of select documents to a *records center* where records may reside until their final disposition is implemented. As a vital component of the selection process, the disposition occurs within the legal, administrative, and social parameters of a records-creating environment. Many guidelines suggest a record's disposition is best applied within the records' natural aggregations determined by use. This level of aggregation is normally a *series*.

Origins

The concept of a record's disposition emerged from the origins of modern *records management*. Attending to the modernist archival challenges of governance, volume, and technology, influential American archival writers P. C. Brooks, Margaret Cross Norton, and T. S. Schellenberg proposed an expanded archival role in the creation and management of records (Schellenberg 1956; Norton 1975; Cook 1997). Brooks and his colleagues introduced the concept of the "*lifecycle* of a record" and the close collaboration of records stakeholders in order to coordinate the selection of records based on the needs of creators, *archivists*, and researchers. Disposition attended to the nature and term of a record's retention within this lifecycle innovation. In one of the earliest published definitions of the term Robert Bahmer credits Brooks with conceptualizing a record's final disposition: "I use the term 'disposition' as Dr. Brooks has defined it to mean everything that is done to records whether it be elimination, transfer to storage or to an archival institution, or reduction by microphotography" (Bahmer 1943, 170).

Conclusion

Records management, selection, and disposition are relatively recent developments built on frameworks of method and practice that carefully attended to issues of modern records volume and use. Recent challenges posed by electronic records—ease of distribution, ambiguous provenance, fragmentation of records' components, voluminous reproduction—highlight the need to build records management practices more closely on theoretical principles of *provenance*. A disposition authority is a useful tool to integrate the research conclusions concerning the creator's context (i.e., provenance) with the resources available for retention, preservation, and disposal (i.e., disposition). Some have argued that the fluid combination of functions and activities rapidly distributed through digital records environments makes disposition authorities too static and detailed to be useful for comprehensive control over an organization's records disposition. But recent records management guidelines (e.g., ISO 15489) illustrate that disposition authority remains the best method to encapsulate all the activities involved in implementing records' disposition: physical destruction; retention periods; transfers of location, storage medium, and control within an organization; and archival preservation. Regardless of the medium, the concept of a record's disposition is the fulcrum for a balance of records value and preservation feasibility.—*Raymond Frogner*

Keywords: selection, records schedule, lifecycle, archives

Bibliography

Bahmer, R. H. "Scheduling the Disposition of Records." *American Archivist* 6 (3) (July 1943): 169–74. http://archivists.metapress.com/content/e2457xl474772377/fulltext.pdf.

Brooks, Phillip C. "The Selection of Records for Preservation." *American Archivist* 3 (4) (1940): 211–34. http://archivists.metapress.com/content/u77415458gu22n65/fulltext.pdf.

Cook, Terry. "What Is Past Is Prologue: A History of Archival Ideas since 1898, and the Future Paradigm Shift." *Archivaria* 43 (Spring 1977): 17–63. DOI 10.1007/BF02435636.

Duranti, Luciana. "The Concept of Appraisal and Archival Theory." *American Archivist* 57 (Spring 1994): 328–45. http://archivists.metapress.com/content/pu548273j5j1p816/fulltext.pdf.

International Standards Organization. *ISO 15489: Information and Documentation—Records Management, Part 1: General.* Geneva, Switzerland: International Standards Organization, 2001.

Schellenberg, T. R. *Modern Archives: Principles and Techniques.* Chicago: University of Chicago Press, 1956.

Shepherd. E., and G. Yeo. *Managing Records: A Handbook of Principles and Practice.* London: Facet, 2003.

DOCUMENT

The popular generic concept of document is that of a written text—information inscribed on a medium, usually paper. The disciplines that study or manage information objects—including *archival science*, *diplomatics*, information science, law, history, and computer science—have developed definitions of document as a conceptual object to meet their particular needs. These definitions vary in scope, from recognizing a narrowly conceived archetype of text handwritten or typed on paper, to a broad functional view of a document as "organized physical evidence" (Briet, quoted in Buckland 1997) that transcends text. This entry outlines the definitions and purposes of the document in these distinct but related fields of study.

The Concept

Document derives from the Latin *docere*, to teach, and *documentum*: lesson, proof, instance, specimen. In medieval Latin the word was used to mean "instrument," "charter," or "official paper." In the twelfth and thirteenth centuries it denoted "lesson" or "written evidence" (old French). Clanchy suggests that the *documentum* may have been an oral instruction (Norman, eleventh century, Clanchy 1993). The use of the word *document* to indicate instruction or warning is found in the early sixteenth century and as late as 1793 (J. Williams, *Life of Earl Barrymore*, 101, "I have heard much document from the Grey Beards of society, delivered to prove . . . ," OED). In common usage document suggests something inscribed or written to provide information or evidence. The writing is commonly assumed to be on paper or equivalent, but exceptions to this abound (A. Jameson 1850, *Legends of Manastic Orders*, 419: "These frescoes . . . have become invaluable as documents," OED).

The simplest definition of document is recorded information. International standards in the field of archival science have defined document as recorded information regardless of medium or characteristics that can be treated as a unit (ISAD-G 1999; ISO 15489-1 2001), or an indivisible unit of information constituted by a message affixed (recorded) to a medium, in a stable, syntactic manner; a document has fixed form and stable content (Duranti 2005; 2009). A more detailed definition for the purpose of diplomatics considers a document as "the written evidence of a fact having a juridical nature, compiled in compliance with determined forms, which are meant to provide it with full faith and credit" (Cesare Paoli 1942, *Diplomatica*, 2nd ed., quoted in Duranti 1998). The rules of representation, or form, of documents reflect the political, legal, administrative, economic, and social contexts in which the

documents are created and are the subject of study of diplomatics in order to evaluate *authenticity*. Of particular concern to *archivists* is the distinction between documents—that is, recorded information—and *records* or archival documents—that is, documents made or received in the course of practical activity and set aside for action or reference.

Documents in Historical Research

Documents are the primary sources of historical research when interviews or direct observation are no longer possible. They are "the traces which have been left by the thoughts and actions of men of former times," regarded as especially valuable to the historian because they were not created for posterity but as testimony of the past (Langlois and Seignobos 1908, *Introduction to the Study of History*, quoted in Scott 1990). The classical historical tradition that concerned itself with a narrow range of documents from state and constitutional origin has influenced modern understanding of a document as a textual object. Distinction has been drawn between a document that is "an instrument in language which has, as its origin, and for its deliberate and express purpose to become the basis of, or to assist, the activities of an individual, an organization, or a community . . . exclusively for the purpose of action" (similar to the archival document or record as defined by archival science) and contemporary literature, which is a residual term for all other written sources (S. and B. Webb 1932, *Methods of Social Study*, quoted in Scott 1990). Historians and social scientists have broadened this narrow understanding to include printed *ephemera*, maps (text embodied in pictorial form), and other images and artifacts, depending on their informational versus aesthetic function. Scott has suggested categorizing documents according to their *access* restrictions (closed, restricted, open-archival, open-published) and authorship (personal, official-private, or official-state) (1990).

Documents in Law

According to *Black's Law Dictionary*, a document is:

an instrument on which is recorded, by means of letters, figures, or marks, matter which may be evidentially used. In this sense the term "document" applies to writings; to words printed, lithographed, or photographed; to seals, plates, or stones on which inscriptions are cut or engraved; to photographs and pictures; to maps and plans. The inscription may be on stone or gems, or on wood, as well as on paper or parchment.

Documentary evidence contrasts with real evidence (physical objects like a gun or knife), and testamentary evidence (verbal statements). In common law environments, documentary evidence must be shown to be relevant and authentic in order to be admitted at trial or in pre-trial hearing. Traditional documentary evidence must satisfy an exception to the hearsay rule that excludes documents as hearsay, such as the business records exception that allows documents created in the usual and ordinary course of business. Documents must adhere to the "best evidence" rule, interpreted as a requirement for the original, unless the original document/record is unavailable for accepted reasons. Digital documentary evidence is challenging traditional norms, and common law jurisdictions are adapting to these challenges with statute and precedent law.

Documents in Computer Science

In the field of computer science, a document is an object created with software, such as a word-processing application, or a computer file that is not an executable file and contains data for use by applications. This conforms to the traditional concept of document as information-bearing object. But digital objects are strings of bits—the medium on which a message is inscribed can no longer be considered an integral attribute of the document. Traditional documents in the digital environment, whether digitized from a physical medium or born digital, are organized and stored in one or more bit streams making up a variety of digital components.

Documents in Information Science

The field of documentation science, or documentation, arose in the early twentieth century to establish new ways of accessing and retrieving the growing body of textual material, primarily scientific and technical literature. By the middle of the twentieth century, the field was increasingly known as infor-

mation science and the nature of the documents to be managed was a subject of much theoretical debate. Documentalists rejected a definition of document based on medium in favor of one based on function. The definition of document was extended from a printed or textual object to include any graphic or written representation of ideas, or "any material basis for extending our knowledge which is available for study or comparison" (Schürneyer 1935, quoted in Buckland 1997). Paul Otlet proposed that any object bearing the graphical or written representation of ideas (natural objects, artifacts, explanatory models, educational games, artworks, etc.) could be considered a document if one is informed by observing them (Otlet 1934, in Buckland 1997). This concept was taken further by Suzanne Briet, who asserted that "a document is evidence in support of a fact," and presented as an example an antelope taken into captivity as an object of study (1951, in Buckland 1997).

Conclusion

Documents are constructs that allow us to organize, navigate, and understand information. The archetypal document as paper or other physical medium inscribed with text is only one such construct. Each information profession refines its definition of document—the form or *function* of the document—according to its specific needs.—*Corinne Rogers*

Keywords: document, information, text
Related Entries: Archival Science; Diplomatics; Record(s)

Bibliography

Brown, John Seely, and Paul Duguid. "The Social Life of Documents." 1996. http://firstmonday.org/htbin/cgiwrap/bin/ojs/index.php/fm/article/viewArticle/466/387.

Buckland, Michael K. "What Is a 'Document'?" *Journal of the American Society for Information Science* 48 (September 1997): 804–9.

Dictionary of Computing. London: A & C Black, 2004.

"Document." In *Black's Law Dictionary Free Online*, 2nd edition. The Law Dictionary, 2012. http://thelawdictionary.org/document (accessed May 28, 2014).

Duranti, Luciana. *Diplomatics: New Uses for an Old Science*. Lanham, MD: Scarecrow Press, 1998.

Duranti, Luciana, and Kenneth Thibodeau. "The Concept of Record in Interactive, Experiential and Dynamic Environments: The View of Inter-PARES." *Archival Science* 6 (1) (2006): 13–68.

Jenkinson, Hilary, Roger H. Ellis, and Peter Walne. *Selected Writings of Sir Hilary Jenkinson*. Chicago: Society of American Archivists, 2003.

Scott, John. *A Matter of Record: Documentary Sources in Social Research*. Cambridge, UK: Polity Press, B. Blackwell, 1990.

DOCUMENTARY EDITING

The editing and publication of historical *documents* has been an activity closely associated with *archives* throughout their history. Archives and historical societies have regularly engaged in the publication of documents in their custody to fulfill the missions of both dissemination and *preservation* of *records*. In the second half of the twentieth century documentary editing emerged as a separate profession significantly removed from its earlier, more direct connection to archives. Recent technological developments, however, may enable archives to once again be more actively involved in editing and publication projects.

The Concept

The interest of historians in having easier access to records and the close alliance between historians and archives led quite early to archival involvement in documentary publications. For example, Ludovico Antonio Muratori, *archivist* and librarian in Modena, assembled *Rerum Italicarum scriptores* (*Writers on Italy*), published in twenty-eight volumes from 1723 to 1751. Similar examples of historians and archivists collaborating on editorial projects can be found in other European countries in the eighteenth and nineteenth centuries.

In the United States and Canada, documentary publication was often carried out by historical societies. Part of the preservation mission of the first such society in the United States, the Massachusetts Historical Society, established in 1791, was the publication of the papers it collected. As its

founder, Jeremy Belknap, had written to Ebenezer Hazard in 1788, "I am sensible that the only sure way to preserve manuscripts is to multiply the copies" (Jimerson 2006, 251). These efforts created a model followed by numerous historical societies in the nineteenth century. Standards for such editorial efforts developed slowly, however, and it was only with the advent of a more scientific approach to history later in the nineteenth century that editors began to adopt more rigorous standards for accuracy of transcription so that published texts would more closely convey the *authenticity* of the archival documents.

The subject of the archivist's role in publishing selected documents in archives often received attention in archival manuals. In their famous Dutch manual, Muller, Feith, and Fruin wrote, "The final duty which is incumbent on the archivist in connection with the archival collection entrusted to his care is the publication of the most important documents" (187). T. R. Schellenberg's *Modern Archives* (1955) devotes a full chapter to publication programs, describing them often as collaborations between historians and archivists.

The law creating the U.S. National Archives in 1934 also created the National Historical Publications Commission (NHPC). Although it was a still-born agency for sixteen years, in 1950 the NHPC began funding documentary editions of many of the papers of America's founding fathers. These projects set a higher standard for care in editing and documentation, ushering in a new era in documentary editing. The length of time that it took for these meticulously edited volumes to be published, however, caused concern in many quarters.

The editing of historical documents should be differentiated from textual, or critical, editing, which also emerged in the twentieth century as a robust field of scholarship focused on the reconstruction of accurate texts of published literary works. In general the aim of critical editors was to ascertain an ideal text based on a collation of surviving manuscripts, proofs, and published editions. Documentary editors, on the other hand, were interested in providing the evidentiary value of the documents themselves. G. Thomas Tanselle, a prominent bibliographer and textual critic, argued in 1978, however, that documentary editors needed to develop more consistent standards along the lines of those used by textual editors. Tanselle's article resulted in documentary editors adopting a more conservative approach in the literal transcription of documents. It also led to the creation of the Association for Documentary Editing, which has sought to bridge the gap between literary editors and historical editors.

After the NHPC was transformed in 1974 into the National Historical Publications and Records Commission (NHPRC), it began funding archival projects as well as editorial projects. Tensions ultimately developed between archivists and editors over NHPRC funding for their different activities, and these tensions pointed to the increased gulf between the two fields. During this time, the archival profession began to distance itself somewhat from its long, close connection with historians, and this shift also contributed to a diminution in archival involvement in documentary editing. Scholar archivists with experience in documentary editing, such as Lester J. Cappon, became a disappearing breed. The World Wide Web and other new technologies, however, have offered possibilities for archivists and documentary editors to forge a more collaborative future and for archives themselves to become more active participants in documentary publications. As archivists meet the increased demand from *users* to make records available online, they can revive an older tradition in which archives were ready collaborators with the historical community in publishing historical records. Documentary editors have become fully engaged in online publication, while still maintaining a commitment to print for selected documents and projects. Archivists can enhance their online presentation of documents by adopting techniques in transcription and annotation developed by documentary editors.

Conclusion

While the editing and publication of documents in their custody has never been a primary focus of archival work, it is an activity in which archivists and historians have collaborated to enhance access to records. It also formerly was a key element in archival preservation during the period in history when archives were at greater risk from fire and other disasters. The demand of dealing with the challenges of information technology has been one factor diverting the attention of archivists away from editorial activities. Paradoxically some of these same technological developments may enable archivists to reengage with documentary editing as they seek new ways to provide access to historical records.—*Philip Eppard*

Keywords: editing, publication, preservation, access

Related Entries: Access/Accessibility; Archival Preservation; Archives and the Web; Auxiliary Sciences; Facsimile; Outreach

Bibliography

Coles, Laura Millar. "The Decline of Documentary Publishing: The Role of English-Canadian Archives and Historical Societies in Documentary Publishing." *Archivaria* 1 (23) (1986): 69–85. http://journals.sfu.ca/archivar/index.php/archivaria/article/view/11367/12308.

Cox, Richard J., ed. *Lester J. Cappon and the Relationship of History, Archives, and Scholarship in the Golden Age of Archival Theory*. Chicago: Society of American Archivists, 2004.

Dow, Elizabeth H., et al. "The Burlington Agenda: Research Issues in Intellectual Access to Electronically Published Historical Documents." *American Archivist* 64 (1) (2001): 292–307. http://archivists.metapress.com/content/y1w62427q7778637/full-text.pdf.

Dunlap Leslie W., and Fred Shelley. *The Publication of American Historical Manuscripts*. Iowa City: University of Iowa Libraries, 1976.

Harvey, P. D. A. *Editing Historical Records*. London: British Library, 2001.

Jimerson, Randall C. "Documents and Archives in Early America." *Archivaria* 60 (60) (2006).

Kline, Mary-Jo, and Susan Holbrook Perdue. *A Guide to Documentary Editing*, 3rd edition. Charlottesville: University of Virginia Press, 2008.

Luey, Beth. *Editing Documents and Texts: An Annotated Bibliography*. Madison, WI: Madison House, 1990.

Tanselle, G. Thomas. "The Editing of Historical Documents." *Studies in Bibliography* 31 (1978): 1–56. www.jstor.org/stable/40371673.

DOCUMENTARY EVIDENCE

As traditionally defined by Black's Law Dictionary, documentary evidence is "evidence supplied by a writing or other document, which must be authenticated before the evidence is admissible" (*Black's Law Dictionary*, 2009), although the phrase *documentary evidence* is sometimes used only to refer to wills, trusts, or invoices, any type of evidence that presents recorded information in some way can be considered "documentary." Accordingly, letters, contracts, deeds, licenses, certificates, tickets, or other writings are also well-recognized, traditional categories of documentary evidence (*West's Encyclopedia of American Law*, 2008). Documentary evidence from written instruments, inscriptions, and documents of all kinds is distinguishable both from "oral" evidence (i.e., that delivered by human beings by voice) and from "real evidence" furnished by things themselves (e.g., material objects, biological evidence). As discussed below, the traditional definition of what constitutes documentary evidence recently has expanded to any form of evidence introduced at trial in the form of *documents*, which may include nontraditional media on which information is preserved (e.g., photographs, films and videos, sound recordings, printed emails, web pages).

Documentary Evidence: The Concept

A piece of evidence is not documentary evidence if it is presented at trial for any purpose other than the examination of the contents of the document. Documents presented for a different purpose, such as proving that they were handled and contain prints from a victim or suspect, are real evidence, but they may be documentary as well if the contents are relevant.

Documentary evidence is subject to rules of *authentication*, including through the testimony of an eyewitness to the execution of the document, or to the testimony of a witness able to identify the handwriting of the purported author. Certain forms of documentary evidence may be "self-authenticating," where a presumption of *authenticity* applies absent objection or challenge. Certain forms of public documents, including under seal or as certified by an official custodian, as well as other forms of official publications, books, newspapers, periodicals, commercial paper, and related documents, may not require sponsoring testimony of any witness to be considered as authentic exhibits at trial.

Documentary evidence is also subject to the best evidence rule, which requires that the original document be produced unless there is a sufficient reason not to do so. The best evidence rule requires that either an original of a document (including a film or other recording) or a reliable duplicate be used. The rule traces back to the eighteenth century, when it was designed to prevent the introduction into evidence of documents that have been altered, manipulated, or obtained fraudulently. With the advent of photocopying and the exponential growth of electronic documents, the best evidence rule has taken on lesser importance, as some courts have adopted "secondary evidence rules" that do not require introduction of an original of a writing.

Documentary evidence is typically admitted at trial as an exhibit. In order to be admitted as an exhibit, the party presenting the documentary evidence must first lay a foundation that explains what the evidence is, where it came from, and that it follows the "best evidence rule." Foundations are typically laid through testimony by a witness familiar with the item and what is in it. If the party trying to admit the evidence doesn't create a proper foundation, the opposing party may object. In increasingly rare instances where the issue is material to the outcome of a lawsuit, a judge may allow a jury to decide if an original ever actually existed or if a copy accurately reflects the original.

In jurisdictions in which parties in litigation engage in pretrial "discovery" of documentary evidence, the rules of discovery recently have expanded the definition of document to accommodate the role technology has played in the making, storing, and retention of evidence for purposes of disclosure and exchange. For example, the term "electronically stored information" was added to the U.S. Federal Rules of Civil Procedure in 2006 to expand the concept of what may constitute discoverable "documents" and, by application, what may be introduced as "documentary evidence" in court. The advisory notes to rule 34 in particular:

> The growth in electronically stored information and in the variety of systems for creating and storing such information has been dramatic. Lawyers and

judges interpreted the term "documents" to include electronically stored information because it was obviously improper to allow a party to evade discovery obligations on the basis that the label had not kept pace with changes in information technology. But it has become increasingly difficult to say that all forms of electronically stored information, many dynamic in nature, fit within the traditional concept of a "document." Electronically stored information may exist in dynamic databases and other forms far different from fixed expression on paper. . . . A common example often sought in discovery is electronic communications, such as e-mail. The rule covers—either as documents or as electronically stored information—information "stored in any medium," to encompass future developments in computer technology. [The rule] is intended to be broad enough to cover all current types of computer-based information, and flexible enough to encompass future changes and developments.

Similar developments in the law have taken place in a variety of common law jurisdictions. See, for example, part 31 of the Civil Procedure Rules of England and Wales, "Disclosure and Inspection of Documents."

The issue of whether documentary evidence in electronic form is deserving of special attention from the perspective of the application of the traditional tests for authentication is an emerging issue in law. One leading commentator on the rules of evidence states:

> In general, electronic documents or records that are merely stored in a computer raise no computer-specific authentication issues. If a computer processes data rather than merely storing it, authentication issues may arise. The need for authentication and an explanation of the computer's processing will depend on the complexity and novelty of the computer processing. There are many states in the development of computer data where error can be introduced, which can adversely affect the accuracy and reliability of the output. . . . Factors that should be considered in evaluating the reliability of computer-based evidence include the error rate in data inputting, and the security of the systems. The degree of foundation required to authenticate computer-based evidence depends on the quality and completeness of the data input, the complexity of the computer processing, the routineness of the computer opera-

tion, and the ability to test and verify results of the computer processing. (Weinstein and Berger 1998)

To the extent that documents in the form of electronically stored information are now increasingly voluminous, legal systems face novel issues in the authentication of documentary evidence given the ease in which specific forms of communications (e.g., e-mail) may be easily altered or modified through either automatic processes or human manipulation (Paul 2008). One method of authenticating documentary evidence in electronic form is through examination of *metadata*. Metadata "includes information about the document or file that is recorded by the computer to assist in storing and retrieving the document or file. The information may also be useful for system administration as it reflects data regarding the generation, handling, transfer, and storage of the document or file within the computer system" (Sedona 2007). To address authenticity concerns arising in the digital age, one leading case in the United States has suggested the use of "hash values" or "hash marks" when making documents (*Lorraine v. Markel Ins. Co.* 2007). A "hash value" is a unique numerical identifier that can be assigned to a file, a group of files, or a portion of a file, based on a standard mathematical algorithm applied to the characteristics of the data set. Examples of algorithms include MD5 and SHA (Federal Judicial Center Pocket Guide 2007).

The *Lorraine* decision summarized the emerging law in this manner: "It can be expected that electronic evidence will constitute much, if not most, of the evidence used in future motions practice or at trial" (2007, 101). Accordingly, parties in litigation and their counsel are well advised to understand how best to authenticate documentary evidence, especially in electronic form.

Conclusion

Traditional notions in the law of what constitutes "documentary evidence," including the requirement that documents be authenticated, continue to have relevance at evidentiary hearings and trials. Increasingly, however, newer forms of electronic records, including on social media, will constitute important documentary evidence in future cases. In the future, as documents are created and preserved in electronic form, lawyers and judges should anticipate the need to authenticate such evidence in the courtroom, including through proper interpretation of metadata.

—*Jason Baron*

Keywords: documents, writings, authentication, electronically stored information

Related Entries: Authentication; Document; Metadata

Bibliography

Black's Law Dictionary, 9th edition. St. Paul, MN: Thompson Reuters, 2009.

Cleary, Edward W., ed. *McCormick on Evidence*. St. Paul, MN: West, 1972.

Lorraine v. Markel American Ins. Co., 241 Federal Rules Evidence Service 446 (District of Maryland, 2007) (Chief Magistrate Judge Paul W. Grimm). www.mdd.uscourts.gov/opinions/opinions/lorraine%20v.%20markel%20-%20esi-admissibility%20opinion.pdf.

Paul, George L. *Foundations of Digital Evidence*. Chicago: American Bar Association, 2008.

Rothstein, Barbara J., Ronald J. Hedges, and Elizabeth C. Wiggins. *Managing Discovery of Electronic Information: A Pocket Guide for Judges*, 2nd edition. Washington, DC: Federal Judicial Center, 2012.

The Sedona Principles Addressing Electronic Document Production, 2nd edition. The Sedona Conference, 2007. https://thesedonaconference.org/download-pub/81.

Weinstein, Jack B., and Margaret A. Berger. *Weinstein's Federal Evidence*, 2nd edition. Edited by Joseph M. McLaughlin. New York: M. Bender, 2011.

West's Encyclopedia of Evidence Law. St. Paul, MN: West, 1998.

DOCUMENTATION PLAN

A documentation plan identifies subjects, organizations, topics, activities, or functions that an archival institution, or group of institutions, commits or proposes to document in its archival holdings. As such it is a proactive archival management tool for both *acquisition* and *appraisal* of *records* using value criteria derived not from the records or records creators, but from society as the object of archival documentation. West German archivist Hans Booms first proposed the concept in 1972, although *documentation strategy* and macroappraisal are related concepts developed independently by other archivists in other countries.

Background

Booms's original 1972 proposal was essentially a response to claims from archivists in the German Democratic Republic (East Germany) that archivists in the West, and in the Federal Republic of Germany (West Germany) in particular, were unable to appraise archives effectively. West German archivists, they contended, had no basis for determining social value, lacking the definitive historical science of dialectical materialism. In a sweeping review, Booms analyzed the history of German appraisal theories: idealism, using the archivist's intuition (*fingerspitzengefuhl*); appraisal based on future research value; and analysis based on the relative importance of original functions (*provenienz*) that created the records. All are shown to be flawed in their essential reasoning. Of course, Booms rejected the deductive communist ideology of East German archivists as largely useless to West German archivists working in a pluralist, liberal society supported by empirically derived public policy.

Documentation Plan Characteristics

As an alternative to previous appraisal theories and methodologies, Booms envisioned developing a "documentation plan" as a hierarchical taxonomy of historical events or phenomena scaled according to societal significance and against which the documentary value of specific archival records could be measured. Although clearly a very preliminary concept, the documentation plan needed to possess certain qualities to make it valid as an appraisal tool:

1. Subject-based: The plan needs to identify documentation objects from society as a whole that can be related to the subjects documented in the records. It cannot simply identify the functions or institutional units that produced the records—instead, this provenance informa-

tion would become one object among the very many available to *archivists* constructing a comprehensive documentation plan of society.

2. Use values of the time: Archivists would need to develop and use a clear standard of values to place documentation objects in a relative order of significance. The values need to be drawn from the society at the time the records under examination were created, using contemporary publications, public statements, and cultural expressions as the main sources, not the records themselves.

3. Liberal/pluralistic context required: In line with Boom's critique of ideologically derived values for appraising records, a valid documentation plan could only be constructed by a team of experts effectively representing all segments of a free society, not a small group within society, or one working within a society dominated by one political group or person.

Reception and Implementation

Ironically, it was archivists in East Germany who in 1984 first completed a documentation plan based on the Booms concept. Working in a time of economic and political collapse, this East German plan was never implemented, nor could it survive the reunification of Germany in 1990 since it was developed using only the political and historical values of the communist state.

Within his own country, Booms's ideas on constructing and implementing a documentation plan were never realized. There was no formal response within West Germany to his proposal until 1989 when a German colleague rejected the concept as too ambitious and demanding of a society that has little interest in archival appraisal and that would be too diverse in its viewpoints to build the required consensus. Others characterized appraisal by documentation plan as "content-based," in many ways working contrary to traditional *archival theory* of analysis based on the *principle of provenance*. With the English translation and publication of Booms's original article in 1987, appraisal by documentation plan entered archival thinking in North American as well, influencing development of macroappraisal tools in the 1990s.

In 1991, Booms reexamined and clarified aspects of his original documentation plan proposal by introducing a step-by-step explanation:

1. Develop an historical chronicle: In place of a rigid hierarchy of events and phenomena, this component of the documentation plan would take the form of a chronicle to guide archivists in their decision-making. To maintain a degree of *objectivity* and distance in this process, the archivist must decide what to include in this chronicle using the values of the society at the time.

2. Analyze and prepare records based on provenance: Assess and maintain records considered for archival *preservation* within their original institutional, functional, and technical context. This process includes documenting the record-creating function and reducing duplication and redundancy. With this step, Booms makes a clear and definitive statement that the documentation plan approach incorporates, not replaces, provenance-based archival preservation and analysis.

3. Identify which records best document the chronicle: With the provenance of proposed records established and informing decision-making, determine which records best represent and document events and phenomena established by the sections of the historical chronicle representing the values of the society at the time the records were created.

Conclusion

The documentation plan provides a comprehensive, systematic, and transparent methodology for archivists to direct and measure how and how well their appraisal decisions are documenting the society within their jurisdiction of operation. The concept proposed by Hans Booms relies heavily on identifying clear and concrete documentation priorities in a taxonomy or chronicle that reflects social values and priorities predominant at the time the records being appraised were created, not those of the present day. With this in place, the archivist uses the documentation plan to acquire or appraise identified records, but only after the provenance of the records have been established and considered as well. The scale of such an effort, the resources required, and the elusive nature of value consensus among archivists, let alone societal representatives, has made archival institutions hesitant to even begin the process of building a documentation plan. At the same time, the concept proposed by Hans Booms has encouraged archivists to acknowledge and attempt to address the larger social implications of their work and to look beyond their traditional professional and research constituency for support in making appraisal decisions.—*Rick Klumpenhouwer*

Keywords: appraisal, selection, macroappraisal
Related Entries: Acquisition Policy; Appraisal; Documentation Strategy; Selection

Bibliography

Aus der Arbeit der Archive: Beiträge zum Archivwesen, zur Quellenkunde und zur Geschichte; Festschrift für Hans Booms. Edited by Friedrich P. Kahlenberg. Boppard am Rhein, 1989.

Booms, Hans. "Society and the Formation of the Documentary Heritage: Issues in the Appraisal of Archival Sources." *Archivaria* 1 (24) (1987): 69–107. http://journals.sfu.ca/archivar/index.php/archivaria/article/view/11415/12357.

———. "Uberlieferungsbildung: Keeping Archives as a Social and Political Activity." *Archivaria* 1 (33) (1991): 25–33. http://journals.sfu.ca/archivar/index.php/archivaria/article/view/11796/12747.

Menne-Haritz, Angelika. "Appraisal or Documentation: Can We Appraise Archives by Selecting Content?" *American Archivist* 1 (57) (1994): 528–42. http://archivists.metapress.com/content/g114464381p11324/fulltext.pdf.

DOCUMENTATION STRATEGY

Documentation strategy is a methodology intended to guide the *selection* and retention of information about a specific topic, ongoing issue, activity, geographic area, or event. It is one of the major archival concepts of the 1980s that developed in response to the changing nature and volume of modern *records*, the *interrelatedness* of *records*, the diversity of information *formats*, and the perceived weaknesses in archival *appraisal* approaches (Samuels 1986). In this methodology, *archivists* are seen as active par-

ticipants in the *creation,* analysis, and selection of records, rather than passive keepers of information (Samuels 1991).

A documentation strategy is an ongoing activity that is usually designed, promoted, and implemented by a partnership involving the mutual efforts of many institutions and individuals who influence both the creation and retention of records. Carrying out a documentation strategy involves choosing and defining the topic to be documented, which includes a subject, functional or geographical analysis that encourages archivists to explore institutions' collections and plan for the appropriate retention of material in its appropriate setting; selecting advisors for the strategy and establishing a permanent base for the activities to be carried out; structuring the inquiry and examining the form and substance of the available documentation (archivists at this stage are concerned with what records should exist, rather than what records currently exist); and placing the documentation, which will determine the appropriate repository capable of storing and preserving the records (Samuels 1991).

Origins of Documentation Strategy

The proposal of documentation strategy was formally put forward in 1984 by Helen Willa Samuels, Larry J. Hackman, and Patricia Aronnson at a time when archivists were deciding whether appraisal should be defined on a basis of set common practices, functions, and principles, or if it should be identified through the roles archivists take on in their institutions when they carry out appraisal (Cox 1994). During the 1980s, the complex relationships between records, records' integrated functions, form, and substance altered significantly by technology, caused archivists to rethink appraisal strategies and refine institutional collection policies.

Earlier discussions of a documentation theory in the archival profession, however, can be traced back to the 1970s as a consequence of the cultural shifts and revolutions of the 1960s that witnessed the increasing demands for records documenting the lives of women, working classes, minorities, and the poor (Hinding 1993). Ultimately, the archival profession failed to provide these documents because they were not in existence in the majority of repositories. Throughout the 1970s, the realization that the majority of society was not adequately represented in archives led to the continuous discussion of how archivists were to close the gaps in the records. Gould P. Colman and Howard Zinn, for example, solidified the opinion that the *archives* were biased toward the rich and elite, leaving those with the most power and wealth in society to dominate the field of knowledge. They believed the lack of guidelines for the *acquisition* of archival materials resulted in a skewed study and representation of culture (Colman 1973; Zinn 1977). In 1972 Hans Booms attempted to create a documentation model that archivists could use to shape a more balanced representation of society (Booms 1987, originally published in German 1972). Gerald Ham continued the discussion in 1975 with his criticisms of the profession's broad collecting mandates, random selection processes, and fragmented, uncoordinated, and at times accidental selection of records (Ham 1975).

The conversation regarding documentation carried on into the 1990s, as contemporary records were in constant flux due to advances in technology, which affected record creation, format, preservation, and storage, and as relationships between records, creators, and institutions became more complex. Archivists realized they had to address all these changes and concerns by adapting old techniques and creating new ones to effectively manage modern records (Marshall 1998). During the 1990s, many case studies were conducted to determine how to take documentation strategy from theory to practice.

Reception by Archival Community

Overall, documentation strategy generated skepticism and concern among archivists, as many thought the strategy violated the basic tenets of *archival theory* and questioned the role of the archivist in the creation of records. Additionally, it left many individuals with more questions than answers to the growing appraisal concerns because it was unclear if archivists were to preserve evidence through the creation of a representative documentation, or if archivists had a broad quest to document all of society (Cox 1994). Lingering issues about the theoretical and practical implications of documentation strategy, such as what was and was not to be documented, how many events or institutions should be involved, how much information was enough, what the ramifications were of choosing to document one topic or area over another, left archivists suspicious and doubtful of the legitimacy of the methodology. Some criticism simply focused on the notion that the foundation of documentation strategy, that of collaboration between archivists and institutions and the necessary analysis and research components of the job, were already long-standing tasks of the profession. Other criticisms included the premise that the results of documentation strategy are an illusion and unachievable.

Despite the prominent dissatisfaction, there were some advocates who believed the discussion prompted by the documentation strategy was an opportunity for archivists to ask more refined questions about appraisal and the influences of records creation and collection. Some understood that documentation strategy is intended to supplement rather than replace traditional methods of appraisal (Cox 1989). In addition, advocates regarded documentation strategy as improving contemporary *archival practices* in ways such as avoiding duplication in collecting. According to advocates, the broad definition of documentation strategy allows it to be adapted to a wide variety of issues, its ongoing process provides flexibility for revision as the nature of the documentation changes, and it affords archivists the opportunity to educate other sectors of society about the importance of archival work (Marshall 1998).

Conclusion

A documentation strategy is composed of four components: an analytical tool that provides a framework for addressing some aspect of the documentary universe; an interdisciplinary process that brings multiple institutions and individuals together; a recognition of the inherent documentary problems; and a plan to determine what formulates appropriate documentation for an area under analysis (Marshall 1998). Documentation strategy has been related to *functional analysis* and macroappraisal, as all three approaches aim to improve the quality of documentation through more effective selection, though they approach appraisal in different ways (Marshall 1998).—*Emily Chicorli*

Keywords: appraisal, selection, documentation
Related Entries: Acquisition Policy; Appraisal; Documentation Plan

Bibliography

Booms, Hans. "Society and the Formation of a Documentary Heritage: Issues in the Appraisal of Archival Sources." *Archivaria* 1 (24) (1987): 69–107. http://journals.sfu.ca/archivar/index.php/archivaria/article/view/11415/12357.

Colman, Gould P. "The Forum." *American Archivist* 36 (3) (1973): 483–86. http://archivists.metapress.com/content/mt802p87l2878684/fulltext.pdf.

Cook, Terry. "Mind Over Matter: Towards a New Theory of Archival Appraisal." In Barbara L. Craig, ed., *The Archival Imagination: Essays in Honour of Hugh A. Taylor*. Ottawa: Association of Canadian Archivists, 1992, 38–70.

Cox, Richard J. "The Documentation Strategy and Archival Appraisal Principles: A Different Perspective." *Archivaria* 38 (1994): 11–36. http://journals.sfu.ca/archivar/index.php/archivaria/article/view/12021/12985.

Ham, Gerald F. "The Archival Edge." *American Archivist* 38 (1) (1975): 5–13. http://archivists.metapress.com/content/7400r86481128424/fulltext.pdf.

Hinding, Andrea. "Inventing a Concept of Documentation." *Journal of American History* 80 (1) (1993): 168–78. www.jstor.org/stable/2079701.

Marshall, Jennifer A. "Documentation Strategies in the Twenty-First Century: Rethinking Institutional Priorities and Professional Limitations." *Archival Issues* 23 (1) (1998): 59–74. www.jstor.org/stable/41101988.

Samuels, Helen W. "Improving Our Disposition: Documentation Strategy." *Archivaria* 1 (33) (1991): 125–40. http://journals.sfu.ca/archivar/index.php/archivaria/article/view/11804/12755.

———. "Who Controls the Past?" *American Archivist* 49 (2) (1986): 109–24. http://archivists.metapress.com/content/t76m2130txw40746/fulltext.pdf.

Zinn, Howard. "Secrecy, Archives and the Public Interest." *Midwestern Archivist* 2 (2) (1977): 14–26. www.jstor.org/stable/41101382.

DONATION

Webster's Dictionary defines donation as "the act or an instance of donating, as in making a gift, especially to a charity or public institution." The Society of American Archivists' glossary is even clearer, noting a donation occurs when "legal title is transferred from one party to another without compensation." Special collections repositories often receive materials via donation. Donors may have any number of reasons for making a gift—a love of history, a love of the repository to which they are donating, the wish to safeguard family materials for future generations, or the accrual of a monetary benefit. What follows discusses the donation of material such as might be received by a special collections repository as opposed to financial gifts.

Donation

Donations to special *collections* repositories should be formalized through a gift agreement (also referred to as a deed of gift). This legally binding document should address both the *transfer* of the physical property rights and the literary rights to the material being donated. Property rights refer to the ownership of the actual material; literary rights refer to the rights to the intellectual property, the copyright, and/or the right to quote from the materials. It is recommended that gift agreements include a simple broad statement by which the donor also signs away their literary rights to future gifts and to items in other collections to which the donor holds the literary rights. For example, the agreement made with Donor A could transfer Donor A's literary rights to letters they had written and sent to Donor B. In such cases, Donor B held the property rights to Donor A's letters, but the literary rights remained with the creator, Donor A.

Monetary benefits to the donor chiefly come through tax benefits. The U.S. Internal Revenue Service (IRS) requires that its Form 8283 be used for "donations of noncash charitable contributions" totaling over $500, and requires a description of the donee organization, the donated property, and its value and cost basis. Form 8283 also requires a statement as to any restriction, "temporary or permanent, on the donee's right to use or dispose of the donated property." A common example of such a restriction is the requirement by the donor that their collection be closed for some set period of time.

Generally, if the gift agreement includes any restriction on the use of the material by the donee, such as imposing a set date before which the collection may not be made available to the public, the IRS will not consider the transfer to be a gift. By requiring the restriction, the donor is withholding certain rights to the materials, albeit only for a specified time period.

In the United States, items valued at more than $5,000 will generally require a declaration of value made by an independent appraiser along with an acknowledgment by the donee organization that it qualifies as a charitable organization. The IRS specifies definite requirements both for the qualifications of the appraiser and for the timing of the appraisal. Tax law is very complex, and donors and/or institutions might want to seek expert counsel when large valuations are involved.

IRS policies regarding "self-generated" materials often greatly limit the tax deduction available to authors and artists donating their own work. Such materials must be appraised only for the cost of the materials used. Thus, an editorial cartoonist might typically sell his or her drawings for $500 each to a ready market. If that artist were to donate 150 cartoons to their alma mater, the IRS will only allow a deduction for the cost of the supplies used in their production, perhaps $10 for paper and ink, rather than the $75,000 the cartoons could have fetched on the open market.

As with any contract, a gift agreement can be as simple or complex as the circumstances dictate. Often an institution will have a simple form used for the bulk of the gifts they receive, and create special agreements for particularly large and/or valuable collections or for complex negotiations. Besides addressing rights issues, the gift agreement will include the name and address of the donor(s), a concise description of the material being donated, and a statement as to the disposition of material not retained by the institution. Such material might include duplicates, cancelled checks, and other items having no historic significance. Some donors wish the return of everything not retained for their collection; others allow the institution to exercise its discretion. In the latter case, much of the material might simply be destroyed while items of value might be transferred to another institution where they are a better fit, perhaps placing ephemera in a museum or published books in a library.

More complex agreements might call for the donor and/or repository to provide special services,

specifying who is to pay for the physical transfer of the *collection* to the repository or how the *arrangement* and *description* of the collection will be funded. As in any negotiation, anything and everything can be put on the table. Also, like any contract, the agreement can be amended at any time with the consent of both parties.

Larger institutions generally have their gift forms and special agreements approved by their legal counsel. At some institutions, only certain individuals have the authority to sign a contract, often a president, director, or secretary of the board.

Some institutions accept materials on *deposit*, a loan without the transfer of property or literary rights. This is not encouraged in the archival world, as those institutions incur expenses in receiving, storing, and perhaps even referencing a collection that may be removed at the depositor's whim. In the event that a collection is accepted on deposit, some clear language is needed in the agreement by which the rights to the material will automatically transfer to the institution at a specific date or, in the case of a certain eventuality, perhaps after five years or upon the death of the depositor. The institution should not be obligated to any onerous expenditure or to uncertainty as to the future of the deposit such as would occur if the depositor were to pass away or move without leaving a forwarding address.

Conclusion

In negotiating a donation, the institution must be alert to the donor's wishes and try to create a result in which both the donor and the institution "win." Most important, the institution must show its appreciation by being a good steward of each donation. That will create the positive environment necessary to encourage future donations.—*Herbert Hartsook*

Keywords: deed of gift, donor, gift agreement

Bibliography

Pease, C. *Managing Congressional Collections*. Chicago: Society of American Archivists, 2008.

Weideman, C. *A Guide to Deeds of Gift*. Chicago: Society of American Archivists, 2002.

E

ELECTRONIC DOCUMENT AND RECORDS MANAGEMENT SYSTEM (EDRMS)

An electronic document and records management system (EDRMS) is part of an evolving class of computer application oriented toward the management of *records* in the digital environment. Rooted in earlier meanings ascribed to document management systems (DMS) and records management systems (RMS), later modified with the addition of *E* for electronic as in ERMS and EDMS, this compound term is an effort to comprise the full spectrum of records for management through the use of digital technology. EDRMS is commonly understood to describe an automated tool to control and track the *creation*, use, modification, management, and disposal of both physical and electronically created *documents* and records, encompassing a workflow capability that extends functionality toward content management (CM) as an aspect of business intelligence (BI) systems. Pragmatic considerations for implementation suggest that it may be more correct to consider the EDRMS as a set of centrally controlled functions applied independently and through integration with a range of applications and systems within an operational context.

Evolution of the EDRMS

Computerization was introduced into the workplace as a means to calculate data on a larger scale in shorter time than human beings could achieve. Data was compiled into hierarchical database structures to enable aggregation, analysis and selective extraction for presentation in documents. This electronic data processing (EDP) within highly structured databases characterized the 1960s, followed by introduction of the relational database model and word processing in the early 1970s. These developments opened the door to extension of information relationships and to the presentation of data content such that documents could be updated with current data and made available simultaneously to a distributed workforce. With recognition of the need to distinguish between documents in progress and those deemed complete, document management systems (DMS) emerged to control and monitor *access* to content so that completed documents suitable to inform action could be identified and disseminated across a distributed network. Evolving iteratively, incorporating technological advances, the electronic document management system (EDMS) controlled and tracked the acquisition, creation, modification, and dissemination of digital and digitized documents. An EDMS enables collaborative development of documents, reducing costs, time, and risk associated with service or product delivery while improving consistency and *accountability*. Benefits of an EDMS are directly related to the operational process and *context* and are not, therefore, generalizable to the management of information resources that pertain to processes outside the EDMS (Johnston and Bowen 2005). *Metadata* is used to denote stages in creation, editing, and update processes as well as to identify actors, approvals, and currency among coexisting versions of the same document and relationships among documents that exist in digital form within a defined workflow. The EDMS does not incorporate a taxonomy to place documents in a broader information context surrounding a given workflow. Rather, it exists within and relies on defined processes that constitute a specific and limited procedural context. Historically, the focus on document creation, use, and dissemination did not extend to *disposition*.

The EDMS as described here is typically a subset of the overall information resource environment within an enterprise. Incorporated within the EDRMS, it constitutes one function set that is specific to the needs of business procedures within predefined workflows. The second function set is the Electronic Records Management System (ERMS) that is derived from the *records management* application and serves to automate *recordkeeping* regardless of the form of record to be managed.

The ERMS emerged as distinct from EDMS in the 1990s to encompass intellectual management of paper-based and other physical records (Adam 2008). The ERMS was designed to manage physical entities, records in analogue form with utility for establishing and managing the relationship between logical entities and their physical manifestation in records stored in physical locations. With time and increased need to manage electronic records, the meaning of the term has been applied inconsistently as "primarily an application for managing electronic records, though it may also be used to manage physical records" (European Commission 2008). Cited in MoReq2, a key though now-surpassed international standard, this qualified definition highlights the quandary. Is it clear that a particular ERMS supports management of electronic records, nonelectronic records, or both, and to what degree? The answer differs in relation to the historical design origins of the software application in question. For example, an ERMS developed from the foundation of a records management application with its focus on applying new technology to traditional records management is more likely to incorporate management of both nondigital and digital records with validity, *authenticity*, and *reliability* over time as a grounding principle of design. In contrast, an ERMS that derives from origin as a document imaging system (DIS) or its successor, the document management application or system (DMS), is more likely to reflect an information technology sensibility that is augmented with functionality to serve both digital and nondigital records management needs, underpinned by a design oriented toward access more than *preservation*. The

distinctions are not readily apparent but are critical in operation. Specific needs of the organizational context set the scope of the ERMS initiative, which, in turn, drives selection of software, procurement, and design of functionality to achieve the requisite level of records management including disposition and *preservation*. Except in the area of data generated as a by-product of functionality, the ERMS is a recordkeeping, not a record-creating, system.

The emergence of EDRMS to represent the combined attributes of an EDMS and ERMS is a recognition that record-creating, workflow-management, and recordkeeping functionalities are required to achieve organizational outcomes and optimize information management.

Terminological Challenges

Terminology, when clear, represents an idea that is grounded in specialized knowledge. When there are overlaps in specialist domains, or when usage becomes colloquial or connotes an imprecise concept, meaning becomes unclear. Term combinations, such as EDRMS, share fundamental elements but are susceptible to interpretation and misrepresentation, inevitably so where the understanding, intent, and practice differ. For example, a content-management system that enables collaboration is neither a document-management system nor a records management system. Conceptually, however, it might be either, or both. A knowledge-management system may be all or none of these.

A further linguistic challenge exists in the terms from which EDRMS derives. The adjective electronic may be understood to modify the words document, records, and management with variable meaning. Electronic may apply to the form of information (document, record); a method of data transmission applicable to both digital and analog data; or the system of control, that is, management of documents and records through electronic means. Variable definitions in numerous texts, standards, guidelines, and policies enable differing interpretations of the EDRMS term combination within and across jurisdictions as observed in Asia, Australasia, Europe, and North America. In addition to grammatical considerations, EDRMS gives equal weight to document and records management in a representation that may reflect a positioning of the information technology and records management domains. In concept and operation, however, the management of documents is subsumed within an overriding records management functionality. Alternatives such as electronic recordkeeping systems (ERKS) avoid this contradiction. Yet, the influential National Archives and Records Authority of the United States has declared *ERKS* to mean the keeping of electronic records, rather than the more grammatically sound recordkeeping through electronic means. As a result, this term also suffers from inconsistent interpretation.

The adoption of enterprise document and records management systems (Sutton 1996) as an EDRMS alternative illustrates the continuing effort to capture the intent and meaning of the term. This variation implies a reach across all information content within an enterprise. As a statement of intent, this approach has value. In practice, however, an enterprise-wide document and records management system demands a shared vision and collaboration among decision makers, practitioners, and vendors that is not yet evident.

Toward Implementation

The specific functional requirements and the implementation of EDRMS software must be defined through analysis of relevant legislation, regulation, strategies for the use of recorded information resources, and such factors that are relevant to the operational environment. These considerations may be international, national, regional, sectoral, and operational. Therefore, selection cannot rely entirely on any standard. Relevant standards such as DOD 5015.2 and MoReq2010, within the frame provided by ISO 15489 and ISO 30301, detail required and optional functions to be incorporated, as appropriate to the specific initiative.

A challenge to the successful implementation of an EDRMS may be the underestimation of necessary pre- and post-procurement work to ensure organizational readiness. The EDRMS is required to interface with operational systems and applications, that is, any process that generates information recorded for a business purpose. As an indication of the scope of work, note that each of these processes must be identified and analyzed to identify and define the metadata through which the integration of ERMS and EDMS functionality is achieved.

Such knowledge is required for effective operation of the EDRMS, yet may reside in operational units outside the purview of those charged to select and procure the EDRMS. Operational units, when engaged, necessarily focus on stating requirements of the as-yet-unknown system ahead of examining implications that system may have on existing practices. Procurement of a technical functionality that is out of sync with applicable juridical and legislative requirements or operational practice is a risk. Additional considerations with a significant effect on workload, timelines, and budget include the development of taxonomies, definition of configurable elements, and identification of need for and design of customization. Knowledge workers are affected by the imposition of controlled access and accountability for modification and disposition in ways that can affect performance, outcomes, and workplace culture.

Conclusion

Successful implementation of EDRMS functionality depends on an unequivocal definition of the term, informed by analysis of required and variable aspects set forth in standards and practices that are relevant to the operational context. This foundation guides assessment of interdependencies among systems with regard to function and interoperability and the definition of metadata elements. Findings of the assessment reveal the nature and degree of configuration and customization requirements necessary for effective use. Early and continuing attention to the management of organizational, practice, and cultural change is required to ensure the viability of an EDRMS that is integral to overall *information management.—John James O'Brien*

Keywords: content management, recordkeeping, terminology
Related Entries: Digital Records; Recordkeeping; Recordkeeping System(s)

Bibliography

Adam, A. *Implementing Electronic Document and Record Management Systems*. Boca Raton, FL: Auerbach Publications, 2008. www.myilibrary. com?id=113570 (accessed November 2013).

CCSDS 650.0-R-1. *Reference Model for an Open Archival Information System (OAIS)*. Draft Recommendation for Space Data System Standards, Magenta Book CCSDS 650.0-R-1. Consultative Committee on Space Data Systems, 2012. http://public.ccsds.org/publications/archive/650x0m2.pdf (accessed November 2013).

DLM Forum Foundation. *MoReq2010: Modular Requirements for Records Systems—Volume 1: Core Services & Plug-in Modules*. 2011. http://moreq2010.eu/pdf/moreq2010_vol1_v1_1_en.pdf (accessed November 2013).

International Standards Organization. *ISO 15489-1: Information and Documentation—Records Management. Part 1: General and Part 2: Guidelines.* Geneva, Switzerland: International Standards Organization, 2001.

Johnston, G., and D. Bowen. "The Benefits of Electronic Records Management Systems: A General Review of Published and Some Unpublished Cases." *Records Management Journal* 15 (3) (2005): 131–40. www.emeraldinsight.com/doi/pdfplus/10.1108/09565690510632319.

Pearce-Moses, R. *A Glossary of Archival and Records Terminology*. Archival Fundamentals Series. Chicago: Society of American Archivists, 2005.

State Records of South Australia. *EDRMS Panel of Products Procurement and Pre-Implementation.* Government of South Australia, 2009. www.archives.sa.gov.au/files/management_guidelines_EDRMS_pandp.pdf (accessed December 2013).

Sutton, M. J. D. *Document Management for the Enterprise: Principles, Techniques, and Applications.* New York: John Wiley & Sons, 1996.

University of Surrey, Department of Computing. *The Importance of Terminology.* www.computing.surrey.ac.uk/ai/pointer/report/section1.html (accessed December 2013).

U.S. Department of Defense. *DoD 5015.2-STD: Electronic Records Management Software Applications Design Criteria Standard.* 2007. www.dtic.mil/whs/directives/corres/pdf/501502std.pdf (accessed November 2013).

Wilhelm, P. *EDRMS Standards—a Critical Evaluation of the Benefits of Superseding National Standards with European Models Focusing on TNA 2002 Replacement by MoReq2.* Northumbria University, UK, 2008.

ENVIRONMENTAL SYSTEMS

Environmental systems are incorporated into buildings to maintain an optimum setting for the long-term *preservation* of the archival and/or manuscript *collections* housed in the facility. They may consist of heating, air-conditioning, fans, thermostats, or filtering or freezing systems. Smaller *archives* may have a single environmental system for their entire building while larger facilities may have a variety of systems designed for a specific use or type of material.

Temperature, Humidity, and Collection Deterioration

Archival collections consist of natural and man-made materials that are subject to continuing deterioration as they age. Storage conditions can enhance or exacerbate deterioration. Twentieth-century research has highlighted the impact of high temperature and humidity on the chemical decline of different types of archival collections. Some types of deterioration, such as embrittlement or color change, are not immediately obvious, while others such as mold or mildew have an immediate effect. Appropriately designed and well-functioning environmental controls can prevent mold and mildew as well as slow other types of collection deterioration by filtering out air pollutants and maintaining appropriate temperature and humidity.

Archival Buildings and Preservation

Archival buildings provide a first level of preservation for archival collections. They protect collections from the outdoor elements as well as provide security from theft. Buildings have the ability to create a separate environment from their surroundings. They can help protect collections from high outside temperatures by eliminating windows and installing vapor barriers and high levels of insulation. However, buildings by themselves cannot slow the inherent deterioration affecting archival collections brought about by heat, humidity, and air pollution. Maintaining collections at constant levels of temperature, humidity, and air filtration requires a variety of environmental controls.

Heating, Ventilation, and Air-Conditioning Systems

Heating, ventilation, and air-conditioning systems (HVAC) are the most common types of environmental controls used in archival *facilities*. Such systems have the ability to maintain constant levels of temperature and humidity and filter out harmful pollutants if properly designed for local conditions. Heat is provided by electricity, burning gas, or oil. Other systems develop warm and hot temperatures by passing air over pipes heated by central hot-water-generating systems. Cooling is achieved by forcing air over refrigerant coils filled with chilled water, which removes moisture from the air. Archives located in areas with high humidity may need to use specialized technologies, such as adding glycol to chilled water or using desiccant equipment, to lower temperatures. The latter technology operates by removing all moisture from the air and then adding an appropriate amount to reach a set humidity level.

Air filtration systems are equally important environmental controls and are especially critical in areas with high air pollution. Passive air filters can remove large and medium-size pollutants passing through the heating and air-conditioning systems. High levels of gaseous pollution may require the installation of gas-phase filtration. Pollution dangers also can be lowered by careful location of outside air intakes and lowering the amount of outside air mixed with recirculated filtered air already in the heating and air-conditioning system.

Heating and air-conditioning systems are controlled by thermostats and humidistats located in various parts of the building. Thermostats control building heating systems by maintaining temperatures within a specific range dictated by mechanical design specifications. Thermostats can gather data at a variety of locations, from individual rooms to specific locations within the heating system. Humidistats measure relative humidity and increase or decrease water chilling to maintain constant levels of relative humidity in a particular space.

Older HVAC systems are controlled by mechanical thermostats using wires and mercury capsules that respond to changes in room temperature and turn heating and air-conditioning on and off. With the advent of the computer, most systems now use direct digital controls to manage heating and air-conditioning systems. These systems are more accurate and can be controlled by computer systems that may be centralized in the facilities-management or maintenance department of the building. Digital controls can carefully balance the levels of temperature and moisture required to maintain a stable environment within very specific parameters. Such systems may be equipped with alarms, which will send a warning when the temperature and/or humidity levels are too high or low. Digital controls have the advantage of allowing a variety of individuals to monitor conditions while only allowing building managers to make temperature or humidity adjustments.

Environmental Systems and Global Warming

The increased cost of energy combined with concerns about green-house gasses and global warming has driven architects and engineers to seek methods of lowering the amount of energy needed to maintain stable temperatures and humidity within archival buildings. Some of these solutions focus on the building itself through careful siting and by increasing the levels of insulation. Strategic placement of the records storage area, which generally uses high amounts of energy, can also lower energy use. Alternate energy sources, such as wind and solar power, are being used to cut costs. The Image Preservation Institute at the Rochester Institute of Technology has carried out detailed research on the impact of temperature and humidity on collection environments and suggested methods of adjusting those levels to reflect the seasonal outside environment while not impacting collection deterioration (http://ipisustainability.org/resources).

Environmental systems are a critical element in the preservation of archival collections. From buildings to heating, ventilating, and air-conditioning systems to their controls, archivists need to be aware of how each interacts in preserving their collections and how to incorporate them so that their collections are stored in optimum conditions ensuring long life for the entire archives.—*Thomas P. Wilsted*

Keywords: buildings, archival facilities, preservation, temperature, humidity

Related Entry: Archival Buildings and Facilities; Conservation; Preservation

Bibliography

International Standards Organization (ISO). *Information and Documentation: Document Storage Requirements for Archive and Library Material.* Geneva, Switzerland: International Standards Organization, 2003.

National Archives and Records Administration. "NARA 1571: Archival Storage Standards." 2002. www.archives.gov/foia/directives/nara1571.pdf.

Pacifico, M., and W. Wilsted. *Archival and Special Collection Facilities.* Chicago: Society of American Archivists, 2009.

EPHEMERA

What is ephemera? In many ways ephemera defies definition: short-lived yet sometimes avidly collected, momentary in purpose yet carrying a wealth of social and historical detail, it has often been given the default label of "miscellaneous" or "fugitive" material. Falling in the crack between books, manuscripts, and artifacts, ephemera challenges traditional library and archival approaches to *description*, discovery, and *preservation*, yet its value to scholars is significant. The explosion of born-digital *documents* has only added to the complexities inherent in this peculiar material.

Definitions

Traditional Definition

Ephemera comes from the Greek ἐπί (epi: "on, for") and ἡμέρα (hemera: "day"), implying something that lasts only a short time. The term *ephemera* in the library sense came into use in the 1960s; shortly thereafter, in 1975, Britain's Ephemera Society was formed "for the conservation, study and presentation of printed and handwritten ephemera," closely followed by the Ephemera Society of America in 1980. One of the earliest documented definitions of ephemera, and the most succinct, is "anything printed for a specific short-term purpose" (Lewis 1976). Examples of ephemera thus run the gamut from bumper stickers to broadsides, menus to matchbooks, postcards to packaging, and everything in between.

A more detailed or precise definition is difficult to establish because the same item may be viewed in different ways by different departments or repositories; the designation of a given item as "ephemera" is to some degree contextual and variable (Makepeace 1944). For example, a general library might class an advertising brochure for a Ford Pinto as ephemera, while a repository specializing in automobile history might view this as a minor publication worthy of cataloging. The Ford Motor Corporation probably did not intend its marketing brochures to be collected and preserved any more than the sender of a text message intends for it to be permanently retained by its recipient.

Expanding the Definition

Later definitions retained the emphasis on ephemera's transitory nature, but expanded it beyond paper to include audio and video. In the early days of television, for example, even regularly scheduled programs were regarded by the networks as ephemera, and it was standard practice to reuse tapes numerous times without any effort to preserve original recordings. Home recordings were often made on low-quality VHS tapes that quickly degraded, rendering them ephemeral regardless of their creator's intention.

With the advent of the digital world and the ubiquitous *e-* prefix (e-mail, e-business, e-shopping, e-learning), we must now also grapple with what one might call "e-phemera." This encompasses not only traditional forms of ephemera that now exist in digital form, such as menus produced as PDFs or electronic greeting cards sent between friends, but also uniquely "e" forms such as Twitter posts, text messages, tribute/memorial pages, pop-up advertisements, chats, email "read" receipts, and e-mails sent purely to convey an attachment. (Interestingly, despite the temporary intention of its creators, e-phemera is frequently retained not by *archivists* for its historical value but by corporations like Amazon for its financial value in targeted marketing.)

Some scholars have argued for a definition of ephemera that includes acts of "public memory," such as the teddy bears, flowers, ribbons, notes, and candles left at sites of tragedy. Since the opening of the Vietnam Veterans Memorial in Washington, DC, for example, visitors have left mementos, notes, cards, flowers, stuffed animals, and so on, that temporarily become part of the memorial. The National

Park Service initially regarded these items as "lost and found," but they later began saving them and making them part of a *collection*, recognizing the vernacular and ephemeral as a valid part of the monumental (Haskins 2007, 401–22).

Value of Ephemera

The fact that an item's creator intended it to have a short life does not mean that ephemera has no interest for collectors or value to the historian or researcher. On the contrary, much can be learned from ephemera (including e-phemera) far beyond its creator's intent. Postcards, business trade cards, catalogs, business letterhead—whether a blank sheet of paper or a Microsoft Word template—and emoticons/abbreviations appearing in text messages ("lol" or >:|) may offer insight into the history of illustration, typography, and page design as well as rhetoric, persuasion, communication, semiotics, and other forms of discourse.

Ephemera is also a snapshot of the cultural *context* in which it was created and embedded. In a sense, its temporary nature is the very thing that gives it historical value. With its focus on the moment, ephemera "inevitably contains facts, prejudices, and other aspects (such as language, art and social organization) reflecting [its] particular time and place" (Ephemera Society of America). Fliers for student rallies in the 1960s provide *evidence* of political activity on college campuses, while Facebook status updates may tell future social historians what people viewed as important enough to share with others. Postcards and Pinterest pages represent what a given era finds inspiring, beautiful, or simply interesting. Product brochures from the 1950s and unboxing videos posted to YouTube supply raw material for the student of technology. Cell phone photos, videos, and text messages document the average citizen's experience of civil unrest or police brutality. Lolcats and other popular memes illuminate the manner in which we play with language. A company's brochures, fliers, and posters may yield information about the *organizational culture*. Ephemera is, in short, a way of capturing "what social reality feels like rather than what it should be like" (Bodnar, quoted in Haskins 2007).

Finally, ephemera can provide valuable data for scholars of marginalized groups. Libraries and *archives* have often neglected ephemera in favor of more formal *records*, but the creation of formal records is usually a result of a formal organization. As a result, "we take the records of big important offices, and ignore small, original, eclectic, powerless social processes. We miss the origins of movements, and . . . the alternatives to nationally significant groups" (Murphy, quoted in Burant 1995). Marginalized groups such as women, working-class people, African Americans, and LGBTs have historically been underrepresented in formal organizations; collecting and preserving ephemera forwards the archivist's goal of representing a wide variety of viewpoints and accurately reflecting cultural history and memory.

The Ephemeral Challenge

Ephemera challenges all aspects of the archival process, from *acquisition* to *preservation*. Because ephemera is the result of nontraditional methods of production and distribution (e.g., concert programs distributed by hand before a performance, fliers stapled to telephone poles or placed on car windshields, text messages sent by cell phone), acquisition can be difficult and sporadic, and may demand extra effort and creativity on the part of curators. Certain types of ephemera such as postcards are avidly collected, so acquisition may occur in large quantities via *donation*. Alternatively, ephemera may come in as single items purchased, donated, or removed from collections as out-of-scope; these items must be individually accessioned and their *provenance* documented. Finally, due to its transitory nature, ephemera must be acquired promptly before it decays or is discarded. Acquisition of e-phemera such as tweets can be even more difficult; at the time of this writing, Twitter offers the option to "request my twitter archive" (but only of one's own account, as a comma-separated file), while many other social media services offer no archiving capability at all. Accurate capture of such material may require either specialized tools or labor-intensive manual effort, and even so the result is likely to be a lower-quality derivative representation rather than a true copy. Finally, concerns about privacy are causing some e-phemera to be aggressively purged and users to choose social media platforms that deliberately do not archive content (e.g., SnapChat).

Lacking traditional bibliographic information such as creator or publisher, the *arrangement* and *description* of ephemera can be difficult. Many repositories take the simplest route, storing individually acquired items in vertical files arranged alphabetically by type (broadsides, pamphlets, programs) and/or topic (political, cultural). While this at least gives researchers a starting point, folder-level description of material that varies so widely in size, content, coverage, and form may place an undue burden on the researcher. In addition, this approach ignores the vast amount of ephemera scattered throughout records and manuscript collections, which remains there due to the archival principle of *respect des fonds*. Tightly bound to a particular time and place, the meaning of a piece of ephemera resides as much in its *context* as in the item itself; while archival description has always endeavored to provide context, it is especially critical—and sometimes especially difficult—with ephemera. Donation of a large quantity of material may demand item-level processing and description, which takes considerable time. In the case of audio, video, or e-phemera, description may require viewing or reading hundreds of individual files, while in the latter case the concept of arrangement may not even be applicable. More often than not, an external system is used to associate *metadata* (subject, date, etc.) with specific digital files.

Because ephemera is not intended for long-term survival, it is often made of cheap, flimsy, or rapidly-decaying materials and therefore may require more preservation or *conservation* effort than other manuscript material, including specialized storage to prevent deterioration. Although there is no such thing as "flimsy" or "lower-quality" bits and bytes, e-phemera as a type of *digital record* poses particular difficulties in that the digital item itself must be preserved, as well as a method of viewing or listening to it. Cell phone messages, for example, may be in .wav or .mp3 format; although today's computers can play either format, this may not always be the case. Preserving e-phemera, therefore, requires specialized strategies, tools, and techniques.

Given that ephemera poses the above challenges while still possessing great research value, repositories need better guidelines for the *appraisal* of potential ephemera collections to help them choose what to acquire. Dan Cohen of the Digital Public

Library of America proposes a "calculus of importance" derived from research in profiling for security purposes, which offers guidance on what to pay attention to and, therefore, how to spend limited resources on saving objects in a digital age. His conclusion is that "we should continue to expend the majority of resources on those documents and people of most likely future interest, but not to the exclusion of objects and figures that currently seem unimportant" (2010, para. 13).

Conclusion

Ephemera, long treasured by collectors, is increasingly attracting the notice and appreciation of scholars and historians despite its resistance to easy definition or categorization. Fragmentary, temporary, easily lost or discarded, each item is "a form of time capsule, a crystallization of another time and place" (quoted in Burant 1995) and as such merits as much attention, both practical and theoretical, as any other archival form.—*Michele Combs*

Keywords: ephemera, digital records, marginalized groups

Related Entry: Acquisition; Appraisal; Collection; Context; Digital Records; Selection; Preservation

Bibliography

Altermatt, Rebecca, and Adrian Hilton. "Hidden Collections within Hidden Collections: Providing Access to Printed Ephemera." *The American Archivist* 75 (1) (2012): 171–94. http://archivists.metapress.com/content/6538724k51441161/fulltext.pdf.

Bee, Robert. "The Importance of Preserving Paper-Based Artifacts in a Digital Age." *The Library Quarterly* 78 (2) (2008): 179–94. www.jstor.org/stable/10.1086/528888.

Burant, Jim. "Ephemera, Archives, and Another View of History." *Archivaria* 40 (1995): 189–98. http://journals.sfu.ca/archivar/index.php/archivaria/article/view/12105/13098.

Chao Center for Asian Studies. "The Ephemera Project." Rice University, 2011. http://chaocenter.rice.edu/ephemera.

Clinton, Alan. *Printed Ephemera: Collection, Organization and Access.* London: Clive Bingley, 1981.

Cohen, Dan. "Digital Ephemera and the Calculus of Importance." Dancohen.org, 2010. www.dancohen.org/2010/05/17/digital-ephemera-and-the-calculus-of-importance (accessed June 2014).

The Ephemera Society. www.ephemera-society.org.uk (accessed June 2014).

The Ephemera Society of America. www.ephemera-society.org (accessed June 2014).

Haskins, Ekaterina. "Between Archive and Participation: Public Memory in a Digital Age." *Rhetoric Society Quarterly* 37 (4) (2007): 401–22. DOI:10.1080/02773940601086794.

Lewis, J. N. C. *Collecting Printed Ephemera.* London: Studio Vista, 1976.

Makepeace, Chris E. *Ephemera: A Book on its Collection, Conservation and Use.* Aldershot, England: Gower, 1944.

Rickards, Maurice. *Encyclopedia of Ephemera.* New York: Routledge, 2000.

ETHNICITY AND ARCHIVES

Until the 1960s immigrant and ethnic groups were neglected by *archives*, except those run by ethnic organizations themselves. The large ethnic collections of today, such as those of the Immigration History Research Center, were developed mostly in the 1970s and 1980s, using a "from the bottom-up" approach to archiving that relied heavily on fieldwork in ethnic neighborhoods. At the same time, the archival profession became aware of the need for more diversity in its ranks and has multiplied efforts to train and recruit members of ethnic minorities. Since the 1990s, new theoretical approaches and web technologies have led to archiving experiments characterized by emphasis on collaboration between *community* and mainstream archives, donors, and curators to achieve a more representative record of history.

Early Initiatives

The first significant attempts to collect materials documenting the history of immigrants and ethnic groups in the United States and Canada were made in the nineteenth century by ethnic historical societies. Until the 1960s, mainstream archives—academic and public archives not managed by ethnic communities—showed little interest in ethnic groups, except as subjects of governmental policy, or components of local history. The concept of ethnicity, now so prevalent, did not become widespread until the 1960s. The word "ethnic" itself was used interchangeably with more popular terms like race, nationality, and immigrant origin until the 1940s, when sociologists started using it to underscore cultural characteristics defining human groups rather than biological traits. In the 1960s, the term expanded to include blacks, Asians, Latinos, and all groups previously designated as racial minorities (Rees 2007).

The relative lack of ethnic materials in mainstream collections is due to numerous factors, among which are Anglo-Saxonism and racism, the ideology of the melting pot—according to which immigrant cultures were destined to disappear through assimilation—and, in the United States especially, the *archivists'* focus on governmental and organizational records and on the elite. Such neglect accounts for the efforts by established ethnic communities to preserve their own cultural heritage. Ethnic historical societies like the Jewish American Historical Society built collections designed to demonstrate their contributions to the nation's history, a phenomenon that historian John Higham has called "ethnic Americanism" (Higham 1994).

The Heyday of Ethnic Archives

As interest in immigration history and ethnicity grew in the 1960s and 1970s, the number of "ethnic archives"—collections of ethnic materials run by ethnic or mainstream institutions—multiplied. Many of today's large collections find their origin in that period: for example, the Immigration History Research Center, recently renamed IHRC Archives; the Balch Institute for Ethnic Studies, now integrated into the collections of the Historical Society of Pennsylvania; the Multicultural History Society of Ontario; and the National Ethnic Archives program of Canada's national archives (Singer 1997). However, such institutions devoted exclusively to ethnic materials remain rare compared to the numerous regional and local archives, public and private, ethnic and mainstream, that include ethnic history in their collections.

The *acquisition* and *appraisal* of these archival *collections* were influenced by a political, social, and academic context marked by challenges to the melting pot, the resurgence of "white ethnics," new scholarship in immigration history, the civil rights movement and its demands for racial equality, and the rise of the "black power" and "black is beautiful" movements. In Canada, new policies of multiculturalism provided significant federal and provincial funding for cultural-heritage programs supporting ethnic history. Archives devoted significant efforts to documenting the history of white ethnic groups coming from immigration, but also Asians, blacks, and Latinos.

Professional archivists thought that entire segments of society had been un- or underdocumented and that archives should provide a more representative view of society. As a result, mainstream institutions expanded their reach to new types of *records* documenting the lives of ordinary people—through artifacts such as letters, diaries, scrapbooks, or photographs—that would meet the needs of social historians who wanted to write history "from the bottom up." They sought out the records of ethnic organizations such as newspapers, fraternal associations, and churches, which formed the bulk of new acquisitions. Those archival collections reflected an understanding of ethnicity as a social construct rather than a set of cultural characteristics one was born with—a product of immigration and adaptation to the host country, rather than the remnants of a culture imported from the "old country." The focus was clearly on experiences during and after immigration, whether in the workplace, the church, ethnic neighborhoods, or the family (Daniel 2010).

This required extensive fieldwork, surmounting suspicions, and establishing trust with ethnic communities. Efforts were challenged by problems that remain acute to this day: the scarcity of archivists speaking relevant foreign languages, the immensity of the task, and the lack of clear collection-development policies that would circumscribe collecting projects. Questions about what made a document "ethnic" were difficult to answer, and most archives selected materials based on self-defined ethnic identities—identities claimed by ethnic organizations and individuals. Collections were, therefore, skewed in favor of the sources that were most easily documented, those produced by actively ethnic organizations and individuals, located in visibly ethnic neighborhoods (Daniel 2013). Collections were also arranged and described based on the same self-defined identities.

Ethnic Archives in the Digital Age

Since the 1970s, archivists and their professional *associations* like the Society of American Archivists (SAA) have become aware of the need to diversify not only their collections but also the profession itself (Adkins 2008). In 1987, the SAA established the Minority Round Table, now the Archivists and Archives of Color Roundtable, which offers conference programs, scholarships, and awards and promotes education and training for minorities. The SAA's 2010 statement on diversity reflects the association's commitment to diversity as one of three high priorities in its strategic plan. Other diversity initiatives include the *Protocols for Native American Archival Materials*, drafted in 2006 by professionals to identify best practices for "culturally responsive care and use" of Indian archives held by mainstream American organizations.

At the same time, since the 1990s, approaches to ethnic diversity have been transformed due to new political voices springing from the surge of immigration from Asia, Latin America, and other parts of the world, and to academics whose interest has shifted from white ethnics to racial minorities and postcolonialism. Ethnic community archives like the Resource Center at the Japanese American National Museum and projects like the Chinese Canadian Stories reflect these new interests. Scholars are now treating ethnicity as one of many factors shaping identities and social experiences, including gender, class, race, and religious affiliations, and have moved away from an inward-looking single-group approach toward intergroup relations and diasporic phenomena.

The influence of postmodernist theories in archival science has also had a significant impact on ethnic archives. It has given a new impetus to the call to recover the voices of the marginalized and powerless and has stimulated the shift away from the traditional conception of the archivist as a neutral custodian of the historical record and toward a new role as an active participant in the shaping of the record. Archivists have challenged the conception of the archival *document* as a static or finished product and study the dynamic process of *record creation* and management. They offer a change of perspective, considering the *transfer* to archives as the beginning, rather than the end, of the life of the record. This approach has led to new models that reconsider the responsibilities of the archivist toward donors from ethnic communities, such as stewardship (Wurl 2005) and *participatory archives* (Shilton and Srinivasan 2007). Such models challenge not only the traditional authority of the archivist but also ethnocentric *archival practices* embedded in the profession.

They put into question the core notion of *provenance*, which attributes record creation to specific individuals or organizations and is based on the values and structures of nineteenth-century European bureaucracies—values that may not be relevant to other cultures that transmit history and memory differently. Some archival scholars contend that archivists should consider societal provenance, namely the societal and cultural contexts in which individuals and organizations create records (Nesmith 2002, 35). Jeannette Bastian has pushed for such an approach in colonial settings, where archives are created and run by the dominant power but the voices of the colonized can still be found if the actors and processes of archiving are considered in their broader context (Bastian 2006).

Today mainstream archives strive to be culturally responsive and to empower communities to "speak" for themselves. Collaboration with ethnic organizations and communities is on the rise. Participatory archiving has been implemented most thoroughly by indigenous archives in Australia, New Zealand, and Canada, and implies incorporating indigenous values in the very governance structures and procedures of archival institutions as well as in access to collections. Recognition that non-Western systems of knowledge have their own ways of transmitting knowledge has led to an expansion of the very concept of archives to include oral histories, artifacts, and even recorded performances and rituals. Some initiatives have also experimented with crowdsourcing and other forms of online user participation to create *arrangement* and *description* of ethnic collections that are more in tune with the cultures of the groups they document (Daniel 2013). Web technologies allow geographically scattered materi-

als to be united virtually and make it possible to add multiple layers of description and arrangement. All these changes challenge the traditional authority of the professional archivist, who takes on new roles in relation to records creators and users.

Conclusion

Today's archivists know not only that ethnicity is a dynamic social construct, but also that ethnic archives contribute to molding it. If archives do not just record ethnic histories, but create them, the development and management of collections have a determining impact on ethnic identities, past and present. Community archives contribute significantly to the recording of neglected ethnic histories, but in North America the archival profession remains dominated by white archivists. Yet, in an increasingly multicultural world, archives encourage diversification of their staff and take advantage of collaboration and digital technologies to represent ethnic histories and memories as the group members see them. Some question the benefits of ethnic community archives' focus on identity in their mission and operations (Paschild 2012). The challenge is that ethnic groups are heterogeneous communities with hazy and shifting boundaries, and ethnic markers cannot be separated from other forms of belonging. The debate continues on how to obtain a representative record of history and to preserve it over the long term.—*Dominique Daniel*

Keywords: participatory archiving, immigrants, identity, cultural diversity, societal provenance

Related Entries: Archives and Memory; Community Archives; Participatory Archives; Principle of Provenance; Web Archiving

Bibliography

Adkins, Elizabeth W. "Our Journey toward Diversity—and a Call to (More) Action." *The American Archivist* 71 (1) (2008): 21–49. http://archivists. metapress.com/content/lv370048r7875175/full-text.pdf.

Bastian, Jeannette A. "Reading Colonial Records through an Archival Lens: The Provenance of Place, Space and Creation." *Archival Science* 6 (3–4) (2006): 267–84. DOI:10.1007/s10502-006-9019-1.

Daniel, Dominique. "Archival Representations of Immigration and Ethnicity in North American History: From the Ethnicization of Archives to the Archivization of Ethnicity." *Archival Science* 14 (2) (2013): 1–35. DOI:10.1007/s10502-013-9209-6.

———. "Documenting the Immigrant and Ethnic Experience in American Archives." *American Archivist* 73 (1) (2010): 82–104. http://archivists.metapress.com/content/k2837h27wv1201hv/fulltext.pdf.

Higham, John. "The Ethnic Historical Society in Changing Times." *Journal of American Ethnic History* 13 (2) (1994): 30–44. www.jstor.org/stable/27501124.

Nesmith, Tom. "Seeing Archives: Postmodernism and the Changing Intellectual Place of Archives." *American Archivist* 65 (1) (2002): 24–41. http://archivists.metapress.com/content/rr48450509r0712u/fulltext.pdf.

Paschild, Cristine. "Community Archives and the Limitations of Identity: Considering Discursive Impact on Material Needs." *American Archivist* 75 (1) (2012): 125–42. http://archivists.metapress.com/content/c181102l71x4572h/fulltext.pdf.

Rees, Richard W. *Shades of Difference: A History of Ethnicity in America*. Perspectives on a Multiracial America Series. Lanham, MD: Rowman & Littlefield, 2007.

Shilton, Kate, and Ramesh Srinivasan. "Participatory Appraisal and Arrangement for Multicultural Archival Collections." *Archivaria* 63 (2007): 87–101. http://journals.sfu.ca/archivar/index.php/archivaria/article/view/13129/14371.

Singer, Lisa. *The Value of Community-Based Ethnic Archives: A Resource in Development*. Master's thesis, University of Manitoba, 1997. http://mspace.lib.umanitoba.ca/handle/1993/1018.

Wurl, Joel. "Ethnicity as Provenance: In Search of Values and Principles for Documenting the Immigrant Experience." *Archival Issues* 29 (1) (2005): 65–76. www.jstor.org/stable/41102095.

F

FACSIMILE

A facsimile is an "exact" copy that attempts to convey the content and material form of a unique source, insofar as it is possible to re-create the physical likeness of an object.

The Concept

A facsimile reproduction may be distinguished from a textual transcription because of the attentiveness in the former to the scale and *format* of its exemplar, as well as to visual cues, such as color, the design of letter-shapes, ornamentation, and illustration. Producers of facsimiles have held different opinions regarding the condition that should be reproduced, some preferring to transmit visible indications of the passage of time, and others opting to reimagine the original in its primordial state by "cleaning up" annotation, damage, and discoloration (Weitenkampf 1943, 129). Duplication in the facsimile is thus selective, and indeed no process of reproduction can imitate the social history of an object, such as a tradition of ownership and handling, by which specific signs of wear were accrued. Perhaps it is for this reason that publishers often discuss their techniques of reproduction in hopes of convincing readers to accept their facsimile as a faithful one. As David McKitterick observes, facsimiles will always raise questions "not only . . . respecting their adequacy for other purposes, editorial or otherwise representative, but also the degree to which the reader can be persuaded to suspend disbelief; to accept some always variable degree of compromise between what he sees before him, and what he perceives as its inspi-

ration" (1993, 164). Worth noting is that facsimile reproductions have generally been focused on the visual replication of the physical form of *documents*, with limited attention paid to the imitation of smells, sounds, and textures that may be present in or elicited by the age, history, or natural properties of the original materials.

Conclusion

Early facsimiles were produced by hand, and employed techniques such as drawing and engraving on blocks of wood, stone, or plates of copper. The quality of such facsimiles depended in part on the skill of the artists and their abilities to interpret and reproduce graphic markings transmitted by the exemplar. In the late-nineteenth century, the advent of photography meant that reproductions could be generated mechanically, although whether mechanization improved the trustworthiness of such facsimiles was contested famously by Erwin Panofsky and Walter Benjamin, who discussed the aesthetic and moral implications of such duplications, and by art critics, bibliographers, *archivists*, and librarians, among others, through the middle of the twentieth century. More recently, the proliferation of online facsimiles and so-called digital surrogates has reignited the debates about the relationship between originals and reproductions, and the authority of copies (Deegan and Sutherland 2009; Latour and Lowe 2011). —*Bonnie Mak*

Keywords: copy, reproduction
Related Entries: Authenticity; Status of Transmission (Records)

Bibliography

Cerquiglini, B. *In Praise of the Variant. A Critical History of Philology*. Translated by B. Wing. Baltimore: Johns Hopkins University Press, 1999.

Deegan, M., and K. Sutherland. *Transferred Illusions. Digital Technology and the Forms of Print*. Farnham, England: Ashgate, 2009.

Latour, B., and A. Lowe. "The Migration of the Aura, or How to Explore the Original through Its Facsimiles." In T. Bartscherer and R. Coover, eds., *Switching Codes: Thinking Through Digital Technology in the Humanities and the Arts*. Chicago: University of Chicago Press, 2011.

McKitterick, D. "Old Faces and New Acquaintances: Typography and the Association of Ideas." *Papers of the Bibliographical Society of America* 87 (1993): 163.

Tanselle, G. T. "Reproductions and Scholarship." In *Literature and Artifacts*. Charlottesville, VA: The Bibliographical Society of the University of Virginia, 1998, 59–88.

Weitenkampf, F. "What Is a Facsimile?" *Papers of the Bibliographical Society of America* 37 (1943): 114–30.

FILE

In general terms the definition of a file can refer both to container and content as in the *Oxford English Dictionary*'s description (1995): "1) a folder or box for holding loose papers together and in order for easy reference; e.g., a file of correspondence, or 2) a collection of information about a particular person or thing; e.g., MI5 were keeping a file on him."

In recordkeeping terms, glossaries generally agree that a file is (1) an organized physical assembly of *documents*, usually held within a folder, that have been grouped together for current use or because they relate to the same subject, activity, or transaction, and (2) usually the basic unit within a record *series*. The IRMT (2009, 18) notes that a file can be found in any format, but the term folder is more commonly used in digital *recordkeeping* environments.

Those focusing on *archival description* have a slightly different emphasis: according to ISAD(G) a file is "an organized unit of documents grouped together either for current use by the creator or in the process of archival arrangement, because they relate to the same subject, activity, or transaction. A file is usually the basic unit within a record series" (ICA 2000, 14).

There is recognition that the term folder more appropriately reflects the traditional function of a file particularly for text-based documents in a computing environment, where a file has different connotations, operating as an object that stores data, information, settings, or commands that are used with a computer program.

The legacy of the functionality and format of the physical file continues to influence practice in the electronic environment despite the increased flexibility and multiple representations that the latter can afford.

Origins

Classification and *arrangement* exists to facilitate *access* whether to the contents of supermarket or library shelves. Documents and *records* in whatever format or media have always required organizing in order to be better understood and accessed. The "file" (or by whatever name it is known) is one way in which this has been achieved.

The function of the file is fundamental to recordkeeping and can be traced from the earliest text-based *recordkeeping systems*. The principle of organizing content has been transmitted through time, encompassing a range of media and formats—clay tablet, wood, papyrus, parchment, paper, and so on through to the digital environment.

Descriptions of recordkeeping in the ancient world, where stone tablets or other media bore the text, suggest that the function of the file, sometimes referred to as a "dossier" in some kind of retrospective allocation of a current term, is long-standing. In a discussion of recordkeeping procedures from the third millennium BCE in Mesopotamia and the Near East, where clay tablet records of receipts and deliveries were organized in relation to subject matter (such as grain, wool, fruit, cattle) Brosius (2003, 14–15) argues, "Clearly, tablets were stored according to different types and labelled containers were marked to denote the 'dossiers' they contained."

While the filing function has a long history across space and time, the term in its modern incarnation itself is more recent. The English word is derived from the Latin *filum*, a thread, cord, or string, and hence the French *fil* and *filer*, a reference to the method of storing documents together on a string or a spike. Schellenberg (1968, 185) notes that file units containing specific types of document were called *Reihenakten* in Germany, *liasse* in France and *Bundel* in the Netherlands, while subject-based ones were known as *Sachakten* in Germany and *dossiers* in France and the Netherlands. Posner (1967, 102) states that in Italy the *fascicolo* or *practica* were terms used for a dossier or case file.

Jenkinson (1966, 23–24) refers to the file as the "simplest of all Archive forms . . . which we use as a generic term for a sack or box or hamper or other receptacle in which are contained, or a string on which are threaded, a miscellaneous collection of scraps of paper or parchment." Like Jenkinson, Heather Wolfe of the Folger Library (2013) also focuses on file as container, noting that bundles, pouches, wooden boxes, drawers, and pigeon holes were used to assist storage and retrieval. Indeed filing can primarily be undertaken to facilitate storage, with access and retrieval being a secondary consideration.

Subsequently eighteenth- and nineteenth-century systems continued to depend on the methodical arrangement of file units, often in registry-based systems. Duchein (1992) notes how the strict European *registratur* system as used in Germany and central Europe required that at the point of its creation or reception, each document belong to a prenumbered file in a predetermined system, registered with a registry number corresponding to an *Aktenplan* or schedule.

Less formal *registry systems* existed elsewhere in Europe that in England were at their peak from the mid-nineteenth to early twentieth centuries. Moss (2012, 866) quotes the English secretary of state for war, asserting in 1855 that "the great desiderata for the easy and efficient discharge of the duty of a public office is a simple and efficient system of registration of the papers of the department." The nineteenth-century British government file grew out of the eighteenth-century *docquet* system. It was introduced into the treasury in the 1850s and had been universally adopted across government by the end of the century.

A typical British government file comprised a cover sheet with a title devised by a registry clerk, and a reference number linking it to a filing plan authorized by the department's central registry. The contents were arranged in chronological order with the earliest at the bottom, with those to be kept being secured on the right, with ephemeral material being filed on the left side of the folder for eventual destruction. Civil servants and ministers consulting the file added their initials and date accessed to the cover (Moss 2012).

The "Ministry of State Control" file in figure F.1, dated 1918, appears to be a caricature: it has been printed and circulated and may have been used to train staff in the creation and management of files. From its topic, "Jonas Rowbottom's Cow-Cake," to the names of the ministers and civil servants who "consulted" it (Sir Tainly Passiton, Mr. Dallymore), it gently mocks the officialdom and procrastination endemic in heavily bureaucratic systems.

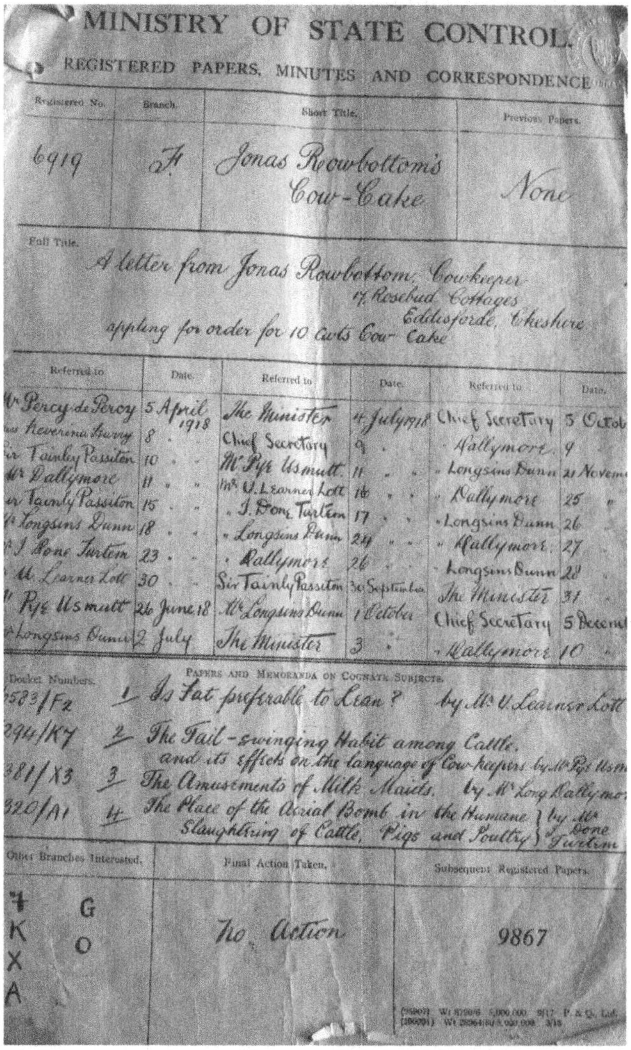

Figure F.1. "Ministry of State Control" file. *Courtesy of the author*

In Recordkeeping—Paper-Based Systems

The longevity of such file units and systems is evidence of their practical value and paper filing systems continue to operate alongside their digital counterparts. A file is an organized unit of documents grouped together because they relate to the same subject, activity, or transaction. A collection of files will be organized to reflect the *functions*, activities, and transactions of an organization. In general terms only policy files may reflect functions, while operational, subject, and correspondence files record activities and projects. At the level of the transaction files may comprise specific types of document (e.g., invoices, bank statements). General files may hold more than one type of document or record more than one transaction, while case files relate to individual instances such as individual employee, client, or patient (project files are sometimes treated as case files). The file, rather than the document, is the unit of retrieval: this provides the user with a comprehensive and browsable view of the *context* and content of activities and transaction.

In terms of file architecture Shepherd and Yeo (2003, 87) suggest that in defining the scope of a physical file unit, the issues to be considered are:

- the need to keep related items together;
- the logical level at which *users* wish to retrieve records;
- the options for the grouping of records; and
- the limitations of file size.

The physical nature of files in paper systems imposes certain requirements. Files will vary in size depending on the nature of the transaction involved: one transaction may be sufficiently complex to require a number of files, yet in simple cases papers from a number of separate transactions can be housed within a single file unit. Efficient retrieval requires that files are organized (both physically and intellectually) in line with an agreed organizational classification scheme, that finding aids (filing lists, classification schemes, indexes) are kept up to date so that it is known what files can be accessed, that retention/destruction requirements are built in to the filing process to prevent unnecessary buildup, and that file titles are used consistently and in accordance with required authority lists for controlling

terms. In paper systems the file *metadata* (description/title, dates, location, access permissions, retention information, and so on) may be maintained separately from the file, often stored electronically.

In Recordkeeping—Digital Systems

Most organizations now create and maintain their files in electronic systems. While many of the principles and business requirements are similar to those applicable in paper systems noted above, automated systems facilitate different approaches to storage, arrangement, and retrieval. Documents are stored in order to maximize the efficient use of disc space rather than to reflect any intellectual or physical relationship. While they can be managed and viewed as a unit (known as a "folder" rather than a file), it is as easy and convenient for them to be managed at the level of the individual item, since the folder/item relationship is a logical rather than a physical one. While physical constraints dictate the number of documents that can be stored in a paper file, e-folders' contents are limitless—any control required is therefore intellectual rather than physical.

Nested folders can be arranged logically according to directories that reflect the hierarchical organizational classification scheme. This replicates the paper environment, allowing hybrid (paper and electronic) systems to be supported within the same intellectual structure. However, schemes that work well in the paper world can restrict access functionality in the electronic, where it is not necessary to arrange items in a single, fixed order within a file/folder. The use of metadata and the application software enable users to view and manage folders as if they were physical rather than virtual entities. However, provided that the appropriate metadata has been attached to an item (using controlled language), there is no need to have predetermined subject or other groupings. In paper systems controlling data at the input stage was a prerequisite for effective retrieval; in electronic systems the user can define terms required for a search at the output stage. End users can use supplied metadata to search for subjects, people (e.g., clients), dates, locations, access permissions, retention/destruction information or combinations of these (Shepherd and Yeo 2003, 94).

In Archival Description

As the ISAD(G) definition provided above shows, a file in archival description remains an organized unit of documents. However the process of archival arrangement and description may lead to some files being reorganized, ceasing to represent exactly what was generated by the originating body, or even created anew or reconstructed for pragmatic purposes.

The *standard* identifies the file as one of the hierarchical levels of description where the *fonds* (archive group) represents the highest level, followed by subfonds, series, files, and individual items. Cook points out that ISAD(G)'s definition of *file* to represent a unit of handling "although intelligible in terms of government archives, in other archive work . . . can be all sorts of things. . . . For example . . . volumes, bundles or boxes, sets of index cards, microfiche etc." (Cook 1999, 112). Files may be described by archivists exactly as they were received from a parent body. On the other hand they may be constructed to make sense of otherwise disparate and disorganized material and arranged along a chronological, functional, or subject basis. If so, new titles will be required, such as "papers relating to the construction of the church hall" or "newscuttings and printed ephemera relating to local elections" for convenience of description and access (Williams 2006, 103).

Conclusion

All definitions serve prescribed and limited purposes, and perceptions of a file are no different. The basic definition provided here may suit recordkeepers, but will not suit all. For Verne Harris a government correspondence file is something asking to be interrogated—with questions that are spaces "suggesting, inviting, or demanding the adjective political" (Harris 2011, 113). For Timothy Garton Ash (1997, 10), a British journalist, "The Stasi's observation report, my diary entry: two versions of one day in a life. The object described with the cold outward eye of the secret policeman and my own subjective, allusive, emotional self–description. But what a gift to memory is a Stasi file. Far better than Proust's madeleine."—*Caroline Williams*

Keywords: file, filing, dossier, record series, registry, digital file

Related Entries: Archival Arrangement; Archival Description; Archival Standards; Authority Control; Digital Records; Recordkeeping; Records Classification; Registry System

Bibliography

Brosius, Maria, Ed. *Ancient Archives and Archival Traditions: Concepts of Record-Keeping in the Ancient World.* Oxford: Oxford University Press, 2003.

Cook, Michael. *The Management of Information from Archives.* Aldershot: Gower and Ashgate, 1999.

Garton Ash, Timothy. *The File: A Personal History.* London: Harper Collins, 1997.

Harris, Verne. "Archons, Aliens and Angels: Power and Politics in the Archive." In Jennie Hill, ed., *The Future of Archives and Recordkeeping.* London: Facet, 2011, 103–22.

International Council on Archives. *ISAD(G): General International Standard Archival Description,* 2nd edition. Ottawa: International Council on Archives, 2000.

International Records Management Trust. "Training in Electronic Records Management Glossary of Terms." International Records Management Trust, 2009. www.irmt.org/documents/educ_training/term%20modules/IRMT%20TERM%20Glossary%20of%20Terms.pdf (accessed July 2014).

Jenkinson, Hilary. *A Manual of Archive Administration,* 2nd edition. London: Percy Lund, Humphries and Co, 1966.

Moss, M. "Where Have All the Files Gone? Lost in Action Points Every One?" *Journal of Contemporary History* 47 (2012): 860–75. DOI: 10.1177/0022009412451291.

Posner, Ernst. *Archives and the Public Interest: Selected Essays.* Edited by Ken Munden. Chicago: Society of American Archivists, 2006 [1967].

Schellenberg, T. R. *Modern Archives,* 4th edition. Chicago: University of Chicago Press, 1968.

Shepherd, E., and G. Yeo. *Managing Records: A Handbook of Principles and Practice.* London: Facet, 2003.

Williams, Caroline. *Managing Archives: Foundations, Principles and Practice.* Oxford: Chandos, 2006.

Wolfe, Heather. "Filing, Seventeenth-Century Style." *The Collation,* blog entry, March 28,

2013. http://collation.folger.edu/2013/03/filing-seventeenth-century-style (accessed July 2014).

FORMAL ANALYSIS

"Analysis is the essence of archival appraisal" (Schellenberg 1956a, 45 [277]). While this is undoubtedly true, and most kinds of analyses in the archival field are currently conducted for *appraisal* purposes, analysis is at the core of all archival functions. Structural and *functional analyses* were undertaken by *archivists* since the beginning of the nineteenth century for *arrangement* and *description* as well as retrieval purposes, and formal analysis served the purposes of identification and *authentication* long before the other types were developed. All these long-proven types of analysis were introduced in the archival discourse about appraisal only at the beginning of the twentieth century by German theorists. They were adopted in North America through the mediation of Brooks and Schellenberg in the 1950s (Brooks 1940; Schellenberg 1956b). Schellenberg identifies formal analysis as one of the three tests by which informational value may be judged and states that formal analysis is meant to identify *records* that are in the most complete, usable, and concentrated form available (Schellenberg 1956a, 256–57).

The Concept

The concept of formal analysis has its origin in *diplomatics* and is based on the idea that the relationship between the records and the actions from which they result is embedded in the records documentary form, which tends to be very repetitive, and can enable us to identify which *functions* and activities generated the records, as well as their meaning and value (Duranti 1991a, 26). Barbara Craig firmly believed this to be true when she wrote:

> The reality of the record base must be an indispensable component of all acts of appraisal. Without an understanding of documents and records, of their forms and of their functions, and of how they were created and used, a plan can be so easily upset by the attractiveness of concentrating on information divorced from the realities of its documentary expression. . . . It is the record which is our special area

of knowledge; it will be a sad day and a dangerous step when faith in planning replaces the study and knowledge of records. (Craig 1992, 179)

Formal analysis, otherwise called "diplomatic criticism," was based on the definition of form as the whole of the rules of representation by which an act is documented or a message is conveyed in writing. It comprises all those characteristics of a record that can be separated from the determination of the particular subjects, *persons*, or places the record is about. Early diplomatists believed that all records are similar enough that it is possible to conceive of one typical ideal documentary form, a template, that encompasses all the possible elements of a record, and that can be used to analyze existing records for the purpose of determining their nature, *provenance*, and trustworthiness. Thus, they built the ideal documentary form by distinguishing the formal elements that determine the appearance of the record and make it effective from those that represent the articulation of the discourse and make the record complete, and calling the former extrinsic elements, and the latter intrinsic elements. Those elements were identified through a process of abstraction and systematization, the aim of which was to see the essential attributes that all records of the same type share and make them transportable to different historical and documentary *contexts*. By decontextualizing and generalizing the essential attributes of every record first, and the attributes of each entity listed in a record typology, the original diplomatists were able to recognize and evaluate records created over several centuries and across different juridical systems (Duranti 1991b).

Although formal analysis originated from the need of discovering, understanding, and assessing existing records, and it is so used by diplomatists and archivists for a variety of scholarly and professional purposes, the body of knowledge about documentary forms that has been accumulated over the centuries can guide the determination of the elements of the records that are to be generated and relate them to action and procedure. The InterPARES (International Research on Permanent Authentic Records in Electronic Systems) research project has focused much of its work on this endeavor, for example, by developing a *Template for Analysis* of digital records (InterPARES 2005). Certainly this work of standardization would support the development of software conducting visual document classification in the context of a *recordkeeping system*. Tests are being conducted that prove that even today's *digital records*, which are usually defined as unstructured information, are very much structured, and their formal structure can be further standardized. "By normalizing documents regardless of the type of file that was used to store or transmit the contents, visual classification is able to consolidate paper and electronic silos of information" (Kerschberg 2014, para. 4).

Conclusion

In the paper environment, formal analysis is mostly carried out to identify records and records *series*, and to establish their meaning and value. In the digital environment, formal analysis is primarily used to assess the *authenticity* of the records destined to continuing *preservation*; to determine which elements of the records form must be maintained through conversions and migrations; and to monitor the records and the system in which the records exist during the period between the initial assessment of value and the implementation of the final appraisal decision (e.g., the transfer to an archival institution). It is very likely that formal analysis will guide the design of software not only for visual classification but also for visual *archival description.—Luciana Duranti*

Keywords: diplomatics, documentary form, appraisal, authentication, identity

Related Entries: Appraisal; Diplomatics; Functional Analysis; Records Function; Structural Analysis

Bibliography

Brooks, Philip. "The Selection of Records for Preservation." *American Archivist* (1940): 221–34. http://archivists.metapress.com/content/u77415458gu22n65/fulltext.pdf.

Craig, Barbara. "The Acts of the Appraisers: The Context, the Plan and the Record." *Archivaria* 34 (1992): 175–80. http://journals.sfu.ca/archivar/index.php/archivaria/article/view/11848/12800.

Duranti, Luciana. "ACA 1991 Conference Overview." *ACA Bulletin* (July 1991a).

———. Diplomatics: New Uses for an Old Science. Part V." *Archivaria* (1991b): 7–24. http://journals.sfu.ca/archivar/index.php/archivaria/article/view/11758/12708.

———. "Structural and Formal Analysis: The Contribution of Diplomatics to Archival Appraisal in the Digital Environment." In Jennie Hill, ed., *The Future of Archives and Recordkeeping: A Reader*. London: Facet, 2010, 65–88.

InterPARES. "Template for Analysis." In Luciana Duranti, ed., *The Long-Term Preservation of Authentic Electronic Records: Findings of the InterPARES Project*. San Miniato: Archilab, 2005. www.interpares.org/book/interpares_book_j_app01.pdf.

Kerschberg, Ben. "Visual Document Classification: Changing the Dynamics of Information Governance." *Forbes*, August 8, 2014. www.forbes.com/sites/benkerschberg/2014/08/19/visual-document-classification-changing-the-dynamics-of-information-governance.

Schellenberg, Theodore R. "The Appraisal of Modern Records." *Bulletins of the National Archives* 8 (October 1956a). www.archives.gov/research/alic/reference/archives-resources/appraisal-of-records.html#note.

———. *Modern Archives: Principles and Techniques*. Chicago: University of Chicago Press, 1956b.

FUNCTION

Records have a fundamental relationship with functions, in that they are the outcome of the fulfillment of functions as well as the means through which functions are accomplished. Understanding functions is therefore essential to grasp the meaning of both the records and the *context* of records creation and use.

Function

The idea that records have a special relationship with organizational functions and must therefore be processed, stored, and accessed differently from any other information artifacts emerged in the professional practice before it was described in the archival literature. Already in some medieval chanceries, records were kept in the order in which they were received or sent and organized according to the activity they referred to. However, the first systematic *classification* of records based on the function they fulfilled appeared in the Prussian state of the seventeenth and eighteenth centuries, and became later an institutionalized practice in most European states under the Napoleonic administration.

In English-speaking countries, Sir Hilary Jenkinson, Margaret Cross Norton, and Theodore Schellenberg are among the first writers who emphasized the absolute relevance of the functional principle in relation to all archival endeavours, as the following quotes show:

- Archive series must always refer to some Administrative Function, because without it they themselves would never have come into existence. (Jenkinson 1937 [1922], 111)
- It is a rule in government that records follow functions. (Norton 1975 [1941], 110)
- Records, as a rule, should be classified according to function. They are the result of function; they are used in relation to function; they should therefore be classified according to function. (Schellenberg 1956, 62–63)

Schellenberg, in particular, provided us not only with a definition of function but also with a first attempt of *functional analysis*. Function is defined as "all the responsibilities assigned to an agency to accomplish the broad purposes for which it was established" (Schellenberg 1956, 53). His method of developing a function-based records classification scheme consists of breaking down the functions identified into two main sets of activities, respectively named "substantive" (i.e., "activities relating to the technical and professional work of the agency") and "facilitative activities" (i.e., "activities relating to the internal management of the agency, such as housekeeping activities") (Schellenberg 1956, 54). Each activity is then further subdivided into transactions, which Schellenberg splits again into two groups, "policy" and "operational transactions," and considers in relation "either to persons, or corporate bodies, or places, or topics" (1956, 54). The functional definitions and hierarchy (function-activity-transaction) as well as the classification model (a.k.a., F-A-T model) devised by Schellen-

berg are still today considered as a useful framework for the analysis of the activities carried out by contemporary organizations.

Early archival scholars saw in the functional approach the advantage of being in line with the nature of records and helping preserve the records context. However, none of them did clearly distinguish between an organization's functions and its structure, as both constructs tended to overlap in the way bureaucracies used to be configured. Until World War II, both public and private bodies were characterized by rather simple, rigid, and stable hierarchical structures, and rational division of labor. Functions, as defined in the organization's mandate, were implemented through repetitive procedures, which were in turn linked to fixed sets of responsibilities (or competencies) assigned to each office or department in accordance with written rules and regulations. Communications flowed one way and downwardly, and decision-making processes were linear and involved few actors, who steadily performed the same tasks. The dramatic societal changes that occurred in the second half of the last century profoundly affected the organization of work and our perception of the internal dynamics of bureaucracy. Faced with multi-hierarchical, networking organizations, where competencies are continuously redefined, archivists started to look at function, rather than administrative structure, as a stable framework for classifying records, but also as a broadly applicable criterion to guide records *appraisal*, a solid principle for archival *arrangement* and *description*, and a powerful *access* point to archives. David Bearman and Richard Lytle (1985–1986), who introduced the notion of "functional provenance" as an effective tool for accessing archival holdings, write:

It is probably more important to relate the records to a particular function than it is to relate them to an organizational component because there may be no relationship between the organization and the function. Functions are independent of organizational structures, more closely related to the significance of documentation than organizational structures, and both finite in number and linguistically simple. (22)

The idea to separate conceptually function and structure, in the light of the ever-changing and integrated nature of modern organizations, is what inspired Helen Samuels's approach to appraisal. In the context of her *documentation strategy* methodology, Samuels (1992) discusses "institutional functional analysis" as the technique that would support archivists in their search for the activities that ought to be documented, "no matter where they occur" (24). The focus on function is the hallmark of Terry Cook's macroappraisal as well. However, in line with the theory of structuration, which provides great insights into social phenomena, Cook's (1992) method did not neglect the role played by an agency's structure, and by the social interactions taking place when records are enacted, in shaping the agency's functions or programs.

Borrowing from Chris Hurley's (1995) terminology, we may say that Cook was looking at functions as "ambient functions," that is, broad, contextual knowledge that would require "external validation" to be meaningful, in that it refers to circumstances that were contemporary to the *creation* of the records and may have become unknown after a while (Hurley 1995, 22–24). The area of archival description is obviously that in which the appreciation of the effects of the passing of time on both records creators and records systems—which may engender a very complicated puzzle, given the different lifespan of either entity—is particularly important. If, on the contrary, one considers "business functions" as they are represented in *recordkeeping systems* that are still in use, there would be no need for the "contextual control" mentioned above. A taxonomic approach to functions, as typically applied in relation to functional classification systems and functions thesauri, would only involve "terminological control," in order to provide consistency to its "hierarchical and logical expressions of predictable relationships" (Hurley 1995, 24–26). Examples of the latter *modus operandi* may be found in the development of the Canadian business activity structure classification system (BASCS) as described by Paul Sabourin (2001), and in the Australian *Keyword AAA* functions thesaurus (New South Wales n.d.).

Most archival traditions recognize that the concept of function and that of structure are inseparable in the intellectual construct of *provenance*. This, however, does not imply that the responsibilities, activities, and tasks of an agency (which lead directly to the meaning of its records) cannot be described separately from the agency's administrative context. In Australia, this intuition brought to the development of the so-called "*Series System,*" where the *integrity* of the whole *fonds* is preserved at the intellectual level only, while physical arrangement is based on the records *series*, as an element that is independent from the broader institutional context. In order to improve archival control and access, Hurley (1993) suggests that all data about records and agencies that are linked to a given function be concentrated in one single point, which he calls "functional unit of description" (214). This would avoid the repetition of functional information for each agency entrusted with the same responsibilities. This idea was picked up by the International Council of Archives, which in 2007 published the International Standard for Describing Functions (ISDF). This standard is meant to complement ISAD(G) and ISAAR(CPF), which are well-accepted international standards for the description of records and the preparation of authority records, respectively. According to the ISDF authors,

> An understanding of the functions of corporate bodies is essential for a full understanding of the provenance. . . . An archival descriptive system which includes descriptions of functions in addition to descriptions of record creators and records will therefore provide a much richer account of the provenance. (ICA 2007, 29)

Although functions are generally more stable than administrative structures and "the relationships between records and functions remain constant" (ICA 2007, 29), functions "do evolve and change" (Hurley 1993, 211). Furthermore, the hierarchies of functions, activities, and transactions on which we build our records management and archival tools are always subjectively constructed. Because of these difficulties, the archival community still has to agree on one common and consistent functional vocabulary, and the meaning of function, activity, business process, and the like has not yet been investigated sufficiently. One of the factors contributing to make the analysis of functions so hard has to do with the relativity of the notions of purpose, or end (usually associated with function), and process, or means (usually associated with activity). How human agents perceive the "means-end hierarchy" depends on their particular location in the organizational hierarchy and their degree of procedural knowledge

(Foscarini 2012). Sociology, social-psychology, theory of administration, management science, and organizational theory (with particular regard to *organizational culture*) are among the disciplinary approaches that may help archivists and records managers get a better understanding of function.

Conclusion

Because records are the product of functions and contribute to the accomplishment of functions, the concept of function is used as a pillar of archival methodology throughout a record's *lifecycle*. Nevertheless, due to the ambiguous nature and complex relationship of function with the other components of a record's context (e.g., structure, human agents), defining what function is and how it relates to any kinds of subfunctions and to the structural features of organizations is arduous and requires further research. —*Fiorella Foscarini*

Keywords: function, activity, transaction
Related Entries: Access/Accessibility; Appraisal; Archival Arrangement; Archival Description; Functional Analysis; Formal Analysis; Records Classification

Bibliography

Bearman, D., and R. H. Lytle. "The Power of the Principle of Provenance." *Archivaria* 21 (1985–1986): 14–27. http://journals.sfu.ca/archivar/index.php/archivaria/article/view/11231/12170.

Cook, T. "Mind over Matter: Towards a New Theory of Archival Appraisal." In B. L. Craig, ed., *The Archival Imagination: Essays in Honour of Hugh A. Taylor*. Ottawa: Association of Canadian Archivists, 1992, 38–70.

Foscarini, F. "Understanding Functions: An Organizational Culture Perspective. *Records Management Journal* 22 (1) (2012): 20–36. DOI:10.1108/09565691211222072.

Hurley, C. "Ambient Functions: Abandoned Children to Zoos." *Archivaria* 40 (1995): 21–39. http://journals.sfu.ca/archivar/index.php/archivaria/article/download/12095/13080.

———. "What, If Anything, Is a Function?" *Archives and Manuscripts* 21 (2) (1993): 208–18.

International Council of Archives (ICA). *International Standard for Describing Functions (ISDF)*. 2007. www.ica.org/10208/standards/isdf-international-standard-for-describing-functions.html (accessed July 2014).

Jenkinson, H. *A Manual of Archive Administration*, 2nd edition. London: Percy Lund, Humphries & Co., 1965 [1937].

New South Wales (NSW) State Records Authority. "Keyword AAA." n.d. www.records.nsw.gov.au/recordkeeping/resources/keyword-products/keyword-aaa (accessed July 2014).

Sabourin, P. "Constructing a Function-Based Classification System: Business Activity Structure Classification System." *Archivaria* 51 (2001): 137–54. http://journals.sfu.ca/archivar/index.php/archivaria/article/view/12797/13999.

Samuels, H. W., ed. *Varsity Letters. Documenting Modern Colleges and Universities*. Metuchen, NJ, and London: Society of American Archivists and Scarecrow Press, 1992.

Schellenberg, T. R. *Modern Archives: Principles and Techniques*. Chicago: University of Chicago Press, 1956.

Thornton W. M., ed. *Norton on Archives. The Writings of Margaret Cross Norton on Archival and Records Management*. Carbondale and Edwardsville: Southern Illinois University Press, 1975.

FUNCTIONAL ANALYSIS

Functional analysis, used as a phrase, has never been treated in the *records* literature as a stand-alone topic, that is, as the title of a dedicated article or standard. Instead, it is associated predominantly with the writings on archival *appraisal*. Less in the form of the exact expression and more in its variations, such as "functional approach" or "*function-based approach,*" the topic is also associated with the management of current *records*, that is, with the control of the *creation*, capture, *classification*, and *disposition* of records. Although the generally promoted notion of understanding or studying the functions of records-creating organizations for other records purposes such as *arrangement, description*, and *access* is also discernible in the literature, this type of discussion lacks a noticeable degree of cohesiveness and synthesis in presenting function-related arguments. For this reason, this entry focuses on functional analysis in the context of archival appraisal and current *records management*, and in particular, within the latter, on *records classification*, as records classification joins together and manifests records creation and capture on the one hand, and serves as foundation for disposition on the other.

Functional Analysis and Archival Appraisal

The term functional analysis was introduced in Helen Samuels's 1992 article, "Improving Our Disposition: Documentation Strategy," along with the qualifying term institutional. To be accurate, the phrase functional analysis appeared earlier in her 1986 article, "Who Controls the Past," published in *The American Archivist*, but only once, and as a general term. The 1992 article, which is primarily based on the introduction section of her book *Varsity Letter, Documenting Modern Colleges and Universities*, formally presented "institutional functional analysis" as "a new tool to supplement archival practice . . . and revamp it." Archival practice here was used to include "appraisal," "selection," "acquisition," and "collection analysis" (Samuels, 128). The term, however, was not accompanied by a definition, nor were its relationships with those *archival practices* specifically explained. The discussion involved general all archival practices, without sufficient differentiation. Moreover, a number of terms such as functional study, functional approach, and functional understanding were seemingly used as synonyms of functional analysis, although the synonym-stance was not explicitly stated and none of the terms are defined or elaborated on. In the article the term institution seems to be used to refer to two types of institutions: a designated archival institution and an organization having an in-house archival program. According to Samuels, functional analysis means to understand what institutions do, irrespective of organizational structures and the content of records. The analysis of organizational structure and records content is considered "traditional" and no longer responsive to archival needs arising from contemporary reality. The arguments for this assertion are built around two main issues: frequently changing structures and unmanageable volume of records. Methodologically, institutional functional analysis is stated as applicable to both

individual organizations and types of organizations, such as scientific institutions and colleges/universities. However, no general methods for carrying it out were introduced. *Varsity Letters* exemplified one procedural step, consisting of deriving categories and terms from "a careful examination of the literature on higher education, and particularly the vocabularies this community uses to describe and evaluate itself," and then consider "the categories and concepts familiar to the archivists responsible for these records" (Samuels, 132).

In contrast, macroappraisal considers "functional analysis" its "theoretical and methodological core." Without the benefit of a dedicated definition, the "theoretical core" likely refers to the assumptions, as reflected by the concept of function, on "what is valuable and what is not, what is worth remembering by society and what is not, what should become archives and what should be destroyed" (Cook 2004, 5–6), and the "methodological core" refers to "researching, understanding and evaluating the degree of importance of the legislation, regulations, policies, mandates, purposes, functions, programmes, decision-making processes and deliberations, the internal organisation and structures, organisational culture and communication patterns, the liberty and flexibility allowed to public servants to interpret policy and thus implement it in varying ways, and, out of all this, the activities and transactions of the record creator (the branch, sector or programme entity covered by the appraisal project)" (Cook 2004, 12). Here, functional analysis, in addition to a methodological usage, acquired a theoretical underpinning, thus differentiating itself from the institutional functional analysis as articulated in the *documentation strategy*, where it is only a "tool" or "technique." Moreover, the analysis component of the macroappraisal functional analysis, as prescribed by its methodology, is much more intensive than that of the institutional functional analysis, as the former includes many aspects not required to be examined by the latter, with "internal organization and structures" being the most noticeable example. Correspondingly, the issue of recurring organizational changes as a supporting argument for functional analysis is no longer present, and the justification for functional analysis becomes primarily the unmanageable volume of records and the "crisis of preserving electronic records" (Cook 2004, 5)

There are other discussions of functional analysis in relation to archival appraisal, presenting rather distinct focuses from the aforementioned two. Gerald Ham explained functional analysis as "an examination of who created the record and for what purpose," and considered it useful for providing "important clues to the value of a record, especially for institutional history," yet less useful in evaluating "what records tell us about people, places, and phenomena with which the institution dealt with" (1993, 51–52), hardly resembling any aspect of the functional analysis as advocated in both Samuels's documentation strategy and the Canadian macroappraisal. Relying on Mintzberg's theory on organizational configuration, Victoria Lemieux proposed to analyze how the structural components of an organizational system function rather than what they specifically do (1998, 37–85). Theoretically subscribing to the same assumptions of macroappraisal, however, the methodological aspect of Lemieux's proposal—that is, the focus on how—differs significantly from the one developed by Cook.

Functional Analysis and Records Classification

As a phrase, functional analysis was first used in the Australian national standard AS 5090-2003, *Work Process Analysis for Recordkeeping,* which was subsequently issued in 2008 as an ISO standard. Functional analysis in this standard conforms theoretically with the requirements of ISO 15489-2001 *Information and Documentation—Records Management,* that is, operates along the lines of the relationship between records and "business activity," with the latter as the sole cause for the creation and use of the former. In the standard, functional analysis constitutes one of the two types of analyses that aim at "the creation, capture and control of records," which "seeks to group together all the processes undertaken to achieve a specific, strategic goal of an organization" (ISO 2008, 2). A (work) process in this context means "one or more sequences of transactions required to produce an outcome that complies with governing rules," and transaction means "the smallest unit of a work process consisting of an exchange between two or more participants or systems" (ISO 2008, 2). Functional analysis, therefore, is expected to uncover relationships among functions, processes, and transactions and, as dictated by its being a top-down approach,

to represent the uncovered relationships in a hierarchical fashion. Unlike process and transaction, the term *function* is not defined, but, as indicated by the prescribed basic steps of functional analysis, linked to the strategic goals of the organization. Functional analysis distinguishes "operational functions" and "administrative functions," with the former defined as those that "meet the unique objectives of the organization" and the latter as those that "support the delivery of the operation functions" (ISO 2008, 8). The standard recommends conducting functional analysis independently of organizational structure and rationalizes the recommendation as due to the consideration that "function may be exercised in more than one location within, or across one or more organizations" (ISO 2008, 6). Structural analysis, however, is not ignored but addressed as part of "contextual review"—"the foundation for undertaking functional analysis" (ISO 2008, 6). The major outcome of the analysis is a high-level relationship representation model, useful for "determining aggregations of records for disposition"—an idea similar to that claimed by functional analysis for appraisal and for a "functions-based classification scheme" (ISO 2008, 8).

A function-based classification scheme in the context of ISO 15489-2001 refers to a logically established system that identifies and arranges business activities or records. The analysis of business activity, therefore, becomes synonymous with functional analysis in this sense. For example, the Step B in the DIRKS manual is termed "Analysis of Business Activity," producing a hierarchical representation of functions, activities, and transactions, which, in turn, serves the need of constructing a function-based records classification (NSW State Records 2007). Another example is the methodology developed by Library and Archives Canada, called the Business Activity Structure Classification System (BASCS), which prescribes a classification structure of function, subfunction, and activity (Library and Archives Canada 2006). These developing methodologies maintain the same theoretical stance, by prescribing the adherence to the operations of an organization embodied in functions as the foundation for classifying records—a recommendation made by Schellenberg in his 1956 book, *Modern Archives: Principles and Techniques,* and already proposed by Campbell in 1941. They, however, differ in the methodology, most noticeably on how to break down or formulate a function (Xie 2006). The most challenging part for users of these methodologies is to determine how specific or at what level the analysis should be. A (true) function-based, or functional, classification system cannot stop at high-level analyses (that is, what constitutes function, subfunction, activity, or process, depending on the methodology being applied), but needs to go further down to the level of transactions—that is, it needs to conduct, for example, the other type of analysis described in ISO 26122-2008 as sequential analysis. It is at the level of transaction that records creation takes place, and, in order to classify records functionally, in particular *digital records*, classification is to be done when and where records are created. In this sense, transactional analysis is at the heart of functional analysis for records classification, and this contrasts sharply with the top-down approach of functional analysis for archival appraisal.

Conclusion

Functional analysis in its current state appears to be an underdeveloped concept, in both its theoretical underpinnings and its methodological implications. This is due to its inherent link to the concept of function, which is abstract and difficult to be defined in a way that allows direct application. The common guidance that functions are derivable from legal and regulatory documentations pertinent to the records-creating organization is simply inadequate for explaining the nature of functions and ineffective in indicating the complexity of the analysis required to reach the pursued goal. Also, there is a lack of recognition by the archival literature on functional analysis of the indispensable role of *records management* in supporting and, in some cases, allowing to conduct archival work. As discussed earlier, all of the functional analyses proposed by *archivists* focus exclusively on guiding archivists to tackle "messy" records in organizations. Messy records are only the symptom of poor records management. In other words, the archival discourse on functional analysis misses the cause of the issues that functional analysis is called to resolve—the lack of a records management program in creating organizations. A strong and effective records management program is one that conducts both top-down and bottom-up analysis, with the

former focusing on developing an adequate understanding of the organization and the latter on synthesizing the lowest level of business actions for the purpose of identifying functions, activities, or processes (Xie 2013). Therefore, the decision of conducting bottom-up analysis should not be left to individual organizations to make—as the functional classification methods typically recommend, but instead, should be strongly advocated if not prescribed as a precondition for good records management. The concept of functional analysis, therefore, requires a further development that takes into consideration these factors.—*Sherry Xie*

Keywords: function-based approach, functional classification, top-down approach, bottom-up analysis, transactional analysis

Related Entries: Appraisal; Formal Analysis; Function; Records Classification

Bibliography

Campbell, E. G. "Functional Classification of Archival Material." *The Library Quarterly: Information, Community, Policy* 11 (4) (1941): 431–41. www.jstor.org/stable/4302884.

Cook, Terry. "Macro-Appraisal and Functional Analysis: Documenting Governance Rather Than Government." *Journal of the Society of Archivists* 25 (1) (2004): 5–18.

Ham, Gerald. *Selecting and Appraising Archives and Manuscripts*. Chicago: Society of American Archivists, 1993. Available online at http://babel. hathitrust.org/cgi/pt?id=mdp.39015024110697;view=1up;seq=21.

International Standards Organization. *ISO/TR 26122:2008: Information and Documentation—Work Process Analysis for Records*. Paris, France: International Standards Organization, 2008.

Lemieux, Victoria. "Applying Mintzberg's Theories on Organizational Configuration to Archival Appraisal." *Archivaria* 1 (46) (1998): 32–85. http://journals.sfu.ca/archivar/index.php/archivaria/article/view/12675/13842.

Library and Archives of Canada. "BASCS Guidance." www.collectionscanada.gc.ca/007/002/007002-2089-e.html#six (accessed December 2013).

NSW State Records. "DIRKS Manual." www.records.nsw.gov.au/recordkeeping/dirks-manual (accessed December 2013).

Samuels, Helen. "Improving Our Disposition: Documentation Strategies." *Archivaria* 1 (33) (1992): 125–40. http://journals.sfu.ca/archivar/index.php/archivaria/article/view/11804/12755.

Xie, Sherry. "Function-Based Records Classification System: A Comparative Study." www.armaedfoundation.org/pdfs/Sherry_Xie_Study.pdf (accessed December 2013).

———. "The Nature of Records and the Information Management Crisis in the Government of Canada." https://circle.ubc.ca/handle/2429/44450 (accessed December 2013).

IMPARTIALITY (RECORD)

In 1922, Hilary Jenkinson, in his seminal book *A Manual of Archives Administration*, identified as the first characteristic of archives their impartiality. In doing so, he was not referring to the relationship between the authors of the *records* constituting the *archives* (or *archival fonds*) and the acts or facts the records put into being, participated to, or talked about. Rather, he referred to the relationship between the records and the use to which those records are put after they are no longer current and active in the activity generating them. Impartiality is therefore not an attribute of *persons* (be they authors, writers, or creators), but a characteristic of records that are part of an archives; it expresses the ability of their form, content, relationships with the other records in the same archives (i.e., the *archival bond*) to reveal facts, acts, and the circumstances of their occurrence. Impartiality is also an attribute of the *archivist* only in the sense that archivists should not be partial to any type of use or *user*; however, the term is not presented here in relation to the archivist, but in relation to the nature of archives and records.

The Concept

All archives, and the records constituting them, are impartial with respect to the purposes for which they will be used in the future because such purposes cannot be predicted by the persons creating them or authoring their content. Records are created in the course of activity as a means for carrying it out and its by-product. Therefore—Jenkinson writes—they are "free from the suspicion of prejudice in regard to the interests in which we now use them . . . because they were not written in the interest or for the information of Posterity" (1937, 11–12).

This characteristic of impartiality makes archives inherently truthful and the most reliable source for both law and history, whose purposes are to rule and explain the conduct of society by establishing the truth (Duranti 1994, 334). In common law, evidence acts consider records to be an exception to the hearsay rule, and to be admissible as *evidence* precisely because of the trustworthiness that derives to them from their creation in the usual and ordinary course of business, for the purposes of the business, by a person responsible for doing so, at the time or close to the time of the fact or act they refer to (Duranti and Rogers 2012, 528).

Conclusion

Records and archives are impartial and the most reliable source of information because they are not the purpose of the activity from which they result, but their by-products. To protect the impartiality of archives and records as well as their evidentiary nature is to protect their capacity to reveal the biases and idiosyncrasies of their creators or authors. The activities supporting this duty of protection, in particular *archival arrangement* and *description*, came to be known as the "moral defence of archives" and are seen as central to the professional ethics of archivists (Jenkinson 1937, 66).—*Luciana Duranti*

Keywords: archives, record, archival document, evidence, reliability

Related Entries: Authenticity; Interrelatedness (Record); Naturalness (Record); Reliability; Uniqueness

Bibliography

Duranti, Luciana. "The Concept of Appraisal in Archival Science." *The American Archivist* 57 (2) (Spring 1994): 328–44. http://archivists.meta-press.com/content/pu548273j5j1p816/fulltext.pdf.

Duranti, Luciana, and Corrine Rogers. "Trust in Digital Records: An Increasingly Cloudy Legal Area." *Computer Law & Security Review* 28 (5) (October 2012): 522–31. http://dx.doi.org/10.1016/j.clsr.2012.07.009.

Eastwood, Terence M. "What Is Archival Theory and Why Is It Important?" *Archivaria* 1 (37) (1994): 122–30. http://journals.sfu.ca/archivar/index.php/archivaria/article/view/11991/12954.

Jenkinson, Hilary. *A Manual of Archives Administration*. London: Percy Lund, Humphries & Co., 1937.

INFORMATION ASSURANCE

The goal of information assurance (IA) is to ensure that "the information flows within a company are confidential; their integrity is safeguarded and available" (U.S. Federal Government Committee; McCumber 1992; Maconachy, Schou, Ragsdale, and Welch 2001). The integrity of the system's architecture and the *authenticity* of its contents are now regarded as of equal importance as the security of its data. Verifying the identity of the creators of information, proving that they are who they say they are and that the information in question has not been altered subsequently, have all proven to be critical success factors in recent court cases. The field of *records management* (RM) has been addressing the issue of what constitutes critical information for an organization for some time. RM is one of disciplines within the broader context of communities with a fundamental stake in IA. Both RM and IA seek to address issues relating to the integrity, authenticity, and security of the content of systems that directly impact our private, organizational, and societal personas.

A key element of RM has always been its ability to provide evidence of an activity. Historically, if evidence could be provided of an event, it was deemed to have happened that way. *Records*, then, are powerful tools in the hands of those who seek recognition of positions of authority and verification of the status quo, for example. Recent archival articles on ethics and the use of records in countries where power structures are shaping and reshaping highlight the danger of misuse. Control of records and therefore evidence enables the construction of external image, affecting standing within the international community and ultimately global power structures. At an organizational level, control of records requires the implementation of RM processes to ensure that records can be provided as evidence.

Records are defined in ISO 15489 (the international standard for RM) as "information created, received and maintained as evidence and information by an organization or *person*, in pursuance of legal obligations or in the transaction of business" (International Standards Organization 2001). It further identifies the RM role as ensuring that records will be accepted as evidence in a court of law, should this be required.

"The principles of good practice in *recordkeeping* are of value, even if the need to produce electronic records in court never arises. The effort and resources required to comply quickly bring business benefits, whether the original is in court or not" (International Standards Organization 2001).

Frank Upward, creator of the Record Continuum Model, highlights "evidentiality" as one of the four axes of recordkeeping (RK) and asks how the use of the term evidence in RK relates to legal evidence (2005).

The tools available to the *records manager* include classification schemes to categorize records in a systematic and consistent way, *appraisal* to determine which records are deemed to have value, retention to determine how long they should be kept, and *disposition* to ensure these decisions are implemented. The authors believe that some of the tried and tested methods honed to international standards in the records management arena can shed light on the management of digital forensics data embedded in systems in order to ensure the preservation of reliable digital evidence for current and future *access*.

Table I.1. Underlying principles of IA vs. RM (Boucher and Endicott-Popovsky, 2008).*

Information Assurance Principles	Records Management Principles
Confidentiality	Integrity
Integrity	Usability
Availability	Authenticity
Authentication	Reliability
Non-repudiation	

Discussion of the Principles of Each

The authors make the case that the goals of both are similar. ISO 15489 states that records must possess content, *context*, and structure. Content reflects the facts about the activity: they should be accurate and complete. Context, that is, the circumstances of creation and use, include the activity, *function*, and administrative context of the record. Structure reflects the relationships within the record and external to it and organizes the content in such a way as to denote context (Shepard and Yeo 2003, 156).

RM has always been about the context in which records are created—that is, if this is not known, the "record" ceases to be relevant and evidential. ISO 15489 further isolates four qualities that records should possess: *authenticity*, *reliability*, integrity, and usability. Authenticity is linked to the accuracy of the records; reliability pertains to the records being a full and accurate representation of the activity/transaction. Integrity relates to the fact that records are complete and unaltered. Finally, usability refers to records being retrievable, presentable, and interpretable. Although the language relates to the "record," increasingly it is accepted that in order to maintain the above characteristics in records, it is the systems and the information architecture that must be proven to meet these requirements.

RM does not explicitly refer to nonrepudiation and confidentiality. It does, however, constantly work within the confines of legislation, particularly freedom of information and data-protection laws. These form a natural tension between what society considers appropriate in terms of *accountability* of organizations and confidentiality demanded by citizens and customers. Access rights and data security are key elements in the management of *digital records*, as is evidenced by their prominence in the recently released MOREQ 2 specification (February 2008) issued for comment on behalf of the Euro-

pean Commission. In some respects, ISO 15489 itself was devised in order to deal with the issues of nonrepudiation. By following the principles and recommendations enshrined in the standard, it would prove more difficult to repudiate records provided as evidence of activities.

In RM, the level of accountability and the operational requirements of the organization and their perception of legal risk, compliance, and business decision making will define which transactions require full evidential protection. These are organizational decisions that the RM team will implement.

ISO 15489 catalogues an eight-stage procedure for RM programs, the first five of which relate to establishing the current position and identifying the requirements for records, before designing a strategy to satisfy these requirements. This common objective of defining what records/information/data are required for evidential and legal purposes is an area that we believe brings the two disciplines closer together. By pre-identifying certain categories of evidence, it would be possible to provide special treatment for those requiring full digital forensics (DF) protection.

Sremack refers to the need for research into "using case specific knowledge of a system to determine what information is critical, thereby minimizing the amount of extraneous information that is collected and analyzed and guarantee that no critical data is missed" (2008, 6). Sommer (2005, 34) calls for "improvements in overall system specific and management process to capture more potential worthwhile evidence."

Records managers have to analyze the processes in an organization before they can identify the record-creating processes. Only then are they able to identify those that require "special treatment" (i.e., *vital records* in current business terms). From a DF point of view, knowing where (i.e., what processes) to apply the techniques more rigorously would be a benefit. From an RM perspective, the ability to prove that techniques have been employed to assist in verifying that a system and, therefore, the records it creates possess integrity and authenticity is a benefit.

The aim of RM is to ensure that the relationships between the essential business entities are apparent and maintained for current and future usage. If RM offers tools that narrow down the number of "information objects" that should be considered "critical," that is, those more likely to be called on in court and therefore have a requirement to be "trustworthy," DF processes could be applied to a more limited set of processes, and NFR may be more achievable.

We can't know how which single *document*/data set/record will be challenged in the future but we can seek to manage those most likely to be required. RM procedures are set up to determine which of these are most likely to be and to capture them into RK systems. Making early decisions regarding risk to the organization and to wider society of keeping or not keeping records and utilizing RM and DF practices and procedures to ensure their reliability and accessibility may reduce discovery and spoliation costs. It may also reduce *digital preservation* costs.

A Comprehensive Model of Information Assurance

Hardware, software, protocols, and operational techniques associated with the process of managing information change at a very high rate. Any stable

information-security model must be based on environmental, organizational, system, and information aspects that remain relatively constant over extended periods of time. The last two decades of tumultuous change and growth in the information-processing and -management area has shown that the Comprehensive Model of Information Systems Security (CMISS) presented in 1991 by McCumber has the basic model components and characteristics that allow this model to remain useful over this extended period of time (McCumber 1992; see figure I.1). The key aspects of the CMISS that provide the foundation of this continual period of application and usefulness are its focus on information along with a model structure that allows human beings the ability to organize and reason about information at the proper level of abstraction.

With a focus on characteristics of information that are independent of implementation technology and organizational structure, the CMISS distills the essence of information-security practices in a manner that is usable by security planners and managers. By arranging primary concepts in groups of three and constraining model relationship views to nine or fewer items, the CMISS also addresses critical cognitive complexity issues associated with the application of these types of models. The stable form presented by the CMISS is of great benefit to seasoned information-assurance professionals that have an extensive background and expert understanding of the information-assurance domain.

Walking through the model, security must be considered for each information state through which

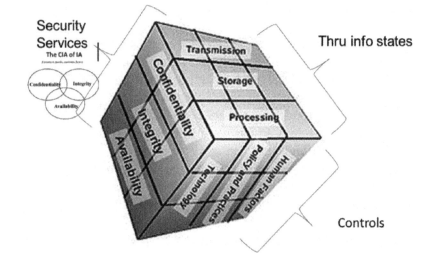

Figure I.1. The McCumber Cube. *McCumber 1992*

information passes in a system: transmission, storage, and processing. In each information state, the required security services of confidentiality, integrity, availability—the so-called CIA of security—are described. Finally countermeasures—human factors, policies and practices, and technologies—are identified and prescribed. Further, changes brought about by networking systems have generated a modified model that incorporates the security services of *authentication* and nonrepudiation into the base CMISS (Maconachy, Schou, Ragsdale, and Welch 2001).

Conclusion

The field of information assurance is in a formative stage that is proceeding with a high rate of change at organizational and technical levels. A fundamental security model that is independent of technology and organizational changes is helpful in thinking through information-security requirements of systems. Using the McCumber Cube, the complete security context for any given situation can be effectively addressed.—*Barbara Endicott-Popovsky*

Keywords: information assurance (IA), records management, McCumber Cube
Related Entries: Archival Standards; Authenticity; Records Continuum; Reliability (records)
*Acknowledgment: The comparison of IA and RM is courtesy of a collaboration between the University of Washington Center for Information Assurance and Cybersecurity and Aberyswyth University, Wales, Adran Astudiaethau Gwybodaeth/ Department of Information Studies (Boucher and Endicott-Popovsky 2008). (See Table I.1.)

Bibliography

Boucher, K., and B. Endicott-Popovsky. "Digital Forensics and Records Management: What We Can Learn from the Discipline of Archiving." Paper presented at Information Systems Compliance and Risk Management Institute, University of Washington, September 2008.
International Standards Organization. *ISO 15489-1:2001: Information and Documentation—Records Management—Part 1: General.* Geneva, Switzerland: International Standards Organization, 2001, 5.1ff.
Maconachy, W., C. D. Schou, Maconachy, Daniel Ragsdale, and Don Welch. "A Model for Information Assurance: An Integrated Approach." Paper presented at the Proceedings of the 2001 IEEE Workshop on Information Assurance and Security, U.S. Military Academy, West Point, NY, 2001.
McCumber, John. "Information Systems Security: A Comprehensive Model." In *Proceedings of the 14th National Computer Security Conference*, Washington, DC, October 1991. Reprinted in *Proceedings of the Fourth Annual Canadian Computer Security Conference*, Ottawa, Ontario, May 1992. Reprinted in *DataPro Reports on Information Security.* Delran, NJ: McGraw-Hill, 1992.
Shepherd, Elizabeth, and Geoffrey Yeo. *Managing Records: A Handbook of Principles and Practice.* London: Facet, 2003.
Sommer, Peter. "Directors and Corporate Advisors' Guide to Digital Investigations and Evidence." Information Assurance Advisory Council, 2005.
Sremack, Joseph. "Formalizing of Analysis: A Proof-Based Methodology." Master's thesis, North Carolina State University, Raleigh, NC, 2004.
Upward, Frank. "The Records Continuum." In Sue McKemmish, Michael Pigot, Barbara Reed, and Frank Upward, eds., *Archives: Recordkeeping in Society.* New South Wales: Charles Stuart University, Centre for Information Studies, 2005, 207.
U.S. Federal Government Committee on National Security Systems Instruction No. 4009. National Information Assurance Glossary.

INFORMATION GOVERNANCE

Information is a vital organizational asset, and information governance (IG) is an integrated, strategic approach to managing, processing, controlling, maintaining, and retrieving information as evidence of all transactions of the organization. Information governance is defined as "the specification of decision rights and an *accountability* framework to ensure appropriate behavior in the valuation, creation, storage, use, archiving and deletion of information. It includes the processes, roles and policies, standards and metrics that ensure the effective and efficient use of information in enabling an organization to achieve its goals" (Gartner n.d.). IG is a high-level, strategic *function* that involves stakeholders from across the organization, each with their own expertise and responsibilities (Franks 2013, 321). A renewed interest in *records* and *information management* has resulted in a call by many to use fundamental *records management* principles as the foundation for sound IG. Records management is just one component of IG, but the processes used to manage records can be leveraged to manage all information (Franks 2013, 29).

Rationale for Information Governance

The realization that an IG strategy is necessary is often the result of the dramatic changes that have taken place due to the growing amount of data and unstructured electronic records; an increased emphasis on e-discovery and compliance; and the lack of sufficient controls over all electronically stored information (ESI).

An IG program enables an organization to manage information securely and effectively; reduce the volume of information retained while meeting its regulatory, legal, and business obligations; and develop an awareness of both the location and nature (sensitive, proprietary, private) of its information assets. Specific benefits of IG are reduced risk; improved e-discovery preparedness; increased transparency, trust, and therefore enhanced reputation; and reduced product and information cycle times due to improved information flows.

Information Governance Components and Reference Model

IG is comprised of the following components: *records lifecycle* management, information risk, policy management, information *access* and security, information capture and classification, and information content governance.

Information Governance Reference Model

Representatives from legal, human resources, information technology, and business units must collaborate in developing the IG strategy as illustrated in the IG Reference Model (see figure I.2).

This model presents an image of the cross-functional groups of key IG stakeholders; not all organizations will have the same mix of stakeholders. Notice the relationship between the value of the information assets that were created and used and the duty the organization has to hold, discover, retain, maintain, store, secure, and dispose of those assets. Cooperation between all stakeholders is necessary to develop policies and processes to achieve effective IG.

Information Governance Framework

Effective IG helps businesses operate more efficiently and mitigate risk. Writing in the *eDiscovery Journal* blog, Barry Murphy explained that IG provides a framework for the "conservative side of information management" (2010).

Every organization must consider its legal and regulatory environment along with its tolerance for risk when determining its governance framework. Questions to be asked include these:

- What records and information are needed to support business processes?
- What steps must be taken to be in compliance with governing laws and regulations?
- What records and information should be destroyed and when?

Records management plays a key role in answering these questions. An IG model can be used to provide context to discussions of an integration of information management, *risk management*, and records management considerations. This framework would address all types of information, whether meeting the requirements for a record or not.

There are three basic elements to an IG framework: policies, processes, and compliance. The IG framework sets out the way the organization handles information, in particular personal and sensitive data. The framework determines how data is collected, stored, used, and shared. Accountability measures in the form of audits and metrics monitor the components of these elements. Records management should be integrated throughout the process.

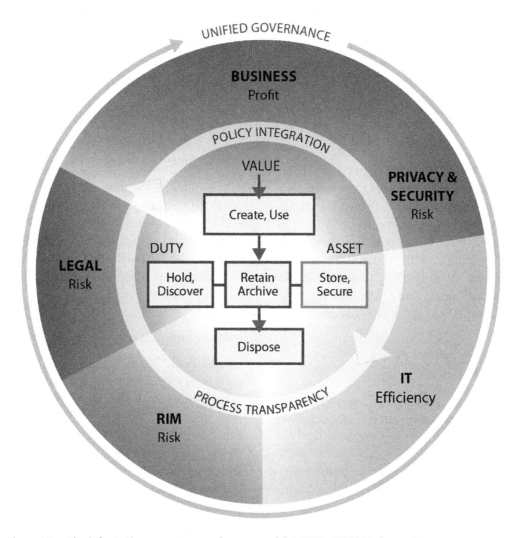

Figure I.2.   The information governance reference model (IGRM). *EDRM (edrm.net)*

ARMA's Principles and Information Governance

ARMA's *Generally Accepted Recordkeeping Principles* can be used to govern both records and information. The eight principles are: accountability, transparency, integrity, protection, compliance, availability, retention, and *disposition* (ARMA n.d.). The principles can be assigned to specific IG stakeholders to ensure that ownership is clear and, in some cases, shared across the organization. For example, the principles of retention and disposition may be "owned" by the records and information management program, compliance may be the responsibility of the legal/risk stakeholders, and integrity and transparency responsibilities could be shared by all stakeholders.

Information Governance, C-Level Management, and the IG Steering Committee

"C-level" is an expression describing high-ranking executive titles in an organization, including chief information officer, chief knowledge officer, chief compliance officer, and chief records officer. Some organizations may use traditional titles, such as president, vice president, general manager, and director. Regardless of the size of the organization or the titles of high-ranking officials, the organization would benefit from the formation of an IG steering committee to develop a strategic plan and provide:

• advice on the organization's information management strategy with regard to quality and integrity, safety and security, and appropriate access and use of records and information assets; and

- assurance in relation to processes for creating, collecting, storing, disseminating, sharing, using, and disposing of information. (Franks 2013, 324)

Each member of the steering committee should have the responsibility for filling a specific role; for example, the chief executive officer may be responsible for information across the organization in his/her role as accountability officer, and the senior IT security specialist may be assigned responsibility for ensuring compliance with information security standards (ISO/IEC 27001-2005). Examples of additional roles are IG lead, data protection and freedom of information lead, and records management lead.

Information Governance Strategy

IG strategy documents must include at a minimum an introduction, a scope statement, and a conclusion. However, most include the following sections:

1. Introduction: Asserts the value of information as a vital asset and establishes IG as the framework for information management.
2. Purpose Statement: Provides the context for the IG plan in relation to other organizational strategies such as risk management and business management.
3. Scope Statement: States the components of the strategy, such as the IG policy and annual action (improvement) plan.
4. Goals: Overarching goals of IG, goal of the strategic plan, and methods to achieve effective IG are stated in this section.
5. Strategic Objectives: Objectives for a specific period of time (e.g., three to five years) are either included in the goals section or immediately follow it. Objectives include monitoring and assessment methods, identification of lead position (not person), and target date for completion.
6. Key Strategic Areas: This section explains the role of the IG steering committee and any subgroups (e.g., project teams).

7. Responsibilities: This section clarifies individual responsibilities, including those for all employees.
8. Conclusion: This section reinforces the importance of the IG strategy, policy, and action plans to ensure efficient information management and risk reduction (Franks 2013, 326).

Information Governance Plan

The IG plan is the first of two required components of the IG strategy. It should be brief and concise and provide actions to be taken to accomplish goals: for example, assign IG roles and responsibilities; approve the IG policy and strategy itself; and refer to additional existing governing policies such as the e-mail policy and confidentiality policy.

Information Governance Strategic Policy

The IG policy is the second required component of an IG strategy. The policy provides details that were not included in the IG plan, including foundational principles, governing legislation, best practices, improvement plan and assessment, auditing and monitoring criteria, implementation and dissemination strategy, responsibility for IG document (steering committee), and any relevant attachments and appendix, such as a list of related policies and procedures (e.g., mobile-computing policy, social media policy, records retention policy).

Change Management, Communication, and Training

Two issues that can have a positive impact on the acceptance of an IG initiative are change management and training. Change management is a structured approach to transition individuals, teams, and organizations from a current state to a desired future state where change can be accepted and embraced. As with other changes, the best approach to implement an IG strategy will depend on the culture of the organization. Success of a change management effort will depend on the organization's ability to establish a clear vision and strategy to stimulate organization-wide buy-in.

These goals, as well as the benefits that will accrue to the organization, must be communicated to all employees. Training can provide an explanation of the IG strategy, expectations for compliance, and penalties for noncompliance. Training platforms and venues might include in-person classes; online modules; on-demand classes; wikis and blogs; a private social media site managed by the organization; and podcasts, videoconferences, and audio conferences.

Assessment Tools and Services

The IG steering committee is responsible for measuring the level of compliance with the norms established for IG. Industry-related IG tools are available and may be required; for example, the United Kingdom National Health Service (NHS) Department of Health issues an IG Toolkit for NHS organizations to conduct mandated self-assessments (NHS n.d.). Other assessments can be voluntary and involve employing an outside organization to conduct an assessment; for example, EMC Corporation will lead a structured discussion to assess the current state of information within an organization using the EMC IG Maturity Model Matrix (EMC² n.d.).

Professional Certification

IG provides a holistic approach to managing all information within the organization. *Recordkeeping* professionals can expand their background in the area of records and information management by earning a new credential—the Information Governance Professional (IGP) designation—that recognizes the expertise of those who possess the knowledge, skills, and abilities to perform competently as an IG professional. Recordkeeping professionals, including *archivists*, can prepare for the 140-item examination administered through ARMA International by acquiring additional knowledge and skills in the areas of *information assurance*, risk management, strategic planning, and information technology (including cloud computing).

However, recordkeeping professionals are not the only stakeholders who would benefit from certification as an Information Governance Professional. Stakeholders from information technology, risk management, and legal professions can also benefit by demonstrating their competence to become involved in IG initiatives by earning the Information Governance Professional designation.

Conclusion

As stated in the introduction, IG is a high-level, strategic function that involves stakeholders from across the organization, each with their own expertise and responsibilities (Franks 2013, 321). IG provides an accountability framework comprised of processes, roles, standards, and metrics designed to encourage desirable behavior that enables an organization to achieve its goals" (Gartner n.d.).

High-level managers must support the IG strategy and are ultimately responsible for its success, but the actual planning is best carried out by an IG steering committee comprised of some senior managers as well as representatives from IT, business units, risk/legal, and records management.

Although records management is a subset of IG, it can provide the foundation for an effective IG Strategy. *Records managers* and other information professionals wishing to move into new positions made available by the transition from records and information management to IG can demonstrate their capabilities by earning the designation of Information Governance Professional.—*Patricia Franks*

Keywords: information assurance, information governance, IG, strategy, information management
Related Entries: Information Assurance; Information Management; Information Policy; Records Management

Bibliography

ARMA International. *Generally Accepted Recordkeeping Principles*. 2014. www.arma.org/r2/generally-accepted-br-recordkeeping-principles (accessed July 30, 2014).

EMC². *EMC Information Governance Maturity Model Assessment*. EMC Corporation, n.d. www.emc.com/collateral/services/consulting/h4905-info-gov-maturity-model-svo.pdf (accessed July 30, 2014).

Franks, P. C. *Records and Information Management*. Chicago: ALA-Neal Schuman, 2013, 29, 321, 326.

Gartner. "Information Governance." IT Glossary, 2013. www.gartner.com/it-glossary/information-governance (accessed July 30, 2014).

Murphy, B. "What Is Information Governance?" *eDiscovery Journal* (blog), March 22, 2010. http://ediscoveryjournal.com/2010/03/what-is-information-governance.

National Health Service. *Information Governance Toolkit*. Department of Health, England, n.d. www.igt.hscic.gov.uk (accessed July 30, 2014).

INFORMATION MANAGEMENT

The nature of information management as a discipline is subject to debate. Information management is a contested concept, with the meaning varying according to the occupational group claiming ownership of it. Its origins can be traced back to the early twentieth century; reflecting on this historical development provides some insight into the current situation.

The Concept

The three modern information ages identified by Ronald Day (2001) provide a useful perspective from which to view the development of particular occupational specialties that arose in order to address specific problems encountered in managing information. The first information age occurred in the late nineteenth century and resulted in the specialty of documentation to manage the explosion of *documents* in the late nineteenth century. From about 1920 in Europe the term "documentation" was used as a comprehensive one encompassing bibliography, *records management*, and archival work (Buckland 1997). Two leading figures in the *Institut International de Bibliographie* (renamed the International Federation for Documentation in 1935), Paul Otlet and Frits Donker Duyvis, showed an integrative view of the management of information resources of a variety of types and in a variety of contexts, including the office as well as library (Buckland 1998).

Williams (1998) describes special librarians as the first documentalists in the United States and quotes Ethel Johnson in 1915 distinguishing special libraries from public libraries by emphasizing the key role of information: "The main function of the general library is to make books available. The function of the special library is to make information available" (174).

In the United States, information science eventually superseded documentation as the preferred term, and the American Documentation Institute, founded in 1937, changed its name to the American Society for Information Science in 1968 (Buckland 1999), eventually becoming the American Society for Information Science and Technology. It has been suggested that the terms information management and information science can be used interchangeably, with either being today's manifestation of documentation (Buckland 1999).

The second information age occurred in the mid-twentieth century. The formation of records management as a distinct profession has been linked to the need to manage the immense proliferation of documents in North America post World War II (Duranti 1989). Today, in the third information age, there is a tendency for *records managers* to emphasize their role as information managers. For instance, the Records Management Association of Australasia has rebranded itself as "Records and Information Management Professionals Australasia." However, corporate information technology professionals may also often refer to themselves as information managers. Librarians also continue to refer to themselves as information managers.

The consequence of these multiple claims for jurisdiction over the domain is that the scope and range of information management can be defined too narrowly, or if broadly, the purposes for which different information types need to be managed may not be recognized. A major contributing factor to the ambiguity associated with information management is the absence of a robust and coherent theoretical basis.

The information continuum model that was developed as a teaching tool by academics at Monash University has the potential to clarify the ambiguity. The model is briefly described as part of a suite of continua (Upward 2000) and provides a theoretical framework that unifies approaches to information management. It is applicable to all information management specialisms and facilitates more in-depth analysis of occupational roles. It has been applied in various settings, including to assess the sustainability of a community information network (Schauder et al. 2005), to investigate information culture (Oliver 2004) and in the development of a university-wide information strategy and *digital repository* (Treloar et al. 2007).

Conclusion

While there is no generally accepted unifying theory underpinning information management, practitioners claiming to be information managers are likely to remain blinkered in their respective silos. In today's third information age when *archivists*, records managers, and librarians are all struggling to demonstrate their relevance, it is essential that each occupation understands their unique focus and contribution. Only then can the key occupations work together coherently to achieve real progress in information management.—*Gillian Oliver*

Keywords: information management, information science, documentation, records management, information continuum
Related Entry: Records Management

Bibliography

Buckland, M. K. "Documentation, Information Science, and Library Science in the USA." In M. K. Buckland and T. B. Hahn, eds., *Historical Studies in Information Science*. Medford, NJ: ASIS, 1998, 159–72.

———. "The Landscape of Information Science: The American Society for Information Science at 62." *Journal of the American Society for Information Science* 50 (11) (1999): 970–74. DOI: 10.1002/(SICI)1097-4571(1999)50:11<970::AID-ASI3>3.0.CO;2-D.

———. "What Is a 'Document'?" *Journal of the American Society for Information Science* 48 (9) (1997): 804–9. www.columbia.edu/cu/libraries/inside/units/bibcontrol/osmc/bucklandwhat.pdf.

Day, R. E. *The Modern Invention of Information: Discourse, History, and Power*. Carbondale and Edwardsville: Southern Illinois University Press, 2001.

Duranti, L. "The Odyssey of Records Managers Part II: From the Middle Ages to Modern Times." *Records Management Quarterly* 23 (4) (1989): 3–11.

Oliver, G. "Investigating Information Culture: Comparative Case Study Research Design and Methods." *Archival Science* 4 (3–4) (2004): 287–314. DOI: 10.1007/s10502-005-2596-6.

Schauder, D., L. Stillman, and G. Johanson. "Sustaining and Transforming a Community Network: The Information Continuum Model and the Case of VICNET." *Journal of Community Informatics* 1 (2) (2005). www.ci-journal.net/index.php/ciej/article/viewArticle/239.

Treloar, A., D. Groenewegen, and C. Harboe-Ree. "The Data Curation Continuum: Managing Data Objects in Institutional Repositories." *D-Lib Magazine* 13 (9/10) (2007). www.dlib.org/dlib/september07/treloar/09treloar.html.

Upward, F. "Modelling the Continuum as Paradigm Shift in Recordkeeping and Archiving Process, and Beyond—a Personal Reflection." *Records Management Journal* 10 (3) (2000): 115–39. www.emeraldinsight.com/doi/pdfplus/10.1108/EUM0000000007259.

Williams, R. V. "The Documentation and Special Libraries Movements in the United States, 1910–1960." In M. K. Buckland and T. B. Hahn, eds., *Historical Studies in Information Science*. Medford, NJ: ASIS, 1998, 173–79.

INFORMATION POLICY

Information policy is a set of often-interconnected principles and strategies (as manifested in laws, regulations, rules, etc.) that guide the production, collection, organization, manipulation, storage, distribution, retrieval, use, *access*, preservation, and destruction of information and *records*. Information policies are developed at the organizational, local, national, and international levels. Policies are necessary in order to address the divergent views of multiple stakeholders regarding the management of information and records; policies privilege a particular approach or "set of value priorities" (Hoberg 2003). Values are embedded in laws, regulations, and norms, and agreed upon by society, disciplines, professions, and so on. Policies govern practice and are embedded in the *context(s)* in which they operate, thus the values, perspectives, and norms of these environments will influence the shaping of policies and the process of policy making.

Information policy, in its current form (both public and organizational), is relatively young. Browne argues that early de facto information policies existed, citing Galileo at the receiving end of papal information policy, but notes that more generally agreed-on beginnings of modern information policies began in the 1960s (Browne 1997), with most countries developing information policies in the 1970s and 1980s and organizational information policy really beginning to take root in the 1990s (Orna 2008). Possibly due to its relative infancy in the policy arena, information policy has a number of definitions at both the public and organizational levels and no common agreed-on universal definition exists (Duff 2004): "there are at least as many definitions of information policy as there are writers on the subject" (Rowlands 1996, 14). There is no all-encompassing policy; rather, information policies tend to address specific issues and, at times, are fragmented, overlapping, and contradictory depending on the issues they seek to address (Hernon and Relyea 2009). Information policy issues include but are not limited to: freedom of information, privacy, censorship, data protection, security and secrecy, *access*, intellectual property and ownership, openness, information infrastructure, and information flows (Duff 2004; Overman and Cahill 1990).

Information policies on the international, national, and organizational levels are subject to power relations involving different groups of stakeholders. There are differences in the relative power held by such groups, for example, individuals and organizations that are subject to legislation that is part of policy and the government that determines such policy; information and communication technology (ICT) vendors and the individuals who must use them within a government or organization; industry that seeks to exploit commercial interest in harnessing scientific research and those who support free access to such research (Orna 2008).

Contemporary information policy discussions are often informed by e-government (electronic or digital government) and the role of ICTs at national and international levels. Governments are increasingly using the Internet and mobile technologies to communicate with citizens, engage in commerce and political activities, and deliver services. The first decades of the twenty-first century are seeing the increased use of these technologies in state surveillance of and information gathering about citizens with varying levels of transparency and reciprocation. Braman argues that the information state has the capacity "to gather and process information about its citizens and about the resources and activities within its space . . . by growing orders of magnitude" while the inverse, citizens learning about what

governments are doing is on the decline (Braman 2006a). Additional topics include open government initiatives, discussion around the collection and use of vast amounts of data on individuals, and issues of Internet infrastructure, governance, and access.

Organizational Information Policy

Organizations, while subject to similar power relations as governments, engage in information policy making to avoid risk, ensure compliance, maximize resources, and take advantage of change and opportunity (Orna 2008). Organizational information policy is predicated on the requirements of an organization to control the way it creates, records, controls, uses, communicates, retains, and destroys information and records in relation to its goals and objectives. External factors such as legislation, standards, social values and norms, and technology are all elements that must be considered in relation to organizational information policy. Organizational information policy guides decision making and actions around the use and management of information within an organization in order to support and achieve the desired outcomes of particular goals. It serves as a framework that situates information within the broader context of the organization and aids it in carrying out its mandate. Ongoing monitoring and evaluation in the application of information policy within an organization allows the organization to evaluate and react to rapid evolutionary changes in the social, economic, political, and technological landscapes. An information policy must be "flexible, dynamic and responsive to changing circumstances" (Rowlands 1996, 15).

Useful organizational information policy includes a number of characteristics, including: the need for policy to be universal in scope, covering all organizational uses of information throughout its lifecycle; an understanding of how information is contextually defined; information as a basis for social decision making that is linked to human behavior; a recognition of the values as well as the issues that result from interaction between society and information technologies; acknowledgment of its interrelationship with other policies, laws, and standards; and an ability to act as a governance framework for information broadly.

Significance of Information Policy to Archival Science

Archival institutions operate within a broader context of a public policy framework, which governs the boundaries of their infrastructure, operations, and funding, and informs their mandated role in a society. *Archivists* have roles in interpreting and understanding the policies under which they operate and how it affects their offices and the services they provide, as well as informing and influencing policy and the policy-making process. In the broader information infrastructure, the role of *archives* as stewards and preservers of society's records and the archivist's training in administering access, protecting privacy, and privileging of a contextual understanding of their holdings positions them to inform information policy making and the infrastructures that support its manifestations.

Just as archivists realized that a greater understanding of the information and records in digital and online environments was necessary in order to effectively preserve and steward them through space and over time, in the contemporary "information state" knowledge of information policy and the social, economic, political, and technological forces that inform and drive it are also necessary and there is a role for archivists to play. State memory of action, inaction, and decision making, and the context in which these operate, are necessary for effective policy making. Braman (2006a) argues that there are significant consequences if the memory of the state is "fragmented, incoherent, [or] non-existent." For:

> knowledge of the past provides insight into the causal forces that have created present circumstances, providing valuable input into future planning. Knowledge of the present serves control purposes but unless archived and made accessible, does not support the planning function. (Braman 2006a, 319)

There is a clear role here for the archivist and archival institutions in contextually preserving reliable records for future policy-making efforts and ensuring knowledge of their existence and facilitating access.

Along with a prominent focus on technologies, information-policy discussions in the early twenty-first century are also occupied with discourses of participation and democratization; however, the rhetoric that surrounds such ideas often conflict with practices in the public sphere. Knowledge production can be hindered by laws and regulations that work to inhibit "the efforts of researchers, preventing the diffusion of knowledge throughout society so that it can be used, and declining to use the results of research as inputs into public decision making" (Braman 2006a, 320). Intervention in the tools of information policy can undermine evidence-based decision-making, which has historically been relied on in the policy-making process (Braman 2006a). An example of this can be found in Canada with the conservative government's 2010 cancellation of the mandatory long-form census, which supports Braman's (2006a) statement that such tools "intervene in agency information collection, processing, and distribution practices" and result in reduced or absent information to support an evidence-based process. Arguably, archivists and archival institutions must articulate a position in this sphere and advocate for the integrity of the information and records they receive, and weigh into debates that affect the existence of the public record.

As the preservers of society's contemporary records, archivists' voices and expertise are necessary in the public dialogue around the systems that create and house digital information and records. Increasing numbers of government-citizen transactions take place on third-party platforms and with proprietary technologies that may impede the effective preservation and access to information and records of government. Additionally, as Braman (2006a) points out, there is a potential conflict between an increased reliance on the technologies of private-sector entities by those who also regulate them. Archivists can play a role in advocating for policies that ensure public records can be effectively preserved and made accessible for future policymakers.

Conclusion

The availability of information is increasing as the global reach of information and communication technologies proliferate and social and economic barriers to access, participation, and engagement are ameliorated. The economic, social, and political value of information as manifested in the increase in and evolution of e-government is informing social and political change broadly. As Simeon argues, policy is not only a matter of problem solving but also a matter of making choices under tight resource constraints. This leads to conflicts due to resource scarcity, choice constraints, and confronted values and needs. "Policy emerges from the play of economic, social and political forces, as manifested in and through institutions and processes" (Simeon 1976, 550). Archival institutions and archives have a role to play in information-policy analysis and development as they continue to develop in the broader socio-technical infrastructure. The archival field must identify strategies to bring their expertise in the field of records, preservation, and access to the policy-making process to ensure the long-term preservation and access to records and information in support of the process.—*Elizabeth Shaffer*

Keywords: information, policy
Related Entries: Acquisition Policy; Archival Policy; Collection Management Policy

Bibliography

Braman, S. "Information, Policy, and Power in the Informational State." In *Change of State: Information, Policy, and Power*. Cambridge, MA: MIT Press, 2006a, 313–28.

———. "An Introduction to Information Policy." In *Change of State: Information, Policy, and Power*. Cambridge, MA: MIT Press, 2006b.

Browne, Mairead. "The Field of Information Policy: 1. Fundamental Concepts." *Journal of Information Science* 23 (4) (1997): 261–75.

Burger, Robert H. *Information Policy: A Framework for Evaluation and Policy Research*. Norwood: Alex Publishing, 1993.

Duff, A. S. "The Past, Present and Future of Information Policy." *Information Communication and Society* 7 (1) (2004): 69–87.

Hernon, P., and H. C. Relyea. "Information Policy: United States." In *Encyclopedia of Library and Information Sciences*, 3rd edition. New York: Taylor and Francis, 2009, 2504–18.

Hoberg, G. "Policy Cycles and Policy Regimes: A Framework for Studying Policy Change." In B. Cashore, G. Hoberg, J. Howlett, J. Rayner, and J. Wilson, eds., *Search for Sustainability: British Columbia Forest Policy in the 1990s*. Vancouver: UBC Press, 2003, 1–30.

Orna, Elizabeth. "Information Policies: Yesterday, Today, Tomorrow." *Journal of Information Science* 34 (4) (2008): 547–65.

Overman, E. S., and A. G. Cahill. "Information Policy: A Study in Values in the Policy Process." *Policy Studies Review* 9 (4) (1990): 803–18.

Rowlands, Ian. "Understanding Information Policy: Concepts, Frameworks and Research Tools." *Journal of Information Science* 22 (1) (1996): 13–25.

Simeon, R. "Studying Public Policy." *Canadian Journal of Political Science* 9 (4) (1976): 548–80.

INTERRELATEDNESS (RECORD)

Interrelatedness is one of the characteristics of archival *documents* (or *records*) identified by Jenkinson in his *Manual of Archival Administration*, the others being *impartiality*, *authenticity*, and *naturalness* (Jenkinson 1937, 11–12). Interrelatedness manifests itself in the *archival bond*.

The Concept

Interrelatedness is explained by Jenkinson as follows: any archival document (or record) "is potentially related closely to others both inside and outside the group in which it is preserved and . . . its significance depends on these relations" (Jenkinson 1937, 12).

Several decades later, Terry Eastwood linked interrelatedness to naturalness, stating that

> [they both trace to the] manner in which the documents accumulate in the course of the transaction of affairs according to the needs of the matter at hand. [The documents] are natural, in the sense that they are not collected for some purpose outside the administrative needs generating them, and not put together according to some scheme to serve other than those needs, as are the objects in a museum or the documents in a library collection. The documents in any given *archives* then have their relationships established by the course of the conduct of affairs and according to its needs. The relationships among the documents and to the affairs make it axiomatic that no single archival document can stand as sufficient memorial of the course of past activity; they are interdependent for their meaning and in their capacity to serve as evidence of the activity that generated them. (Eastwood 1994, 127–28)

Thus, archival documents or records are linked among themselves by a relationship that arises at the moment in which they are made or received and saved by the creator of the archives (or *archival fonds*) and is determined by the reason for which they are created. This relationship is necessary to very existence of the records, to their ability to accomplish their purpose, to their meaning for the activity in which they participate, and to their capacity of being used as evidence. Because of this cohesiveness, an archives can be regarded as a whole of relationships as well as a whole of documents.

A corollary of interrelatedness is the characteristic of *uniqueness*, which derives to each archival document (or record) by the fact that it has a unique place in the structure of the group in which it belongs (Duranti 1994, 335).

Conclusion

Interrelatedness is the characteristic of archival documents (or records) that determines the dependence of their meaning or *context*. Its manifestation is the archival bond, often expressed in a classification code or a registry number, and revealed by documentary procedures and workflows.—*Luciana Duranti*

Keywords: naturalness, records, archives, archival bond

Related Entries: Archival Bond; Archives (Material); Authenticity; Context; Impartiality (Record); Naturalness (Record); Objectivity (Archivist); Principle of *Respect des Fonds*; Records Classification; Uniqueness

Bibliography

Duranti, Luciana. "The Concept of Appraisal and Archival Theory." *American Archivist* 57 (2) (Spring 1994): 328–45. http://archivists.metapress.com/content/pu548273j5j1p816/fulltext.pdf.

Eastwood, Terry. "What Is Archival Theory and Why Is It Important?" *Archivaria 1* (37) (1994): 122–30. http://journals.sfu.ca/archivar/index.php/archivaria/article/view/11991/12954.

Jenkinson, Hilary. *A Manual of Archive Administration*. London: Percy Lund, Humphries & Co., 1937.

INTRINSIC VALUE

The U.S. National Archives and Records Administration's influential internal paper by the Committee on Intrinsic Value begins with this brief definition:

> Intrinsic value is the archival term that is applied to permanently valuable *records* that have qualities and characteristics that make the records in their original physical form the only archivally acceptable form for *preservation*. Although all records in their original physical form have qualities and characteristics that would not be preserved in copies, records with *intrinsic value* have them to such a significant degree that the originals must be saved. (Committee on Intrinsic Value 1982, para. 3)

Although the language of this definition implies that the concept had been universally accepted, in fact this source is always cited when the concept is discussed in archival *context*. The history and possible continuing relevance of the concept in the digital realm are worth revisiting.

The Concept as Used by Archivists

The language of much current archival discourse in the English-speaking world, especially that around the practice of *appraisal* of materials for archival *selection* and preservation, is full of the term *value* in that the archival appraiser is seen to be obliged in practice to balance many kinds of value in making choices in an environment of scarce resources, whether concerned with organizational or private materials. It is therefore important to understand how the concept of intrinsic value fits in.

Historically, the foregrounding of intrinsic value in Western archival discourse has been related to two *archival practices*: that of manuscript collecting and that of assertion of archival authority and expertise. In addition, and crosscutting the two practices, there have been two epochs in the concern with intrinsic value, both correlated with changes in *recordkeeping* technologies. These four important backgrounds of the concept are not, however, neatly correlated temporally.

Preservation of unique manuscripts in places of learning and in private (usually family or ecclesiastic) *archives* dates to the Middle Ages and was founded on the need to communicate information and to preserve proofs of possession (Clanchy 2013). Such usages, such as when preservation was carried out by creators, made the manuscripts themselves especially interesting to historians and led to manuscript collecting by historians, which persisted until historians moved in the late nineteenth century to form university and *private archives* to support the professionalization of their pursuits. The result of these collecting activities was what is often referred to as a manuscript collection or *collecting archives*, which served the needs of antiquarian interest or research. What came to be known as "artificial collections" were often made meaningful as much by the collector as by the content of the collections (Burnette 1969).

But this was not the end of the value motivations of manuscript collecting. By the beginning of the twenty-first century archival thinking was taking up issues of memory, identity, and community as important to the work of archives; the Canadian archives had fully implemented the *total archives* concept; and the American national archives had been parenting presidential libraries. These departures from the organizationally oriented focus on evidence and *accountability* opened archival consideration to a wider range of values once more, especially as this development was increasingly paired with the challenge to *archivists* of the preservation of *digital records* (Cook 2013).

History of the Concept

Much of the original spate of North American archival discussion around intrinsic value emerged in a government context, in the form of response to the issuance of a staff paper by the American National Archives and Records Service (NARS) in 1982. This paper, which distinguished nine "qualities and characteristics of records with intrinsic value," included a section on the application of the concept and provided general guidelines for the use of NARS staff, including three case studies. Little attention has been paid to the significance of the situation that prompted this paper, but it is useful to mention it. In 1979, the General Services Administration (GSA), to which NARS was then subordinate, ordered NARS to *microfilm existing holdings and then destroy the paper* as an economy measure. This

prompted NARS to form a Committee on Intrinsic Value and to issue what became known as "the 1982 report" in September of 1980. The upshot was that NARS was able to assert its expertise in choosing what should be microfilmed and destroyed and what should be preserved in original form. The staff paper became not only a part of American *archival history*, but also a source of practical guidance for archivists and indeed filtered into NARA practice in the form of, for example, advice that materials with intrinsic value should be given special treatment for preservation.

According to the original *document*, the nine qualities of records exhibiting intrinsic value are:

1. Physical form that may be the subject of study if the records provide meaningful documentation or significant examples of the form.
2. Aesthetic or artistic quality.
3. Unique or curious physical features.
4. Age that provides a quality of *uniqueness*.
5. Value for use in exhibits.
6. Questionable *authenticity*, date, author, or other characteristic that is significant and ascertainable by physical examination.
7. General and substantial public interest because of direct association with famous or historically significant people, places, things, issues, or events.
8. Significance as documentation of the establishment or continuing legal basis of an agency or institution.
9. Significance as documentation of the formulation of policy at the highest executive levels when the policy has significance and broad effect throughout or beyond the agency or institution. (Committee on Intrinsic Value 1982)

These nine qualities represent a motley collection, including aspects of Schellenberg's approach to value assignment and multiple qualities drawn from the *manuscript tradition*. Yet it is questionable whether that practical advice as to how to defend the retention of records in their original form was originally intended to be used as an appraisal practice: the original records threatened in 1979 by replacement reformatting were already deemed permanent. McRanor's (1996) essay certainly assumed that the nine qualities were criteria intended to apply to *ap-*

praisal, however, and both the Society of American Archivists basic manuals on appraisal have included mention of the concept since the document was written (Ham 1993; Boles 2005).

If the context of the creation of the NARS report is considered, it is clear why the concept of intrinsic value has come up again some twenty years later. In 2000 Angelika Menne-Haritz observed: "Intrinsic value has up to now played a minor role in *archival science* and library literature." The second event that brought it to archival attention started similarly with the emergence of the idea that paper materials could be converted to digital form and the originals destroyed. A parallel phenomenon, the concern with preserving born-digital materials with qualities that preclude replacement reformatting, led to a practice now referred to as preservation of "significant properties" of the original. These issues were addressed in a broad study on the preservation of both paper and born-digital materials by Menne-Haritz and Brubach at the Archiveschule, providing a detailed analysis of the preservation of the "testimony" of born-digital materials in 2000 that drew significantly on the NARS document. For the authors, "Intrinsic value is given [assigned] when the testimony of the original relevant for its consultation is not completely preserved on conversion to a different medium" (Menne-Haritz and Brubach 2000). This position was echoed by a Council on Library Information Resources study in 2001, which also focused on preservation and how best to preserve both physical and digital materials to keep their research values intact (Council on Library and Information Resources 2001). Both of these studies drew on the NARS document.

The notion of preserving born-digital materials was early driven by the now mostly rejected practice of converting records materials with similar functions to a few standard formats, maintaining only the "significant properties" of the records, in order to simplify the work of preserving them. Perhaps the strongest response to this suggestion, which has come from several directions, all rested on the fact that the original format of a digital object is part of its authenticity, which takes the preservation of original form past the special consideration of intrinsic value and into the fundamental requirement of documentary authenticity and the increasing adoption of digital forensic methods to guarantee

it. This is where the concerns of collecting archives especially came into play again, since increasing understanding of the "media materiality" of artistic and entertainment-related digital materials made it clear that all the qualities and characteristics of such materials might be important (Yeo 2010).

Conclusion

As has been the case with many archival issues, the generalization of the concept of intrinsic value into the idea of significant properties has exposed another way in which meeting the challenges of digital recordkeeping has led to an expansion of archival thinking. The claim of archival expertise in detecting intrinsic value prompted the process of examining the characteristics of special categories of original records that could not be replicated on microfilm. As further technological change ushered in the digital age, archivists were faced with a new situation in which all preservation of permanent records would eventually entail replication. This more pervasive problem forced all archivists to begin to consider what values—and significance—would have to be preserved and how that would be done.

—*Pat Galloway*

Keywords: value, materiality, significant properties
Related Entries: Appraisal; Manuscripts Tradition; Secondary Value

Bibliography

Boles, Frank. *Selecting & Appraising Archives & Manuscripts*. Chicago: Society of American Archivists, 2005.

Burnette, O. Lawrence, Jr. *Beneath the Footnote: A Guide to the Use and Preservation of American Historical Sources*. Madison: The State Historical Society of Wisconsin, 1969.

Clanchy, M. T. *From Memory to Written Record: England 1066–1307*, 3rd edition. Hoboken, NJ: Wiley-Blackwell, 2013.

Committee on Intrinsic Value. "Intrinsic Value in Archival Materials." National Archives and Records Service Staff Information Paper 21. National Archives and Records Service, 1982. www.archives.gov/research/alic/reference/archives-resources/archival-material-intrinsic-value.html.

Cook, Terry. "Evidence, Memory, Identity, and Community: Four Shifting Archival Paradigms." *Archival Science* 13 (2013): 95–120. DOI: 10.1007/s10502-012-9180-7.

Council on Library and Information Resources. *The Evidence in Hand: Report of the Task Force on the Artifact in Library Collections.* November 2001.

Ham, Gerald. *Selecting and Appraising Archives and Manuscripts.* Chicago: Society of American Archivists, 1993.

McRanor, Shauna. "A Critical Analysis of Intrinsic Value." *American Archivist* 59 (4) (1996): 400–411. http://archivists.metapress.com/content/hw1x875811u11671/fulltext.pdf.

Menne-Haritz, Angelika, and Nils Brubach. "The Intrinsic Value of Archive and Library Material." *Microform & Imaging Review* 29 (3) (2000): 79–95. DOI: 10.1515/MFIR.2000.79.

Yeo, Geoffrey. "'Nothing Is the Same as Something Else': Significant Properties and Notions of Identity and Originality." *Archival Science* 10 (2010): 85–116. DOI: 10.1007/s10502-010-9119-9.

MANUSCRIPTS TRADITION

In the United States, the manuscripts tradition (also known as the historical manuscripts tradition) was an antiquarian approach to collecting personal and public records that emerged in the early nineteenth century. Because many government agencies did little to care for their records, many historical societies and libraries sought to acquire, preserve, and publish private and public records that focused on "great Americans" and documented the revolution and new democracy. The *records* were often acquired individually and venerated because of their associational value or autographs, rather than their content. As the records lacked contextual relationships, the collections were more random than systematic. The manuscripts tradition was dominant through the 1950s, when the increasing size of collections and a shift from historical to modern records caused curators to adopt methods from the *public records tradition* for physical and intellectual control (Berner 1983, 11, 20).

The Concept

In 1835, Joseph B. Felt, librarian of the Massachusetts Historical Society and later public records commissioner for Massachusetts, arranged manuscripts and records chronologically within broad subjects. New Hampshire and Connecticut followed Felt's method, making it a model for physical and intellectual control (Schellenberg 1965, 36). In 1897, Herbert Friedenwald devised a similar approach, largely based on the massive collection of Peter Force acquired by the newly established Manuscripts Division of the Library of Congress (Cole 1979, 62). Records were organized chronologically under geographic headings, with separate headings for noteworthy individuals. In 1904, Worthington C. Ford, chief of manuscripts at the Library of Congress, noted that collections of *personal records* were sometimes arranged alphabetically by the writers' names but preferred chronological organization (Cutter 1904, 136). In 1913, John C. Fitzpatrick (1913) described Friedenwald's approach in *Notes on the Care, Cataloguing, Calendaring and Arranging of Manuscripts*. Fitzpatrick noted that "the strict chronological arrangement by years, months, and days is the only perfectly satisfactory one," after observing that "an arrangement and indexing born of administrative necessity" was "in no wise competent to answer the needs of the historical investigator" and "useless and faulty . . . for students of history and economics" (1913, 8) A chronological arrangement is beneficial because it "presents a complete picture of the daily course of events as the life of the past was lived; it satisfies the instincts of the investigator by placing the records before him in unbroken sequence of time" (1913, 14). Howard H. Peckham of the Clements Library observes, "The chronological arrangement often brings unrelated *documents* together, it has the virtue of offering the papers to the reader in the order in which they 'happened,' or were written" (Peckham 1938, 218). Given the relatively few records and the lack of meaningful order, chronological arrangement made the sequence of events comprehensible and provided a primary *access* point.

Records were typically described individually. Ford briefly codified descriptive practice in Cutter's *Rules* (1904, 135), and Fitzpatrick's *Notes* served as a manual for use by other institutions, with subsequent editions in 1921 and 1928. Description was limited to essential details, including the date, writer, recipient, place, and format. A separate calendar might summarize content. However, such detailed description was impractical. Fitzpatrick (1913, 15) describes an ideal in which "every single manuscripts under the *archivist's* care is represented by a card" and notes, "desirable as this is and devoutly as it may be wished, it is as often not. . . . There are always arrears, and there are apt to be formidable accessions."

The emergence of *archives* as a new profession in the early twentieth century signaled a different approach to managing records in the United States. In 1899, the American Historical Association established a Public Archive Commission "to investigate and report on the character of the historical public archives in each state" (Berner 1983). Waldo G. Leland, who had studied at the École des Chartes and was then secretary of the Association, organized the First Conference of Archivists in 1909 to address concerns that historical societies and libraries collected only a few, select public records and that the management of these records resulted in the loss of important historical context. At the conference, he argued for archivists to follow European *principles of provenance* and to follow the practices that Muller, Feith, and Fruin described in their 1905 Dutch Manual. "Archives should be classified according to their origin; they should reflect the processes by which they came into existence. . . . Nothing is more disastrous than the application of modern library methods of classification to a body of archives" (Leland 1909).

Conclusion

The manuscript and public records traditions coexisted well into the twentieth century. Practice at the Library of Congress served as the basis for rules to describe manuscripts in both the 1967 and 1978 editions of *Anglo-American Cataloging Rules*. During the twentieth century, ever-growing collections of records were acquired as aggregates, rather than individually. Because these large, organic collections had a structure similar to collections of public records, historical societies and manuscript libraries

began to adopt principles from the public *records* tradition, including respect for provenance and original order, and hierarchical arrangement and description. Steven L. Hensen's *Archives, Personal Papers, and Manuscripts*, first issued in 1983 with a second edition in 1989, was a modern codification of descriptive practice that began to harmonize the two traditions and ultimately served as the foundation of modern standards of *archival practice* for private and public records, including *Encoded Archival Description* (1998, 2002) and *Describing Archives: A Content Standard* (2004, 2013).

—*Richard Pearce-Moses*

Keywords: personal records, arrangement, and description

Related Entries: Archival Arrangement; Archival Description; Collecting Archives; Personal Records; Principle of Respect for Original Order; Public Records Tradition; Records Classification

Bibliography

Berner, Richard C. *Archival Theory and Practice in the United States: A Historical Analysis.* Seattle: University of Washington Press, 1983.

Birdsall, William Forest. *The American Archivists Search for Professional Identity.* Ann Arbor, MI: University Microfilms International, 1973.

Cole, John. *For Congress and the Nation: A Chronological History of the Library of Congress.* Washington, DC: Library of Congress, 1979. Cited in Robert D. Reynolds Jr. "The Incunabula of Archival Theory and Practice in the United States: J. C. Fitzpatrick's Notes on the Care, Cataloguing, Calendaring and Arranging of Manuscripts and The Public Archives Commission's Uncompleted 'Primer of Archival Economy.'" *American Archivist* 54 (4) (1991): 467–69.

Cutter, Charles Ami. *Rules for a Printed Dictionary Catalog*, 4th edition. Washington, DC: U.S. Bureau of Education, 1904.

Fitzpatrick, John C. *Notes on the Care, Cataloguing, Calendaring and Arranging of Manuscripts.* Washington, DC: Manuscripts Division, Library of Congress, 1913. Republished in 1921 and 1928.

Hensen, Steven L. *Archives, Personal Papers, and Manuscripts: A Cataloging Manual for Archival Repositories, Historical Societies, and Manu-*

script Libraries, 1st edition. Washington, DC: Manuscripts Division, Library of Congress, 1983; 2nd edition: Chicago: Society of American Archivists, 1989.

Leland, Waldo G. "American Archival Problems. Presented at the First Conference of Archivists, 1909." Cited in Peter J. Wosh. *Waldo Gifford Leland and the Origins of the American Archival Profession*. Chicago: Society of American Archivists, 2011.

Muller, S., J. A. Feith, and R. Fruin. *Anleitung zum Ordnen und Beschreiben von Archiven*; Leipzig: Otto Harrassowitz; Gronigen: Erven B. van der Kamp, 1905.

Peckham, Howard H. "Arranging and Cataloguing Manuscripts in the William L. Clements Library." *American Archivist* 1 (4) (October 1938): 218. http://archivists.metapress.com/content/14l5102465r27084/fulltext.pdf.

Schellenberg, T. R. *The Management of Archives.* Foreword by Jane F. Smith. New York: Columbia University Press, 1965.

METADATA

Often defined as "data about data," metadata is much more complex than these words imply. Metadata is, indeed, data about data, but there are different kinds of data and thus different kinds of metadata. Metadata is best defined in terms of metadata types, metadata structures, metadata standards, metadata usage, metadata administration, and metadata management. All metadata describes data that constitute an aspect or aspects of a data object or resource. The U.S. National Information Standards Organization (NISO) defines metadata as "structured information that describes, explains, locates, or otherwise makes it easier to retrieve, use, or manage an information resource" (2004, 1). A common metadata implementation with which many are familiar is the public library card catalog or public library online public-access catalog. Each of these tools provides *access* to library resources through the use of various metadata elements that collectively constitute a metadata record. Each metadata record is a set of elements that describe a library object, such as a book or periodical. Common metadata elements in a metadata set describing library objects are the element's title, author, publisher, and date.

Types of Metadata

Definitions of *metadata* generally hold that metadata falls into two or three classes or types: structural metadata, descriptive metadata, and administrative metadata. (In some circles, administrative metadata is sometimes subsumed as a part of structural metadata.) Some of these metadata types have subtypes, added by particular metadata user communities. Metadata that constitutes data describing a data object's container and the complexities of a data object such as different parts or components is structural metadata. Metadata that describes what a data object holds or is about, whom or what created it, and its purpose, is descriptive metadata. Metadata that facilitates a data object's use, management, and preservation is administrative metadata. In the class of administrative metadata are such subtypes as rights management metadata, preservation metadata, *authentication* and encryption/decryption metadata, audit and use data objects, as well as the data objects themselves, for as long as needed. Data objects can be associated with all of these types of metadata and metadata can be of more than one type. Employment of all types of metadata provides the best environment for organization and identification of data objects, optimum retrieval of data objects in response to queries, maximum interoperability between data objects in different systems, and the best chance to archive and preserve data objects.

Metadata Creation

Metadata can be generated by a machine or authored by a human, unstructured or structured and simple or complex. Metadata can be created to reflect varying degrees of granularity in the description of a data object. The data objects that metadata describe largely determine metadata generation, structure, and complexity in a given *context* and domain. Metadata user communities have initiated the development of metadata structures as well as modification of existing metadata structures used for data objects within their community of interest. Metadata structures are created according to a particular syntax encoding, a set of rules that specify metadata fields or elements within a metadata structure. For example, many metadata implementations for web-based data objects have been expressed in HTML/XHTML, XML, and RDF (DCMI 2013).

Metadata Standards

Metadata development has produced a number of metadata standards and element sets. Metadata standards or sets can be locally adopted or intended for national and international use within a user community, domain of interest, or other social-juridical context. The Dublin Core metadata element set (DC) is an example of an established international metadata standard, used to describe networked data objects (such as webpages) across many domains. DC is used as a base metadata structure for many public and private organizations and is modified, extended, and used as a data model to describe data objects in numerous implementations throughout the world. AGLS is an example of a metadata structure for government data resources published and used in Australia.

Metadata in Use

Metadata is created and employed by many organizations and user groups throughout their computing and data enterprise. *Metadata application profiles* are developed within and between organizations to allow automated management of user access to specific data objects and their metadata based on defined user profiles. Metadata's most basic and fundamental use is to enable the right users to find, use, and manage data resources.

The administration and management of metadata occur whether metadata is embedded as a part of a data object, detached from a data object and managed separately, or a combination of both. Since metadata is necessary to the management of data objects over time and metadata accrue to a data object as it is created, used, and maintained, storage and management of metadata are critical to the long-term preservation of, and access to, data objects. Embedding metadata within the resource is easily achieved in certain data object formats but not in others. Some metadata is better maintained independently of a data object, such as in a database or registry, and links to a described object are provided from within a metadata record. Each storage method

has advantages and disadvantages and storage methods may change over time as conditions warrant.

Conclusion

Metadata as a concept is older than modern web-driven computer technology. Its application does not have to be in a strictly electronic environment. Metadata fulfills its greatest potential in networked electronic environments, however, and is the foundation of semantic web research and technologies. In our desire to provide and control access to as much data and information as possible, metadata plays a vital role in the organization, discovery, management, *authenticity*, and preservation of data objects.—*Lori Lindberg*

Keywords: description, metadata, standards
Related Entries: Metadata Application Profiles; Recordkeeping Metadata

Bibliography

Baca, Murtha. *Introduction to Metadata: Pathways to Digital Information*. Los Angeles: Getty Information Institute, 1998.

"Dublin Core User Guide." Dublin Core Metadata Initiative, Wikipage, last modified 2011. http://wiki.dublincore.org/index.php/User_Guide (accessed December 23, 2013).

"Understanding Metadata." National Information Standards Organization (NISO). Bethesda, MD: NISO Press, 2004.

Zeng, Marcia Lei, and Jian Qin. *Metadata*. New York: Neal-Schuman, 2008.

METADATA APPLICATION PROFILES

In contemporary practice, metadata application profiles define which *metadata* properties (sometimes called elements) are used in a particular instance. The rationale for this is the wide range and variety of metadata schema standards. We can think of a metadata application profile as a mixing of only those relevant properties from different (and perhaps diverse) standard metadata schemas, combined for the purpose of describing resources (e.g., *records, documents*) in a particular *context*.

One of the most common metadata schema standards comes from the Dublin Core Metadata Initiative. Originally designed to be parsimonious with only fifteen metadata properties, the concept of "core" was an attempt to be lightweight and versatile. The intention was to allow anyone to describe anything and put that description on the web so that anyone using the web could find anything. However, the one-size-fits-all appearance of the schema has been a source of criticism (Harper 2010).

One amelioration that has been proposed is to extend or supplement the Dublin Core metadata set with other properties either from other standard metadata schemas or by inventing semantically unique properties for a particular implementation. These innovations are then formalized to become metadata application profiles.

History of Metadata Application Profiles

Metadata application profiles surfaced in the information and archival studies spaces in the early 2000s. They were a response to the attempt to build a web-based metadata standard that fit different communities (Lagoze 1996). Designers at the time realized that one size does not fit all; the proposed solution was to mix and match metadata from different schemas. From this first realization, researchers, professionals, and technical experts have discussed the requirements, affordances, and constraints of metadata in the newly emerging World Wide Web (the web).

The concept was debated in the Dublin Core Metadata Initiative (DC-General) and refined to the form of a recommended specification (Coyle and Baker 2009). There is now a strong relationship between Dublin Core Metadata (which are now called DCMI Metadata Terms) and the Resource Description Framework (RDF Working Group 2014) of the World Wide Web Consortium (W3C). This has influenced the vocabulary used to talk about application profiles in this context. In non-DCMI contexts, language may differ, but the basic design requirements are similar. Coyle and Baker (2009) codify these requirements, which now stand as the best practice when designing and implementing metadata application profiles.

Metadata Application Profiles

When implementing metadata in information or archival systems, it is rare that any given metadata schema works perfectly. We know this by analyzing the requirements of the system in context. These requirements lead us to choose metadata elements from schemas. All of this is documented in the application profile. An application profile is a document or set of documents that contains: (1) functional requirements, (2) domain model, (3) description set profile, and (4) syntax guidelines and data formats.

Functional requirements are what the metadata implementation is supposed to accomplish. This is usually an activity or set of activities. In the archival context, we are interested in documenting the context of creation, the documentary form, the identity of the record(s), their integrity over time and in the full range of technological and juridical contexts, and action taken to preserve records. These allow us to keep authentic records in digital systems for the long-term.

The domain model identifies the materials, agents, and context of the implementation. Again, in the archival context we have records, aggregations of records, and attributes of records as materials. Agents include creators, *records managers*, and *archivists,* as well as users of records. Creation, *recordkeeping*, and *preservation* are the three major contexts identified by the InterPARES research project (Duranti and Preston 2008), but there could be more or fewer depending on the particular implementation.

The description set profile enumerates the elements that will be used in the implementation based on the functional requirements and the domain model. The DCMI Metadata Terms are an example of this (DCMI 2012), as is the listing of terms in appendix III of the InterPARES Authenticity Metadata Application Profile (Rogers and Tennis 2012). Examples might include author, documentary type, or subject. These would then have a value associated with them in the implementation. In the application profile the designer lists these elements and then specifies whether they are required or not, and what values they are allowed to take.

Because metadata implementation is carried out in a digital context, we also must specify syntax guidelines and data formats. These encode the semantics of the elements into machine-readable form.

Examples of data formats include XML, RDFXML, HXTML, and JSON. While there are modeling commitments that are tied to the choice of encoding, they are separate considerations from the main work of creating an application profile.

Authenticity Metadata as an Example

While many *metadata* schemas are available for resource discovery (e.g., DCMI) and for preservation (e.g., PREMIS), there is a need for metadata to help *archivists* and records managers preserve authentic records, where authentic means we know the identity and integrity of the records in as complete a manner as possible. To that end we can see that while DCMI and PREMIS might be useful, they do not offer a complete set of metadata to fit the functional requirements that surface from the needs of archivists and records managers.

The InterPARES 3 Project defined a set of functional requirements, built domain models, and outlined a description set profile for authenticity metadata called the IPAM. While we were able to pull in many elements from Dublin Core and PREMIS, we also required unique elements because our domain models and functional requirements were different from either of these complementary schemas. What the IPAM provides is an element to mark records as authenticated.

Other examples of applications profiles exist, such as the Scholarly Works Application Profile (Allinson and Powell 2006) and the Describing Core Collections Application Profile (DCMI 2007).

Conclusion

In the context of archival work, metadata that works for the needs of our institutions is essential. While some metadata schemas are widely used, they may not meet all of our needs. Metadata application profiles can be constructed to fit our needs by combining different aspects of existing metadata schemas and creating our own where needed to fit our functional requirements, domain context, and implementation context.—*Joseph T. Tennis*

Keywords: metadata, preservation, recordkeeping
Related Entries: Metadata; Recordkeeping Metadata

Bibliography

Allinson, Julie, and Andy Powell. "SWAP: Scholarly Works Application Profile." 2006. www.ukoln.ac.uk/repositories/digirep/index/Eprints_Application_Profile.

Coyle, Karen, and Tom Baker. "Guidelines for Dublin Core Application Profiles." 2009. http://dublincore.org/documents/profile-guidelines.

"DC-General Mailing List." www.jiscmail.ac.uk/cgi-bin/wa.exe?SUBED1=dc-general&A=1.

DCMI. "Dublin Core Collections Application Profile." 2007. http://dublincore.org/groups/collections/collection-application-profile.

"DCMI Metadata Terms." 2012. http://dublincore.org/documents/dcmi-terms.

Duranti, Luciana, and Randy Preston. *International Research on Permanent Authentic Records in Electronic Systems (InterPARES 2): Experiential, Interactive, and Dynamic Records.* Cleup, Padova, 2008. www.interpares.org/ip2/book.cfm.

Harper, Corey. "DCMI: Beyond the Element Set." *Information Standards Quarterly* 22 (1) (2010): 20–28. http://dx.doi.org/10.3789/isqv22n1.201004.

Lagoze, Carl. "The Warwick Framework: A Container Architecture for Diverse Sets of Metadata." *D-Lib* (July/August 1996). www.dlib.org/dlib/july96/lagoze/07lagoze.html.

Nevile, Liddy. "Adaptability and Accessibility: A New Framework." In *Proceedings of the 17th Australia Conference on Computer-Human Interaction: Citizens Online: Considerations for Today and the Future*, 1–10. Computer-Human Interaction Special Interest Group (CHISIG) of Australia, 2005. http://dl.acm.org/citation.cfm?id=1108413 (accessed February 4, 2009).

RDF Working Group. "Resource Description Framework." 2014. www.w3.org/RDF.

Rogers, Corinne, and Joseph T. Tennis. *General Study 15—Application Profile for Authenticity Metadata.* InterPARES 3 Project, 2012.

MONETARY APPRAISAL

Monetary appraisal can contribute to the *acquisition* of more and better holdings of private *documents* for institutions interested in keeping private fonds. While in many countries, *archivists* do not participate in the *monetary appraisal*, the Canadian practice provides for the involvement of archivists in the process.

Monetary appraisal of *archives* is the process of determining the pecuniary value of a grouping of archival *records*. It is used for several purposes, notably the purchase of archival documents directly or at auctions, tax deductions or exemptions for *donations* of archival material, insurance for transportation or exhibition of documents, and estate settlement.

In many countries, archivists are discouraged from any involvement in the process of archival monetary appraisal. In the SAA *Guide to Donating Your Personal or Family Papers to a Repository*, for example, it is stated that "archivists cannot give tax advice, nor are they permitted to appraise the monetary value of a collection" (see www2.archivists. org/publications/brochures/donating-familyrecs, para. 22). In Canada, archivists have been involved from the early beginning of the formalization of the process with the creation of the Document Appraisal Committee of the Canadian Historical Association in 1971. As a result, they have been able to take into consideration such factors as research value and significance of the records.

Responding to the need to obtain credible evaluations of archival records, the Canadian National Archival Appraisal Board (NAAB) was established formally in 1974 as an independent body composed of archivists, researchers, and dealers, to evaluate archival records donated to repositories across the country at reasonable costs to institutions. The main objective of the NAAB consists of providing monetary evaluations acceptable to fiscal authorities for archival donations to public archival institutions. Since the implementation of the Cultural Property Export and Import Act in 1975, the Canadian Cultural Property Export Review Board (CCPERB) supervises the overall process for the revenue agencies; it is responsible, among other tasks, for "certifying cultural property for income tax purposes and for establishing the fair market value of donations to designated Canadian museums, art galleries, archives and libraries" (www.appointments-nominations. gc.ca/prflOrg.asp?OrgID=PER&lang=eng). In this role, the CCPERB not only reviews the conclusions of NAAB's and private appraisers' reports for important donations of *archival fonds* but also provides the basic ground rules used for archival evaluations.

The Process of Monetary Evaluation

For all *appraisals*, the process of monetary evaluation aims to determine the "fair market value" of a group of records, whether sold or donated. *Fair market value* is defined by CCPERB as "the highest price, expressed in terms of money, that a property would bring, in an open and unrestricted market, between a willing buyer and a willing seller who are both knowledgeable, informed, and prudent, and who are acting independently of each other" (Gordon 1972, 62).

The main steps of an appraisal are fairly straightforward:

1. An institution desiring the monetary appraisal of a fonds or collection of archival records prepares a full description of the donated material, including all the main groupings (*series* and subseries, when relevant) of the records to be evaluated with a proper arrangement, making sure to record the quantities of the various types of documents.

2. An appraiser or an NAAB appraisal committee examines the records and drafts an appraisal report containing a summary description, the monetary value of the fonds (and its main components), and a justification outlining the basis for the conclusions.

3. When warranted by the importance or significance of the accession and if eligible, the institution makes an application for certification by the Cultural Property Import and Export Board, which when approved, exempts the donor from the capital gain provisions and confirms on behalf of Revenue Canada the value of the gift and the resulting exemptions. When the institution is not designated by CCPERB or for any other gift in kind, the donor can still benefit under the provisions of donations to charitable organizations.

4. Using the NAAB evaluation report or the CCPERB certificate as a basis, the archival institution or its sponsoring body produces an income tax receipt for an amount not exceeding that indicated in the evaluation report.

The prospect of better compensation for significant records or more valuable historical insights can only encourage more people to keep more and better private records and to control more effectively their destruction habits for material that otherwise they would discard as unimportant drafts, lapsed or unimportant working papers, or old photographs, films, or tapes. Indeed, the notion of historical recognition used almost exclusively in the past to stimulate the preservation of valuable records can only be effectively complemented by adequate compensation to those who keep good research records to be used eventually by a public increasingly interested in archival sources.

Conclusion

Unlike other heritage-preservation institutions, which can build their collections mainly through regular purchase, archival institutions can still acquire from private sources through donations without spending budgetary resources needed for processing and preserving their holdings. Monetary appraisal, then, can be part of the acquisition strategy of all archival institutions interested in donations of private fonds and collections.—*Marcel Caya*

Keywords: acquisition, appraisal, evaluation, monetary

Related Entries: Acquisition; Appraisal

Bibliography

Applications for Certification of Cultural Property for Income Tax Purposes. Information and Procedures, revised edition. Ottawa: Heritage Canada, Canadian Cultural Property Export Review Board, 2010. www.pch.gc.ca/eng/1358368698299/13583 68860650.

Caya, Marcel. "Évaluation monétaire." In Normand Charbonneau and Mario Robert, eds., *La Gestion des archives photographiques*. Sainte-Foy: Presses de l'Université du Québec, 2001, 63–81.

———. "L'évaluation monétaire: un instrument d'acquisition." *Archives (Revue de l'Association des Archivistes du Québec)* 28 (1) (1996–1997): 49–58.

Cook, Terry. "Bucks for Your Bytes: Monetary Appraisal for Tax Credit of Private-Sector Electronic Database Records." *Archivaria* 62 (2006): 121–25.

"Gifts and Income Tax." Canada Revenue Agency, 2000. Last updated January 2014. www.cra-arc.gc.ca/E/pub/tg/p113/p113-06e.pdf.

Gordon, R. S. "Document Appraisal Committee." *The Canadian Archivist* 2 (3) (1972): 62–63. http://journals.sfu.ca/archivar/index.php/ca/article/viewFile/13078/14317.

Kula, Sam. *Appraising Moving Images: Accessing the Archival and Monetary Value of Film and Video Records*. Lanham, MD: Scarecrow Press, 2003.

Silversides, Brock. *Preparing for Monetary Appraisals: A Guide for Canadian Archival Institutions*. Ottawa, Ontario: ACA, 2003, 1–30.

Walden, David. "The Tax Credit System: Blessing or Burden?" *Archivaria* 18 (1984): 84–90. http://journals.sfu.ca/archivar/index.php/archivaria/article/view/11080/12016.

N

NATURALNESS (RECORD)

Archival writers have since the seventeenth century acknowledged the fact that archival *documents* or *records* accumulate over time progressively and continuously, like the sediment of geological stratifications or the residues of a running river on a riverbed (Bautier 1961, 1120). Jenkinson wrote, "Archives are not documents collected artificially, like the objects in a museum . . . but accumulating naturally in offices for the practical purposes of Administration" (Jenkinson 1937, 12). Thus, naturalness is, together with *interrelatedness, impartiality*, and *authenticity*, one of the characteristics of *archives* (material).

The Concept

Archives have been traditionally regarded as a natural accumulation of documents kept for the practical purposes of their creator, as opposed to an artificial collection. Archival documents (or records), different from other types of documents (e.g., a published book), are one of the means by which a *person* or organization carries out its activity, rather than the purpose of the activity itself. Being instruments for their creator's purposes, records carry with themselves, since their origin, the bond of a common destination and constitute a *universitas*, a whole, the components of which derive their meaning from each other and their interrelationships. This aggregation is natural and necessary because it results from the functionality itself of each document with respect to the others. The fact that archival documents are not contrived outside the direct requirements of the conduct of affairs—that is, that they accumulate naturally, progressively, and continuously, like the sediments of geological stratifications—provides them with an element of spontaneous yet structured cohesiveness (Duranti 1994, 334).

Conclusion

Naturalness is the characteristic of archival documents (or records) most often referred to as "organicity" or "involuntariness," meaning that archival documents grow spontaneously from one another and are not the purpose of the activity that generates them, but its residue, similar to the bed of a river or the roots of a tree, all metaphors used in archival literature.—*Luciana Duranti*

Keywords: archives, creation, interrelatedness, records
Related Entries: Archival Bond; Archives (Material); Authenticity; Impartiality; Interrelatedness; Principle of Respect des Fonds; Record Creation; Record(s); Reliability

Bibliography

Bautier, Robert-Henri. "Les Archives." In *L'histoire et ses methods*. Paris, 1961.
Duranti, Luciana. "The Concept of Appraisal and Archival Theory." *American Archivist* 57 (2)

(1994): 328–45. http://archivists.metapress.com/
content/pu548273j5j1p816/fulltext.pdf.

Eastwood, Terry. "What Is Archival Theory and
Why Is It Important?" Archivaria 1 (37) (1994):
122–30. http://journals.sfu.ca/archivar/index.php/
archivaria/article/view/11991/12954.

Jenkinson, Hilary. *A Manual of Archives Administration*. London: Percy Lund, Humphries & Co,
1937. Reprint 1965.

Livelton, Trevor. *Archival Theory, Records, and the
Public*. Lanham, MD: Scarecrow Press, 1996.

OBJECTIVITY (ARCHIVIST)

The idea of objectivity as the ethical stance of the *archivist* surfaced in Europe in the early twentieth century in relation to *appraisal* and in direct connection with the debate about an appraisal methodology based on content analysis and the *principle of pertinence* versus one based on *structural analysis* and the *principle of provenance* (Booms 1987, 85). Although sometimes the term used, especially in the German context, was *impartiality*, meaning that the archivist should not be partial to any type of use or user, the trust of the idea was that the archivist should not serve any interest other than that of protection of the characteristics of the *records*. In the words of Felix Hull: "How dangerous a word is 'interest.' As an archivist I should not have 'interest' for I must be 'all things to all *archives*' irrespective of age or provenance—how difficult then for me to make judgements affecting the existence of archives—yet I must!" (Hull 1980, 289).

The difficulty of carrying out appraisal without being influenced by one's own interests, that is, objectively, and by others' interests, that is, impartially, was evident since the beginning of this endeavor, but nowhere else was it as pervasive as in German and British literature. In contrast, the American writers have not been concerned with either objectivity or impartiality, as shown, for example, by Schellenberg's reliance on the archivists' subjectivity, which is considered a strength, because the resulting diverse judgments "may well assure a more adequate social documentation" (Schellenberg 1956, 149), and his choice of equating value with use and involving scholars of specific disciplines in the *selection* of the records that would best serve them (Schellenberg 1956, 148–56).

The Concept

In the past century, archival literature has based the function of appraisal on several points of principle: appraisal must be impartial (i.e., not partial to any type of use or user), objective (i.e., not influenced by the personal outlook and interests of the person carrying it out), professional (i.e., the ultimate responsibility for it must be the archivist's), contextual (i.e., it must be based on knowledge of the records environment), and holistic (i.e., it must aim at providing the complete picture of society). While the first two attributes represent the British contribution to the discussion on appraisal, the others are German and North American contributions (Duranti 1994, 330).

The concept of objectivity as first envisioned by Jenkinson was based on the so-called "non-evaluational" nature of archival work deeply rooted in the characteristics of impartiality, *authenticity*, *naturalness*, and *interrelatedness* of archival material, all features that the archivist has the responsibility to protect (Duranti 1994, 337). The primary duty of the archivist—Jenkinson believed—is to the evidentiary nature of archival material, and the activities supporting this duty, which came to be known as the "moral defense of archives," are central to the archival professional ethics. Such activities do not include appraisal. At the first International Congress of Archives meeting, in Paris, Jenkinson stated that the task of the archivist is to be the servant of truth, of the simple truth, not of that truth that can please him or serve the views of the one or the other school of thought (*Archivum* I 1951, 47). In his *Manual of Archives Administration,* he wrote: "For the Archivist to destroy a *document* because he thinks it useless is to import into the collection under his charge what we have been throughout most anxious to keep out of it, an element of his personal judgement" (Jenkinson 1937, 128).

In the United States, the only writer who upheld the centrality of the moral defense of archives in an explicit way was Margaret Cross Norton. She wrote that archivists are bound "to protect the integrity of . . . records," and even if "historical" archives may appear to have no value for current affairs, this "does not release the custodian from his legal and moral responsibilities" (Mitchell 1975, 26).

Methodology

Jenkinson's articulation of the characteristics of archives that must be protected by the archivist (i.e., impartiality, authenticity, naturalness, and interrelatedness) established the theoretical framework for appraisal. In fact, his "golden rule" for creating and maintaining records is a strong argument for an efficient *record management* program capable of maintaining the traces of all activities while continuously disposing of the superfluous (Jenkinson 1937, 153). His ideas were implemented in Great Britain by the Public Records Act of 1958, following the recommendations of the Grigg Report. The report stated that the preservation of archival value, that is, of the probative nature of the records as found in the "unselfconscious" and "impartial," is of paramount concern (Grigg Report 1954, 111). Based on the report, Great Britain established an appraisal procedure consisting of a two-tiered review process that combines a first review of the records at five years from the closure of the *files* and a second review at twenty-five years. The first review was to be done by each creator's record officer to destroy those records that are no longer needed for the creator's purposes. The second review was to be done by the record officer together with the archivist and was meant to examine all the records that survived the first review and destroy those considered to be of no further relevance. Here, continuing value was equated with long-term administrative value, understood in the broadest sense, and its assessment was to be based on the structural analysis of the records using the *functions* and activities of the creating body as an objective method. In 1986, Michael Cook commented that the methodology introduced by the Grigg Report is still valid today and wrote: "The historical record should reflect the biases and idiosyncracies of the administration of the day, and not those of the academic researchers of the time, or of a later time" (Cook 1986, 70). Thus, the British appraisal methodology rests on the principle that there is a broad correspondence between administrative values and research values and on what Felix Hull called the "principle of movable responsibility," where, over time, the interest of the creator gives way to the competence of someone "more fully capable of objective assessment," the archivist, who is the only one capable of preserving the whole picture. "The whole picture, not a partial or biased one, is the ideal and the archivist's motto should be 'always objective' so that he endeavours to achieve the ideal" (Hull 1980, 288).

However, this methodology may work well for the appraisal of the records of structured administrations, both public and private. What about the records of families and individuals? "Things—those we can be dispassionate about; people—seldom, and our sense of judgement may be so easily influenced," but, by using "perfectly correct methods we may so easily produce a grey impression and in the interests of proper objectivity emasculate the record" (Hull 1980, 291). Obviously, there is no easy answer.

Conclusion

Objectivity is a value that permeates all European writings on appraisal (e.g., in Germany and Italy) but is at the core of British appraisal methodology, which in part realizes it through its procedures for the *selection* of organizational records but encounters intense difficulty when dealing with *personal records.*

Contemporary archival writers in North America are divided in two groups: those who recognize that objectivity is a nice ideal but, being impossible to achieve, should either be ignored or simply regarded as something to strive for, and those who believe that objectivity is in conflict with the mission of the archivist. The former group mostly comprises public records archivists, who rely on systematic appraisal procedures to protect the integrity and evidentiary nature of records, while the latter group mostly comprises archivists responsible for the *acquisition* of private records, who consider their cultural function to be engineering a comprehensive record of the past capable of giving voice to those who never expressed it in writing or in formal records.

Archivists in general believe that they need to adhere to some conception of how to preserve a truthful memory of the past without keeping every record, so that they can anchor the integrity of *archival practice* to an ideal stance. To this day they have not found an agreement, but, in the words of Heather MacNeil, "There is something to be said for an approach to truth that acknowledges alternative perspectives, embraces persistent debate, and tolerates imperfect solutions" (2001, 47).—*Luciana Duranti*

Keywords: archivist, appraisal, impartiality
Related Entries: Appraisal; Archivist; Authenticity; Impartiality; Interrelatedness; Naturalness

Bibliography

Booms, Hans. "Society and the Formation of a Documentary Heritage: Issues in the Appraisal of Archival Sources." Translated by Hermina Joldersam and Richard Klumpenhouer. *Archivaria* 1 (24) (1987): 69–107. http://journals.sfu.ca/archivar/index.php/archivaria/article/view/11415/12357.

Cook, Michael. *The Management of Information from Archives*. Hants, England: Gower, 1986.

Duranti, Luciana. "The Concept of Appraisal in Archival Science." *The American Archivist* 57 (2) (1994): 328–44. http://archivists.metapress.com/content/pu548273j5j1p816/fulltext.pdf.

Hull, Felix. "The Appraisal of Documents: Problems and Pitfalls." *Journal of the Society of Archivists* 6 (5) (1980): 287–91. DOI:10.1080/00379818009514154.

Jenkinson, Hilary. *Manual of Archives Administration*. London: Percy Lund, Humphries & Co., 1937.

MacNeil. "Trusting Records in a Postmodern World." *Archivaria* 1 (51) (2001): 36–47. http://journals.sfu.ca/archivar/index.php/archivaria/article/view/12793/13991.

Mitchell, Thornton W., ed. *Norton on Archives: The Writings of Margaret Cross Norton on Archival and Records Management*. Carbondale: Southern Illinois University Press, 1975.

Report of the Committee on Departmental Records, a.k.a. The Grigg Report. Great Britain. Parliament. Cmnd. 9163. London: HMSO, 1954.

Schellenberg, Theodore R. *Modern Archives: Principles and Techniques*. Chicago: University of Chicago Press, 1956, 133–60.

ORGANIZATIONAL CULTURE

In the 1990s, a number of archives researchers such as Bearman (1992) and Yakel (1996) urged for more empirical research on organizational culture and its effects on *recordkeeping* as well as a more detailed investigation on the sociocultural *context* on how *records* are created and used. Since then, there has been a growing body of research and literature on organizational culture in the *archival science* discipline. For example, the doctoral research by Oliver (2007) and Foscarini (2010) demonstrates how organizational culture can provide a lens through which *archivists* and records professionals can critically analyze *information management* and recordkeeping issues.

Definitions of Organizational Culture

Organizational culture is an interdisciplinary construct that spans across several disciplines including organizational management, sociology, cultural anthropology, and information science.

One perspective of organizational culture views it at a cognitive level in terms of a system of ideas, beliefs, and practices. For example, Hofstede (2001, 373) defines organizational culture as the "differences in collective mental programming found among people from different organizations, or parts thereof, within the same national *context*." Hofstede views national and organizational cultures as being manifested at two different levels as "a nation is not an organization, and the two types of culture are of different kinds" (2001, 373). Hofstede's perspective has been criticized because he views culture in deterministic terms and also because he views organizational culture as a monolithic concept.

Oliver utilizes Hofstede's approach of analyzing culture at different levels. She defines organizational culture in three layers: national culture, occupational culture, and corporate culture. The national culture is described as the "values acquired growing up from family and school [which] influence attitudes and behaviour" (Oliver 2011, 26). Occupational culture is described as those "values and practices which have been learned in the course of vocational education and training," while corporate culture is defined by the "sector or industry that the organization is engaged in" and the "occupational groupings working inside the organization" (Oliver 2011, 26).

Culture can be reflected in visible structures and symbols such as legislation and policies relating to recordkeeping and preservation. Culture is also based on the process of interaction with other individuals at both a group and interpersonal level, and it is that process that reveals the unitary and fragmentary aspects of organizational dynamics.

In recognition of the process of negotiation and interaction among organizational members that can take place in Weberian bureaucracies and in more participatory form of organizations, the International Research on Permanent Authentic Records in Electronic Systems (InterPARES) Project adopts a pluralistic perspective. The project defines organizational culture as "a system of shared values, assumptions, and beliefs that may be explicit or implicit in nature; practices and ways of working; an organization's sociocultural system, processes, and technology, and the interaction of values and assumptions of various stakeholders" (InterPARES 3 Project Terminology Database).

Typologies of Organizational and Recordkeeping Culture

Five types of organizational culture were constructed based on a mapping of two models from organizational theorists Handy (1978) and Cameron and Quinn (1988). They are "power," "role," "task," "*person*," and "market" culture (International Council on Archives and InterPARES Project). These five types of culture can exist within different groups in an organization, such as at a departmental or working group level, and as such, "different cultures may exist simultaneously within the same organization" (Shepherd and Yeo 2003,

43). In a power culture, personal relationships and networks are valued more than written policies and procedures. Most of the key decisions are communicated orally rather than documented through records. The key decision-makers in the organization also tend to rely on their own information channels, which are segregated from the overall *recordkeeping system*. In contrast, a role-based culture relies less on verbal communication. A role-based culture tends to document work processes, policies, and procedures. It is also based on a hierarchical structure, where there are clear lines of authority. In a task culture, decision making is based on a lateral system. The knowledge and resources necessary to complete any given task is valued more than the years of seniority or the designation of the staff. Since the culture values collaboration and innovation, individuals will actively utilize collaborative tools to share and disseminate information to their team members. There is also a smaller presence of standardized policies and procedures or standardized documentary forms to govern the work, which tends to be more experimental in nature. In a person culture, individualism and autonomy of a person is respected, since the expertise of the individual is of importance to the organization. A person culture tends to have a fluid organizational structure, and individuals tend to enjoy a high degree of independence in their work. Administrative responsibilities, including *records management*, are viewed as administrative burdens. In such a culture, there are difficulties in distinguishing between a personal and a corporate record. Compared to the other types of culture, the market culture is one that is most attuned and responsive to the external environment. In such a culture, individuals work at a fast pace because the culture is achievement oriented and places an emphasis on meeting and exceeding targets. There also tends to be an emphasis on using records and information to forecast business opportunities and trends in the market.

According to Shepherd and Yeo (2003), "no single approach is right for all organizations" and the "*records manager* should adopt a strategy that will work within the prevailing culture" (45). In a power culture, records managers need to work very closely with influential individuals and the key decision-makers in the organization who have their own separate information system that is segregated from the rest of the organization (International Council on Archives and InterPARES Project). In a role-based culture, records managers need to ensure that the records management program is aligned with the overall strategic directions and business processes of the organization. In both the task and the person culture, records managers need to work with individuals on a personal basis or in small groups. Records managers also need to pitch records management initiatives in terms of supporting collaborative work, since these cultures tend to be resistant to requirements that interfere with their creativity. Finally, in a market culture, records management should be marketed as a means to enhance the competitive advantage of the organization and as a means to fulfill the regulatory requirements imposed by an external body (International Council on Archives and InterPARES Project).

Organizational Culture as Symbols

Organizational culture can also be expressed in terms of symbols, which are the "words, gestures, pictures and objects that carry often complex meanings recognized as such only by those who share the culture" (Hofstede 2001, 10). For example, the language used by various stakeholders in an organization; the visible manifestations of culture in the form of mission statements, strategic plans, and directions of the organization; and the use or modification of a technology all reflect the culture of an organization. Records managers need to be sensitive to the use of technical jargon by specific groups of stakeholders and to clarify the use of specific terminology in policies and in their interaction with other stakeholders. Different groups of stakeholders may define specific archival terminology such as records, *archives*, and *file* differently from the archives profession or they may use different terms to convey the same meaning. For example, IT professionals may refer to specific fields entered into a database as records, whereas records managers would refer to it as *metadata* (International Council on Archives and InterPARES Project). Even within the archives and records management community, there are varying definitions of the term records, and this is partly dependent on the organizational *context*. As noted by Oliver and Foscarini (2014, 80), "Even the most technical languages come from a complex history of

negotiations of meanings and are subject to continuous renegotiation."

The adoption, use, and modification of a technology, such as an *electronic document and records management system* (EDRMS), can both enable and constrain an individual's action and behavior. Even though a records manager may work closely with the vendor and the information technology professional to design specific functionalities of the system, employees in an organization would not passively accept the inherent properties of the technology. Instead, employees will draw on their own experiences and assumptions, which can affect how they perceive and interact with the system. Such experiences and assumptions may be commonly shared at a group level, such as the occupational culture of an employee. For example, the values inherent in an EDRMS may conflict with the overall values of a particular occupational culture. If an EDRMS promotes the sharing and easy *access* of records in an organization, such a system may be perceived as a threat to a culture that rewards "information hoarding" and competition among their employees (Oliver and Foscarini 2014, 62–63). At the same time, how employees interact with the system is also dependent on their unique experiences such as their previous job, personal values, and beliefs. Consequently, employees may use the system in ways unanticipated by records managers or even bypass the system. Records managers need to act as mediators in order to effectively monitor how users adapt and use the system to fulfill their business needs, to provide training to users, and to adjust the system based on feedback from users.

Conclusion

Organizational culture comprises the shared values, assumptions, and practices of a group. At the same time, organizational culture is characterized by underlying conflicts and tensions among various interest groups and individuals. Archivists and records managers need to pay attention to both the shared and divergent understandings and assumptions of stakeholders and to adopt a more people-centric approach in the development and implementation of records management policies and systems.—*Elaine Goh*

Keywords: culture, values, assumptions, symbols, interaction

Related Entries: Archives (Material); Context; Electronic Document and Records Management System (EDRMS); File; Metadata; Record(s)

Bibliography

Bearman, David. "Diplomatics, Weberian Bureaucracy, and the Management of Electronic Records in Europe and America." *American Archivist* 55 (1) (1992): 168–81. http://archivists.metapress.com/content/240053825k3v3648/fulltext.pdf.

Cameron, Kim S., and Robert E. Quinn. *Diagnosing and Changing Organizational Culture: Based on the Competing Values Framework*. Menlo Park, CA: Addison Wesley Longman, 1998.

Foscarini, Fiorella. "Understanding the Context of Records Creation and Use: 'Hard' versus 'Soft' Approaches to Records Management." *Archival Science* 10 (4) (2010): 389–407. DOI: 10.1007/s10502-010-9132-z.

Handy, Charles B. *Understanding Organizations*. Middlesex, England: Penguin Books, 1976.

Hofstede, Geert H. *Culture's Consequences: Comparing Values, Behaviors, Institutions, and Organizations across Nations*, 2nd edition. Thousand Oaks, CA: Sage, 2001.

International Council on Archives. "Digital Records Pathways: Topics in Digital Preservation—Module 3: Organizational Culture and Its Effects on Records Management." www.ica-sae.org (accessed July 6, 2014).

International Research on Permanent Authentic Records in Electronic Systems (InterPARES) 3. "The InterPARES Project Terminology Database." www.interpares.org/ip3/ip3_terminology_db.cfm?term=673 (accessed July 6, 2014).

Oliver, Gillian. "Implementing International Standards: First, Know Your Organization." *Records Management Journal* 17 (2) (2007): 82–93. www.emeraldinsight.com/doi/pdfplus/10.1108/09565690710757887.

———. *Organisational Culture for Information Managers*. Oxford, UK: Chandos, 2011.

Oliver, Gillian, and Fiorella Foscarini. *Records Management and Information Culture: Tackling the People Problem*. London: Facet, 2014.

Shepherd, Elizabeth, and Geoffrey Yeo. "Analysing the Context for Records Management." In *Managing Records: A Handbook of Principles and Practice*. London: Facet, 2003, 30–71.

Yakel, Elizabeth. "The Way Things Work: Procedures, Processes, and Institutional Records." *American Archivist* (4) (1996): 454–64. http://archivists.metapress.com/content/c1545152u4218314/fulltext.pdf.

OUTREACH

There is today an increasing recognition that *archivists* need to focus more of their resources on raising public awareness of their repositories and increasing use of their collections—that is, on the activities traditionally referred to as outreach. While promoting collections has always been part of the archivist's role, changing technologies and assumptions about possible users have changed how professionals reach out to new audiences. Outreach today is more active, wide-ranging, and varied than in the past. While it is related to activities usually classified as *advocacy*, public relations, and even donor relations, the goals for outreach are usually broader and the related activities more diverse.

Outreach as an Evolving Facet of the Profession

Reporting on the results of a 1976 survey of U.S. archival repositories, the author concluded:

> The fact that 30 percent of the institutions responding reported that they had no outreach programs confirms the general reluctance among archivists to view outreach as a worthwhile, much less essential, archival *function*. Those archivists who included outreach activities in their programs seemed to consider them as extras or one-shot affairs. (Pederson 1978, 160)

The respondents to the A*CENSUS survey of U.S. archivists conducted in 2004 were individuals rather than institutions, and so the results aren't specifically comparable to the data gathered in 1976. However, information from this group reflects what seems to be a greater emphasis on outreach in professional practice:

- The mean percentage of the respondent's time spent on outreach, advocacy, or promotion was 6.5 percent.

- The number of respondents citing outreach as among "the three most important issues" was 9.8 percent (higher than appraisal, ethics, salaries/better pay, standards, and leadership, among others).
- When asked to rank their interest in continuing education and training topics, outreach ranked twenty-second out of thirty-eight topics (16.8 percent of respondents) (see tables, Walch 2006).

In the decade since the A*CENSUS survey was taken, the need for effective outreach and advocacy has become a constant theme in the professional discourse. However, this heightened awareness of the importance of outreach has not resulted in an increase in the literature devoted to the general topic. While articles and books about specific outreach activities—such as exhibitions, instruction, and the use of social media—are common, publications about outreach as a whole are not. Perhaps because it has only comparatively recently become the subject of more attention, the professional literature lacks extensive discussion on the meaning or purpose of "outreach."

The definition provided in the 2005 glossary produced by the Society of American Archivists is a narrow one: "The process of identifying and providing services to constituencies with needs relevant to the repository's mission, especially underserved groups, and tailoring services to meet those needs" (Pearce-Moses 2005). While accurate, the emphasis on "services" does not take into account the wide range of activities designed to increase awareness, which most archivists would classify as outreach. Indeed, some would argue that any and all interactions an archivist has with members of the public are a type of outreach—from answering reference questions to chatting with strangers at a social event about what it is that he or she does for a living.

Outreach Goals and Activities

Leaving personal interactions aside, all outreach activities have as their primary goal promoting an archivist's own repository, and secondarily or as a by-product, increasing awareness about *archives* in general. Outreach is also usually intended to encourage use of a repository's collections, as well

as making people feel more comfortable visiting the archives and more inclined to make a *donation*. While the terms outreach and advocacy are often used in tandem, and many people may think them interchangeable, they are separate but complementary concepts. Raising public awareness and increasing use of collections through outreach can lead to more effective advocacy, but advocacy focuses on a narrow body of people with more specific goals in mind.

However, outreach is also commonly thought of in terms of activities rather than overarching goals. Among the most basic forms of outreach are publications and tools that convey information about an archives—either general or specific. A well-designed and useful website or brochure, interesting newsletters, and timely well-crafted press releases are all good forms of outreach. Many forms of social media, including blogs, Facebook, Twitter, Tumblr, Pinterest, Flickr, and Instagram, lend themselves well to sharing information and images about an archives and its collections, as do apps for mobile devices. Videos may also be shared using those platforms, as well as YouTube and Vimeo. These tools allow an archives to share information about recent acquisitions and upcoming activities, as well as a chance to look "behind the scenes" at how archivists do their work.

Sharing information about items in the collection, as well as sharing the items themselves, is also part of outreach. Traditionally this has been done through print publications and physical exhibitions, but online exhibits and social media tools provide new channels to bring collections to the attention of the public. Using new platforms like Wikipedia and Historypin, archivists can integrate images of and information about collections into tools the public uses to search for information. Anything that raises the visibility of *archival collections*—from promotional items like customized pencils and paper, to prominent well-placed signage, to images from the collection displayed in diverse locations with appropriate credit lines—can be considered types of outreach.

More active or participatory forms of outreach have long been used to promote awareness and use of collections. Public programs such as lectures, workshops, symposia, tours, and open houses have long been staples of outreach programs. Educational programs, ranging from simple "show and tell" sessions to active participation in instruction, are among the most common forms of outreach. However, new forms of active outreach—some dependent on technology, some not—are increasingly popular alongside traditional public programs and instruction. Archives are hosting Wikipedia edit-a-thons, scan-a-thons, and "history harvests," all with the aim of using face-to-face sessions to increase awareness of archival resources.

Similarly, social media tools enable archivists to engage with new and existing audiences as never before. These platforms allow for direct communications and exchanges with people across the globe. Posting simple comments and replies, providing information or *context* about an image, and transcribing a *document*—using social media tools in these ways—not only allow archivists to share information but also allow audiences to provide information in return. Many outreach activities—in-person as well as online—are now designed to engage people by allowing them to share their own knowledge.

Collaborations of all kinds are modes of outreach, as they can be used for promotion, education, collection sharing, as well as building relationships that will encourage the use of the archives in the long term. Many archivists in academic settings seek to collaborate with faculty on digital humanities projects. New and emerging local, organizational, and *community archives* can often benefit from expert advice or outside support. Within an institution, activities like working with a public affairs office or departments in need of speakers on historical topics builds a foundation for ongoing outreach programs.

Many archivists are also using outreach opportunities to shatter the public image of archives as dusty forbidding places and archivists as stuffy and old-fashioned. Such institutions are hosting activities like sleepovers for children, sponsoring contests on social media, showing films and hosting musical events, and encouraging artists to use collections for new creative works, all with the goal of promoting the archives as a place of engagement for people who might not have thought of archives as attractive or welcoming places. Outreach also often takes place outside of the archives itself, as many organizations seek to have a presence at community events and festivals. More active and targeted documentation initiatives can be seen as a form of outreach

too, as they convey the message that the archives is interested in collecting materials about events or parts of the community that the public might find surprising. All of these constitute an "opening up" of the archives that is essential to many organizations' outreach programs.

As the possible range of activities under the umbrella of outreach has become more diverse, so have the audiences at which those activities are directed. Many outreach activities have a specific audience in mind, such as K–12 students or historically underrepresented communities. But many activities are launched with no target audience in mind; this is especially true of social media activity, which has the potential to attract anyone with web access. Rather than target a specific audience, such broad strategies allow anyone interested in the archival content or subject to participate and learn. While broad-based web outreach presents an exciting opportunity, archivists must always keep in mind the need to balance virtual outreach with in-person activities, and "high tech" with "no tech," to ensure reaching people of all ages, incomes, and demographic factors. However, targeting specific segments of a community may also be a goal of an outreach program. In such cases decisions may be made to favor activities that will be easily accessible and attractive to those audiences.

Conclusion

While outreach programs across repositories have the same essential goals, the way those goals are pursued is more varied today than ever, and technology and creativity will mean that the forms outreach takes will continue to become even more diverse. One factor that most outreach programs have in common is that their activities have become more participatory, in every sense. Archivists themselves are more active participants in many outreach activities, and many activities are designed for people to engage in active participation with the archives. Whether transcribing online, engaging in an archives-related craft or art project, bringing in a family document to be scanned, adding a personal history to a collection, or just making a comment about an online image, outreach today often seeks to allow people to engage in meaningful experiences and share knowledge, while at the same time spreading awareness and breaking down stereotypes. — *Kate Theimer*

Keywords: promotion, public relations, public programs
Related Entries: Advocacy; Participatory Archives

Bibliography

Bain, G. W., J. A. Fleckner, K. Marquis, and M. J. Pugh. "Reference, Access, and Outreach: An Evolved Landscape, 1936–2011." (Session 406). *The American Archivist* 74 (supplement 1) (2001): 1–40. http://archivists.metapress.com/content/l4625w7459q3g2lu/fulltext.pdf.

Ericson, T. "Preoccupied with Our Own Gardens: Outreach and Archivists. *Archivaria* 1 (31) (1990): 114–22. http://journals.sfu.ca/archivar/index.php/archivaria/article/view/11724/12673.

James, R. D., and P. J. Wosh. *Public Relations and Marketing for Archives*. New York: Neal-Schuman and Society of American Archivists, 2011.

Pearce-Moses, R. *A Glossary of Archives and Records Terminology*. Chicago: Society of American Archivists, 2005. www2.archivists.org/glossary/terms/o/outreach.

Pederson, A. E. "Archival Outreach: SAA's 1976 Survey." *The American Archivist* 41 (2) (1978): 155–62. http://archivists.metapress.com/content/l2070166pt18j487/fulltext.pdf.

Theimer, K., ed. *Outreach: Innovative Practices for Archives and Special Collections*. Lanham, MD: Rowman & Littlefield, 2014.

Walch, V. I. "A*CENSUS: A Closer Look." *The American Archivist* 69 (2) (2006): 291–419. http://archivists.metapress.com/content/d474374017506522/fulltext.pdf.

P

PARTICIPATORY ARCHIVES

The concept of participatory archives is still in the process of evolving, incorporating many different models for *archival practice* in the twenty-first century. Proposed definitions and usages range from including users as full participants in the creation and management of an *archives* to incorporating aspects of participatory culture into selected archival *functions*, particularly description and *outreach*. While the archival community has yet to settle on any one formal definition, acceptance of some aspects of the principles of participatory archives appear to be widespread, building on earlier calls for greater openness and transparency in archival practice. Changes in technology and the broad adoption of new tools also allow archives to interact more directly with a broad range of users and take advantage of their knowledge and enthusiasm.

Participatory Archives and Archival Authority

In 2008 Isto Huvila put forward what is commonly credited with being the first articulation of a concept of the participatory archive: an archive implementing decentralized curation, radical user orientation, and contextualization of both *records* and the entire archival process (Huvila 2008). In 2011 Elizabeth Yakel expanded on Huvila's concept, framing a participatory archives as "a space where information is co-represented, credibility norms co-established, knowledge co-created, authority co-negotiated, and control is shared" (Yakel 2011). In the model of the participatory archive described by both these definitions, the critical element is the sharing of authority and control/curation between the *archivist* and a body of users who self-identify as stakeholders in the archives' content. In such a model it would also be possible for there to be no involvement from anyone with formal archival training or affiliation—in other words there would be no "archivist."

This model for participatory archives has been used in approaching the records of indigenous Australian communities, as articulated by Livia Iacovino: "A participatory archive is one that acknowledges all parties to a transaction as immediate parties—co-creators—with negotiated rights and responsibilities in relation to ownership, *access* and privacy" (2012, 6). Iacovino further observes that this model is "a useful tool for preserving diverse cultures whether it is for the purpose of setting the record straight for past wrongs or for preserving and promoting cultural identity" (2012, 6). This concept of an archives, in which authority and power over the management of the archives is shared, is a useful one when considering many different types of communities who may be reluctant or unable to relinquish control of their records to a traditional archives. In this sense, participatory archives have much in common with *community archives*, which function with varying levels of formal archival control.

Another sense in which participatory archives has been used is to describe collections—usually digital—which are created in whole or in part based on the suggestions and submissions of users. In this model the contributors to and users of the archives are not considered to have authority equivalent to the archivist, but the archives is created largely from their efforts. Examples of this kind of participatory archive are commonly associated with specific events, such as the Egypt Revolution and Politics collection created by the American University in Cairo (Runyon 2012) and various collections documenting the March 11, 2011, disasters in Japan ("Opportunities and Challenges" 2013). Another participatory aspect of these collections is the active solicitation of *metadata* such as comments, tags, and ratings.

A broader definition for participatory archives was proposed by Kate Theimer in 2011: "An organization, site or collection in which people other than the archives professionals contribute knowledge or resources resulting in increased understanding about archival materials, usually in an online environment" (slide 9). This definition was designed to incorporate the more specific models of participatory archives but also to describe the incorporation into archival practices of a range of participatory activities, such as crowdsourced transcription, tagging, and description. Public participation in core functions such as *appraisal* (Shilton and Srinivasan 2007), determining *digitization* priorities, and gathering input on policies regarding access are also characteristics of this conception of participatory archives.

Conclusion

The move toward participatory archives—of any definition—is the result of trends in the archival profession toward greater transparency, collaboration with record-creating communities, and engagement with users, combined with larger societal shifts toward a more participatory culture. This move is also made possible by changes in technology that have expanded the way people are able to use the web. This combination of trends in the profession with advances in technology have made participatory archives a popular, if not clearly defined, concept. The degree and type of participation in the activities of an archives will vary from instance to instance, from co-creation and shared authority, to the active solicitation of contributions and descriptions, to input in specific and limited aspects of the work of the archives. However, we can expect that the future will bring expansion of the ways in which archives allow participation as well as dialogue about the changing role of the archivist and archival authority in these participatory archives.—*Kate Theimer*

Keywords: authority, engagement, social media
Related Entries: Community Archives; Digital Archives; Outreach

Bibliography

Eveleigh, A. "Welcoming the World: An Exploration of Participatory Archives." Paper presented at the International Council on Archives Congress, Brisbane, Australia, August 2012. http://ica2012.ica.org/files/pdf/Full%20papers%20upload/ica-12Final00128.pdf (accessed February 22, 2014).

Huvila, I. "Participatory Archive: Towards Decentralized Curation, Radical User Orientation, and Broader Contextualization of Records Management." *Archival Science* 8 (1) (2008): 15–36. DOI: 10.1007/s10502-008-9071-0.

Iacovino, L. "Reshaping Identity and Memory: Balancing Competing Human Rights in the Participatory Archive." Paper presented at the International Council on Archives Congress, Brisbane, Australia, August 2012. http://ica2012.ica.org/files/pdf/Full%20papers%20upload/ica12Final00092.pdf (accessed February 22, 2014).

"Opportunities and Challenges of Participatory Digital Archives." Lessons from the March 11, 2011, Great Eastern Japan Disaster, January 24–25, Harvard University, 2013. http://projects.iq.harvard.edu/digitalarchivesconference (accessed February 22, 2014).

Runyon, C. "Revolutionary Digitization: Building a Participatory Archive to Document in the January 25th Uprising in Egypt." *Microform & Digitization Review* 41 (2) (2012): 60–64. DOI: 10.1515/mir-2012-0007.

Shilton, K., and R. Srinivasan. "Participatory Appraisal and Arrangement for Multicultural Archival Collections." *Archivaria* 63 (2007): 87–101. http://journals.sfu.ca/archivar/index.php/archivaria/article/view/13129/14371.

Theimer, K. "Exploring the Participatory Archives." Paper presented at the Society of American Archivists Annual Meeting, Chicago, IL, August 2011. www.slideshare.net/ktheimer/theimer-participatory-archives-saa-2011 (accessed February 22, 2014).

Yakel, E. "Credibility in the Participatory Archives." Paper presented at the Society of American Archivists Annual Meeting, Chicago, IL, August 2011.

PERMANENCE

Permanence and the associated term permanent value are symbolic concepts by which *archivists* measure their commitment to the long-term care of archival *records*. Historically, the terms became part of the archival profession's lexicon as a response to the need for permanent safe-keeping in secure archival facilities, the search for a permanent reproduction medium, and the perceived professional imperative to assign permanent value to a small subset of records produced by twentieth-century organizations. James O'Toole writes that "the idea of *permanence* as it is understood by archivists has changed considerably over time, passing from an unattainable desire to an absolute value within the realm of achievement to an extremely relative notion of little clarity" (O'Toole 1989, 23). The digital revolution of the second half of the twentieth century has largely eliminated the meaning of the concept of "permanent value." Instead archivists have adopted alternative concepts, such as enduring or continuing value, that recognize the ongoing responsibilities of archivists and the relational nature of value itself. Today, permanence and permanent value are little-used terms that sustain the power of archival imagination but lack an actionable capacity.

Keeping Archives

Until the emergence of modern corporations and government bureaucracies in the nineteenth century, archival records survived by accident or serendipity. Clerical, political, and business elites kept *documents* of peculiar interest or value and passed them from generation to generation without regard for archival principles. Purpose-built archival facilities, designed for security, fire-protection, and permanent storage, served as a practical antidote to the risks of natural and human-made disasters that all-too-commonly struck wood-frame courthouses and government or business workplaces. The function of twentieth-century governments—democratic and totalitarian alike—to document their actions in permanent *archives* symbolized their aspirations for permanent governance. A commitment to permanent storage plays out still in the maintenance of archival facilities but extends also to the physical environments within these buildings. Permanence

in the care of archival holdings today takes the form of robust environmental controls in archival facilities that are designed to extend the life expectancy of physical (organic) media by retarding their rate of deterioration, thus buying time for the records to fulfill their use value or for the application of *conservation* treatment or reproduction technologies (Reilly 1995).

Media Longevity

No storage medium lasts forever. The physical media that are integral components of the archival record are inherently unstable and have rarely been engineered explicitly for longevity. The search for a permanent storage medium for the archival record has been a driving ambition of materials scientists and the archival profession for the better part of the twentieth century. Beginning with William Barrow's diagnosis of acidic degradation of paper fibers in the 1950s, archivists have collaborated in the development of alkaline paper products, archival quality adhesives, and thirty-five millimeter preservation microfilm. In arguing for the use of robust and stable storage media for archival records, where possible, archivists recognize the *intrinsic value* of some original archival records but also accept that periodic transfer of archival records to media with greater predicted life expectancies is a core principle of effective archival management. David Levy highlights the essential link between media and information value in the form of ever-changing documents: "All documents, regardless of technology, are fixed and fluid—fixed at certain times and fluid at others. Indeed, they exist in perpetual tension between these two poles—fixing content for periods of time to serve particular human needs, and changing as necessary to remain in synch with the changing circumstances of the world" (1994, 6). Media's longevity today involves remaining alert to the weakest link in a system of interlocked elements that make up any information-storage environment (Besser 2000).

Assigning Value

For much of the twentieth century, archivists have attempted to assign permanent value to a segment of records produced in the normal course of organizational or personal behavior and to deem such records as worthy of permanent retention. Theodore Schellenberg's influential *Modern Archives* (1956) codified procedures as well as established the professional mandate to discern the informational and evidentiary properties inherent in the archival record. In the intervening decades, archivists have pursued multiple strategies and methodologies— with marginal success—to make the *appraisal* of permanent archival value a more objective and measurable process. Brien Brothman is one of the last archivists to argue for the existence of permanent archival value, but he does so by placing primary emphasis on *archival practices*: "As they make determinations about archival or historical value, archivists in effect create, initiate or perpetuate an axiological commitment which is manifested in the permanence of the order that emerges . . . during the archival process, not before or after" (1991, 4). Archivists may only know, and perhaps measure, the subjective values that communities and individuals assign to the records they create. Today, judgments about archival value have taken on the relativistic perspective that also governs the commitment of space for *archival collections* and the longevity of archival media.

Digital Sustainability

Archives in digital form further challenge the expectations for long-term availability. In the place of permanency and permanent value archivists now strive for sustainability and enabling ongoing judgments of value by successive cohorts of users. Digital sustainability recognizes the inherent instability of physical storage media, the rapid obsolescence of most aspects of digital technologies, the need for active management of archival data, and the periodic and more frequent migration of data across storage and delivery systems. Kevin Bradley notes the profound change in perspective that is required for *digital archives*: "What distinguishes the contemporary sustainability approach from earlier aspirations to a 'permanent' solution is the concentration on systems architectures and schemas that will aid in future management of digital information, rather than on the solution itself" (2007, 161). The permanent value of archives thus resides in the development of tools that future users will need to facilitate *access* to digitally encoded content to help these future users make decision about its worth. Geoffrey Yeo circumscribes the world of archives untethered from intrinsic value: "When interacting with records, as with other boundary objects, each community will bring its own perspectives, its own ideas of what is significant and its own criteria of identity" (2010, 98).

Conclusion

In the course of a half century, archivists have transformed the concepts of permanence and permanent value from absolutes of professional practice to disavowed abstract concepts. In their place archivists have adopted the interchangeable concepts of enduring or continuing value, which recognize the limited lifecycle of value judgments themselves. In qualifying value, archivists have shifted emphasis from identifying the qualities or properties of archival records worthy of retention to certifying the potential value of the records relative to past, present, and hypothesized future use. Along with embracing a concept of archival value that is conditioned by time, space, and the perspectives of users, the archival enterprise has also reduced its reliance on the symbolism of building architecture and yielded on its insistence on durable storage media as a foundation for long-term *records management*. Ultimately, archivists' renewed confidence in the very long, if not permanent, survival of digital archival records turns on renewed attention to the durability of storage media systems.—*Paul Conway*

Keywords: permanence, permanent value, enduring value, longevity, sustainability

Related Entries: Appraisal; Archives (Material); Digital Preservation; Intrinsic Value

Bibliography

Besser, H. "Digital Longevity." In *Handbook for Digital Projects: A Management Tool for Preservation and Access*. Andover, MA: Northeast Document Center, 2000, 164–75. www.nedcc.org/assets/media/documents/apnssg.pdf (accessed April 2014).

Bradley, K. "Defining Digital Sustainability." *Library Trends* 56 (1) (2007): 148–63. DOI: 10.1353/lib.2007.0044.

Brothman, B. "Orders of Value: Probing the Theoretical Terms of Archival Practice." *Archivaria* 32 (2) (1991): 78–100. http://journals.sfu.ca/archivar/index.php/archivaria/article/view/11761/12711.

Conway, P. *Preservation in the Digital World.* Washington, DC: Commission on Preservation and Access, 1996.

Levy, D. M. "Fixed or Fluid?: Document Stability and New Media." In *ECHT '94: Proceedings of the 1994 ACM European Conference on Hypermedia Technology.* New York: Association of Computing Machinery, 1994, 24–31.

O'Toole, J. M. "On the Idea of Permanence." *American Archivist* 52 (1) (1989): 10–25. http://archivists.metapress.com/content/3x85283576r43387/fulltext.pdf.

Reilly, J., D. W. Nishimura, and E. Zinn. *New Tools for Preservation: Assessing Long-Term Environmental Effects on Library and Archives Collections.* Washington, DC: Commission on Preservation and Access, 1995.

Schellenberg, T. R. *Modern Archives: Principles and Techniques.* Chicago: University of Chicago Press, 1956.

Yeo, G. "'Nothing Is the Same as Something Else': Significant Properties and Notions of Identity and Originality." *Archival Science* 10 (2) (2010): 85–116. DOI: 10.1007/s10502-010-9119-9.

PERSON

In *archival theory*, the term person refers to a legal entity endowed with rights and duties Physical or juridical *persons* are involved in *records* creation (Duranti, Eastwood, and MacNeil 2002, 15). A physical person is a human, or natural, individual. A juridical person may be a succession of single physical persons (e.g., the CEO of an organization), or a collection of physical persons who together have the capacity to act legally within the system of law or rules that they are bound and abide by (e.g., an institution, a committee) (Duranti, Eastwood, and MacNeil 2002, 15).

In *diplomatics*, persons are considered to be the central element of a *document*, serving as the tie between documents and the juridical systems in which the documents exist. This is because persons, having rights and duties, are able to act within a legal system and be recognized for their activity; their actions include the creation of records.

The Concept

The concept of person is rooted in diplomatics, which requires that three persons be involved in the creation of any given archival document or record (Gilliland-Swetland 2002, 201). These persons fulfill distinct roles, those of author, writer, and addressee (MacNeil 2000a, 87). According to Duranti, the author of a record is the person(s) competent for the making of the record, which is issued by it, or by its command, or in its name; the *addressee* of a record is the person(s) for whom the record is intended (as opposed to the recipient, who can be any person receiving the record); and the writer of a record is the person(s) responsible for the tenor and articulation of the writing. These three persons may be three individuals or even the same individual (e.g., one can write a cheque to oneself, thereby being its author, addressee and writer), but they play different roles with respect to the record (Duranti 1998, 5–14; Duranti 2002, 16–17).

In addition to the author, addressee, and writer, other persons may be involved in the creation of a record, and may have various functions with respect to it (Duranti 1998, 5–14). Regarding electronic records, Duranti identifies the originator as a relevant person; this term refers to a physical or juridical person who is assigned the electronic address associated with where the record has been generated (Duranti and Rogers 2012, 524). Duranti also notes that, in order to see each record in its documentary *context*, a key person that must be identified is the creator of the *archival fonds* in which the record belongs, who is the creator of the record because it made or received it and included it in its archival fonds (Duranti 2002, 15–17). For electronic records, the creator must be explicitly identified, as it may not immediately be obvious, which is usually the case with traditional records, as creators "are usually obvious from the location of the record" (MacNeil 2000a, 94). Also witnesses are key persons for records that require their signatures, such as last wills and testaments, and contracts.

Conclusion

Identification of the persons involved in the creation of a record is a necessary process, both for understanding the context of a record while carrying out archival functions like arrangement and description and for assessing its *authenticity*. Alongside other attributes, such as date(s) of issuing and receipt and the name of the action in which the record participates, the names of the persons involved in the creation of a record are what uniquely characterizes and identifies a record (Gilliland-Swetland 2002, 206). Identification of the persons involved in the creation of a record is also used to aid in establishing provenance and support *authentication*.

As it concerns the persons involved in the creation of records in the digital environment, Duranti and Rogers state:

Many digital objects that can be identified as records are generated by the interaction of technologies without direct input from human actors, thus the persons involved in their creation are to be identified in terms of systems ownership and use. (Duranti and Rogers 2012, 524)

Person is a key concept in archival theory for purposes of record identification, evaluation, description, and retrieval and for the assignment of intellectual, economic, and other rights.—*Victoria Ostrzenski*

Keywords: addressee, authenticity, author, creator, diplomatics, writer

Related Entries: Archival Fonds; Authority Control; Diplomatics; Document; Principle of *Respect des fonds*; Record(s)

Bibliography

Duranti, Luciana. "The Concept of Electronic Record." In L. Duranti, T. Eastwood, and H. MacNeil, eds., *Preservation of the Integrity of Electronic Records*. Dordrecht, the Netherlands: Kluwer Academic, 2002, 9–22.

———. "Concepts, Principles, and Methods for the Management of Electronic Records." *The Information Society* 17 (4) (2001): 271–79. DOI:10.1080/019722401753330869.

———. "Part III." In *Diplomatics: New Uses for an Old Science*. Lanham, MD: Scarecrow Press, 1998, 5–14.

Duranti, Luciana, and Corinne Rogers. "Trust in Digital Records: An Increasingly Cloudy Legal Area. *Computer Law and Security Review* 28 (2012): 522–31. DOI:10.1016/j.clsr.2012.07.009.

Gilliland-Swetland, Anne J. "Testing Our Truths: Delineating the Parameters of the Authentic Electronic Record." *The American Archivist* 65 (2002): 196–215. http://archivists.metapress.com/content/f036wp74710g1483/fulltext.pdf.

MacNeil, Heather. "Creating and Maintaining Trustworthy Records in Electronic Systems: Archival Diplomatic Methods." In T. Eastwood, L. Duranti, M. Guerico, and M. Piggott, eds., *Trusting Records*. Dordrecht, the Netherlands: Kluwer Academic, 2000a, 86–112.

———. "Providing Grounds for Trust: Developing Conceptual Requirements for the Long-Term Preservation of Authentic Electronic Records." *Archivaria* 50 (200b): 52–78. http://journals.sfu.ca/archivar/index.php/archivaria/article/view/12765/13955.

PERSONAL RECORDS

Personal *records*/personal *archives* are *documents* created by individuals or family groups in the course of their activities. Despite having a long history of records creation and active *acquisition*, these archives were dealt with by *archival theory* only in recent decades. The current *context* for personal records shows a multidisciplinary focus and complex issues resulting from technology, networking, and social media that overturn conceptions and/or broaden understanding.

The Concept

Personal archives/records comprise documents whose provenance is an individual or a family group. The term personal archives emphasizes the collectivity of an *archival fonds* while personal records emphasizes the *functions* of individuals and families creating records and these documents' qualities as records. The second term came into play as *archivists* accommodated *digital records* and with the broader discourse on *recordkeeping.*

Personal records typically consist of: correspondence and communications (business and personal); diaries, journals, daybooks, and calendars; photographs; recordings; *ephemera*/memorabilia; and drafts of creative, scholarly, business, or other types of work produced by individuals. The concepts of personal archives and personal recordkeeping hinge on the relationship between the documents and the activities and development of their creator.

The Manuscript Tradition

As Ernst Posner remarked, examples of archives of individuals and families (particularly of family business affairs) survived from the ancient world and were often housed separately from business or public records by their creators (Posner). There are also many examples of estate archival holdings for prominent families held throughout the Middle Ages and Renaissance. A tradition focusing on acquisition of archives of particular individuals by research repositories developed much later in the Western world, mainly as a post-Enlightenment phenomenon.

In the nineteenth and twentieth centuries, there was a trend toward acquisition of personal documents, which were generally referred to as "personal papers" in the English-speaking world. In many countries, personal papers of individuals were acquired by universities as well as national libraries and cultural museums, whereas the official records of government were kept by government archival institutions (Berner 1983). There are also cases of private or state-sponsored research institutes based around personal archives of particular individuals (e.g., the Goethe and Schiller Archives, Germany). Acquisition of personal papers often focused on well-known individuals and particularly on cultural figures such as literary authors, artists, and politicians. This type of acquisition supported research in the humanities and social sciences and followed mandates to preserve cultural heritage. In Canada, where the total archival approach had significant adoption, acquiring *private archives* (i.e., archives from the private sector, personal archives, and those from private industry/organizations) was held to be equally important as the official records of govern-

ment, which meant personal archives were also acquired in *total archives* settings. This being said, across the globe there is still a large proportion of personal records held in library special collections. Acquisitions strategies also contributed to broadening scope and more comprehensive acquisition of personal records, somewhat tempering the "canonical" focus on important individuals.

Because personal archives are acquired directly from individual creators or family groups or their estates, a less structured, more personal approach to *appraisal* and acquisition has predominated. Archivists rely on a network of personal connections to elicit archival acquisitions and make site visits to discuss the archives with the creator or family in their own settings.

Developing Theory

Foundational archival theorists tended to dismiss personal archives. The *Dutch Manual for the Arrangement and Description of Archives* by Muller, Feith, and Fruin (1898) claims that only those documents received by an official body constitute archives. The manual treats family archives in a cursory fashion, stating that these family *archival collections* "do not form a whole" and "the rules for ordinary archival collections, therefore, cannot be applied to family archives." In 1922 Sir Hilary Jenkinson wrote that "archives are documents which formed part of an official transaction and were preserved for official reference." He acknowledged that collections of a personal or private nature could be subject to "exactly the same rules of keeping, arranging and inventorying" as archives, although the same rigid archival qualities did not seem to apply to these records. In 1956, Theodore Schellenberg focused on the evidential and informational value of records of public agencies.

In response to the lack of theory or practical advice provided by archival literature, a discussion of personal archives began to emerge in the 1990s with the publication of a special issue of the Australian journal *Archives and Manuscripts*. The issue touched on the history of Australian acquisition of personal papers; the historical separation between the acquisition of government records and the work of collecting archivists (referred to as the manuscripts tradition in North America); functional requirements for acquisition of personal records; memory, personal records, and broader social contexts; precustodial intervention for electronic records; and arrangement and description practices as well as possibilities and constraints for interpretation of personal archives. Further publications in the 1990s and 2000s (including a special section [2001] and special issue [2013] of the Canadian journal *Archivaria*) centered on the particular qualities of personal records, personal recordkeeping, and broader social contexts and broached the digital. Trends emerged: some authors emphasized the similarities of personal archives to other types of records; others focused on their differences in order to address the particular needs of these records and record-creating situations. Some discussions questioned the boundaries of the archival fonds and its overlap with other archival entities; other authors explored the social and temporal contexts of recordkeeping, aligning the discussion with broader developments in archival theory. This deepening scholarly debate brought an increased interest in personal archives/records worldwide and resulted in specific research into appraisal, arrangement, and description. *I Digital* (2011) addressed the issues for personal digital recordkeeping building on earlier themes as well as digital forensics and human computer interaction research.

Multidisciplinary Interest

Since the 1990s, there has been interest by researchers in the humanities and social sciences in the concepts of archives ("the Archive") within those disciplines' responses to postmodern theory. Writings by Michel Foucault and Jacques Derrida brought scholars to discuss archives and significantly reexamine their relationship with actual archival materials. There was a return to the archives within humanities and social-science-based research, particularly literature, history (women's history, counter-histories), and gender studies, alongside a focus on the everyday. This development placed personal archives and recordkeeping in a multidisciplinary context in terms of theory, and broadened discussion.

Digital Forensics and Digital Humanities

Considerations of born-digital records focused on personal archives examples, perhaps in part because these archives are smaller in size and scope. These archives were addressed with new tactics in the digital realm. The Paradigm (Personal Archives Accessible in Digital Media) project by the libraries of the Universities of Oxford and Manchester was one of the earliest to develop parameters for the appraisal, treatment, and storage of born-digital records. The Paradigm approach to appraisal involved close discussions with records-creators (British politicians) to examine the creation and use of the records, and Paradigm provided guidelines for records-creators as well as pioneering digital forensic treatment and long-term storage.

The traditional appraisal of the records and coordination with their creator played a key role in this phase of the intake of born-digital records. Because personal archives are often less structured than records found in organizations, this aspect will probably continue as archivists move to recover records created with diverse devices and stored on dispersed platforms.

In digital forensics, considerations from digital humanities melded with the archival endeavor. Many prominent digital humanities partnerships emerged, including at the Maryland Institute for Technology in the Humanities, Emory University, Stanford University, the Harry Ransom Centre at the University of Texas, and the British Library. Centering again on the records of individual figures, digital humanities projects approached digital forensics and storage in ways which explore original order and interest in the personal contexts of records creation and keeping found in archival theory. In particular, there has been a focus on digital materiality: the connection between document creation and the parameters/constraints provided by technologies and more traditional archival supports (Kirschenbaum et al. 2013). For artistic works, these parameters and constraints offer insight into the creative process and therefore the meaning of the documents. In the case of Emory University's Salman Rushdie Digital Archives Project, the repository chose emulation to provide researchers a direct experience of Rushdie's Macintosh Performa 5400 computer. There is an emphasis as well on saving physical media and hardware to retain the physical materiality of objects in this context. Digital humanities projects also linked creators' physical workspaces to these conceptions of materiality by documenting workspaces with high-definition or interactive photography, which is then linked to *archival description* (e.g., Stanford University and the British Library). This forensic archival focus was bridged to digital humanities advances in data modeling and mining such as mapping email activity among correspondents.

In these ways, digital humanities brought fresh considerations of individuals' contexts of *record creation* and their influence on the biographical or developmental interpretations of those archives.

Human Computer Interaction and the Computer Industry

Personal record creation and *archival practice* also became a focus of human computer interaction theory. The late 2000s and early 2010s saw keen interest from the computer industry to study personal recordkeeping and archiving practices from the standpoint of individual users of technology in order to develop useful tools for self-archiving. Catherine Marshall and others at Microsoft contributed significantly to the literature on personal recordkeeping by studying creators' attitudes and approaches to their digital belongings. Key to these discussions was Marshall's assertion in 2008 that the sentiment of "benign neglect" in personal records' creators operates even in a context of multiple devices, distributed storage, and potentials for large-scale loss of digital belongings. These scholars studied individuals' conceptions of record creation and keeping and their activities within virtual workspaces in ways that align the discussion with developments in digital humanities and archival theory.

Interdisciplinary digital lives conferences emerged to investigate the role of technology in daily life. New fields such as biometrics offer chances to trace human functions in minute detail using technology, and this area is dovetailing with human computer interaction interests in the active and passive roles of document creators.

Complex Digital Context for Personal Records in the Present

The trend within social media of sharing personal information widely on the Internet and employing different levels of *access* has complicated notions of personal archives and blended personal records with notions of the public sphere. In addition, blurring between personal and professional lives has been further enhanced by portable digital technologies, making boundaries between personal and professional documentation even hazier. Thirdly, opportunities for collaboration offered by digital platforms supplement effects like co-ownership of research data (particularly within the sciences) or co-authorship. Group document creation complicates a clear boundary for personal archives and personal provenance because documents do not display qualities of single origin, nor do they reside only in one context or location.

Interesting questions remain as to how the archival discipline is going to adapt ideas of personal context to the now-decentralized creation and storage of personal records on multiple devices and platforms or whether these considerations have been eclipsed by broader notions of networked recordkeeping and concepts of *records function* within society and across temporal divisions. The existing theory indicates perhaps that parallel investigations of the particular and the broader contexts of personal records will continue.

Conclusion

Personal archives/recordkeeping were not considered within early archival theories but have since elicited scholarly discussion from archivists. This discussion merged with the interdisciplinary dialogue about archives, personal archives, digital recordkeeping, and digital living. These developments shaped archivists' understandings of the qualities of personal records and opened up further avenues for investigation. The decentralized nature of digital lives, in particular, may further distinguish personal records from other types of records qualitatively, while the ability to co-create, share, and network presents greater possibilities to link personal records with broader social and temporal reconceptions of provenance and context.

—*Catherine Hobbs*

Keywords: personal archives, personal papers, personal recordkeeping, digital lives

Related Entries: Acquisition; Archival Theory; Archives (Material); Record(s); Total Archives

Bibliography

Archives and Manuscripts 24 (1) (May 1996). Australian Society of Archivists, special issue on personal recordkeeping.

Archivaria 52 (Fall 2001): 126–83. Association of Canadian Archivists, special section on personal archives.

Archivaria 76 (Fall 2013). Association of Canadian Archivists, special issue on personal archives.

Berner, Richard. *Archival Theory and Practice in the United States: A Historical Analysis.* Seattle: University of Washington Press, 1983.

Jenkinson, Hilary. *A Manual of Archive Administration.* London: Percy Lund, Humphries and Co., 1965 [1922].

Kirschenbaum, Matthew G., et al. "Approaches to Managing & Collecting Born-Digital Literary Materials for Scholarly Use." White Paper to the NEH Office of Digital Humanities Start-Up Grant, May 2009. http://drum.lib.umd.edu/bitstream/1903/9787/1/Born-Digital%20White%20Paper.pdf (accessed November 28, 2013).

Lee, Christopher A., ed. *I, Digital: Personal Collections in the Digital Era.* Chicago: Society of American Archivists, 2011.

Marshall, Catherine C. "Rethinking Personal Digital Archiving, Part 1: Four Challenges from the Field." *D-lib Magazine* 14 (3/4) (2008a). http://academic.research.microsoft.com/Publication/46886464/rethinking-personal-digital-archiving-part-1-four-challenges-from-the-field (accessed: November 28, 2013).

———. "Rethinking Personal Digital Archiving, Part 2: Implications for Services, Applications, and Institutions." *D-lib Magazine* 14 (3/4) (2008b). http://academic.research.microsoft.com/Publication/46886465/rethinking-personal-digital-archiving-part-2-implications-for-services-applications-and (accessed: November 28, 2013).

Muller, S., J. A. Feith, and R. Fruin. *Manual for the Arrangement and Description of Archives.* Translated by A. Leavitt. New York, 1940 [1898].

Odom, William, Abigail Sellen, Richard Harper, and Eno Thereska, "Lost in Translation: Understanding the Possession of Digital Things in the Cloud." Presented at the ACM SIGCHI Conference on Human Factors in Computing Systems, May 5, 2012. http://research.microsoft.com/apps/pubs/default.aspx?id=158029 (accessed: November 28, 2013).

"Paradigm Project." Universities of Oxford and Manchester. www.paradigm.ac.uk/index.html (accessed: November 28, 2013).

"Personal Archives: Bibliography." Special Interest Section on Personal Archives, Association of Canadian Archivists. http://personalarchivesbibliography.pbworks.com/w/page/16005219/FrontPage (accessed November 28, 2013).

Posner, Ernst. *Archives in the Ancient World.* Chicago: Society of American Archivists, 1972.

Schellenberg, Theodore R. *Modern Archives: Principles and Techniques.* Chicago: University of Chicago Press, 1956.

PHOTOGRAPHIC RECORDS

For more than 150 years, photographs have been an integral part of human communication. They have complemented, supplemented, and even supplanted the written word. They have been used as visual arguments and supporting evidence. They have been created to express feelings and evoke lived experience. They have been employed to do things: to show, describe, confirm, contest, validate, authorize, subvert, inspire, conspire, consider, calculate, conclude. Photographs now preserved in *archives* were once "working objects in their own time" (Frizot 1998, 12) used to supply the *context*, furnish the subtext, and corroborate the text of written and oral communication. However, the way photographs are managed in archives reveals that they are understood more for their informational/historical value(s) than their evidential/archival value(s) or functional origin(s).

Discussion

Like the digital revolution of the late twentieth century, the advent and rapid spread of photography in the mid-nineteenth century brought about changes in *records* creation and *recordkeeping*. Soon after the 1839 public announcements of two very different processes for fixing an image directly from nature, photographs began to enter archives in government reports as well as in official and personal correspondence. Between the late eighteenth and late nineteenth centuries, as lithography, photography, the steam press, and photo-mechanical reproduction spawned new and hybrid forms of materials destined for archives, traditional *archival theory*, based on the experience of European nations with centuries of written, printed, and cartographic records, was ill-equipped to deal with the products of these increasingly complex, intertwined technologies of visual and print culture. Photographic structure did not conform to strict diplomatic analysis, and neither the Dutch Trio nor Sir Hilary Jenkinson explicitly acknowledged photographs as integral to the mission of archives.

Throughout most of the twentieth century, photographs were largely ignored in archival theory, crammed awkwardly into textual models of archival organization, or relegated to the status of "special media" with unreasonable expectations of item-level description and *access*. The first clear statement on "pictorial records" was articulated by Theodore Schellenberg in his *Manual of Archival Management*. His claim that "the provenance of pictorial records in some government agency, corporate body or *person* is relatively unimportant, for such records do not derive much of their meaning from their organizational origins" (1965, 325) only validated the long-established content-based framework for dealing with photographs.

If Schellenberg misread the source of photographic meaning and underestimated the influence of pictorial records, William Leary's *The Archival Appraisal of Photographs: A RAMP Study with Guidelines* further compromised understandings of photographic archives. Declaring the negative the "truest record of the information captured by the camera," Leary stressed "the importance of *uniqueness* in appraising archival records" and claimed that the "concentration upon the negative as the 'record copy' is an important characteristic distinguishing archives from some picture libraries and virtually all art museums" (1985, 46). This privileging of negative over print, uniqueness over provenance, and information content over functional origins further entrenched the practice of content-based, item-level cataloguing, undermined the preservation of archival meaning of photographs, and justified the destruction of untold numbers of valuable vintage prints. More important was the appearance of the seminal volume *Archives & Manuscripts: Admin-istration of Photographic Collections* (Ritzenthaler, Munoff, and Long 1984), which did much to foster greater care and consistency in the treatment of photographs in archives.

In response to Luciana Duranti's challenge to apply *diplomatics* to modern records, Joan Schwartz (1995) advocated a broadly contextual approach to photographs that reconciled traditional archival principles with emerging scholarly writing on representation. Of critical importance was her assertion that what distinguishes a photograph as archival is its nature as a *document* created by an author, for a purpose, to convey a message, to an audience. In subsequent writings, Schwartz drew on the work of Taylor, Cook, Brothman, Samuels, and other archival theorists, as well as writings in the history of cartography and visual anthropology, to explore photographs in archives in terms of functional origins and evidential value, descriptive standards, materiality, institutional practices, disciplinary perspectives, digital surrogates, and power (Schwartz 2000, 2002, 2011; Cook and Schwartz 2002).

As the "visual turn" increased interest in photographs across a range of scholarly disciplines and heightened the demand for online access, the archival profession was confronted with the proliferation of born-digital images. Together, these raised new theoretical issues and new practical questions about the preservation of electronic images on the one hand and the scanning of analogue images on the other. Joanna Sassoon tackled the thorny issue of "photographic meaning in the age of digital reproduction" (1998/2004), and Tim Schlak published a bibliographic overview that surveyed the professional literature on photographic archives (2008), while others addressed analogue photographs and digital images, and visual and material literacy from a distinctly archival point of view.

Despite such advances, rules for *archival description* have not kept pace with new thinking about photographs in archives and have not acknowledged fundamental differences between visual media of record. Photographs wield rhetorical power and function as devices of memory in ways that are distinct from paintings, prints, drawings, or other "graphic materials"; they are created for different reasons, employed to different ends, and underpinned by different assumptions, prime among them "truth value." Recent challenges posed by born-digital images and scanning for online access have only exacerbated long-standing problems created by content-driven, library-based descriptive practices, and call for a basic theoretical rethinking of the nature and needs of photographic archives.

The Photograph in the Archive: Concept, Principles, and Practices

The term "photographic" encompasses myriad presentational forms: daguerreotypes, glass-plate negatives, albumen prints, roll film, 35mm slides, snapshots, transparencies, Polaroids, and even digital images. All are found in archives, each with its own capacity to convey information and produce effects. All carry information in their subject content; some also command attention for their aesthetic qualities. Because a negative or electronic *file* is capable of yielding multiple original prints, the same image can, simultaneously and legitimately, exist comfortably as art in a gallery, fact in a library, and artifact in a museum. However, archives preserve photographs for reasons different from those guiding collecting and preservation initiatives in galleries, libraries, and museums. Photographs are prized in archives, not simply as discrete facts nor for their artistic merit, but rather because of the role(s) they played in various processes—empirical, cognitive, and imaginative—integral to human thought, communication, negotiation, decision-making, *accountability*, and remembering. Not only indexical, but also instrumental, they offer information about and also constitute evidence of these processes. As active participants in both the life of business and the business of life, photographs take their rightful place in archives. What, then, makes photographs archival in both principle and practice?

Save for human intervention, natural disaster, or chemical deterioration, the content of photographs is fixed but their meaning is not. Indeed, photographic meaning is neither inherent nor observable, neither singular nor stable. The facts communicated in visual form by photographs are neither inert nor neutral. The meaning of the subject content of a photograph is historically situated, socially constructed, and culturally constituted. Moreover, because most photographic processes are able to produce multiple originals, the same visual facts, contained in dif-

ferent prints from the same negative, can deliver different messages depending on their contexts. To understand photographs in archival terms, as embodying evidence of authorial intentions, having functional origins, wielding rhetorical power, and producing effect(s), photographs must be returned to the action in which they participated. Such contextualization begins with the *principles of provenance* and original order, which are fundamental to all *archival practice*.

Provenance is more than simple attribution to the photographer; as a marker of authorial intention, provenance must be traced more fully to persons and institutions "concurring in the formation of the document." Similarly, original order applied to photographs may refer to the place of an image in a *series* of negatives, prints, or stereoscopic views; the relationship of a photograph to other photographs in an album or to other materials in a scrapbook; or the juxtaposition of photographs, maps, and text in an official report or private diary, or, indeed, to the privileged location of a framed portrait on a wall.

Until the advent of digital imaging, photographs were physical objects, the tangible elements of which governed their geographical reach and shouldered part of the burden of the messages they carried. Dimensions, shape, materials, and format each represent purposive choices, made at the time of creation that influenced the ways in which photographs were transmitted and received. Equally, the documentary universe—their placement in albums or series, printed reports, handwritten journals, or personal letters—refers to the context(s) in which photographs were circulated and viewed, and forms an inseparable part of the meaning(s) they were intended to convey.

What archival photographs present to researchers, onsite or online, is also very much shaped by institutional and professional practices. For this reason, best practices of description and *digitization* must respect those attributes and contexts of photographic meaning-making. However, institutional approaches to photographs continue to be shaped, far too often, by understandings that remain overwhelmingly content-based, and item-level access, especially in the digital world of crowd-sourcing and social media, is devoid of any but the most superficial contextual *metadata*.

Conclusion

Photography has had a profound effect on our strategies of seeing, engaging, and understanding the world. Like all archival documents, photographs must be situated in the multiple contexts in which they participated, and where they can be understood within the social, cultural, technological, and material evolution of human communication. Treated as such, they must be acquired for the meanings they communicated within the contexts in which they first appeared and were subsequently used.

If a photograph is conceived as the visual residue of an act of human communication, then its presence in an archive is predicated not simply on its truth value as a realistic representation of some part of the natural or material world, nor on its store of historical facts, nor on its display of aesthetic qualities, although each of these attributes may contribute to the meaning it conveyed from author to audience. That meaning cannot be discerned by gazing only at image surface and content. Rather, it is bound up in the complexities of visual facts, physical form, functional origins, and documentary universe of circulation. Returned to the action in which they participated, and re-presented to researchers through words and surrogates that reveal their meaning(s), photographs emerge as the powerful tools they once were and—if properly preserved in an archive—remain for the communication of information, ideas, feelings, values, and beliefs.

New digital technologies of information creation, transfer, and storage, new critical thinking about reality and representation, and new scholarly approaches to materiality and meaning demand that archival theory recognizes, and archival practices respect, all media of record as valid participants in the information economy of human communication. Accordingly, archival principles governing arrangement, description, and access must be reconceptualized if archival photographs are to maintain and transmit the meanings invested in them by their creators with undiminished strength and clarity.

Archivists need to ask a new set of questions. Rather than focus solely on what photographs show or look like, or who took them, we must also ask why they were taken; what they were meant to convey and to whom; and what they succeeded in communicating and how. As technologies of information and media of record continue to evolve, new best practices can only emerge from a more thorough understanding of photographs as fundamentally archival—as evidence of societal and institutional frameworks of understanding, and as having functional origins, authorial intentions, and purposive effect(s). As scanned photographs and born-digital images are made increasingly available online and are accessed without direct interaction with archivists, it becomes ever-more important to maintain those links to the contexts of production, circulation, and use through which photographic images, both analogue and digital, reveal themselves to be one player, among many, fully engaged in the archival mission.—*Joan M. Schwartz*

Keywords: photography, visual, graphic, images, photographic meaning

Related Entries: Artistic Records; Audio-Visual Records

Bibliography

Cook, Terry, and Joan M. Schwartz, eds. "Archives, Records, and Power." *Archival Science* 2 (1–4) (2002). DOI: 10.1007/BF02435628.

Frizot, Michel, ed. *A New History of Photography.* Köln: Könemann, 1998; French edition, Paris: Bordas, 1994.

Leary, William H. *The Archival Appraisal of Photographs: A RAMP Study with Guidelines.* Paris: UNESCO, 1985.

Ritzenthaler, Mary Lynn, Gerald J. Munoff, and Margery S. Long. *Administration of Photographic Collections.* Basic Manual Series. Chicago: Society of American Archivists, 1984. Republished in revised and expanded form as Ritzenthaler, Mary Lynn, Diane L. Vogt-O'Connor, with Helena Zinkham, Brett Carnell, and Kit A. Peterson. *Photographs: Archival Care and Management.* Chicago: Society of American Archivists, 2006.

Sassoon, Joanna. "Photographic Meaning in the Age of Digital Reproduction." *LASIE: Library Automated Systems Information Exchange* 29 (4) (1998): 5–15. Republished in expanded form as, "Photographic Materiality in the Age of Digital Reproduction." In Elizabeth Edwards and Janice Hart, eds. *Photographs Objects Histories: On the Materiality of Images.* London: Routledge, 2004, 186–202. http://search.informit.com.au/document Summary;dn=753187057136599;res=IELHSS.

274 *Postcustodialism*

Schellenberg, Theodore R. *The Management of Archives*. New York: Columbia University Press, 1965.

Schlak, Ti. "Framing Photographs, Denying Archives: The Difficulty of Focusing on Archival Photographs." *Archival Science* 8 (2) (2008): 85–101. DOI: 10.1007/s10502-009-9081-6.

Schwartz, Joan M. "The Archival Garden: Photographic Plantings, Interpretive Choices, and Alternative Narratives." In Terry Cook, ed., *Controlling the Past: Documenting Society and Institutions. Essays in Honor of Helen Willa Samuels*. Chicago: Society of American Archivists, 2011, 69–110.

———. "Coming to Terms with Photographs: Descriptive Standards, Linguistic 'Othering,' and the Margins of Archivy." *Archivaria* 54 (2002): 142–71. http://journals.sfu.ca/archivar/index.php/archivaria/article/view/12861/14092.

———. "'Records of Simple Truth and Precision': Photography, Archives, and the Illusion of Control." *Archivaria* 50 (2000): 1–40. http://journals.sfu.ca/archivar/index.php/archivaria/article/view/12763/13951.

———. "'We Make Our Tools and Our Tools Make Us': Lessons from Photographs for the Practice, Politics, and Poetics of Diplomatics." *Archivaria* 40 (1995): 40–74. http://journals.sfu.ca/archivar/index.php/archivaria/article/view/12096/13082. Published in an abridged and revised version as "To Speak Again with a Full Distinct Voice: Diplomatics, Photographs, and Archives." In *Archivi fotografici: Spazi del sapere, luoghi della ricerca*, a special issue of *Richerche di Storia dell'Arte* 106 (2012): 7–24.

POSTCUSTODIALISM

Since the early 1980s a growing number of archival writers and practitioners have subscribed to the philosophy of postcustodialism. The philosophy asserts that the archival mission should not be limited to traditional notions of managing archival holdings in custodial arrangements, but should embrace a much wider and more proactive range of programs involving *outreach*, collaboration, and documentation of and support for *records* in distributed custody. Sometimes conflated with noncustodialism, the philosophy does not in fact reject centralized custody as a valid archival strategy.

F. Gerald Ham and the "Postcustodial Era"

In 1981 F. Gerald Ham presented a set of archival strategies for what he called "the postcustodial era." He characterized *archives* in the custodial era as being passive and introspective and almost exclusively concerned with the custodial management of archival holdings. He argued that archives and *archivists* could not afford to persist with this narrow custodial mind-set, especially if they were to both survive the challenges of and take advantage of the opportunities presented by automation and the growth of born-digital information and online networks.

Ham characterized the postcustodial era as featuring a decentralized computer environment where every individual will become their own *records manager*. In such an environment, archivists would need to be much more active and interventionist if they were to have any hope of fulfilling their mission. He called for much greater levels of inter-institutional cooperation between archives programs, the development of strategies for providing easy and centralized *access* to increasingly complex and decentralized archives, and greater archival involvement in the process of information creation and management.

Importantly, Ham did not argue that archives should stop managing custodial holdings but rather that archives needed to expand their repertoire of strategies in order to navigate the increasingly complex realities of the late twentieth century. This expansion of archival strategies was not a renunciation of custody but rather a recognition that custody on its own was insufficient to ensure future archival success. Ham was not recommending a "noncustodial era," but a "postcustodial era" where *archival programs* and archivist self-image would not be defined by custody alone.

Archives as a Place

How does the vision of the postcustodial archive sit with resilient notions of archives as a place of secure deposit? Throughout the ages one of the regularly recurring functions of archival institutions has been to provide a secure place for the safekeeping of valuable records to guarantee the ongoing legal *authenticity* of those records. Luciana Duranti (1996) has highlighted the importance of this *function* in archives stretching back to the days of the Justinian Code and the Tabularium in Ancient Rome. One of Sir Hilary Jenkinson's more influential contributions to the archival discourse is the related notion of the need to guarantee an uninterrupted transmission of custody from records creator to archival institution—the physical and moral defense of the record. Duranti has argued that when records "cross the archival threshold" they are attested to be authentic and henceforth guaranteed to be preserved as such by an archives that is independent from the records creating office and for which the preservation of the authenticity of its holdings is its *raison d'être*.

While this is a common theme in the history of archival institutions, it is not a universal one. Duchein (1992) has argued that there are many countries in which the notion has never existed, including France, "where the fact of its being preserved in a public archival repository does not give a *document* any guarantee of authenticity." Similarly, while the preservation of authenticity is undoubtedly an objective of most collecting/historical archives, it cannot be said to be their sole *raison d'être*. More recently, archivists who agree with Duranti and Jenkinson about the absolute importance of guaranteeing the authenticity of records have disagreed with Duranti's argument that this can only be achieved by means of archival institutions taking physical custody of the records. To these critics adequate control of records to guarantee authenticity in the digital age can be achieved without the need for archives to provide a physical place of safekeeping. In the digital age the very physicality of records is superseded by a virtual concept or "performance" where the idea of a record having a set physical location becomes meaningless. They argue that the *archival bond* and subsequent guarantees of authenticity should commence at the point of records creation, which by definition cannot be physically in the archives. If the archival bond is achieved and guaranteed at the point of records creation, the decision when or whether to perform a physical act of custodial transfer to an archives becomes a minor administrative consideration, not a matter of central significance (Cook 1994; Hedstrom 1991; Upward and McKemmish 1994). In the online world the development of virtual archives is

considered desirable, if not essential, for continued relevance and survival. Many users will wish to be assured of authenticity but may not care about the existence of or necessity for places of custody.

Skeptics argue that it is naïve for postcustodialists to assert that technological change has made it possible, much less essential, for *digital records* to be archivally captured, described, and controlled in such a way as to guarantee the long-term authenticity and integrity of the records from the instant of creation onward. Perhaps the closest archivists have come to achieving this vision is with the "VERS encapsulated objects" (or VEOs) of the Victorian Electronic Records Strategy (VERS). VEOs are versions of records captured into a standardized archival file format and locked with a digital signature to guarantee authenticity. The vision, however, remains an unproved—though appealing—hypothesis. The problem is convincing creating agencies to capture all of their records as VEOs at the point of records creation, as only a small proportion of the records of an agency need to be retained for long-term archival purposes. The overheads for this commitment are high and may often be viewed as a case of "the archival tail wagging the business dog."

David Bearman's "Indefensible Bastion" and Australian Responses

During the 1990s, in the midst of a fevered discourse on electronic records, Ham's postcustodial vision reemerged as a divisive fault line in the archival community. In this context there was no figure more divisive than American David Bearman. Bearman reshaped Ham's call to arms as a visceral polemic that reverberated for years to come. Bearman (1991) argued that not only should archives adopt strategies based on distributed custody but they should also avoid (except as a last resort) taking any custody at all of electronic records. According to Bearman there were "few imaginable advantages and considerable disadvantages to the *archival custody* of electronic records." He argued that in a networked world "if archives have intellectual control over the records that are deemed archival, it doesn't matter much where records or users are."

In a commentary published simultaneously with Bearman's polemic, Margaret Hedstrom (1991) demurred. While agreeing with Bearman's call for an expanded role for archival programs and that there would be many circumstances where custody of records by archives would be "unnecessary and even ill-advised," she did not agree that custodianship was always going to be incompatible with these broader imperatives and strategies. Hedstrom presented some criteria to help archives decide whether or not it was best to take custody of electronic records. There will be times, Hedstrom argued, when creating agencies will be much better prepared than any archives to take physical custody of archival records in electronic form—for example, agencies whose primary mission is data collection and analysis. In any case, until archives develop the requisite technical capacity, the archival mission would be better served by temporarily leaving electronic records in the custody of the creating agency. To Hedstrom, such issues ultimately were trivial matters of implementation and timing. What was more important was for archival institutions to become sources of expertise in digital media, formats, management, preservation, and dissemination.

Hedstrom's rejoinder to Bearman's provocative paper should probably have been an end to the matter. Instead, however, Bearman's "noncustodial" arguments gained significant traction in Australia, traction that served largely as a distraction in the context of the broader postcustodial discourse. In 1994 the then Australian Archives (now National Archives of Australia) announced a distributed custody policy for electronic records that was, for all intents and purposes, Bearman's indefensible bastion paper in the guise of official *archival policy*.

Within seven years the National Archives of Australia (NAA) officially moved on from its policy of noncustody of electronic records when it established a *digital preservation* project and an accompanying custody policy that argued that archival value digital records should ideally be transferred to archival custody sooner rather than later. In retrospect the NAA was simply doing what Margaret Hedstrom had recommended in 1991, namely to leave electronic records in the custody of creating agencies until such time as the archives had the necessary technical capacity to receive and preserve digital records. Had the NAA said clearly in 1994 that "distributed custody" was merely an interim measure, few would have objected. Instead, its 1994 announcement was accompanied by elaborate and contentious justifica-

tions for a policy regime that had the appearance of being a long-term commitment and in retrospect may be seen as a misguided attempt to make a virtue out of a necessity. As such, postcustodial became confused with noncustodial in the minds of many observers and participants in the discourse.

Moving beyond Custody . . . to the Records Continuum

At the same time as the National Archives of Australia found itself embroiled in a largely sterile debate about custody, it and many other Australian archival programs, educators, and practitioners were exploring the "postcustodial" terrain first envisaged by Gerald Ham. For some years Frank Upward and Sue McKemmish of Monash University had been endeavoring to reconcile the emerging new paradigm with Jenkinsonian principles. Jenkinson's requirements for unbroken chains of custody and the physical and moral defense of records had, according to Upward (1993), been honored by the Australian Archives during the 1960s when it attempted to implement a universal system of documentation for all Australian Government records, "without regard to location or the designation of permanency." The father of the Australian *series system* for intellectual control and *archival description*, Peter Scott, together with his colleague and mentor Ian Maclean, were acclaimed as the first postcustodialists. Scott's groundbreaking 1966 article on the series system argued crucially that the archivist is essentially "a preserver and interpreter of *recordkeeping systems*" and that "series registration may be extended to cover *series* not yet in archival custody" (Scott 1966). According to Upward (1993, 44), "Jenkinson's concept of custody is that of guardianship, not imprisonment, and can be readily extended out from the archival institution." While the realities of limited resources meant that this brave experiment was only ever partially successful, it nevertheless pointed the way ahead toward a truly postcustodial *recordkeeping* paradigm.

Validation of emerging Australian postcustodial thinking came from the Canadian Terry Cook (1994). According to Cook, archivists needed to "stop being custodians of things and start being purveyors of concepts" and to reorient themselves from "records to the acts of recording." Cook argued that the future of archives was as access hubs and "virtual archives without walls." In prefiguring the following decade's dominant archival discourse about the power relationships that are integral to all information systems and related social and organizational systems, Cook managed to simultaneously applaud Australian postcustodial thinking while at the same time question some of its neo-Jenkinsonian foundations.

Today's Postcustodial Realities in Archival Programs

To what extent has the vision of postcustodial archives been realized? From the comfort of 2015 there seems little doubt that what once was a radical new vision is now almost archival orthodoxy. The functions of many archival programs have expanded greatly since Gerald Ham added the term postcustodial to our professional lexicon. Most larger archival programs now allocate significant resources to inter-institutional cooperation, including the development of cooperative online access services for distributed holdings, and to "front-end" engagement with records creators (often through influencing the design and implementation of recordkeeping systems). While traditional custodial functions have been retained, albeit often with proportionately fewer resources, archives are now usually far more proactive and outwardly engaged—with records creators, with other archives and documentation programs, and with an expanding base of users in cyberspace.

Archives and archivists are far less introspective and holdings-focused than was the case a generation ago. For most archives user services, access and public outreach are at least as important as the physical and moral defense of records. *Digitization* programs abound and users vote with their fingers in cyberspace in far greater numbers than has ever been the case with users voting with their feet in visiting reading rooms. The community expects its information sources to be available online and increasingly regards anything that is not online as being irrelevant.

Nevertheless, despite the explosion in online access to archives, physical custody of holdings remains the stated preference of the overwhelming majority of archival programs, both for traditional format and for digital records. Why has a preference

for old-fashioned archival custody proved to be so resilient? In recent years the notion of *trusted digital repositories* has achieved widespread acceptance. This reflects a recognition of the fragility of digital information objects and the need for reliable infrastructure and professional curation skills to ensure the authenticity, integrity, accessibility, and longevity of those objects. Digital curation is emerging as a specialist field in its own right, partly perhaps as a reaction against the notoriously short-term perspectives of the great majority of ICT professionals. Experience has taught archivists that, except for a small minority of exceptional cases, creating agencies cannot be relied on to manage born-digital archival value records over the long term. Agencies may maintain legacy systems for a certain period of time or may export or migrate business critical data from such systems into replacement systems, but it is not their core business to ensure the long-term preservation of records that have broader societal or historical value but little or no ongoing legal/administrative value. That is the core business of archives—core business that is most effectively carried out by transferring archival value digital records into archival custody at the earliest possible convenience, when the archives in question has the technical capacity to preserve those records.

None of which means that archives should be disconnected from current recordkeeping in records creating environments, or that archives should not maintain a strong interest in documenting and assisting the sound management of records that are in agency custody. Nor does it mean that archives should not support those agencies that have good business reasons for retaining and preserving digital records over the medium to long term when they can be relied on to do so. The UK National Archives' Digital Continuity Service is an example of postcustodial innovation, expert outreach, and cooperation by an archival institution that nevertheless remains committed to taking archival value digital records into archival custody at the earliest possible opportunity.

Conclusion

There is little doubt that the archival paradigm shift into the postcustodial era envisaged by Gerald Ham a generation ago has occurred. Archives are very different institutions nowadays and archivists, by and large, think and operate in very different ways. Archives have different priorities and different partnerships and use very different tools and processes. Archivists are less inclined to see themselves and their role as being passive and objective defenders of records created by other people and instead recognize the significance of their own role in shaping records. Being flexible, open-ended, and postcustodial is seen as a more attractive orientation for archives than being rigid, narrow-minded, and passively focused on custodial considerations and operations. Over the past thirty years archivists worldwide have come to recognize this and have been busy putting the new outlooks and mind-sets into operation.—*Adrian Cunningham*

Keywords: custody, outreach, records continuum
Related Entries: Outreach; Records Continuum

Bibliography

Bastian, J. "Taking Custody, Giving Access: A Post-custodial Role for a New Century." *Archivaria* 53 (2002): 76–93. http://journals.sfu.ca/archivar/index.php/archivaria/article/view/12838/14058.

Bearman, D. "An Indefensible Bastion: Archives as a Repository in the Electronic Age." Technical Report. *Archives and Museum Informatics* 13 (1991): 14–24.

Cook, T. "Electronic Records, Paper Minds: The Revolution in Information Management and Archives in the Post-custodial and Post-modernist Era." *Archives and Manuscripts: Journal of the Australian Society of Archivists* 22 (2) (1994): 300–328.

Duchein, M. "The History of European Archives and the Development of the Archival Profession in Europe." *The American Archivist* 55 (1992): 14–25. http://archivists.metapress.com/content/k17n44g856577888/fulltext.pdf.

Duranti, L. "Archives as a Place." *Archives and Manuscripts: Journal of the Australian Society of Archivists* 24 (2) (1996): 242–55.

Ham, F. G. "Archival Strategies for the Post-custodial Era." *The American Archivist* 44 (3) (1981): 207–16. http://archivists.metapress.com/content/6228121p01m8k376/fulltext.pdf.

Hedstrom, M. "Archives: To Be or Not to Be: A Commentary." Technical Report. *Archives and Museum Informatics* 13 (1991): 25–30.

The National Archives, U.K. "Managing Digital Continuity." www.nationalarchives.gov.uk/information-management/our-services/digital-continuity.htm (accessed January 2014).

Scott, P. "The Record Group Concept: A Case for Abandonment." *The American Archivist* 29 (4) (1966): 493–504. http://archivists.metapress.com/content/y886054240174401/fulltext.pdf.

Upward, F. "Institutionalizing the Archival Document—Some Theoretical Perspectives on Terry Eastwood's Challenge." In S. McKemmish and F. Upward, eds., *Archival Documents: Providing Accountability through Recordkeeping*. Melbourne: Ancora Press, 1993, 41–54.

———. "Structuring the Records Continuum Part One: Post-custodial Principles and Properties." *Archives and Manuscripts: Journal of the Australian Society of Archivists* 24 (2) (1996): 268–85.

Upward, F., and S. McKemmish. "Somewhere Beyond Custody." *Archives and Manuscripts: Journal of the Australian Society of Archivists* 22 (2) (1994): 136–49.

PRIMARY VALUES

Schellenberg writes (1956, 16) that "public *archives*, then, have two types of values: the primary values to the originating agency and the *secondary values* to other agencies and to non-government users." He goes on to say that "record officers and the other agency officials are mainly responsible for judging primary values" (1956, 28). He suggests that record officers should cooperate with *archivists* when assessing secondary value ("evidence of an agency's organizational *function* and development, or for their social, economic or other information"). Schellenberg's taxonomy of *record* values (primary and secondary values) was influential during the following half century and forms the basis of many records *appraisal* processes even in contemporary organizations. This article will consider the first of these: primary values.

Discussion

T. R. Schellenberg's views on the management of archives were captured in a seminal book, *Modern Archives,* which drew on his experience working as an archivist in the federal government of the United

States and were developed during his tour of Australia as a Fulbright lecturer in 1954. The demands of World War II, the massive increase in record production, including mechanical production, and detrimental war drives such as the waste paper collections in the UK, led archivists to consider carefully the need to select modern records systematically, both for permanent preservation as archives (secondary value) but also to select records not worthy of permanent preservation for destruction. One approach to record *selection* decision-making was to develop systematic practices based on principles of appraisal. Most approaches to appraisal sought to identify "value" in records or in the *context* of their creation and capture: Schellenberg's taxonomy of record values was designed to help frame appraisal decisions for government records. He suggests that primary value represented the importance of records to the organizations that created them, while secondary value was to users outside the originating organization, such as historians and other scholars who were interested in information and evidence found in the records. This subdivision provided a practical approach to records appraisal and could be used to guide the work of record officers (*records managers*) and of archivists in appraising value in records.

Schellenberg suggests that agency officials and record officers, who "focus on the primary value of records," should be responsible for judging primary value since they keep records for their current use "and are therefore prone to judge their value only in relation to such use" (1956, 28). Schellenberg also writes that "officials keep records for their current use —administrative, legal and fiscal." Schellenberg does not examine these three divisions in any detail; even so, the subdivision was widely adopted in the *records management* literature. Primary value is defined by many authors (e.g., Penn, Pennix, and Coulson 1994) as comprising three subvalues: administrative—that is, records that support the ongoing business activities of the organization; legal—that is, records that establish legal obligations and protect legal rights; and fiscal—that is, records that document the receipt and use of funds.

Schellenberg was not alone in writing about record values in the 1940s and 1950s. P. C. Brooks, at the National Archives of the United States, considered values of records for selection and the development of retention schedules in the context of new legislation for records disposal (Brooks 1940, 1948), while Emmett Leahy wrote about the different approaches to the "reduction of public records" adopted in the United States and in European countries. Leahy concluded that the administrator had an important role in the selection for destruction of public records but that "in every instance an archivist supervises the reduction programme" (1940, 32).

In the UK, and in contrast with the North American approaches, Hilary Jenkinson articulated a long-held European view that the *authenticity* of records derives in part from their interrelationships and that appraisal based on artificial assignment of record values impairs their *impartiality* as evidence. Jenkinson, therefore, in contrast with Schellenberg and Leahy, wrote that the archivist had no role in the selection of records: "For the Archivist to destroy a *document* because he thinks it is useless is to import into the collection . . . an element of his personal judgement; for the Historian to destroy . . . is even more destructive of the Archives' reputation for impartiality . . . ; but for an Administrative body to destroy what it no longer needs is a matter entirely within its competence . . . provided always that the Administration proceeds only upon . . . the needs of its own practical business" (Jenkinson 1922/1966, 149–50). It can be argued that what Jenkinson describes as the "needs of its own practical business" is in many ways similar to Schellenberg's idea of records kept by officials "for their current use" (1956, 27–28) and that the two traditions are not entirely dissimilar in their approach to assigning primary value.

In the UK, ideas of primary value were embedded into public records management practices following the recommendations of the Grigg Committee (established in 1952, reporting in 1954) and enshrined in the UK Public Records Act of 1958. The Grigg Committee's objective was to "review the arrangements for the preservation of the records of government Departments in the light of the rate at which they are accumulating." Although Jenkinson is often credited with influencing the Grigg Committee, in fact he was seen by the treasury as an obstruction and was not invited to be a member of the committee. Jenkinson found the committee's recommendations unpalatable, and he retired in 1954, leaving the implementation of the new system to his successor as deputy keeper of the Public Record Office (PRO), David Evans.

The Grigg Committee recommended a new approach to the review of government administrative files. *Files* that concerned policy, legal, financial, and other general administrative issues were to be subject to a two-tier system of review, while *case files* (sometimes called particular instance papers) were normally to be destroyed as soon as they were no longer current. Administrative files passed through a "First Review" (to be undertaken not later than five years after the file had been closed and passed out of current use) on the basis of administrative need, followed by a "Second Review" (twenty-five years after the opening date of the file), which considered both administrative and historical use. Records that passed Second Review on account of their historical value were then transferred to the PRO and opened up to the public when they were thirty years old.

First Review owes something to Schellenberg's ideas of primary values, since it requires creating departments to judge the current value of their files, and to help them do so, they had to appoint a departmental record officer, much like the U.S. government's record officers, who would undertake the evaluation of current use. Although the new UK system only applied by law to public records (i.e., those created by national ministries and courts), it was also influential over the practices of local government organizations, such as London County Council, who were beginning to develop systematic records management programs including record retention reviewing and appraisal in the 1950s and 1960s. Subsequently many public organizations adopted versions of two-tier record review, often combined with elements from Schellenberg's taxonomy, as a basis for record retention and archival appraisal decisions. The system largely remained in place until the late 1990s, when it began to be replaced with archival *acquisition* and operational selection policies (Simpson and Graham 2002), influenced by North American ideas of macroappraisal (Cook 1992).

Conclusion

Schellenberg (1956) established a taxonomy of record values (which he divided into primary and secondary values) that proved to be very influen-

tial in framing *record* selection approaches in the English speaking world in the second half of the twentieth century. Record officers faced with the accumulation of paper files in government ministries following World War II found the taxonomy a practical and useful basis for decision making about the destruction of records. Primary values, the subject of this entry, were generally subdivided into three types of value: administrative value for current business use, legal value to establish legal obligations and rights, and fiscal or financial value, which relates to the receipt and use of funds. However, as the paper-based *registry systems*, which enabled file-by-file selection based on record values to be operated, were largely abandoned in favor of hybrid and *digital record* systems, so also fixed ideas of primary values found in records were supplanted by more complex and nuanced approaches to appraisal.

—*Elizabeth Shepherd*

Keywords: appraisal, archival value, administrative value, legal value, fiscal value

Related Entries: Appraisal; Public Records Tradition; Record(s); Registry System; Secondary Value

Bibliography

Brooks, P. C. "Archival Procedures for Planned Records Retirement." *American Archivist* 11 (4) (1948): 308–15. http://archivists.metapress.com/content/h5311622113r8j21/fulltext.pdf.

———. "The Selection of Records for Preservation." *American Archivist* 3 (4) (1940): 221–34. http://archivists.metapress.com/content/u77415458gu22n65/fulltext.pdf.

Cook, T. "Mind over Matter: Towards a New Theory of Archival Appraisal." In B. L. Craig, ed., *The Archival Imagination. Essays in Honour of Hugh A. Taylor*. Ontario: ACA, 1992.

Grigg, J. *Report of the Committee on Departmental Records (Grigg Report)*. London: HMSO, Cmd. 9163, 1954.

Jenkinson, H. *A Manual of Archive Administration*. London: Lund Humphries, 1966 [1922].

Leahy, E. J. "Reduction of Public Records." *American Archivist* 3 (1) (1940): 13–38. http://archivists.metapress.com/content/928725x784741064/fulltext.pdf.

Penn, I. A., G. Pennix, and J. Coulson. *Records Management Handbook*. Aldershot, Hants, England: Gower, 1994.

Schellenberg, T. R. *Modern Archives: Principles and Techniques*. Chicago: University of Chicago Press, 1956.

Simpson, D., and S. Graham. "Appraisal and Selection of Records—a New Approach." *Comma, International Journal on Archives* 1–2 (2002): 51–56.

PRINCIPLE OF PERTINENCE

The principle of pertinence is defined as "a principle, now mostly rejected, for the arrangement of *archives* in terms of their subject content regardless of their provenance and original order" (Project Group on Terminology of the International Council on Archives [ICA], "Dictionary of Archival Terminology III," n.d.), though it has also frequently been invoked as a criterion for *appraisal* and reappraisal. The consequence of arranging or appraising by pertinence is the loss of the *records'* original *context*, and in some cases increased difficulty for the researcher because, instead of being guided by the records' provenancial context, the users must contend with the new context imposed upon them by the *archivists'* rearrangement.

In the modern history of archives, the principle of pertinence was at various times a contender for a method of arranging and describing and/or appraising archival materials. Although eventually supplanted by the now widely accepted *principle of provenance*, arrangement and description based on pertinence still exist in pockets.

Historical Practice: Pertinence in Arrangement and Description

From the seventeenth to the early nineteenth century, archivists' approaches to arrangement were influenced by libraries' classification methods, so that arrangement schemes based on subject headings (pertaining to names of *persons*, places, and thematic keywords) were adopted, and provenance and original order were disregarded (Miller 1997). This made the task of arranging and describing extremely onerous: since the creators of the records

had not arranged them according to subject, it was necessary to physically dismantle and rearrange the records after accessioning (Miller 1997). As a result, it was impossible for researchers to detect the relative importance of individual *archival fonds* within this new classification scheme, while, from a purely practical point of view, the allotment of storage space could not be determined in advance, and finding aids could never be finished, because accruals could be added to any section of the records, rendering the finding aid instantly out of date (Miller 1997). With the growth in complexity of administrative practices in the nineteenth century and the concomitant explosion of *recordkeeping*, the new government-run archives in France and Prussia found themselves overwhelmed by records, so that it was necessary to reassess the practicability of arranging records by pertinence (Miller 1997).

At the same time, theoretical doubts were expressed, most notably by the Dutch archivists Muller, Feith, and Fruin in their *Manual for the Arrangement and Description of Archives* (1898), which echoed the earlier calls of Natalis de Wailly and other European archivists (particularly during the administrative upheavals caused by the Napoleonic wars) for the adoption of provenance as the principle of arrangement, and provided it with a theoretical underpinning while also emphasizing its practical aspects (Horsman 1994). The principle of provenance quickly achieved dogmatic status throughout Europe, replacing the principle of pertinence, although its reception in the United States was slower and more uneven, due to significant influences from history and library science, which pulled in favor of pertinence as an arrangement principle, and a characteristic unawareness that provenance should also be applied to private papers (Barritt 1993).

Pertinence in Appraisal: Germany

The records crisis of World War I brought a new focus on appraisal to Europe. There was fleeting support for a return to pertinence in arrangement from some archivists, such as Weibull in Sweden, who suggested that archivists should primarily consider historical research interests and base their arrangements on subject (Horsman 1994). A particularly rich debate on provenance versus pertinence developed in Germany. In 1937, the records crisis prompted the formation of a reappraisal committee by the Prussian archival administration (Landwehr 1996). The committee's chief movers were Meisner and Meinert. Informational content (pertinence) was one of Meisner's three value criteria for appraising records, along with the records' age and the rank of the records' creator in the administrative hierarchy, although his approach overall emphasized provenance. Meinert later expanded on the pertinence element of Meisner's theory, arguing that *selection* for informational content should be reflective of three large themes—*volk, staat,* and *kultur* (people, state, and culture)—an approach later criticized by Booms as impractical. In contrast to Meisner's approach, Meinert's theory was dominated by pertinence, although provenance was seen as an important starting point for appraisal. This parallelism between provenance and pertinence was typical of German approaches to appraisal in the 1930s, and little effort was made to reconcile them (Landwehr 1996).

In the post-war period, Zimmermann argued for pertinence as the main criterion for archival appraisal from 1958 until the 1970s (Couture 2005). Like the American archivist Bauer, he believed that a document's content principally determined its value, so that the demands of its potential users should be the primary consideration, rather than provenance (Couture 2005). Significance of informational content should be determined in the light of the broader society's needs and activities, and with an eye to future research interests, extrapolated from statistical analyses of current research use and identified in consultation with the relevant research professions. Zimmermann foresaw assigning grades of archival value according to the importance of the records' informational content, though he did not specify how such values should be assessed (Landwehr 1996).

Pertinence also surfaced in Booms's theory, first developed in the 1960s, that records must be selected in accordance with the values of the creating society and thus be pertinent to topics that such society regarded as important. These were to be identified through a study of contemporary sources (such as newspapers) to form the basis of a *documentation plan* developed in collaboration with other archivists and perhaps in consultation with representa-

tives of different public interests (Booms 1987). Contemporary politics were reflected in Booms's insistence that, in order to be reliable, the sources examined must have been produced in a democratic political environment, a criticism of the Marxist-Leninist appraisal strategies of East German archivists (Booms, 1987). Ironically, while Booms's approach was never adopted in West Germany and was vociferously attacked in East Germany, it became an important influence on the development of the complex, pertinence-focused East German documentation profile. In 1979, Zimmermann developed a new approach, influenced by Haase's arguments for frequency of use as an appraisal criterion, in which provenance would be the primary value in the initial appraisal stage, but use (linked to informational content) would be the criterion for reappraisal, since it would indicate the records' usefulness as sources (Landwehr 1996). There was an overall difference between levels of government in Germany: archives at the federal level were more likely to adhere to provenance in appraisal, while those at lower levels of government often preferred an older approach to appraisal based on the value of records to historians (Landwehr 1996).

In 1991, there was a confrontation between provenance and pertinence-based approaches at a conference in East Berlin, the former advocated by West German attendees, the latter by East German delegates (notably Papendieck) who attempted to salvage some aspects of the documentation profile, while Booms distanced himself from his previous advocacy of pertinence, turning instead to provenance (Landwehr 1996). Menne-Haritz's presentation highlighted the archival profession's dependence on history for its identity as the source of (in her view) misguided pertinence-based appraisal theories oriented to historians' needs. Drawing heavily on Schellenberg, whose writings she had recently translated into German, she highlighted the provenance-based aspects of his approach but argued that pertinence could play a supplementary role in increasing evidence's *accessibility* (Menne-Haritz 1994).

Following reunification, the pertinence-based approach was decisively rejected in favor of a strictly provenancial, taxonomical approach known as horizontal and vertical appraisal (Treffeisen 2003). Nevertheless, in recent years Terry Cook's *macroap-*

praisal theory and the American *documentation strategy* have exerted influence on some German theorists, most notably Kretzschmar, who has argued for the reintegration of Booms's documentation profile to counterbalance what he views as an overly provenancial emphasis. Pertinence-based ideas can also be detected in the 2004 and 2011 position papers by the Society of German Archivists' Working Group. There is, however, an important exception at the municipal archive level, where documentation profiles are often used to thoroughly document notable local persons and events.

Pertinence in Appraisal: The United States and Canada

Around 1948, American archivist Philip Bauer advocated for a use- rather than origin-based approach to appraisal that emphasized informational content (Couture 2005). In 1956, Schellenberg responded to the governmental records crisis with an appraisal theory that attempted to integrate both provenance and pertinence. In fact, the *secondary value* of records includes research value (based on the documents' informational content) in addition to evidential value in terms of historical proof, and the importance of the document's informational content (along with form and *uniqueness*) is one factor that archivists must consider in appraising based on this criterion (Schellenberg 1956).

The sophisticated documentation strategy advocated by Helen Samuels in the 1980s was at first dominated by a focus on informational values, although she afterward added a *functional analysis* component in order to determine the *functions* to be documented, thereby orienting her approach more toward provenance and making the pertinence element supplementary (Samuels 1992). Boles and Young integrated numerous criteria relating to informational content into their appraisal model for university records (which featured thirty criteria in total) (Couture 2005).

In the 1960s and 1970s documentation strategies were particularly popular with archivists connected to the labor movement and multicultural archives, given its potential to address the imbalance of records on disadvantaged groups through proactive documentation of their experiences. In 1975, Ham's

"The Archival Edge," influenced by the social historians Zinn and Bass Warner, argued vigorously for the adoption of an approach to appraisal dominated by pertinence, to be focused on capturing important social movements and trends. In Canada, Hugh Taylor similarly argued that appraisal should aim to document the whole of society, and Cook's macroappraisal theory, while involving an ambitious functional analysis component, requires the archivist to evaluate records for their reflection of citizen-state interactions and thus integrates a strong emphasis on pertinence (Couture 2005).

Pertinence in Appraisal: Great Britain

Archivists in the United Kingdom have contributed little to appraisal theory, preferring to follow Jenkinsonian orthodoxy and leave selection decisions to the recordkeepers themselves. The Second World War records crisis forced a reevaluation of this attitude, and in 1958 the Grigg Committee attempted to find a suitable appraisal methodology. It suggested a two-step process: first, appraising the administrative value of documents five years after their creation (provenance-focused), and, after twenty-five years, evaluating the historical value of the records left after this initial destruction (pertinence). Although this approach was pronounced a failure in 1981 by the Wilson Report and the Keeper of Public Records (Couture 2005), it endured to this day.

Today: Pertinence in Arrangement

Survival of the principle of pertinence in arrangement and description can be found in collections of private manuscripts, particularly in the United States, where they are often kept in research libraries rather than in archives. This results in pressure to apply bibliographic description to facilitate research use by historians.

A few archives, such as the International Tracing Service (ITS) in Bad Arolsen, still arrange their holdings according to the principle of pertinence. In the case of the ITS, this is consistent with its *sui generis* primary purpose, which is humanitarian rather than historical: facilitating users' searching for family members.

Conclusion

In the context of arrangement, the advent of new forms of technology as described by Duranti in "Structural *Formal Analysis*" may eliminate the requirement to choose between provenance and pertinence, providing users with the benefits of being able to search by subject while maintaining the traditional emphasis on the records' generative context (Duranti 2010). In appraisal, however, provenance's dominance seems assured.—*Isabel Taylor*

Keywords: appraisal, arrangement, pertinence, provenance

Related Entries: Appraisal; Archival Arrangement; Archival Description; Documentation Plan; Functional Analysis; Primary Values; Principle of Provenance; Principle of *Respect des Fonds*; Principle of Respect for Original Order; Secondary Values; Selection

Bibliography

Barritt, Marjorie Rabe. "Coming to America: Dutch *Archivistiek* and American Archival Practice." *Archival Issues* 18 (1) (1993): 43–54. www.jstor.org/stable/41101846.

Booms, Hans. "Society and the Formation of a Documentary Heritage: Issues in the Appraisal of Archival Sources." *Archivaria* 1 (24) (1987): 69–107. http://journals.sfu.ca/archivar/index.php/archivaria/article/view/11415/12357.

Couture, Carole. "Archival Appraisal: A Status Report." *Archivaria* 1 (59) (2005): 83–107. http://journals.sfu.ca/archivar/index.php/archivaria/article/view/12502/13624.

Duranti, L. "Structural and Formal Analysis: The Contribution of Diplomatics to Archival Appraisal in the Digital Environment." In Jennie Hill, ed., *The Future of Archives and Recordkeeping: A Reader*; *Hill*. London: Facet, 2010, 65–88.

Horsman, P. "Taming the Elephant: An Orthodox Approach to the Principle of Provenance." In *The Principle of Provenance*. Stockholm: Swedish National Archives, 1994, 51–63.

Landwehr, Regina. *The German Archival System 1945–1995*. Master's thesis, University of British Columbia, 1996.

Menne-Haritz, Angelika. "Appraisal or Documentation: Can We Appraise Archives by Selecting Content." *American Archivist* 57 (3) (1954): 528–42. http://archivists.metapress.com/content/g114464381p11324/fulltext.pdf.

Miller, Thea. "The German Registratur." Master's thesis, University of British Columbia, 1997.

Samuels, Helen W. "Improving Our Disposition: Documentation Strategy." *Archivaria* 1 (33) (1991–1992): 125–40. http://journals.sfu.ca/archivar/index.php/archivaria/article/view/11804/12755.

Schellenberg, Theodore R. *Modern Archives, Principles and Techniques*. Chicago: University of Chicago Press, 1956.

Treffeisen, Jürgen. "The Development in German of Archival Processing—the Vertical and Horizontal Appraisal." *Archival Science* 3 (4) (2003): 345–66. DOI: 10.1007/s10502-004-2273-1.

*The author's thanks are due to Dr. Nicole Bickhoff and Dr. Wolfgang Mährle of the Hauptstaatsarchiv Stuttgart.

PRINCIPLE OF PROVENANCE

Archivists base their work on the idea that the origin of archival *documents* or *records*, or their provenance, must be known if the purposes of *archives* are to be achieved. The overriding archival purpose is to maximize the usefulness of records by enhancing the records' meanings. The meanings of records whose origin is unknown, mistaken, or partially known are limited, sometimes severely. Archivists begin to apply the principle of provenance when they identify records. Thus the most widely accepted definitions of the principle stress that the records of a given origin, whether an institution or private individual or family, must neither be misidentified as those of a different *creator* nor be physically intermixed by archivists with records made by other creators. These missteps would either destroy at worst or obscure at best the records' provenance and undermine the purposes of archives.

The Concept

The application of the principle of provenance results in division of archival holdings into particular groups of records linked to their creator. These groups become the primary objects of attention of archival *functions*—such as *description*, which becomes the basis of reference work. Preservation involves awareness of information about the records' provenance that is embedded in their material features. And much *appraisal* work is driven by assessment of the significance of the functions and impact of the creator of records. The overall management of an archives is at heart management of the application of the principle of provenance.

Users of archives thus typically encounter records grouped and described in relation to their accumulation by their creator: whether an institution and/or its subunits; a private *person*; or a family. The formation by archivists of the main components of these groups of records is also guided by the principle of provenance. These subgroups (for example, established around one or more formal *recordkeeping* systems, usually called *series*) are often the focus of the internal arrangement of the group because they are key physical expressions and evidence of the process that produced the records. A variety of record-creating acts involved in compilation of the records is at the core of this process: their inscription by their compiler; the compiler's accumulation of records inscribed by others; and/or the compiler's maintenance and use of these records. The relationship between the records created in this process is often called their "original order" or the sequence in which they may have been inscribed and maintained. Archivists attempt to maintain this order as another key aspect of their commitment to protecting knowledge of the records' provenance or creation processes.

The History

We lack a detailed history of the place of the principle of provenance in archival work. The above widely adopted Western view of provenance arose largely from European archival experience. It emerged from sometimes heated debates in the nineteenth century, especially among archivists, historians, other scholars, and government administrators and recordkeepers over the best basis for work in expanding newly established state-administered archives. The debate turned on the question of what approach to archival work conveys the most accurate and accessible understanding of the past. Some argued that arranging records according to their information content (e.g.,

on the basis of alphabetical, subject, chronological, geographical, or other categories such as record type) would reflect best what actually happened and ease retrieval of that information. Others argued for a provenance-based approach—that retrieval of records and understanding what happened in the past depends more on protecting the records' relationship to their creator and the interrelationships it established between records. Key contributions to the debate in support of the principle of provenance came from France in the 1840s, Germany in the 1880s, and the Netherlands in the 1880s and 1890s. In 1841, archivist and historian Natalis de Wailly declared on behalf of the French government that the best ordering of archives is achieved when the records' relationship to their creator is maintained. The group of records that resulted from this relationship he called a fonds. This gave major impetus to the idea that archival work must abide by *respect des fonds*. De Wailly articulated the idea that the origin of a body of records mattered greatly. But the principle was initially applied in certain limited ways in France—grouping the records of merely similar institutions into one fonds, and only applying the concept to certain records.

While others in Belgium, Italy, and elsewhere contributed to the discussion, German archivist-historians refined the principle in two ways—emphasizing the importance of the relationship of a fonds to its specific administrative creator (which they called the provenienzprinzip) and preserving the original order of the records within fonds (the registraturprinzip). Dutch archivists made a pivotal contribution to consolidation of the principle of provenance in 1898 with the publication under the auspices of the Netherlands Association of Archivists of *The Manual for the Arrangement and Description of Archives*. The *Manual* not only accepted the French emphasis on the origin of fonds and the two German components of the principle of provenance, but also responded to the then-most-important practical questions arising from problems in applying them. Drawing on this groundwork, the 1910 International Congress of Archivists and Librarians held in Brussels formally and unanimously endorsed the principle as the best basis for *archival arrangement* and description and historical research in archives. Over the next half century, the widespread influence of the *Manual* and of writings by leading archivists who believed in the principle of provenance, such as Hilary Jenkinson of Great Britain and Theodore Schellenberg of the United States, marked its acceptance in virtually all major Western archives for institutional as well as personal or family records. Although its adoption moved at an uneven pace and in differing ways, including stunning blind spots (Schellenberg maintained that the principle of provenance need not apply to pictorial records), the view that archival work should be based on the principle now prevails in Western cultures and many areas influenced by them.

This consensus emphasized certain key things about the principle of provenance, above all that archivists should link records to the primary creator of them, which was usually deemed to be their initial inscriber, accumulator, and user. The contextual descriptive information in finding aids about their creator (beyond its mere identity) then focused on the formal administrative units and their formal overall functions or the personal and family activities of that single primary creator as the cause of the creation of the records.

The Principle of Provenance Today

Since the mid-twentieth century, critics of this view of provenance have voiced different understandings of its meaning and application. They have not sought to overthrow the principle but to apply it more fully or faithfully by bringing to light what is implicit in the concept itself. Their answers have broadened and deepened it. They have contributed to the changing understandings of the principle that mark its entire history. Particular statements about the provenance of particular records can now be seen as arising from an ongoing process of interpretation and reinterpretation of knowledge drawn from the complex history of the records that produced them. In the 1960s, Australian Peter Scott brought to the fore that institutional records often have multiple creators, rather than a single primary one, as records come under the consecutive control of various units across time. His work launched the Australian *series system* of arrangement and description, which is based on recognition of the multiple creators of record series. The idea that a series could have multiple simultaneous creators also received greater examination. These insights into institutional records

have been accompanied by a growing awareness of the impact on personal and family records of their often complex custodial histories, which had usually been seen as mere ownership and/or passive keeping until the records were handed off to an archives.

Personal and family record-creating activities, however, have not yet received the scrutiny institutional functions have had, as archivists deepened the conventional general understanding of the latter by urging closer examination of their particular types, components, and interrelationships. The limits of institutions' formal definitions of their functions and administrative structures as means of understanding *record creation* have also received attention. This led to exploration of the *organizational cultures* that shape the less formal ways in which work may well be done and records thereby created. Some suggest that the personal life experiences and values of institutional officials ought to be seen as factors in "formal" organizational record-creating behavior. It is also suggested that archivists pursue the provenance of personal archives beyond the activities that appear to have produced them into the deeper psychological motivations people may have for creating records.

Recordkeeping systems and information technologies have also received more attention with increased awareness of their power to shape the creation of records. Detailed study of record creation processes in institutions, and of particular types of records, received greater attention through renewed interest in *diplomatics*, particularly in response to the challenges to understanding the provenance of often unstable digital communications. The similar notions of societal, parallel, and community provenance have also been advanced. They reflect an increasing awareness of the impact of various societal conditions on records creators and record creation processes at any given time and place across the records' history. Some extend this interpretation to a territorial notion of provenance that maintains that records created in a certain place should be archived as closely as possible to it. For their provenance to be understood, thus their meanings conveyed and retrieval in research facilitated, records need to be seen as products of societal forces and interactions.

This broadening of the idea of provenance in the West to include its societal dimensions was prompted in part by interaction with indigenous people. They are at the origin of the large volumes of information in nonindigenous archives provided by them to or taken from them by Western record makers. Yet this key aspect of the provenance of such records has been largely ignored in archival work in the Western tradition. This interaction, however, has thrown light on the importance of the idea of provenance in indigenous archival thinking. Being able to assign its provenance to its archives is a powerful act of affirmation for any community. And it allows indigenous people to retell their often discounted story from their archives in their way, which they believe is essential to withstand the ongoing pressures of cultural assimilation, to pursue redress of past justices, and work toward more equitable relationships with nonindigenous people. Thus indigenous communities have long created and maintained their own archives. Some now also seek to acquire copies of records about them in state and other Western archives so that they can reestablish them as archives under indigenous provenance and control. This societal idea about the origin of records has led to calls for a more participatory approach by such Western archives to the *acquisition* of provenance information from indigenous people. This approach obviously can also extend to others in society.

Some archivists have broadened the concept of provenance to include the actions of archivists and users of archives as formative influences on the creation of the records. In effect, these actions can be understood as extensions of the acts of inscription, accumulation, and use that frame the traditional view of provenance. When archivists decide what records are (either archival or not), describe them in certain ways, rather than others, and indeed say what their provenance is or is not (such as by welcoming or resisting intercultural participatory engagements), or reformat records (e.g., through particular approaches to *digitization*), they join the initial inscribers and subsequent prior controllers of the records in making them what they then also become in archival control. Users of archives at various places and times all along the history of the records do similar things. They, like archivists, animate the record into new life, in ways shaped by what may be known of its history by them. As the above-mentioned indigenous example shows, different people can have very different views of what

the provenance of a record is, and thus what the record is and means. The outcomes of such debate can influence subsequent understandings of the record in a society, and thus archivists' understandings of it, which then affect again its re-creation by them as archival or not, having this or that provenance.

Conclusion

We can say that provenance is an ongoing process in which records are created and re-created, arising from knowledge of the history of the records as shaped by the various formative influences outlined above—from initial inscription to acquisition and use in archives, perhaps centuries later. This process causes a record to exist as what it is thought to be in a given archives at a given point in time. It is thus its provenance. Like the origin of any human creation, the origin of records is equally multifaceted and ever open to new insights and explanations.—*Tom Nesmith*

Keywords: archival arrangement, principle of *respect des fonds*, archival history

Related Entries: Archival Arrangement; Archival Description; Archival History; Archival Method; Archival Theory; Archives (Material); Principle of Respect des *Fonds*; Principle of Respect for Original Order

Bibliography

Bastian, Jeannette Allis. "Reading Colonial Records through an Archival Lens: The Provenance of Space, Place, and Creation." *Archival Science* 6 (3–4) (2006): 267–84. DOI 10.1007/s10502-006-9019-1.

Cook, Terry. "What Is Past Is Prologue: A History of Archival Ideas since 1898, and the Future Paradigm Shift." *Archivaria* 1 (43) (1997). http://journals.sfu.ca/archivar/index.php/archivaria/article/view/12175/13184.

Douglas, Jennifer. "Origins: Evolving Ideas about the Principle of Provenance." In T. Eastwood and H. MacNeil, eds., *Currents of Archival Thinking*. Santa Barbara, CA: Libraries Unlimited, 2010, 23–43.

George-Shongo, David. "Deerskin Archiving." A presentation to Sharing the Truth: Creating a

National Research Centre on Residential Schools, National Research Centre Forum, Vancouver, March 2, 2011. www.trcnrc.ca/websites/NRC/index.php?p=189 (accessed February 28, 2014).

Hurley, Chris. "Parallel Provenance (1): What, If Anything, Is Archival Description?" *Archives and Manuscripts* 33 (1) (2005): 111–45. http://search.informit.com.au/documentSummary;dn=200601141;res=IELAPA.

———. "Parallel Provenance (2): When Something Is *Not* Related to Everything Else." *Archives and Manuscripts* 33 (2) (2005): 53–91. http://search.informit.com.au/documentSummary;dn=200606879;res=IELAPA.

International Council of Archives. "Multilingual Archival Terminology." http://www.ica.org (accessed February 28, 2014).

Millar, Laura. "The Death of the Fonds and the Resurrection of Provenance: Archival Context in Space and Time." *Archivaria* 1 (53) (2002): 1–15. http://journals.sfu.ca/archivar/index.php/archivaria/article/view/12833/14048.

Nesmith, Tom. "The Concept of Societal Provenance and Records of Nineteenth-Century Aboriginal-European Relations in Western Canada: Implications for Archival Theory and Practice." *Archival Science* 6 (3–4) (2006): 351–60. DOI 10.1007/s10502-007-9043-9.

———. "Still Fuzzy, But More Accurate: Some Thoughts on the 'Ghosts' of Archival Theory." *Archivaria* 1 (47) (1999): 136–50.

PRINCIPLE OF *RESPECT DES FONDS*

Respect des fonds is a fundamental principle that guides the arrangement and description of *archives* and defines the distinctive practice of the archival profession. Formulated in the nineteenth century by European *archivists*, the principle is "the most important intellectual development in the history of the archival profession" (Nesmith 1993, 1), and it has led to the establishment of the core of modern *archival science*. From its first articulation in a government circular issued in France in 1841 to its rediscovery in North America in the last quarter of the twentieth century, the principle has been steadily enriched in its theoretical connotations and practical applications. The essence of the principle is to connect archival *documents* or *records* to the *functions* and activities in the course of which they are accumulated and to the entity that is responsible for the execution of those functions and activities. This way, records will not be separated from the *context* and purpose of their creation and can be preserved as authentic and reliable evidence of the life and work of individuals, organizations, and communities for the comprehension and use of posterity.

The Concept

An *archival fonds* can be defined as "the whole of the documents of any nature that every administrative body, every physical or corporate entity, automatically and organically accumulate[d] by reason of its function or of its activity" (Bureau of Canadian Archivists 1985, 7). Guided by the principle of *respect des fonds*, archivists keep all records of the same origin together and retain them in their natural, organically developed order of creation and use. In some countries, the practice of respecting the boundaries and internal order of an archival fond has been referred to as one method guided by two subprinciples, the *principle of provenance* and the *principle of original order*. Respect des fonds is, however, the overarching principle guiding the multilevel hierarchical arrangement of archives and embedded in all major international and national archival descriptive standards, such as *General International Standard Archival Description* (International), *Describing Archives: A Content Standard* (United States), *Rules for Archival Description* (Canada), and *Manual of Archival Description* (United Kingdom). In the digital world, the principle of *respect des fonds* can be implemented by conceptual representation rather than by physical arrangement of records.

The necessity of arranging and describing archives did not become evident until the birth of modern archives in the aftermath of the French Revolution. The establishment of the National Archives of France in the last decade of the eighteenth century created a nationwide public archives that collected and preserved "the documentary heritage of the past" and made it accessible for public use (Posner 1940, 161–62). In the first few decades, efforts were made to arrange records into a predefined subject schema designed to facilitate the scholarly and public use of the archives. The breakthrough came in 1841, when the French Ministry of the Interior issued a circular authored by French archivist Natalis de Wailly, which introduced a new way of organizing archives: "To assemble the different documents by fonds, that is to say, to form a collection of all the documents which originate from a body, an organization, a family or an individual, and to arrange the different fonds according to a certain order" (Ministère des Affaires Culturelles 1970, quoted in Bartlett 1992, 107).

The principle of *respect des fonds* as applied in the early French practice kept records of old and new regimes separate but considered it necessary to arrange them within a fonds by subject matters devised by archivists. During the second half of the nineteenth century, when the principle started to be applied to records of existing government bureaucracies in several European countries, the new notion was developed that records within an archival fonds should be maintained in the order derived from the *recordkeeping system* of the creating agency. The regulations issued by the Prussian Privy State Archives in 1881 created a combined notion of keeping all the records of each creating agency together (*provenienzprinzip*) and maintaining them in the order given by the registry office of the agency (*registraturprinzip*) (Schellenberg 1956, 174). The idea of arranging the records according to their provenance and original order was finally formulated into specific rules and introduced to the rest of the world with the publication of the so-called Dutch manual by three Dutch archivists: Samuel Muller, Johan Feith, and Robert Fruin, in 1898 (2003).

The concept of *respect des fonds*, along with its development in the principles of provenance and original order, was introduced to North America through intellectual contacts of American archivists in the early twentieth century with their European counterparts, the publication of the English translation of the Dutch manual in 1940, and the writings of T. R. Schellenberg (Barritt 1993). When the National Archives was established in the United States in 1934, the concept of *record group* was adopted to organize a voluminous mass of modern records generated by a large and complex governing body of federal agencies. Record group numbers are flexibly designated to specific agencies based on the volume of records. This way, the concept of fonds could be applied at any level of the administrative hierarchy,

and several small fonds could be grouped to form a collective record group. Within the record group, there is a multilevel arrangement of *series*, *file*, and item. The practice ensures that "each document has its place, a natural place, so that its association and relation with all other documents produced or received by the creating agency remain clear" (Holmes 1964, 21).

The "long-established principles of *respect des fonds* (*Provenienzprinzip*) and respect for original order (*Registraturprinzip*)" are the theoretical foundation on which Australian archivist Peter Scott based his critique of the record group concept in a 1966 article (493). Scott argues that if records belonging to multiple fonds are forced to be transferred to a single record group, the practice actually fails rather than fulfills the objectives of the principles of *respect des fonds* and original order. A more appropriate approach would let records follow *functions* and functions follow administrations. The Australian *series system*, implemented in the Australian Commonwealth Archives Office in the 1960s, uses the record series as the primary category of classification of archives so that they can be linked to multiple administrative agencies responsible for their creation and maintenance. The system offers new insights into the relationships between fonds and series—the latter being traditionally regarded as subordinate to the former.

Archival researchers and professionals continued to explore the theoretical implications and practical applications of the principle of *respect des fonds* in the second half of the twentieth century. In 1983, French archival theorist Michel Duchein's 1977 article "Theoretical Principles and Practical Problems of *Respect des Fonds* in Archival Science" was translated into English and published in *Archivaria*, the journal of the Association of Canadian Archivists (ACA). Duchein's article provides a fresh view of the historical definition, theoretical justification, and practical application of *respect des fonds*. The translation and publication of Duchein's article in *Archivaria* marked the beginning of a revival of the principle of *respect des fonds* in the English-speaking archival community. The concept of archival fonds and the principle of *respect des fonds* as discussed by Duchein and other Canadian archival thinkers became the theoretical foundation for the Canadian standardization of *archival description* and resulted in the publication of the Canadian *Rules for Archival Description* (RAD) in 1990 and its theoretical companion, *The Archival Fonds: From Theory to Practice* in 1992.

The Canadian rediscovery of *respect des fonds* explores the boundary and structure of the archival fonds. It reiterates the importance of fonds as the highest level of archival control and develops strategies to deal with the complexity of modern bureaucracies. The structural view of the archival fonds, that is, the study of its external and internal dimensions, highlights the organic connection of authorities, functions, activities, and records—the essence of the principle of *respect des fonds*. This journey of rediscovery also examined a notion of archival fonds capable of expressing a multiple, dynamic interconnection between records and their creators.

Moving into the twenty-first century, new developments in the interpretation and application of the principle of *respect des fonds* continue to emerge. Researchers in the past decade have looked into new theoretical and practical implications of the principle in electronic records and *digital archives* environments. The networked world makes it possible for archivists to go beyond the boundary of individual *repositories*. The concept of archival fonds, traditionally associated with a group of archival material stored in one single repository, can now still hold when records of the same creator are located in several repositories. Challenges (and opportunities) also arise when *digital records* are made directly accessible on the web where digital content can easily get disconnected from its context. For years, archivists from multiple countries have had issues with a single view of the archival fonds and the fixed structure characterizing the traditional archival fonds. They have wished for an enhanced system enabling them to express the rich and dynamic relationships between records and their context while at the same time meeting the information needs of a variety of users. It is very likely that such a system will soon be developed.

Conclusion

Since its initial articulation in France, the principle of *respect des fonds* has been incorporated into various practices throughout the world. In spite of variations in *archival practice*, the essence of the principle remains unchanged and reflects the consensus among archivists that the meaning of records as evidence is closely associated with the context in which they are created and used. The principle of *respect des fonds* requires archives to preserve and make accessible records within their original documentary context so that their meaning is not lost or misinterpreted. Archivists around the world today continue to apply the principle while researching ways of bringing it to meet and support the digital environment of the twenty-first century.—*Jane Zhang*

Keywords: archival arrangement, archival description, provenance, original order

Related Entries: Archival Arrangement; Principle of Provenance; Principle of *Respect des Fonds*; Principle of Respect for Original Order; Record Group; Series System

Bibliography

Barritt, Marjorie R. "Coming to America: Dutch Archivistiek and American Archival Practice." *Archival Issues* 18 (1) (1993): 43–54. www.jstor.org/stable/41101846.

Bartlett, Nancy. "*Respect des Fonds*: The Origins of the Modern Archival Principle of Provenance." *Primary Sources & Original Works* 1 (1992): 107–15. DOI: 10.1300/J269V01N01_07.

Bureau of Canadian Archivists. *Toward Descriptive Standards: Report and Recommendations of the Canadian Working Group on Archival Descriptive Standards*. Ottawa, ON: Bureau of Canadian Archivists, 1985.

Duchein, Michael. "Theoretical Principles and Practical Problems of *Respect des Fonds* in Archival Science." *Archivaria* 1 (16) (1983): 64–82. http://journals.sfu.ca/archivar/index.php/archivaria/article/view/12648/13813.

Eastwood, Terence. *The Archival Fonds: From Theory to Practice*. Ottawa, ON: Bureau of Canadian Archivists, Planning Committee on Descriptive Standards, 1992.

Holmes, Oliver Wendell. "Archival Arrangement: Five Different Operations at Five Different Levels." *American Archivist* 27 (1) (1964): 21–41. http://archivists.metapress.com/content/1721857117617w15/fulltext.pdf.

Muller, S., J. A. Feith, and R. Fruin. *Manual for the Arrangement and Description of Archives*. Chicago: Society of American Archivists, 2003.

Nesmith, Thomas. "Archival Studies in English-Speaking Canada and the North American Rediscovery of Provenance." In Thomas Nesmith, ed., *Canadian Archival Studies and the Rediscovery of Provenance*. Metuchen, NJ: Scarecrow Press, 1993, 1–28.

Posner, Ernst. "Some Aspects of Archival Development since the French Revolution." *American Archivist* 3 (3) (1940): 159–72. http://archivists.metapress.com/content/q64h3343h663402j/fulltext.pdf.

Schellenberg, Theodore R. *Modern Archives: Principles and Techniques*. Chicago: University of Chicago Press, 1956.

Scott, Peter J. "The Record Group Concept: A Case for Abandonment." *American Archivist* 29 (4) (1996): 493–504. http://archivists.metapress.com/content/y886054240174401/fulltext.pdf.

PRINCIPLE OF RESPECT FOR ORIGINAL ORDER

The publication in 1898 of the Dutch *Manual for the Arrangement and Description of Archives* (Muller, Feith, and Fruin 2003) established among Western *archivists* the idea that materials preserved in an *archives* should be kept in provenance-based groups representing a more or less "organically" cumulated *fonds* (or archive group or *record group*) and where possible should be preserved in "original order." The Dutch manual included but did not entirely replicate the insights of French theory (which considered original order as the "internal order" of a fonds) and German theory (where the concept revealed its origin in registry practice by its name: *registraturprinzip*). All of these concepts were developed primarily for government *records* at that time being brought fully under rational discipline by national archives. Since then the concepts have come to be applied broadly to all kinds of archival materials and have made their way into the terms of art of North American *archival practice*. According to Pearce-Moses in *A Glossary of Archival and Records Terminology* (www.archivists.org/glossary/index.asp), original order is defined as "the organization and sequence of records established by the creator of the records." In this definition the term "sequence" is key. Holmes and Schellenberg, for example, construct sequences by level from record group down to *file* unit and even *document* (Holmes 1964; Schellenberg 1961). Where record groups have been abjured in favor of *series*, the need to shelve physical records still forces sequence.

Original order, however, is ironically seldom easily achieved. Beginning with Muller, Feith, and Fruin, archival theorists have repeatedly asserted that lacking a perfect order from recordkeepers, archivists must take on the responsibility of restoring original order, following any perceptible filing practices and rationalizing any minor departures from it (See also Cook, "What Is Past Is Prologue," http://journals.sfu.ca/archivar/index.php/archivaria/article/view/12175/13184). Although Muller, Feith, and Fruin asserted repeatedly that any such changes must be a last resort and fully documented, in practice these warnings have frequently been ignored, thus erasing the actual dialogic use of ordering in practice by real records creators.

The Development of the Concept

The development of the concept of original order through its reception and application by leading archivists shows a variety of applications. In Muller, Feith, and Fruin (2003, chapter 2, "The Arrangement of Archival Documents"), the authors begin by laying down the principle: "16. The system of arrangement must be based on the original organization of the *archival collection*, which in the main corresponds to the organization of the administrative body that produced it"—they then immediately advise methods to use in clearing away prior arrangements of earlier archivists (52). Jenkinson, on the other hand, forbids any change in the order of documents as they arrived at the archives and required the preservation of old lists and any numeration on the documents themselves. He further advises the addition of an accession numeration of all documents in the order received, precisely to preserve that order in case any rearrangement might be found to have been mistaken. Jenkinson's detailed description of working with records in "order of arrival" suggests that elaborate notes were also accumulated during the remainder of the arrangement process. Finally, Jenkinson instructs his reader that the goal is to "establish or re-establish the original arrangement" (Jenkinson 2004, 66).

Less wedded to original order than his predecessors, Schellenberg keeps provenance sacrosanct but considers original order as variously applicable and completely disposable if it did not assist use (Schellenberg 1998). For Schellenberg, the order of series within a record group was simply a matter of usability and coherence, while the ordering of items within series might be preserved if it reflected administrative process, but he considered that standardized filing systems in government use generally provided no evidence of specific activity and could be freely rearranged for use (Schellenberg 1961). This break in concern for order at the lower levels of documentation marked not only a change in theoretical stance but also a change in the quantity and state of the records received.

Series of filed materials have thus come to be fitted into an archivally created structure deemed to represent in some sense the functional structure of the creating body at some ideal past time or historical present. Even here opinions have been varied on how materials should be restored to original order; in dealing with ancient records, at least, archivists all had idiosyncratic institutions to replicate—so the writing on this topic tends to be very much case-based. In modern practice it becomes clear that original order is primarily taken to refer to what Holmes considers the lower levels of arrangement: filing units in a series and documents within filing units. From *A Glossary of Archival and Records Terminology*:

> Original order is not the same as the order in which materials were received. Items that were clearly misfiled may be refiled in their proper location. Materials may have had their original order disturbed, often during inactive use, before transfer to the archives (see restoration of original order).

Archivists today rarely follow Jenkinson's advice in recording precisely what changes were made to which records in the reordering, since the overhead of the reordering is already burdensome. Hugh Taylor even observes, "For straightforward series it is a waste of time" (1980, 24). Most often, a series of standard practices is outlined in a processing manual, and reordering is silently carried out. It is therefore very difficult or impossible for the researcher to restore any archivally modified order and thereby to understand more about the work practices represented by it (MacNeil 2008). In the case of individuals' records, special collections archivists have frequently taken even more drastic measures, since such records often come to them upon the death of the creator. Records are overtly arranged for the convenience of the user and often according to local categories. In arriving at original order in normal processing practice, whether in the archival or *manuscript tradition*, it has also been customary to "weed" duplicates and other unwanted categories of materials while this arrangement is taking place, though Jenkinson far precedes current minimal processing ideals in pointing out how laborious and impractical this practice really is.

Thus in spite of the early complaints of misguided *archival arrangements*, archival practice has now been following for nearly a century handbooks in which logical tweaking or even replacement of original order is portrayed as permissible and even called for. We have already seen what Muller, Feith, and Fruin; Jenkinson; and Schellenberg have to say. Since 1977 the Society of American Archivists has been producing basic manuals of archival practice, and in spite of lip service to "original order," the practice of ignoring any "order as received" in order to create a "usable" order has been consistently advised. For Schellenberg, preserving filing errors, though it might be advisable in the case of the peccadilloes of the famous, would ordinarily be "obviously carrying logic too far" (Schellenberg 1956, 101).

Yet every archivist who has worked with a "disordered" body of records knows that it is nearly impossible for the "disorder" to extend to true randomness or complete chaos. Instead, there are likely to be many loci of order within such *archival fonds*. Further, if the creator was a messy filer, why should the archivist presume to turn him into a neat one? Textual editor Thomas Tanselle brought a needed correction to historical editing practice in the 1970s when he reminded people that correcting George Washington's spelling did nothing for the *authenticity* of a historical edition of his letters (MacNeil 2005). These archival "norms" are clearly the result of serving two masters—archival convenience and least-common-denominator user requirements—while ignoring the needs of two others: archival managers who want to cut down on processing costs and researchers who want to approach the records with as little intermediation as possible. MacNeil (2008) has pointed to multiple case studies in which historians and archivists alike have proved the historical worth of detective work to uncover the biography of the multiple orderings of a fonds, both while in use and while in the hands of different custodians.

Most bodies of documentary materials arrive at the archives in an order that may reflect any number of events that happened to the materials since they were created, and archivists have begun to consider capturing these states. Long before *digital records*, Peter Scott articulated the notion of "order as last found," since most records have usually undergone rearrangements in use, and the contemporary Australian *records continuum* approach does recognize the necessity to build the ability to record these complexities into digital *recordkeeping systems* (Smith 1986, 1987). Debra Barr goes further, calling for preserving strict original order in "accession units" of continuing series so as to signal piecemeal transfer of materials (Barr 1989). The preference of the minimal processing approach also favors acceptance of order(s) as accessioned with no more processing if at all possible (Greene and Meissner 2005).

Conclusion

Why is order so important an abstract aspect of archival work? Various commentators from Max Weber to Verne Harris have pointed out that the Enlightenment heritage of modern archival practice and its respect for abstract/logical order grew from reinforcing an idea of the stability of a system of statist discipline (the practices Muller, Feith, and Fruin were rationalizing were all about supporting such systems). In the programmatic literature of archival practice in government there has been little explicit consideration of the meaning that may be present in multiple orders, because the assignment of authority to high levels has erased the existence of low-level file handlers and their work practices, while the affordances of paper have hidden much filing system reorganization. From this perspective the interaction between filers and their filing and classification technologies and the resulting modification of these technologies over time were seen as disorder, to be expunged if possible to preserve stasis/stability.

The need for a single order also assumes physical custody of paper records. The necessity of handling large quantities of paper to find a misplaced item has made paper records less manageable than digital records may potentially be. With digital *recordkeeping*, efforts have been made to construct systems so that order as created might be permanently preserved, yet this very characteristic has made it impossible to dictate orderly recordkeeping without constant surveillance and training. At the same time, archival research with digital records has shown that it is possible and desirable to take advantage of affordances of digital systems to create and preserve the multiple orders about which archivists as early as Jenkinson have dreamed, thereby capturing a fonds' historical ordering from creation through its entire existence.—*Pat Galloway*

Keywords: order, arrangement, recordkeeping
Related Entries: Archival Arrangement; Archives (Material); Principle of Provenance; Principle of *Respect des Fonds*; Principle of Respect for Original Order; Record Group; Records Continuum

Bibliography

Barr, Debra. "Protecting Provenance: Response to the Working Group on Description at the Fonds Level." *Archivaria* 1 (28) (1989): 141–45. http://journals.sfu.ca/archivar/index.php/archivaria/article/view/11575/12521.

Greene, Mark, and Dennis Meissner. "More Product, Less Process: Revamping Traditional Archival Processing." *American Archivist* 68 (2) (2005): 208–63. http://archivists.metapress.com/content/c741823776k65863/fulltext.pdf.

Holmes, Oliver W. "Archival Arrangement—Five Different Operations at Five Different Levels." *American Archivist* 27 (1) (1964): 21–41. http://archivists.metapress.com/content/l721857l17617w15/fulltext.pdf.

Jenkinson, Hilary. *A Manual of Archive Administration Including the Problems of War Archives and Archive Making.* London, 2004 [1937].

MacNeil, Heather. "Archivalterity: Rethinking Original Order." *Archivaria* 1 (66) (2008): 1–24. http://journals.sfu.ca/archivar/index.php/archivaria/article/view/13190/14459.

———. "Picking Our Text: Archival Description, Authenticity, and the Archivist as Editor." *American Archivist* 68 (2) (2005): 264–78. http://archivists.metapress.com/content/01u65t6435700337/fulltext.pdf.

Muller, S., J. A. Feith, and R. Fruin. *Manual for the Arrangement and Description of Archives*, 2nd edition. Translated by Arthur H. Leavitt. Chicago: Society of American Archivists, 2003 [1940].

Schellenberg, T. R. "Archival Principles of Arrangement." *American Archivist* 24 (1) (1961): 11–24. http://archivists.metapress.com/content/l330351406231083/fulltext.pdf.

———. *Modern Archives: Principles and Techniques*. Chicago: Society of American Archivists, 1998 [1956].

Smith, Colin. "A Case for Abandonment of 'Respect.'" *Archives and Manuscripts* 14 (2) (1986): 154–68.

———. "A Case for Abandonment of 'Respect,' Part II." *Archives and Manuscripts* 15 (1) (1987): 20–28.

Taylor, Hugh. *The Arrangement and Description of Archival Records*. Munich: K.G. Saur, 1980.

PRIVATE ARCHIVES

In their most elemental form, private archives are noncurrent *records* created and maintained in non-public settings. Within this broad definition, the phrase private archives can take a variety of meanings, depending on the context.

Discussion

Private organizations, such as corporations; colleges, universities, and private secondary schools; religious groups and congregations; nonprofit service organizations; labor unions; political *advocacy* groups; cultural groups; and many others maintain noncurrent records of their activities. Some of these organizations manage sophisticated and robust *archival programs* with the primary goal of contributing to the broader mission of their parent organization. These *archives* serve their internal audiences first and foremost and therefore *access* to records can be carefully guarded. Corporate archives, for instance, can hold trade secrets, whose release would have a detrimental impact on the economic health of the company. Archives of religious organizations and cultural groups can hold records sacred to their members and adherents, with strict prohibitions on *access* by outsiders. Not subject to public records laws that govern access to archives in the public sector, private archives self-determine their access policies.

Some other types of institutions, as well as families and individuals, create and preserve (whether consciously or not) archival records outside of a formal archival structure. Private archives can also refer to such records. Recognizing the archival value and/or historical significance of their records but without the resources or mandate to preserve and facilitate access to them, private organizations, families, and individuals commonly donate or occasionally sell their records to an archival repository in an academic or public history setting. Private entities transfer their archives to such repositories so that they can be properly preserved, arranged, described, and used in order to promote historical and cultural understanding. Examples of this phenomenon range from major corporate archives such as the Hudson Bay Trading Company records held by the Provincial Archives of Manitoba to the records of a local environmental group donated to the archives and library of a university or historical society.

Yet another meaning of private archives is of private repositories that, rather than preserving their own records, instead acquire and preserve the archives of private organizations, businesses, families, and individuals. Such *acquisition* is, or at least should be, guided by an *acquisition policy*, such that the overall collections of such a private repository are connected to one or more clear themes or topics. These private archives can set their own policies regarding access to the holdings they acquire. Such policies can require researchers to have exclusive membership in the repository's parent institution or, to the contrary, the repository may allow unfettered access to all researchers.

Finally, private archives can refer to the papers or records of families and individuals that hold enduring historical value, whether or not the papers or records ever will be held and managed within a formal archival structure. In some nations such collections, managed archivally or not, are considered part of the country's cultural patrimony, and they cannot be donated or sold to a collector or repository (private or public) outside the nation (e.g., under the Open General Export License [Objects of Cultural Interest] dated May 1, 2004, issued by the Secretary of State of Great Britain).

As a phrase, private archives is more commonly employed in countries and archival communities whose practice and discourse have primarily a public records bent, including Europe and Australia. It is used less frequently by *archivists* working in North America.

Conclusion

Using any definition, private archives contribute to the archival endeavor by acquiring, preserving, and maintaining records with archival value. In many cases, private archives later become public, or at least more broadly accessible, allowing subsequent generations to understand and learn from past actions and events.—*Tom Hyry*

Keywords: corporate archives, private repositories, historical records
Related Entries: Archival Collection; Archives and Memory; Participatory Archives

PROTOCOL REGISTER

From the very beginning of writing, humankind has attempted to keep track of the *documents* made and received both from a legal and a management point of view. Throughout the Middle Ages and up to the Modern Age, the registration of documents was performed in an integral or "extended" way. In other words, either the entire content or an excerpt of the most significant portions was transcribed in one or more books, called a register. These transcripts served to verify *authenticity* as their duplicate content was held in the *archives* of the relevant authority.

During the Napoleonic period, due to the increasing documentary production, it was decided to substitute the integral or extended transcription of the documents with a "synthetic transcription" of the main identifying information. The data recorded in the register, usually, related to both the content and the *context* of the *record*. This information was taken from the initial part of the document, called protocol (from the Greek *proto-* [first] and *kolon* [part]). The protocol register (in Germany *registratur*, in France *registre*, in Italy *protocollo* or *registratura corrente*, in Spain *registro*, in Portugal *cota*) was introduced toward the end of the eighteenth century, first in Austria, France, and Germany, and from these countries into Italy and beyond. In the early years of the nineteenth century, especially between 1803 and 1820, several European governments and their courts of control formalized, through regulations and procedures, the use of the protocol register, asking for increasing attention to the compilation of the data elements and introducing, at the same time, embryonic business *records management* through filing plans and classification systems, usually organized either by *function* or by structure.

Throughout the nineteenth and until the end of the twentieth century, the protocol was a paper register held by a dedicated public office. The register was divided into two parts: the page on the left contained information pertaining to incoming documents and that on the right contained information related to sent documents.

With the advent of new technologies, especially at the turn of the twenty-first century, many countries have established that the protocol register must be maintained digitally. In Italy, for example, the Decree of the President of the Republic October 20, 1998, no. 428, ordered its compulsory use for all public authorities since January 1, 2004. In Spain, the law of June 22, 2007, no. 11, which regulates the right of citizens to use digital technologies for government services, required a digital protocol register for all administrations.

The Concept

The protocol register is a tool for the legal and procedural control of current archives. It has two main functions:

1. a notarial function, as it certifies the effectiveness of administrative action;
2. a management function, which pertains to *recordkeeping*.

From the notarial function point of view, the protocol register has the nature of a public record of absolute trustworthiness and is the main instrument of transparency in administrative action. As it regards the second function, recordkeeping, the register is the most important management tool that is contemporary to the records themselves. From both viewpoints, the fundamental (constitutive) parts of the protocol register can be divided into three categories, as follows:

1. elements of serving evidence and *reliability*
2. elements serving records management
3. elements serving business, activities, procedures, and processes

Elements Serving Evidence and Reliability

Today, as in previous times, both in traditional and digital environments, the protocol register records two types of information which are critical for its effectiveness as a source of evidence, reliability, and enforceability against third parties: the exact date and provenance of the record. This information as included in the register is guaranteed reliable by the trusted third party who records it as part of its notarial function of public officer: the *archivist/ records manager*.

There are six data elements of evidentiary relevance that must be recorded:

1. protocol number (i.e., the consecutive number of the registration);
2. date of registration;
3. name of sender for incoming records and of the addressee for outgoing records;
4. subject matter or action;
5. number of attachments, if applicable; and
6. description of the attachments, if applicable.

Registration Number and Date of Registration

The transition from a paper to a digital register has expanded the forms of protection with respect to the register itself and the records manager to serve administrative transparency. In the paper environment it was possible to illegally alter registration numbers or date of registration. In the digital environment, since the control on the number and date of registration is independent of human intervention, illegal recording of additional numbers or the establishment of a different sequence is practically impossible.

Similarly, since the date is linked to the Coordinated Universal Time (UTC), in digital the environment is no longer possible to include a date different from that of the actual recording. The digital protocol register also helps to avoid an old, not so uncommon, bad practice, called "to jump" protocol, which consisted of leaving blank numbers or even blank pages in the register, waiting for a possible later recording.

Persons

All the names of the key *persons*, namely the sender(s) for incoming records and the addressee(s) for sent records and for records transmitted to offices belonging to the same administration (the so-called "internal protocol") must be stored in a database. The database must allow for the efficient identification of the persons, who are divided into physical persons (individuals with last name and first name) and juridical persons (entities, business name, etc.). These data must be entered by following a defined standard.

Standardization plays an important role in defining the set of rules for data entry and preventing the proliferation of incorrect personal data. The names of persons are stored in a database that is not dynamically connected to the records, in order to make it impossible to make changes to the registered records. Thus, the old versions of the persons log will be found in the protocol registrations, and this makes it unnecessary to maintain an authority file of them. The archivist/records manager is also responsible for eliminating background noise caused by an uncontrolled overgrowth of persons' names and their variations.

Subject Matter or Action

The subject matter or action is the main searchable structured field and, therefore, must be recorded carefully and consistently to ensure the effectiveness of information retrieval.

It is necessary to find the right balance between two conflicting requirements: synthesis and need for details. This is important for providing in an accurate and unambiguous way all the information required by all possible interested parties by simply reading the summary of what the record is about.

Thus, the subject must be conceived as a kind of abstract, that is, a synthesis in which the legally relevant elements of the record are highlighted, so that expected and potential users will be able to retrieve a specific record. It is important to record some keywords in the record and order them in the abstract with the greatest precision possible.

The archivist/records manager has the intellectual responsibility for the abstract, also in terms of linguistic suitability. The abstract must not be a mere transcription of the subject of the incoming document, but a conceptual elaboration in a concise way. This requires knowledge of the needs of the users, standardization of language for the same types of records, and explicit identification of relevant data, thereby avoiding the so-called "dumb referrals" to previous recordings.

These abstracts are used by governing and management bodies to understand, day after day, the progress of legal, business, or administrative processes or to keep their data current. Thus, from a management point of view, the most important function of the protocol register is to support, by providing legal evidence, the decision-making processes.

Finally, these abstracts are essential to reconstruct the content of records that have been destroyed, are unavailable, or have been otherwise disposed of. The retention and disposal schedules, in fact, provide for the permanent retention of all protocol registers.

Number and Description of Attachments

If a record has one or more attachments, it is very likely that the main information meant to be conveyed is included in them. The number and description of the attachments are therefore essential to the effectiveness of the registration.

Indeed, very often the administrative interest and, consequently, the legal relevance of records as evidence is provided by attachments (e.g., a contract, a regulation, it must supply a note) and not by the record transmitting them, which acts mostly as cover letter.

If there are no attachments to a record, it is important to enter the value 0 (zero). In this way, we note the absence of attachments is audited and certified by the archivist/records manager.

Elements Serving Records Management and Archival Functions

The elements serving records management and archival functions are, typically, the following: dates of receipt and transmission, time of registration, details on the postponement of the registration (so-called "delayed protocol"), type of delivery, relationship with previous and subsequent records, indication of attachments in electronic form, name of the copied persons (other recipients), subject of the administrative procedure, deadline for completing the administrative procedure, status and timeline of partial procedures of the administrative activity, type of administrative record, indication of type of *access* or deferred access, and computer image of the document.

As far as the recordkeeping/archival system is concerned, the required elements to be included in the protocol are: the classification of the record using the classification schema of the organization; statement date for the *file*, file number, number of the subfile; number of inserts, closing date of the file; customized code for recognizing the matter and/or the record; type of record with indication of the terms for preservation and disposal; and deadlines schedule.

Elements Related to Business Activities and Processes

The elements related to business activities and processes are usually the following: further information on the persons (full legal name, male/female, etc.), full address (street, number, zip code, city, county, state), registration number (if employee or student), tax code and VAT, telephone number, fax address, email address, and public key of digital signature.

In terms of administrative responsibilities, the most important elements are the identification of the office responsible for handling the matter and the name of the office of primary responsibility for maintaining the records and the file until the transfer into the *recordkeeping system*/archives.

Conclusion

In an effective records system, the length of preservation of files is identified at the time of registration of the records in the protocol register. The *selection* of records for permanent preservation, therefore, starts with the registration process, due to the function of neutral third party fulfilled by the archivist/records manager who carries out the registration in the protocol register. This is the reason why, in the countries using it, the protocol register is at the core of every *archival fonds* and guarantees the reliability, accuracy, and authenticity of all the records and record aggregations contained in it.—*Gianni Penzo Doria*

Keywords: current archives, current records, register, registry, records management

Related Entries: Person; Recordkeeping; Records Management; Registry System

Bibliography

Brenneke, Adolf. *Archivkunde: Ein Beitrag zur Theorie und Geschichte des europaischen Archivwesens*. Leipzig, 1953.

Doria, Gianni Penzo. "Profili archivistici del protocollo informatico." *Archivi & Computer* 15 (1) (2005): 91–109.

Lodolini, Elio. *Archivistica. Principi e problem*. Milano: Franco Angeli, 2012.

PUBLIC RECORDS TRADITION

In the United States, the public records tradition refers to a system for physical and intellectual control of *records* that is based on European principles of provenance, respect for original order, and hierarchical control of aggregates of *records*. Although these principles are taken for granted today, they were not part of the *manuscripts tradition*, an approach used by many *archivists* throughout much of the twentieth century. The public records tradition grew out of efforts to ensure that government records were preserved for historical research. Although originally focused on government records, the public records tradition has largely replaced the manuscripts tradition in contemporary *archival practice*.

The Concept

In the nineteenth century, Alexander de Tocqueville commented on the state of *records* in the new na-

tion: "No methodical system is pursued; no *archives* are formed; and no *documents* are brought together when it would be easy to do so. Where they exist, little store is set upon them" (1839, I 207). Writing about the history of public records in Indiana, although typical of other states as well, Christopher Coleman observed, "Various officers of the state at different times showed little appreciation of the importance of preserving public documents and little discrimination in their care" (1938, 201).

Fearing a loss of records and the information they contained, many historical societies and individuals built collections that included the personal papers of "great Americans" as well as public records (Berner 1983, 11). Most repositories arranged the records chronologically under a few broad geographic or topical headings, although literary papers were sometimes organized alphabetically by writer. This approach, based on library principles and commonly called the manuscripts tradition, is generally credited to Joseph B. Felt's work at the Massachusetts Historical Society starting in 1835. It continued to be used well into the twentieth century.

In 1899, the American Historical Association created the Public Archives Commission "to investigate and report on the character of the historical public archives in each state" (Berner 1983, 13). The commission focused on surveys of state archives, publishing reports to make the records accessible. The commission also sought to preserve the records by advocating that each state centralize its records in an archives (Birdsall 1973).

A second objective of the commission was "the unification and improvement . . . of methods of . . . arranging and preserving official documentary material" (Evans 1966, 4). Several members of the commission sought to introduce European archival principles. At the first Conference of Archivists in 1909, Waldo Gifford Leland promoted the use of European principles based on the Dutch manual. "Nothing is more disastrous than the application of modern library methods of classification to a body of archives" (Leland 1909). At the Fourth Annual Conference in 1912, he argued that American archivists had to abandon the "opinion that seems to be entertained, to the effect that American conditions differ so fundamentally from conditions in Europe that the results of European experience can have but a limited application with us. A careful examination of the differences, however, makes it clear that they are superficial and not fundamental" (Leland 1912, 89).

In addition to introducing new principles, the conferences set the stage for the rise of a new profession of archivists. The conferences, which William Birdsall (1973, 173) described as "little more than a study group," set the stage for the formation of the Society of American Archivists in 1936. The chance for individuals whose primary concern was the administration of *archival collections*, rather than historical research based on those collections, to meet together gave them the opportunity to discover a nascent professional identity. The society provided a forum for the evolution of ideas resulting in a consensual agreement of professional practice.

Through the conferences, and later the society's meeting and papers, archivists began to move away from preserving records for their historical value to their preservation for legal and administrative value. Margaret Cross Norton (1930, 4) argued that, rather than being servants to historians, "the real function of an archivist, however, is that of custodian of legal records of the state, the destruction of which might seriously inconvenience the administration of state business." Christopher Crittenden (1949, 4) observed, "When attention had been given to the subject, the idea for the most part was one involving repositories of rare and valuable historical manuscripts, something in the nature of treasure houses for the historian and the antiquarian rather than agencies which would serve a broad public need. There was no full comprehension of the problems involved, especially that of dealing with vast quantities of records, running into millions of cubic feet." The archives was no longer exclusively for historical research, but "an agency of the government whose primary function was to perform certain official duties" (Crittenden 1949, 5).

Conclusion

The manuscripts and public records traditions coexisted throughout much of the twentieth century as the profession matured. Many saw a clear distinction between the two types of records, not least the authors of the Dutch manual (Mueller, Freith, and Fruin 1905) and Hilary Jenkinson (1922). Others saw similarity and, continuing Leland's calls begun

in 1909, argued that for some organic manuscripts, their organic, archival nature was "their most important attribute" (Cappon 1956, 110). T. R. Schellenberg asserted that "the principles and techniques now applied to public records may be applied also, with some modification, to private, records, especially to private manuscript material of recent origin, much of which has the organic character of archival material" (1965, xxix). By the 1960s, the nature of acquiring *personal records* had changed, focusing more on large, contemporary collections rather than on select, older items (Berner 1983, 1). As a result, manuscript archivists began adapting principles from the public records tradition.

—*Richard Pearce-Moses*

Keywords: public records, arrangement and description, archival profession in the United States, Society of American Archivists

Related Entries: Archival Arrangement; Archival Associations; Archival Method; Archival Practice; Archives (Institution); Manuscripts Tradition; Principle of *Respect des Fonds*; Record(s)

Bibliography

Berner, Richard C. *Archival Theory and Practice in the United States: A Historical Analysis.* Seattle: University of Washington Press, 1983.

Birdsall, William Forest. *The American Archivists' Search for Professional Identity.* Ann Arbor, MI: University Microfilms International, 1973.

Cappon, Lester J. "Historical Manuscripts as Archives: Some Definitions and Their Application." *American Archivist* 19 (2) (1956): 101–10. http://archivists.metapress.com/content/4402r63w3t257gv8/fulltext.pdf.

Coleman, Christopher B. "Indiana Archives." *American Archivist* 1 (4) (1938): 201. http://archivists.metapress.com/content/g163457n140n2673/fulltext.pdf.

Crittenden, Christopher. "The Archivist as Public Servant." *American Archivist* 12 (1) (1949): 3–8. http://archivists.metapress.com/content/g163457n140n2673/fulltext.pdf.

De Tocqueville, Alexis. *Democracy in America.* Translated by Henry Reeve. Original preface and notes by John C. Spencer, 3rd American edition. New York: George Adlard, 1839.

Evans, Frank B. "Modern Methods of Arrangement of Archives in the United States." *American Archivist* 29 (2) (1966): 241–63. http://archivists. metapress.com/content/7j27l2p346860442/full-text.pdf.

Leland, Waldo G. "American Archival Problems." Presented at the First Conference of Archivists, 1909. Reprinted in Peter J. Wosh, ed. *Waldo Gifford Leland and the Origins of the American Archival Profession.* Chicago: Society of American Archivists, 2011.

———. "Some Fundamental Principles in Relation to Archives." Presented at the Fourth Annual Conference of Archivists, 1912. Reprinted in Peter J. Wosh, ed. *Waldo Gifford Leland and the Origins of the American Archival Profession.* Chicago: Society of American Archivists, 2011.

Norton, Margaret Cross. "The Archives Department as an Administrative Unit of Governments." National Association of State Libraries, *Papers and Proceedings, Thirty-Third Annual Convention.* Los Angeles, CA, June 23–27, 1930.

Norton, Margaret Cross, Thorton W. Mitchell, Ernst Posner, and Randall C. Jimerson. *Norton on Archives: The Writings of Margaret Cross Norton.* Chicago: Society of American Archivists, 2003.

Schellenberg, T. R. *The Management of Archives.* Washington, DC: National Archives, 1988 [1965].

PUBLIC SERVICE

Public service is an overarching term encompassing two interrelated archival *functions* concerned with accessibility of, and communication about, *archives*: (1) the provision of archival reference services, and (2) archival *outreach* and public programming. Public *access* to archival material is of eighteenth-century origin. While this area of archival activity has received relatively little attention in archival literature, interest in it has increased in recent years. Nowadays, the delivery of archival public services is viewed as a critical archival function, with new forms of digital media technology (e.g., social media and mobile platforms) transforming community engagement with archives.

What Is Archival Public Service?

It is necessary to turn to definitions of archival reference service and archival outreach and public programming in order to understand archival public service. The Society of American Archivists' (SAA) glossary defines reference service as "a service to aid patrons in locating materials relevant to their interest" (Pearce-Moses 2005). Mary-Jo Pugh adds that "reference services, broadly conceived, are the activities by which *archivists* bring users and *records* together to meet user needs . . . they encompass a wide variety of activities and call upon intellectual, administrative and interpersonal skills" (2005, 24). Pugh goes on to suggest that reference services provide: information about the repository; information about the holdings; information from the holdings; information about the records creators; referrals to other repositories and resources; information about laws and ethics regarding the use of information; instruction on the use of records; education about the research process; and physical access to holdings (2005, 23). Wendy Duff, in an essay on archival mediation, takes a more limited view of archival reference services, focusing on services that provide information about the repository, holdings, and records creators, as well as information *from* the holdings, and one-on-one instruction on the use of archives and archival material, which she characterizes as the responsive approach to promoting and facilitating use of records (2010, 116–17). J. E. Cross describes the reference process as proceeding "through the stages of registration, identification, orientation, the initial reference interview, continuing interaction during the user's research, and then finally the exit interview" (1997, 7).

The related area of archival outreach, according to J. E. Cross, "is closely linked to reference because it is seen as a way of meeting user needs that cannot be satisfied effectively by one-on-one interaction at the reference desk. It can also be used to encourage use and promote the archival mission. A strong element of user education . . . is often found in such programs" (1997, 10). Ann Pederson writes of educational programming as "a planned sequence of projects and activities which inform the wider community about [archival] holdings and services and involve its members directly with their documentary heritage" (1993, 306). The SAA glossary describes outreach as "the process of identifying and providing services to constituencies with needs relevant to the repository's mission, especially underserved groups, and tailoring services to meet those needs," including such services as exhibits, workshops, publications, and educational programs (Pearce-Moses 2005). Duff generally characterizes these activities as falling under the proactive approach to promoting and facilitating use of archival records (2010, 116).

Evolution of Archival Public Service

The notion of archival public service can be said to have taken root with the French decree of July 25, 1794, when the *documents* of defunct administrative bodies held in the National Archives of France were declared the patrimony of the nation and made accessible to the public (Posner 1940). Prior to that time, access and use of archives were the exclusive purview of sovereigns or rulers and their servants (Posner 1940).

Archives were open to the public following the French decree, though access was still quite limited in reality. During the Enlightenment, access and use of archives was the almost exclusive purview of historical scholars, and archives evolved to become repositories of historical sources (Posner 1940). The twentieth century saw users of archives expand from traditional scholar-historians to include amateur local historians, university students, genealogists, school children, and members of the general public. As a result, archivists needed to know more about the information-seeking behavior of diverse users of archives, resulting in publication of many user studies on historians, genealogists, and other users of archives (Duff 2010). During the last half of the twentieth century, freedom-of-information laws provided broader access to records in some public repositories as well. Simultaneously, North American society, aiming to reduce prejudice based on race, class, education, gender, sexual orientation, and ability, further opened access to its cultural institutions. Demand for access to archives from a wider range of users coupled with the rise of an archival profession distinct from that of the profes-

sional historian provided the conditions for the role of the specialist reference archivist to emerge. Concomitant with this development was the emergence of a body of archival literature concerned with the knowledge and skills of the reference archivist (Duff 2010). Most notably, Elizabeth Yakel and Deborah Torres (2003) proposed the notion of archival intelligence as being an important factor in the successful provision of reference services.

More recently, the tide of access and use within public archives has begun to turn away from increasing openness amid concerns about the protection of personal privacy that have seen the introduction of laws that restrict access to some archival documents. Today, most public archival institutions still serve a wide variety of publics, however, providing open access subject to the limitations of privacy laws, copyright, and/or other legal and donor-specified restrictions. *Private archives* (i.e., those not established by the state and/or publicly funded), on the other hand, still very much operate to serve their sponsoring organizations, which may or may not permit access and use by scholars or other members of the public.

Discourse on the Role of Archival Public Service

One of the persistent themes in the archival literature related to archival public service concerns its priority in relation to other archival functions. Perspectives on the importance of archival public service as an archival function vary, from those that place relatively little importance on it to those that see it as of the utmost importance. Reflective of a more traditional, pre-public archives view, Sir Hilary Jenkinson has written that "in the first place [the archivist] has to take all possible precautions for the safeguarding of his Archives and for their custody, which is the safeguarding of their essential qualities. *Subject to the discharge of these duties* he has in the second place to provide to the best of his ability for the needs of historians and other research workers. But *the position of primary and secondary must not be reversed*" (1965, 19, italics added). Theodore Schellenberg, on the other hand, has written, "The end of all archival effort is to preserve valuable records and make them available for use"

(1965, 224). In more recent times, Ann Pederson has suggested that "all of us who keep archives and other historical material have two equally important responsibilities. The first is to identify, acquire and preserve records of lasting value. The second is to make these materials available for use" (1993, 306). J. E. Cross summed it up well in saying that "finally the archivist must balance access and use with the need to protect the integrity of the holdings" (1997, 10). According to Pugh, "The archival profession has moved from a custodial role, in which the archivist's primary duty was to protect repository collections by limiting use, to a more activist role promoting the wider use of archives" (2005, 21). Critical perspectives on archival public service have led to greater self-awareness among archivists of the extent to which they mediate between the user and the historical record and to calls for greater transparency and openness (Cross 1997, 6; Schwartz and Cook 2002). Archivists continue to hold varying views on the role of archival public service, including what constitutes the correct balance between preservation and access, passive and proactive public service, and mediation and direct access (see Duff 2010).

Archival Public Service in a Digital World

Increasing societal use of digital media technology is transforming archival public service, providing the means for unprecedented access to the holdings of archives and reshaping traditional archival reference and outreach practices. *Digitization*, for example, allows greater access to archival materials while at the same time raising questions about the way in which it alters the interpretations and meanings of archives (Conway 2010). The rise of so-called Web 2.0 technologies has produced the first experiments in making archival material accessible online and incorporating user-provided content into *archival description* to enhance, or—intersecting with critical archival discourse—even supplant, traditional archival mediation. The capabilities of digital media technologies have encouraged archivists to consider more deeply how *digital archives* may promote community engagement and create cultural awareness and collective collaboration. Contemporary digital media practices associated with visualization, mobile media, online storytelling, gaming, open

data, and performance represent emerging themes in the literature related to archival public service (see, e.g., Theimer 2011).

Conclusion

Archival public service operates as an amalgam of the provision of reference services and the offering of outreach activities and public programs that promote understanding and use of archives. It is increasingly recognized as a core archival function, though debates continue as to the extent to which archivists should prioritize the provision of public services over other archival activities and how archivists might best balance preservation of the integrity of archives with access and use. In recent times, the affordances of digital media technologies and digital strategies for providing access to archival materials have transformed how public service is conceived of and carried out, opening up debates about the archivist's role as mediator and activist that are reshaping traditional archival functions and, arguably, the role of the archives in society.—*Victoria L. Lemieux*

Keywords: archival reference, outreach, public programming, reference service

Related Entries: Access/Accessibility; Advocacy; Archival Ethics; Archival History; Community Archives; Digitization

Bibliography

Conway, P. "Modes of Seeing: Digitized Photographic Archives and the Experienced User." *American Archivist* 73 (2) (2010): 425–62. http://archivists.metapress.com/content/mp275470663n5907/fulltext.pdf.

Cross, J. E. "Archival Reference: State of the Art." *The Reference Librarian* 26 (56) (1997): 5–25. DOI:10.1300/J120v26n56_02.

Duff, W. "Archival Mediation." In T. Eastwood and H. MacNeil, eds., *Currents of Archival Thinking*. Santa Barbara, CA: ABC-CLIO, 2010, 117–36.

Jenkinson, H. *A Manual of Archival Administration*. London: P. Lund, Humphries, 1965.

Pearce-Moses, Richard. *Glossary of Archival and Records Terminology*. Chicago: Society of American Archivists, 2005. www2.archivists.org/glossary (accessed November 25, 2013).

Pederson, A. "User Education and Public Relations." In Judith Ellis, ed., *Keeping Archives*, 2nd edition. Melbourne, Australia: Australian Society of Archivists, 1993.

Posner, Ernst. "Some Aspects of Archival Development since the French Revolution." *American Archivist* 3 (3) (1940): 159–72. http://archivists.metapress.com/content/q64h3343h663402j/fulltext.pdf.

Pugh, M. J. *Providing Reference Services for Archives and Manuscripts*. Chicago: Society of American Archivists, 2005.

Schellenberg, T. R. *Modern Archives: Principles and Techniques*. Chicago: University of Chicago Press, 1965.

Schwartz, Joan M., and Terry Cook. "Archives, Records, and Power: The Making of Modern Memory." *Archival Science* 2 (3–4) (2002): 1–19. DOI 10.1007/BF02435628.

Theimer, K. "What Is the Meaning of Archives 2.0?" *American Archivist* 74 (1) (2011): 58–68. http://archivists.metapress.com/content/h7tn4m4027407666/fulltext.pdf.

Yakel, E., and D. Torres. "AI: Archival Intelligence and User Expertise." *American Archivist* 66 (1) (2003): 51–78. http://archivists.metapress.com/content/q022h85pn51n5800/fulltext.pdf.

R

RECORD CREATION

Record creation is the first activity that formally captures decisions made by individuals who undertake transactions and make decisions as part of the day-to-day business for which they are responsible and accountable, in both the *record life cycle* and *continuum* models.

Record creation looks at what record creation is, what triggers and influences decisions around record creation, who creates *records*, and when record creation happens. It also considers the *context* of creation, how it is influenced, and in what form creation happens. Specific organizational scenarios for record creation cannot all be described in detail; however, supporting references from projects and research studies are provided.

What Is Record Creation?

Creation implies the start of something, although it does not mean that it is an act in isolation. In fact, creation of a record, from both an archival and recordkeeping perspective, is the result of business activities and processes undertaken by individuals and organizations as part of day-to-day business operations. The term creation as it applies to records requires an understanding of the who, what, when, where, why, and how record creation takes place because record creation does not just "happen." Record creation is dependent on, interacts with, and also impacts other recordkeeping actions including capture, manage, use, preserve, and dispose.

Record creation is the formation of the record as part of the first phase/dimension of the *record* life-cycle/continuum models, in which a record is created/made or received to document actions taken and decisions made in the transaction and as evidence of an organization's business *functions* and activities.

Record creation involves people, policies and procedures, processes, and technology and is the result of an activity with which the record is associated. Record creation captures details about the activity that created it, decisions made to support that activity, the business process, record composition standards (e.g., completing forms, following formats for writing project reports, capturing minutes of meetings) surrounding it, and the individual/organization involved. The creation of the record results in evidence of the business transaction and related decisions made to support it.

Record creation activities and requirements are documented in the policies and procedures supporting the business function and the *recordkeeping system*. The policies and procedures address record creation requirements and define roles and responsibilities to ensure the records are created, methods of creating (record composition) and capturing records, the required forms and formats for record creation, and associated methods of applying classification schemes, retention period, *metadata*, and taxonomies to ensure preservation, ongoing use, and availability of the record to meet immediate and future needs.

Defining the Need for Record Creation

Each organization is governed by legal, regulatory, and business needs that require it to create records to document its activities as evidence of transactions and decisions made every day. For example, a yogurt manufacturer is required to create records about its manufacturing plant operations and its quality-control practices to meet Food and Drug Administration requirements; an elevator company must create and keep records about its elevator manufacture and installation to meet safety and quality-control requirements; a pharmaceutical business creates records to document its research about drug development and clinical trials in accordance with Food and Drug Administration regulations.

The need to create records is based on organizational mandates, business drivers, and operational strategies. An organization introduces new business activities to support its strategy. A project team (which should include those involved in recordkeeping) determines what the business activities will involve. The steps in a business activity will define who (record *creator*) is involved in what activity, which transactions must be documented, what records are to be designed and created as part of the process, and when, where, and how they are to be created. Roles and responsibilities are documented, as are the record composition needs. Specific forms are designed, metadata and attributes are assigned to the forms and where technology is used to create an online record, and technological considerations are included to ensure that records are authentic, reliable, and have integrity.

The following example shows how decisions about record creation are made.

Each year, XYZ holds its annual meeting, attended by staff, members of the senior executive, key stakeholders, and the public. Policies and procedures govern how the annual meeting is staged and hosted. Before the meeting takes place, meeting rooms are booked, hotel and transportation arrangements are made for board members and senior management, and agendas and related reports are created and sent to interested parties. Resolutions are presented and voted on, and minutes document decisions made at the meeting.

Each of the activities associated with the annual meeting involves individuals or groups who, as part of their activity, create records of the transactions they undertake. The secretary, who books meeting rooms and makes hotel booking and travel arrangements, creates records that confirm those arrangements, such as meeting room and hotel confirmations and flight reservations. Individuals and departments create reports and resolutions that form part of the agenda. The meeting secretary creates an agenda, based on received reports and resolutions. At the meeting, as resolutions and reports are presented, a record of votes is created. Throughout the meeting, the meeting secretary takes notes of the discussions, decisions made, and final outcomes. Following the meeting, the notes are summarized and the minutes of the annual meeting are created.

Each individual within this scenario has a role to play and defined responsibilities, which include creating records at specific points to document the activity and related decisions.

Who Creates Records?

The record creation process involves record creators who generate records as outputs from their business activities to document actions (minutes of meetings, reports) and ensure that actions take place (e.g., through letters/contracts). It also involves stakeholders such as *records managers* and *archivists*, who provide oversight in the design and implementation of record creation policies, procedures, and standards. The record creation process may involve:

- individuals who create *personal records* such as income tax returns, wills, personal photographs;
- individual employees and/or collaborative teams who create records as evidence of their daily work activities in an organization;
- managers at all levels who ensure that record creation policies and procedures are followed and implemented; and
- *information management* professionals (including archivists and record managers) who develop such tools as classification schemes and retention schedules, forms/templates, and document composition formats to support record creation, based on the business activity supported.

Organizations require an accurate, reliable, and authentic record to carry out their business, fulfill legal functions, understand previous activities, ensure continuity, and ensure that record creation policies and procedures are in place and adhered to as part of an organization-wide recordkeeping system.

Determining Why Record Creation Happens and When

The record creation process happens every day as individuals and organizations carry out their business activities to meet the defined mission and strategic direction of the organization. The need to create a record is determined by the business and takes into consideration the cost of creating a record against the risk of not creating a record.

Record creation ensures that the organization/individuals support business transactions and document decisions made in completing the business transactions to:

- address external legal, regulatory, compliance, risk and financial requirements;
- capture details about a business function and its related activities as proof and evidence of decisions made and actions taken by the record creator;
- document and protect the rights and obligations of organizations, stakeholders, and individuals; and
- ensure *accountability* to the public in the case of government organizations.

In analyzing business transactions, consideration is given to such things as: Does a record of the transaction need to be created? What is the risk of not creating a record? How will record creation happen? Who will be involved in record creation?

When record creation happens is dependent on the process that supports the business activity and the point at which decisions are reached, contracts are agreed to, policy documents are signed off, and minutes of meetings are approved. In other words, a record is created at the point in time when transactions are completed, documents are considered final, and decisions have been made. One requirement, from a legal perspective, is that the record creation process must happen close to or at the same time (contemporaneously) as the business transaction takes place.

Record Creation and Technology

In the twenty-first century workplace, the majority of record creation activities take place in various hardware and software environments, thereby creating *digital records*. The purpose for record creation and the record content and context remain the same as in the nondigital workplace. However, creating digital records through such means as online forms, word-processing software, spreadsheets, emails, and social media, or as digital formats for music, books, and movies requires an additional set of record creation issues to be addressed through the policies and procedures.

In a digital environment, the record creation process must ensure that the record has integrity; is authentic, reliable, and trustworthy; continues to be accessible and retrievable; and is managed and preserved until it is no longer required as evidence of a transaction or of a decision made. In addition, there may be privacy, security, and *access* considerations that must be addressed at the time the record is created. To address these requirements the record creation process is managed as part of an overall recordkeeping system.

The record creation policies and procedures are addressed in requirements for proposed technology solutions to ensure that records can be reassembled over time, as required, to meet business and evidentiary requirements.

Conclusion

In summary, the record creation activity is the beginning of a journey for the record as it supports the organization's business needs and accountability and transparency requirements and addresses external legal, compliance risks, and regulatory needs. Record creation is supported by policies and procedures that define roles and responsibilities for record creation, methods for creating records, and standards for *document* creation and capture. Without clearly defined record creation practices, organizations are at risk of noncompliance with legal and regulatory requirements.—*Christine Ardern*

Keywords: record creation, creator, business activity, policies and procedures
Related Entries: Records Lifecycle; Records Continuum

Bibliography

Archives New Zealand. "S7 Create and Maintain Recordkeeping Standard." n.d. http://archives.govt.nz/s7-create-and-maintain-recordkeeping-standard (accessed December 2013).

Cardin, Martine. "Part Two—Records Creation and Maintenance: Domain 1 Task Force Report." In Luciana Duranti and Randy Preston, eds., *International Research on Permanent Authentic Records in Electronic Systems (InterPARES) 2: Experiential, Interactive and Dynamic Records*. Padova, Italy: Associazione Nazionale Archivistica Italiana, 2008. www.interpares.org/ip2/display_file.cfm?doc=ip2_book_part_2_domain1_task_force.pdf.

Department for Education and Child Development. "Creation and Capture of Official Records." Government of South Australia, last Modified September 25, 2014. www.decd.sa.gov.au/rmp/pages/cg0000941/creation-capture/?reFlag=1 (accessed December 2013).

Duranti, Luciana, Jim Suderman, and Malcolm Todd. "Appendix 19: A Framework of Principles for the Development of Policies, Strategies and Standards for the Long-term Preservation of Digital Records." In Luciana Duranti and Randy Preston, eds., *International Research on Permanent Authentic Records in Electronic Systems (InterPARES) 2: Experiential, Interactive and Dynamic Records*. Padova, Italy: Associazione Nazionale Archivistica Italiana, 2008. www.interpares.org/ip2/display_file.cfm?doc=ip2_book_appendix_19.pdf (accessed December 2013).

Guercio, Maria. "Principles, Methods, and Instruments for the Creation, Preservation, and Use of Archival Record in the Digital Environment." *The American Archivist* 64 (Fall/Winter 2001): 238–69. http://archivists.metapress.com/content/n88455np210p8j5v/fulltext.pdf.

Hare, Catherine, and Julie McLeod. *How to Manage Record in the e-Environment*, 2nd edition (formerly titled *Developing a Record Management Programme*). London: Routledge, 2006.

Hurley, Chris. "Relationship in Record." *New Zealand Archivist* (Summer 2001–Summer 2004). Monash University, Information Technology. http://infotech.monash.edu/research/groups/rcrg/publications/ (accessed December 2013).

InterPARES 2 Project. "The InterPARES 2 Project Glossary." In Luciana Duranti and Randy Preston, eds., *International Research on Permanent Authentic Records in Electronic Systems (InterPARES) 2: Experiential, Interactive and Dynamic Records*. Padova, Italy: Associazione Nazionale Archivistica Italiana, 2008. www.interpares.org/ip2/display_file.cfm?doc=ip2_glossary.pdf&CFID=4365173&CFTOKEN=70993861.

Pearce-Moses, Richard. "A Glossary of Archival and Records Terminology." Chicago: Society of American Archivists, 2005. www.archivists.org/glossary/index.asp.

Shepherd, Elizabeth, and Geoffrey Yeo. *Managing Records: A Handbook of Principles and Practice*. London: Facet, 2009.

RECORD FORMAT

A record format, also referred to as a data format, is a means of encoding data to contain information about its structure, organization, and contents so it can be interpreted for future use in storage, retrieval, processing, presentation, manipulation, and transmission activities. There are thousands of formats in existence, each with different structures, degrees of openness, and intended interpreters, but in all cases some combination of "technical mediation" (Abrams 2004, 49)—that is, hardware, operating system, software—is required to interact meaningfully with the encoded data. Because of this, and due to the complexities involved in maintaining *access* to formats over time, the proper management of formats is considered a critical aspect of long-term *digital preservation*.

The Concept

A record format is distinct from a physical format or medium—many record formats are medium-independent, and can readily be transferred between multiple physical carriers (e.g., data tape, CD-R and DVD-R, hard disk, flash drive, etc.). Data may be internally structured in a variety of methods (e.g., in chunks or directories, using file headers or magic numbers, etc.), but the format must maintain a logical method to identify and organize its component *files*, bitstreams, or bytestreams for future interpretation.

A format may contain a single *file* or bitstream (e.g., many image formats), or it may be comprised of multiple discrete components. Sometimes referred to as wrappers, the latter format type may contain complementary diverse components, each in their own format, such as a textual *document* with embedded images, or the discrete audio and video bitstreams in a video format, which may also contain subtitle text, multiple language channels, and further *metadata*. Still other formats are designed to act as containers facilitating storage and transmission, and may encapsulate diverse data encoded in a variety of other formats. Sometimes known as bundling formats, this format type may be a simple and generic means of aggregating content into a directory structure (e.g., ZIP, TAR), or it may be self-describing, containing additional technical, descriptive, and administrative metadata listing component parts, relationships, and specifications (e.g., METS, BagIt).

Additionally, some formats may make use of compression algorithms to encode information using fewer bits, thereby reducing storage and transmission requirements. This data compression can be either lossy or lossless. A lossless compression algorithm will exploit statistical redundancies to encode a less verbose representation of the data, which can be uncompressed without losing information. A lossy compression algorithm, in contrast, will discard information considered "nonessential" (based on the limits of human ability to perceive subtle bit-level variations) to conserve space during compression. Because the data integrity of the digital object is altered when it is compressed, lossy compression formats are generally considered unsuitable for long-term preservation. Some formats will allow the user to choose whether its contents are stored in an uncompressed or compressed form; in others, the compression algorithm is inherent.

A format or its components (such as the compression algorithms used, embedded fonts and spacing tables, etc.) may be proprietary or public, and its specifications may also be open or unpublished, either because they are considered a trade secret (i.e., closed specifications), and/or because the format was never properly documented. Some formats have been accepted as standards, either through *formal analysis* and recommendation by national and international standards bodies (i.e., de jure standards), or through widespread adoption and use (i.e., de facto standards). A format may be an open standard while still being proprietary in nature. Many proprietary formats with closed specifications can be interpreted by other commercial or open source applications,

but without full access to the specifications, aspects of fidelity and/or functionality may be compromised during rendering. For this reason, well-documented, standardized public formats with open specifications are often considered preferable for long-term preservation.

Sustainability Considerations for Formats

There is a wide and ever-growing proliferation of formats for digital content, whose sustainability is impacted by a number of intersecting technological and human factors that must be considered. Beyond the human and economic cost factors involved in ongoing preservation is the risk of obsolescence. Format obsolescence occurs when there is no software available capable of adequately interpreting a target format's bits. This may occur due to a variety of interrelated factors, including: a format being superseded by newer incompatible versions or newer formats; a lack of initial or sustained public use and market penetration; changes in the availability of interpreting software; and/or the proprietary and unpublished nature of a format inhibiting its use and the development of software capable of interpreting it. Where open standard formats have been used and open-source rendering tools exist, the risk of format obsolescence is greatly reduced, but if these supporting standards and software are not themselves maintained and preserved, future attempts to access obsolete formats may be prohibitively expensive or impossible. Factors that can influence the sustainability of a digital format include (but are not limited to):

- Openness: the degree to which complete and authoritative specifications and tools for format validation are available. The impact of format or component patents on long-term preservation must also be considered.
- Adoption: the degree to which a format is currently in use by producers, preservers, and consumers of digital content.
- Complexity: The degree of human readability of content; availability of basic tools for analysis; and the number of features supported by the format. Features adding complexity can include technical protection measures such as encryption, digital rights management, password protection, etc.

- Interoperability: The degree of data mobility between platforms, interpreters, format versions, subtypes, etc., and fidelity of the interpreted data across multiple systems.
- External dependencies: the degree to which a format depends on particular hardware, operating system, or software for its rendering, access, and intended functionality.
- Self-documentation: the degree to which a format can contain technical, descriptive, and administrative metadata of its specifications and/or all component objects, and whether this metadata is automatically derived, user-defined, or both.

Format Preservation Strategies

The Open Archival Information System (OAIS) Reference Model outlines specific information about a record format that must be preserved meaningfully if the information contained therein is to remain accessible. It calls this "representation information," whose purpose "is to convert the bit sequences into more meaningful information. It does this by describing the format, or data structure concepts, which are to be applied to the bit sequences and that in turn result in more meaningful values such as characters, numbers, pixels, arrays, tables, etc." (CCSDS 2012, 4–22). Other representation information may be required about the standards used or software necessary to interpret and access the format, and representation information about the encoded digital objects and their significant properties or specific characteristics (i.e., technical metadata) must also be collected to ensure long-term preservation and access.

To support the gathering of such a daunting amount of information, a growing number of tools and resources have been created to support format preservation activities. Format registries attempt to collect comprehensive format specifications and make them available for reference and to support future preservation actions. Format identification and characterization tools aim to automate the process of identifying the presumptive format of a digital object based on its extrinsic and intrinsic elements and by extracting metadata about the properties (or characteristics) of a given format significant to its

ongoing preservation. Format validation tools assess the conformance of a given object against the formal specifications of its presumptive format. Format assessment tools are intended to automate preservation workflows by determining the suitability of a format for preservation, based on locally defined preservation plans where format sustainability factors have been considered and policies for preservation actions determined. *Archivists* have also begun adapting digital forensics tools and techniques, originally developed by law enforcement, to support preservation activities on digitally formatted information without altering the data integrity of the bits or their associated metadata.

At present, most preservation actions undertaken to mitigate the risk of format obsolescence can be loosely grouped into two broadly defined strategies, each with many variations: migration and emulation. Migration entails the transformation from one format to another with a perceived greater degree of sustainability—for example, a more recent version, or one that is more widely adopted, interoperable, open, etc. It can be performed as a preventative measure in advance of obsolescence, or at the time of access. Such transformations inevitably involve some alterations to the original bitstreams, and data may be lost, or even added—especially if migration is performed iteratively. Normalization is a specific migration strategy at ingest into a digital preservation system or repository, guided by local preservation policies. By normalizing to more sustainable formats and reducing the overall number of formats maintained in a preservation environment, it is hoped that the costs and technological challenges associated with digital preservation can be reduced. To avoid loss of fidelity as new technologies and preservation paths appear, the original format is generally preserved along with migrated or normalized formats. With emulation, content is both preserved and presented on future access in the original format, and hardware and/or software is used to virtualize the original operating environment across diverse platforms. Emulation depends, in some regards, on a preservation approach known as encapsulation, advocated in the OAIS Reference Model. It implies packaging digital objects with all the necessary information to access them meaningfully in the future, including reference, representation, provenance, fixity, and *context* information. Encapsulation ensures all relevant information is available so that the original computing environment of a digitally formatted object can later be virtualized—although it is a preservation strategy applied to both migration and emulation-based policies. With both migration and emulation, care must be taken by the preservation agent to monitor changes in relevant format sustainability factors that might require intervention—for example, emulators can require migration as their dependencies become obsolete, and early migrations to new formats may squander resources if the formats do not achieve maturity.

Conclusion

Ultimately, it would appear that there are no formats currently in existence that will not eventually risk obsolescence without intervention. New technological innovations will continue to appear, some of them revolutionary in their capabilities, which will alter the way in which we create, access, and preserve information. To maintain access to the digital information currently in existence and to prepare for future paradigm shifts, format preservation activities will undoubtedly continue to be a primary area of concern for digital archivists. Recent successes in browser-based emulation, decentralized registries, and open-source preservation systems suggest promising gains, but unless the proliferation of formats stabilizes considerably, constant vigilance and adaptability will continue to be required to maintain long-term access to digitally encoded information.—*Dan Gillean*

Keywords: data, digital information, encoding, migration, emulation

Related Entries: Digital Preservation; Digital Record; Digital Records Forensics; Metadata

Bibliography

Abrams, Stephen. "File Formats." In S. Ross and M. Day, eds., *DCC Digital Curation Manual*, October 2007, 53. www.dcc.ac.uk/sites/default/files/documents/resource/curation-manual/chapters/file-formats/file-formats.pdf (accessed December 20, 2013).

———. "The Role of Format in Digital Preservation." *VINE* 34 (2) (2004): 49–55. DOI: 10.1108/03055720410530997.

Arms, Caroline R., and Carl Fleischhauer. "Digital Formats: Factors for Sustainability, Functionality, and Quality." Paper presented at *IS&T Archiving 2005* conference, Washington, DC, April 29, 2005. http://memory.loc.gov/ammem/techdocs/digform/Formats_IST05_paper.pdf (accessed December 15, 2013).

Reference Model for an Open Archival Information System (OAIS). Magenta Book. Consultative Committee for Space Data Systems. Issue 2, June 2012. http://public.ccsds.org/publications/archive/650x0m2.pdf (accessed December 20, 2013).

Folk, Mike, and Bruce R. Barkstrom. "Attributes of File Formats for Long-Term Preservation of Scientific and Engineering Data in Digital Libraries." In *Joint Conference on Digital Libraries* (JCDL), Houston, TX, issue 1, 2003. http://ftp.hdfgroup.org/projects/nara/Sci_Formats_and_Archiving.pdf (accessed December 15, 2013).

Park, Eun G. "Examining the Criteria for Open Standard File Formats." *InterPARES 3* Project, TEAM Korea, General Study 20. www.interpares.org/ip3/ip3_general_studies.cfm#gs20 (accessed October 25, 2012).

Pearson, David, and Colin Webb. "Defining File Format Obsolescence: A Risky Journey." *The International Journal of Digital Curation* 3 (1) (2008): 89–106. DOI: 10.2218/ijdc.v3i1.44.

Rog, Judith, and Carolina Van Wijk. "Evaluating File Formats for Long-Term Preservation." *Koninklijke Bibliotheek* 2 (2008). www.kb.nl/sites/default/files/docs/KB_file_format_evaluation_method_27022008.pdf (accessed December 15, 2013).

Rosenthal, David S. H. "Format Obsolescence: Assessing the Threat and the Defenses." *Library Hi Tech* 28 (2) (2010): 195–210. http://lockss.stanford.edu/locksswiki/files/LibraryHighTech2010.pdf (accessed December 19, 2013).

Rosenthal, David S. H., Thomas Lipkis, Thomas S. Robertson, and Seth Morabito. "Transparent Format Migration of Preserved Web Content." *D-Lib Magazine* 11 (1) (January 2005). www.dlib.org/dlib/january05/rosenthal/01rosenthal.html (accessed December 7, 2013).

RECORD GROUP

In the process of *archival arrangement*, records are linked to their *creator* and to associated *functions*, events, places, and/or chronological periods (external provenance), as well as to the *recordkeeping system* in use by the creator (internal provenance). Modern archival arrangement schemes construct these layers intellectually and physically by consecutively nesting sets of records within hierarchical levels that relate to their external (record group and subgroup) and internal (*series*, subseries, and *file*) *contexts*.

- Record group/fonds/collection: records of an entity/from the same provenance
- Subgroup/sous-fonds: subset of records with a distinct external provenance
- Series: group of similar records created, received, or used in the same function or activity, and filed accordingly
- Subseries: a set of records within a series, distinguished from the whole by a filing arrangement such as type, form, or content
- File: set of records related to the same matter or event

The notion of establishing physical and intellectual control over records, through order, continues in the archival process of description. Traditionally, description is seen as dependent on arrangement, with the descriptive finding aid mirroring the levels of arrangement in the hierarchical and linear way in which collections are described. *Archival description* thus acts as a form of representation of arrangement and, in explaining the nature and context of archival material, helps promote its *accessibility*.

The Concept

In the archival arrangement hierarchy, a record group is comprised of records relating to an entity that, due to its "separate or distinct functional responsibilities," can be treated as a self-contained unit (Schellenberg 1988, xxxvi). A subgroup is a division of the record group corresponding to a subordinate unit or, alternatively, to some other external facet (e.g., place, chronology, event, structure, or function) that helped shape the documentary

material. The record group also generally forms the broadest level of description, with subsequent levels only seen as meaningful in light of the description of the entire record group.

The notion that *archivists* would organize and describe records according to a standardized hierarchical structure emerged at the turn of the twentieth century. The process began with attempts to divide the totality of government records into manageable units for archival administration and access. Following the archival profession's adoption of the *principle of respect des fonds*, records were to be inextricably linked to their creator, and the top level or set in the archival arrangement hierarchy was deemed to be a group of records from the same administrative unit. However, differences in the history, size, and organization of government across these national spheres resulted in conflicting notions of what constituted this chief unit of arrangement. In the United States, this level or set of records came to be known by the term record group, and by the terms fonds and archive group in France and the United Kingdom respectively.

In France, the term *fonds d'archives* was used to indicate the body of records from an administrative unit, with the fonds representing "any subordinate office that kept records, no matter how small" (Holmes 1964, 26). In Great Britain, Hilary Jenkinson defined the archive group as "the Archives resulting from the work of an Administration which was an organic whole, complete in itself, capable of dealing independently, without any added or external authority, with every side of any business which could normally be presented to it" (Jenkinson 1966, 101). The manner in which respect des fonds was applied to government records in Great Britain resulted in "a division much wider, much less strictly defined then the Fonds" (Jenkinson 1966, 102).

The Development of the Record Group Concept

In the United States, it was the Finding Mediums Committee, established to look into the adequacy of finding aids at the National Archives, which was given the task of figuring out how to demarcate distinct groupings when federal records were accessioned. A memorandum, published in February 1941, included the first formal definition of the term record group. With a nod to their European archival counterparts, the record group was established with due regard to the *principle of provenance*. However, unlike in France and in Great Britain, this chief archival unit was not chiefly tied to any consideration of the nature of government administration, but rather to the idea of bringing records under physical control. The strong pragmatic streak of American archivists was clear in the acknowledgment that the record group was established somewhat arbitrarily due to concerns that the unit be "of convenient size and character for the work of arrangement and description and for the publication of inventories" (Schellenberg 1996, 181). In order to create records groups, the National Archives divided the records of large agencies (such as departments) into groupings usually at the bureau level and, in turn, the National Archives united the records of subordinate offices under their superior offices, up to this bureau level. By 1944, 206 record groups were in existence at the National Archives.

Further treatments of the record group and subgroup were articulated in National Archives staff information circulars published in 1950 and 1951, and their widespread dissemination influenced practices at other American archival institutions (Berner 1983, 25–38). Staff information circular no. 14 ("The Preparation of Preliminary Inventories," 1950) focused on the preparation of initial finding aids (called preliminary inventories) at the record group and subgroup level. Containing information to both identify and describe the record group, the main components of the preliminary inventory were designated as the introduction (containing an analysis and description of the origins of the record group) and associated entries on subordinate units of records. In setting out which aspects of the record group to describe (history, structure, functions, and major classes of records in the record group), and articulating what archivists needed to know to carry out this work, a foundation was set for the creation of descriptive finding aids at this and other archival repositories.

Staff information circular no. 15 (titled "Control of Records at the Record Group Level") highlights the fact that adaptations to the original concept of the record group were necessary in order to ensure that groupings continued to be of a convenient size for both archival work and for subsequent access. A "general" record group was put in place to bring together aggregations of records pertaining to the overall administration and functioning of the executive level of an agency, and its subordinate units. A "collective" record group could be created to bring together the records of a number of small independent agencies, provided the agencies had certain characteristics in common ("The Control of Records at the Record Group Level," 1950, 5).

Staff information circular no. 18, written by Theodore Schellenberg (1951), outlined principles of arrangement at the National Archives, and provided insights into how record groups were divided at the subgroup level. The logical relationship of subgroups to each other was also elucidated, with rationales provided as to when the order among subgroups should follow along hierarchical, chronological, functional, geographical, or subject lines. According to Schellenberg, it was preferable to form subgroups along organizational lines, particularly when the record group encompassed smaller subordinate organizational units with distinct filing systems. Alternatively, if the function of an administrative unit had stayed more stable than its organizational structure, subgroups could be created along functional lines. Finally, if neither subordinate units or functions but rather record types were a defining feature of the materials, then Schellenberg states that subgroups could be formed around specific genre/formats. By considering material type as a possible means of creating subgroups, Schellenberg blurred the traditional distinction between subgroups (representing the external context of records creation) and series (representing the records themselves).

The role of the record group as the primary unit for both archival arrangement and description was solidified in the publication of Oliver Wendell Holmes's five-part model in 1964. This model delineated a set of nested hierarchical levels: depository, record group, subgroup, series, filing unit, and *document*. This model of combining creator and record descriptions in a hierarchical structure formed the basis of modern multilevel data structure standards for archival description (and their associated data content standards), including Encoded Archival Description (EAD) and the International Council on Archive's General International Standard for Archival Description (ISAD[G]).

Although the record group has been in place for over seventy years, theoretical and practical objections to the concept, and all it entails, have been raised. At the most basic level, the "very arbitrariness of the concept" has been sufficient to make some archivists question its usefulness (Scott 1966, 497). The fact that workplace efficiency and physical storage concerns were the driving force behind the National Archives' creation of the record group unit has only served to undermine the notion that the concept had theoretical appeal. One prominent objection to the record group concept relates to concerns that the traditional hierarchical model of arrangement and description neither accurately nor fully documents the network of relationships in which bodies of records are created and used. As Cook puts it, "The classic mono-hierarchical theory of bureaucracy elucidated by Max Weber, in which each subordinate unit is responsible to one superior unit, has long been a thing of the past" (Cook 1993, 31). Instead, modern bureaucracies are seen as dynamic and unstable entities, with structures and functions that change in and over time. Thus, the traditional hierarchal model is seen as limiting— limiting the relationships between provenancial and *recordkeeping* contexts to a linear, static, and hierarchical relationship rather than reflecting the true complexity of these relationships.

Based on these, and other criticisms, a number of archivists, including Australian Peter Scott and American archivist Max Evans, have suggested and implemented alternatives to the record group concept, both of which involved the development of separate but linked systems for dealing with information about key external contexts and about the records themselves. Peter Scott (1966) was one of the first to argue that the strict and fixed hierarchy of archival arrangement, where record series were assigned to one and only one record group, often misrepresented the true relationships between creators and their records. In effect, Scott argued that the record group concept (as it was instantiated in archival arrangement and description) was violating the principle of provenance by assuming that record group and series always maintained a one-to-one relationship. Scott's answer was the *series system*, in which the record series replaced the record group as the primary unit of arrangement and description. This, however, did not mean that elements relating to provenance were divorced from the series system. In fact, provenance and record elements were

reimagined as separate but interrelated networks of relationships that could be instantiated and represented through non-hierarchical descriptive systems.

In the 1980s, Max Evans (1986) built on this call to abandon the record group as the primary unit of arrangement. Evans's main critique of the record group concept was his belief that it inserted a static and artificial grouping of records into the arrangement scheme, arbitrarily bringing a number of record series together in a hierarchy and in a manner that simply facilitated their management and control. Like Scott, Evans also believed that the one-to-one relationship that the arrangement hierarchy imposed between records and record agencies failed to reflect the complexity of modern bureaucracies. In its place, Evans introduced archival *authority control* as the solution for archivists trying to describe such complex systems, with information about creators captured in separate authority records instead of within the descriptions of the records themselves.

Conclusion

Overall, the record group concept feeds into the notion that there are certain contexts (both external and internal to recordkeeping systems) that must be captured as part of archival arrangement and description in order to ensure that bodies of records can serve as evidence of their creator's functions and activities. The record group has functioned as the chief unit of arrangement for organizational records, serving to reinforce the archival concern for provenance. However, the continuing evolution of archival notions about the nature of context and how arrangement and description schemas should capture and represent it, will likely bring further scrutiny of the concept of the "record group" in years to come. — *Ciaran Trace*

Keywords: arrangement, provenance, original order
Related Entries: Archival Arrangement; Archival Collection; Archival Description; Principle of Provenance; Principle of *Respect des Fonds*

Bibliography

Berner, Richard C. *Archival Theory and Practice in the United States: A Historical Analysis.* Seattle: University of Washington Press, 1983.

"The Control of Records at the Record Group Level." National Archives Staff Information Circulars, no. 15. Washington, DC, July 1950.

Cook, Terry. "The Concept of the Archival Fonds in the Post-Custodial Era: Theory, Problems, and Solutions." *Archivaria* 35 (1993): 24–37. http:// journals.sfu.ca/archivar/index.php/archivaria/article/view/11882/12835.

Evans, Max J. "Authority Control: An Alternative to the Record Group Concept." *American Archivist* 49 (3) (1986): 249–61. http://archivists.metapress.com/content/0862585240520721/fulltext.pdf.

Holmes, Oliver Wendell. "Archival Arrangement—Five Different Operations at Five Different Levels." *American Archivist* 27 (1964): 21–41. http://archivists.metapress.com/content/l721857l17617w15/fulltext.pdf.

Jenkinson, Hilary. *A Manual of Archive Administration*. London: P. Lund, Humphries, 1966.

"The Preparation of Preliminary Inventories." National Archives Staff Information Circulars, no. 14. Washington, DC, May 1950.

Schellenberg, Theodore R. *The Management of Archives*. Washington, DC: National Archives and Records Administration, 1988.

———. *Modern Archives: Principles and Techniques*. Chicago: Society of American Archivists, 1996.

———. "Principles of Arrangement." National Archives, Staff Information Papers, no. 18. Washington, DC, June 1951.

Scott, Peter. "The Record Group Concept: A Case for Abandonment." *The American Archivist* 29 (4) (1966): 493–504. http://archivists.metapress.com/content/y886054240174401/fulltext.pdf.

RECORD(S)

In English-speaking countries, records are widely perceived as the materials with which archival principles and practices are concerned. Archival professionals agree that records are made and accrued in the course of the activities of organizations or individuals, and are closely connected with the activities in which they are made, but beyond this there is little consensus. Archival literature variously characterizes records as evidence of, information about, or representations of activities, transactions, or events, or as *documents* made or received in the course of these phenomena. There are different understandings of what constitutes a record as well as divergent uses of terminology.

History of the Term and Concept

Until the late twentieth century, both the term and the concept of record were confined to countries whose legal and administrative systems have English origins. They remain distinctive to English-language discourse and have no equivalent in most other linguistic cultures. Record derives from Latin *recordari* (to remember); derivatives of this Latin word in other European languages connote remembrance, but their meanings do not correspond to English usage of record.

The origins of this usage lie in English common law, where record was originally a formal oral recollection of court proceedings. After oral methods of recalling judicial business began to be superseded by writing in the twelfth and thirteenth centuries, the term record was applied to their written successors. By the seventeenth century, the term had also come to be used more widely for writings of English church and state institutions. When the Public Record Office was founded in London in 1838, it was intended for the preservation of court records (i.e., records in the narrower legal sense), but its scope soon expanded to include records of government departments. The narrower meaning of record survives in law, but is now rare in archival discourse.

In mid-twentieth-century Britain, the terms records and *archives* (the latter supposedly newly introduced from continental Europe) were considered largely synonymous. In the early twenty-first century, they are still sometimes used synonymously; many British local government repositories are called "record offices" and refer to their holdings as "records," but in most other countries (and increasingly in twenty-first-century Britain) such repositories and their holdings would usually be called "archives." Like archives, the term records has traditionally been associated with governmental settings, and increasingly also with nongovernmental institutions; its usage is now often extended to embrace records of families, individuals, and social groups.

In the twentieth century, the growing bulk of organizational records led archival practitioners to reject notions that all records could be preserved and to attempt to identify *appraisal* criteria for selecting records for long-term preservation. American practitioners developed lifecycle models, which indicated that records are created and initially used in business *contexts*, and at some later moment a decision is made either to destroy them or to maintain them indefinitely for historical purposes. When lifecycle models are followed, the term *records management* is used to denote control systems for records in the early stages of their life, and records are said to "become" archives when designated for long-term retention or entrusted to a dedicated archival repository. While most European countries make no distinction between "records" maintained for business purposes and "archives" with longer-term cultural objectives, in most English-speaking countries only records that have undergone a *selection* process and been judged to have continuing value are now termed "archives."

The Concept of Record Today

Today, many lifecycle models posit a transformation at an earlier stage, when items previously labeled documents or content are said to become records. Proponents of these models note that documents may be changeable over time, while records are stable and unchanging (or need to be made so). Capturing records within a formal records management system assists in securing them against loss, damage, alteration, or premature destruction, besides supporting their continuing accessibility. In the pre-digital world, public-sector organizations in many countries operated "registration" procedures, whereby papers were acknowledged as records when they were placed on file, while papers not formally filed were deemed to require less stringent protection. Particularly in the United States, preliminary drafts, working notes, and casual messages have often been termed "non-records." In digital environments, documents may be "declared" as records when they cease being volatile and are captured in an electronic records management system. Promoters of this approach usually restrict the term records to materials formally captured within a records management system and assert that documents become records at the moment when they are designated for secure preservation or pass into corporate control.

Some also assert that, by stabilizing the records and bringing them into relation with other records, formal capture helps protect the records' *authenticity*, *reliability*, and integrity.

A different view of records is taken by those (especially in Australia) who reject lifecycle models and propose *records continuum* theories that eschew artificial boundaries based on decisions about custody. Continuum proponents usually accept that few organizations need to manage every record with equal stringency, and that judgments are often required about which records should be subject to formalized control systems and which records can be overseen less rigorously or summarily destroyed. However, they deprecate notions that records warranting protection should first be captured into a records management system and later moved to a separate system for *archival management*. Instead, they often argue that such records should be maintained in a comprehensive *recordkeeping system*; they also usually insist that record status is not determined by crossing the threshold of such a system, and even *ephemeral* records and informal communications have evidential characteristics that qualify them as records. More recently, continuum proponents have affirmed that some records are most appropriately maintained within business systems that offer recordkeeping functionality, and that assumptions about the need to transfer records to specialist preservation environments are becoming outmoded. Rejecting rigid divisions between documents, records, and archives, they usually employ records as an inclusive term.

Underlying these debates are questions about when records come into existence. Is a record formed when an inscription is made or when someone decides to set it aside and make explicit its linkage to other records? Does record status depend on associations with organizational or personal activity or is it achieved by acts of designation or selection? The view that record status is independent of management procedures is often associated with *postcustodialism*, but it is not necessary to reject custodial practice to perceive that records are distinguished by their relationships to actions and events rather than by decisions about their capture. Professional literature often notes that the idea that record status depends on formal designation rarely reflects the working of the law. For legal purposes, all records (including drafts, casual messages, and records that survive by happenstance) can be subject to discovery or disclosure. Selection decisions are fallible; evidence of past actions can be obtained from a plenitude of records, not merely from those selected for systematic retention.

Definitions of records in professional literature evince these varying perceptions. Some characterize a record as a kind of document (typically as a document that has been made or received and set aside in the course of activity). Others prefer to define records in terms of evidence or information. Australian writings often emphatically characterize records as evidence of business activities. Many others define records as a kind of information; one such definition (records are "information created, received, and maintained . . . by an organization or *person*, in pursuance of legal obligations or in the transaction of business") appears in ISO15489, the international *records management standard*, and is widely used.

Another interpretation suggests that evidence and information are better understood as affordances that a record can supply to users, and that records may be more suitably characterized as persistent representations of activities, transactions, and other temporal phenomena, made by participants in or observers of the phenomena concerned. Such representations operate in different ways. In some cases, including those where diplomatists call records "dispositive" (see *Records Function*), a transaction or other activity is achieved by the creation and transmission of a written representation of the activity itself. The writer of a business letter, for example, can make a commitment, statement, order, or request by creating a representation of that activity and transmitting it to the appropriate recipient; when the representation has accomplished this task, its continuing existence provides evidence of what has occurred. Other records, including those diplomatists call "probative," are not intrinsic to an activity, but are constructed separately. Traditionally, separately constructed records were made after the activity was ended; a participant or observer made a written assertion that the activity had been performed and perhaps also described the manner of its performance. However, mechanical recording devices increasingly allow separately constructed records to be made contemporaneously with the activities they represent. In all cases, the representation persists after the activities have ceased.

Some definitions, especially legal ones, attempt to characterize records by listing specific media formats, but archival discourse generally affirms that records can be created using any media. From the Renaissance to the twentieth century, written records in Western societies were usually on paper, but by the early twenty-first century, computing technologies had brought new means of creating records, and increasing numbers of records are now maintained digitally. The persistence of a *digital record* lies in its capacity for repeated presentation: more precisely, in the continuing possibility of using technological tools to locate and assemble its components and present the resulting record to a user.

Whether digital or analog, the archetypal record probably takes the form of a unit of text, more or less in narrative style, though possibly also containing graphics or images. Photographic images can represent what happened in the past, and many would argue that drawings, sketches, and other graphical and artistic forms fulfill a similar role. But records need not be inscribed text or static images; they can also include films and sound recordings. In preliterate or semiliterate societies, records have often taken the form of notched sticks, tokens, knotted strings, or other three-dimensional artifacts. Archival professionals sometimes affirm that "any" artifacts—laboratory specimens, fabric samples, publications, or advertising materials, for example—can become records when used or transmitted in business activity or systematically associated with records of activity. In recent years, critics sympathetic to *postmodernism* or *postcolonialism* have proposed reconceptualizing records to include landscapes, oral traditions, and ritual performances. If objects that are not in documentary form can be records, and if records need not employ written text, it is arguable that notions of a record as a kind of document merely reflect practices predominant in Western cultures at particular periods of history. Nevertheless, textual (and perhaps visual) records remain central to most understandings of archival work.

One reason for capturing records in a structured system is to formalize their relations with other records; the systematic association of related records adds contextual wrapping that may be critical to their interpretation. Some archival professionals believe that realization of records' *interrelatedness* in formally structured aggregations is essential to their status as records. Others argue that record status derives from a connection with activity rather than from juxtaposition to other records, and that a record is a record irrespective of whether it is kept with other records or stands alone.

Where aggregations are concerned, many professionals use the term records primarily to refer to entities at item level. Some insist that a record can only be a single item and identify it with the "archival document" that forms the traditional object of study in *diplomatics*. Others, however, assert that records need not be equated with items or documents, and that records exist at collective as well as unitary levels. From this viewpoint, a record can be a part of a document (e.g., an entry in a ledger) or comprise several documents (e.g., an e-mail message and its attachments). Some argue that records are possible at multiple levels of aggregation; in organizational contexts, records are generated at the level of a single activity or transaction and these "elementary" records can be aggregated to form records of business processes and *functions* at higher levels. From these perspectives, records and documents have different logical characteristics. A "record" is perceived as a relational term: a record "of" some activity, transaction, process, or function.

Because they are generated in the course of business or daily life, and are not usually designed to disseminate knowledge or opinion to humanity at large, records have traditionally been thought to possess objective qualities of *naturalness* and *impartiality* that underpin their credibility. Many archival professionals and scholars maintain these traditional understandings, but others affirm that records are shaped by the decisions and actions of their originators and of *records managers* and *archivists*, and that elementary records are rarely as natural or impartial as was once believed. The naturalness of record aggregations is also disputed. Some assert that, even if elementary records are sometimes created more or less naturally, record aggregations are purposeful constructions. Paper aggregations usually have a stable physical form, but aggregations in digital environments need not be immutable, and it is sometimes argued that it should be possible to construct record aggregations representing, for example, different perceptions of process boundaries, as they are required.

In the twenty-first century, increasing numbers of records are made using data and database applications. Some professionals contend that the shift toward "data-centric" records invalidates attempts to define records as a subset of documents, while others have sought to expand definitions of documents to embrace data. It can also be argued that database technology offers a paradigm for understanding record aggregations in the digital era. In a database, data may be grouped in multiple ways to form different record aggregations, but these can only be constructed if appropriate frameworks are available. The persistence of any digital record aggregation depends on its continuing potential for realization, which in turn demands the continuance of a system that allows sets of elementary records to be collated and displayed to users.

Conclusion

Records provide rich resources for individuals, organizations, and wider communities. According to ISO 15489, they have (or should have) qualities of authenticity, reliability, integrity, and usability. With these qualities, records supply the ability to refer back to or corroborate what was said and done in the past. As durable representations, they can protect the powers and privileges of governments, institutions, and commercial corporations; they can also safeguard individual rights, promote a sense of personal or social identity, and enable scrutiny of those in positions of responsibility. Some commentators note that records can have multiple meanings and fulfill aesthetic and symbolic as well as memorial, evidential, and informational roles. Records can be kept by almost anyone, and users employ or interpret them in different ways. Although created in the first instance to serve legal, administrative, or domestic purposes, or to meet compliance and *accountability* requirements, they also support cultural understanding, study, and research.—*Geoffrey Yeo*

Keywords: documents, archives, lifecycle, continuum, records management, recordkeeping system
Related Entries: Archival Bond; Archival Theory; Archives (Material); Captured Records; Digital Record; Diplomatics; Document; Impartiality (Record); Interrelatedness (Record); Naturalness (Record); Personal Records; Postcustodialism;

Recordkeeping, Recordkeeping System(s); Records Continuum; Records Function; Records Lifecycle; Records Management

Bibliography

Abukhanfusa, Kerstin, Ed. *The Concept of Record: Second Stockholm Conference on Archival Science and the Concept of Record, 30–31 May 1996.* Stockholm: Riksarkivet, 1998.

Brothman, Brien. "Afterglow: Conceptions of Record and Evidence in Archival Discourse." *Archival Science* 2 (3–4) (2002): 311–42. DOI: 10.1007/BF02435627.

Clanchy, M. T. *From Memory to Written Record: England 1066–1307,* 2nd edition. Oxford: Blackwell, 1993.

Duranti, Luciana, and Kenneth Thibodeau. "The Concept of Record in Interactive, Experiential and Dynamic Environments: The View of InterPARES." *Archival Science* 6 (1) (2006): 13–68. DOI: 10.1007/s10502-006-9021-7.

International Standard Organization. *ISO 15489-1:2001, Information and Documentation: Records Management. Part 1: General.* Geneva: International Standards Organization, 2001.

Livelton, Trevor. *Archival Theory, Records, and the Public.* Lanham, MD: Scarecrow Press, 1996.

Meehan, Jennifer. "The Archival Nexus: Rethinking the Interplay of Archival Ideas about the Nature, Value, and Use of Records." *Archival Science* 9 (3–4) (2009): 157–64. DOI: 10.1007/s10502-009-9107-0.

Reed, Barbara. "Records." In S. McKemmish, M. Piggott, B. Reed, and F. Upward, eds., *Archives: Recordkeeping in Society.* Wagga Wagga, Australia: Charles Sturt University, 2005.

Yeo, Geoffrey. "Bringing Things Together: Aggregate Records in a Digital Age." *Archivaria* 74 (2012): 43–91. http://journals.sfu.ca/archivar/index.php/archivaria/article/viewArticle/13407.

———. "Concepts of Record (1): Evidence, Information, and Persistent Representations." *American Archivist* 70 (2) (2007): 315–43. http://archivists.metapress.com/content/u327764v1036756q/fulltext.pdf.

———. "Rising to the Level of a Record? Some Thoughts on Records and Documents." *Records Management Journal* 21 (1) (2011): 8–27.

www.emeraldinsight.com/doi/pdfplus/10.1108/09565691111125071.

RECORDKEEPING

Recordkeeping is a broad framework for making and managing evidence and memory that is brought into specific application by discrete processes serving multiple purposes and operating through time. In practice, recordkeeping describes a plurality of coherent, iterative, and inter-dependent processes by which *records* are created, captured, organized, described, managed, and made accessible for multiple purposes over multiple time periods. Recordkeeping is a synthesis of *records management* and archival concerns. Recordkeeping does not represent a fundamental rupture with traditional *archival practice* as it foregrounds traditional archival principles such as provenance, evidence, recordness, and contextuality, but it does reorient practice away from approaches based on physical record objects and management cycles. Recordkeeping can be applied equally to paper-based and *digital records* and *archives* in any environments.

Competing Definitions

In some jurisdictions the term recordkeeping is used interchangeably with the term records management and is defined as "the systematic creation, use, maintenance, and *disposition* of records to meet administrative, programmatic, legal, and financial needs and responsibilities" (Society of American Archivists 2005). In other environments it has a very granular process and object-based definition, defined in the *Cambridge Dictionary* as "the activity of organizing and storing all the *documents, files,* invoices . . . relating to a company's or organization's activities."

Predominantly, however, recordkeeping is understood as a broad term describing the framework for "making and maintaining complete, accurate and reliable evidence of business transactions in the form of recorded information" (Standards Australia 1996, clause 4.19). In this usage, recordkeeping is defined as "a critical function which is performed through the collective action of individuals and systems throughout all organizations. Recordkeeping is not the province of archivists, records managers or systems administrators alone but an essential role of all employees and of individuals in their private lives" (Bearman 1994, 295).

Evolution of the Term Recordkeeping

The 1950s

The broad understanding of recordkeeping was referenced in archival literature in the 1950s by North American archivist T. R. Schellenberg and Australian Commonwealth Archivist Ian Maclean.

In the post–World War II era, Schellenberg and Maclean were working in an administrative environment where rates of annual *record creation* were escalating rapidly and where traditional *archival methods*, derived originally to describe small extant collections of legacy records, were increasingly difficult to apply to large volumes of contemporary archives.

In *Modern Archives: Principles and Techniques*, Schellenberg critiqued the failures in contemporary recordkeeping which he argued were affecting the *selection* and management of archives in North America. He wrote:

> While most records developed by European governments are organized in registry offices before their release to archival institutions, many records of the Federal government of the United States are left in a disorganized state. Several attempts have been made to bring about uniformity on a national scale in the recordkeeping procedures of government agencies, but the only result has been the adoption of systems which have tended to complicate rather than to simplify the organization of the records of any particular agency. (Schellenberg 1956, 192)

In Australia, and influenced by the work of Schellenberg (specifically his *advocacy* of archival involvement in the *appraisal* and management of current records), Ian Maclean at the Commonwealth Archives Office (CAO) developed a "theory of recordkeeping" and implemented a registrar's training program across Australian Commonwealth government departments in 1958. Through this program Maclean sought to use recordkeeping—broad record creation and management frameworks—to deal with the profusion of modern records and to implement effective archival management. His intention

was to implement "comprehensive public records administration" across the public sector (Maclean 1959, 390–416). (Maclean's program employed and trained registrars in each government department and developed extensive guidance for registrars on classification, disposal and filing, naming, numbering, and indexing conventions.)

Critical to Maclean's understanding of recordkeeping was his definition of documents as "pieces of paper constituting evidence of particular administrative actions of which they formed a part" (Maclean 1959, 400), and his theory of recordkeeping emphasized processes to support the preservation of the evidential characteristics of records. His recordkeeping strategies prioritized the management of records of ongoing value to business activity and rejected selection criteria based on the informational value of records or their value to current historical research interests.

At the CAO (now the National Archives of Australia), Keith Penny and Peter Scott embedded Maclean's theory of recordkeeping into the organization's archival description systems and strategies (primarily embodied by the Commonwealth Record Series [CRS] System). These approaches integrated contemporary and *archival description* in the one descriptive framework and separated descriptions of records from descriptions of provenance in order to better represent the evidential history of records.

The 1990s

Recordkeeping provided an influential management framework in Australia for many years, but it reemerged as a critical and international professional concern in the 1990s. In this era, the advent of information technologies caused a fundamental revolution in the very nature of records and in the structure of digital business environments. Rather than being fixed, paper-based, and impermeable, records were now digital, fragile, and subject to multiple technological dependencies. In business environments individual staff were responsible for creating and storing their own records, traditional centralized registries or filing systems broke down, and primarily non-records-based information technology staff became responsible for designing the diverse and complex environments used for record creation and management.

For records managers and archivists, existing management strategies based on the control of physical record objects now had limited applicability. Archival selection and management techniques based on post hoc transfer of legacy collections were also in jeopardy as a consequence of virtual and vulnerable information.

In this era of significant flux, threat, and risk, recordkeeping was broadly adopted as an approach for the creation and management of contemporary records and for identifying and protecting records of archival value at or even before their creation through system design and active management strategies. The term recordkeeping professional was also coined to emphasize the role of records managers and archivists in the strategic management of contemporary digital information, not simply paper record legacies. Electronic recordkeeping became a widespread term, used to mean the application of recordkeeping strategies to digital records and systems.

Within Australia, the reemergence of recordkeeping approaches was directly associated with the rearticulation of the continuum theory spearheaded by Frank Upward and Sue McKemmish. There is a fundamental relationship between recordkeeping and continuum-based management approaches. In explaining the continuum, Upward and McKemmish have said it is "a concept of *records* which is inclusive of records of continuing value (archives) which stresses their uses for transactional, evidentiary and memory purposes, and which unifies approaches to archiving/recordkeeping whether records are kept for a split second or a millennium" (Upward 1996, 40).

There were also significant North American influences on continuum theory and recordkeeping strategies from the mid-1980s onward. Jay Atherton's article "From Life Cycle to Continuum" triggered significant reassessments of lifecycle-based approaches to records and archives management, and Hugh Taylor's arguments for the return of registrar programs highlighted the need for coherent and consistent management frameworks across business and archival environments. The work of David Bearman, however, was fundamental for identifying the scope and potential of recordkeeping strategies and for grounding them in core archival principals such as provenance, evidence, and *context*. His advocacy of

revised appraisal and descriptive frameworks, functional requirements for recordkeeping, provenance in the digital business era, and capacity and risk in digital business frameworks continue to impact on contemporary recordkeeping strategies today.

Recordkeeping and Standardization

With its emphasis on proactive, coherent, and strategic approaches, its relationship to system design, and its close connections to evidentiality and *accountability*, recordkeeping is often supported by standardization initiatives aimed at making its processes routine, standardized, and systematic. David Bearman and the team at the University of Pittsburgh were leaders in this area with their project, "Functional Requirements for Evidence in Recordkeeping."

The first national standard on records management, Australian Standard AS4390 (1996), embodied and codified recordkeeping strategies, processes, and requirements. The International Standard on Records Management, ISO 15489 (2001), was based on AS4390 and rearticulated these requirements for an international audience.

The definition and standardization of aspects of recordkeeping continues today; for example, in ARMA International's Generally Accepted Recordkeeping Principles.

Critiques of Recordkeeping Approaches

Recordkeeping is sometimes criticized as a concept that applies best to government business environments where more formal management rules and frameworks can potentially be applied. Its emphasis on records as evidence is also criticized as diminishing alternative cultural, historical, informational, or other values that can apply to records and archives (Cook 1997, 42–43). It should be noted that social and memory dimensions are valid and appropriate components of recordkeeping frameworks, but they are seldom considered in organizational recordkeeping strategies.

Other critiques come because recordkeeping requires very interventionist approaches. Effective recordkeeping strategies recommend that archives are identified and that appropriate systems for their management are designed even before records are created. As Terry Cook states, archivists "have evolved from being, allegedly, impartial custodians of inherited records to becoming intervening agents who set recordkeeping standards" (Cook 1997, 46), and this evolution is at odds with traditional non-interventionist approaches to records creation and management.

Recordkeeping could also be critiqued for failing to sufficiently adapt to the extreme complexity of the contemporary digital world. Its reinvention in the 1950s and the 1990s has not been followed by a parallel contemporary leap forward. It could be argued that recordkeeping professionals are not sufficiently involved in defining records in today's online, complex, interdependent, and data-rich world and are therefore not yet developing the recordkeeping strategies required to identify, support, and manage these complex records through time.

The Future of Recordkeeping

As the digital information revolution continues to permeate every aspect of society and culture, recordkeeping is less frequently referenced as a specific term in professional discourse. While conceptually it is more valid than ever before, the need to explain records and recordkeeping to multidisciplinary audiences has led to broad terms such as *information management* and *information governance* frequently being used as substitutes.

These terms, however, describe broad professional practices and communities, much of which is beyond the scope of records, and they do not natively embody the core archival principles fundamental for forming evidence and memory. It has been argued that "without the adequate presence of the single minded concentration on the recordkeeping processes that produce evidence of actions within the framework of broader information management, we will be left with information sludge, and an environment of increasing chaos" (Upward et al. 2013, 40). Recently therefore the term "recordkeeping informatics" has been adopted to describe "the way we capture, archive and disseminate recorded information as evidence using modern communication and information technologies" and to ensure that the notion of recordkeeping is not lost in today's complex information environments (Upward et al. 2013, 40). The future of managing evidence and memory in complex digital environments lies in communicating core records and archives management principles to multidisciplinary collaborators in diverse business, informational, and technological environments, and the discipline of recordkeeping informatics may provide frameworks for enabling this communication.

Conclusion

Recordkeeping refers to the series of processes that make and manage evidence and memory, now and through time. It applies in all environments where records and archives are made, kept, and managed.—*Kate Cumming*

Keywords: records management, archives management, continuum, evidence, accountability

Related Entries: Recordkeeping System(s); Records Continuum; Records Management; Series System

Bibliography

Bearman, D. *Electronic Evidence: Strategies for Managing Records in Contemporary Organisations*. Pittsburgh, PA: Archives and Museum Informatics, 1994.

Cook, T. "What Is Past Is Prologue: A History of Archival Ideas since 1898, and the Future Paradigm Shift." *Archivaria* 1 (43) (1997): 17–63. http://journals.sfu.ca/archivar/index.php/archivaria/article/view/12175/13184.

Maclean, I. "Australian Experience in Record and Archives Management." *American Archivist* 22 (4) (1959): 387–418. http://archivists.metapress.com/content/cu4242717578022t/fulltext.pdf.

Schellenberg, T. R. *Modern Archives: Principles and Techniques*. Chicago: University of Chicago Press, 1956, 192.

Society of American Archivists. "A Glossary of Archival and Records Terminology." 2005. www2.archivists.org/glossary (accessed October 4, 2013).

Standards Australia. "Australian Standard: Records Management." AS 4390. Homebush, 1996, part 1.

Upward, F. "Structuring the Records Continuum—Part One: Postcustodial Principles and Properties." 1996. www.infotech.monash.edu.au/

research/groups/rcrg/publications/recordscontinuum-fupp1.html (accessed November 30, 2013).

Upward, F., B. Reed, G. Oliver, and J. Evans. "Recordkeeping Informatics: Re-figuring a Discipline in Crisis with a Single Minded Approach." *Records Management Journal* 23 (1) (2013): 37–50. http://dx.doi.org/10.1108/09565691311325013.

RECORDKEEPING METADATA

Recordkeeping metadata (see *Metadata*) is structured information used to manage all aspects of the use and management of *records*, including the preservation thereof, in a *recordkeeping* environment. The use of good recordkeeping metadata can improve efficiency and *access*, maintain compliance to laws and other mandates, reduce risk, and support good *information governance*. Recordkeeping metadata is an essential tool used to describe records, the activities that produce records, and the people who create and use records. According to Gilliland et al. (2008), recordkeeping metadata is

> all types of structured information . . . that is created manually or automatically by *recordkeeping systems*, including metadata that documents the juridical-administrative, business and technical *contexts* within which records are created; identifies records and delineates how the records behave, their *function* and use; identifies and describes the relationships within and between records and other information objects; and expresses and supports how records should be managed, and what happens to them over time.

Purposes

Australian Kate Cumming identified seven roles and purposes for recordkeeping metadata, and in her doctoral thesis codified these roles and purposes in a scheme: the Classification of Recordkeeping Metadata by Purpose Scheme (Cumming 2007). According to Cumming, recordkeeping metadata support reliable and authentic records and recordkeeping systems by:

- identifying all entities (record, agent, business, recordkeeping business) at all levels of aggregation;
- establishing connections between related entities;
- sustaining record structure, content, and accessibility through time;
- administering recordkeeping business;
- documenting the history of recordkeeping events;
- facilitating discovery, understanding, retrieval, and delivery; and
- documenting metadata attribution.

Recently, recordkeeping metadata research has evolved from research with a primary focus on the automated creation of metadata that is managed and reused primarily for support of digital recordkeeping to a research focus on how recordkeeping metadata can be used to support not just the traditional bureaucratic context but larger societal contexts as well. These societal contexts not only include the customary Western-leaning concepts of records and recordkeeping but also include support for such contexts and initiatives as "emergent nations and post-conflict societies; empowering multiple ethnic communities within individual nations; building strong, sustainable communities; and supporting social justice, human rights, and social inclusion agendas" (Gilliland and McKemmish 2011, 107).

Use

Recordkeeping metadata has proven its value in a variety of information environments from eBusiness and eGovernment to eScience. Each environment has its own recordkeeping requirements, derived from a study of its specific contexts, mandates, and the records necessary to properly document functions and activities and any changes in them over time. These recordkeeping requirements are facilitated via recordkeeping metadata. Capturing necessary recordkeeping metadata, maintaining it over time, and adding metadata when necessary, supports the *authenticity* of the records the system manages and maintains their integrity, thus sustaining the records' use as evidence of activity.

Standards

A number of recordkeeping standards have recordkeeping metadata implications. *DOD 5015.2—the*

United States Department of Defense Records Management Applications Design Criteria Standard, ISO 15489—Information and Documentation—Records Management, its companion standard *ISO 23081-1—Information and Documentation—Records Management Processes—Metadata for Records*, and *ISO 9000—Quality Management Systems—Requirements*, all address metadata either directly (ISO 23081-1) or indirectly (all others) in their basic principles and requirements for such recordkeeping practices as identification of records and records creating agents and activities, audit trails, version control, and application profiles.

Implementations

Locally implemented recordkeeping metadata standards have been created and utilized in many jurisdictions throughout the world. Some of the most cited and modeled implementations are the Archives New Zealand "S8: Electronic Recordkeeping Metadata Standard," the "Australian Government Recordkeeping Metadata Standard," and the "Minnesota Record Keeping Metadata Standard" from the state of Minnesota in the United States.

Conclusion

Recordkeeping metadata is designed specifically for recordkeeping contexts and ensures that records it describes are, and remain, authentic and reliable evidence over time for many important purposes. *Records managers* and *archivists* rely on its use to perform their work and to ensure all stakeholders in the records' content that what they are using is a true record, representative of the activity that produced it.—*Lori Lindberg*

Keywords: records, recordkeeping, metadata, recordkeeping metadata, description
Related Entries: Metadata; Metadata Application Profiles

Bibliography

Cumming, Kate. "Purposeful Data: The Roles and Purposes of Recordkeeping Metadata." *Records Management Quarterly* 17 (3) (2007). www.emeraldinsight.com/doi/pdfplus/10.1108/09565690710833099.

Gilliland, Anne, Lori Lindberg, Victoria McCargar, Alison Langmead, Tracy Lauriault, Monique Leahey-Sugimoto, Joanne Evans, Joe Tennis, and Holly Wang. "Investigating the Roles and Requirements, Manifestations and Management of Metadata in the Creation of Reliable and Preservation of Authentic Electronic Entities Created by Dynamic, Interactive and Experiential Systems: Part VI." In Luciana Duranti and Randy Preston, eds., *InterPARES 2: Experiential, Interactive and Dynamic Records.* Padova, Italy: Associazione Nazionale Archivistica Italiana, 2008. www.interpares.org/ip2/book.cfm (accessed June 8, 2014).

Gilliland, Anne, and Sue McKemmish. "Recordkeeping Metadata, the Archival Multiverse, and Societal Grand Challenges." From the Proceedings of the International Conference on Dublin Core and Metadata Applications, Kuching, Sarawak, Malaysia, September 3–7, 2012.

RECORDKEEPING SYSTEM(S)

Both the term *recordkeeping* and the term systems invoke different interpretations in different contexts. Placed together, these terms have specific meanings in some usage that are not clear for other users. This entry identifies three usages of recordkeeping systems: firstly as a component of *information governance*, secondly as a set of functionality delivered by software systems, and thirdly as a contextual entity for understanding and interpreting records.

Recordkeeping System as a Component of Information Governance

Recordkeeping Systems are organized sets of people, policies, processes, tools, technologies, ongoing education, and maintenance required to establish and support the infrastructure for recordkeeping within an organization (NSW State Records 2001). Used in this sense, the recordkeeping system operates at the same level as the concept of fonds or *archives*. Within Australian practice, recordkeeping system is formally equated to the usage of records system in the International Standard ISO-15489, "Records Management," via an explicit equivalence stated in the preface to the Australian edition of that standard (Standards Australia 2002).

Increasingly, a recordkeeping system is a component of the broader framework of information governance deployed by organizations to provide an *accountability* framework for management of all information assets. As a component of information governance, recordkeeping systems define and identify recordkeeping requirements and allocate responsibility to ensure that appropriate *records* are made and managed. Within the concept of recordkeeping system is the understanding that records are critical to organizational functioning and may, or may not, require one or more technology systems dedicated to ensuring the storage, management, and *accessibility* of records. Increasingly the conceptualization of recordkeeping informatics is proposing to incorporate some or all of the characteristics of records into the management of all information assets, regardless of the conditions of their creation and the systems that manage them. Identifying those information assets requiring additional management layers is a matter of organizational risk undertaken within the framework provided by the recordkeeping system.

As the foundation for implementation of good, sustainable recordkeeping within an organization, the recordkeeping system must be flexible and capable of adapting to changing organizational priorities and ever-changing technologies used as the basis for business transactions. Key to this are the requirements for:

* a strong conceptual understanding of recordkeeping;
* a sustainable analytic framework defining recordkeeping requirements; and
* a flexible and agile implementation methodology.

The equivalence of recordkeeping system to the ISO terminology records system points to well-developed, internationally accepted guidance available in the suite of ISO standards, in particular:

* ISO 15489, *Records Management*; and
* ISO 30300 series of standards on *Management Systems for Records*.

Within those standards, a recordkeeping system consists of:

* the framework of analysis;
* the definition of recordkeeping requirements;
* the records control tools (such as metadata schema, business classification, access and security model, and disposal rules);
* the specific technology deployed; and
* the records processes (*appraisal*, registration, classification, storage, use, migration, and disposal).

Recordkeeping System as Software

The phrase recordkeeping system is often used to refer to business systems that manage records—that is, systems that capture, maintain, and provide access to records over time. When system is used in its broad sense of people, processes, and technologies, this usage is not incompatible with the primary usage outlined above. And it was this broader usage that David Bearman employed in his 1993 essay "Recordkeeping Systems," which reintroduced the term to wide professional use. The articulation and discussion in this seminal essay was embedded within the context of information systems theory and design, originally a technological context. It articulated the differences between electronic information systems and electronic systems that manage records; summarized by Terry Cook:

> Information systems by definition contain data that is timely; efficient from a technical perspective; interchangeable for many differing uses or views; manipulable; and non-redundant—old data is bad data, and is therefore replaced by new, updated, correct data. Recordkeeping systems are just the opposite: they contain records that are time-bound and context-stamped; inefficient technically; directly connected to every use and its animating function through controlling metadata; inviolable and unchangeable once created; and redundant—old data is not condemned as outdated and therefore deleted, but is viewed as being just as valuable as new data. (Cook 1997, 23)

In this way, recordkeeping systems are often equated to the specific technology employed to capture, manage, or access records, at the expense of the broader framework that surrounds any such technology. It is common to find discussions of EDRMS (*electronic document and records management systems*) as recordkeeping systems. Increasingly we are finding discussions of business information systems as recordkeeping systems where these possess the capabilities to manage records. The equation of specific technology and system is common here. It is this usage that is perhaps most often encountered in colloquial use.

Recordkeeping System as Context

A third major strand to the use and understanding of the phrase recordkeeping system is found within Australian usage. As early as 1959, Ian Maclean identifies the theory of recordkeeping that was developed early in 1958 during a course for *record* managers in Commonwealth Government Departments. Discussing the theoretical grounding of education for recordkeepers, Maclean articulated professional study as "the study of the characteristics of record materials, the comparative study of past and present recordkeeping systems, and the classification problems associated with them" (Maclean 1959, 389).

This articulation defining the centrality of understanding recordkeeping systems predates the development of the establishment of the Commonwealth Archives Office (Australia's predecessor a few times removed from its National Archives), the *records continuum* theory, and the *series system* of records control. However, Maclean's seminal influence in these events (Upward 1994) makes the centrality of his thinking about recordkeeping systems one of the core building blocks of Australian recordkeeping theory and practice.

Recordkeeping systems as a concept resonate through Australian archival literature (Bearman 1993, footnote 3). In the series system implemented at the Commonwealth Archives Office, whether an organization possessed an independent recordkeeping system was the criteria determining its registration as an independent agency (National Archives of Australia). The recordkeeping system was documented exactly through relationships of *series*: the correspondence system related to all its indexes, registers, and past and present iterations of the control records. Recordkeeping systems as such were not regarded as entities for independent registration

within the series system, but as has been argued in more recent times (Hurley 2008), incorporating these as entities would require only a very minor adjustment to the system fundamentally designed by Peter Scott.

In this conceptualization of recordkeeping system, the understanding of the functioning of the system becomes a key component in understanding the *context* of the creation of the record. These conceptualizations were done for a paper-based world, and reinvented by David Bearman for a digital world in the "Recordkeeping Systems" and "Documenting Documentation" articles. Bearman writes:

> Archives appraise and accession recordkeeping systems, not individual records, because recordkeeping systems do not just passively reflect how the creating organization used information, they actively determine it. As such, recordkeeping systems are an organic whole. (Bearman 1992, 22)

When used as contextual entities, recordkeeping systems are broader than a single technology implemented. The relationships between various technology components need to be identified and documented to record the recordkeeping context. For example, an EDRMS is not always a single recordkeeping system but may need to be documented with all its embedded links to related systems—perhaps the personnel system that may detail the user permissions and roles, or the business systems to which it interfaces. Together all these linked technology systems would form the recordkeeping system as context. Failing to understand the importance of these relationships in the conceptualization of recordkeeping systems will negate one of the purposes of recordkeeping systems:

> Quality recordkeeping systems retain the information content and structure of records in reconstructable relations, and also enable records to be retrieved at a later date in a form that represents their original structure and in a way that reflects their context of creation and use. (McKemmish 1994, para. 34)

Conclusion

Recordkeeping system possesses different interpretations according to different cultures and contexts. Care needs to be taken to position the understanding of usage. Three of the most common usages of recordkeeping systems are: firstly as a component of information governance, secondly as a set of functionality delivered by software systems, and thirdly as a contextual entity for understanding and interpreting records.—*Barbara Reed*

Keywords: recordkeeping system, records system, information governance, context, software

Related Entry: Electronic Document and Records Management System (EDRMS)

Bibliography

AS/ISO 15489, "Records Management. Part 1: General." Standards Australia, 2002.

Bearman, D. "Documenting Documentation." *Archivaria* 34 (1992). http://journals.sfu.ca/archivar/index.php/archivaria/article/view/11839/12791.

———. "Recordkeeping Systems." *Archivaria* 36 (1993). http://journals.sfu.ca/archivar/index.php/archivaria/article/view/11932/12886.

Cook, T. "The Impact of David Bearman on Modern Archival Thinking: An Essay of Personal Reflection and Critique." *Archives and Museum Informatics* 11 (1) (1997). DOI: 10.1023/A:1009035121019.

CRS Manual. National Archives of Australia, 1960s. http://naa12.naa.gov.au/manual/Provenance/AgencyDefinition.htm (accessed December 2013).

Hurley, C. "What, If Anything, Is the Australian Series System? Part 3, Understanding a 'Series.'" 2008. www.infotech.monash.edu.au/research/groups/rcrg/hurley.html (accessed December 2013).

"Introducing the DIRKS Methodology." State Records NSW, 2001. www.records.nsw.gov.au/recordkeeping/dirks-manual/introducing-the-dirks-methodology/recordkeeping-systems (accessed December 2013).

International Standards Organization. *ISO 15489-1:2001: Information and Documentation—Records Management—Part 1: General.* Geneva, Switzerland: International Standards Organization, 2001.

International Standards Organization. *ISO 30300:2011: Management Systems for Records.* Geneva, Switzerland: International Standards Organization, 2011.

Maclean, I. "Australian Experience in Records and Archives Management." *American Archivist* 22 (5) (1959). http://archivists.metapress.com/content/cu4242717578022t/fulltext.pdf.

McKemmish, S. "Are Records Ever Actual?" In S. McKemmish and M. Piggott, eds., *The Records Continuum: Ian Maclean and Australian Archives: First Fifty Years.* Clayton, Victoria, Australia: Ancora Press, 1994. www.infotech.monash.edu.au/research/groups/rcrg/publications/smcktrc.html.

Upward, F. "In Search of the Continuum: Ian Maclean's 'Australian Experience' Essays on Recordkeeping." In S. McKemmish and M. Piggott, eds., *The Records Continuum: Ian Maclean and Australian Archives: First Fifty Years.* Clayton, Victoria, Australia: Ancora Press, 1994.

RECORDS CENTER

In the United States and Canada, the *records lifecycle* is an important concept based on the idea that *records* lose their usefulness as time passes. The phases or stages of the life of a record vary from country to country and through time but correspond to the lifecycle of an organism: birth (creation phase), life (maintenance and use phase), and death (*disposition* phase). At times, the lifecycle of a record is divided into phases to allow for different storage options: creation, active records, semi-active records, inactive records, and final disposition (destruction or transfer to another department, organization, or an *archives*).

In the international context, there is no universal term to define the semi-active and inactive phases of records; nevertheless, the procedures for the legal maintenance of *documents* are almost the same in all countries. On one hand, the definition "current record" and "historical record" are commonly accepted; on the other hand, in North America and Europe the second stage (semi-active/inactive) of records is defined according to different terms and concepts. In France, for instance, we talk about *archives intermédiaires* instead of records centers, while the term *documents semi-actifs* refers to *documents* and papers; Italians and Romanians use the definitions *archivio di deposito (arhiva de deposit)*, Germans *Altregistratur*, and the Anglo-Saxon *semi-*

active records. Apart from the nomenclature, the specific functions are rather very well defined.

Internationally, the term archives as an institution harkens back to *recordkeeping* activities carried out in the ancient world. The term may be applied to institutions that house permanent records or institutions that store semi-active records (e.g., *archives intermédiaires*). In the United States, the term records *center* is used to describe facilities that store records that have *primary value*, and the term archives is used to describe facilities that store records based on their *secondary* (historic or research) *value*.

Semi-active and Inactive Records

The integrity and *authenticity* of records become more vulnerable to external risks as their use declines. As soon as all practical tasks are accomplished, records are legally stored in a sort of "limbo," which is much more often conceptual than physical. Those that are referred to as semi-active are referred to only occasionally because of their primary value. In larger organizations, those that are referred to less than once in a month are considered semi-active. Inactive records are those that are no longer needed for current business but have not yet met the end of their retention period (Franks 2013, 281).

The task of *records managers* is not only to manage the proper storage and maintenance of records but also to appraise records for legal disposal or long-term preservation. All tasks have to be performed by highly qualified personnel with a wide knowledge of the institutional history of the creator, the filing plans and *records schedules*, the organization models, and all legal implications related to the preservation or disposal of specific record *series*. At times records may not be physically moved but may remain in the same location they were stored while used for current business. At other times, they are moved for storage to a loft or in a basement, a sort of no man's land where they can be accessed by anyone (or no one). This is a serious matter, in particular when one has to deal with *appraisal* for long-term preservation. For this reason, it is necessary to create environmental, juridical, technological, and safety storage conditions.

Organizations may decide to retain semi-active records onsite so that they are available when needed, but inactive records are most often trans-ferred to an offsite records center. As experience in North America (Canada and the United States in particular) shows, storage of inactive records should meet these three requirements:

1. The decision to dispose of records has to be revised periodically by the *archivists* and the creator (the office in charge and its officials), so that any choice made at a certain point can be reviewed according to an historical point of view, as well as considering the creator's and the referring community's new needs (like in OAIS);
2. Workspaces for records handling have to be maintained so that all cleaning, disinfection, and dusting operations can be fulfilled in an adequate environment; regarding *digital archives*, all operations concern security, logical data integrity, copying, migration, and conversion; and
3. Staff training must be continuous, in particular for the personnel dealing with digital archives; training must concern formats, software, and conceptual models for filing.

History of Records Centers in the United States and Canada

The U.S. National Archives and Records Administration (NARA) was created in 1934, but it was not until 1950 that the Federal Records Centers (FRCs) were created with seventeen branches in nine states. More recently (2005), the Electronic Records Archives (ERA) was launched as part of NARA's mission to provide ready *access* to essential evidence. Today the FRCs hold 27 million cubic feet of records for nearly four hundred federal agencies and are able to complete 13 million reference requests annually. The ERA held 380 TB of electronic records at last count, many of which come from the Bush administration, various federal agencies, and Congress. Also within the ERA is a tool called Online Public Access (OPA), which has provided researchers the ability to look at descriptions of at least 75 percent of NARA's holdings.

In Canada, semi-active records are stored in archives; the first main archive was founded in Ottawa (1956), followed by branches in Toronto (1965), Montreal (1966), Vancouver (1972), and additional locations.

Early records centers maintained the physical memory of a creator; today, *digital records* are also stored. The goal is to maintain and preserve all records in a safe and secure environment. Services offered by records centers, whether managed in-house or by a third party, can carry out any combination of the following:

a) Organize the transfer of records from the creator to the nearest Records Center and ensure the preservation of them in a suitable environment;

b) Fulfill legal disposal through records schedules agreed with the creator;

c) Make, on demand, the *records delivery* with the exhibition of the original or by sending a copy, by web, e-mail, mail, etc.;

d) Transform paper copies in digital copy or microform;

e) Destroy, for security reasons and for preserving personal data, all records containing very personal information even recycling traditional formats, with particular attention to the environment;

f) Fulfill the conversion and migration of digital documents; and

g) Provide expert advice to creator.

When the creator transfers custody of its semi-active or inactive records to an in-house records center, expenses for staff and facilities (e.g., purchase or rent, cleaning, furniture) can be substantially reduced. Because most records centers are located outside of city centers, the prices for properties are much lower than the value of properties in the city center, where most of the public offices are located. It is clear that such decisions can be financially advantageous, inducing economies of scale.

Commercial Records Centers

Although semi-active and inactive records can be stored in-house in a private records center, an attractive alternative is to send them to a commercial records center. Commercial records centers (CRCs) provide a way to store, access, and retrieve records while retaining the ability to track them and destroy them when their retention period has been met. CRCs are equipped with environmental controls and

security measures to make sure their clients' records are kept safe.

History

The history of CRCs in the United States starts with a gentleman named Emmett J. Leahy. He held numerous positions over the course of his life, but from 1935 to 1941, he worked for the National Archives, followed by becoming the director of records coordination for the Department of the Navy for the duration of World War II. In 1948, he became the executive director of the National Records Management Council. In this capacity, Leahy was able to provide advice to the federal government and help lead the way on legislation that would reduce paper-record waste. He also started the Business Archives Center, which is considered by some to be the first CRC in the United States. It was not until 1953 that Leahy created his own *records management* consulting and storage businesses, thus beginning these services in the private sector.

Services

Most CRCs provide some combination of six services. These services are hardcopy storage, media storage, shredding, imaging/*digitization*, e-backup/electronic vaulting, and cloud service. Many people are familiar with hardcopy storage because paper records have been around for millennia. The records are typically stored in record carton boxes that have a barcode transfixed to them so that the boxes can always be tracked by the inventory management system. Media storage requires a greater degree of environmental control because temperature, especially heat and humidity, can do major damage to these items. Therefore, media items are usually placed in vaults so that they can have their greater protection schemes. For most records centers, media storage is comprised of CDs, DVDs, and magnetic tapes, though this can be expanded to include things like SD cards and hard drives.

When it comes to shredding services, there are usually three choices. The first choice is onsite shredding. This option enables organizations to have confidential documents destroyed onsite, usually with someone from the organization watching the proceedings. The second choice is to have a bin-rotation program. This enables workers to deposit materials that can be shredded into bins that the records center will pick up to be destroyed on a scheduled basis. Destruction can be done either onsite or at the records facility. The third choice is the destruction of items stored in the records center that have come to the end of their retention period and have no archival value. This service is carried out in the records facility. In the case of the Federal Records Centers (FRCs), a notice will be sent out ninety days before the scheduled destruction. Once the notice is returned signed, destruction will commence. Other companies will complete the destruction based on what was agreed on when the contract was signed. Some companies, like National Records Centers, provide a certificate of *disposal* after these methods are carried out.

The last three services have been born out of the digital age. Imaging/digitization allows documents to be transformed into a machine-readable *file* that allows for indexing and features such as Optical Character Recognition (OCR), which makes a document's text searchable. Also included under this is something the National Records Centers calls Scan-on-Demand. This makes it possible for organizations to send certain documents between branches without having to send the physical files. Similarly, the FRC offers a service called SmartScan, which acts as a reference request for an organization's documents to be scanned and sent to them electronically.

Electronic backups store the organization's records and information onto tapes or disks that are then sent off to the records center. Should a disaster hit, this allows for organizations to resume operations fairly quickly, usually within seventy-two hours. Electronic vaulting, on the other hand, allows the organization's data to be at the ready 24/7, because the information is transmitted directly to the records center.

Cloud storage is much like electronic vaulting in that information is available anywhere at any time. The main differences with cloud storage are that the information is under the control of a third party and that it may be stored on multiple servers and, therefore, in multiple locations. In spite of perceived risks, cloud storage is growing in popularity due to the promise to reduce infrastructure and management costs while improving data accessibility.

Conclusion

Semi-active records are those that are referred to infrequently based on their primary value. They may be stored onsite or in a records center. Inactive records are those that are no longer needed for current business but have not yet met the end of their retention period. They are likely candidates for storage in an offsite organization-owned or third-party records center. Benefits can be derived from moving inactive records to a less-expensive storage facility. Records and information managers may be involved in planning and designing in-house record storage spaces or in identifying and recommending commercial storage services.—*Lacey Ryan Banks and Gianni Penzo Doria*

Keywords: compliance, records, information, management
Related Entries: Primary Values; Records Lifecycle; Secondary Value

Bibliography

ARMA International. "Who We Are." 2014. www.arma.org/r2/who-we-are.

Business Records Management. "What Is a Commercial Records Center?" n.d. http://brmabilene.com/commercialrecords.html.

The Emmett Leahy Award. "Emmett J. Leahy (1910–1964)." www.emmettleahyaward.org/leahy-bio.html.

Faber, M. "Brief History of Commercial Records Management." PRISM International, n.d. www.prismintl.org/Learn-About-PRISM/learn/brief-history-of-commercial-records-management.html.

Franks, Patricia. *Records and Information Management*. Chicago: Neal-Schuman, 2013.

National Archives and Records Administration. "Electronic Records Archives." 2014. www.archives.gov/era.

———. "Federal Records Centers." 2014. www.archives.gov/frc.

Records Centers. "Education." 2013. http://record-center.com/education.

Vanguard Archives. "Compliance & Privacy." 2014. www.vanguardarchives.com/compliance-privacy.

RECORDS CLASSIFICATION

Records classification systems are ideally organized according to *functions*, but most employ a hybrid approach that takes into account organizational structure, records formats and media, and/or subject headings. Some challenge the value of function-based classification and the need for detailed records classification schema, especially in the born-digital records era; they espouse instead reliance on *metadata*, automatic classification, "big bucket" categories, and/or use of software applications for enterprise content management (ECM).

Discussion

Records classification is the logical structuring of an organization's records into predetermined categories that serve its business requirements and represent the relationships among *records, files,* and *series*. A records classification system is used by staff when setting aside records to be filed in the *recordkeeping system*, and when retrieving them to serve the functions and activities of the organization. An effective records classification system ensures that each record is placed in its proper context, to ensure it can be located and used both for its original purpose and to ensure *accountability* over time.

A very simple means of organizing records is by format or type, that is, minutes, reports, and correspondence (traditionally broken down into "incoming" and "outgoing" and arranged chronologically, also possibly indexed by names and subjects). Media can also enter the picture—for example, a "photographs" category. However, the increasing volume of records in various formats and media requires most modern organizations to employ a system with meaningful classification categories that accurately reflect the ongoing value of the records, as well as the functions, activities, and purposes they document.

Classification systems that are subject-based tend to become very detailed and require constant updating to maintain their relevance in the current operational structure. They can break down without the discipline of a controlled vocabulary.

Leading archival theorists from Theodore Schellenberg to Luciana Duranti have traditionally emphasized a functional approach, and this continues to be espoused in international standards that address the management of electronic records, including ISO 15489 and MoReq2.

Schellenberg (1956) outlined the basic elements of a records classification system as follows:

- Direct or indirect *access*: Direct access uses words, which are easily browsed but provide poor search results in the absence of a controlled vocabulary; while indirect access uses alphabetical and/or numeric codes that require an index and may be arranged in blocks using two or more sets of characters to denote an organizational unit and a specific file series (i.e., the block numeric system).
- The system may be detailed (standardized and codified) or flexible (relatively simple and easy to expand). A detailed system may prove difficult to maintain over time if rooted in the organizational structure (as reorganizations wreak havoc); however, if based on thorough analysis of ongoing functions, it can actually prove to be surprisingly flexible, as in British Columbia's ARCS and ORCS system (Meyer zu Erpen 1991). Where this is not the case, the "big bucket" approach, discussed further below, seems an appealing option.
- Centralized vs. decentralized: The former approach provides uniformity of filing and contributes to the standardization of an organization's processes, whereas the latter is convenient for users but can make records searches difficult and can lead to inconsistent practice. A combined approach is possible—for example, policy and procedures may be centralized and other records managed in individual offices. These days, high-value records are often managed in an *electronic document and records management system* (EDRMS) and records with short-term value are maintained in individual drives, e-mail folders, and collaborative tools (e.g., SharePoint sites). The risk here is that high-value records may not ever make their way into the recordkeeping system. This very common problem needs to be addressed through the development of viable, effective, and simple schemas/systems.

Until the late twentieth century, organizations commonly employed professional file clerks, who were responsible for filing the *documents* created and received. File clerks were essentially the "gate-keepers" of an organization's accountability as well as of its corporate memory. Nowadays there are few file clerks, and increasingly the gatekeeper is an automated system (an EDRMS). While the system may offer a variety of search capabilities, records *creators* become frustrated by the decision-making and knowledge requirements of good filing. They want automated, flexible, easy-to-use classification structures that include fewer categories and require less time and thought. Can keyword search capabilities, automated classification, and "big buckets" meet their needs?

Automated classification is a component of ECM systems developed to help manage the information in "unstructured data" (i.e., records not contained in structured databases). It involves automatically extracting "index, category, and transfer data . . . based on predefined criteria or a self-learning process" at the time records are entered into the system (i.e., the "capture" phase) (Kampffmerger 2006, 36). Automated classification is a concept in its early stages and may have great potential; however, this is yet unproven. This approach may reduce records filing effort but requires a significantly greater information technology infrastructure than standard classification systems (replacing those long-lost file clerks with systems staff).

The issues of cost and efficiency also arise when the interesting idea of abandoning classification and even the creation of files in favor of reliance on records metadata is floated (Bak 2012). While metadata linked to the titles and contents of records, files, and series can be a tremendously powerful means of bringing together records for a variety of purposes, detailed metadata can make the system cumbersome. This renders long-term maintenance unwieldy, especially from the perspective of the archival repository that must preserve those records. These conditions give birth to exactly the complex, user-unfriendly environment we are trying to escape. The *information governance* landscape becomes less effective, and its value is called into question. Most importantly, records maintained without the *context* of a file or series will lose their *archival bond* with related records and become

difficult or impossible to schedule. Any grouping of records that is created using metadata becomes an aggregation created for reference purposes; the original purpose of the record is obscured, as is the relationship it had to other documents created for that purpose. Thus the document is reduced to data with much of its meaning lost forever. "The creation of virtual files 'on demand' should not replace the 'fixed' arrangement that provides evidence of the way records had originally accumulated in the course of business" (Foscarini 2009, 58).

"Big buckets" (the concept of using a few or several categories to cover a large group of records that share a retention schedule and some other features, as an alternative to assigning multiple specific classification codes) may be appropriate for low-value records that do not document significant actions and decisions but are needed for reference purposes for a few months or years. Most email correspondence, project documentation, and reference materials would be eligible for these big buckets, if the buckets are keyword searchable. These buckets essentially serve the needs met by "crutch files," "day files," and subject-based reference files in the paper-based era. However, big buckets cannot obviate the needs for more detailed management and retrieval tools (Montana 2008) and for a function-based classification system that places these records in the context of their creation, showing their relationship to other records and to electronic systems and the data they contain. It is especially valuable for government organizations to have such systems for purposes of accountability and transparency ("open government").

Classification schemes are also extremely valuable when integrated with *records schedules*, thus ensuring minimal effort is required to move records from one stage of their lifecycle to another. Records eligible for *disposition* or long-term storage can be easily identified; "offsite" storage is an important option for high-volume records series of physical records, and secure "nearline" storage is becoming an issue for *digital records* that may not become inactive for decades due to sensitive legal or other issues (e.g., records relating to children in care that need to be available throughout the individual's lifetime). Functional classification systems combine especially well with records schedules, as the resulting categories can be used not only for filing, search, and retrieval, but also for defining the *lifecycle* timetable for the records (Meyer zu Erpen 1991).

Have functional classification systems been given a real chance to succeed in the electronic era? Researchers suggest that we need proper studies of the *user* experience, explicit detailed manuals for developing the systems, and perhaps also standard taxonomies (Foscarini 2009; Guercio 2002); we should also exploit the discipline of *diplomatics* to ensure that the *functional analysis* of archival records is not only "top down" (i.e., analyzing laws, regulations, and related materials to gain an understanding of the creator's functions and organization) but also "bottom up" (i.e., analyzing the records themselves) (Duranti 1998).

The effectiveness of any classification system depends on three main factors: flexibility (with broad, high-level categories that encompass records in all formats and withstand organizational change), integration with records schedules (the records in each category should share the same retention schedule, a natural fit if it reflects existing records series), and harmony with the organization's actual *recordkeeping* practices (to reflect the way records creators are creating and using the records). Considerable consultation and functional analysis is required to achieve this. The result should not be a snapshot of file titles currently in use, but rather a synthesis that employs plain language and function-based classification terms. It should also provide indexes and other metadata that provide terminology and explanatory text to assist both expert and new users to locate the file series relevant to their search. In addition, a system needs to be practical, efficient, user-friendly, and the classes of documents must be mutually exclusive.

Conclusion

Modern organizations need classification systems to meet their business needs. The ideal system may be a hybrid of high-level functional classification categories and, within records series, lower-level arrangement according to organizational structure, records format, or subject. Good metadata enhances access to the records but cannot adequately reflect the manner in which an organization uses its information to conduct actions and make decisions, unless it is rooted in a set of stable relationships among records, files, and series classified in a recordkeeping system.—*Susan Hart*

Keywords: big buckets, block numeric system, classification, enterprise content management (ECM), records management

Related Entries: Case File; Context; Digital Record; Diplomatics; Electronic Document and Records Management System (EDRMS); File; Function; Functional Analysis; Interrelatedness (Record); Metadata; Organizational Culture; Recordkeeping Metadata; Recordkeeping System(s); Records Function; Records Management; Records Schedule; Registry System; Series; User Behavior

Bibliography

Bak, Greg. "Continuous Classification: Capturing Dynamic Relationships among Information Resources." *Archival Science* 12 (3) (2012): 287–318. DOI: 10.1007/s10502-012-9171-8.

Duranti, Luciana. *Diplomatics. New Uses for an Old Science*. Lanham, MD, and London: The Society of American Archivists and Association of Canadian Archivists in association with Scarecrow Press, 1998.

Foscarini, Fiorella. *Function-Based Records Classification Systems. An Exploratory Study of Records Management Practices in Central Banks*. PhD dissertation, University of British Columbia, 2009. https://circle.ubc.ca/bitstream/handle/2429/9310/ubc_2009_fall_foscarini_fiorella.pdf.

Guercio, M. "Records Classification and Content Management: Old Functions and New Requirements in the Legislations and Standards for Electronic Record-Keeping Systems." In *Proceedings of the DLM-Forum*, 2002, 432–42.

International Standard Organization. *ISO 15489: Information and Documentation—Records Management. Part 1: General*, 1st edition. September 2001.

Kampffmerger, Ulrich. "Enterprise Content Management—Definitions, Components and Challenges, 2006." White Paper for *DMS Expo*. http://project-consult.net/Files/ECM_White%20Paper_kff_2006.pdf (accessed December 2013).

Meyer zu Erpen, Walter. "British Columbia's Integrated System of Records Classification, Records Scheduling, and Archival Appraisal." Paper presented at the annual conference of the Association of Canadian Archivists, Banff Alberta, May 1991. www.islandnet.com/~wmze/BC_records_management_and_archival_appraisal.htm (accessed December 2013).

"Model Requirements for the Management of Electronic Records." DLMForum, MoReq2, specification sponsored by InforesightLimited, 2009. www.moreq2.eu (accessed December 2013).

Montana, John. "Legal Implications for Using Big Buckets." *Information Management Journal*, Hot Topic Supplement (2008): 13–15.

Schellenberg, Theodore R. *Modern Archives: Principles and Techniques*. Chicago: University of Chicago Press, 1956.

RECORDS CONTINUUM

John Keane argues in his book *The Life and Death of Democracy* that we should always regard the languages, characters, events, institutions, and effects of democracy as thoroughly historical. Keane points to the essence of the continuum perspective. The ways things are formed are essential to understanding them, and those things are always in motion. The same can be said of any institutionalized ways of governing our web of relationships, and *archives* are crucial to the study of the process of governance, its movement, and its operation in particular times and places.

Discussion

The study of ongoing motion underpinned many of the philosophies of emergence that mushroomed at the end of the nineteenth century and in the first three decades of the twentieth. Philosophically such approaches can be labeled "continuum thinking" if they emphasize process, fluidity, and the expansive effects of interaction of moments in spacetime. Readers interested in developing their own overviews of such philosophies might like to look at *Wikipedia* entries for Gabriel Tarde, Henri Bergson, Albert Einstein, Edmund Husserl, Samuel Alexander, A. N. Whitehead, John Dewey, C. S. Peirce, William James, Georg Simmel, Max Weber, Herman Minkowski, Georg Cantor, Kurt Gödel, T. S. Eliot, and/or J. M. Keynes.

It is an impressive list. Each of these men has shaped intellectual currents and in the manner of great minds of their era almost all were generalists who transcended disciplinary fragmentation. The sociology of emergence suggested by Georg Simmel has genetic links to more recent sociologists such as Erving Goffman, Zygmunt Bauman, Pierre Bourdieu, Bruno Latour, and Anthony Giddens. Henri Bergson's ideas were complexified by Jacques Derrida, Gilles Deleuze, Michel Foucault, and others. Continuum mathematicians like Gödel and Cantor have influenced later theorists including Imre Lakatos and Benoit Mandelbrot.

Can a case be established that such seminal thinkers had any impact on *archival practice*? If we look at Great Britain and Sir Hilary Jenkinson's *Manual of Archives Administration* the answer to that question would seem to be yes. The first edition of the manual was produced in 1921 at the height of discussions about the work of Albert Einstein and Samuel Alexander in Britain. Jenkinson was interested in continuous custody and the forensic examination of source, transmission, and the organic formation of archives in particular times and places. The founding and early operation of the U.S. national archival authority in the 1930s and 1940s added clinical approaches to forensic study and provides an even clearer example of continuum thinking. The development was supported by much of the archival discourse at the time. Memorable federal and state archivists such as Phillip Brooks and Margaret Cross Norton helped set up management structures for, and wrote about, the full lifespan of *records*. Ernst Posner noticed the strength of this administrative strand of archival thought when he ended his first article as an American academic archivist with the assumption that *archivists* will become the nation's experts who must be consulted in all questions of public record-making and *recordkeeping*.

This is a form of records continuum thinking, although the label was not used widely until the 1980s. In Australia it was used to describe an approach to archival administration in alignment with Posner's advocacy of the need for a single record-keeping mind, which was put in place by the Commonwealth Archive Office (CAO) during the 1950s and 1960s. The main architects were Peter Scott and Ian Maclean. Maclean, Australia's chief archivist, had studied the complexity of the parts. He analyzed file types and records *series* inside and outside of the government's administrative registries, paying particular attention to patterns for forming sets of records. The sets, whether they were deemed to be permanent or temporary, could be transferred to the archival authority whenever it was deemed convenient to do so (McKemmish and Piggott 1994). The management of "temporary" records, logically, is as much part of any continuum approach as the management of records deemed to be of enduring value.

Scott provided the systematic whole that could sit above the complexity and fluidity of the movement of series and sets. He developed a control system that involved registering agencies, registering the series they produced, and establishing a matrix of relationships between both as they moved through spacetime. His framework could be applied no matter where the *series* was located, how old it was, or what type of material was involved (Cunningham 2010).

For a number of reasons the system did not survive in the Australian government in a continuum-based form. In the 1980s Australian Archives (the successor to the CAO) began to follow more traditional custodial strategies. Its legislation was broad but its mandatory powers were focused on permanent records after the lapse of at least twenty-five years from their creation. Scott's system when applied forensically sets up a heavy descriptive workload. For it to be manageable, description needs to be built up progressively, continuum fashion.

The single-minded recordkeeping approach (a mind capable of thinking about making and keeping records in past, present, and future moments) has continued to develop in Australia, but it has done so outside of the Commonwealth government. Today its strongest manifestations can be seen in various university archives and state government operations, especially State Records NSW, in International Records Management Standards and Guidelines, which were first developed in Australia in the 1990s, in consultancy organizations, and in discussion groups such as the Recordkeeping Roundtable and the Monash University Records Continuum Research Group.

Conceptually, while criticisms of continuum theory can come from outside the paradigm, two major types of criticism can be made from within. One type is topographical, critiquing applications for their adequacy or otherwise for particular times and places. For example, Maclean and Scott put together an adequate approach at the tail end of the paper era, but it failed to sustain itself through the changes involved in electronic and digital recordkeeping.

The other type of major critique is topological. Are records continuum approaches actually in tune with continuum thinking? One facet of the shape of such thinking is that the space-time continuum is a generator of expansion, difference, and diversity. This cardinal feature of any philosophy of emergence connects ideas from space-time–based studies of motion and expanding complexity with ideas about the galloping continuum of recorded information that is such a feature of our emerging digital recordkeeping era. But are we making the connections?

A second facet of the shape of continuum thinking, illustrated in the above discussion of practices introduced by Scott and Maclean, is the relationship between the whole and the part. Gabriel Tarde and Alfred Whitehead, for example, both regarded the whole as a continuum in which a vast number of entities entered in one way or another into the constitution of every other. Underneath that simple view of the whole, as Tarde argued, the parts are more complex, a "confusing plasma composed of myriads of monads, a chaos, a brew" that constitutes that complexity (Latour 2012). Whitehead recommended using scientific method as a way of bringing some order to that chaos. How well are we managing the whole, and are we effectively using *archival science* to come to terms with the brew?

A third facet of the shape of continuum thinking is the deeply sensible notion of T. S. Eliot that only time can conquer time, a theme he set out poetically in *Burnt Norton* published in 1936 (Ketelaar 2004). Larry Stillman and I have called this archival time (see figure R.1). The information continuum element of the cone (the capture, organization, and pluralization elements) indicates the way archival action affects the amplification of a moment that might otherwise be unnoticed amid billions of other moments. This idea has provided the basis for my own information continuum modeling (Upward 2005).

Archival time is pragmatic, dealing with antecedents, conditions, causes, results, and future moments. It is always remaking things, often in an

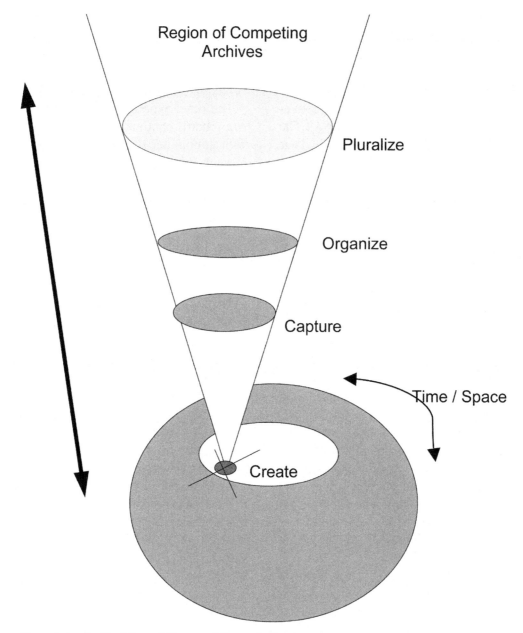

Figure R.1.   Archival Time. *Stillman and Upward, after Bergson*

atmosphere of contestation. In records continuum theory managing it is our only way of future proofing ourselves to use a term coined by David Roberts within reports and programs at State Records, NSW.

Are archivists carrying out their future proofing role effectively, bearing in mind that in continuum theory expanding complexity means that the goal is adequacy, not perfection? This requires archivists to be in tune with motion, complexity, and archival time in their own time and place. Many Australians claim Scott and Maclean were in tune when they

made their major contributions but their contributions remained time-bound.

Continuum practices to be longlasting need to evolve from a stable base such as an acceptable records continuum model. One such four-dimensional model was developed at Monash University in 1996 (see figure R.2). Its first dimension refers to how we represent traces of action, the second with capturing those representations, the third with how we organize an archive, and the fourth with the plurality of the whole. The axes in the model represent how

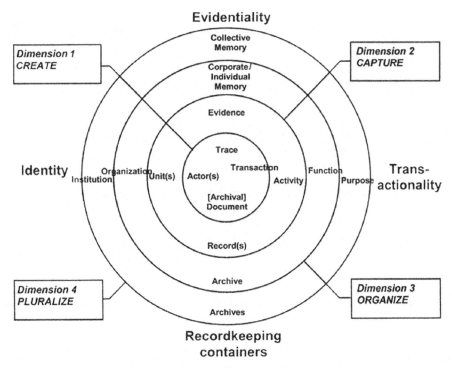

Evidentiality

Dimension 1
CREATE

Dimension 2
CAPTURE

Collective
Memory

Corporate/
Individual
Memory

Evidence

Trace

Transaction

Identity

Institution Organization Unit(s) Actor(s) Activity Function Purpose Trans-actionality

[Archival]
Document

Record(s)

Archive

Dimension 4
PLURALIZE

Dimension 3
ORGANIZE

Archives

**Recordkeeping
containers**

Figure R.2.   The Records Continuum Model. *Upward 1996*

basic recordkeeping techniques can help us store evidence of our actions.

The model has helped promote an informatics approach. Informatics as a term covers studies of the computational, cognitive, and social aspects of the way we represent, process, and communicate information. Three major strands have emerged at Monash University. One is community informatics, which of course is not just an Australian development. In the United States and Great Britain it is increasingly present in archival studies that address community archiving processes and the archival multiverse ("Pluralizing the Archival Curriculum Group," 2011).

A second strand, recordkeeping informatics, is under construction. It is emerging from the collaboration of Australasian teachers and trainers and aims to reestablish recordkeeping as a specialization based on using time to conquer time and to make this role clear to other *information management* specialists (Upward, Reed, Oliver, and Evans 2013). The third and necessarily international strand is the most complex and can be called juridical informatics, within which archivists will need to help establish protocols for communications in the changing information spaces of their time and place. Those protocols will need to be compatible with the capture of quality records and the formation of a useful and usable archive over time, goals that can be present in all forms of informatics.

Conclusion

Records continuum archivists have helped keep the ideal of a space-time approach alive in the face of massive changes to our information and communication technologies. The developments in digital recordkeeping currently grouped together under the labels of cloud computing and social media mean that a new generation of archivists, if they wish, can now begin to find recommencements. For their approach to be coherent, however, they will have to come to terms with the complexity and fragmentation of the parts and the expanding breadth of the whole. They also face the challenge of convincing people all over again that only time conquers time.—*Frank Upward*

Keywords: archival time, informatics, recordkeeping

Related Entries: Archival Science; Information Management; Recordkeeping

Bibliography

Cunningham, A. *The Arrangement and Description of Archives amid Administrative and Technological Change: Essays and Reflections by and about Peter Scott*. Brisbane: Australian Society of Archivists, 2010.

Ketelaar, E. "Time Future Contained in Time Past: Archival Science in the 21st Century." *The Journal of the Japan Society for Archival Science* 1 (2004): 20–35. http://hdl.handle.net/11245/1.227317.

Latour, B. "The Whole Is Always Smaller Than Its Parts: A Digital Test of Gabriel Tarde's Monad." www.bruno-latour.fr/node/330 (accessed on July 31, 2012).

McKemmish, S., and M. Piggott. *The Records Continuum: Ian Maclean and Australian Archives: First Fifty Years*. Melbourne: Ancora Press in association with Australian Archives, 1994.

"Pluralizing the Archival Curriculum Group: Educating for the Archival Multiverse." *American Archivist* 74 (1) (2011): 69–101. http://archivists.metapress.com/content/hv3396471274 5684/full-text.pdf.

Upward, F. "Continuum Mechanics, Memory Banks and the Making of Culture." *Archives and Manuscripts* 33 (1) (2005): 84–109; 33 (2) (2005): 18–51. http://search.informit.com.au/documentSummary;dn=200606902;res=IELAPA.

Upward, F., B. Reed, G. Oliver, and J. Evans. "Recordkeeping Informatics: Re-figuring a Discipline in Crisis with a Single Minded Approach." *Records Management Journal* 1 (2013): 37–50. http://dx.doi.org/10.1108/09565691311325013.

RECORDS FUNCTION

In *diplomatics*, the way in which a record relates to an action is considered to be the *function* of the record. There are six possible record functions: dispositive, probative, supporting, narrative, instructive, and enabling. The first two produce *records* whose written *form* is required by the legal system in the *context* of which they are created and are the only functions identified by classic diplomatics (Duranti 1989–1990). The second couple of functions were identified by modern diplomatics for records whose written form is discretionary (Duranti 2009a). The last two functions were added in the course of research on *digital records* with reference to certain structured records in electronic systems (Duranti and Thibodeau 2006).

The Concept

Classic diplomatics considered to be records only those *documents* that participate in action, and categorized them according to the way they relate to action, that is, their function. The chosen categories reflected the types of records existing at the time they were developed. Thus, in the seventeenth century, diplomatists called *notitia* a record that was meant to provide evidence of an act that came into existence and was complete before being manifested in writing, and *charta* a record that was meant to put the act into being and was therefore the essence and substance of the act. Later on, the former category came to be called "probative records," and the latter "dispositive records." Both categories comprise records whose existence and written form are required by the juridical-administrative system within which they are created. These are therefore legal records, capable of serving as authentic evidence of the matter they talk about. Examples of probative records are birth certificates, land registries, court transcripts, and receipts. Examples of dispositive records are contracts of sale, grants, job applications, and money orders.

With the increase in literacy and in amount of written documents made and received in the course of activity, legal records came to be a very small part of the entire documentary production. Thus, it became important to diplomatists to identify and categorize these new types of nonlegal records. They began by dividing the nonlegal records into two categories: "supporting records," whose function is to guide the activity in which they take part; and "narrative" records, whose function is simply to convey information. While both categories of records participate in some kind of action, neither is able to carry out an action or provide evidence of it by itself. Examples of supporting records are teaching notes and maps, and examples of narrative records are informal correspondence, unsolicited reports, and accounts of events.

In the 1990s, research aimed at the understanding and control of digital records decided to use diplomatics as a methodology, and test its records categorization on the entities found in electronic applications and systems. This process was perfected during the second phase of the InterPARES (International Research on Permanent Authentic Records in Electronic Systems) Project (see www.interpares.org) and resulted in the identification of two additional categories of records, which clearly existed also in a traditional environment, but were not as pervasive: "instructive" records and "enabling" records. Instructive records are those that indicate the way in which external data are to be formally presented (e.g., regulations, manuals of procedure, forms with embedded instructions for filling them out). Early examples of this type were music scores, and scripts for plays, as well as traditional instructions attached to paper forms. Enabling records are those that allow for the execution of business transactions (e.g., interacting business applications), the conduct of experiments (e.g., a workflow generated and used to carry out the experiment of which it is instrument, by-product, and residue), or analysis of observational data (e.g., interpreting software), and performance of artworks (e.g., software patches). Early examples of this type were numeric conversion tables. The salient characteristic of these two categories of records in the electronic environment is that, in both cases, the record as it is stored in the system differs from the record as it is manifested on the computer screen, and sometimes the stored record has no corresponding manifested record (e.g., software) (Duranti and Thibodeau 2006).

Conclusion

Diplomatists identify the function of records with respect to the action in which they participate in order to assess the evidentiary capacity of the records and their ability to reveal the development of the action. However, the understanding that derives from a *functional analysis* of the records themselves also helps to identify the *archival bond* among the records participating in the same activity, the way the records were used, and the importance of preserving intact specific elements, features, and capabilities of the records (Duranti 2009b).—*Luciana Duranti*

Keywords: records, diplomatics, records types, evidence

Related Entries: Archival Bond; Diplomatics; Record(s)

Bibliography

Duranti, Luciana. "Diplomatics: New Uses for an Old Science. Part II." *Archivaria* 1 (29) (1989): 4–17. http://journals.sfu.ca/archivar/index.php/archivaria/article/view/11605/12552.

———. "Diplomatics." In Marcia Bates, Mary Niles Maack, and Miriam Drake, eds., *Encyclopedia of Library and Information Science*. New York: Marcel Dekker, 2009a.

———. "From Digital Diplomatics to Digital Records Forensics." *Archivaria* 68 (68) (2009b): 39–66. http://journals.sfu.ca/archivar/index.php/archivaria/article/view/13229/14548.

Duranti, Luciana, and Kenneth Thibodeau. "The Concept of Record in Interactive, Experiential and Dynamic Environments: The View of InterPARES." *Archival Science* 6 (1) (2006): 13–68. http://dx.doi.org/10.1007/s10502-006-9021-7.

RECORDS INVENTORY

The records inventory is a "detailed listing that identifies all of an organization's records" and "includes data about the types of *records*, locations, dates, volumes, equipment, classification systems and other relevant information about the records" (ARMA International 2012). A records inventory is prepared for planning and analysis purposes to determine the characteristics of an organization's *recordkeeping systems* (Saffady 2011). The data gathered in an inventory will enable the evaluation, *appraisal*, and organization of records, so that *records management* instruments such as classification schemes, retention schedules, or security requirements can be developed. An inventory can also identify vital or critical records and is a key tool for preparing backup and disaster recovery planning and procedures. In addition, the inventory can provide the baseline data from which a data map of an organization's electronically stored information is developed.

Inventory Method

The method for conducting an inventory consists of the following steps: developing an inventory plan, preparing a survey instrument to collect the inventory data, conducting the inventory according to the plan, and collating and evaluating the inventory results (Saffady 2011).

Inventory Plan

The inventory plan outlines the steps of the inventory, including determining the scope, span, and duration of the inventory project, determining any requirements for identifying and surveying electronic information resources, and determining who will perform the inventory. The purpose is to identify the organizational units and the records generated. The inventory plan also includes development of the procedures and training of personnel for conducting the inventory.

One of the key planning decisions is the determination of how extensive and how much time the inventory will take to complete. Ideally, the inventory should encompass all organizational units and all of the records held within. However, in specific circumstances, a less intensive method of reviewing records may be undertaken by conducting a records survey. The scope of the inventory, including the organizational units and types of records to be covered, must be practical in scale and time, to provide useful data. Assigning more human resources to complete the inventory, conducting the inventory in phases by work groups, or scaling back the scope of the inventory to key organizational units, will ensure that the plan can be completed in a timely fashion and provide relevant data useful for analysis and planning. Management approval and support for the inventory are crucial, as the project will touch all parts of an organization as the organization's information assets are surveyed.

Survey Instrument

The survey instrument is the data-gathering tool that will be used to collect the data from the inventory. Using a formal survey form (inventory form) will ensure that the data collected are useful, uniform, and complete. Records should be described according to the program unit or work group where they are created and according to the record *series*, the logical grouping related to the business *functions* of the work unit. The organizational units and physical locations of information should be mapped, with temporary location numbers to enable specific data entry and analysis (Bennick and Sitton 2014, 36). Whether in physical or electronic format, the inventory form identifies the elements and characteristics of the records, and ensures consistency of data collection. The specific data elements to be collected include the following sets: fundamental information such as the program unit, the record series, location, and purpose of the records; other items include *record format*, filing method, security requirements, creating body or individual, date range and physical extent of the records, and additional information such as how often the records are referenced, and whether there are regulations governing the records (Saffady 2011, 43–54). Additional data about electronic records includes the system from which the records are generated, the software and hardware requirements, frequency of updates, type of database, linkages to related systems, reports generated, and duplication or relationship to physical records formats (ARMA International 2005; Bennick and Sitton 2014, 36–40).

A paper form can be carried by staff on clipboards as they interview staff and explore the various locations to be inventoried. An electronic form on a tablet will save keyboarding time, if the organization has an electronic forms-management program, enabling the inventory data to be readily uploaded into an inventory database (Bennick and Sitton 2014, 50). Samples of inventory forms will provide useful sources from which to determine the specific elements to be collected (ARMA International /Society of American Archivists 2002) (Saffady 2011, 38–39). A database that compiles inventory results should be developed as part of the development of the forms, and a method of quality control for review of the inventory data and data entry should be developed as part of the preparations for the inventory.

Conducting the Inventory

Conducting the inventory takes time and attention to detail. The inventory must be conducted systematically, efficiently, and according to procedures. Ensuring that the inventory is completed according to the timetable developed in the plan ensures that the data gathered is timely and useful for planning. Taking too long to complete an inventory means that the data collected will be outdated and possibly irrelevant as the collected data will be rendered obsolete by the continuing accumulation of records accrued through organization activities.

The inventory data can be collected by distributing the inventory form as a survey, using designated records coordinators in the work groups or departments. Alternatively, the data may be gathered directly by trained records management teams examining records and consulting with users. Depending on the time available, a combination of both methods may be used. Generally, the survey will enable quicker collection of information, whereas the direct collection will take more time but permit the inventory staff to query the users, observe practices, and clarify any questions. In all circumstances, the inventory project manager must clarify the answers to ensure completeness of information.

The amount of time taken to complete an inventory will depend on the size and scope of the organization, as well as the survey approach used. A *sampling* of work activity will provide a benchmark for identifying how long it will take to complete the inventory (Bennick and Sitton 2014, 32–33). In addition, a calculation of time required can be developed, based on the number of work groups to be reviewed, as follows: one preliminary visit, followed by the data collection (estimated at ten minutes per records series), and then follow-up to review any questions. Each set of activities is estimated to take three hours of time. Following the data collection, an additional amount of time should be allocated for the tabulation, analysis, and summary of the information collected in each work unit (Saffady 2011, 40–41).

Surveying Electronic Records

Electronic records must be included in the inventory to ensure completeness of the data collection. Electronic records are found in various systems, and assistance from information technology staff may be required to determine the nature and extent of the various types and locations of electronic records. Repositories can include: centralized information systems such as electronic mail servers, network file shares, enterprise application servers, and legacy systems; dedicated information systems for specific functions within defined work groups; personal work stations and storage devices including personal computer hard drives, laptops, tablets, smartphones, digital cameras, and removable media; and third-party service providers and external locations such as social media sites and cloud service providers (Franks 2014, 5).

Depending on the architecture and systems products, electronic records are identified and described as systems, rather than individual records series. The ownership of these systems may be a central agency such as the information technology department operating on behalf of the organization. Systems-generated records should be described as part of the information system from which they are produced, and then at the series level if the records that are produced can be so described. Data about the information system should include the application software, the input and output data from the system, including data, text, digital images, and other formats, as well as the purposes for which the electronic records are used (Saffady 2011, 41). Relationships with records in hard-copy formats should also be described. Unstructured electronic records in repositories and file shares may be described at the series level. Other data to be collected about electronic records includes the supporting files, backup procedures, provisions for migration, as well as retention requirements, use restrictions, and *vital records* status (Franks 2014, 5).

Data Mapping

Data mapping is a recent term associated with the records inventory, and has become as significant as the activity to identify records series. A data map is defined as a

> comprehensive and defensible catalog of an organization's electronically stored information (ESI), that includes the relevant information technology systems and media (online and off line), and the responsible business units, data stewards and custodians. It goes beyond typical hardware and software inventories, and includes scope, character, organization, formats and limits on *accessibility*. (Bennick and Sitton 2014, 82)

This system information can be identified as additional questions for collection on the survey form, described by users to the survey teams, and used to prepare the data map as an additional product of the inventory process.

Inventory Analysis

The analysis of inventory results is the final step taken to complete the inventory. As the inventory forms and data are collected, the *records manager* or project manager should ensure that all information collected is clear and complete. Following correction or clarification, the data should be transcribed into the inventory database or other electronic tool for analysis and use in preparing records retention schedules, classification systems, or other records management instruments. It is recommended that as each interview or work-group evaluation is completed, a set of minutes or notes is prepared, and provided to the department or work group for confirmation and clarification if any data are not clear. This clarification will ensure the accuracy of the data collected and enable appropriate decisions going forward (Saffady 2011, 56).

Conclusion

The records inventory has evolved from a survey of physical records to a comprehensive survey and analysis of all of the information assets of an organization. The completed inventory, provided it has been well planned and executed, will provide data on which to base decisions about the records instruments needed by the organization, as well as enable the organization to produce evidence in compliance with regulations regarding the management of electronically stored information (ESI).—*Alexandra Bradley*

Keywords: records inventory, inventory plan, survey instrument, data map
Related Entries: Records Function; Records Management; Records Schedule

Bibliography

ARMA International. *Glossary of Records and Information Management Terms*, 4th edition. ARMA TR22-2012. Overland Park, KS: ARMA International, 2012, 43.
———. *Retention Management for Records and Information Management.* ANSI/ARMA 8-2005. Overland Park, KS: ARMA International, 2005, 9.
ARMA International/Society of American Archivists. *Sample Forms for Archival and Records Management Programs.* Overland Park, KS: ARMA International, 2002, II.
Bennick, Ann, and Judy Vasek Sitton. "File System Development—the In Depth Records Inventory."
In *Managing Active Business Records*, 2nd edition. Overland Park, KS: ARMA International, 2014, 31–51, 82.
Franks, Patricia. "Part 3: ERM Program Fundamentals, Slide 5." In *Electronic Records Management.* www.statearchivists.org/seri/STEP/ERM-3/index.htm.
Saffady, William. "Preparing Retention Schedules I: Inventorying Records." In *Records and Information Management: Fundamentals of Professional Practice*, 2nd edition. Overland Park, KS: ARMA International, 2011, 31–56.

RECORDS LIFECYCLE

The idea that *records* have a life is linked to the qualities of organicity and *naturalness* that archival authors have traditionally associated with the concept of *archives*. This idea recurs in the international literature of *records management* and *archival science* since the 1940s but finds its origin in the United States, although Europe had toyed with the concepts of "live archives and dead archives." The phases or stages of records' life have since varied from country to country and through time, as have the criteria determining which they are, but everywhere the concept of records lifecycle involves a progression, a sequence, a beginning, and an end. This is in contrast with circularity of the concept of *records continuum* developed in Australia in the 1980s adopting an expression first used by Canadian author Jay Atherton (1985) to embody a records view articulated a couple of decades earlier by Australian writer Peter Scott.

From Life History to Life Span to Lifecycle

In 1940, American author Philip Brooks argued that "the several steps in the life history of a given body of *documents*" involve creation, filing, *appraisal*, and either destruction or permanent preservation, that "the earlier in the life history of the documents the *selection* process begins is the better for all concerned. And the earlier in that life history that co-operation between the agency of origin and the agency can be established, the easier will be the work of all" (Brooks 1940, 223–26). Thus, the record's life moves from the responsibility of the "office manager" to that of the *archivist* in a seamless way through the exercise of the appraisal function. Although we already encounter in the writings of Brooks the expressions "current" and "noncurrent record," they are linked to frequency of use and not yet to changes in jurisdiction on the records themselves.

In was only after the end of the second world war that records creating agencies and national archival institutions in North America and Europe began to be concerned with "dormant" records, that is, with records that were no longer current ("active" in Canada) and not yet noncurrent ("inactive" in Canada). In response to this concern, various administrations created *records centers* that would store records that were semi-current ("semi-active" in Canada) and host the appraisal process. While in the United Kingdom and other European countries, like Italy, these variously named units were under the jurisdiction of the creating agency (Posner 1972), in North America they were placed under the jurisdiction of the archival institution, preferring, in the words of Schellenberg, the purgatory concept to the British limbo (Atherton 1979, 55):

> Records management is thus concerned with the whole life span of most records. It strives to limit their creation, and for this reason one finds "birth control" advocates in the records management field as well as in the field of human genetics. It exercises a partial control over their current use. And it assists in determining which of them should be consigned to the "hell" of the incinerator or the "heaven" of an archival institution, or, if perchance, they should first be held for a time in the "purgatory" or "limbo" of a record center. (Schellenberg 1956, 37–38)

Following further elaborations of Brooks's and Schellenberg's ideas, the life of the records came to be regarded as developing at the same time through three stages, with regard to the frequency of use and related management activities, and through two phases and eight stages, with regard to jurisdiction/responsibility and management activities, as outlined:

Criterion: Frequency of Use
1. Current or Active Records: creation, filing, maintenance, use, scheduling, disposal
2. Semi-current or Semi-active Records: transfer to record center, identification and organization, administration of reference, disposal

3. Noncurrent or Nonactive Records: selection/*acquisition*, arrangement and description, preservation, *conservation*, reference service

Criterion: Jurisdiction
1. Records management stage (carried out by the creator for its administrative purposes)
   Phases:
   Creation or receipt
   Classification/filing
   Maintenance and use
   Disposition
2. Archival stage (carried out by the archivist for the public's research purposes)
   Phases:
   Selection/acquisition
   Arrangement and description
   Preservation
   Reference and use

It was in relation to the growing dichotomy between records management and archival management that the expression "records lifecycle" began to be used within the national archives of the United States first and throughout North America later. And it is to this dichotomy that Jay Atherton objected when he proposed that such expression be substituted by a "records management-archives continuum" in four phases, where the guiding criterion is service, as follows (Atherton 1985–1986, 51):

1. Ensure the creation of the right records, containing the right information in the right format.
2. Organize the records and analyze them to facilitate availability.
3. Make the records available promptly to those who have a right and a requirement to see them.
4. Systematically dispose of records that are no longer required.
5. Protect and preserve the information for as long as it may be needed.

Jay Atherton's continuum is very similar to Philip Brooks's records life history in that it envisions an ongoing collaboration between the creator and the designated preserver since the creation of the records and presents a sequence of integrated activities that begins at creation and ends at preservation—very different from the Australian circular concept of records continuum.

Interpretations of the Records Lifecycle Concept

In the past half-century, North America has settled on the concept of the records lifecycle as articulated in the mid-1950s while in practice moving toward Atherton's concept of the continuum, primarily because of the need to acquire control of "machine readable," "electronic," and today *"digital" records* of enduring value as soon as possible after creation and, possibly, even before then, by designing reliable *recordkeeping systems.* During the same time span, several initiatives have reexamined the lifecycle concept, giving it different spins, albeit often maintaining its name.

France, in the 1960s, developed the theory of the record's three ages (Duchein 1970), based on to whom the records are useful, as follows:

1. Administrative age: usefulness to the creator
2. Intermediate age: decreasing usefulness to the creator, increasing usefulness to others
3. Historical age: general usefulness

A decade later, most continental Europe moved toward the idea of structuring the records lifecycle on the basis of the records location, de facto supporting the North American dichotomy between the management of the records for the purposes of the creator, and the management of the records selected for permanent preservation for general purposes, as follows:

1. Records in the creating office
2. Records in the central registry (creator)
3. Records in the intermediate archives/records center (preserver)
4. Records in the historical archives

Great Britain, with the Grigg report issued in 1954, established the principle of collaboration between the *record manager* and the archivist since the beginning of the lifecycle, especially in relation to appraisal. Discussing the British situation, in 1980, Felix Hull developed the theory of "movable responsibility," according to which record manager

and archivist work together throughout the lifecycle but the responsibility of the former gradually diminishes as the responsibility of the latter grows. Indeed, this approach is very similar to Atherton's continuum, and it is fully implemented for public records.

In the 1990s, the issues presented by records created in electronic systems began to dominate the discourse related to the records lifecycle. Instead of renouncing the concept though, it was preferred to change its meaning and to design its stages so that it would serve the identified need. Thus, the United Nations ACCIS Report of 1990, although still naming the newly conceived process as a records lifecycle, described the functional requirements of an information system in relation to the following idea of the lifecycle:

1. Records Creation and Identification
2. Appraisal
3. Control and Use
4. Disposition

A few years later, in 1997, the International Council on Archives (ICA) Committee on Electronic Records decided to rewrite in its guidelines for the management of electronic records the stages of the records lifecycle using as criterion "the archival *function*." Accordingly, the stages were reduced to three:

1. Conception of Records (including the design of the records creating and keeping system)
2. Creation of Records
3. Maintenance of Records (including Preservation and Use)

If one considers carefully the UN and the ICA models, one realizes that, regardless of their name, they are not a reworking of the lifecycle model but are two different expressions of the Australian records continuum model. In fact, differently from those models, the concept of records lifecycle involves a shifting of responsibility for the records from the creator to the preserver—no matter how seamless, and regardless of ongoing collaboration—and is based on the use and location of the records, on the purpose of the activities carried out on the records, and on the *person* responsible for those activities: the creator or the preserver. Does this mean that the concept of lifecycle had by this time fulfilled its function and finished its usefulness? Perhaps not.

Clearly, by the late 1990s, the focus of the concept was firmly established on electronic records. Simultaneously to the ICA, the UBC/DOD Project (1994–1997) developed its own version of a lifecycle for electronic records that was later embedded in the DOD Standard 5015.2 (1998). The criterion determining the stages of the lifecycle was the *reliability* and authenticity of the record system (Duranti, Eastwood, and MacNeil 2002):

1. Creation in office space (before transmission): make, send, and set aside
2. *Recordkeeping* in a central space (after transmission): receive from outside and from inside the organization, and set aside
3. Classification and scheduling
4. Maintenance activities of all kinds and use
5. Disposition
6. Record-preservation in a central preservation space: preservation activities of all kinds
7. Dissemination activities of all kinds

While in this model the shifting of responsibility from the creator to the preserver is blurred by the fact that the electronic system is regarded as one entity with separate spaces and separate *access* privileges to such spaces, in the model developed a few years later by the first phase of the InterPARES Project (www.interpares.org, 1999–2001), the division between the two stages of the lifecycle following under the responsibility of the creator and the preserver could not be sharper. The criterion on which the InterPARES concept of lifecycle is based is the *status of transmission* of the records. The model includes two stages, the first regarding the records of the creator, and the second regarding the authentic copies of the records of the creator.

It is generally accepted that it is not possible to preserve electronic records. It is only possible to preserve the ability to reproduce them. This is because every time one retrieves a record, a copy of such record is generated. However, when copies are produced by the creator in the course of its activity, as soon as they participate in further activity and reference, they are again original records in the cre-

ator's *context*. They behave and have to be treated as originals every time they are used and acted on. This implies that any management activity carried out on those items is carried out on the creator's records.

When the records of the creator are no longer needed for the ordinary course of activity and are passed on to the preserver, they cannot any longer be treated as originals because the creator has never used or acted on the copies produced by the preserver for long-term storage and preservation. These are authentic copies of the original records. If the records were to be reactivated for the use of the creator, then we would again have the records of the creator.

The implications of the different status of transmission of the records are key to the way they are managed. The creator can decide at any given time to give to its records the most useful, accessible, interoperable form, or the form that best serves its present and projected needs, and have as a result entities that we can call the records of the creator. In contrast, the preserver can only manage what it receives from the creator by making an authentic copy of it and has no right to alter its documentary form, only its format.

Conclusion

The concept of records lifecycle has supported the management of records for several decades and its usefulness is not diminishing, especially at a time when records are increasingly created and maintained in online environments, and might have to be preserved in hybrid environments (i.e., in in-house as well as online records preservation systems). While, at the time the concept was developed, the shifting of responsibility from the creator to the designated preserver involved a flow of records from the physical custody of the creating office to that of a records center and later of an archives, in the future, this shifting of responsibility might involve simply the passage of the legal and intellectual control on records that continue to exist in the same online environment.—*Luciana Duranti*

Keywords: current records, noncurrent records, archival management

Related Entries: Appraisal; Record(s); Records Continuum; Records Management

Bibliography

Advisory Committee for the Coordination of Information Systems (ACCIS), United Nations. *Management of Electronic Records: Issues and Guidelines.* New York: United Nations, 1990.

Atherton, J. "From Life Cycle to Continuum: Some Thoughts on the Records Management–Archives Relationship." *Archivaria* 1 (21) (1985): 43–51. http://journals.sfu.ca/archivar/index.php/archivaria/article/view/11233/12172.

———. "The Origin of the Public Archives Records Centre 1897–1956." *Archivaria* 1 (8) (1979): 35–59. http://journals.sfu.ca/archivar/index.php/archivaria/article/view/10728/11607.

Brooks, P. C. "The Selection of Records for Preservation." *The American Archivist* 3 (4) (1940): 221–34. http://archivists.metapress.com/content/u77415458gu22n65/fulltext.pdf.

Duchein, M. "Le pre-archivage: quelques clarification necessaires." *La Gazette des Archives* 71 (4.e trimester) (1970): 225–36.

Duranti, L., T. Eastwood, and H. MacNeil. *Preservation of the Integrity of Electronic Records.* Dordrecht: Kluwer Academic, 2002.

Great Britain, Parliament. *Report of the Committee on Departmental Records.* Cmnd. 9163. London: HMSO, 1954. (Known as "The Grigg Report.")

Hull, F. "The Appraisal of Documents: Problems and Pitfalls." *Journal of the Society of Archivists* 6 (5) (1980): 287–91. DOI:10.1080/00379818009514154.

International Council on Archives, Committee on Electronic Records. *Guide for Managing Electronic Records from an Archival Perspective.* Paris: International Council on Archives, 1997.

International Research on Permanent Authentic Records in Electronic Systems (InterPARES). InterPARES 1 Book. www.interpares.org/book/index.cfm.

Posner, E. "Introduction." *Archives in the Ancient World.* Cambridge, MA: Harvard University Press, 1972.

Schellenberg, T. R. *Modern Archives.* Chicago: University of Chicago Press, 1956.

RECORDS MANAGEMENT

A centuries-old practice yet a twentieth-century construct, records management is concerned with the processes and controls for the creation, capture, and management of an organization's *records* to support that organization's operations. It is also the term used for the professional practice of managing records. Its relationship with *archival science* has been the subject of much debate over the last century, and perspectives on this remain divided.

A Brief History

There is evidence of *recordkeeping* societies dating back at least to the Sumerians in 3500 BCE. The evolving principles of records administration, implying a controlled and strategic approach to the management of records, have been understood in many countries over the centuries. For example, the Romans had aerariums for managing legal dictats sent across Europe; the Normans in England developed the scaccarium (or exchequer) to control the management of finances; and in the middle ages across Europe, registries or chanceries evolved to log proprietary records and track their movements. In many cases where a transaction was worthy of capture through recording, surrounding systems of administration evolved to authenticate and make accessible that recorded information through time (Clanchy 2013). These administrative systems sought to deliver information that was trustworthy, and hence records have often been associated with concepts surrounding evidential information for the law and societal *accountability* for current and past events.

With the growth and formalization of governments in the West, the extent and centralization of records resulted in concepts of archives separate from the operation of daily government at both national and regional levels. The first national archives was the Archives Nationales established by decree in France in 1794 following the gathering up of records in the wake of the French Revolution of 1789. In 1838, in London, the Public Record Office Act was passed to "keep safely the public records." Over time, regimes and legislation were developed in many countries that required officials to pass on records designated for permanent preservation and to make these publicly available in archives.

Until the 1930s the approach to managing records (records administration) had been to "keep track of it all," often through very effective *registry systems* such as those established during World War I in the UK's Treasury Department by the chancellor and later Prime Minister Lloyd George to support operations and management. However, as the volume of records grew, it became clear that a new approach was required. During the 1930s and 1940s there were discussions across the globe about what to destroy and what to keep; some European countries were implementing records destruction processes. The discussions led to new concepts that underpin records management theory and practice. Instrumental in these debates were developments in the United States where Brooks (1940) outlined key ideas on *appraisal* and the model of lifecycle ("life history") management, the latter building on Leahy's view (1940) that more effective control of "records making" was needed. Their work is considered by many to be the foundation of contemporary records management. During this period Leahy chaired a number of committees including the 1948 "Records Management Task Force" to address the requirements for federal records management and their relationship with the nation's archives. Part of the Hoover Commission contributed to the precise term "records management" being enshrined in legislation for the first time when the U.S. government passed the Federal Property and Administrative Services Act in 1949, which provided for "an economical and efficient system" for, among other things, records management.

In the 1950s two significant publications were the Grigg Report (Great Britain Parliament, *Report of the Committee on Departmental Records*, Cmnd. 9163 [London: HMSO,1954]), which considered the management of the UK government's records and made key recommendations about their appraisal and transfer to the national archives; and Schellenberg's book (1956), which became a handbook for twentieth-century records management. Schellenberg did not define the concept of records management, but did explicitly state that it is "concerned with the whole life span of most records" (1956, 37). As such the lifecycle concept of managing records from birth to death, during the different phases of their life, was further developed, and it worked well in the paper paradigm. In the 1980s, an alternative model for managing records was first made explicit by Atherton at the annual conference of the Association of Canadian Archivists (Atherton 1985), although its antecedents were later traced

by Ian Maclean to the 1950s. Atherton proposed a continuum approach that emphasized the complex interrelationship between records management and archives. The continuum concept was significantly developed in Australia by Upward (2005, 205) in his *records continuum* model, which tries to "cater for both an object approach and a systems-based process approach to recordkeeping."

At the heart of the evolution of many of these ideas was a debate about the relationship between archives and records management. The "Dutch Manual" (Muller, Feith, and Fruin 1898) had presented a management system for records that was separate to that of archival management, and later Jenkinson (1922), then deputy keeper of the UK Public Record Office, similarly advocated for an approach to managing records whereby *archivists* would take an active role only from a point at which the custodianship of the records was transferred to the archives. In the United States, a running debate about the relationship between archivists and administrators and the processes for selecting records was published in *The American Archivist* (Scanlan 2011). The protagonists included Brooks, Grover, Leahy, and Posner; the case for linking the two was won largely by Leahy.

In the latter half of the twentieth century, records management was increasingly defined within textbooks and journals, notably often written by archivists. In the final decade and the early twenty-first century the term was defined and enshrined in standards.

Contemporary Records Management

The international *records management standards* contain the text that is the closest representation of an international consensus in regards to what contemporary records management is and should be, viz.:

> the field of management responsible for the efficient and systematic control of the creation, receipt, maintenance, use and *disposition* of records, including processes for capturing and maintaining evidence of and information about business activities and transactions in the form of records. (ISO 30300 2011, 11)

This is a slightly wordsmithed version of the original definition in ISO 15489 (2001, 3) and, additionally, ISO 30300 contains a note that records management is also called recordkeeping.

If one consults these standards and the range of records management handbooks that are available, one can conclude that the value of records management lies in supporting an organization to conduct its "business" efficiently, effectively, and economically, over the short, medium, and longer term, by providing evidence in the form of information contained in records to support its internal business activities and decision making in line with business and legal requirements, and for internal and external accountability. It helps protect the interests of the organization and the rights of its stakeholders. It ensures that information is available when it is required but equally that it is held securely and accessed only by those with the appropriate permissions. In most instances contemporary records management is conducted within organizations devoid of any connection or consideration for archival concerns, focusing solely on supporting current business functions and processes.

Reflecting an increasing recognition of the value of managing records as an information asset, the term has been widened to "records and information management" or "information and records management" to include such information that may not have strong evidential characteristics but is nonetheless created and/or used in the course of an organization's business activities. Records management is increasingly linked to corporate governance requirements, *risk management*, and compliance programs, particularly in the context of the audit culture and ethical accountability. In this context many records management requirements have been enshrined in legislation and codes of practice. And, in the digital world, records management is enabled by its intrinsic link to information systems and information and communications technology.

The Practice of Records Management

While records management has been carefully defined in standards, the systems and processes for its delivery are not prescribed. However, they must be reliable, secure, compliant, comprehensive, and systematic (ISO 30300, 3). Well-established and accepted tools, or controls, exist that enable the efficient and systematic control of the creation, re-

ceipt, capture, maintenance, use, and disposition of records. These include classification and indexing; *metadata*; access controls; storage and tracking; retention and disposal schedules; and risk management including business continuity planning. Good records management leads to authoritative records that have the necessary characteristics of *authenticity*, *reliability*, integrity, and usability as required by the organization. Not all business information needs to be captured as an evidential record and as such records (and information) management systems ensure that information is appropriately managed with resources proportionately directed in accordance with organizational requirements.

It is widely recognized that records management systems need to be based on organizational requirements, which will differ. Taking these into account, risk assessment is vital. Approaches need to be proportionate, based on information cultures within the organization, legal requirements, and wider societal expectations, as records management is not an end in itself but rather supports operational activities and processes. The benefits and drawbacks of different approaches and practices are discussed within the literature. Records management systems need to provide for business needs and be adaptable to new challenges and records *contexts*. In the digital world it is increasingly possible to automate records management processes and achieve the goals via different mechanisms, but a key challenge is the dispersal of information across systems and different legal domains where interoperability and ownership may be complicated. The information, the technology, the business processes, and the people (stakeholder) aspects of records management are inextricably linked, and the importance of people in successful records management cannot be underestimated (McLeod, Childs, and Hardiman 2011).

Professional and Scholarly Discipline

Although records management governs the practice both of *records managers* and of any *person* who creates or uses records in the course of their business activities (ISO 15489 2001, 4), it is also the term associated with the professional practice of managing records. While different occupations have undertaken records management work, for instance, UK civil service registry clerks, records management was first identified as a distinct occupation in the early nineteenth century and more widely recognized as such following the establishment of the U.S. National Archives in the 1930s. Those who lead the records management function, developing strategy, policies, and processes rather than being involved in the administration on the ground are often termed records managers. Through the foundation of professional societies in many countries, creation of ethical/professional codes of conduct, the development of degree-level qualifications often accredited by professional bodies, and the publication of professional literature, records management has established itself as a profession. The development of a body of knowledge and theory from academic research means that records management is also now recognized as a scholarly discipline.

Conclusion

Centuries old, records management was born out of supporting effective administration and government and providing evidential information. Its contemporary development evolved with the rise of administration in the nineteenth and twentieth centuries and then the information explosion, fueled by technological innovation of many kinds and the desire and drive for global connections that digital technologies enable. Perhaps because many of its early architects were archivists, records management has been perceived as a handmaiden to archives administration. In fact the reverse is true since the vast majority of records are not retained permanently in any archives, public or private. The raison d'être of contemporary records management is to support an organization in its business conduct. It should therefore be aligned with business and information systems, *information governance*, and risk management—not trapped in an archival paradigm. It must add value for an organization and be an enabler as well as a protector.—*Julie McLeod and Elizabeth Lomas*

Keywords: information asset management, systematic control, recordkeeping

Related Entries: Appraisal; Archival Science; Archival Standards; Record(s); Recordkeeping; Records Continuum; Records Lifecycle; Records Management (RIM) Standards

Bibliography

Atherton, J. "From Life Cycle to Continuum: Some Thoughts on the Records Management—Archives Relationship." *Archivaria* 1 (21) (1985): 43–45. http://journals.sfu.ca/archivar/index.php/archivaria/article/view/11233/12172.

Brooks, P. C. "The Selection of Records for Preservation." *The American Archivist* 3 (4) (1940): 221–34. http://archivists.metapress.com/content/u77415458gu22n65/fulltext.pdf.

Clanchy, M. *From Memory to Written Record. England 1066–1307*, 3rd edition. Oxford: Wiley-Blackwell, 2013.

International Standards Organization. *ISO 15489-1: Information and Documentation—Records Management. Part 1: General* and *ISO/TR 15489-2: Information and Documentation—Records Management. Part 2: Guidelines.* Geneva, Switzerland: International Standards Organization, 2001.

———. *ISO 30300: Information and Documentation Management Systems for Records—Fundamentals and Vocabulary* and *ISO 30301: Information and Documentation Management Systems for Records—Requirements.* Geneva, Switzerland: International Standards Organization, 2011.

Jenkinson, H., Sir. *A Manual of Archive Administration Including the Problems of War Archives and Archive Making.* Oxford: Clarendon Press, 1922. Digitized version available at www.archive.org/details/manualofarchivea00jenk_bw.pdf (accessed January 2014).

Leahy, E. "Reduction of Public Records." *The American Archivist* 3 (1) (1940): 13–38. http://archivists.metapress.com/content/928725x784741064/fulltext.pdf.

McLeod, J., S. Childs, and R. Hardiman. "Accelerating Positive Change in Electronic Records Management: Headline Findings from a Major Research Project." *Archives & Manuscripts* 39 (2) (2011): 66–94. http://search.informit.com.au/documentSummary;dn=201205682;res=IELAPA.

Muller, S., J. Feith, R. Fruin. *Manual for the Arrangement and Description of Archives*, 1898. Translated by A. Leavitt. New York: HW Wilson, 1940.

Scanlan, K. "ARMA v. SAA: The History and Heart of Professional Friction." *The American Archivist*

74 (2) (2011): 428–50. http://archivists.metapress.com/content/b52104n3n14h8654/fulltext.pdf.

Schellenberg, T. R. *Modern Archives: Principles and Techniques*. Reissued in 2003 with new introduction by H. G. Jones. Chicago: Society of American Archivists, 2003. www.archivists.org/publications/epubs/ModernArchives-Schellenberg.pdf (accessed Jan 2014).

Upward, F. "The Records Continuum." In Sue McKemmish, Michael Piggott, Barbara Reed, and Frank Upward, eds., *Archives: Recordkeeping in Society*. Wagga Wagga, New South Wales: Centre for Information Studies, Charles Sturt University, 2005, 205.

RECORDS MANAGEMENT (RIM) STANDARDS

Records management—also known as *records* and *information management* or *recordkeeping*—is "the field of management responsible for the efficient and systematic control of the creation, receipt, maintenance, use and *disposition* of records, including processes for capturing and maintaining evidence of and information about business activities and transactions in the form of records" (ISO 30300 2011, 11). Even when the ultimate responsibility for managing records is assigned to a *records manager*, other individuals within the organization can be expected to participate in the process.

Standards facilitate consistency during the recordkeeping process by providing codification of practice, the development of explicit rules from implicit methodologies, the accumulation of a body of common knowledge, consistency in practice and quality, interoperability and interconnectivity of systems, and efficiency in operations (Manning 2011, quoted in Franks 2013). The use of standards adds credibility to a RIM program and provides a "baseline of generally accepted principles, methods, and tools that can be relied upon to produce desirable results" (Dearstyne 2008, 45). Standards can overlap, and more often than not, several standards work together to achieve the defined goals. The appropriate mix of standards will be unique to each organization (Franks 2013).

Standards can be classified in several ways. Two types of standards are of value to records and information managers: de jure and de facto standards.

De Jure Standards

De jure standards are those adopted by an official standards-setting body, such as the International Standardization Organization (ISO), the American National Standards Institute (ANSI), and the British Standards Institution (BSI). Examples are ANSI/ARMA 18-2011, *Implications of Web-Based, Collaborative Technologies in Records Management*, and ISO 16175, *Principles and Functional Requirements for Records in Electronic Office Environments*.

Records Management Standards

The first national records management standard (AS4390) was published in Australia in 1996. The Australian standard laid the foundation for the first international standard, ISO 15489-1:2001, *Information and Documentation, Records Management—Part 1: General*, and the accompanying document, and ISO 15489-2:2011, *Information and Documentation, Records Management—Part 2: Guidelines*. Part 1 provides guidance for managing records of originating organizations, whether public or private, for internal and external clients. The following topics are addressed in the standard: policy and responsibilities; records management requirements; design and implementation of a records system; records management processes and controls; and monitoring and auditing. Part 2 offers implementation guidelines for the standard to be used by those responsible for managing records within their organizations. The guidance provided parallels the topics in part 1 as follows: policies and responsibilities; strategies, design, and implementation; records processes and controls; monitoring and auditing; and training. ISO 15489 can be useful to an organization when developing records and information management policies and procedures.

Metadata is used to identify and authenticate records and information, as well as the people, processes, and systems that create, maintain, and use them. ISO 23081 provides a guide to understanding, implementing, and using the metadata needed to manage records within the framework of ISO 15489. ISO 23081-1:2006: *Information and Documentation—Records Management Processes—Metadata for Records—Part 1: Principles* covers the principles that underpin and govern records management metadata. "These principles apply through time to records and their metadata; all processes that affect them; any system in which they reside; and any organization that is responsible for their management" (ISO 23081-1 2006). ISO 23081-2:2009: *Information and Documentation—Managing Metadata for Records—Part 2: Conceptual and Implementation Issues* "establishes a framework for defining metadata elements consistent with the principles and implementation considerations outlined in ISO 23081-1:2006" (ISO 23801-2 2009).

ISO/TR 23081-3:2011: *Information and Documentation—Managing Metadata for Records— Part 3: Self-Assessment Method* "provides guidance on conducting a self-assessment on records metadata in relation to the creation, capture, and control of records" (ISO 23801-3 2011).

In 2012, a working group was established to produce a revised draft of ISO 15489, part 1, to be published in 2015 or soon after. The need for a revision arose from the fact that, although the standard was written to be technology neutral, some of the guidance is rooted in a paper-based perspective that is no longer useful, such as the distinction between *documents* and records and the boundaries between *archives* and records management.

Standards for Management Systems for Records (MSR)

Although a revision of ISO 15489 was contemplated in 2006, the ISO subcommittee responsible for leading the work on the standard (TC46/SC11) decided that it was not warranted at that time. Consequently, the ISO subcommittee published ISO 30300 and ISO 30301 (2011), the first two in a series of standards for management systems for records (MSR). ISO 30300:2011: *Management Systems for Records—Fundamentals and Vocabulary* "defines the terms and definitions applicable to the standards on management systems for records (MSR). It also establishes the objectives for using a MSR, provides principles for a MSR, describes a process approach and specifies roles for top management." It is applicable to any type of organization that wishes to "establish, implement, maintain, and improve a MSR to support its business and assure conformity with its stated records

policy" (ISO 30300 2011). ISO 30301:2011: *Information and Documentation—Management Systems for Records—Requirements* "specifies requirements to be met by a management system for records (MSR) in order to support an organization in the achievement of its mandate, mission, strategy and goals" (ISO 30301 2011). ISO/DIS 30302—*Information and Documentation—Management Systems for Records—Guidelines for Implementation* was under development as of September 2014. This set of standards supports the technical, operational content of ISO 15489, but upgrades the approach that senior management should take to manage records at a policy and risk-assessment level by managing procedures and technology, conducting routine audits, and utilizing continual improvement processes.

Standards for Records in Electronic Office Environments

ISO 16175 was originally developed by a multinational team under the auspices of the International Council on Archives (ICA) between 2006 and 2008. Since the ICA project team included some individuals who were also active within ISO TC46/SC11, the three parts were proposed as ISO standards (Cunningham 2012). Parts 1 and 3 were approved and published by ISO in 2010, and an amended part 2 was published in 2011. ISO 16175 supports ISO 15489 by providing internationally agreed-upon principles and functional requirements for software used to create and manage digital information in office environments. This standard is divided into three parts:

- Part 1: *Overview and Statement of Principles*, which sets out the fundamental principles for the management of records in a digital environment.
- Part 2: *Guidelines and Functional Requirements for Digital Records Management Systems*, which defines the functional requirements for software systems designed principally to manage records.
- Part 3: *Guidelines and Functional Requirements for Records in Business Systems*, which defines the functional requirements for the management of information held in business systems.

Related Standards

Depending on the needs of the organization, records managers may be involved in selecting a trusted third-party *digital repository* or assessing and mitigating risks related to records processes and systems. ISO/TR 17068:2012, *Information and Documentation—Trusted Third Party Repository (TTPR) for Digital Records*, describes services and processes to be provided by a TTPR. ISO/TR 18128:2014, *Information and Documentation—Risk Assessment for Records Processes and Systems*, can be used by records professionals and auditors or managers who have responsibility for *risk management* programs related to records processes and systems.

The standards available to records managers are not just those that are considered records management standards. Records managers use other standards based on the needs of the organization and the task at hand. For example, three additional ISO standards that may prove useful are ISO 31000:2009: *Risk Management—Principles and Guidelines*; ISO 10005:2005: *Quality Management Systems—Guidelines for Quality Plans*; and ISO/IEC 27001:2005: *Information Technology—Security Techniques—Information Security Management Systems—Requirements* (Franks 2013, 41).

While records management has been carefully defined in standards, the systems and processes for its delivery are not prescribed. However, they must be reliable, secure, compliant, comprehensive, and systematic (ISO 30300, 3).

De Facto Standards

De facto standards emerge when industry best practices or standards developed for one organization are adopted for widespread use. Some de facto standards are adopted by standards-setting bodies to become de jure standards. Two examples of de facto standards are the Department of Defense standard *DoD 5015.2-STD Electronic Records Management Software Applications Design Criteria Standard* and MoReq2010 commissioned by the European Commission. Both of these standards set forth jurisdiction-specific requirements based on legal requirements within that jurisdiction.

DoD 5015.2 was developed as a U.S. Department of Defense standard, endorsed by the National Archives and Records Administration (NARA) for all U.S. government agencies, and referred to by private organizations within the United States. This standard was originally developed to provide implementation and procedural guidance on the management of records in the U.S. Department of Defense (JITC n.d.). The Joint Interoperability Test Command (JITC) tests products and makes information about certified records management application (RMA) products available through product registers.

MoReq2010 was prepared for the European Commission and has been widely accepted within the European Union. It provides a comprehensive but simple set of requirements for a records system intended to be adaptable and applicable to divergent information and business activities, industry sectors, and types of organization. It establishes a definition of a common set of core services that are shared by many different types of records systems, but that are also modular and flexible, allowing them to be incorporated into highly specialized and dedicated applications that might not previously have been acknowledged as records systems (MoReq2010 2010, 14).

Conclusion

Standards that are directly relevant to the field of records and information management can be used to develop new records management programs or improve existing ones. The overarching de jure records management standard is ISO 15489, *Information and Documentation, Records Management—Part 1: General*, with guidance provided in ISO 15489-2:2011, *Information and Documentation, Records Management—Part 2: Guidelines*. De facto standards have been developed to provide guidance in specific jurisdictions, such as DoD5015.2-STD, *Electronic Records Management Software Applications Design Criteria Standard*, and MoReq2010. Related standards are also of use to records management professionals. They include standards related to risk management, quality management, and security and privacy. Records managers should also refer to *archival standards*, including preservation and metadata standards, to provide guidance when managing records for long-term *preservation*.

—Patricia C. Franks

Keywords: standards, International Organization for Standardization, MoReq2010, DoD5015.2-STD, ISO 15489
Related Entries: Archival Standards; Digital Repository

Bibliography

Cunningham, Adrian. "Relationship between the ISO 16175 Series of Standards and Other Products of ISO/TC46/SC11: Archives/Records Management." ICA.org International Council on Archives. www.ica.org/?lid=12984&bid=1029.

Dearstyne, Bruce, ed. *Leading and Managing Archives and Records Programs*. New York: Neal-Schuman Publishers, 2008.

DoD 5015.2-STD. "Electronic Records Management Software Applications Design Criteria Standard." JITC Records Management Application. http://jitc.fhu.disa.mil/cgi/rma/standards.aspx.

Franks, Patricia. *Records and Information Management*. Chicago: Neal-Schuman/American Library Association, 2013.

Joint Interoperability Test Command (JITC). "Records Management Application." http://jitc.fhu.disa.mil/cgi/rma/ (accessed December 6, 2012).

MoReq 2010. *Modular Requirements for the Management of Records*. "Purpose and Objective," section 1.2.1, 14. http://moreq2010.eu/pdf/moreq2010_vol1_v1_1_en.pdf.

RECORDS MANAGER

The records manager is defined as "the individual within an organization who is responsible for systematically managing the records and information generated and received by the organization" (ARMA 2012, 44). In particular, the records manager is responsible for all aspects of the program, including the design, implementation, and operation of systems and for training and working with users on *records management* programs as they affect individuals (ISO). The term "records and information management (RIM) professional" is also used to describe the records manager, and implies a span of responsibility for all information assets, including digital assets, as expressed in the standard.

Depending on the jurisdiction and type of organization, the job title may vary, and the span of responsibilities may also include privacy protection and compliance, information technology services, knowledge management, legal compliance, or internal audit. Where an organization also houses an *archives*, responsibilities may be shared, with records managers assuming responsibilities for current records, and *archivists* taking control of the historic records. In some jurisdictions, records management is considered a division of archives. Government regulations and bylaws may also identify specific responsibilities of records management professionals.

Within the records management work group, staff members may have diverse titles depending on their defined role and level of responsibility. Such titles include director of records and information, records and information officer, records administrator, records coordinator, and records clerk (ARMA 2008, 76–91).

Competencies and Professional Knowledge

Competencies for records management roles have been identified, and the skills and tasks, while varying with the size and scope of the organization, have been described in various jurisdictions and within professional organizations. ARMA International, representing RIM professionals in North America and other parts of the world, published a detailed model that aligns six domains of knowledge and four levels of experience (ARMA 2007, 2–5). The domains of knowledge include: general business *functions*, common to all organizational functioning, including supervision and budgeting; RIM practices, encompassing all techniques required to manage information assets through lifecycles; *risk management*, including risk assessment and risk mitigation; communications and marketing, including speaking and writing to champion the program; information technology, including the selection and implementation of appropriate electronic tools for records management, as well as the analysis of new technology formats; and leadership, including motivation and leadership for the program. Levels of experience include level 1 (entry level with no previous experience), level 2 (having prior knowledge of RIM techniques and projects), level 3 (an experienced professional who has worked at the enterprise level and possesses extensive knowledge and skills), and level 4 (executive level, responsible for strategic decisions) (ARMA 2007, 2–5). Companion job descriptions provide examples of position titles and detailed role descriptions covering a diverse spectrum of records management responsibilities (ARMA 2008, 76–91).

An example of other competency statements includes the government of Canada's standard for competencies of the federal government information management community (CGSB). The Records and Information Management Professionals of Australasia, jointly with the Australian Society of Archivists, have also identified a Statement of Professional Knowledge, against which individuals can be tested and certified (RIMPA).

Education and Certification

Records managers possess diverse educational backgrounds and training. Depending on the country or region, records managers may have undergraduate or graduate level courses in records management subjects. However, individuals with legal, library, information technology, archival, and business degrees are also occupying records management roles. As demand for professionals with records management skills is increasing, there are a growing number of courses and degrees available, both in place at educational institutions as well as in online or distance education models.

Postgraduate testing and certification are common methods by which records managers obtain professional credentials (ICRM) (IGP) (RIMPA). To qualify for certification, a candidate must meet a combination of education and working experience requirements. Once certified, the individual will be required to earn continuing education units to maintain certification.

Conclusion

Given the growing complexity of information creation and transmission technologies, as well as the associated information regulatory and governance issues, the records manager is a professional with an imperative for extensive and continuous learning about all aspects of information creation, capture, use, and retention or *disposition*. Records mangers

can use their skills and knowledge to develop and implement enterprise records management training that will help the organization minimize risk, streamline its business processes, and meet its business goals.—*Alexandra Bradley*

Keywords: records and information management (RIM) professional, certified records manager (CRM), information governance professional (IGP), records management competencies

Related Entries: Archival Education; Archivist; Records Management

Bibliography

ARMA International. *Glossary of Records and Information Management Terms*, 4th edition. Overland Park: ARMA International, 2012.
———. *Job Descriptions for Records and Information Management*. Overland Park: ARMA International, 2008.
———. *Records and Information Management Core Competencies*. Lenexa, KS: ARMA International, 2007, 2–5.
Canadian General Standards Board. *Competencies of the Federal Government Information Management Community CGSB-192.2-2009*. Ottawa: Canadian General Standards Board, 2009.
Institute of Certified Records Managers (ICRM). www.icrm.org.
International Standards Organization (ISO). *ISO/TR15489-1: Information and Documentation—Records Management—Part 2: Guidelines*, 1st edition. Geneva, Switzerland: International Standards Organization, 2001, 2.
Records and Information Management Professionals of Australasia (RIMPA). www.rimpa.com.au.

RECORDS SCHEDULE

A records schedule is a policy document that provides certain descriptive information about a given set of *records*, including retention and *disposition* decisions. Records schedules were first used to authorize the retention and disposition of federal government records in the nineteenth century. Over the years, other public institutions and the private sector incorporated scheduling into their *records management* programs. Early records schedules were structured by department, often leading to duplicated record *series* and the need for schedule updates due to frequent organizational change. In response to this, functional schedules based on the use and purpose for keeping a record series became widespread. Born digital records challenge these conventions, and recent methodology includes the big bucket approach and identifying high- and low-value records.

Records schedules protect the interests of an organization by ensuring that official business records are kept for as long as needed, changing to meet shifting records creation, retention, and storage needs. In the governmental *context*, statutory law often dictates retention and disposition requirements, although recent legislation, such as the Sarbanes-Oxley Act (2002), has had a profound impact on American private-sector records management practices.

Records Schedule

Due to voluminous records creation, concern for records safety and security, and the need for public *accountability*, federal governments have played a pivotal role in records schedule development. Early methods of records disposition included disposal lists, special authorizations, and records schedules, which became the preferred disposition vehicle due to provisions for storage and preservation (Mohan 1994). Over the past three centuries, the governments of Great Britain, the United States, and Canada developed legislation relating to records management. For example, in the United States the Federal Records Act (1950) made documenting government decisions mandatory, and the scope of schedules expanded from records disposition to include filing methodology, identification of records of continuing value, utilization of federal *records centers*, designating record versus nonrecord copies, and developing rationales (legal, administrative, historical value) for authorized dispositions. General schedules provided for the scheduling of an agency's routine records, permitting *archivists* to evaluate and schedule the program records or "archival core" (Perlman 1952). Common or administrative records were disposed of first, followed by unique or operational records and, over time, one-time schedules were largely replaced with ongoing schedules.

Traditional records schedules consist of a description of a records series, followed by retention and disposition decisions. Retention periods are usually divided into active, semi-active, and final disposition. The active period describes the phase in which the records series is in use and physically held in the office of creation; semi-active is when the records series has been closed but may still be referenced and is often stored offsite; and final disposition determines whether the records series will be destroyed or transferred to the *archives*. Records schedules are traditionally used by records managers, but in some jurisdictions records creators apply the schedules during their regular course of business. When preparing records for offsite storage, records managers use the schedule as a tool to box records of the same retention and disposition together, simplifying the off-siting and disposal processes. At the scheduled time, records managers work closely with the disposition authority, a person or agency formally authorized to approve final disposition decisions, to effectively destroy records with no lasting historical or evidential value or transfer records to *archival custody*. With most functional schedules the records are appraised by an archivist once the transfer is complete; in some cases such as integrated *records classification* and scheduling systems, archivists are involved in records schedule development and *appraisal* decisions are imbedded in the schedule. When archivists develop schedules, for example, in the British Columbia government, they have a unique opportunity to conduct records appraisal in the office of creation. The benefit to this model is that appraisal decisions are made for all records, not just those considered to have lasting archival value. Appraisal decisions are recorded in the schedule and provide context and a greater understanding of the retention and disposition rationale. This expedites the transfer process and ensures that records of archival value are identified early in the *records lifecycle*.

Records schedules may be developed by records creators, records managers, dedicated schedule developers, or archivists. Each of these players has a different agenda: the records creators and managers want authority over the records and to have efficient disposition methods, while archivists are most interested in using schedules to retain historically valuable records. The development process includes a combination of records analysis, background research, and interviews with records creators to determine the office's operational requirements for records retention. Final approval is often contingent on legal review and formal sign-off at the executive level. In some jurisdictions such as the British Columbia government, records schedules must be approved by the legislature, while in many other provinces or states and at the federal level the state/federal archivist is responsible for approving records schedules. The process of legal and legislative review safeguards the records creators from litigation. Both the public and private sector need to comply with various statutory requirements. When legislation does not specify a retention period, scheduling information is determined based on a study of the branch's operational needs and risk analysis to determine if there are any other legal requirements to retain the records series. In the absence of legislation, schedule developers assess the history of litigation connected to a records series and determine how long the record must be kept to mitigate risk of future legal disputes. When statutory requirements such as privacy legislation or an act directly related to branch operations designate a minimum retention period, the organization must comply and be able to produce the records in court if required. Organizations that do not purge records that are due for destruction are required to disclose all related records during document discovery. In addition to the financial burden, this could lead to legal action against the records creators.

Due to government propensity for organizational change, departmental schedules have largely been replaced with more flexible, functional schedules that focus on the *functions* and activities that lead to records creation and the records that support business decisions. The following two types of functional schedules are widespread in government: common or general schedules pertain to common functions practiced government-wide such as administration, policy and program planning, legal services, communications, and executive management, while program-specific or operational schedules cover mandated or unique functions of a branch or ministry division. Public institutions such as universities often emulate this government model. In Canada, records schedule development at the provincial level was influenced by Frost and Corbett's 1983 Public Archives of Canada (PAC) study, which found that records schedules

failed to effectively identify and *transfer* records of long-term value to the archives due to a disconnect between records management and *archives*. In response to this, British Columbia and Nova Scotia developed integrated records classification and scheduling systems, fusing records schedules and file-classification plans and reintroducing the archivist to schedule development (Ware 1996).

Many institutions continue to apply traditional paper-based scheduling models to records stored in their *Electronic Document and Records Management System (EDRMS)*. The concept of a semi-active retention period is less pertinent to born-digital records as they are not subjected to the same physical movements as hard-copy records. The end result is that records will live out both their active and semi-active periods as one, at which point they are destroyed or transferred to an *archives* or a trusted *digital repository*. Integrated records classification and scheduling systems have a place in the electronic environment where the *classification* and scheduling information becomes searchable *metadata* that assists with document discovery and *disposition* and retention processing. This intrinsic connection between the scheduling information and the records differs from the paper-based world, where the schedule is often separate from the classification schema (Bak 2012).

Increasingly, corporations and other government institutions are exploring new methods for scheduling records including the big-bucket approach and identifying high-value and low-value records. These are an alternative to traditional schedules, which are often criticized as being labor intensive and not intuitive to users. In order to help lessen the workload of schedule developers, NARA implemented a "flexible scheduling" approach that uses big buckets/large aggregation schedule items for temporary records combined with flexible retention periods. Scheduling records into big buckets means narrowing an organization's record series from thousands to hundreds, or it can mean a much more extreme approach, merging all the records into as few as six buckets (for example, one bucket each for one year, three years, five years, ten years, twenty-five years, and indefinite). This big-bucket approach is being promulgated by various technology vendors as a way to optimize storage and *access* to records in a cost-effective manner; conversely, it has been noted that this approach "may be useful in managing data storage costs; however, it is not recommended for retention management because it does not effectively address event-driven conditional retention periods and is not granular enough to adequately address federal and state requirements for record retention" (John Isaza in Cisco, 2008, para. 10). Supporters of the big-bucket approach argue that benefits include ease of user-driven classification, correct application of retention periods, and quicker approvals for records disposition, as well as cost savings associated with reduced need for training and records schedule maintenance. However, these benefits can lead to a misperception that using the big-bucket strategy helps organizations avoid the need for granular classification. This is not the case: classification is still necessary, but if it is not included in the schedule, it is done elsewhere, in an indexing scheme or list system that is related and linked to the schedule (Montaña, 2008).

In recent years, there has been increased pressure on private companies to develop records schedules as part of a records management program. The Sarbanes-Oxley Act (SOX) of 2002 was introduced as a reaction to a number of major corporate and accounting controversies in the United States. Among other considerations, the act demands that certain *recordkeeping* and reporting standards be met. The act has resulted in heightened awareness surrounding SOX compliance, but it has also led to a greater understanding of corporate records management and consistent documentation of records management programs, including records destruction (Myler 2006). Documentation comes in the form of an approved schedule describing the records and outlining the records lifecycle, including final disposition. More so than in the public sector, private companies are implementing records schedules to safeguard them from the risk of litigation as there is rarely legislation guiding their records management practices. In recognition of the time and effort required to develop schedules, some records management experts suggest that companies start by scheduling the records that are high risk or likely to be subject to investigation or audit, initially leaving low-priority records out of the scheduling process.

Conclusion

The purpose of records schedules has changed very little from its initial conception. Scheduling contin-

ues to be essential for government and corporations to effectively manage large aggregates of records and regularly apply retention and disposition decisions. When departmental schedules became unwieldy, most government and public organizations shifted to functional schedules. However, as both the public and private sector seek out safe and effective storage of *digital records*, records managers and archivists will continue to experiment with other scheduling systems. This includes the big-bucket approach, and over time the current methods will be revised in response to changing recordkeeping practices.—*Genevieve Weber and Sarah Jensen*

Keywords: schedule, disposition, retention, authorization

Related Entries: Appraisal; Archival Custody; Archivist; Authority Control; Digital Record; Disposition (Records); Electronic Document and Records Management System (EDRMS), Metadata; Records Classification; Records Lifecycle; Records Management; Records Manager; Records Transfer; Series

Bibliography

Bak, Greg. "Continuous Classification: Capturing Dynamic Relationships among Information Resources." *Archival Science* (2012): 287–318. DOI: 10.1007/s10502-012-9171-8.

Cisco, Susan. "How to Win the Compliance Battle Using 'Big Buckets.'" *Information Management* 42 (4) (2008). http://content.arma.org/imm/JulyAug2008/How_to_win_the_compliance_battle. aspx (accessed October 2013).

Fischer, Laurie. "Condition Critical: Developing Records Retention Schedules." *The Information Management* 40 (1) (2006): 26–34. www.arma. org/bookstore/files/Fischer1.pdf.

Frost, Eldon. "A Weak Link in the Chain: Records Scheduling as a Source of Archival Acquisition." *Archivaria* 33 (1991–1992): 78–86. http://journals.sfu.ca/archivar/index.php/archivaria/article/view/11800/12751 (accessed October 2013).

Meyer zu Erpen, Walter. "British Columbia's Integrated System of Records Classification, Records Scheduling, and Archival Appraisal." Paper presented at the annual conference of the Association of Canadian Archivists, Banff, Alberta, May 1991.

Mohan, Jennifer. *Origin and Development of Records Scheduling in North America.* Master's thesis, University of British Columbia, January 1994. https://circle.ubc.ca/bitstream/handle/2429/4948/ubc_1994-0116.pdf?sequence=1 (accessed October 2013).

Montaña, John. "Legal Implications for Using Big Buckets." *Information Management Journal* Hot Topic Supplement (2008), 13–15. http://connection.ebscohost.com/c/articles/34731396/legal-implications-using-big-buckets.

Myler, Ellie. "The ABC's of Records Retention Schedule Development." *E-doc Magazine* 20 (3) (2006): 52–56. http://connection.ebscohost.com/c/articles/20920851/abcs-records-retention-schedule-development.

Perlman, Isadore. "General Schedules and Federal Records." *The American Archivist* 15 (1) (1952): 27–38. http://archivists.metapress.com/content/l43t803005802nq1/fulltext.pdf (accessed October 2013).

Ware, Reuban. "Multi-level Records Systems in British Columbia and Nova Scotia, Canada." Paper presented at the annual meeting of the Society of American Archivists, San Diego, CA, session 30, August 1996.

RECORDS TRANSFER

As a noun, a transfer is "a conveyance of property, a right, or a responsibility to another," or "an act of moving something or someone to another place, organization, etc." (OED 2007). In an archival environment a transfer refers to the exchange of intellectual and physical elements of a *record*. Records transfer occurs when responsibility and/or location of records passes officially from one *person* or office, which may represent the records creator, to another person or office. A transfer may include physical possession, legal rights, or both. The act of transferring records to an archival repository addresses the *appraisal* values assigned to the records and the *selection* of records based on the combined criteria of creators and preservers. An archival transfer attends to these distinctions and documents the details of an abstract and/or physical exchange. The careful details and formality of an archival transfer support the *authenticity* of records.

Modern Era

The transfer is a fundamental and timeless archival activity. But records transfer did not critically and substantially enter archival thought until the modern era. In the nineteenth century elements of modernity influenced the governance of society and its creation of records. These elements included interventionist authority, information technologies, and the distributed jurisdiction of modern bureaucracy. As volumes and varieties of records increased exponentially, problems and tentative archival solutions evolved. At the turn of the twentieth century, archival theorists spoke of records transfer in relation to the movement of *functions* as part of bureaucratic reorganizations. Muller, Feith, and Fruin (2003) note that, as a function originating in one office moves to a successor office, the records related to that function should be transferred as well. Hilary Jenkinson echoes these principles, viewing it as a question of custody when functions are created, transferred or cease within an administrative office (1967, 33–40). Jenkinson (11) views *archivists* as part of "an unblemished line of responsible custodians," essentially acting as extensions of the records creators themselves. This is the moment when the activity of transfer becomes closely associated with records authenticity.

By the 1930s the increasing influence of *records management* theory on archival administration described the concept of records transfer as a formal and documented activity within a records management system. The activity was associated with the physical transfer of records from a creating office to an offsite storage facility, often through the authority of approved records retention schedules. In *Modern Archives*, Schellenberg (1956) discusses records transfer within the context of *disposition*, with physical transfer to a records storage center serving as an intermediate step in the disposition process, which results in either destruction of the records once they have met their retention period or final transfer to the legal custody of the designated archival institution of that creating office.

Although the records have been physically removed from the office that created them, Couture and Rousseau 1987, 118) that the creating office initially still retains ownership and legal custody of the records until the records have met their defined retention period according to the records retention schedule. The issue of custody and control over an office's records is important in jurisdictions with "*access* to information" legislation, where an office with custody and control over records must respond to requests for information. When records possessing ongoing value have met their retention period, they are transferred to the custody and control of an archival institution and accessioned as part of the holdings of the *archives*. Once the archival institution has accessioned the records, the creating office no longer has authority over the records.

Although it is a familiar concept in the field of records management, records transfer can also occur in archival institutions that acquire records created by individuals or organizations that are not previously affiliated with that archival institution. In contrast to the process documented through *records schedules*, records transfer from individuals or records creators not affiliated with the archival institution can take place through bequest in a will, purchase, or *donation* through a deed or certificate of gift. In these cases, the transfer of the records represents a transfer of physical ownership to the archival institution and may include the transfer of copyright and other legal rights to the material. It is desirable to include the transfer to the archival institution of all legal rights to the records, as it will facilitate administration of these rights by the archival institution instead of requiring ongoing contact with the original records creator.

The impact of the digital era has introduced additional complexities to the process of transferring records from a creator to a preserver. In order to ensure the authenticity of the records over time, there must be controls over the transfer of electronic records to *archival custody*. These controls include procedures for registering the records transfer; verifying the authority to transfer; examining of the records to determine that they correspond to the terms and conditions of the authority governing their transfer; and accessioning the records (Eastwood 2013).

Conclusion

Although it can be viewed as a strictly administrative activity of moving records from a creator to an archival institution, the concept of transferring records is central to the archival principles of preservation and authenticity. By documenting key components of records during their conveyance from the creator to the preserver, the archival institution ensures that the records remain authentic evidence of the creator's actions.—*Michael Gourlie*

Keywords: archives, appraisal, selection, disposition

Related Entries: Appraisal; Donation; Selection; Disposition

Bibliography

Bailey, Catherine A. "Turning Macro-Appraisal Decisions into Archival Holdings: Crafting Function-Based Terms and Conditions for the Transfer of Archival Records." *Archivaria* 61 (2006): 147–79. http://journals.sfu.ca/archivar/index.php/archivaria/article/view/12539/13683.

Couture, Carol, and Jean-Yves Rosseau. *The Life of a Document: A Global Approach to Archives and Records Management.* Translated by David Homel. Vehicule Press: Montreal, 1987.

Eastwood, Terry, chair. "Appraisal Task Force Report: Interpares Project I." www.interpares.org/book/interpares_book_e_part2.pdf (accessed December 18, 2013).

Jenkinson, Hilary. *A Manual of Archive Administration.* London: Percy Lund, Humphries & Co., 1965.

Livelton, Trevor. *Archival Theory, Records, and the Public.* London and Lanham, MD: Society of American Archivists and Scarecrow Press, 1996.

Muller, S., J. A. Feith, and R. Fruin. *Manual for the Arrangement and Description of Archives*, 2nd edition. Translated by Arthur H. Leavitt. Chicago: Society of American Archivists, 2003.

Schellenberg, T. R. *Modern Archives: Principles and Techniques.* Chicago: University of Chicago Press, 1956.

Shepherd, Elizabeth, and Geoffrey Yeo. *Managing Records: A Handbook of Principles and Practice.* London: Facet, 2003.

REGISTRY SYSTEM

A registry system is a means of keeping track of *documents* through use of a register. Having such a basic and important *function*, registry systems have existed in many forms since ancient times. Today they are commonly represented by database systems. Within the context of *recordkeeping*, a registry system is simply one that makes use of a register to keep track of documents. A register, in turn, is to be thought of as some device, external to the record keeper, which serves to record essential information about the documents it is used for. In a very simple form, this can be pictured as follows: A letter comes to me, and I make a note of it in a list I keep of all letters that come in to me for the current year. The note consists of the current date, the name of the sender of the letter, and a few words describing the content.

Registry systems can take many forms, as can the register itself. Even in the example just given, the register can easily be imagined as being kept on paper with handwriting, or digitally in a computer file or database. The system may be applied to individual documents, to files of documents, or even to the business matters that generate the documents. Accordingly, what is considered essential information can vary as well. If a filing plan is being used, the essential information may be just a date and *file* number. It can be helpful for understanding the nature of the registry system to examine it through the history of its use.

The Registry System and Its Use

Approximately five thousand years ago Mesopotamian administrators put their *records* (in the form of clay tablets) in earthenware containers sealed with a baked strip of clay describing the contents. These seals were effectively registers and served quite simply to attest and summarize the content of the tablets within. Later, in Roman administration, registers such as *commentarii* and *gesta* were used not only to attest and summarize but also to report individual transactions to other offices (the senate, for example). In medieval Europe, registers appeared as books of different kinds, such as books for incoming and for outgoing correspondence, land books (real estate transactions), and monastic books recording gifts and *donations*. These books served not only to attest to the transactions recorded, but also to guarantee their *authenticity*, such that no individual document (diploma) could be regarded as authentic if it was not duly recorded in the issuer's register.

From the renaissance period on, registers tended either to maintain this authenticating role, or to revert to a simpler reporting or summarizing role. In German-speaking countries, however, a new twist was added. By the eighteenth century, the Prussian government had made the transition from registering documents or transactions to registering actual business matters. This transition was enabled by the adoption of the so-called "action file" system, in which a file is constituted by all of the documents pertaining to the resolution of a single business matter. In this kind of system, the register assumed a new role; not only did it serve to authenticate, but it also enabled administrators to quickly determine at what stage any particular business matter was. This, in turn, proved invaluable in business evaluation and planning.

Contemporary recordkeeping—in Europe, North and South America, and elsewhere—continues to make use of the registry system in traditional forms. However, the widespread use of computers in office environments, and the consequent production of electronic files, has led to the development of digital registers, chiefly in the form of databases. These databases, which along with associated software are often packaged and marketed as recorded *information management* (RIM) solutions, greatly facilitate both the handling and management of large numbers of files (electronic or physical) and the retrieval of relevant information contained in them. However, their use is accompanied by at least two serious issues. Where the development of traditional registers was part of the work of the recordkeeper, the development of digital registers is a product of software engineers, who have little or no understanding of recordkeeping. Further, such databases almost invariably tend to be document-centric and therefore not useful for other recordkeeping approaches, such as that represented by the traditional German *Registratur*.

Conclusion

The registry system is fundamental to modern recordkeeping, and it is anticipated that approaches in the near future will continue to rely on both physical and digital models, with continuing refinement of digital systems to address a broader range of recordkeeping needs.—*Thea Miller*

Keywords: registry, records management, record-keeping

Related Entries: Document; Protocol Register; Record(s); Recordkeeping; Recordkeeping Metadata; Recordkeeping System(s)

Bibliography

Miller, Thea. "Action, Transaction and *Vorgang.*" *Archival Science* 3/4 (2003): 413–30. DOI 10.1007/s10502-004-0042-9.

RELIABILITY

One of the three concepts by which the trustworthiness of a *record* is assessed, and, along with *authenticity,* one of the two concepts by which the genuineness of a record (i.e., "the quality of a record that is truly what it purports to be" [InterPARES 2, "Glossary"]) can be indirectly assessed, the reliability of a record is its capacity to be trusted as a faithful representation of the juridical fact it speaks of, that is, it is the degree to which a record "can be treated as the fact of which it is evidence" (Duranti 1995, 6). As defined by the *diplomatics*-based ontologies of InterPARES 2, the reliability of a record is evaluated by examining its completeness (i.e., "the presence within [a record] of all the elements required by the creator and juridical system for it to be capable of generating consequences") and the documentary procedure generating it (i.e., "the body of rules governing the making of an archival *document,*" where "the more standardized and rigorous the procedure, the more reliable the record is presumed to be" [InterPARES 2, "Glossary"]). How the requirements for the completeness and documentary procedure of reliable records have manifested themselves within different juridical contexts has varied: societies bestow "some methods of *recordkeeping* and record creating with an authority or 'warrant' for generating reliable records" (Duff 1998, 88), and the criteria for assessing the "truth-value" of records, as well as what counts as true, "are themselves the product of historical, cultural, and political choices" (MacNeil 2001, 45); however, as variously manifested as they may be, these are the central two concepts that determine the reliability of records (Duranti 1995). Whereas authenticity is associated with transmission and preservation of records and is the shared responsibility of the record creator and their legitimate successors, the reliability of a record is associated only with its creation and "is the sole responsibility of the physical or juridical *person* making the record" (Duranti, Eastwood, and MacNeil 2002). It is therefore not possible to increase the reliability of a record after it has been created through *authentication* or any other means. Consequently, a notable development is that the ease and autonomy with which electronic records can be produced has posed significant challenges to creating defensibly reliable records for many organizations.

Reliability, Authenticity, and Trustworthiness

As stated by Wendy Duff, "the legal, administrative, fiscal, or information value of records is dependent upon the degree of trust society places in records as reliable testimony of evidence of the acts they purport to document" (Duff 1998, 88). The social trust in records to represent juridical facts is not a quality inherent to the record, but rather the result of social confidence in the validity of the methods and procedures used to create and maintain them. A record resulting from methods and procedures that have little social confidence is still a record, but its capacity to serve as evidence is lessened. Within Duff's statement we may isolate two related concepts of trustworthiness that are distinct: reliability, to trust a record as a statement of fact; and authenticity, to trust a record to be what it purports to be, that is, to trust the record as a record. As an example of this difference, in the Roman tradition, a record attesting to a juridical fact would be considered reliable if written in a regular procedure of creation by a trusted authority, such as a notary or public officer, and possessed the signatures or other signs by those involved in the action (including the countersignature of the writer) required by the juridical system to be considered complete (Duranti 1995). The record would be considered authentic through time if it could be demonstrated that it had remained exactly as it was when it was first created, which was accomplished through the inclusion of seals and special signs only accessible to the appropriate authorities and sequestering the records away in locked chests or other inviolable spaces with *trusted custodians* (Duranti 1995). In other words, "to declare a document authentic means to say that it is precisely as it was when first transmitted or set aside for preservation, and that its reliability, or the trustworthiness it had at that moment, has been maintained intact" (Duranti 1996, 247). Although diplomatic theory reasons that reliability can be inferred from authenticity, this is because the discipline was developed in "a time when the procedures, rules and routines for records creation were so rigorous, and the means of authentication so inaccessible to anyone other than the persons entitled to use them that it was practically impossible to generate documents formally correct other than in the competent chancery, records office, or notary office" (Duranti, Eastwood, and MacNeil 2002). With the means to create records now widely accessible, particularly with the introduction of electronic systems to record-making procedures, this assumption has been necessarily dispensed with and has given way to analyzing the reliability of records to determine their credibility as evidence.

Completeness and Documentary Procedure

As the concept of reliability is rooted in observational principles, reliability is assessed "in relation to the proximity of the observer and recorder to the facts recorded." Because a record is assumed to reflect an event, its reliability depends on the claim of the record-maker to have been present at that event" (MacNeil 2001, 40). As such, the concepts of documentary procedure and completeness may be viewed as "approaches to ensuring the truth-value of records, both of which attempt to compensate for the fact that bureaucrats must rely on records that report events they have not personally witnessed or participated in" (MacNeil 2001, 41). The first approach, control on documentary procedure, focuses on ensuring the reliability of those who compile records through clearly documented procedural (and increasingly technological) controls over *record creation* in the course of practical activity. These documented controls establish the persons with the capacity to concur in records' creation, the person(s) responsible for the record, the procedural workflow associated with records creation, the actions and decision-making processes in which records participate, and the handling of records as they are compiled, completed, and filed (Duranti,

Eastwood, and MacNeil 2002). The procedure itself may also have its credibility assessed against the requirements (or "literary warrant") for creating socially trusted records set out in laws, regulations, standards, customs, and best practices (Duff 1998). The more rigorous the documentation and oversight (including supervision and audit logs), the more demonstrable that the record was generated in a regular procedure in the course of business activity, which forms a part of the requirements for business records to be accepted as evidence in both common and civil law. The second approach, which relates to completeness, has to do with "conceiv[ing] of the record itself as the event" where "records are evaluated, not in terms of their effectiveness in mirroring external events, but rather in terms of their completeness in accordance with bureaucratic standards" (MacNeil 2001, 42)—that is, it includes the elements of intellectual form required for it to generate the consequences intended by the creator and the juridical system. These elements typically "include the date, the mention of the necessary persons involved in the creation of the record and of the action or matter to which the record relates, and some manifestation of the *archival bond*, whether a classification code or any other identifier capable of placing the record within its documentary *context*" (Duranti, Eastwood, and MacNeil 2002). Although a reliable record "will be one that appears to be reliable by anyone looking at it" (MacNeil 2001), an incomplete record may also be considered reliable to a degree depending on its documentary procedure, and two records that are both at their maximum degree of completeness may have different degrees of reliability accorded to them.

Reliability in Digital Forensics

There is yet another kind of reliability that needs to be considered when treating electronic records as *documentary evidence*. In digital forensics, reliability is defined as "the trustworthiness of a record as to its source, defined in a way that points to either a reliable person (for computer-stored documents) or a reliable software (for computer-generated documents), or both" (Duranti and Rogers 2012). For example, for records created within an *electronic document and records management system (EDRMS)*, reliability may be in part demonstrated through embedded *access* privileges, audit logs of all activities within the system, and automated procedural controls, but only if there is trust that the system and associated software continuously function properly. This trust is established through audits, and is more easily established if the software is open source, as access to the source code allows for forensic authentication of results from a process or system (Duranti and Rogers 2012).

Conclusion

Because reliability is associated with records creation, the ease and autonomy with which *digital records* may be created has made it difficult for organizations to create defensibly reliable records: "too many persons and too many records forms generated in too many different contexts participate in the same transaction; too much information is recorded; too many duplicates are preserved; and too many different technologies are used" (Duranti 1995, 9). As it is not possible to later increase the reliability of a document by any means, business procedures and recordkeeping must be highly structured and regulated to ensure that records are created in such a way that they are defensibly reliable so that they may stand as the facts of which they are evidence.—*Kevin Owen*

Keywords: reliable record, trustworthiness, genuineness, documentary procedure, completeness

Related Entries: Authenticity; Record Creation; Recordkeeping

Bibliography

Duff, Wendy. "Harnessing the Power of Warrant." *American Archivist* 61 (1) (1998): 88–105. http://archivists.metapress.com/content/j75w-k8152n5u7r52/fulltext.pdf.

Duranti, Luciana. "Archives as a Place." *Archives & Manuscripts* 24 (2) (1996): 242–55. http://search.informit.com.au/documentSummary;dn=970505404;res=IELAPA.

———. "The Concepts of Reliability and Authenticity and Their Implications." *Archivaria* 39 (1995): 5–10. http://journals.sfu.ca/archivar/index.php/archivaria/article/view/12063/13035.

Duranti, Luciana, and Corrine Rogers. "Trust in Digital Records: An Increasingly Cloudy Legal Area." *CLSR* 28 (5) (2012): 522–31. http://dx.doi.org/10.1016/j.clsr.2012.07.009.

Duranti, Luciana, Terry Eastwood, and Heather MacNeil. *Preservation of the Integrity of Electronic Records*, 1st edition. Dordrecht: Kluwer Academic, 2002.

InterPARES 2 Project. "Glossary." http://interpares.org/ip2/ip2_terminology_db.cfm (accessed December 2013).

MacNeil, H. *Trusting Records: Legal, Historical, and Diplomatic Perspectives*, 1st edition. Dordrecht: Kluwer Academic, 2000.

———. "Trusting Records in a Postmodern World." *Archivaria* 1 (51) (2001): 36–47. http://journals.sfu.ca/archivar/index.php/archivaria/article/view/12793/13991.

REPLEVIN

Replevin is a form of civil action employed to recover personal property taken or withheld without permission. The term also describes the court order, or writ, authorizing the recovery of personal property by the *person* entitled to possess it. The origins of replevin can be traced to the thirteenth century when tenants employed a civil legal action to recover goods and chattels distrained, seized to satisfy a claim, by a landlord for nonpayment of rent. Eventually the remedy evolved to cover situations outside of the landlord and tenant relationship. In the United States, replevin actions were historically part of a state's common law, but today more efficient laws of civil procedure are used in most states to recover personal property. The United Nations Education, Scientific and Cultural Organization (UNESCO) supports the right of all nations to replevin public *documents* and other cultural materials that have gone astray.

Origin and Early History

The remedy of replevin was employed in common-law countries to secure the return of goods and chattels (i.e., inanimate or animate personal property) taken by a landlord for nonpayment of rent without the tenant's consent. A subsequent trial would answer the question of title to the property, and restitution to the recognized owner would be considered final.

Two versions of the early remedy exist. One, documented by Henry de Bracton, a thirteenth-century medieval jurist and priest, held that the tenant was entitled to legal redress under the plea and procedure of *de vetito namii* (i.e., *vee de nam* in French) only if faced with a refusal by the lord to redeliver the chattels taken as a distress when offered substituted security and a promise to bring suit to ascertain the parties' rights (i.e., gage and pledge; Woodbine 1944).

The second description is an earlier view by Ranulf de Glanvill in the *Treatise on the Laws and Customs of the Kingdom of England*, likely written in the late twelfth century during his tenure as justiciar of the Court of Justice under Henry II. The treatise contained two writs related to the remedy of replevin. The first recognized the need for gage and pledge but also included the requirement that the goods and chattels were taken unjustly. The second referred to taking a subtenant's cattle for dues, which he claims he does not owe since he is a free tenant. In this case, the sheriff is required to return the chattel without gage and pledge (Brennan 2007). Glanvill's description goes more directly to the existence of a debt rather than the refusal to return chattel upon the offer of substitute collateral (Hall 1965). Eventually, these early remedies evolved into the replevin action.

Other remedies for recovery of damages for wrongful taking of personal property exist, including *trover*, a form of lawsuit in common-law countries for the recovery of the value of the items taken; *trespass*, in tort law an action to compel the defendant to compensate the plaintiff for injury due to trespass on real property or injury to personal property; and *detinue*, in tort law an action to recover personal property wrongfully taken or the value of that property.

The remedy of replevin was eventually invoked for *conversion*—wrongful taking or withholding of personal property in general. The significant feature of replevin is the return of the property taken or withheld and not its monetary value. Among the property subject to replevin actions in the past are sheep (*Hopkins v. Hopkins*, 10 Johns. 369 [N.Y. Sup. Ct. 1813]), sugar (*Clement v. Jones*, 12 Mass. 60 [Mass. 1815]), and slaves (*Dickinson vs. Noland* [ARK. Sup. Ct.1845]).

In *A Practical Treatise on the Law of Replevin as Administered by the Courts of the United States*, J. E. Cobbey (1890) provides the basis for replevin actions by governments and cultural-heritage institutions by asserting that the U.S. government and not the person in charge of the public *archives* is the custodian of the archives. Although, as Cobbey (46) states, "replevin is not the proper remedy to obtain possession of papers filed in public offices," replevin can be used to recover public records held in private hands.

Replevin and Public Archival Materials in the United States

"Replevin actions for public archival estrays sustain a historical view and belief that official *records* belong to the people as represented by their governments" (O'Neil 1979, 29). "In 1853 Congress passed an act making it illegal to destroy any federal records" (Dow 2012, 4), including *captured records* of the Confederacy that were sent to Washington, DC.

In 1939, Randolph G. Adams touched on the question of the legal status of archival estrays in his account of the case of a general order to the "First Philadelphia City Cavalry" written by General George Washington on January 23, 1777. Samuel Morris, the troop's captain, took the document home. In 1823, the troop noted that the Washington document was in the possession of Captain Morris's son and resolved that it had no claim to it. When, in 1870, the troop brought suit to retrieve the document, Justice Sharswood of the Supreme Court of Pennsylvania ruled that the troop gave up all claim to the document in 1823. Adams draws the conclusion that "the *archivist* must think and act in time" to reclaim public documents (1939, 91).

The North Carolina case of the *State v. B. C. West Jr.* for the recovery of eighteenth-century public documents purchased lawfully by the defendant, an autograph dealer, on the open market became the modern replevin precedent in the United States. In 1975, the attorney general's office filed a civil complaint for the return of two documents signed in 1767 and 1768 by William Hooper, who later signed the Declaration of Independence. The Superior

Court upheld the defendant's claim of ownership because the state could not prove the documents left its possession unlawfully. However, both the North Carolina Court of Appeals (1976) and the North Carolina Supreme Court (1977) ruled in favor of the state based on proof the documents had been docketed in the King's Court under the authority of King George III and the belief that sovereignty does not lapse and that the sovereignty of the crown became the sovereignty of the state (Price 1978).

On its website, the U.S. National Archives declares its legal authority to retrieve lost and stolen documents through replevin. It further describes the consequences of lost and stolen documents for dealers, repositories, and individuals who have bought, traded, or otherwise acquired alienated U.S. government historical documents.

While recovery of the materials is the goal, punishment for a crime can result in imprisonment and/ or fines. In 2005, Howard Harner was sentenced to two years in prison, a two-year probation, and a $10,000 fine for stealing more than one hundred Civil War–era documents from the National Archives building in Washington, DC, between 1996 and 2002. Only 42 of the 103 documents were recovered.

Some of the missing documents may be in the hands of private collectors, and recovery efforts may fail, but others may be in the possession of individuals who seek to profit from their private or public sale. The emergence of the Internet provides a convenient venue for the sale of alienated public records. In 2008, Daniel Lorello, a former archives and records management specialist for the New York State Department of Education, was convicted of selling stolen artifacts on eBay, sentenced to two to six years in prison, and required to pay $129,500 in restitution.

A number of states—including California, Georgia, Maine, Michigan, New Jersey, New Mexico, Pennsylvania, South Carolina, Tennessee, Texas, and Virginia—have laws and regulations governing the sale of official government records. The New York State Archives also issued a records advisory listing steps to retrieve alienated records, including replevin, which is conducted under the terms of article 71 of the *Civil Practice Law and Rules* (CPLR). Because criminal proceedings require proof of intent in New York, the civil action

is a more convenient remedy. If a replevin action is instituted, the courts merely require documentation that the records are public records belonging to the government. In some cases, the courts may order the government agency to compensate the defendant for the purchase price of the records and the cost of their care.

California Safe Harbor Provision

Only California protects institutional holders of public documents through the Safe Harbor provision of its replevin law, which is mainly concerned with the unlawful possession of public records (Dow 2012). The law enables state and local government agencies to recover public records not in government custody that are being held unlawfully. The holder of a public record is not entitled to compensation but, if the record is returned, will receive a certified copy or digital image of the record produced by the Secretary of State or local government agency.

The Safe Harbor provision recognizes that many organizations have custody of public records obtained through noncriminal actions and allows some to retain custody if they meet two requirements. They must preserve, care for, and manage the records in accordance with professional practices as recommended by the Society of American Archivists, and they must make the records available to the public according to the California Public Records Act (Government Code 6250-6276.48).

Displaced Archives and Replevin Laws

"Displaced archives" are items missing from any *archival fonds*. Every country has holes in its collective memory due to missing public documents, and many countries, especially in Western Europe and Northern America, have foreign public documents in their repositories. Countries seeking the return of missing public documents use any private or legal means at their disposal, including a request for return, negotiation, purchase, offering alternatives such as microfilm or photocopies, and replevin. The 1985 RAMP study written by Eric Ketelaar for UNESCO states that public archives are public property and, as such, inalienable and imprescriptible. Therefore, "the National Archives should have a right to replevin (or, at least, a right to make copies) of public archives which have gone astray" (Ketelaar 1985, 104).

A state's replevin laws can be employed by plaintiffs outside of the United States to retrieve cultural heritage materials. In 1990, the *Greek-Orthodox Church of Cyprus and the Republic of Cyprus* brought a successful replevin action to reclaim four Byzantine mosaics removed without the church's authorization (*Autocephalouos Greek Orthodox Church of Cyprus v. Goldberg and Feldman Fine Arts, Inc.*). Although the defendants purchased the mosaics in good faith, the district court found that the church had met the elements of replevin under Indiana State law and was entitled to title and possession (Hoffman 2006).

Whether the remedy of replevin will be available in the future is questionable. In a 2001 article in the *Liverpool Law Review*, John Kruse asked, "Replevin—Repeal or Retain?" The author described the remedy as little used in Great Britain and Northern Ireland and questioned the necessity of its retention in light of equivalent remedies that have fewer disadvantages. By 2007, the *Tribunals, Courts and Enforcement Act* included a number of changes to bailiff law to remove archaic and complex legislation, and section 65 of the act abolished the old common law rules of replevin and rescuing goods (Baldwin and Cunnington 2010, 164).

Conclusion

The foundation for the common-law remedy of replevin can be traced back to the thirteenth century when tenants used it to recover goods and chattels (most often cattle) from a landlord. The remedy expanded over the years to include the recovery of all types of personal property, including sugar and slaves. Today, other remedies to retrieve personal property exist, but in some jurisdictions replevin remains a viable remedy for archivists seeking the return of public records and other cultural-heritage materials alienated from their archives.—*Patricia Franks*

Keywords: public records, civil action, Rules of Civil Procedure
Related Entries: Archival Fonds; Archives (Institution); Captured Records

Bibliography

Adams, Randolph G. "The Character and Extent of Fugitive Archival Material." *The American Archivist* 2 (2) (1939): 85–96.

Baldwin, John, and Ralph Cunnington. "The Abandonment of Civil Enforcement Reform." *Civil Justice Quarterly* (2010): 2.

Brennan, David J. "Replevin and the Paradox of English Chattel Property." *Common Law World Review* 36 (4) (2007): 343–44.

Cobbey, Joseph E. *A Practical Treatise on the Law of Replevin as Administered by the Courts of the United States*. Chicago: Callaghan and Company, 1890, 46.

Dow, Elizabeth. H. *Archivists, Collectors, Dealers, and Replevin: Case Studies on Private Ownership of Public Documents*. Lanham, MD: Scarecrow Press, 2012, 4.

Hall, George D. G. *The Treatise on the Laws and Customs of the Realm of England Commonly Called Glanvill*. London: Nelson, 1965, as quoted in David J. Brennan. "Replevin and the Paradox of English Chattel Property." *Common Law World Review* 36 (4) (2007): 337–54.

Hoffman, Barbara T., ed. *Art and Cultural Heritage: Law, Policy, and Practice*. New York: Cambridge University Press, 2006, 171–72.

Ketelaar, Eric. *Archival and Records Management Legislation and Regulations: A RAMP Study with Guidelines*. Paris: United Nationals Educational, Scientific and Cultural Organization: 1985.

Kruse, John. "Replevin—Repeal or Retain?" *Liverpool Law Review* 23 (1) (2001): 95–115.

O'Neil, James E. "Replevin: A Public Archivist's Perspective." *College & Research Libraries* 40 (1979): 26–30. DOI:10.5860/crl_40_01_26.

Price, William S., Jr. "N. C. v. B. C. West, Jr." *The American Archivist* 41 (1) (1978).

Woodbine, George E. "A Case of Misnomer." *Columbia Law Review* 44 (2) (1944): 65–68.

RISK MANAGEMENT (RECORDS)

Risk management is defined as the set of coordinated activities to direct and control an organization with regard to risk (International Standards

Organization 2009). Risk has no single accepted definition, but generally comprises the combination of a probability of an event and its consequences (International Standards Organization 2009). Since the early 2000s, the application of risk management principles in *archives* and *records management* has grown almost exponentially with a perceived rise in risk to *records* primarily as a result of the expanding use of digital technologies to create, communicate, and store records. Today, risk management is seen as a critical component of *information governance.*

Historical Developments

Over the past twenty years, the terms *records* and risk management have become tightly intertwined. So tightly coupled have the terms become that it has even been posited that records management is almost synonymous with risk management. To what may this records-risk nexus (Lemieux 2010) be attributed?

Some attribute growing attention to risk and risk management to the rise of the Risk Society. This is a term first introduced in the 1980s by two sociologists, Ulrich Beck and Anthony Giddens, to describe the way in which modern society organizes around the concept of risk. Anthony Giddens (1999, 3) describes the Risk Society as "a society increasingly preoccupied with the future (and also with safety), which generates the notion of risk," while Ulrich Beck (1992, 260) defines it as "a systematic way of dealing with hazards and insecurities induced and introduced by modernisation itself." Notions of risk, however, pre-date what Beck and Giddens define as modernity: the word risk has been traced, variously, to the seventeenth-century Italian words *risco, riscare,* and *richiare,* the sixteenth century, and pre-modern Portuguese and Spanish maritime ventures (Lemieux 2010). Similarly, risk management is said to be an ancient practice dating from the Tigris-Euphrates Valley c. 3200 BC (Lemieux 2010). Beck and Giddens have argued that modernity has given rise to three important changes that distinguish risk management in modern times from its manifestation in earlier periods: the notion of man-made or manufactured risks versus those purely arising from acts of God or natural causes; the idea of human agency in the production, identification, and mitigation of risk (giving rise to the notion of risk management

itself, wherein people set out to manage and control risks); and the idea that by reflexively undertaking the management of risk, society alters the production and processes of risk.

Whether one accepts Beck's and Gidden's shared thesis, the rise of a modern records-risk nexus must also be set against the increasing importance of governance, risk, and compliance (GRC) frameworks in the field of records management. In September 1992, the four-volume report entitled *Internal Control—Integrated Framework* was released by the Committee of Sponsoring Organizations (COSO 1992, updated 2013). The COSO framework was embedded into U.S. law with the introduction of the Sarbanes-Oxley Act following the Enron scandal, which broke in October 2001 and eventually led to the bankruptcy of Enron Corporation, an American energy company based in Houston, Texas, as well as the de facto dissolution of Arthur Andersen, which was one of the five largest audit and accountancy partnerships in the world at that time. The introduction of the Sarbanes-Oxley Act began the GRC era. COSO's *Internal Control—Integrated Framework* was followed in 2004 by publication of its *Enterprise Risk Management—Integrated Framework* (COSO 2004). Other GRC frameworks that have since emerged include *Control Objectives for Information and Related Technology* (COBIT) (ISACA 2012), a framework created for information technology (IT) management and IT governance and, in the field of records management, ARMA International's *Generally Accepted Recordkeeping Principles* (ARMA International 2012).

The Nature of Risk

Like the definition of a record, risk is defined and described differently in different *contexts* and from different epistemological perspectives, from those that privilege mathematical and positivist orientations to those that see risk as a social construction. Each field of practice with which the subject of risk intersects has its own interpretation of the meaning of the term. The ARMA guideline on evaluating and mitigating records and information risks relies on a definition from ISO Guide 73 as follows: "Risk is defined as the combination of a probability of an event and its consequences" (*Evaluating and Mitigating Records and Information Risk*).

Finally, ISO 31000, *Risk Management—Principles and Guidelines*, defines risk as "the effect of uncertainty on [organizational] objectives" (International Standards Organization 2009), noting that an effect is a deviation from the expected—either positive and/or negative.

Though definitions vary, it is possible to extract some common ideas associated with the notion of risk. Risk is a concept that only exists as a future state that has a probability greater than zero of occurring. Once the expected event occurs, it is no longer a risk. Risk is often characterized by a trigger event linked to certain consequences (International Standards Organization 2009). Indeed, references to risk frequently associate it with the combination of the probability of an event's occurrence and its consequences (International Standards Organization 2009). From the field of IT security, it is possible to extrapolate the additional concept of a threat combined with a vulnerability that triggers a risk event (Lemieux 2010). Often, the consequences of a risk event are associated with losses or a negative outcome. On the flip side, however, lies the notion of opportunity associated with the early Portuguese root of the word *risk*: "to dare" (Lemieux 2010). Probability theory helps define the relative likelihood of gains over losses. Reference to probability links the concept of risk to the notion of uncertainty, which the International Standards Organization (ISO) risk management standard defines as "a state, even partial, of deficiency of information related to, understanding or knowledge of an event, its consequence, or its likelihood" (ISO 2009).

Although the above definitions convey objectivity in the notion of risk and risk-based decision making, in the psychology and behavioral economics literature, risk and risk-based decision making have been framed as incorporating perceptions of a combination of factors including: numeric probability, context, and the nature of the potential outcome. While models of risk-based decision making do exist, as discussed in Kahneman (2011), there is a lack of a basic understanding of how relevant these models are in the context of records-related risk analysis. It may be that the models only tell part of the story and that, through studying risk-based decision making, we can learn much more about the representation of risk and processes of risk-based reasoning as applied to records.

In an effort to begin to understand representations of risk within the discourse on archives and records management, Lemieux undertook a study in 2010 to discover what types of records and information risks are most commonly discussed; how different writers engage with the subject of risk; how different writers conceive of risk in relation to records and records management; whether the discourse on risk has changed over time, and if so, how; and whether there are disciplinary differences in the discussion of risk. She identified references to risk in several hundred articles from archival and records management journals and analyzed these articles (using visual analysis) to develop a typology representing discourse on risk in relation to records. The typology identifies several categories of articles as follows:

- Articles that discuss various risks to records (e.g., natural and manmade disasters and long-term preservation);
- Articles that discuss how records can be causes of other types of risk (e.g., litigation risk, reputational risks);
- Articles that discuss changes to the record that pose a risk to the profession if the profession does not adapt, most notably in connection with the rise of electronic or *digital records*;
- Articles about risks associated with how traditional archival *functions* are carried out, again in connection with electronic or digital records or in connection to specific populations or groups;
- Articles concerning records management or *recordkeeping* techniques as a strategy for mitigating risks (e.g., use of retention scheduling to control litigation risks);
- Articles that discuss applying risk management processes to manage records and information risks; and
- Articles that discuss using records to explore other types of risk (e.g., limitations of existing search and retrieval strategies).

Lemieux also noted a general trend toward increasing references to risk in archives and records management discourse. Her research identified that the years 2001 and 2002 saw significant numbers of articles on risk, including those concerned with risks associated with the collapse of Enron and the 9/11 terrorism attack in the United States. The year 2006 also saw a high number of publications discussing risk, which Lemieux suggests is the result of the confluence of two separate narratives on risk: concern with the risks of managing and preserving new digital forms of records, such as instant messages and web resources, coupled with a rising concern with e-discovery and litigation risk. Although archival and records management literature still pay close attention to traditional areas of concern, such as risk to records from natural disasters or environmental conditions, discussion of risks associated with new forms of digital communication continue to rise. The link between IT security and risk to records has surfaced in recent years. With a growing move to cloud technology for creation and storage of records, new concerns about records in the cloud (e.g., privacy, ownership and control, and preservation) have emerged (Lemieux 2010). The sources and types of risk to records continue to expand, perhaps proving Beck and Gidden's theory about modernity and the creation of a Risk Society.

Concomitant with the rise in mention of risks in literature related to archives and records has been introduction of the notion that records professionals could control risks through the application of risk management. Lemieux's 2004 publication, *Managing Risks for Records and Information*, was one of the first to outline how *records managers* could apply risk management principles to managing records-related risks. Risk management generally includes: context and values assessment; risk identification; risk analysis; risk evaluation; risk treatment (or mitigation); and risk communication (ISO 2009). In her 2004 book and a later 2004 publication, Lemieux also outlines two risk-management methodologies: a traditional events-based approach and a newer, requirements-based approach that is more strategic in focus. The "Digital Repository Audit Method Based on Risk Assessment" (DRAMBORA) was the first to apply risk management to support the assessment of *digital preservation* repositories. In 2010, ARMA International published a guideline on *Evaluating and Mitigating Records and Information Risks*. This guideline provides a framework for establishing systems to evaluate information risks and describes a process for framing a risk management system using a risk quadrant of four basic types of risk: administrative risks—threats related to managing the RIM program (information governance, change management, and emergency management); records control risks—*records classification*, records retention and *disposition*, records storage; legal/regulatory risks; and technology risks—information security, electronic communications, and software applications.

Conclusion

Risk management operates as a central pillar of records management practice, being, as it is, part of governance, risk, and compliance frameworks that increasingly dominate records management thinking. Whether one believes that risks are objectively on the rise, or, as Beck and Giddens suggest, are the outcome of modernity, there is no question that discourse about risk in the archival and records management literature has increased dramatically since the early 2000s. During this period, the connection between records management (or information governance) as a risk-management-oriented practice along with IT security, *information assurance*, and data protection, has grown stronger in recent years, largely as a consequence of the rise of new digital forms of records creation, communication, and storage.—*Victoria L. Lemieux*

Keywords: risk, risk management, information governance, records management

Related Entries: Audit and Certification (Trusted Digital Repositories); Digital Preservation; Digital Record; Disaster Plan; Information Assurance; Information Governance; Record(s); Records Classification; Records Management; Vital Records

Bibliography

ARMA International. *Evaluating and Mitigating Records and Information Risk*. Overland Park, KS: ARMA International, 2010.

———. *Generally Accepted Record Keeping Principles*. Overland Park, KS: ARMA International, 2012. www.arma.org/r2/generally-accepted-br-recordkeeping-principles (accessed November 2013).

Beck, Ulrich. *Risk Society, Towards a New Modernity*. London: Sage, 1992.

Committee of Sponsoring Organizations. *Enterprise Risk Management—Integrated Framework.* New York: American Institute of CPAs (AICPA), 2004.

———. *Internal Control—Integrated Framework.* New York: American Institute of CPAs (AICPA), 2013.

The Digital Curation Centre. "Digital Repository Audit Method Based on Risk Assessment." 2004. www.dcc.ac.uk/resources/repository-audit-and-assessment/drambora (accessed November 2013).

Giddens, Anthony. "Risk and Responsibility." *Modern Law Review* 62 (1) (1999): 1–10.

International Standards Organization. *31000:2009: Risk Management—Principles and Guidelines.* Geneva, Switzerland: International Standards Organization, 2009.

ISACA (formerly Information Systems Audit and Control Association). *COBIT 5: A Business Framework for the Governance and Management of Enterprise IT.* Rolling Meadows, IL: ISACA, 2012. www.isaca.org/cobit/pages/default.aspx (accessed November 2013).

Kahneman, Daniel. *Thinking, Fast and Slow.* New York: Doubleday, 2011.

Lemieux, Victoria L. "The Records-Risk Nexus: Exploring the Relationship between Records and Risk." *Records Management Journal* 20 (2) (2010): 199–216.

———. *Risk Management for Records and Information.* Lenexa, KS: ARMA International, 2004.

S

SAMPLING

Sampling is a technique for both appraising the value of collections and selecting content for retention. It was born out of the need to manage a tidal wave of twentieth-century *records* created by bureaucracies, especially governments. Best suited for homogenous bulk records of minimal value, sampling can help reduce the volume of material retained while minimizing costs and *selection* bias, although it should be used with caution and only in the proper circumstances, if at all.

Discussion

Sampling provides a means of representing an entire collection from a limited number of records. Only certain records are suitable for sampling: voluminous records similar in content and format, and of some value to warrant archiving, although not of enough value to save them all. *Case files* produced by governments and businesses are often referenced in the sampling literature.

Multiple types of sampling are available. Random sampling provides every record an equal chance for selection. Records are selected at random, without respect to internal characteristics or outside influence. Systematic samples are drawn from every *n*th record, with selection based on the order or physical characteristic of the record; every fifth record or every *file* larger than five inches, for instance, might be selected. Subjective or purposive sampling selects only the exceptional records. Mixed-mode samples combine more than one type of sampling to augment results.

While sampling can produce objective and cost-effective results under the proper circumstances, it is a sensitive procedure that warrants cautious and measured use, if it is used at all. Heterogeneous, unique, or incomplete records do not make good candidates for sampling. Improper or incomplete samples can bias collections by making the retained sample not generalizable to the original collection, thereby skewing any future analytic or informational value.

Conclusion

Sampling can help appraise records, reduce selection bias, and ultimately remove unnecessary bulk. Still, healthy skepticism abounds within the literature, with numerous recommendations that sampling be adopted as a last resort and only if there is no alternative. Careful planning is essential, along with full documentation of the sampling methodology and steps taken.—*Jared Lyle*

Keywords: sampling, selection, appraisal
Related Entries: Appraisal; Selection

Bibliography

Boles, Frank. "Sampling in Archives." *The American Archivist* 44 (2) (1981): 125–30. http://archivists.metapress.com/content/a5458p2p62873437/fulltext.pdf.

Bradsher, James Gregory, and Bruce I. Ambacher. "Archival Sampling: A Method of Appraisal and a Means of Retention." *Mid-Atlantic Regional Archives Conference Technical Leaflet Series*, no. 8 (1992).

Cook, Terry. "'Many Are Called, but Few Are Chosen': Appraisal Guidelines for Sampling and Selecting Case Files." *Archivaria* 32 (1991): 25–50. http://journals.sfu.ca/archivar/index.php/archivaria/article/view/11759/12709.

———. *The Archival Appraisal of Records Containing Personal Information: A RAMP Study with Guidelines.* Prepared for the General Information Program and UNISIST. Paris: United Nations Educational, Scientific and Cultural Organization, 1991.

Hull, Felix. *The Use of Sampling Techniques on the Retention of Records: A RAMP Study with Guidelines.* Prepared for the General Information Program and UNISIST. Paris: United Nations Educational, Scientific and Cultural Organization, 1981.

Kepley, David R. "Sampling in Archives: A Review." *The American Archivist* 47 (3) (1984): 237–42. http://archivists.metapress.com/content/kj041746214p6u1v/fulltext.pdf.

Lewinson, Paul. "Archival Sampling." *The American Archivist* 20 (4) (1957): 291–312.

Sly, Margery N. "Sampling in an Archival Framework: Mathoms and Manuscripts." *Provenance, Journal of the Society of Georgia Archivists* 5 (1) (1987): 55–73. http://digitalcommons.kennesaw.edu/provenance/vol5/iss1/7.

SECONDARY VALUE

Secondary value refers broadly to any and all ongoing value adhering to archival *records* not inherent in the circumstances of their creation or the intentions of their authors or creators. It is broadly conflated with the terms informational value, archival value, or historical value, which refer more specifically—and more or less synonymously—to the value conferred on archival materials by their content, rather than by their documentary form, the use for which they were intended by their creators or authors, or the procedural or juridical *context* within which they originate. Secondary value is generally the chief criterion informing archival *appraisal* or *selection*.

Concept of Secondary Value

The concept of secondary value emerges fully in the work of T. R. Schellenberg. Discussing the notion

in a 1956 bulletin explicitly rooted in his work on behalf of the U.S. government—and of government more generally—he stated that "public records are preserved in an archival institution because they have values that will exist long after they cease to be of current use, and because their values will be for others than the current users . . . this [is] lasting, secondary usefulness." He goes on to further divide secondary values into strict "evidential" and "informational" categories, positing that the former derive from "the evidence they contain of the organization and functioning of the Government body that produced them," while the latter consist of "the information they contain on *persons*, corporate bodies, things, problems, conditions, and the like, with which the Government body dealt." After detailing various "tests" by which these precisely quantified values may be ascertained by the discerning *archivist*, he goes on to assert rather boldly that "modern archivists are generally trained as historians, and it may therefore be assumed that they are competent to appraise the value of public records for historical research. Most archivists are likely to preserve all records that relate significantly to important personages, episodes, or events."

The precise academic demography of the archival profession has shifted somewhat since Schellenberg's time, and in recent decades a rather broader sense of secondary value has emerged even as Schellenberg's distinction between information-about-subjects and information-about-creators has eroded somewhat. This more inclusive sense of secondary value tends to encompass not only the informational value of archives' content as it contributes to the study and construction of historical narrative—whether this relates to the bodies that produce records or the events and persons to which they refer, although this sense is certainly still present—but also a wider notion of what Gerald Ham characterized in 1993 as "values that some records have because of the uses, often unforeseen, to which they can be put by individuals other than those for whom the records were originally created" (7). This notion of "the unforeseen" was nominally present in Schellenberg's writings but tended to be glossed over somewhat. Ham also echoes Schellenberg in asserting that these secondary values are "the main concern of the archival appraiser." It should be noted that these articulations are not unique to archival studies in a narrow sense; both Schellenberg's and Ham's sense of this concept are also embraced by the discipline of *records management*, as echoed by David Stephens and Roderick Wallace in 2001: "Research or historical values are generally designated as secondary values. Legal value can be either a primary or a secondary value, depending on the purpose and *function* of a record" (6).

In this latter assertion Stephens and Wallace draw our attention to a curious phenomenon: the intended function of a record can do much to determine where the distinction between primary and secondary value lies, and in some cases may not be apparent even to the most astute appraiser. Consider, for example, records falsely—but exactly—conforming to prescribed documentary forms that are intended by their creators to provide misleading evidence about the creators' activities; clearly in such a situation distinguishing primary from secondary value is challenging at best. Resolving such concerns has traditionally been the purview of archival *diplomatics*. Considering such ambiguities also draws us back to Ham's mention of "the unforeseen," which was presaged by Schellenberg's own assertion that "the archivist preserves records for unknown uses." One scarcely imagines that Schellenberg could have conceived the notion of the Truth and Reconciliation Commissions so important to South Africa, Canada, and other countries. These painful but essential processes, which rely very heavily on archival materials, have seen records put to uses that neither their creators nor the archivists who have preserved them could possibly have foreseen.

Conclusion

Early conceptions of "evidentiary value" and "informational value," while still extant, have largely coalesced into a more inclusive and unified sense of "secondary value" that encompasses not only the worth of information regarding historical events that may be contained in archival materials but also the other uses—some more obvious, some less so—to which archival materials may be put by users. Assessing these manifold potential uses, and the ability of records to serve them, is the chief concern of archival appraisal and selection. These processes require no small degree of creativity and rigor since

the possible secondary value of records may be conceived of so broadly.—*Myron Groover*

Keywords: secondary value, archival value, informational value, evidentiary value, enduring value, research value, reference value
Related Entries: Intrinsic Value; Primary Values

Bibliography

Ham, F. Gerald. *Selecting and Appraising Archives and Manuscripts.* Chicago: Society of American Archivists, 1993.

Schellenberg, T. R. "The Appraisal of Modern Public Records: Informational Values." *Bulletins of the National Archives* no. 8 (1956). www.archives.gov/research/alic/reference/archives-resources/appraisal-of-records.html.

Stephens, D., and R. C. Wallace. "Electronic Records Retention: Fourteen Basic Principles." *ARMAil Central New York* 10 (4) (2001): 1–10. www.questia.com/magazine/1G1-67373678/electronic-records-retention-fourteen-basic-principles.

SELECTION

Selection commonly means to set apart, "to carefully choose as being the best or most suitable" (*Oxford English Dictionary* 2007). In an archival *context*, selection is a *function* designed to choose certain *records* from a single creator and secure their safekeeping in an archival repository. Often equated with *appraisal*, assigning value to records, selection is more specifically the process of securing records in an *archives* by bridging their appraised value with an institution's plans and policies for records' *acquisition*. Selection thereby integrates the concerns of the creator, the preserver, and the social jurisdiction where selection is performed. In contemporary practice an appraisal of the records informs archival selection, validating recorded values worthy of archival care. In this way, archival selection brings logical and physical consequence to the act of archival appraisal. Selection coordinates a broad set of constituencies within the particular context of an archives' mission and archival acquisition goals (Ham 1975).

Organized societies necessarily reference certain memorialized activities; some kind of records selection for preservation is a timeless pursuit. However, it was not until the modern era that records selection defined the work of *archivists* to such a fundamental degree. This is because in contemporary archives, selection is an inescapable response to the massive, uncoordinated scale of records creation and the unprecedented diversity of their use. Archivists address this modern dilemma with a variety of criteria and methods constructed to deliver *accountability* and consistency in selection within the mission of an archival institution. But some have observed that archival records possess fundamental probative values inhering through their creation and use (Duranti 1994). Archival selection, by implementing appraisal's subjective attribution of worth, attenuates these values (Jenkinson 1937). Viewed this way, archival selection is a professional conceit that has turned the concept of archival value on its head, since it is by the archivist's selection, not the creator's use, that records become archives (Dancy 1998; Livelton 1996). The archivist is no longer a preserver of records but rather a selector for preservation (Norton 1975).

Whatever the values applied, archival selection must be done through the information concerning the records' provenance—creators, records, and their contexts—and the cultural and administrative policies and procedures to administer the records' *disposition* (InterPARES, n.d.). Archival selection will increase in proportion to the dilemmas of accumulation and use. Recognizing this, selection must strive to be consistent and accountable in light of the needs of society and the mission of the archival institution. Ultimately, archival selection, properly administered, delivers an archives both physically manageable and intellectually usable, safeguarding authentic and reliable records, agnostic of format, and embodying evidence of values considered enduring within the contemporary context of creation and purposeful use.

Applying Selection

Premodern

Archival selection arrived recently on the archival landscape to bring managerial consistency, democratic accountability, and theoretical clarity to the process of choosing from an overabundance of records. In Roman and medieval practice, "only the persons or corporations vested with sovereign power had the right to establish [an archives] in their jurisdiction" (Duranti 1994). For centuries selection served the purposes of the sponsoring entity. An appraisal to attribute value was unnecessary since archival purposes were few: to enshrine jurisdiction, underscore rights and privilege, and memorialize certain social values. Modern interpretive selection values of provenance (values of source context) and pertinence (values of subject context) originate in this period.

Early Modern Practice

Modern archival selection emerged from the democratic principles expressed in the French Revolution (Posner 1940; Lokke 1968). Sovereign authority could no longer preserve archival records in privileged *access* to prove legal jurisdiction or promote self-serving historical narratives. Democratic governance required probative accountability found in publically administered and accessible national archives designed to care for the nation's collective documentary heritage. At the height of the revolution's ideological furor, records of pre-revolutionary feudal privilege were selected for destruction to enshrine the new civil authority. As democratically governed nation states formed across Europe, publically administered repositories emerged devoted to documenting an ideological concept of "the people" and provide evidence for accountable governance.

As national repositories assembled a new kind of "public" record, methods of organization and destruction emerged chaotically. Incidents of uncoordinated destruction and loss of valuable records suggested a need for well-formed theory on the value and administration of public archives. Sir Hilary Jenkinson, British Public Records Office archivist, fashioned an early modern conceptualization of records selection. For Jenkinson, an organization created archival records value through the processes of creation, use, and setting aside of records in daily affairs. Administrators *in situ* were best positioned to select records for their probative (i.e., archival) values because of their intimate relationship with the processes and functions records documented (Jenkinson 1922). Jenkinson described the need to safeguard these probative archival values as "the moral defense of the archives" (Jenkinson 1922). Only as records volumes expanded with technological and bureaucratic advances did writers question the role of archivist as passive custodian and expand on the ideas of selective archival disposition and levels of destruction, ideas anathema to nineteenth-century British archivists titled "keepers of records" (Cook 1997).

Modern Practice

Elements of modernity impacted *archival practice* and gave archives a new identity in the postwar twentieth century. These elements included interventionist governance, information technologies, forms of recorded information, and the distributed authority of modern bureaucracy. Archivists confronted not only new volumes but also new genres and uses of records. The *case file* emerged to embody the selection challenge for new types of government records. Archivists in the United States responded in the 1930s and 1940s with the creation of the *records management* profession and the concept of a *record's lifecycle*. Developed for practical concerns of bulk, archivists encouraged collaboration with *records managers* to select records in an early period of their creation and use. These selection decisions were articulated in a new device: the *records schedule*. In fashioning a practical management response to bulk accessions, much of the contemporary European debate over archival values was glossed over. T. Schellenberg, an archival writer in the U.S. National Archives, refashioned the traditional definition of archives in the North American environment, suggesting that archival selection creates archives: he incorrectly argued it is through the archival selection that records are transformed into archives. Schellenberg thus conceived of a new, more dogmatic division of values: *primary values* documenting the creator's context and *secondary values* of evidence and information for researchers. Although Schellenberg's work advocated selection as a collaboration between records managers and archivists, the result was more an unfortunate division of professional responsibilities: records managers attended to the primary administrative values and archivists the secondary research values. Professional historiography increasingly shaped the

interpretive parameters for archival selection. Somehow the users of these secondary values would not be interested in the primary or original values of administrative provenance (Livelton 1996). In chasing historiographical fashion, modern archival selection practices in North America have left a somewhat-confused assemblage of records across public archives (Ham 1975). This discontinuity and fragmentation in archival selection practices was not professionally addressed until the 1970s.

Postmodern Practice

It may be argued that contemporary archival selection has come full circle to the democratizing values of the French Revolution. The discomforting realization that embedded government administrators should not bear sole responsibility for selection of the records of their activities, and the reality that professional historiography inconsistently renews its values, has driven archivists to turn to society-sanctioned values to anchor their archival selection. German archivist Hans Booms articulated this approach most forcefully: "Public opinion sanctions public actions, essentially generates the sociopolitical process, and legitimizes political authority . . . should not public opinion . . . legitimize archival appraisal?" (Booms 1987, 104). Booms highlighted social context and provenance as the framework for archival selection. Canadian archivists refined this concept by emphasizing social functions and processes to document social values and emphasize the organic process of knowledge creation and use. Canadian archivist T. Cook described this approach as macroappraisal (Cook 1992). This movement toward societal provenance and the cultural interplay of social values documented in programs, institutes, and societies brought with it the postmodern privileging and social fragmentation common across the humanities. It also meant that archival selection concentrated on the broad purposes and functional context of an organization at the expense of records appraisal at the level of records accumulation.

By the 1990s it became clear that professional archivists were confronted with developments in governance and information technology that highlighted both strengths and weaknesses in the social provenance paradigm. Distributed governance fragmented records aggregations as more local offices applied policies of citizen-state interaction; administrative responsibilities moved fluidly across departments decentralizing provenance; freedom-of-information policies demanded closer control of records creation and distribution; while IT promoted an opposing ability to create and distribute records with limited control. Macroappraisal's organic model of governance as social process addressed the fluid distribution of functional responsibilities in modern administration; however, the increasingly detailed legislation required for transparent, public access to records of governance forced archivists to recognize the utility of Jenkinson's evidential paradigm of archival values. Archival selection soon attended to preserving evidence of the *impartiality* and *authenticity* of records as probative documentation of an agency's activities. As first observed in the 1954 Public Records Office's *Grigg Report* on British public records, social values would theoretically emerge in the interaction of citizens with state functions and policies. This work required systematic methods of appraisal, accountable documentation of decisions, and "operational measures" to implement decisions of records retention and destruction (Shepherd and Yeo 2003).

Conclusion

The very notion of selection of records for long-term preservation indicates there is a plurality of histories, relative truths, and diverse media. Three conclusions follow. First, archival selection must understand and relate the different concerns of creator and preserver: how the resources and objectives of an archival institution can accommodate the appraised values of provenance. Second, selection for subject content will forever be an ideological balance that can only be administered through well-documented, accountable practice. Third, selection must attend to both "the intellectual item and its physical carrier" (Dancy 1998) and must therefore be media agnostic. This requires the selection to attend to the records generating environment and relate this to the requirements of an appropriate carrier for the intellectual content.

Finally, some archivists argue for archives as a depiction of "the human experience"; others view archives as evidence of a sponsor's administrative and legal accountability. In the former sense public institutions deliberately select for an inclusive, socially relevant depiction of the culture and identity of a society. In the second approach, the purpose of selection is to witness purposeful use to supply probative accountability, and over time a representation of society's values will emerge.—*Raymond Frogner*

Keywords: appraisal, disposition, preservation, archives
Related Entry: Appraisal

Bibliography

Booms, H. "Society and the Formation of a Documentary Heritage: Issues in the Appraisal of Archival Science." *Archivaria* 1 (24) (1987): 69–107. http://journals.sfu.ca/archivar/index.php/archivaria/article/view/11415/12357.

Cook, T. "Mind over Matter: Towards a New Theory of Archival Appraisal." In B. L. Craig, ed., *The Archival Imagination: Essays in Honour of Hugh A. Taylor*. Ottawa: ACA, 1992, 38–70.

———. "What Is Past Is Prologue: A History of Archival Ideas since 1898, and the Future Paradigm Shift." *Archivaria* 1 (43) (1997): 17–63. http://journals.sfu.ca/archivar/index.php/archivaria/article/view/12175/13184.

Dancy, R. "Case Files: Theory, History, Practice." Master of Archival Studies Graduating Paper, University of British Columbia, Vancouver, 1998.

Duranti, L. "The Concept of Appraisal and Archival Theory." *American Archivist* 57 (2) (1994): 328–45. http://archivists.metapress.com/content/pu548273j5j1p816/fulltext.pdf.

Ham, F. G. "The Archival Edge." *American Archivist* 38 (1) (1975): 5–13. http://archivists.metapress.com/content/7400r86481128424/fulltext.pdf.

InterPARES. "Appraisal Task Force Report." N.d. www.interpares.org/book/interpares_book_e_part2.pdf (accessed February 8, 2015).

Jenkinson, H. *A Manual of Archive Administration*. London: Percy Lund, Humphries, 1965.

Livelton, T. *Archival Theory, Records, and the Public*. Lanham, MD: Society of American Archivists and Scarecrow Press, 1996.

Norton, M. C. "Records Disposal." In Thornton W. Mitchell, ed., *Norton on Archives: The Writings of Margaret Cross Norton on Archives and Records*

Management. Chicago: Society of American Archivists, 1975, 231–46.

Posner, Ernst. "Some Aspects of Archival Development since the French Revolution." *American Archivist* 3 (3) (July 1940): 159–72. http://archivists.metapress.com/content/q64h3343h663402j/fulltext.pdf.

Schellenberg, T. R. *Modern Archives: Principles and Techniques*. Chicago: University of Chicago Press, 1956.

Shepherd, E., and G. Yeo. *Managing Records: A Handbook of Principles and Practice*. London: Facet, 2003.

SERIES

Series link *records*, keeping intact connections that result from action, maintaining structure, and preserving links with *context* and with other records. Random or topical groupings that do not reflect origin or use are not series but are sometimes so treated for convenience. As *Merriam Webster's* online dictionary defines, the term is used outside *archival science* to denote, inter alia, "a number of things or events of the same class coming one after another in spatial or temporal succession."

How Archivists Conceive of Series

A record series is a body of documentary objects deliberately treated as a unit (e.g., when papers are brought together into *files* or dockets and serially maintained) and purposefully kept apart from other objects—for example:

> a body of file units or *documents* arranged in accordance with a unified filing system or maintained by the records creator as a unit because of some relationship arising out of their creation, receipt, or use.

A series may also come together incidentally as a result of action or circumstances to which they relate. Organization of the contents may support management and use, but the essence of a series derives not from the arrangement imposed by the hand of a records-maker, but from the interconnectedness of the activities being documented. A series excludes extraneous matter that is not part of the interconnected activity even if the subject matter is the same. *Archivists* preserve this "interior structure" or composition (physically or intellectually in their descriptions) as a way of understanding the meaning of each component item.

Connections between the series and the records-maker that distinguished series from each other by provenance were critical for the early authorities. Though sparing in his use of the term, Jenkinson lays great weight on the organization of records as a reflection of the "administrative *function*" (1966, 104–16). Muller, Feith, and Fruin also held that organization of the records would "in the main correspond to the organization of the administrative body that produced it" (1968, 52–59). This is the exterior structure or context, linking series to the circumstances of creation, management, and use and to other series. At its simplest, provenance is origin or derivation from a common creator (records-maker). The Society of American Archivists uses both elements: "similar records . . . arranged according to a . . . system" (interior structure) and "the result of being created, received, or used in the same activity" (exterior structure).

For some, a series is understood to be a layer within a hierarchy of "levels" of arrangement:

- part of a fonds that is the whole of the records of an organization, family, *person*, and so on (that may contain other series);
- generated within a formal *recordkeeping system* that may be represented hierarchically as a super-series or a *sous*-fonds;
- belonging to an organizational, familial, or functional framework that provides a structure to the fonds and binds the series-maker contextually with other aspects of the fonds;
- composed of subordinate layers of organization (subseries) that arrange its contents (e.g., sets of cards, files, sets, classification, volumes);
- containing documentary traces of action or circumstance (items) authored by agents, servants, or actors working for or having dealings with the series-maker.

Information content may be differently organized at each level—for example, papers arranged chronologically within files organized numerically.

How Archivists Use Series

Initially, series were thought of less as output from a recordkeeping system and more as a way of gathering materials resulting from the same recordkeeping process. Archivists permitted themselves to gather dissimilar materials into the same series and to organize miscellaneous material into sequences of their own devising—what Jenkinson calls artificial series and Schellenberg refers to as made series. There was broad agreement, however, on *respect for provenance* and keeping records of common origin together within a fonds or *archief*. The French allowed component parts of a fonds to be organized with less regard for original internal placement than the Prussians and the Dutch, who placed more emphasis on preserving the order imposed by the registry (see discussion in Schellenberg, *The Management of Archives* [New York: Columbia University Press, 1965], 169–86). The Dutch authorities identified series as primary elements in the internal construction of the *archief* corresponding to the skeletal outline of the administration that formed the records (Muller, Feith, Fruin 1968, 57–73). Jenkinson (1966, 104–14) believed that "invertebrates" or *pièces isolées* were more numerous than the Dutch allowed and could be organized by the archivist, as the French advised, provided the unity of provenance and transmission were preserved.

Newer traditions coming from North America and Australia, having to deal with large volumes and closer to the process of records making, developed definitions based on characteristics of internal structure (Cunningham 2010, 315–18, 330–33). These definitions could be applied in terms of observable features given to materials by the systems in which they were generated:

> Documents arranged according to a filing system or kept together because they relate to a particular subject or function, result from the same activity, document a specific kind of transaction, take a particular physical form, or have some other relationship arising out of their creation, receipt, or use (such as restrictions on *access* or use).

The idea that series result from a recordkeeping system or process (whether formal or informal) that can be represented separately from descriptions or provenance permits the successive, and even simultaneous, attribution of a series to multiple provenance statements.

By the 1990s, archivists were developing descriptive standards both nationally and internationally. Adopting a common view supports standardized presentation of information, data exchange and Internet searching, and collaborative work on automated descriptive tools such as the ICA's AtoM software. The series was once widely depicted as a "level of description" within a hierarchy of elements—"a recognisable subdivision of records, with a title peculiar to itself which is commonly used in the office where it is kept" (Cook 1977, 31). It was a component particle—"identify[ing] or establish[ing] series within an archival group or manuscript collection . . . involv[ing] a breakdown of a whole into its parts" (Schellenberg 1965, 89). The *ISAD(G)* definition of series began from that starting point but now aligns more closely to modern Australian and North American parlance:

> Documents arranged in accordance with a filing system or maintained as a unit because they result from the same accumulation or filing process, or the same activity; have a particular form; or because of some other relationship arising out of their creation, receipt, or use. A series is also known as a records series.

Evolving Ideas about Series

Significant alterations to the original conception in the ICA's descriptive standards, including allowance for separating descriptions of records from those of agents of action ("authorities") and functions, permission to multiply relationships between entities outside of strict hierarchies of containment, and the (foreshadowed) development of descriptive rules for relationships between entities open the way to further reconceptualization. In consequence, the idea that series are component parts of something else (defined by incorporation and boundaries) rather than elements in an integrated constellation (defined by relationships with other entities) is weakening.

Other archivists, such as the International Association of Sound and Audio-visual Archivists (IASA), acknowledging that their use of series is different, define it as a group of separate items related to one another by collective features (marks). The items may be intended for use in the sequence they are produced or not, and may be numbered or unnumbered, in production, broadcasting or other forms of publication. Such a group of items may be a finite series (complete) or an open-ended series (ongoing and therefore incomplete).

This definition concentrates more on the process (closed or continuing) and less on an imposed arrangement received or devised by the archivist. Audio-visual archiving techniques may be more relevant to management of digital materials than lessons learned in handling physical artifacts. Film archivists, for example, focus on the enduring image rather than the original medium on which it is first rendered. They have to deal with multiple renderings of the "same" record. Their ideas may assist in our evolving understanding of personal recordkeeping and the digital series.

Records in a fonds have many creators. Only by privileging one (viz. the hand that made the series) to the exclusion of all others have archivists been able to maintain the conception of a single "creator." The series takes the form given it by those responsible for organizing documentary materials—in effect, file clerks who are servants of the organization and viewed by archivists as surrogates for the organization when creation is attributed. This harks back to European ideas about how records are organized by means of an *archief* or registry. But that idea is increasingly anachronistic in modern administrative arrangements and electronic recordkeeping. The authorship of documents, the authorities and permissions to act within a digital environment, the arrangements for shared access and assignment of rights and responsibilities both within and across traditional organizational boundaries all make older ideas about who "creates" a series inapplicable.

Into the Future (Digital Series)

Archivists' ideas about series were first propounded at a precise moment in European and Anglophone recordkeeping arrangements, reflecting the actual state of records that archivists handled, including legacy records from earlier centuries. Will it still be a useful concept as *recordkeeping* moves into a digital environment?

Data "files" are organized into a database (for structured data) or into a directory structure (for digital objects). It is far from clear that these arrangements are a digital equivalent of what archivists mean by series. Organizing digital objects by means of stand-alone computerized record management software (requiring documents to be "checked in"—the same way that physical records were checked into *registry systems*) may be regarded as a passing phase. Instead, it is likely that recordkeeping functionality will be incorporated into IT systems if needed—indeed, business systems with recordkeeping functionality are becoming the norm.

Electronic records need to be managed at the granular level and described at the aggregate level(s) (Zhang 2012, 188–91). The digital series will not be found in the world of database administration but rather in data management—including data governance and data quality; data architecture, analysis, and design; reference data (e.g., taxonomies); business intelligence; *metadata* management; contact data management; and business analysis. Instead of focusing on the organization of the data, those seeking out digital series will find them in the uses made of the data—views (actual, potential, and formulated)—in the functionality that supports those views, in the links made (or permitted) with other records, and with identity data. Some of the knowledge needed to understand and manage a digital series will be found in documentation about the system, the circumstances of the data's generation, migration, and use, and in metadata belonging to each instance recorded.

Conclusion

The focus of archival thinking about electronic records has been too much beguiled by technology, the physical preservation and management of electronic artifacts, and too little focused on management of enduring content (too much attention to the plumbing and too little to water quality). On this view of the series in a digital environment, a single item or instance (each transactional record, for example) will belong, or be capable of belonging, to many uses or views of the data simultaneously. Just as the series itself cannot be understood, as it once was, by containment (within a fonds) but rather through its integration with related entities, so the item will no longer be conceived of merely as the component part of a series (Hurley 2011, 3). In the digital world, the same item may belong to many series, simultaneously or successively, and archivists will learn to think nothing of it.—*Chris Hurley*

Keywords: arrangement, filing, system
Related Entries: Principle of *Respect des Fonds*; Principle of Respect for Original Order; Recordkeeping System(s); Series System

Bibliography

Cook, Michael. *Archives Administration: A Manual for Intermediate and Smaller Organizations and for Local Government*. Folkestone: Kent Dawson, 1977.

Cunningham, Adrian. *The Arrangement and Description of Archives amid Administrative and Technological Change: Essays and Reflections by and about Peter J Scott*. Brisbane: Australian Society of Archivists, 2010.

"Frequently Asked Questions about Federal Records Management." Records Managers, National Archives and Records Administration. www.archives.gov/records-mgmt/faqs/federal.html (accessed April 3, 2013).

Hurley, Chris. "The Hunting of the Snark (Looking for Digital 'Series')." Recordkeeping Roundtable, Sydney, October 25, 2011, 3–13. www.descriptionguy.com/images/WEBSITE/hunting-of-the-snark-search-for-digital-series.pdf.

ISAD(G): General International Standard Archival Description, 2nd edition. International Council on Archives (ICA), 2000. www.ica.org/10207/standards/isadg-general-international-standard-archival-description-second-edition.html (accessed April 3, 2013).

Jenkinson, Hilary. *A Manual of Archive Administration*. London: Percy Lund Humphries, 1966.

Miliano, Mary. "The IASA Cataloguing Rules: Appendix D." International Association of Sound and Audio-visual Archivists (IASA), 1999. www.iasa-web.org/cataloguing-rules/appendix-d-glossary (accessed April 3, 2013).

Muller, S., J. A. Feith, and R. Fruin. *Manual for the Arrangement and Description of Archives Drawn Up by Direction of the Netherlands Association of Archivists*. Translated by Arthur H. Leavitt. New York: H. W. Wilson, 1968.

Pearce-Moses, Richard. "A Glossary of Archival and Records Terminology." The Society of American Archivists. www2.archivists.org/glossary/terms/s/series (accessed April 3, 2013).

"Record Series Definition." U.S. Department of Energy, Berkeley Labs. https://commons.lbl.gov/display/aro/Record+Series+Definition (accessed April 3, 2013).

Schellenberg, T. R. *Modern Archives: Principles and Techniques*. Chicago: Society of American Archivists, 2003.

Suderman, Jim. "Defining Electronic Series: A Study." *Archivaria* 53 (Spring 2002): 31–47.

Zhang, Jane. "Original Order in Digital Archives." *Archivaria* 74 (Fall 2012): 167–94. http://journals.sfu.ca/archivar/index.php/archivaria/article/view/12835/14052.

SERIES SYSTEM

First developed and implemented at the Commonwealth Archives Office (now National Archives of Australia) in the early 1960s, the Series System is a method of describing *records* and their *contexts* of creation and management over time. Now widely implemented in Australia and New Zealand and in some *archival programs* further afield, the defining feature of the Series System is the creation and maintenance of separate but interlinked descriptions of records and context entities such as creating agencies or *persons*. Fundamental to the system is an understanding that relationships between entities are contingent and time-bound, rather than fixed and timeless, and that the contingent nature of these relationships has to be accommodated and reflected in archival control systems. The approach became known as the Series System because implementations use the *series* as the highest level of intellectual control and descriptive input for records entities. Descriptions at fonds or *record group* levels may be generated as outputs, but descriptions at these levels are not created and maintained as descriptive inputs to the control system.

Origins of the Series System

During the 1950s and 1960s staff of the Australian Commonwealth Archives Office were developing an *archival management system* for a newly created government archives. In endeavoring to apply the descriptive rules of the 1898 Dutch Manual of Muller, Feith, and Fruin, they struggled to accommodate the complex realities of frequent administrative change in government. With government agencies being regularly renamed and/or restructured, and with responsibility for government *functions* frequently moving from one agency to another, identifying, describing, and controlling all of the records of a given records creator proved to be extremely difficult. Applying the record group concept—which had become accepted in other parts of the world—as the primary locus of intellectual control of records was problematic from a practical point of view given the frequency of machinery of government change in Australia. It also served to obscure rather than accurately reflect the administrative context in which records were created and managed. The assumption of fixed, unitary provenance that underpins the Dutch manual was contradicted by the reality of multiple provenance, where a given body of records could be managed successively over time by a variety of different creating and controlling agencies.

During the early 1960s, Commonwealth Archives Office staff Ian Maclean, Keith Penny, and Peter Scott devised an alternative approach to describing and controlling records. The underlying concept developed by Maclean and Penny sought to shift the descriptive perspective away from *archival deposits* to the *recordkeeping* processes that produce records, some of which may be deposited in an archives. Scott's contribution was to devise an approach to implementing the concept that involved separating descriptions of creating agencies from descriptions of records, and documenting the interrelationships between these entities through a system of interlinkages and cross-references. Descriptions within each of these two main entity types (*context/provenance* entities and records entities) could reflect the different kinds of entities that exist within each group. Context entities could be organizations, agencies, persons, or families (and later functions), while records entities could be *series*, items (or *files*), and *documents*.

The essential difference between the Series System and traditional approaches to *archival description* is that the series is not defined by being contained within a single larger entity (fonds or record group) but rather is a part of a much wider network of contingent and dynamic relationships. This more flexible approach to archival description and control enables a more accurate representation of the complex realities of administrative change and multiple provenance. Although the approach abandoned the creation and maintenance of fonds-level or record group descriptions, Scott and his colleagues were firmly of the view that the Series System was entirely consistent with archival principles, most particularly the *principle of respect des fonds*.

Responses to Peter Scott's Proposal and Later Developments

Peter Scott first explained his new approach to the wider profession in a 1966 article in *The American Archivist*, "The Record Group Concept: A Case for Abandonment." Initially, this article attracted surprisingly little international attention—although over time its significance became more widely recognized. Since 1966 Scott's proposals have attracted some specific criticism (e.g., Polden 1968; Fischer 1973), but more generally have been treated with a mixture of suspicion, misunderstanding, and indifference. Some of the criticisms argued that, rather than attempt to describe and control records while they are still being created by successive agencies, it is preferable for *archivists* to wait for the "archival dust to settle" before deciding the fonds or record group to which records should be allocated.

While highlighting the critics' attachment to traditional approaches to archival description, these criticisms also served to highlight a fundamental feature of the Series System: a desire for an archival control system that was integrated with, rather than disconnected from, the world of current recordkeeping. As a precursor of later *records continuum* thinking, Australia's first national archivist, Ian Maclean, was a lifelong opponent of any tendency to disconnect *records management* from archives. Indeed, Scott recalls that Maclean was "elated" by Scott's proposal, not only because it offered an elegant solution to the problem of administrative change, but also because it offered a vision of archival control that was not limited to describing records in formal *archival custody* (Scott 2010).

Following the publication of his 1966 article, Scott extended and expanded his descriptive model—most notably in a monumental five-part series of coauthored articles published in *Archives and Manuscripts* between 1978 and 1981 (reproduced in Cunningham 2010). Other Series System practitioners added to this corpus as the system was gradually adopted and implemented by all the public records institutions in Australia and New Zealand and by a number of other archival programs in Australasia and elsewhere (McCausland 1994). Over this time the system evolved to incorporate ideas and approaches developed by *archivists* who either worked with or were inspired by Scott, Maclean, and Penny. The most prominent, articulate, and prolific of these has been Chris Hurley, whose numerous writings on archival description have been conveniently collected together on Hurley's website, DescriptionGuy (www.descriptionguy.com/description.html). Of particular interest has been Hurley's development of Scott's thinking on synchronic or simultaneous multiple provenance: the phenomenon whereby more than one creator can simultaneously participate in the creation of a body of records. More recently, Hurley has developed this thinking even further to encompass the related concept of parallel provenance (Hurley 2005).

The emergence of automation in archival control and *access* systems made the practicalities of implementing the Series System much more approachable. As the data model for the Series System resembles that of a relational database system, its development in many respects prefigured the spread of such systems. Moreover, as the archival profession addressed the challenge of electronic records during the 1980s and 1990s, influential northern hemisphere commentators such as David Bearman and Terry Cook emphasized the flexibility of the Series System in coping with the complexities of describing and controlling digital *recordkeeping systems* (Bearman and Lytle 1985–1986; Cook 1997).

During the 1990s the development of international standards for archival description under the auspices of the International Council on Archives sought to codify a rigid traditional approach to description that was hostile to the Series System. In response, Australian archivists mobilized to advocate for descriptive standards that accommodated Scott's and Maclean's views on how *respect des fonds*

could be achieved. Chris Hurley, as Australia's first representative on the ICA's Ad Hoc Commission on Descriptive Standards (later the Committee on Descriptive Standards), led the crusade for international understanding and acceptance (if not adoption) of the Series System. Over time these efforts achieved a measure of success, as the second editions of ISAD(G) (2000) and ISAAR(CPF) (2004) together accommodated—albeit imperfectly—the Series System. The struggle to gain international acceptance and understanding of the Series System continues, with misinterpretation, incomprehension, and hostility toward the system still commonplace among many archivists who adhere to more traditional approaches.

The Series System data model has also proven to be enormously influential in the development of frameworks and standards for *recordkeeping metadata*. This work commenced with the so-called "SPIRT" recordkeeping metadata research project led by Sue McKemmish at Monash University during the late 1990s (McKemmish et al. 1999). The findings of the SPIRT project in turn influenced the development of recordkeeping metadata standards in various Australasian jurisdictions and later was fundamentally influential in the development of the International Standards Organization's standard for *Records Management Processes for Metadata*, ISO 23081, particularly the 2007 part 2 of that standard, *Conceptual and Implementation Issues*.

Understanding and implementation of the Series System was for many years hampered by the absence of a formal manual for, or codification of, the system for general usage. This gap was filled in 2007 when the Australian Society of Archivists Committee on Descriptive Standards published *Describing Archives in Context: A Guide to Australasian Practice*. More recently, in 2010, the Australian Society of Archivists published the collected writings of Peter Scott in a landmark volume that was strengthened by a major new essay by Scott himself together with reflections by leading Australian archivist Barbara Reed and Canadian archival consultant Laura Millar (Cunningham 2010).

While most of the criticism of the Series System over the years has focused on the philosophical issue of abandoning fonds- or record-group-level control as the primary focus of description, other more practical issues may inhibit archivists from implementing the system. First, for an established program, making the transition from a traditional system of archival description to the Series System can be expensive and labor intensive, and the perceived benefits may not outweigh the likely costs. Second, because Series System descriptions reflect complex realities, user interfaces may be bewildering to the novice end user, with too many relationships and cross-references for the average user to comprehend easily. The challenge here is to design friendly and intuitive user interfaces that make complex relationships apparent without them being a barrier to use, discovery, and understanding.

Describing Functions as Entities

Archives are created when people or organizations perform functions and activities. Increasingly, Series System practitioners regard functions as entities in their own right—entities that require separate descriptions, with links both to the records that document the function and to the records creators that perform the function. Functions are not mere aspects of the life of a records creating entity; on the contrary, records *creators* such as government agencies can often be regarded as nothing more than episodes in the life of a function (Hurley 1993). The

relationships between the three recordkeeping entities can be illustrated as shown in figure S.1.

In terms of archival description, this model can be represented as illustrated in figure S.2.

Within implementations of the Series System, each of the three main entities—business, agents, or records—may be described at different levels of granularity, with relationships between the different levels described accordingly (see figure S.3).

Conclusion

The key feature of the Australian Series System that distinguishes it from other systems of descriptive control is the separation of record description and contextual description. This approach implements a concept of archival description that focuses on describing recordkeeping systems and processes rather than archival relics; the Series System recognizes that those systems and processes exist within a complex world of contingent and dynamic interrelationships rather than an environment of fixed and static hierarchies. In practice three main entities are most commonly described using the Series System: (1) records; (2) the persons or organizations that create and manage records; and (3) the business performed by persons and organizations and documented in the

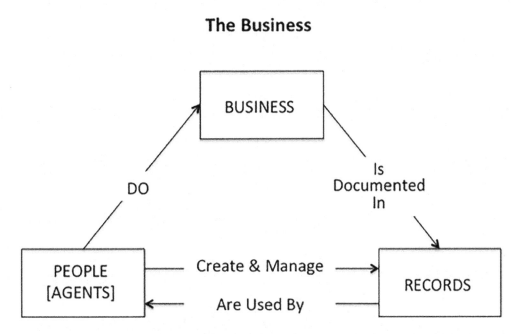

Figure S.1. Conceptual Model—the Business. *www.infotech.monash.edu.au/research/groups/rcrg/projects/spirt/deliverables/conrelmod.html*

The Description

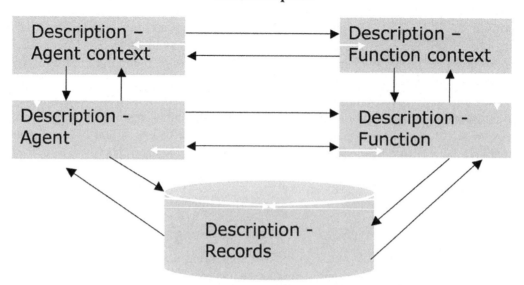

Figure S.2.   Conceptual Model—the Description. *www.infotech.monash.edu.au/research/groups/rcrg/projects/spirt/deliverables/conrelmod.html*

Entities

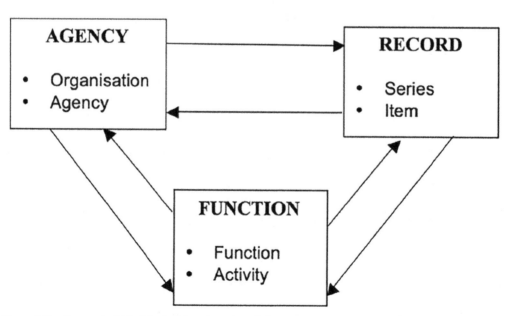

Figure S.3.   Conceptual Model—Entities. *Courtesy of the author*

records. Individual descriptions of manifestations of each of these three entities are registered in the system, and the many interrelationships between them over time are documented as fully as necessary to enable the discovery, use, understanding, and persistence of the records.—*Adrian Cunningham*

Keywords: archival description, context, relationships, administrative change, multiple provenance

Related Entries: Archival Description; Principle of *Respect des Fonds*; Record Group; Recordkeeping System(s); Series

Bibliography

Australian Society of Archivists, Committee on Descriptive Standards. *Describing Archives in Context: A Guide to Australasian Practice*. Canberra: Australian Society of Archivists, 2007.

Bearman, David, and Richard Lytle. "The Power of the Principle of Provenance." *Archivaria* 21 (Winter 1985–1986): 14–27. http://journals.sfu.ca/archivar/index.php/archivaria/article/view/11231/12170.

Cook, Terry. "What Is Past Is Prologue: A History of Archival Ideas since 1898, and the Future Paradigm Shift." *Archivaria* 43 (Spring 1997): 17–63. http://journals.sfu.ca/archivar/index.php/archivaria/article/view/12175/13184.

Cunningham, Adrian, ed. *The Arrangement and Description of Archives Amid Administrative and Technological Change: Essays and Reflections by and about Peter J. Scott*. Brisbane: Australian Society of Archivists, 2010.

Fischer, Gerald L. "The Australian ('Series') System: An Exposition." In Sue McKemmish and Michael Piggot, eds., *The Records Continuum: Ian Maclean and Australian Archives First Fifty Years*. Clayton, Victoria: Ancora Press in Association with Australian Archives, 1994, 150–72.

———. "Letting the Archival Dust Settle: Some Remarks on the Record Group Concept." *Journal of the Society of Archivists* 4 (October 1973): 640–45. DOI:10.1080/00379817309514014.

———. "Parallel Provenance, Part 1: What If Anything Is Archival Description?" *Archives and Manuscripts* 33 (1) (2005): 110–45. http://search.informit.com.au/documentSummary;dn=200601141;res=IELAPA.

———. "What, If Anything, Is a Function?" *Archives and Manuscripts* 21 (2) (1993): 208–20. http://infotech.monash.edu/research/groups/rcrg/publications/whatif.html.

McCausland, Sigrid. "Adapting the Series System: A Study of Small Archives Applications." In Sue McKemmish and Michael Piggott, eds., *The Records Continuum: Ian Maclean and Australian Archives First Fifty Years*. Clayton, Victoria: Ancora Press in Association with Australian Archives, 1994, 173–86.

McKemmish, Sue, Glenda Acland, Nigel Ward, and Barbara Reed. "Describing Records in Context in the Continuum: The Australian Recordkeeping Metadata Schema." *Archivaria* 1 (48) (1999): 3–43. http://journals.sfu.ca/archivar/index.php/archivaria/article/view/12715/13890.

Polden, Kenneth A. "The Record Group: A Matter of Principle." *Archives and Manuscripts* 3 (1) (1968): 3–7.

Scott, Peter J. "Introduction." In Adrian Cunningham, ed., *The Arrangement and Description of Archives amid Administrative and Technological Change: Essays and Reflections by and about Peter J. Scott*. Brisbane: Australian Society of Archivists, 2010, 8–95.

———. "The Record Group Concept: A Case for Abandonment." *The American Archivist* 29 (4) (1966): 493–504.

STATUS OF TRANSMISSION (RECORDS)

The status of transmission of a *record* refers to its degree of perfection (Duranti 1991–1992, 8). A record is classified as an original, *copy*, or draft. An original has the greatest authority because it carries the most elements that allow proving its *authenticity*. The degree of perfection of the record is established on the basis of its primitiveness, completeness, and effectiveness.

The Concept

A record's status of transmission conveys its degree of perfection "in terms of its completeness, primitiveness, and effectiveness" (Xie 2011, 583). Of the three possible statuses of transmission, the original has the highest degree of perfection, in that it is complete—contains all required components and information; has absolute primitiveness—is the first instance of that record; and is effective—capable of achieving the purposes for which it was generated. Thus, an original is defined as "the first complete *document* capable of producing consequences" (Duranti 1995, 7).

A draft is incomplete and lacks effectiveness; it is intended for development and revision, and is not meant to have consequences. A copy lacks primitiveness, as it is a reproduction of an original record, a draft, or another copy. Identifying a record as the original endows it with trustworthiness because "an original is always more trustworthy than its drafts and copies" (Xie 2011, 583).

Status of Transmission in the Electronic Environment

In *archival science*, the medium of a record serves as the carrier of the message of the record, but also contributes to its meaning (Duranti 2002, 12). With physical records, the medium and the record's message cannot be separated, and the medium is an essential component of the record and the one that would reveal its status of transmission. In the electronic records, however, this is not the case, and the medium—while still necessary to the existence of the record, in that even bitstreams need to be affixed to a carrier to exist—is not part of the record, which does not depend on it for its identity or status of transmission.

Due to its nature, an electronic record manifests all three qualities of completeness, primitiveness, and effectiveness only when first accessed by the person receiving it. When a record is first generated by its author, it may be the first complete electronic record, but is not yet effective if it has not crossed "either time, space, or both, to reach its intended recipients" (Xie 2011, 583). In order to be sent to its addressee (also when it coincides with its author if transmission is intended through time rather than space), a record internally generated must first be saved to a physical storage medium. However, this action makes it lose the characteristic of primitiveness, as the act of opening, or viewing, the record on the part of the addressee (i.e., the same person saving it or another person) will require it to be reproduced,

and further reproduced for each instance that it is accessed. The very process of end-to-end transmission through a medium negates a record's claim to primitiveness. A *digital record* is only primitive when it is first manifested on an electronic device screen, prior to it being saved, and it is also complete and effective when it is first manifested to its intended recipient, prior to being saved. Each rendering of an electronic record—that is, the process of opening an electronic record for viewing—creates a copy of the original *file*. The original electronic record, therefore, does not exist in the same way as the original physical record.

The term "original" is better applied only to traditional records (Xie 2011, 583). In the case of electronic records, one might speak of the native format of the record, but the original proper only exists for a nanosecond, if it is ever generated and there is not a directed progress from draft to copy.

Thus, electronic records are used and maintained in the status of copy. In consideration of the fact that electronic records are reproduced when they are accessed, any such copy made by opening a current record is a "copy in the form of original," that is, a complete and effective record lacking the quality of primitiveness. In contrast, any copy made after the record is no longer current, or for purposes of distribution, dispersal, or redundancy, is an "imitative copy," a record that looks like the original, but the act of remaking the record is not intended to support the activity in which the saved record was intended to participate, merely preserving the information in its documentary form (Duranti 1991–1992, 10). It is important to remember that in the electronic environment one can only copy what one can see, which means that copies are rarely complete (i.e., identical) to the record being copied. If one wishes to generate a complete reproduction, one has to make an image.

Copies and the Physical Record

Returning to the realm of physical records, where the medium is a component of the record, which is permanently affixed to the original support, we can categorize copies as follows:

- A *facsimile* is a copy that perfectly reproduces the record and all the details of its appearance, not in order to deceive, but mostly for exhibit purposes.

- A copy in the form of the original appears identical to the original and has the same effects, but is generated subsequently.
- A conformed copy transcribes portions of a record in an exact manner while replacing others that could not be or were not transcribed with written explanations.
- An imitative copy reproduces the content and form of the record being copied in such a way that it is always possible to tell the copy from the record being copied.
- A simple copy only reproduces the content of a record, either partially or completely.
- An authentic copy is a copy declared to conform to the record being copied by an authorized official.
- An insert, *vidimus* or *inspeximus*, is a transcription of a record made by a public officer who has seen the original record and declares to have done so.

Thus, a general definition of *copy* could be "a duplicate of a record resulting from a reproduction process" (Xie 2011, 584).

Conclusion

The status of transmission of a record refers to its degree of perfection. Status of transmission differs with regard to physical and electronic records, in response to the characteristics and constraints of the environments in which each form exists. The physical record is able to convey the highest degree of perfection as an original, that is, a complete, primitive, and effective record. Due to the nature of the digital environment, an electronic record is most often used and maintained in the status of a copy and therefore essentially lacks completeness and primitiveness as understood in the traditional records environment, but can still have effectiveness.—*Victoria Ostrzenski*

Keywords: authenticity, copy, draft, electronic record, original
Related Entries: Digital Record; Diplomatics; Record(s)

Bibliography

Duranti, Luciana. "The Concept of Electronic Record." In L. Duranti, T. Eastwood, and H. MacNeil, eds., *Preservation of the Integrity of Electronic Records*. Dordrecht, The Netherlands: Kluwer Academic, 2002, 9–22.

———. "Diplomatics: New Uses for an Old Science, Part VI." *Archivaria* 1 (33) (1991): 5–24. http://journals.sfu.ca/archivar/index.php/archivaria/article/view/11795/12746.

———. "Reliability and Authenticity: The Concepts and Their Implications." *Archivaria* 1 (39) (1995): 5–10. http://journals.sfu.ca/archivar/index.php/archivaria/article/view/12063/13035.

Xie, Sherry L. "Building Foundations for Digital Records Forensics: A Comparative Study of the Concept of Reproduction in Digital Records." *The American Archivist* 74 (1) (2011): 576–99. http://archivists.metapress.com/content/e088666710692t3k/fulltext.pdf.

STRUCTURAL ANALYSIS

This entry discusses the role of structural analysis as a theoretical and methodological framework in *archival science*, especially in *appraisal*. It focuses on Germany, where structural analysis has been notoriously influential at least since the beginning of the twentieth century. This entry also points out the role of structural analysis in contemporary appraisal in Canada.

The Concept

Structural analysis in appraisal literature refers mostly to the analysis of the organizational and administrative structure of records creators in order to make appraisal decisions. Its main focus is the administrative *context* of creators, not *records* themselves or records content and subject. This approach is based on the ideas that the value of records descends from the value of their respective creators and records worthy of permanent preservation are those that best represent the activities and roles of their creators. In addition, structural analysis refers to the analysis of structure of an *archival fonds*. In this case, the focus is on records, and the analysis is therefore related to *formal analysis*.

State of the Art

Bibliography—or literature reviews—on structural analysis per se are scarce. Hans Booms's critique of appraisal in Germany—originally published in German in 1972, and later translated into English and published in *Archivaria* in 1987—and Luciana Duranti's proposal of the use of *diplomatics* to appraise *digital records*, published in 2010, are the most comprehensive interpretations of the role of structural analysis in appraisal theory. Before offering his own *documentation plan* proposal, Booms examines the development of appraisal in Germany since the beginning of the twentieth century, and highlights how structural analysis has been central to appraisal theory and practice in this country (Booms 1987). Duranti shows how structural and formal analysis have been present in appraisal theory in several countries, before introducing the contributions of diplomatics to understand records structure, *functions*, and activities (Duranti 2010).

Structural Analysis since 1950

Germany has a strong tradition of structural analysis. Until WWII, structural analysis, along with *functional analysis*, guided appraisal decisions to a great extent. This was a consequence of: (i) the existence of registries (see *Registry System*), which made the administrative structure of records creators and the organicity of *archives* easily identifiable; (ii) the wide acceptance of the *principle of provenance*, which acted as a theoretical framework for appraisal; and (iii) the rejection of the *principle of pertinence* or subject-based approaches to appraisal (Klumpenhouwer 1988, 46–47, 139; Booms 1987, 87–88).

After the Second World War, the need to deal with huge volumes of records gave new nuances to the role of structural analysis in appraisal. Prominent supporters were George Wilhelm Sante, Wilhelm Rohr, and Johannes Papritz. In the thirty-fifth German Archival Conference in 1957, Sante suggested that *archivists* should choose to preserve records from the most significant government agen-

cies, and that the significance of agencies would depend on their administrative role. At the same conference, Rohr suggested that the agencies higher up in the administrative hierarchy would be the most significant ones, and therefore, the ones that should contribute with the most valuable records to the archives (Booms 1987, 88–90).

In 1965, Papritz reaffirmed the central role of structural analysis in appraisal by focusing on the structure of records themselves (*strukturtype der schriftgutes*) and on their relationship with the organic structure of the whole body of records (*strukturformen der schriftgutkörper*). He also advocated for the development of criteria to select the particular or peculiar (*das besondere*), as well as the typical or characteristic (*das typische*), by choosing samples (Papritz 1965).

Still in the 1960s, structural analysis was central to appraisal also in the German Democratic Republic (GDR). The analysis of the place of records creators in the administrative hierarchy, of the functions creators performed, and of their role in East Germany socialist society were to guide archivists' decisions regarding the value of records (Booms 1987, 97).

Criticisms of the use of structural analysis in Germany, as synthesized by Hans Booms in the 1970s, point to: (i) its simplistic emphasis on governmental and other institutional (administrative and organizational) activities, at the expense of informal ones; (ii) its overrating of the importance of records creators and underrating of the value of records themselves and their content; (iii) the challenges presented by the constant changes in the structure of records creators (Booms 1987, 90–91, 97–98, 101).

Outside Germany, archivists in different countries have stressed different aspects of structural analysis in appraisal: for example, Brooks and Schellenberg in the United States in the 1940s and 1950s respectively; Grigg, in the Grigg Report from the Committee on Departmental Records in the United Kingdom in 1954; and, decades later, Lodolini in Italy in the 1980s (Duranti 2010).

Structural Analysis in the Past Two Decades

Structural analysis is still influential in Germany, as well as in other countries. For German archivist Angelika Menne-Haritz, structural analysis is central to appraisal and comprises the analysis of agencies and their missions, the functions they perform, and how they use and organize their records (Menne-Haritz 2001, 455). In addition, the stress on procedural context suggested by structural analysis is also present in the "vertical and horizontal appraisal" methodology that has been used in Germany since the middle of the 1990s for appraising government records at the federal, provincial, and municipal levels. This methodology initially evaluates the tasks, functions, and responsibilities of each agency, compares various agencies, and then proceeds to a structural analysis of records per se (Treffeisen 2003).

Furthermore, structural analysis is key to macroappraisal, as proposed by Terry Cook in Canada. Cook argues that appraisal should rather focus on the context and processes of records creation rather than on the records themselves. Archivists, he continues, should perform appraisal by concentrating on the interaction between records creators (called structure) and citizens in order to accomplish a purpose (called function) (Cook 1991; 1992, 6).

Finally, structural analysis is, along with formal analysis, central to the work of the InterPARES project in Canada. Using diplomatics to elaborate the fundamentals of *digital preservation*, InterPARES proposes, among other activities, that appraisal of digital records involves their management since creation until they become inactive (Duranti 2010, 9). The project suggests that appraisal decisions are to be based on a "structural analysis of the functions and activities" of records creators, as well as of records systems (Duranti 2010, 15).

Conclusion

This entry showed the role of structural analysis in appraisal theory and practice since the 1950s. It stressed its influence on German appraisal history and contemporary Canadian appraisal approaches. It also highlighted that structural analysis is related to functional and formal analysis, as well as to the *principle of provenance*.—*Lara Mancuso*

Keywords: appraisal, records creators
Related Entries: Appraisal; Formal Analysis; Functional Analysis; Principle of Provenance

Bibliography

Booms, Hans. "Society and the Formation of a Documentation Heritage: Issues in the Appraisal of Archival Sources." *Archivaria* 1 (24) (1987): 69–107. http://journals.sfu.ca/archivar/index.php/archivaria/article/view/11415/12357.

Cook, Terry. *The Archival Appraisal of Records Containing Personal Information: A RAMP Study with Guidelines*. Paris: UNESCO, 1991.

———. "Mind over Matter: Towards a New Theory of Archival Appraisal." In Barbara Craig, ed., *The Canadian Archival Imagination: Essays in Honour of Hugh Taylor*. Ottawa: Association of Canadian Archivists, 1992.

Duranti, Luciana. "Structural and Formal Analysis: The Contribution of Diplomatics to Archival Appraisal in the Digital Environment." In Jennie Hill, ed., *Re-appraising Archives*. London: Facet, 2010.

Klumpenhouwer, Richard. *Concepts of Value in the Archival Appraisal Literature: As Historical and Critical Analysis*. Master's thesis, University of British Columbia, 1988.

Menne-Haritz, Angelika. "Archivische Bewertung. Der Prozess der Umwidmung von geschlossenem Schriftgut zu auswertungsbereitem Archivgut." *Schweizerische Zeitschrift für Geschichte* 51 (2001): 448–60.

Papritz, Johannes Von. "Methodik der archivischen Auslese und Kassation bei zwei Strukturtypen der Massenakten." *Der Archivar* 2 (May 1965): 117–32.

Treffeisen, Juergen. "The Development in Germany of Archival Processing—the Vertical and Horizontal Appraisal." *Archival Science* 3 (2003): 345–66. DOI: 10.1007/s10502-004-2273-1.

SUBJECT FILES

This entry discusses the role of subject files in archival institutions and in the *records management context*. It focuses respectively on *public service* and on subject classification systems.

The Concept

Subject files are used: (i) to provide reference service in archival institutions; and (ii) for classification and filing purposes in a records management context.

Subject Files for Archival Reference Service

When used in the archival reference service context, subject files—also referred to as subject vertical files—are *files* that contain published and unpublished materials (e.g., newspaper clippings, posters, brochures) about a specific topic. These materials are collected, maintained, and updated by *archivists* for the purpose of improving patrons' experience when they engage in archival research.

For researchers, subject files provide background information around certain topics. They can potentially guide patrons in the process of choosing which *records* and files they are to consult, and can make the context of records, *case files*, and *archival fonds* easier to grasp. For archivists, subject files offer support to answer reference questions.

Archivists usually choose materials and organize them into subject files according to research needs of patrons who consult the *archives*. Subject files can also be compiled when *outreach* activities are organized. Therefore, subject files to a certain extent reflect current and past research interests and user needs, as well as archivists' efforts to promote and increase *access* and improve service delivery.

Subject Files for Records Management

In the context of records management, subject files are used in subject classification systems. ARMA's *Glossary of Records and Information Management Terms* defines a subject classification system as "a plan for the classification and coding of *documents* by subject." The same glossary defines subject filing as "a file system in which each document relates to a specific subject matter and is arranged in alphabetic order by subject" (ARMA 2012, 51).

In this context, subject files are, as suggested by Terry Cook, "files which contain documents relating to a specific subject or topical matter." The author mentions that subject files can, for example, contain records that are relevant or that relate to whole *series* of case files. He also considers *policy files* as a subcategory of subject files (Cook 1991, 14).

Besides policies, subject files can also include correspondence, memos, directives, and reports. They contain, therefore, operational records, which reflect specific missions and mandates of organizations or business units. These files can incidentally contain personal information, for example, in statistical reports or when a specific case file is converted into a subject file because it sets a precedent that impacts policies and procedures. Records professionals are to observe legislation regarding privacy and confidentiality when dealing with subject files (Cook 1991, 27–28).

Subject files are subject to retention periods as specified by the respective retention schedules. Retention periods are determined and applied according to the type of records subject files contain.

Finally, when it comes to arranging records within series, files arranged based on, for example, commodities or clients, can also be thought of as subject files. In this case, they are rather subject groupings, that is, files containing records that refer to a particular transaction involving a specific client or commodity. Subject grouping is an option determined by considerations regarding storage and retrieval. The main goal is to facilitate retrieval within a functional classification system (Shepherd and Yeo 2003, 81–85).

Conclusion

Subject files are used within subject classification systems in records management, in which case they usually contain policies, correspondence, memos, directives, and reports. They may also be used within functional classification systems in order to facilitate retrieval. In archival institutions, subject files are used in order to improve users' experience by providing background and contextual information on topics related to specific archival holdings or fonds. In this case, subject files contain published and unpublished materials such as newspaper clippings, magazine articles, posters, and brochures.
—*Lara Mancuso*

Keywords: reference service, subject classification system

Related Entries: Public Service; Records Classification; Records Management

Bibliography

ARMA International. *Establishing Alphabetic, Numeric, and Subject Filing Systems*. Lenexa, KS: ARMA International, 2005.

———. *Glossary of Records Management and Information Management Terms*, 4th edition. Overland Park, KS: ARMA International, 2012.

Cook, Terry. *The Archival Appraisal of Records Containing Personal Information: A RAMP Study with Guidelines*. Paris: UNESCO, 1991.

Shepherd, Elizabeth, and Geoffrey Yeo. *Managing Records: A Handbook of Principles and Practice*, 1st edition. London: Facet, 2003.

T

TEXTUAL RECORDS

At the most elementary level of explanation, the notion of textual records refers to a general medium and classification of *records* whose content is predominantly composed of "writing," expressing words, language, vocabulary, and meaning through forms and formations of alphabetic characters, numerals, punctuation, and other symbols. Predominantly is the operative word, since textual records can and often do incorporate content from other types of records—for example, plans, maps, drawings, photographs, illustrations, and digital links—both within single *documents* and within functional administrative aggregates of documents (e.g., *files*), which, considered on their own, would typically be distinguished from textual records, for example, as *photographic records*, cartographic records, *audiovisual records*, or *architectural records*. In this entry, the intention is to probe more deeply below the surface of textual records conceived simply as a generic concept of communication medium to explore the multiple layers and dimensions of classification complexity, analysis, taxonomy, and typology that have emerged over time to explain their functionality within both organizations and private life (*personal records*). As the concept of personal records is treated elsewhere, our focus here will be on the functional *context* and classification of the textual aggregates commonly known as administrative records and business records.

The Concept

It is important to recognize that there is currently some ambiguity and uncertainty around the qualification of records as "textual" at the first level of conceptual statement, and how this particular adjective actually signifies, shapes, or influences the general meaning of the combinative noun. For example, postmodern thinking and especially poststructuralist theories challenge many of the conventions and precepts that have generally explained the attributes and elements that have traditionally given text its "textuality" and coherence as a type of constituent whole (texture, context, structure, content) from philosophic, semantic, and semiotic perspectives (see *diplomatics*). This includes basic questions about the nature of text conceived as language and discourse or even more fundamentally the notion that "everything"—whether physical, nonmaterial, or intellectual—actually constitutes text. Further, new modes, forms, and formations of writing continuously evolving through technological innovation (e.g., e-mail, blogs, wikis, social media) and the dynamic intertextuality of text within the digital infosphere (including the ubiquitous presence of text produced via acts of texting and tweeting) have also become problematic, especially for records administration. Intertextuality pushes the boundaries and dimensions of textual records in ways that confound their functional identification, aggregation, and declaration from a corporate perspective, notably from the prospect of what constitutes and/

or meets the documentary requirements of "record-ness" for records within organizational *recordkeeping systems*. Nonetheless, the functional schemes and taxonomies that have evolved over the years to classify textual records once they have been designated as such—especially over the last twenty years or so—within the operational domains of organizations remain conceptually intact and enormously important to business administration.

Another key conceptual issue concerns archival approaches to *appraisal, acquisition*, custodial management, reference, and other services based on the form, format, and substance of the recording medium rather than on the functional and administrative unity of records considered in reference to their operational and transactional provenance regardless of their communications medium. In many *archives*, maintaining and managing textual records in physical and intellectual isolation from records in other recording media is a common practice, even if they were originally produced and kept together within the same administrative environment by creators and recordkeepers because they served common intentionality and functions. In the wake of acquisition, records medium-focus can even lead to the physical extraction of plans, maps, drawings, and photographs by archives from the administrative files of government institutions (notably central registry files) and business organizations toward their dispersal to medium-related special collections or *archival fonds*. Medium-based records appraisal and acquisition also remains an active alternative to broader institutional strategies.

There are various schools of thought for and against archival interventions based on the form, format, and substance of the recording medium. However, most public records administrators and *archivists* (including this writer) would contend that archival interventions of any nature based on the recording medium as documentary or cultural object—especially within an administrative or business context—constitutes a fundamental contravention of the archival *principle of provenance* with very serious consequences. Within these particular environments, failure to observe the principle of provenance—which forbids the separation of records from their functional roots under any circumstances—in all aspects of its archival application conspicuously undermines our capacity to

understand the continuity of records within their respective administrative and business domains; makes decisions about archival and other values very difficult if not wholly untenable; destroys the evidential value and authority of records residing in their original order and documentary association; and distances society even further from the intentions and purposes of the original creators and administrators to the detriment of historical meaning and understanding.

Looking at textual records in more detail, there is a certain amount of competing terminology currently in place to distinguish, describe, and classify them between and within various administrative and business jurisdictions at national, regional, state, municipal, and organizational/institutional levels around the world. Depending on local domain laws, policies, regulations, protocols, and business operations, and the nature and scale of the organization involved—including the physical and intellectual extent of its documentary productivity—there are also significant practical differences relating to the granularity of their identification, aggregation, and classification according to functional type or class as expressed in *recordkeeping* methodology and taxonomy. However, regardless of the methodologies and nomenclatures under which jurisdictions or organizations have decided to identify, describe, organize, and classify their documentary output, there are several very fundamental understandings regarding the form, structure, content, and context of textual records across many administrative and business domains. One element is the consistency of definition, meaning, purpose, and intention present in underlying nomenclatures through the distinctions between and descriptions of functional contexts and documentary types irrespective of how many classes or categories of documents and records have been articulated. This is perfectly evident in the latest records *disposition* authorities in place for the classes and categories of common administrative records at the national level in, for example, Australia, Canada, and the United States. Another element of major consensus is the recent notion that administrative and business records should be identified, arranged, and classified within the functional context of their operational or transactional provenance through the use of business systems analysis rather than by applying subject taxonomies or categorizing them by attributes or characteristics via records typologies.

Functional classification represents the latest phase in a long history of textual records distinction, identification, arrangement, description, and categorization, beginning with the early documentary typologies of the High Middle Ages in Western Europe. It is important to note that many of these early documentary types or at least their formal documentary protocols—which were generally based on notarial and chancellery prescriptions in combination with the evolution of the documentary elements intrinsically necessary to conduct administrative business within nascent bureaucratic organizations—continue to inform current documentation standards. Even if the functional classification systems proposed for textual (and other) records place emphasis on administrative provenance as the guiding principle to structure their functional organization, arrangement, and description as business objects, and in the process eschew necessarily documentary type or subject in favor of functional business contexts, elements of both typology and subject grouping remain intact within in the deeper granularity of their corresponding schematic articulations. Many functional classification plans for textual records are largely hybrids of *function*, subject, and records types, reflecting a gradual transition to provenance- and business-activity–based identification and classification.

In most contemporary organizations or institutions, a very basic and critical distinction is made between administrative records and business records—that is, textual documentary production is commonly subdivided into two generic unities based on their functional intentions and transactional purposes. Administrative records represent the documentary output related to all of the activities and transactions that every organization or institution must normally undertake in order to secure and provide the resources and infrastructure necessary to conduct business in any form at a corporate level. This broad administrative functionality includes activities such as developing and managing human resources; obtaining business capital and managing a budget (financial management or comptrollership); the management of real property (land and buildings) and material (equipment, supplies, contracts, technology); and general administrative services (administrative support, including information resource development and management). Administrative records generally have an inherent consistency and constancy internally within particular functional or activity domains across organizations and institutions. They are heavily process-driven to the extent that they are often formulaic in terms of form and format, and their documentary content is frequently indicated by documentation standards residing in enabling legislation and corresponding policy and regulatory requirements.

For instance, three of the major subclasses commonly identified by organizations under the rubric of administrative records (financial, legal and property records) are all highly formulaic and very content-specific, insofar as their functional context of administrative creation and their intrinsic elements are almost entirely prescribed by law, legislation, policies, regulations, and other authorities. Many are simply completed preset templates or forms, the sole distinction between them being their informational and transactional detail. Typically one encounters intrinsic documentary consistency among the categories and types of documents and files produced within their various functional contexts. This kind of constancy has allowed records administrators to develop common approaches to the definition, distinction, creation, classification, management, and disposition of textual records.

By contrast, business records comprise the documentary output representing the substantive functions and activities an organization or institution undertakes to accomplish its own business mission or mandate. Unlike administrative records, business records are largely organization or institution specific, and they are frequently corporately and culturally idiosyncratic even when created broadly within the frame of existing industry or business standards and/or laws and regulations. While there are some circumstances where business records must be created prescriptively because certain documentary elements reside in the public interest and are required under law to be presented in a particular order and format of organization and description (e.g., the investigation of transportation accidents in reference to safety standards; the advocacy and approval process for pharmaceutical drugs), the vast majority of business records are indigenous to the organization and its specific business context(s). Further, the documentary content one encounters lends itself to much further organization-specific subdivision along functional lines, essentially between (a) business activity documentation, that is, the compulsory outputs or products in the nature and form of records or documents that must be created in order for an institution to transact mandated or mission-critical business, (b) ancillary business records, that is, the records or documents that must be created to satisfy the requirements of *accountability*, stewardship, audit, investigation, and litigation at the corporate level, and (c) contextual business records, that is, records or documents that individuals or groups create, accumulate, capture, and exchange to support business at the operational level. All textual records within these business contexts are typically created in various forms (e.g., memoranda, reports, studies, correspondence) and with varying levels of formality and documentary rigor.

Conclusion

Today, the elements that establish the nature and substance of textual records are not primarily related to the intrinsic requirements of formulaic expression necessary to satisfy typological distinctions or to distinctions of type based on the subject matter of their documentary content. Rather, they are preeminently related to the provenance-based functional context of their creation expressed and understood through the transactional purposes of their documentary intention as business objects; the goals and objectives of creators; and institutional or organizational expectations conceived through the corporate reception and use of information resources via documentary exchange. In conclusion, this entry has indicated that functional interpretations and contextual applications of the concept of provenance are critical to any understanding and treatment of textual records within contemporary administrative and business domains. It remains to be seen whether current notions of provenance and functional *records classification* can evolve further to accommodate the new textuality and intertextuality of text within the environs of the digital infosphere.—*Richard Brown*

Keywords: administrative records, business records, functional classification, records administration

Related Entries: Architectural Records; Audio-Visual Records; Context; Diplomatics; Photographic Records; Principle of Provenance; Records Classification

Bibliography

Brown, Richard. "Macro-Appraisal Theory and the Context of the Public Records Creator." *Archivaria* 1 (40) (1995): 121–72. http://journals.sfu.ca/archivar/index.php/archivaria/article/view/12102/13094.

Caron, Daniel J., and R. Brown. *Creating Documentation Standards for Government Programs, Services and Results: A Developmental Framework and Guide for Business Managers and Information Resource Specialists*. Consultation Draft, Library and Archives Canada, 2008. www.collectionscanada.gc.ca/obj/007001/f2/007001-5000.1-e.pdf (accessed December 2013).

Chosky, Carol. *Domesticating Information: Managing Documents inside the Organization*. Lanham, MD: Scarecrow Press, 2006.

Hill, Jenny, ed. *The Future of Archives and Recordkeeping: A Reader*. London: Facet, 2010.

International Standards Organization. *ISO/TR 15489-1-2:2001: Information and Documentation—Records Management—Part 1: General; Information and Documentation—Records Management—Part 2: Guidelines.* Geneva, Switzerland: 2001.

———. *ISO/TR 26122:2008: Information and Documentation—Work Process Analysis for Records.* Geneva, Switzerland: 2008.

Library and Archives Canada. *Multi-Institutional Disposition Authorities (MIDA).* 2004. www.collectionscanada.gc.ca/government/disposition/007007-1008-e.html (accessed December 2013).

National Archives and Records Administration of the United States. *General Records Schedules (GRS).* 2012. www.archives.gov/records-mgmt/grs/ (accessed December 2013).

National Archives of Australia. *Administrative Functions Disposal Authority (AFDA).* 2010. www.naa.gov.au/records-management/publications/afda.aspx (accessed December 2013).

Shepherd, Elizabeth, and Geoffrey Yeo. *Managing Records: A Handbook of Principles and Practice.* London: Facet, 2002.

TOTAL ARCHIVES

The Canadian concept of total archives advocates that archival institutions should facilitate the management of current *records* of their sponsoring institution or level of government and acquire a small portion of these as permanent historical records, and acquire as well the records of private individuals, groups, and organizations that complement these institutional holdings, in both cases for all recording media. Total archives grew more by historical accident than conscious theory, was codified during the 1970s to enjoy its heyday, and then from 1980 onward was subjected to significant criticism. Despite certain practical limitations in its implementation, the holistic vision of total archives is an important Canadian contribution to archival thinking; it was the harbinger of more inclusive, integrated approaches to theory and practice that later flourished in the archival world.

The Concept

Total archives originated at the national level in Canada, and was eventually adopted by most other *archives* in the country: provincial and territorial, municipal, university, corporate, private and nongovernmental organizations, and educational and religious institutions. By contrast, most national archives in the developed world primarily acquire records from their sponsoring governments; private-sector records and personal papers are typically acquired by libraries, thematic- or media-based documentation centers, or university archives.

This anomaly reflects the historical evolution of Canada's cultural and information infrastructure. Five years after Confederation in 1867, which created the Dominion of Canada, the federal government established the Archives Branch in 1872 as the de facto national archives. In the absence initially of a national museum, national gallery, or national library, the Archives Branch was the focus of the nation's cultural activities. The Records Branch, in another department, was responsible for contemporary post-Confederation government records through a nascent *records management* program. The Archives Branch focused by contrast on acquiring pre-Confederation colonial-era records, copying French and British records overseas relating to

Canada, and collecting private-sector historical records. The two programs were merged in 1903, thus creating "total archives" in reality if not in name, an arrangement formalized in law in 1912 as the Public Archives of Canada (PAC). As with its Archives Branch predecessor, however, the overwhelming emphasis of the PAC remained, until well after the Second World War, on private textual manuscripts, especially those reflecting the colonial, pioneering, and romantic era of early Canadian history. Records management activities and archival government records were largely ignored.

With the growth of government activities (and thus records) in the two world wars and Great Depression, public-sector records management programs gradually expanded. A network of regional records centers was opened across the country for storing dormant federal government records. New *records management standards* and training programs were launched under PAC guidance. The new Public Records Order (1966) prohibited the destruction of any government record without the authorization of the dominion (later national) *archivist* of Canada, following *appraisal* of the records by PAC archivists. These policies, standards, and guidelines increased very significantly the flow of government records having historical value to the permanent archival holdings of the Public (later National) Archives of Canada.

Parallel to these developments with government records, a new National Library of Canada (NLC) was created in 1953. The roles of the PAC and the NLC, and thus the application of total archives, was blurred from the start. Considerable overlap of *acquisition* occurred between published (library) and unpublished (archives) documentary heritage. The NLC deeply resented that, unlike most national libraries, the long head start by the PAC in collecting private manuscripts severely curtailed the NLC's mandate in this area. Resulting tensions and program duplication eventually led to the merger of the PAC/NAC and the NLC in 2004 to form Library and Archives Canada, a total archive in the broadest sense and one more suitable for a digital environment.

But before these tensions were fully manifested, total archives enjoyed a golden age when its key concepts flourished with considerable imagination and operational flair. In 1971–1972, dominion archivist Wilfrid Smith finally named the comprehensive approach that had been evolving since 1872 as the total archives concept. For Smith, total archives involved not only acquiring every medium of record (text, film, photographs, maps, machine-readable) from the government or public sector and from private, personal sources, but also managing, for government records, the "front end" of the *records lifecycle* through records management programs and the "back end" for those records appraised as having archival or historical value.

While Smith labeled total archives, it was one of his chief lieutenants, Hugh Taylor, who made the concept come alive in intellectual substance and organizational change. Taylor transformed total archives from an acquisition strategy to an archival ideal. He explored the deeper theoretical meanings of various recording media, reflecting the contemporary thinking of Canadian media philosopher and international academic celebrity Marshall McLuhan. Taylor asserted that the character of recording media and their patterns of communication were an integral part of the *context* of records. The traditional archival *principle of provenance* that linked records structurally to the *person* or office that created or accumulated them was expanded to include the functional *interrelatedness* and material sensibilities of the media themselves. To develop such specialized media knowledge, Taylor took three media divisions he inherited (one very large one for *textual records* of private and government provenance, and two much smaller ones for pictures and maps), and expanded them to seven much larger media-based divisions.

Many division- or media-specific exhibitions, symposia, and publications were produced by the PAC in the 1970s and early 1980s. Moreover, each division had its own identifying brochures and descriptive guides, even wall posters. Each evolved its own means of first arranging, and then describing, its archival holdings. Each established its own computer systems to describe its particular media holdings. Each developed specialized researcher clienteles, and evolved different ways and places for serving them. Knowledge about different recording media and its contexts of creation and use thereby expanded exponentially.

For the "front end" records management dimension of Smith's total archives, there was also considerable progress: more regional record centers were opened, centralized microfilming services for all departments was implemented, records scheduling and archival appraisal were very much expanded, and extensive training and publication guidance was launched in Ottawa and the regions. Moreover, new centralized public policies of the government of Canada in the 1980s around freedom of information, privacy, and control of records destruction, in the formulation of which the PAC was closely involved, as well as new empowering legislation for the archives itself, gave these *information management* initiatives a considerable boost. Government archival records programs within the PAC grew accordingly in budgets, staff, holdings, and internal influence. From having no internal unit solely responsible for archival government records until 1965—some ninety-three years after the PAC was established and in such direct contrast to all other first-world countries—the Government Archives Division by the 1980s was the largest and most powerful.

Despite this records management growth and archival government records sophistication, total archives as a concept inside the PAC, and in the profession literature, still focused primarily on the all-media dimensions of its definition. And for all the undeniable success of media-based total archives, its PAC implementation caused a serious fragmentation of total archives that generated much debate. Launched by this author, Terry Cook, a government records archivist, his "The Tyranny of the Medium" attacked media-based archival structures for dividing the integrated nature of the *archival fonds*. Respecting the archival principle of provenance required keeping together (virtually if not physically), in one archival fonds, all records in all media created by, or received from, each records creator. Total archives as implemented at PAC and often elsewhere violated this with incompatible finding aids between divisions, lost or nonexistent cross references between media that were transferred from one division to another, mishandling of multimedia files, and no acquisition coordination across media.

Photographic archivist Andrew Birrell fired back with his "The Tyranny of Tradition," claiming that applying Cook's traditional archival principles would thwart media acquisition sensibilities and their specialized curatorial and reference needs. The text-based dominance of Western culture should no longer be allowed to choke off visual *documentary evidence* just as this was finally gaining greater acceptance in the archival world. Aesthetic and artistic values in visual records, normally associated with holdings of art galleries, were no less significant than classic textual evidence. Five archivists from the PAC's National Film, Television, and Sound Archives Division agreed with Cook in their "Total Archives Come Apart," arguing that "media solitudes" reduced audio-visual archivists to technicians running media-viewing machines and related technology, and managing special storage facilities for oversized or sensitive recording media, rather than being cross-media scholars who understood the fuller context linking their particular medium to all other media of the same records creator and to the same activities, functions, ideas, and circumstances animating their creation. This debate closed with Cook's uncompromising "Media Myopia," affirming the value of the new media as archives to be sure, and their specialized storage and handling requirements, but reasserting the need for contextual linkages across media solitudes if new media were indeed to be treated as evidence rather than mere illustration.

No small part of the PAC agenda in the later 1980s and early 1990s, under a new dominion/national archivist, would attempt to bring cohesion to this fragmented world, by implementing common descriptive standards and finding aids, where all records from a single creator would be described in one all-media fonds; creating common, shared, and thus more integrated computer platforms; establishing centralized and cross-media reference services; expanding records management from its text-dominated files to all media, including electronic or digital formats; and implementing all-media and multimedia appraisal concepts, strategies, and methodologies, such as macroappraisal. Theoretically, the holistic, integrated vision of total archives, if not its practical implementation, continued to inspire, at least in part, new archival thinking in the 1990s based on various strands of postmodernism, deconstruction, and critical theory about "the archive."

Conclusion

By the new century, while total archives remains the Canadian archival profession's "creation myth," in Laura Millar's phrasing, it has been followed more in spirit than letter, transforming itself gradually into an "archival system." Except in the smallest one- or two-person archives, where perforce each archivist must perform all functions in all media, across the whole lifecycle of records, archival functions are now too complex to be implemented in isolation repository by repository, or by each archivist. Millar highlights the need for a sustainable, collaborative, multi-institutional, community-based archival system, networked nationwide, to overcome the polarities between text and audio-visual media, public and private records, and records management and *archival programs* that still exist uneasily within total archives.

In the digital world, the custodial and curatorial model of institution-based total archives will need to be further transformed into a virtual total archive system of shared functions, skills, resources, networks, and standards, community-centered and collaborative. In such a framework, archivists will focus more on archiving as a participatory "total" process in society, rather than necessarily acquiring the "total" archives in their institutions. —*Terry Cook*

Keywords: archival theory, media in archives, Canadian archival system

Related Entries: Acquisition; Appraisal; Audio-Visual Records; Digital Record; Principle of *Respect des Fonds*; Records Lifecycle; Records Management

Bibliography

Birrell, Andrew. "The Tyranny of Tradition." *Archivaria* 1 (10) (1980): 249–52.

Cook, Terry. "Evidence, Memory, Identity, and Community: Four Shifting Archival Paradigms." *Archival Science* 13 (2–3) (2013): 95–120. DOI 10.1007/s10502-012-9180-7.

———. "Media Myopia." *Archivaria* 1 (12) (1981): 146–57. http://journals.sfu.ca/archivar/index.php/archivaria/article/view/10891/11814.

———. "The Tyranny of the Medium: A Comment on 'Total Archives.'" *Archivaria* 1 (9) (1979): 141–50. http://journals.sfu.ca/archivar/index.php/archivaria/article/view/12566/13724.

Ernest, J. Dick, Jacques Gagné, Josephine Langham, Richard Lochead, and Jean-Paul Moreau. "Total

Archives Come Apart." *Archivaria* 1 (11) (1980): 224–27. http://journals.sfu.ca/archivar/index.php/archivaria/article/view/10848/11765.

Millar, Laura. "Coming Up with Plan B: Considering the Future of Canadian Archives." *Archivaria* 77 (2014).

———. "Discharging Our Debt: The Evolution of the Total Archives Concept in English Canada." *Archivaria* 1 (46) (1998): 103–46. http://journals.sfu.ca/archivar/index.php/archivaria/article/view/12677/13846.

———. "The Spirit of Total Archives: Seeking a Sustainable Archival System." *Archivaria* 1 (47) (1999): 114–35. http://journals.sfu.ca/archivar/index.php/archivaria/article/view/12697/13871.

Taylor, Hugh A. *Imagining Archives: Essays and Reflections by Hugh A. Taylor*. Edited by Terry Cook and Gordon Dodds. Lanham, MD, and Oxford: Scarecrow Press, 2003.

Wilfred, I. Smith. "Total Archives: The Canadian Experience." *Archives et bibliothéques de Belgique* 57 (1–2) (1986). In Tom Nesmith, ed., *Canadian Archival Studies and the Rediscovery of Provenance*. Metuchen, NJ, and London: Scarecrow Press, 1993, 133–50.

TRUSTED CUSTODIAN

Whereas a custodian is defined as "the individual or organization having possession of and responsibility for the care and control of material" (Pearce-Moses 2005), a trusted custodian in *archival science* is "a preserver who can demonstrate that it has no reason to alter . . . preserved *records* or allow others to alter them and is capable of implementing all of the requirements for the authentic preservation of records" (InterPARES 2, "Creator Guidelines"). A trusted custodian would ideally be a professional (or group of professionals) educated and trained in *records management*, archival science, and preservation who traditionally accepts custody of records set aside for continuing preservation by their creators or legitimate successors, although some contemporary conceptions of trusted custodianship now extend to trusted management of active records and do not involve custody. As a responsible steward over the records, a trusted custodian should take all precautions necessary to safeguard the *authenticity* of the records ("the trustworthiness of a record as a record; i.e., the quality of a record that is what it purports to be and that is free from tampering or corruption" [InterPARES 2, "Glossary"]), which includes ensuring not only the security of the records against purposeful or accidental *suppressio veri* and *suggestio falsi* (Jenkinson 1937), but also the preservation of their unique identity within their physical and intellectual *context*, and the preservation and perpetuation of their interrelationships or *archival bond* ("the network of relationships that each record has with the records belonging in the same records aggregation" [InterPARES 2, "Glossary"]). The social confidence in an inactive record as a record is contingent on our knowledge of the transparency of its preservation, security, and stability (Duranti 1996) throughout its custodial history, which is in turn related to trust in the expertise and *impartiality* of custodians in the discharge of their duties. As such, an unblemished line of trusted custodians is regarded by Sir Hilary Jenkinson and others as essential to ensuring the sanctity of evidence afforded by records.

Archives and the Preserver as Trusted Custodian

The importance of the role held by preservers as trusted custodians can be traced back to the Roman Tabularium (InterPARES 2, "Authenticity Task Force Report"), whose guardians, the *questores*, possessed what is referred to as the "archival right," that is, "the right to keep a place capable of conferring authority to the documentary by-products of action by endowing them with authenticity" (Duranti 1996). Once *documents* crossed the archival threshold of the Tabularium and came into its custody, they were granted the capacity to serve as trustworthy evidence and continuing memory of actions. However, as noted by German jurist Ahasver Fritsch in 1664, the documents' acquisition of authenticity was somewhat more complicated than simply crossing the *archii limes*; it was rather that:

1. the place to which they were destined belonged to a public sovereign authority, as opposed to its agents or delegates, . . .
2. the officer forwarding them to such a place was a public officer, . . .

3. the documents were placed both physically (i.e., by location) and intellectually (i.e., by description) among authentic documents, and . . .

4. this association was not meant to be broken. (Duranti 1996, 3)

The first two points place the preservation of records out of the hands of those who may be held accountable through them, thereby removing suspicion of tampering or corruption, and allowing for the aforementioned transparency of preservation (Duranti 1996). The Tabularium thus impartially "sustained and lent credibility to contractual relationships between citizens," and this role is comparable to the contemporary role of neutral third-party record keepers in electronic contracting (InterPARES 2, "Authenticity Task Force Report"). The third point has to do with the continued protection of the identity and integrity of records, and the preservation of their archival bond with the records belonging in the same aggregation. The fourth point is concerned with the reasonable probability of the custodian's continued existence and the indefinite preservation and security of the records. The essentials of the points outlined by Fritsch are largely echoed by Jenkinson centuries later in his set of conditions for a custodian to preserve records in a way that safeguards their *impartiality* and authenticity, requiring an unbroken chain of custody, application of the rules of *archives* management, reasonable probability of the custodian's continued existence, and the custodian taking the records *en bloc* (Jenkinson 1937). Although the theory of the authenticating function of archives, their capacity to hold creators accountable to themselves and society, and the *en bloc* acceptance of records have for various reasons become disassociated with archives in practice, archives are still regarded as trustworthy custodians of records for their long-standing mandate to impartially preserve them indefinitely and the social confidence in their knowledge and ability to do so.

Commercialized Trusted Custodianship of Digital Records

Archives and historical societies are prototypical examples of trusted custodians. However, with the complexities of maintenance and preservation posed by *digital records*, the ongoing preservation and care of valued information assets can be beyond the capabilities of many organizations. As a result, commercialized digital third-party repository services are presenting themselves as solutions that assist clients in maintaining and transmitting reliable and authentic digital records. As commercial services, their trustworthiness, impartiality, and longevity as custodians may be questioned, as the interests of the financial well-being of the service provider's ownership may not always align with the requirements for preserving authentic records, which introduces an element of doubt into the transparency of their preservation. A model of trust in records, as explained by Duranti and Rogers, suggests that the trust bond is based on the reputation of the custodians, the perceived quality of their performance in meeting their responsibilities, confidence in their conduct, and their perceived competence in the discharging of their duties (Duranti and Rogers 2012). For third-party repositories, this trust bond may be established through rigorous *audit and certification* processes by trusted authorities, which monitor and ensure the continued stability, expertness, neutrality, and overall *accountability* of the service providers (ISO 17068). Although there remain lingering issues surrounding these digital third-party repositories, early examples have successfully garnered social trust as custodians (Park 2009). Since the long-term preservation of digital records must begin at the point of their creation, it is important for creators to implement a preservation strategy and identify a trusted custodian as soon as possible.

Conclusion

Although the role of trusted custodians has somewhat changed since Roman antiquity, the neutrality and professional knowledge of the keepers of the records remain important qualities to ensure that the authenticity of materials entrusted to them does not degrade with time.—*Kevin Owen*

Keywords: authenticity, trustworthiness, archivist, trusted third party

Related Entries: Archives (Institution); Archivist; Authenticity; Digital Record; Postcustodialism

Bibliography

Duranti, Luciana, and Corrine Rogers. "Trust in Digital Records: An Increasingly Cloudy Legal Area. *CLSR* 28 (5) (2012): 522–31. http://dx.doi.org/10.1016/j.clsr.2012.07.009.

InterPARES 2 Project. "Authenticity Task Force Report." http://interpares.org/book/interpares_book_d_part1.pdf (accessed December 2013).

———. "Creator Guidelines: Making and Maintaining Digital Materials: Guidelines for Individuals." http:// interpares.org/ip2/display_file.cfm?doc=ip2(pub)creator_guidelines_booklet.pdf (accessed December 2013).

———. "Glossary." http://interpares.org/ip2/ip2_terminology_db.cfm (accessed December 2013).

Jenkinson, Hilary. *A Manual of Archive Administration*, 2nd edition. London and Bradford: Percy Lund, Humphries & Co, 1937.

Park, Eun G. "Certified e-Document Authority (CeDA): Final Report." InterPARES 3, 2009. www.interpares.org/ip3/display_file.cfm?doc=ip3_korea_cs02_final_report.pdf (accessed December 2013).

Pearce-Moses, Richard. *A Glossary of Archival and Records Terminology*, 1st edition. Chicago: Society of American Archivists, 2005.

U

UNIQUENESS

Uniqueness was not among the characteristics of archival *documents* or *records* identified by Jenkinson: *naturalness, interrelatedness, impartiality*, and *authenticity* (Jenkinson 1937, 11–12). However, it is often mentioned in archival literature as part of records' nature. For example, Vicenta Cortes Alonso attributes four characteristics to archival documents: "unicidad" (uniqueness), "integridad" (integrity), "autenticidad" (authenticity), and "ingenuidad" (naturalness) (Alonso 1982, 44). A North American discussion of the characteristics of archival documents including the concept of uniqueness can be found in the writings of Terry Eastwood and in an article by James O'Toole that explores how the idea of uniqueness has evolved, especially in relation to the changing records-creation technologies, and speculates on the future usefulness of the concept for *archival theory* and practice. O'Toole emphasizes the distinction among "the uniqueness of records themselves; the uniqueness of information in the records; the uniqueness of processes that produce records; and the uniqueness of aggregations of records" (O'Toole 1994, 657).

The Concept

The characteristic of uniqueness derives to each archival document (or record) by the fact of its having a unique place in the structure of the aggregation in which it belongs (e.g., *file, series*, subgroup, fonds) and in the documentary universe. Even when an identical version of the same document exists in another aggregation inside the same archives (*archival fonds*), or in another archives, the complex of its relationships with the records within and outside the aggregation of which it is part is always unique. Each archival document (or record) is unique in its place, in its documentary *context*. Being there signifies its relationship to activity and to the other records accumulated in the course of that activity. For example, a letter of appointment of a professor at a university may be issued in five originals: one goes to the professor, one to the department, one to the faculty, one to financial services, and one to the university president's office. The five documents by themselves are identical, but the archival documents (or records)—that is, the documents with their *archival bond*, the documents in context, are different—carry out a different *function*, participate in a different activity, serve a different purpose, and convey a different meaning.

Terry Eastwood notes that "the information or content of any given archival document, seen as intelligence of the world, may or may not be unique. . . . Nowadays . . . so much of the intelligence that can be gleaned from archives is available elsewhere, usually in more convenient and accessible forms. This only reinforces the view that archives cannot be treated solely or even primarily for the information they bear" (Eastwood 1994, 128). Archival documents (or records) are not only evidence of the actions in which they participate but also a material part of them, and as there are not two identical actions, there cannot be two identical records. This is the reason why most archival theorists worldwide consider uniqueness one of the essential characteristics of records' nature.

Conclusion

Uniqueness is the most commonly identified characteristic of archival documents (or records), a characteristic directly linked to context, as there might be several identical documents that, placed in different contexts, are unique archival documents (or records). The digital environment is challenging the notion of uniqueness because of the accepted practice of dispersal, distribution, and redundancy of multiple duplicates of aggregations of records, that is, of documents kept within their own unique context. However, if the context relevant to uniqueness is considered more broadly than the file or the series, and includes location and jurisdiction, then the concept of uniqueness continues to hold true also in the digital environment.—*Luciana Duranti*

Keywords: archival bond, context, interrelatedness, records

Related Entries: Archival Bond; Archives (Material); Authenticity; Context; Interrelatedness; Record(s)

Bibliography

Alonso, Vicenta Cortes. *Manual de archivos municipales.* Madrid: Associacion espanola de archiveros, bibliotecarios, museologos y documentalistas, 1982.

Duranti, Luciana. "The Concept of Appraisal and Archival Theory." *American Archivist* 57 (2) (1994): 328–45. http://archivists.metapress.com/content/pu548273j5j1p816/fulltext.pdf.

Eastwood, Terry. "What Is Archival Theory and Why Is It Important?" *Archivaria* 37 (2) (1994): 122–30. http://journals.sfu.ca/archivar/index.php/archivaria/article/view/11991/12954.

Jenkinson, Hilary. *A Manual of Archives Administration.* London: Percy Lund, Humphries & Co., 1937. Reprint 1965.

O'Toole, James. "On the Idea of Uniqueness." *American Archivist* 57 (4) (1994): 632–58. http://archivists.metapress.com/content/6l8x444kn3966v00/fulltext.pdf.

USER BEHAVIOR

In the last two decades researchers have become increasingly interested in the information behavior of archival users, including how users interact with archival systems, services, and *records*. This new focus on users' behavior has shed light on how some user groups search for and use archival sources. The majority of research has focused on one type of user: historians and family history researchers. Other studies have highlighted challenges users face when they interact with finding aids and systems.

Definitions

Wilson defined "human information behavior" as "the totality of human behavior in relation to sources and channels of information, including both active and passive information seeking, and information use" (2000, 49). Following Wilson, we define "archival user behavior" to include the totality of human behavior in relation to archival sources and systems of information and records, including active and passive information seeking, information use, and information production. Further, we define "information-seeking behavior" as purposive seeking of information to satisfy goal(s), which may include active searching for information using a manual or online system or by browsing sources or archival access systems. "Information use" is "the physical and mental acts involved in incorporating the information found into the person's existing knowledge base" (Wilson 2000, 50).

Archival Systems and User Research

Yakel and Torres (2003) identify three broad types of requisite knowledge for archival research: domain knowledge, artifactual literacy, and archival intelligence, which they define as "researchers' knowledge of archival principles, practices, and institutions." Archival intelligence encompasses knowledge of archival access systems, and research indicates that users often experience problems when they try to navigate archival information systems (Yakel and Torres 2003). Daniels and Yakel (2010) suggest that users had problems formulating search queries. Research suggests users value descriptive information about dates, location of the material or call number, title, documentary form, an overview of the collection, and subject headings, though some users find subject headings confusing (Edmunson-Morton 2008).

Historians

Scholars have researched historians' information behaviors extensively. Duff and Johnson's (2003) model presents the historians' information-seeking behaviors as nonlinear and consisting of four major activities: becoming oriented to the *archives* and access systems, building contextual knowledge, searching for known items, and identifying relevant material. In carrying out these activities, historians talk to *archivists*, browse finding aids, conduct name and subject searches, and read and scan archival records. Rhee (2012) also suggests that historians' activities can be grouped into four stages: starting, accessing, processing, and ending. At each stage historians engage in tasks such as chaining, browsing, differentiating, orienting monitoring, extracting, accessing, constructing contextual knowledge, verifying, and information-managing activities.

Many researchers have investigated the tools and sources historians consult to locate information. Historians use a variety of methods to *access* material: they consult findings aids and archivists (Duff, Craig, and Cherry 2004) as well as citations in publications (Tibbo 2003; Chassanoff 2013). Duff and Johnson (2003) conclude that a historian's success in identifying, locating, and using sources is linked to his/her background and contextual knowledge. Recent studies suggest that historians use a wide variety of online tools as well.

Historians' information-use behavior has received far less study. Historians are expert readers, and they scan large volumes of records, annotating photocopies and making notes. Cole (1998) suggests that cognitive processes can affect the information that PhD students extract from records. Duff, Monks-Leeson, and Galey's (2012) study of book history students surmises that meaning making follows three stages: asking, guessing, and following hunches about the existence and content of records; conceptualizing the material according to a predetermined framework; and building connections of relevancy within the records according to the participants' identified research topic. Recent research, however, suggests that historians' research practices are changing because of technological developments, such as the digital camera and the growth in digital resources available on the Internet. While archivists remain a critical component of the research process, the "use of digitized finding aids, digitized collections, and digital cameras have altered the way that historians interact with primary sources. While the centrality of archives to the research process remains, the nature of interactions with archival materials has changed dramatically over time; for many researchers, activities in the archives have become more photographic and less analytical" (Rutner and Schonfeld 2012, 8).

Family History Researchers

Information-seeking studies suggest that family history researchers (FHRs) follow common research practices, as the models of Darby and Clough (2013) and Duff and Johnson (2003) indicate. Duff and Johnson identify three different stages in the family history research process: (1) collecting names of family members; (2) gathering detailed information on family members; and (3) contextualizing the detailed information by learning about broader history. Darby and Clough (2013) identify eight distinct phases in the family-tree creation process: (1) trigger event; (2) collect items; (3) learn the process; (4) getting started; (5) fill out tree—easy; (6) fill out tree—medium; (7) fill out tree—hard; (8) push back (finding more obscure family members and sources). Darby and Clough's model assumes that FHRs learn a basic approach to research; however, the easy access to genealogical data on the web may mean individuals are building family history content with little or no knowledge of the research process (Willever-Farr and Forte 2014).

In addition to these studies, scholars have researched FHRs' cooperative behaviors related to information sharing and production of family history content. Duff and Johnson (2003) found that genealogists often worked around archival access systems and relied more on their own social networks than on information professionals to obtain information. FHRs share information, advice, and instructional guidance either virtually or in face-to-face meetings. For example, Yakel and Torres (2007) have found that in face-to-face settings, FHRs helped others learn the research process by engaging in "group problem solving" (Yakel and Torres 2007, 101). However, Willever-Farr, Zach, and Forte have found that in virtual contexts "the abundance of online genealogical data and the affordances of web technologies" appeared to discourage FHRs from providing one another with instructional guidance and inhibited group problem solving in their online exchanges (2012, 303). A lack of online spaces for collaborative problem solving and instruction may be contributing to the production of inaccurate and poor-quality biographical content on family history production websites (Willever-Farr and Forte 2014).

Conclusion

In the last decade, research has shed light on the information behavior of archival users and led to the development of a number of models. Overall the research indicates that user groups share some information behaviors, but often exhibit different information needs, suggesting that archives may need to tailor archival access points and services to meet those disparate needs. It also suggests novices and experts use different strategies; archival terminology, the hierarchical structure of finding aids, and a lack of archival intelligence create barriers for some users; but specific descriptive elements facilitate relevancy judgments, and contextual description supports access and interpretation of records. Finally, as increasing numbers of archives employ Web 2.0 tools, more research about user production behaviors is needed to support users in these participatory settings.—*Wendy M. Duff and Heather Willever-Farr*

Keywords: family history researchers, historians, information seeking, information use

Bibliography

Chassanoff, Alexandra. "Historians and the Use of Primary Source Materials in the Digital Age." *American Archivist* 76 (2) (2013): 458–80. http://archivists.metapress.com/content/lh76217m2m376n28/fulltext.pdf.

Cole, Charles. "Information Acquisition in History PhD Students: Inferencing and the Formation of Knowledge Structures." *The Library Quarterly* 68 (1998): 33–54. www.jstor.org/stable/4309179.

Daniels, Morgan G., and Elizabeth Yakel. "Seek and You May Find: Successful Search in Online Finding Aid Systems." *American Archivist* 73 (2) (2010): 535–68. http://archivists.metapress.com/content/p578900680650357/fulltext.pdf.

Darby, Paul, and Paul Clough. "Investigating the Information-Seeking Behaviour of Genealogists and Family Historians." *Journal of Information Science* 39 (1) (2013): 73–84. DOI: 10.1177/0165551512469765.

Duff, Wendy M., Barbara Craig, and Joan Cherry. "Historians' Use of Archival Sources: Promises and Pitfalls of the Digital Age." *The Public Historian* 26 (2) (2004): 7–22. www.jstor.org/stable/10.1525/tph.2004.26.2.7.

Duff, Wendy M., and Catherine A. Johnson. "Where Is the List with All the Names? Information-Seeking Behavior of Genealogists." *American Archivist* 66 (1) (2003): 79–95. http://archivists.metapress.com/index/l375uj047224737n.pdf.

Duff, Wendy M., Emily Monks-Leeson, and Alan Galey. "Contexts Built and Found: A Pilot Study on the Process of Archival Meaning-Making." *Archival Science* 12 (1) (2012): 69–92. http://link.springer.com/article/10.1007/s10502-011-9145-2.

Edmunson-Morton, Tiah. "Northwest Digital Archives, Executive Summary: Usability Testing Round 4." Orbis Cascade Alliance, 2008. http://oldsite.orbiscascade.org/index/usability-design-working-group-reports.

Fulton, Crystal. "Quid Pro Quo: Information Sharing in Leisure Activities." *Library Trends* 57 (4) (2009): 753–68. http://muse.jhu.edu/journals/lib/summary/v057/57.4.fulton01.html.

Rhee, Hea Lim. "Modelling Historians' Information-Seeking Behaviour with an Interdisciplinary and Comparative Approach." *Information Research* 17 (4) (2012). http://informationr.net/ir/17-4/paper544.html.

Rutner, Jennifer, and Roger C. Schonfeld. "Supporting the Changing Research Practices of Historians." Ithaka S+R, December 7, 2012. Accessed September 8, 2014. www.sr.ithaka.org/research-publications/supporting-changing-research-practices-historians, 8.

Tibbo, Helen R. "Primarily History in America: How U.S. Historians Search for Primary Materials at the Dawn of the Digital Age." *American Archivist* 66 (1) (2003): 9–50. http://archivists.metapress.com/index/b12037011g718n74.pdf.

Willever-Farr, Heather, and Andrea Forte. "Family Matters: Control and Conflict in Online Family History Production." In *Proceedings of Computer-Supported Cooperative Work and Social Computing*. New York: ACM, 2014.

Willever-Farr, Heather, Lisl Zach, and Andrea Forte. "Tell Me about My Family: A Study of Cooperative Research on Ancestry.com." In *Proceedings of the 2012 iConference*, 303.

Wilson, Thomas D. "Human Information Behavior." *Informing Science* 3 (2) (2000): 49.

Yakel, Elizabeth, and Deborah A. Torres. "AI: Archival Intelligence and User Expertise." *American Archivist 66* (1) (2003): 51–78. http://archivists. metapress.com/index/Q022H85PN51N5800.pdf.

———. "Genealogists as a 'Community of Records.'" *American Archivist* 70 (1) (2007): 101.

V

VITAL RECORDS

The term vital records has two distinct definitions according to the Society of American Archivists: (1) *records* that document significant life events, including births, deaths, marriages, divorces, and public health matters; vital statistics; and (2) emergency operation records immediately necessary to begin recovery of business after a disaster, as well as rights-and-interests records necessary to protect the assets, obligations, and resources of the organization, as well as its employees and customers or citizens; essential records (SAA n.d.). The first definition is used specifically within the government sector to refer to a records *series* that can be used to produce statistics about the population for practical purposes. The second definition is used more broadly to describe records that are vital to the continued operation of the organization and to protect the rights of the organization and its stakeholders.

Vital Records and Vital Statistics

The terms "vital records" and "vital statistics" are not synonymous but are often used interchangeably. During the pre-Christian era, civil authorities in Egypt, Greece, and Rome required the registration of births and deaths to gather statistics that could be used for tax purposes and to determine potential military personnel. With that exception, however, the early practice of recording "vital events" fell to ecclesiastical authorities, who had the responsibility for officiating over the ceremonial practices of baptisms, burials, and weddings. These records were often incomplete and did not record the actual events: births, deaths, and marriages (United Nations 1995). Once the value of vital records as a source of health-related information became apparent, medical associations and government officials encouraged legislation that required births, deaths, and marriages to be recorded. Today there are laws in virtually every country for the recording of vital events to serve both legal and statistical purposes.

Vital Records in the United States

Early vital records in the United States were originally registered with churches. Today, vital records are the property of the local government and should be housed in the government office that has control over them.

States that attempted to control the registration of life events met numerous obstacles. For example, the state of Virginia enacted a 1632 law, based on English precedent, requiring the recording of births, deaths, and marriages to be made by ministers or churchwardens of each Parish and presented at a yearly meeting of court. A similar Virginia state law was enacted in 1659 and again in 1713. Few records exist from that time, however, because people were not interested in registering life events, and parish clerks were not properly trained in recording and transmitting them. After the American Revolution, *recordkeeping* of vital statistics became a family obligation due to the disestablishment of the Anglican religion in Virginia and the rise of other religious denominations. On April 11, 1853, the Virginia General Assembly passed a law requiring the systematic statewide recording of births and deaths by every commissioner of revenue at the time that property taxes were ascertained. The commissioners supplied the information to the clerk of court in each locality, which was then included in an alphabetical list with a copy sent to the Auditor of Public Accounts. The law was repealed in 1896 because the state lacked the resources to enforce it. Consequently, between 1896 and 1912, there were no statewide recordings of births and deaths. Statewide registration began again in June 1912 (Library of Virginia 2000).

Vital records contain the type of event and the date, the name of the individual involved in the event, and the location where the event took place. Additional information may be in included; for example, birth records usually contain the parents' full names, and marriage records often record the names and birthplaces of each individual's parents. Birth certificates are permanent legal records that can be used to provide proof of age, parentage, and citizenship. They can be used to obtain passports and driver's licenses as well as enroll in benefits programs. Death certificates are used to settle estates and terminate Social Security benefits for the deceased. Since they usually contain the cause of death and the age of the deceased, they can be used to calculate population growth, identify health risk factors, measure health outcomes, plan and evaluate health programs, and conduct research (Missouri n.d.).

At this time, the legal authority for the registration of vital events—births, deaths, marriages, divorces, and fetal deaths—resides individually with the fifty states, two cities (Washington, DC, and New York City), and five territories (Puerto Rico, the Virgin Islands, Guam, American Samoa, and the Commonwealth of the Northern Mariana Islands). But the Centers for Disease Control and Prevention hosts an intergovernmental data-sharing site where it collects and disseminates the nation's official vital statistics (Centers for Disease Control and Prevention n.d.).

Vital records are an important source of information for individuals seeking to understand their ancestry. Thanks to advances in technology and the work of organizations like *FamilySearch* (established as the Genealogical Society of Utah in 1894), data is gathered through vital records and other sources, such as U.S. Federal Census data, so that individuals across the globe can learn about their ancestry through free online *access* to historical data.

Preservation Strategies

Vital records have long-term preservation requirements. Master copies of physical records, microfilm, microfiche, and *digital records* may be stored in vaults (often in underground storage facilities) designed for controlled-environment storage. The measures taken to secure these records include media validation and media refresh, migration to new technologies and formats, and OAIS-compliant (see *Digital Repository*) conversion and preservation processes. On occasion, copies made for permanent preservation have been used to replace an original destroyed by a natural or man-made disaster.

Vital Records and Business Resumption

A records disaster is a sudden and unexpected event that results in the loss of records and information essential to an organization's continued operation. Natural or man-made disasters—fires, floods, earthquakes, tsunamis, epidemics, terrorist incidents, and riots—can result in the loss of records essential to business continuity for the individual organization and a disruption of normal economic activity for the region (Franks 2013). Operations must be restored to normal as soon as possible.

The loss of information included in vital records can be more devastating to the continuation of an organization's operations than damage to or the loss of physical space or equipment that is often insured and replaceable (Saffady 2004, 124).

The loss of vital records can result in:

- disruption of essential customer services,
- exposure to unplanned expenses of financial settlements or loss of revenue,
- increased vulnerability to litigation, and
- loss of productivity due to gaps in information.

Business resumption requires developing and carrying out an approved course of action to deal with the impact of the event. The actions to be taken can be found in the business-continuity plan, the disaster-preparedness and recovery plan, and the vital-records program. Identifying the vital records essential to the organization's continued operations is the first step toward developing both a disaster-recovery plan and a business-continuity plan (Franks 2013).

Vital (Essential) Records

Typically only 3 to 7 percent of all records held by an organization are considered vital records. Records may be classified according to their value to the organization: vital, important, and useful.

- *Vital records* play an essential role in disaster recovery and business continuity. They are essential both during and immediately after a crisis.
- *Important records* are necessary to the continued life of the business, but they can be replaced or reproduced after a disaster.
- *Useful records* are also replaceable. Their loss could cause a temporary inconvenience.

Vital records typically document delegation of authority and lines of succession and include legal documents and contracts, financial records, and other *documents* that establish the rights and obligations of the organization, its employees and customers, stockholders, and citizens (SAA n.d.).

An organization that has suffered a disaster must continue to meet its business obligations even while recovering from the crisis. Current accounts payable, accounts receivable, customer or client files, contracts and agreements, and unaudited financial records are examples of records essential to business continuity as well as for legal or audit purposes that must be protected.

The ANSI/ARMA 5-2010 standard, *Vital Records Programs: Identifying, Managing, and Recovering Business-Critical Records* recommends separating vital records into three categories that can be prioritized for protection and recovery:

- Essential for emergency operations: Physical records must be stored close to the disaster-response site or team for quick access. Electronic replication methods must be available for immediate access to information. Examples include the emergency action plan, business-continuity plan, vital records manual, architectural drawings, and personnel security-clearance lists.
- Essential for immediate resumption and continuation of business: Physical records stored close to the site for quick business resumption. Electronic replication methods are accessible, and backups can be quickly restored. Examples

include current client files, accounts payable and accounts receivable, and research documentation.
- Essential for legal or audit purposes: Physical records stored outside of the disaster area. Electronic replication methods provide access to information once the previous categories of records have been restored. Examples include existing contracts and agreements and unaudited financial records.

Vital records status should be accorded only as long as those records can fulfill the requirements. Once they have fulfilled their role and are no longer considered essential, they should be reclassified.

Vital Records Protection

Don't confuse vital records with permanent records. The goal of protecting vital records is not long-term or permanent preservation. It is to use the simplest, most economical method of protecting essential records that fits the circumstances. Two methods of protection that apply to both physical and electronic records are:

- Duplication and dispersal: Copies of records can be kept in one or more locations apart from original records. This can occur during normal operations (routine dispersal), by making copies specifically for protection purposes and storing them off-site (planned or designed dispersal), and by spreading copies through the use of the Internet and Web 2.0 technologies as a direct by-product of the information age (derivative dispersal). This last method cannot be relied on but may be increasingly possible, as records are shared virally. Examples include WikiLeaks documents and tweets preserved by the Library of Congress.
- Protective storage: Dispersal does not promise protection. Vital records can be protected onsite in a vault, fireproof cabinet, or fireproof container that conforms to the rating requirements of the National Fire Protection Association (NFPA) standards. They can also be protected in a company-owned or commercial offsite storage facility in a variety of media, including paper, microfilm, tapes, and disks. Given

the volume of digital data managed by today's organizations, it is likely that vital records will take the form of electronically stored information (ESI). Data centers to accommodate vital electronic records can be managed by the organization or outsourced. Increasingly, organizations turn to cloud-based disaster-recovery and business-continuity services to enable faster recovery of critical IT systems without incurring the infrastructure expense of a second physical site.

Conclusion

Vital records can be defined in two ways: (1) records such as birth and death certificates that record information used to derive vital statistics of use to governments and their citizens; and (2) records such as current contracts and accounts receivables and payables that contain information required by the organization to re-create its legal and financial status and to preserve the rights and obligations of stakeholders, including employees, customers, investors, and citizens.

Vital records that document events in an individual's life are important to the individual in establishing his/her identity in order to qualify for benefits. The government can use the vital statistics derived from these vital records in its planning process. For example, a rise in the number of births during a particular year will require additional resources for education at the time the youngsters start school.

Vital records essential to the continued operations of an organization must be identified, protected, and made accessible during and immediately after a natural or man-made disaster. Along with a business-continuity plan and a disaster-preparedness and recovery plan, a vital records program is an essential component of a business resumption strategy.

—*Patricia C. Franks*

Keywords: business continuity, disaster recovery, emergency operations records, essential records, vital statistics

Related Entries: Archival Preservation; Record(s)

Bibliography

ARMA/ANSI. *Vital Records Programs: Identifying, Managing, and Recovering Business-Critical Records*. Overland Park, KS: ARMA International, 2010.

Centers for Disease Control and Prevention. *National Vital Statistics System*. Last updated November 2014. www.cdc.gov/nchs/nvss.htm.

FamilySearch. "Intellectual Reserve." 2013. https://familysearch.org/archives.

Franks, P. C. *Records and Information Management*. Chicago: Neal-Schuman/ALA, 2013.

Library of Virginia. "Using Vital Statistics Records in the Archives at the Library of Virginia (Research Notes Number 2)." 2000. www.lva.virginia.gov/public/guides/rn2_vitalstats.htm.

Missouri Department of Health & Senior Service. *Vital Statistics*. n.d. http://health.mo.gov/data/vitalstatistics.

Moses, Richard Pearce. "A Glossary of Archival and Records Terminology." Society of American Archivists, 2005. www2.archivists.org/glossary.

Saffady, William. *Records and Information Management: Fundamentals of Professional Practice*. Lenexa, KS: ARMA International, 2004, 124.

United Nations. *Handbook of Vital Statistics Method*. New York: Statistical Office of the United States, 1995. http://unstats.un.org/unsd/demographic/standmeth/handbooks/Series_F7en.pdf.

WEB ARCHIVING

Web archiving consists of identifying, selecting, acquiring, preserving, and making accessible information resources from the Internet for current and future users. Use of the term archiving in this context refers to the lifecycle processes necessary for keeping digital content independently available and interpretable over time. A web archive generally refers to a collected corpus of web content, along with various *metadata*, kept under managed control. National libraries and other large institutions do the bulk of web archiving, but smaller organizations are becoming increasingly active.

The web archiving process involves collecting interlinked digital objects that make up websites and other Internet information resources. Typical objects include text, style elements, scripts, and a variety of digital formats, including images, videos, and *documents*. Relationships among all these objects must be maintained so that users can, to the greatest extent possible, view archived web content in a manner similar to how it was originally presented on the live web. Metadata documenting when content is collected, where it was found, and other actions taken by the collection steward is also typically generated and preserved, and is used to establish the original *context* of the information.

Web Archiving Drivers

Two principle drivers underpin web archiving activities. The first is meeting legal obligations for evidential *recordkeeping* purposes. Information on the Internet can meet the definition of a *record* for documenting the activities and *functions* of an organization. Entities operating under public records statutes and other legal mandates must manage electronic records (The National Archives of the UK 2011). In such cases, institutions must consider all appropriate recordkeeping requirements, including *authenticity*, trustworthiness, and authorized *disposition* for management of Internet-based information resources. The imperative for applying appropriate recordkeeping measures is proportionate to the extent that an organization relies on the Internet to publish reports and otherwise transact and document official business. Other legal mandates, most especially those relating to national copyright deposit, may also govern the submission and retention of web content.

The second driver for web archiving is for documenting knowledge, creativity, and innovation (International Internet Preservation Consortium 2012). The Internet is a rich source of detail about many things, and some portion has research or other value that should be kept accessible for an extended time. Websites are typically unique in that no hard copy or other versions exist. Libraries, *archives*, and other institutions that aim to compile and keep detailed research resources may be compelled to collect information from the live Internet.

The extent of web archiving activities is tied to collection development policies or mandates. A web archive can be built around themes, such as political elections, natural disasters or other topics of interest. A collection many also focus on a single institution, a large group of related entities, or even an entire national domain. Collecting may also focus on subsections of the Internet, such as in the form of specific social media services.

Challenges

A major concern for web archiving is the speed at which Internet content is revised, updated, or otherwise changed. While the average rate of change is open to question—the life span of a web page has been variously estimated at forty-four, seventy-five, and one hundred days (Pennock 2013)—it is clear that most content is short-lived. This means institutions have to develop a collecting strategy that is time-based, both in terms of when a website is initially collected and how often it is necessary to revisit the site to capture any changes in content. This could be less of an issue for organizations that operate under a legal mandate, as they may have the authority to compel creators to document content changes. But in many cases it is up to collecting institutions to determine when and how often to gather information.

Scale and scope present a special challenge for web archiving. If a collecting organization decides to focus on a single website with limited content that changes infrequently, the effort involved can be relatively straightforward. In many cases, however, web archiving activities deal with content that is interlinked at different levels and is spread across many different sites. This requires defining and maintaining artificial boundaries for collections. Detailed quality assurance is needed to ensure that the correct files have been gathered and that they present an accurate portrayal of the original content. These tasks grow increasingly complex with the number of sites that fall within collecting interest.

Copyright is a significant issue. Some nations have a legal mandate that permits collecting institutions to archive Internet content without first obtaining owner consent, but others, including the United States, do not (Grotke 2011). Absent a mandate, it may be necessary to first identify site owners so as to seek permission to capture content and to make it independently available to users. Intellectual property law is hazy in many jurisdictions in connection with web archiving (as well as *digital preservation* in general), and it is not uncommon for institutions to consult closely with legal staff in connection with the activity.

The Internet is constantly evolving in terms of the technology used to deliver content. This means ongoing web archiving programs need to regularly adjust their strategies, tools, and infrastructure. Many websites deploy sophisticated content-management systems that dynamically deliver different content for different users at different times. Sites may draw customized content from external sites using a variety of web services that are transparent to the user. A proliferation of social media services is available, each of which has a unique mix of technical underpinnings, and new social media platforms are introduced frequently. Existing social-media tools continue to evolve and change, often without notice, requiring constant monitoring of terms-of-service agreements that may result in updates to the web archiving strategy. A shift toward more video content on the web also has vastly increased some archive storage needs, as video files are typically much larger than other kinds of content.

Methods and Tools

The two basic operational approaches to web archiving center on who does the various tasks required. A third party can be contracted to do some or all of the work, such as crawling and aggregating web content; some third-party providers also can provide customized tools and services to support institutional efforts. The other operational approach is "in house," which involves an institution doing the work itself.

In terms of technical strategies for web archiving, there are four (Pennock 2013):

1. Client-side
2. Transactional
3. Server-side
4. RSS updates

The most common is a client-side approach, which involves using a web-crawling tool such as Heritrix to copy content available on the web via HTTP protocol. Web crawlers use a seed URL to follow links and copy content to a predetermined level of linkage for each website. The result is a partial duplicate of content as it originally appeared on the live web.

Transactional archiving captures a successive series of client-side interactions with the live web. This is useful for documenting dynamic transactions between a client (e.g., a web browser) with servers that deliver different kinds of content depending on user requests or content change over time. Tools such as SiteStory archiving software and the Memento protocol allow all the versions of a website requested by browsers over time to be captured and stored in a web archive. This approach requires installation of special software on web servers; the resulting collection is managed by those who control the server content.

Similarly, server-side archiving involves copying files directly from servers while bypassing the HTTP protocol. As with transactional archiving, explicit intervention by the server owner is required. This method is especially useful for capturing deep-web resources, such as databases, that are difficult to crawl using client-side tools. The approach also may collect the software and scripts used to run the web server, which allows for perhaps the most complete documentation of a site possible. On the downside, rendering the captured content may be difficult, most particularly for dynamic-generated sites that rely on scripts or complex content-management systems.

A fourth method employed by some involves use of RSS feeds to determine when content changes on a site and also pull new content into an archive. Several projects are currently exploring this method, which can be used separate from or in conjunction with a web crawler.

A common method for storing web archives is through the use of the Web ARChive file format standard, or its precursor, the ARchive Container format, both of which store an aggregation of captured files along with related metadata (Taylor 2013). In terms of *access*, the most widely used method involves using the Wayback Machine interface software from the Internet Archive (Taylor 2012). A variety of additional tools and services supporting web archiving are also available (International Internet Preservation Consortium n.d.).

The Internet Archive, a nonprofit organization, is closely associated with web archiving. It has been collecting and serving web content since 1996, and has collected a great deal of information on behalf of national libraries and other cultural-heritage organizations as a third-party provider. The organization also plays a role in terms of developing tools and providing infrastructure support. Institutions from around the world also work together through membership in the International Internet Preservation Consortium.

Conclusion

Web archiving has made great strides in recent years in terms of tools, scale, and infrastructure. The practice is also a highly successful example of practical results flowing from collaboration among the international community of cultural-heritage institutions.—*William LeFurgy*

Keywords: Internet, recordkeeping, web archive
Related Entries: Digital Archives; Digital Preservation; Recordkeeping

Bibliography

Australian Government. "Archiving Websites." Last modified September 4, 2012. http://webguide.gov.au/recordkeeping/archiving-a-website.

Bragg, Molly, and Kristine Hanna. "The Web Archiving Life Cycle Model." The Archive-It Team, Internet Archive, 2013. www.archive-it.org/static/files/archiveit_life_cycle_model.pdf.

Grotke, Abigail. "Web Archiving at the Library of Congress." Information Today, 2011. www.infotoday.com/cilmag/dec11/Grotke.shtml.

International Internet Preservation Consortium. "Web Archiving. Why Archive the Web?" 2012. http://netpreserve.org/web-archiving/overview.

Library and Archives Canada. "Capturing the Digital Universe." *Governance and Recordkeeping around the World* 4 (8) (2013). www.bac-lac.gc.ca/eng/services/government-information-resources/information-management/Documents/september-2013.pdf.

The National Archives of the UK. "Web Archiving Guidance." 2011. www.nationalarchives.gov.uk/documents/information-management/web-archiving-guidance.pdf.

Niu, Jinfang. "An Overview of Web Archiving." *D-Lib Magazine* 18 (3/4) (2012). http://dlib.org/dlib/march12/niu/03niu1.html.

Pennock, Maureen. "Web-Archiving. Digital Preservation Coalition Technology Watch Report." 2013. www.dpconline.org/component/docman/doc_download/865-dpctw13-01pdf.

Reyes Ayala, Brenda. "WebArchiving@UNT: Web Archiving Bibliography." UNT Libraries, 2013. http://digital.library.unt.edu/ark:/67531/metadc172362.

Taylor, Nicholas. "Anatomy of a Web Archive." The Signal Blog, Library of Congress, November 5, 2013. http://blogs.loc.gov/digitalpreservation/2013/11/anatomy-of-a-web-archive.

———. "Using Wayback Machine for Research." The Signal Blog, Library of Congress, October 26, 2012. http://blogs.loc.gov/digitalpreservation/2012/10/10950.

"Web Archiving." The British Library, n.d. www.bl.uk/aboutus/stratpolprog/digi/webarch.

defense systems, 74

de jure standards, 350

deontological ethics, 46

deposits: agreement, 8; archival, 38–39; transfer, 14–15

Describing Archives: A Content Standard (DACS), 41, 88; context and, 151

description: archival fonds and, 50, 52; of ephemera, 204; manuscripts tradition and, 242; pertinence and, 281–83; policy, 71; public records tradition and, 298–99; record, Series System and, 383; record group and, 312; recordkeeping metadata and, 324; *respect des fonds* and, 288; Series System and, 383. *See also* archival description

descriptive metadata, 243

design records, 18–19, *19*. *See also* architectural records

destruction: CRCs and document, 329–30; of deaccessioned material, 156

deterioration, 200

digital archives, 157–59; ethnic, 206–7

digital archiving, 158

digital archivist, 167–68

digital authentication, 117–19

digital case file, 133

digital collections, 159

digital context for personal records, 269

digital diplomatics, 167, 179

digital evidence, 169

digital file, 212

digital forensic investigator, 167–68

digital forensics, 124–26; functions, 167–68; personal records and, 268–69; reliability in, 362–63

digital humanities, personal records and, 268–69

digital imaging technology, 173

digital information: encoding of, 160; record format and, 311

digital lives, personal records and, 269

digital materiality, 169

digital media, public service and, 302

digital preservation, 75, 114, 118, 160–63; CoP and, 133; lifecycle considerations for, 168; long-term considerations for, 168; record format and, 308; standards, 87–89; TDR and, 171

digital recordkeeping systems, 212

digital records, 62, 163–66; accessibility of, 4; acquisition and, 8; archival education and, 44; archival standards and, 87; archives (institution) and, 94–95; audio-visual archives, 111–13; authenticity and, 120, 133; diplomatics and, 338–39; ephemera and, 203–4; forensics, 166–69; original order and, 23–24, 293; personal records and, 267; postcustodialism and, 277; preservation of, 114; record creation and, 307; reliability of, 4; repositories for, 114

digital repository, 133, 170–72

Digital Repository Audit Method Based on Risk Assessment (DRAMBORA), 171

digital series, 379–80

digital signature, 117–19

digital storage media, 160

digital surrogates, 209

digital sustainability, 264

digitization, 173–75; workflow, collection-management policy and, 143

digitized materials, websites and, 158–59

digitized records, 62; accessibility of, 4; reliability of, 4; websites and, 158–59

diplomatic criticism, 177–79; formal analysis and, 214

diplomatics, 107, 124–26, 176–79; archival history and, 55; authenticity and, 119–20, 121; context and, 151–52; digital, 167; digital records and, 338–39; digital records forensics and, 166; document and, 184; formal analysis and, 214; person and, 265; records and, 318; records function and, 338; textural records and, 393

direct reading, 55

disaster plan, 180–82; archival policy and, 72; training, 72

disaster preparedness, 180

disaster recovery, 180–81; vital records and, 410

discipline: archival, 85–86; archival method and, 67–68; archival science, 85–86; auxiliary sciences, 125–26; or records management, 347–48

displaced archives, 365–66

disposal: archival legislation and, 61; CRCs and, 330; of deaccessioned material, 155–56

disposition: EDRMS and, 198; records, 182–83; records schedule and, 354–55, 357; records transfer and, 358; selection and, 374

dispositive records, 338

diversity initiatives, 206

DMS. *See* document management systems

document, 183–85; analysis of, 178; ancient documents exception, 117; archival, 223; archival bond and, 28; archives (material) and, 96; CRCs and destruction of, 329–30; enemy, captured, 128–29; personal records and, 266; records and, 315, 316, 318

documentary editing, 186–87, 292

documentary evidence, 188–90

documentary form, formal analysis and, 214

documentary procedure, reliability and, 362

documentation, information management and, 232

documentation plan, 16, 190–92; pertinence and, 282

documentation strategy, 16, 192–93; acquisition and, 7; documentation plan and, 190

documenting, 54

document management systems (DMS), 197

About the Editors

This first edition of *Encyclopedia of Archival Science* was developed under the editorship of Dr. Luciana Duranti, chair and professor of archival studies at SLAIS, University of British Columbia, and Dr. Patricia C. Franks, program coordinator for the Master of Archives and Records Administration program in the School of Information, San José State University.

Luciana Duranti is the director of the Centre for the International Study of Contemporary Records and Archives (CISCRA, www.ciscra.org), under whose umbrella she leads several research projects, including the InterPARES Project (1998–2018), the largest and longest-living international research endeavor on the preservation of authentic electronic records. She has published widely on diplomatics and archival theory and methods, and digital recordkeeping and preservation.

Patricia C. Franks, a certified archivist, certified records manager, and information governance professional, is a member of the InterPARES Trust Project. Her research focuses on the impact of emerging technologies, including social media and cloud computing, on recordkeeping procedures and practices. She was team lead for the ANSI/ARMA standard, *Implications of Web-Based Collaborative Technologies in Records Management* (2011), and is the author of *Records and Information Management*, published by ALA/Neal-Schuman (2013).

About the Contributors

Anderson, Karen
Professor, Archives and Information Science
Mid Sweden University and Oslo and Akershus University of Applied Science

Karen Anderson (PhD) researches and teaches in digital recordkeeping at Mid Sweden University's Centre for Digital Information Management, at Oslo and Akershus University College and prior to 2008 at Edith Cowan University. She is an editor-in-chief for *Archival Science*, is director of the InterPARES Trust European Team, and was president of the International Council on Archives' Section for Archival Educators 2000–2004.

Entry: Archival Education

Ardern, Christine
Principal Consultant
The Information Specialists

Christine Ardern is a consultant in archives and records management program development and implementation. She was manager of archives and records management for CIBC, the Art Gallery of Ontario, and the Salvation Army, Canada and Bermuda. She is a past president and fellow of ARMA International and an instructor at the iSchool Institute, University of Toronto.

Entry: Record Creation

Bailey, Catherine A.
Senior Archivist
Library and Archives Canada

Catherine A. Bailey is a senior government archivist at Library and Archives Canada (LAC). She holds an honors BA in Canadian History (UBC, 1986) and a Master's of Archival Studies degree (UBC, 1988). General editor of *Archivaria* from 2007 to 2008, she has written and presented widely on archival appraisal, especially the development of macroappraisal within the Canadian federal government.

Entry: Case File

Bak, Greg
Assistant Professor
Master's Program in Archival Studies, University of Manitoba

Greg Bak is an assistant professor of history at University of Manitoba, teaching in the Master's program in archival studies. Previous to July 2011 he worked as a digital archivist and manager at Library and Archives Canada. His research interests include digital recordkeeping, digital culture, and the use of digital archives as tools for social justice.

Entry: Digital Repository

Banat-Berger, Françoise
Deputy Director at the Department of Archives de France
France, ministère de la Culture et de la communication, service interministériel de Archives de France
Françoise Banat-Berger is a French state curator of heritage and director of National Archives. She works about topics of archival policy and the evolution of the archivistic practical in digital environments, policy of records management, digital preservation, evolution of the legal framework, and over all of the new uses of digital technology into the professions concerning heritage.
Entry: Archival Fonds

Banks, Lacey Ryan
Student/Graduate Research Assistant
San Jose State University
Lacey grew up in northwest Georgia before moving to Atlanta for undergrad in 2005. She completed her Bachelor's of Arts in history at Georgia State University. She is currently expected to complete her Master's degree in archives and records administration in May 2015.
Entry: Records Center

Baron, Jason R.
Office Counsel, Drinker Biddle & Reath, LLP
Adjunct Faculty, University of Maryland
Jason R. Baron, Esq., a lawyer at Drinker Biddle & Reath, LLP, serves as adjunct faculty at the University of Maryland, College of Information Studies. Prior positions include trial lawyer at the U.S. Department of Justice and director of litigation at the U.S. National Archives and Records Administration. Mr. Baron's scholarship is in the area of e-discovery and e-recordkeeping.
Entry: Documentary Evidence

Bradley, Alexandra E.
Adjunct Professor,
iSchool@UBC, School of Library, Archival, and Information Studies
University of British Columbia
Alexandra has been teaching records management courses since 1985 and has been a Canadian records management consultant since 1983, specializing in all aspects of records and information-management program development. She has written records management publications and journal articles and is a frequent speaker. She is a certified records manager and fellow of ARMA International.
Entries: Records Inventory; Records Manager

Brown, Caroline
Deputy Archivist and Program Leader, Archives and Family History
Centre for Archive and Information Studies, University Dundee
Caroline Brown is program leader, archives and family history, at the Centre for Archive and Information Studies at the University of Dundee, where she is also deputy archivist. She is a member of a number of national and international professional bodies. Recent publications include guest editions of *Archival Science* and editor of *Archives and Recordkeeping: Theory into Practice* (Facet, 2014).
Entry: Archival Retrieval

Brown, Richard
Independent Consultant, Information Governance and Public Administration
Library of Archives Canada (retired)

Dr. Brown worked at the Library and Archives Canada for over thirty years, primarily in the domain of public records administration. He began as a government records archivist and later filled numerous executive positions, including special advisor to the deputy head and librarian and archivist. Richard has published and presented extensively on archival and public records issues.

Entry: Textual Records

Burant, Jim

Library and Archives Canada (retired)

Jim Burant earned a Master's in Canadian studies from Carleton University. He worked at Library and Archives Canada in the area of art and photography archives from 1976 until he retired in 2011. He has published and lectured on archival issues in North America, Great Britain, Australia, and New Zealand. He was awarded the Queen's Golden Jubilee Medal in 2003.

Entry: Artistic Records

Carmichael, Matt

Archivist, Digital Curator, Historian

Episcopal Diocese of Eastern Oregon and the History Museum of Hood River County

Matt has worked on a digitization and digital-preservation project for the History Museum of Hood River County since June 2011. He has written articles on digitization and digital curation for the Oregon Heritage Commission's Heritage Bulletins. In September 2013, he was appointed archivist and historian for the Episcopal Diocese of Eastern Oregon.

Entry: Digitization

Caya, Marcel

Professor (retired)

Université du Québec à Montréal (UQAM)

Marcel Caya is an historian and an archivist. Now retired, he taught records and archives management at UQAM until 2011, after serving as McGill University archivist (1977–1994). A member of the NAAB since 1978, he served as national chairman from 1993 to 2007. He has participated in and conducted many hundreds of appraisals of various types of archival records.

Entry: Monetary Appraisal

Chicorli, Emily

Graduate Student

The University of British Columbia

Emily Chicorli is completing a Master's degree in archival studies at the University of British Columbia. She is a graduate research assistant for InterPARES and the coordinator for the Association of Canadian Archivists UBC chapter.

Entry: Documentation Strategy

Combs, Michele

Lead Archivist

Syracuse University Special Collections Research Center (SCRC)

Michele Combs received her MS/LIS in 2004 from Syracuse University. She is a member of the Society of American Archivists and of its Technical Subcommittee on Encoded Archival Description. The SCRC's holdings include a number of ephemera collections on topics such as American radicalism and African Americans.

Entry: Ephemera

Conway, Paul
Associate Professor
University of Michigan School of Information
  Paul Conway conducts research and teaches courses on archival science, digitization practices, and the ethics of new technologies. He has also served as a senior administrator for the libraries at Yale and Duke universities. He holds a PhD from the University of Michigan and is a fellow of the Society of American Archivists.
  Entry: Permanence

Cook, Terry (1947–2014)
Formerly of Clio Consulting, Ottawa, CA
  Terry Cook taught archival studies at the University of Manitoba, following a long career at the Public (later National) Archives of Canada. He consulted and lectured internationally, and published extensively on archival theory, appraisal, postmodern archives, and the history of archives. He was the first scholar of archival science to be elected a fellow of the Royal Society of Canada.
  Entry: Total Archives

Corbett, Bryan Eldon
Coordinator, North American Archival Network of ICA (NAANICA)
Chair, Branch Chairs, ICA (retired)
  Bryan Corbett, MA—archivist and manager, Public Archives of Canada; coordinator, records management, Petro Canada; university archivist, University of Alberta—held positions in the Association of Canadian Archivists (ACA), the Archives Society of Alberta, the Canadian Council of Archives, the International Council on Archives (ICA), and ARMA International. He is an ACA fellow; coordinator, North America Archival Network of ICA; and chair, ICA Branches.
  Entry: Archival Associations

Craig, Barbara L.
Professor
Faculty of Information, University of Toronto
  Barbara Craig is an expert in archival appraisal, ethical professional practice, and a historical understanding of records and recordkeeping. She teaches in these areas. Continuing research targets contemporary and historical appraisal practices and the history of records keeping in the British Civil Service with a particular emphasis on the impact of the First World War.
  Entry: Appraisal

Cumming, Kate
Records and Information Manager
City of Sydney
  Dr. Kate Cumming is the manager of records and information at the City of Sydney in Australia. She received her PhD from the School of Information Management and Systems at Monash University. Kate is a co-founder of the Recordkeeping Roundtable discussion group and is actively concerned with developing strategies for effective long-term digital records and information management.
  Entry: Recordkeeping

Cunningham, Adrian
Director, Digital Archive and Government Recordkeeping
Queensland State Archives
  Adrian Cunningham has worked at the National Archives of Australia, National Library of Australia, and State Library of New South Wales. He was secretary of the ICA Committee on Descriptive Standards (2002–

2004), was president of the Australian Society of Archivists (1998–2000), and is a fellow of that society. He was awarded the 2010 Emmett Leahy Award for contributions to records management.

Entries: Postcustodialism; Series System

Daniel, Dominique
Humanities Librarian for History and Coordinator of Archives and Special Collections
Oakland University

Dominique Daniel is humanities librarian for history and coordinator of archives and special collections at Oakland University. She has a Master of Science in information from the University of Michigan and a doctorate in American studies from the University of Paris–Denis Diderot. She has published several articles on ethnic archival institutions and collections and their history.

Entry: Ethnicity and Archives

Dearstyne, Bruce W.
(retired)

PhD, history, Syracuse University. Program director, New York State Archives, 1976–1997. Associate professor, 1997–2000, professor, 2000–2005, adjunct professor, 2005+, College of Information Studies, University of Maryland. Editor of *Leading and Managing Archives and Records Programs* (2008), author of several books and numerous articles. Executive director, National Association of Government Archives and Records Administrators, 1983–2001. Areas of expertise: leadership, management.

Entry: Archival Programs

Driskill, Mark
Writer/Researcher
Self-Employed

Driskill is a recent graduate of San Jose State University's School of Information (May 2014). He holds a BA in American history and a Master's degree in archives and records administration. He currently works as a freelance writer, researcher, editor, and consultant. His areas of research and professional interests include informatics, information governance, corporate archives, and electronic information systems.

Entry: Archival Policy

Duff, Wendy M.
Professor, Faculty of Information
University of Toronto

Dr. Wendy Duff is a professor at the University of Toronto's iSchool. She is a founding member of AX-SNet, an international team of researchers interested in facilitating access to primary materials. Her current research focuses on archives and social justice, archival users, and access to archival material.

Entry: User Behavior

Duranti, Luciana
Professor, the School of Library, Archival, and Information Studies (SLAIS)
The University of British Columbia (UBC), Vancouver, BC, Canada

Dr. Luciana Duranti is chair and professor of archival studies at SLAIS, UBC, and teaches archival science and diplomatics. She is director of the InterPARES Project and several other research projects focusing on the preservation of authentic electronic records. She has published widely on diplomatics and archival theory, the nature of records, appraisal, and digital recordkeeping and preservation.

Entries: Archival Bond, Archives (Material); Formal Analysis; Impartiality (Record); Interrelatedness (Record); Naturalness; Objectivity (Archivist); Records Function; Records Lifecycle; Uniqueness

Eaton, Fynnette
Archivist (retired)
National Archives and Smithsonian Institution

Fynnette Eaton spent more than twenty-five years working with electronic records, participated in the InterPARES research projects, and is currently working as a contractor for two U.S. government agencies, assisting them in meeting requirements of the Managing Government Records Directive. She is also an adjunct instructor at the University of Wisconsin at Milwaukee School of Information Sciences.
Entry: Archival Deposit

Endicott-Popovsky, Barbara
Research Associate Professor with the Information School
Academic Director for the Masters in Infrastructure Planning and Management
Director for the Center of Information Assurance and Cybersecurity
University of Washington

Dr. Endicott-Popovsky's academic career follows a twenty-year career in industry marked by executive and consulting positions in IT architecture and project management. She earned her PhD in computer science/computer security from the University of Idaho and holds a Master's of Science in information systems engineering from Seattle Pacific University and a Master's of Business Administration from the University of Washington.
Entry: Information Assurance

Eppard, Philip B.
Professor of Information Studies
University at Albany, State University of New York

Philip B. Eppard is professor of information studies at the University at Albany, where he has taught since 1988. He was editor of the *American Archivist* from 1996 to 2006 and co-chair of the U.S. research team participating in the first two phases of the InterPARES Project. He has also been chair of the SAA's Committee on Ethics and Professional Conduct.
Entries: Archival Ethics; Documentary Editing

Fisher, Rob
Senior Archivist
Library and Archives Canada

Rob Fisher, a senior archivist at Library and Archives Canada, has extensive experience in the field of private archives. He has a BA in history from the University of Toronto and an MA in public history from the University of Waterloo. His writings have appeared in *Archivaria, Family Chronicle, The Northern Mariner, Canadian Military History, Legion Magazine*, and other publications.
Entry: Acquisition

Flinn, Andrew
Reader in Archival Studies
University College London

Dr. Andrew Flinn is a reader in archival studies and director of the Archives and Records Management Masters program at University College London. Andrew is the vice-chair of the UK Community Archives and Heritage Group, and has written extensively on issues relating to participatory approaches to archival practice and community-based heritage and archive activity.
Entry: Community Archives

Foscarini, Fiorella
Assistant Professor, Faculty of Information, University of Toronto (on leave)
Department of Media Studies, University of Amsterdam

Fiorella Foscarini holds an assistant professor position with the Faculty of Information at the University of Toronto and one with the Department of Media Studies at the University of Amsterdam. Her PhD in archival studies is from the University of British Columbia. She has been investigating the concept of function since the time of her PhD dissertation research.

Entry: Function

Franks, Patricia C.
Associate Professor, School of Information, and Coordinator
Master of Archives and Records Administration program
San José State University

Dr. Franks, author of *Records and Information Management*, is a certified archivist, certified records manager, information governance professional, and fellow of ARMA International. She was team lead for the ANSI/ARMA standard, *Implications of Web-Based Collaborative Technologies in Records Management*, and leads two InterPARES Trust research projects: *Social Media and Trust in Government* and *Retention and Disposition in a Cloud Environment*.

Entries: Disaster Plan; Information Governance; Records Management Standards; Replevin; Vital Records

Frogner, Raymond
Archivist
Royal BC Museum

Raymond Frogner has worked as a professional archivist for thirteen years. He has a Master's degree in archival studies from the University of British Columbia and a Master's degree in history from the University of Victoria. He wrote the private-records acquisition guidelines for the University of Alberta Archives. He has published on aboriginal records and archival value.

Entries: Disposition, Records; Selection

Galloway, Patricia
Professor, School of Information
University of Texas at Austin

Patricia Galloway teaches courses on appraisal and digital archives at the School of Information, University of Texas–Austin. She holds PhDs in comparative literature and anthropology from the University of North Carolina–Chapel Hill. From 1979 to 2000 she worked at the Mississippi Department of Archives and History, where she was the first IT manager and established the state electronic records program.

Entries: Intrinsic Value; Principle of Respect for Original Order

Gillean, Dan
AtoM Product Manager/System Analyst
Artefactual Systems Inc.

Dan Gillean completed his dual MAS/MLIS degree at the University of British Columbia's School of Library, Archival, and Information Studies, and currently serves as AtoM (Access to Memory) product manager for Artefactual Systems Inc. He resides in Vancouver, British Columbia (Canada).

Entry: Record Format

Goh, Elaine
PhD Candidate
University of British Columbia

Elaine Goh is a doctoral candidate at the School of Library, Archival, and Information Studies at the University of British Columbia in Vancouver, Canada. Her research interests are archival legislation, organizational culture, and records management. She is a graduate research assistant in the International Research on Permanent Authentic Records in Electronic Systems (InterPARES) Trust project.

Entries: Archival Legislation; Organizational Culture

Gordon, Heather M.
City Archivist
City of Vancouver

Heather Gordon joined the City of Vancouver Archives in 2005 and was appointed city archivist in July 2013. Prior to 2005, she served as the City of Coquitlam's records management coordinator and before that as archivist for the religious Hospitallers of St. Joseph in Kingston, Ontario. She holds a Master's of Archival Studies degree from the University of British Columbia.

Entry: Archival Exhibit

Gourlie, Michael
Government Records Archivist
Provincial Archives of Alberta

A graduate of the University of British Columbia MAS program, Michael Gourlie works at the Provincial Archives of Alberta as a government records archivist. From 1997 to 2012, he was the executive director/archives advisor for the Archives Society of Alberta. In addition to other committee work, he served as the vice president of the Association of Canadian Archivists from 2013 to 2015.

Entry: Records Transfer

Greene, Mark A.
Director, American Heritage Center
University of Wyoming

Mark A. Greene has directed the American Heritage Center, University of Wyoming, since 2002. The AHC is a seventy-five thousand cubic-foot manuscript repository and the university's archives. Greene oversaw development of the center's first collection development and collection management policies. Previously, Greene was curator of manuscripts acquisitions at the Minnesota Historical Society. Greene is a fellow and former president of SAA.

Entries: Acquisition Policy; Archival Collection; Collection-Management Policy

Groover, Myron
Archives and Rare Books Librarian
McMaster University

Myron Groover is an archivist and librarian keenly interested in how information policy shapes political discourse within contemporary and historical states. He holds an MA (Hons) in history from the University of Aberdeen in Scotland and completed his MAS and MLIS in Canada at the University of British Columbia.

Entry: Secondary Value

Guercio, Maria
Professor of Archival Science
University of Rome, La Sapienza, Digilab

State archivist in the Ministry of Cultural Heritage (1979–1998); full professor of archival science, University of Rome La Sapienza; partner in international projects for digital preservation, director of InterPARES team Italy; co-investigator on digital authenticity for European project APARSEN (2011–2014); component of ICA Programme Committee; author of many articles and manuals on Archival Science; winner of the 2009 Emmet Leahy Award.

Entry: Auxiliary Sciences

Hackman, Larry J.
(Retired)
First director of the NHPRC records grant program (1975–1981), director of the New York State Archives and Records Administration (1981–1995), director of the Truman Presidential Museum and Library (1995–2000). SAA fellow and former member of SAA council and annual meeting program chair. Main writings on advocacy, leadership, the development of archives as organizations, national historical records policy, and public policy and practice regarding presidential libraries.
Entry: Advocacy

Hart, Susan
Archivist, Government Records Service
Government of British Columbia
Susan Hart's career in the BC government has enabled her to explore all aspects of the archival profession, especially archival appraisal and selection, records management policy, and records classification and scheduling. Susan has a Master's of Archival Studies from the University of British Columbia (1989), as well as a BA and MA in folklore from Memorial University of Newfoundland.
Entries: Records Classification

Hartsook, Herbert J.
Director, South Carolina Political Collections
The University of South Carolina
Hartsook has over thirty years of experience in the archival field. He has been active in a number of professional associations and chaired the Society of American Archivists' Manuscripts Section, Oral History Section, and Congressional Papers Roundtable. He has developed and presents workshops training archivists in the collecting of political and legislative papers, oral history, donor relations, and development.
Entry: Donation

Hill, Rosaleen
Assistant Professor, Master of Art Conservation program
Queen's University, Kingston, Canada
Rosaleen Hill is assistant professor in the Master of Art Conservation program at Queen's University in Kingston, Canada. She has extensive experience in paper, photograph, and digital conservation. She has taught at the University of Canberra and the University of British Columbia, and has developed and taught many mid-career preservation and conservation courses.
Entry: Conservation

Hobbs, Catherine
Literary Archivist (English), Senior Archivist
Library and Archives Canada
Catherine Hobbs is responsible for the archives of writers and other figures/organizations in Canadian literature; chairs the Special Interest Section on Personal Archives of the Association of Canadian Archivists; is a steering committee member, ICA Section on Literary and Artistic Archives; teaches and publishes on literary and personal archives; and is an adjunct professor for the Public Texts Programme at Trent University.
Entry: Personal Records

Hoffman, Hans
Hans Hoffman has had a long career as senior advisor recordkeeping at the Nationaal Archief of the Netherlands. He is involved in standards development in ISO TC46/SC11. He acts as the liaison between ISO and the International Council on Archives (ICA). He has given numerous presentations and written articles on topics like digital preservation, recordkeeping metadata, and digital records.
Entry: Archival Standards

Horsman, Peter

(Retired)

Peter Horsman worked successively with the Municipal Archives of Dordrecht, the National Archives of the Netherlands, the Netherlands Archives School, and the University of Amsterdam, from which he retired in 2012. He worked on recordkeeping systems, both traditional and electronic. He is currently working as an independent consultant.

Entry: Archival History

Hurley, Chris

Information and Archives Specialist

Commonwealth Bank of Australia

With over forty years' experience working in public and business archives, Chris Hurley has headed the government archives programs in New Zealand and in Australia. He has been associated with the Records Continuum Research Group (Monash University), InterPARES2 Project, and the Center for Information as Evidence (University of Southern California). He has published on archives legislation, description, and accountability.

Entry: Series

Hurley, Grant

School of Library, Archival and Information Studies

University of British Columbia

Grant Hurley is in the third year of the Dual Master of Archival Studies and Master of Library and Information Studies program at the University of British Columbia. He also holds a Master of Arts in English from UBC. His past research includes published works on biodiversity data and Canadian community archives.

Entry: Archival Reappraisal

Hyry, Tom

Florence Fearrington Librarian

Houghton Library, Harvard University

Tom Hyry is Florence Fearrington Librarian of Houghton Library, Harvard University, a position he has held since September 2014. Prior to moving to Harvard, he served as director of UCLA Library Special Collections; head of the Manuscript Unit, Beinecke Rare Book and Manuscript Library, Yale University; and head of Arrangement and Description, Manuscripts and Archives, Yale University.

Entry: Private Archives

Jackson, Laura Uglean

Associate Archivist, American Heritage Center

University of Wyoming

Jackson began working at the American Heritage Center in 2007 on a reappraisal/deaccessioning project and from 2009 to 2012 chaired the SAA development and review team to create guidelines for reappraising and deaccessioning archival collections. She is currently a processing archivist and university archivist. She holds an MLIS from Simmons College and a BA in art history from Colorado State University.

Entry: Deaccessioning

Jansen, Adam

Director

Praxeum Group Consulting

Adam Jansen is an information-management consultant pursuing a PhD in archival studies at the University of British Columbia. He holds an interdisciplinary MS from Eastern Washington University in business administration and computer science and has been a part of the InterPARES research project since 2008. His research focuses on the preservation and forensic analysis of trustworthy digital records.

Entries: Audit and Certification (Trusted Digital Repositories); Chain of Preservation

Jensen, Sarah

Archivist, Government Records Service, BC Government

Sarah Jensen is an archivist with the BC government. She appraises government records and writes Operational Records Classification Systems (ORCS). Sarah completed her MLIS at McGill University (2006). Previously, she worked as an archivist for the McGill University Archives and the Archives of Ontario. Sarah also completed an MA in English literature at the University of British Columbia in (2002).

Entry: Records Schedule

Jimerson, Randall C.

Professor of History and Director of the Graduate Program in Archives and Records Management Western Washington University, Bellingham, Washington

Randall C. Jimerson is a fellow and past president of the Society of American Archivists. He is a former president of New England Archivists, which presented him the Distinguished Service Award in 1994. He is author of several works including *Archives Power: Memory, Accountability, and Social Justice* and *Shattered Glass in Birmingham: My Family's Fight for Civil Rights, 1961–1964.*

Entry: Archives and Memory

Ketelaar, Eric

Professor Emeritus

University of Amsterdam

Eric Ketelaar is professor emeritus at the University of Amsterdam, where from 1997 to 2009 he was professor of archivistics in the Department of Media Studies. From 1992 to 2002 he held the chair of archivistics in the Department of History of the University of Leiden. He is currently writing a book on the social history of Dutch archives. See www.archivistics.nl.

Entry: Archival History

Klumpenhouwer, Richard

Privacy and Information-Management Consultant and Firm Partner, Cenera, Calgary, Canada

Richard Klumpenhouwer is a graduate of Calvin College, University of Western Ontario, and the University of British Columbia, earning a Master's degree in history in 1982, and a Master of Archival Studies in 1989. He translated and published Hans Booms's 1972 article as part of his thesis on archival appraisal concepts.

Entry: Documentation Plan

Kozak, Greg

Enterprise Records Specialist

British Columbia Hydro and Power Authority (*or BC Hydro*)

Greg Kozak is a graduate of the Master of Archival Studies program at the University of British Columbia. After graduation, he has held several roles in administering freedom of information and privacy legislation and records management. He also teaches as an adjunct professor at UBC's School of Library, Archival, and Information Studies.

Entry: Access/Accessibility

LeFurgy, William G.

Digital Initiatives Project Manager

Library of Congress

LeFurgy is with the National Digital Information Infrastructure and Preservation Program, Library of Congress. The program engages with a network of partners to expand national capacity for digital stewardship.

He worked previously at the National Archives and Records Administration, where he focused on electronic records appraisal and accessioning. He also served as Baltimore City Archivist and Records Management Officer.

Entry: Web Archiving

Lemieux, Victoria
Associate Professor, Archival Studies
University of British Columbia

Dr. Victoria Lemieux, associate professor of archival studies at the University of British Columbia, has previously held positions as a professional archivist, records manager, and risk manager within the public and private sectors. She is author and editor of several publications, including *Risk Management for Records and Information* and *Managing Records in Global Financial Markets: Ensuring Compliance and Mitigating Risk.*

Entries: Public Service; Risk Management (Records)

Léveillé, Valerie
Student (MAS & MLIS Candidate), iSchool of Archival, Library, and Information Studies (SLAIS)
University of British Columbia

Valerie is a dual Master's student at the iSchool of Archival, Library, and Information Studies in Vancouver, BC. She is currently involved as a graduate research assistant for both the *Records in the Cloud* and *InterPARES Trust* SSHRC funded projects. Her main research interests are in open government and open data.

Entry: Cloud Archives

Lindberg, Lori A.
Lecturer/Consultant
San Jose State University

Lori Lindberg is a lecturer at San Jose State University's School of Library and Information Science. Lori is also an archival consultant, having work relationships with entities large and small. As a graduate student researcher with InterPARES II, Lori's focus was on recordkeeping metadata. She is an active member of the Society of American Archivists (SAA) and other professional associations.

Entries: Metadata; Recordkeeping Metadata

Livelton, Trevor
City Archivist
City of Victoria, British Columbia, Canada

Having served the City of Victoria as archivist for more than two decades, Trevor Livelton (MAS, Brit. Col., 1991) abides with his family in Saanich, British Columbia, cultivating a modest garden, while watching for signs of Platonic renewal.

Entry: Archival Theory

Lloyd, Tina
Senior Archivist
Library and Archives Canada

Tina Lloyd is senior reappraisal archivist at Library and Archives Canada. She has an Honors B.Comm, an Honors BA, and a Master of Arts degree in Canadian history from Carleton University. An expert on case files and reappraisal, Tina was the lead author for LAC's Operational Case Files MIDA, and has presented these topics at several international conferences.

Entry: Case File

Lomas, Elizabeth
Research Fellow and Lecturer
Northumbria University

Dr. Elizabeth Lomas is an archivist, records manager, and curator with special expertise in information-rights law. She has put in place heritage and information-governance programs for a range of organizations. She sits on the Lord Chancellor's Council on Archives and Records. She is a research fellow and lecturer at Northumbria University, teaching records management and information-rights law.

Entry: Records Management

Lowell, Waverly
Curator of Environmental Design Archives
University of California, Berkeley

Lowell has held positions as director of the National Archives–Pacific Sierra Region and curator of manuscripts at the California Historical Society. Her publications include *Living Modern: A Biography of Greenwood Common* and *Architectural Records: Managing Design & Construction Records* (co-authored with T. R. Nelb). A fellow of the Society of American Archivists, she is an archival consultant, historian, exhibit curator, and educator.

Entry: Architectural Records

Luckow, Randal
Director of Archives and Asset Management
Home Box Office Inc.

Luckow holds a Master's in information science, focusing on archive administration, from the University of Wisconsin–Madison. He has worked primarily as an archivist in the entertainment business, managing physical and digital media collections ranging from motion picture studios to broadcast television. His work linking enterprise metadata-management strategy and moving-image content description makes viable contextual advertising in cable television.

Entry: Audio-Visual Records

Lyle, Jared
Associate Archivist
The Inter-university Consortium for Political and Social Research (ICPSR)

Jared Lyle is director of curation services at ICPSR, where he is responsible for developing and maintaining a comprehensive approach to data management and digital preservation policy.

Entry: Sampling

Mak, Bonnie
Associate Professor of Library & Information Science
Associate Professor of Medieval Studies
University of Illinois

Bonnie Mak is assistant professor, University of Illinois, jointly appointed in the Graduate School of Library and Information Science and the Program in Medieval Studies. Her research explores the production, design, and circulation of knowledge across time and technologies, especially as it regards writing, libraries, and archives. Her first book, *How the Page Matters*, was published in 2011.

Entries: Authenticity; Facsimile

Mancuso, Lara
Fraser Health Authority

Lara Mancuso works at the Clinical Policy Office at Fraser Health Authority in Surrey, Canada. She holds a PhD in history from El Colegio de México and a Master of Archival Studies from the School of Library, Archives, and Information Studies at the University of British Columbia, Vancouver, Canada.

Entries: Structural Analysis; Subject Files

McDonald, John
Executive Director
Information Management Consulting and Education
   John McDonald is an independent consultant specializing in records and information management. While with the National Archives of Canada and later as a consultant he has advised public-sector organizations on the management of records in a digital environment. He has also delivered numerous workshops and course programs in universities, community colleges, and government training centers.
   Entry: Digital Record

McLeod, Julie
Professor, Records Management
Northumbria University
   Dr. Julie McLeod's research focuses on people, processes, and systems aspects of managing records including the AC+erm (accelerating positive change in managing electronic records) and DATUM (managing research data) projects. She is editor of the *Records Management Journal,* and a member of BSI/ISO records management standards committees. She holds the 2014 Emmett Leahy Award.
   Entry: Records Management

Michetti, Giovanni
Assistant Professor, Archival Science
University of Rome, La Sapienza
   Giovanni Michetti is assistant professor of archival science at the University of Rome "La Sapienza." He has also taught at the University of British Columbia and the University of Urbino. His research area is focused on contemporary and digital archives, and his main research interests are records management, archival description, and digital preservation.
   Entries: Archival Method; Archives and the Web

Miller, Thea
(Retired)
   Thea Miller completed her Master of Archival Studies (MAS) degree at the University of British Columbia in 1997 and her doctorate in information studies at the University of Toronto in 2007. Aside from her work on women's archives, she is chiefly known for her study of the German Registratur (a specialized form of registry system). She retired in 2010.
   Entry: Registry System

Montgomery, Bruce
Professor/Faculty Director of Archives and Special Collections
University of Colorado at Boulder
   Bruce P. Montgomery is professor/faculty director of archives and special collections at the University of Colorado, Boulder. He is the founding director of the UCB Human Rights Initiative and has consulted for the Institute for Defense Analysis and the Conflict Records Research Center in Washington, DC. He is the author of three books and numerous journal articles.
   Entry: Captured Records

Nesmith, Tom
Associate Professor, Master's Program in Archival Studies, Department of History
University of Manitoba, Winnipeg, MB, Canada

Tom Nesmith is an associate professor at the University of Manitoba and founder of the Master's Program in Archival Studies in the Department of History. He has published widely on archival concepts and issues and has been editor of *Archivaria*. He is a fellow of the Association of Canadian Archivists.

Entries: Archives (Institution); Principle of Provenance

Nougaret, Christine
Professor, Institutional History, Archival Science, and Diplomatics of the Contemporary Period
Ecole natioale des Chartes (Paris, France)

Christine Nougaret worked in local and government archives for twenty-five years. She was an expert of the International Council on Archives and chaired the Ad Hoc Commission on Descriptive Standards, which produced the General International Standard Archival Description ISAD (G). She had published extensively in the areas of archival description, archives legislation and history, and private papers.

Entry: Archival Fonds

O'Brien, John James
Senior Partner
Information Resource Management (IRM) Strategies

John James O'Brien brings multisector experience to the challenge of effectiveness, accountability, and learning to his practice in managing the knowledge-centered enterprise. He led the restructuring of the Hong Kong government records service to position it for electronic recordkeeping across the region and teaches records governance in the digital environment. He is now an independent advisor based in Canada.

Entry: Electronic Document and Records Management System (EDRMS)

Oliver, Gillian
Academic, Archives and Records Management
University of Wellington, New Zealand

Gillian Oliver is an archives and records management academic at Victoria University of Wellington in New Zealand. She is editor of Archifacts and coeditor-in-chief of archival science. Her professional practice background spans information management in the United Kingdom, Germany, and New Zealand. Her research interests reflect these experiences, focusing on the information cultures of organizations.

Entry: Information Management

Ostrzenski, Victoria
Analyst, Records and Information Management
First Nations Health Authority

Ostrzenski holds a Master of Archival Studies from SLAIS at the University of British Columbia. Her research examines the preservation of digital records. She has been a researcher for the Records in the Cloud Project and has published on cloud computing. She received the 2012 ARMA AIEF award for her research examining the characteristics, challenges, and requirements of e-commerce records.

Entries: Person; Status of Transmission (Records)

Owen, Kevin J.
Records Management Analyst
Musqueam Indian Band

Kevin Owen is a recent MAS graduate from the School of Library, Archival, and Information Studies, University of British Columbia, and holds a Bachelor of Arts from the University of Alberta. He is currently working with the Musqueam Band Administration as a records management analyst. In the past, he has performed contract work in public archives and consulting records management.

Entries: Reliability; Trusted Custodian

Pacifico, Michele F.
Archival Facilities Consultant
Self-employed
   Michele F. Pacifico has worked in government and private-sector archives for over thirty years. Since 1987, she has worked as an archivist specializing in archival facilities. She is the coeditor and sections author of the Society of American Archivists' standard for archival and special collections facilities, which was approved in 2009 and was revised for a 2014 publication.
   Entry: Archival Buildings and Facilities

Pan, Weimei
InterPARES Project and Records in the Cloud Project
The University of British Columbia
   Weimei Pan is an archival PhD student at the School of Library, Archival, and Information Studies at the University of British Columbia. She has a dual background of Chinese archival science and Western archival science. Her research interests focus on the archival concept of context, records creation in a cloud environment, diplomatics, and the development of Chinese archival science.
   Entry: Context

Pearce-Moses, Richard
Director, Master of Archival Studies Program
Clayton State University, Morrow, Georgia
   Pearce-Moses has worked with state and local government records in Texas and Arizona, and with personal records at Arizona State University and the Heard Museum. He was the principal author of *A Glossary of Archival and Records Terminology* (Society of American Archivists, 2005). He served as president and is a fellow of the society, and is a certified archivist.
   Entries: Archival Preservation; Manuscripts Tradition; Public Records Tradition

Penzo Doria, Gianni
General Manager
University of Isurbria, Varese, Italy
   Gianni Penzo Doria is general manager of the University of Insubria (Varese, Italy). Previously he was in the same position at the University of Trieste and at the University of Padua (archivist, then general manager). He directed the Titulus project, and chairs the education program UniDOC/PROCEDAMUS. He produced inventories of historical archives and tools for current records (records schedules and filing plans).
   Entries: Protocol Register; Records Center

Reed, Barbara
Consultant
Recordkeeping Innovation Pty Ltd
   Barbara Reed of Recordkeeping Innovation is a consultant in the field of records, archives, and information management with more than twenty-five years of industry experience in Australia and the Asia Pacific region. Previously she has been an academic in recordkeeping at Monash University. Areas of special interest include digital recordkeeping strategies, recordkeeping metadata, and standards development for whole of government initiatives.
   Entry: Recordkeeping System(s)

Rogers, Corinne
Adjunct Professor/Doctoral Candidate
School of Library, Archival and Information Studies
University of British Columbia

Corinne Rogers is an adjunct professor and doctoral candidate at the University of British Columbia, School of Library, Archival, and Information Studies. She is project coordinator of InterPARES Trust—international multidisciplinary research into issues of trust in digital objects in online environments—and a researcher with the Law of Evidence in the Digital Environment Project (Faculty of Law, UBC).
Entries: Digital Records Forensics; Diplomatics; Document

Schwartz, Joan M.
Associate Professor, Department of Art History and Art Conservation
Queen's University, Kingston, Ontario, Canada
Joan M. Schwartz is an associate professor (history of photography) in the Department of Art History and Art Conservation, Queen's University, Canada. A specialist in photography acquisition and research at the National Archives of Canada from 1977 to 2003, she was elected a fellow of the Society of American Archivists in 2008.
Entry: Photographic Records

Shaffer, Elizabeth
PhD Candidate/Archivist
University of British Columbia/Vancouver Holocaust Education Centre
Elizabeth Shaffer is a PhD candidate at the iSchool at the University of British Columbia and archivist at the Vancouver Holocaust Education Centre. Her research, informed by archival theory, focuses on record creation in social media/online environments, e-government, and information policy. She has published and presented on issues related to digital preservation and copyright, web 2.0/social media, and policy development.
Entry: Information Policy

Shepherd, Elizabeth
Professor, Archives and Records Management
Department of Information Studies, University College London
Dr. Elizabeth Shepherd is professor of archives and records management at University College London, Department of Information Studies, where she teaches in the Master's program. Her research interests include records management and information policy and the history of the archive profession. She has published many articles and two books: *Managing Records* (2003) and *Archives and Archivists in 20th-Century England* (2009).
Entry: Primary Values

Suvak, William J.
Will Suvak is a recent graduate of the Master of Archival Studies program at the University of British Columbia with a background in information technology. His approach to archival work is strongly influenced by his work in software engineering and data processing. His primary areas of interest are archival management systems, digital preservation, and nontextual records.
Entry: Authentication

Taylor, Isabel
Assistant
Universitätsarchiv, Tübingen; Lehrstuhl für Staats- und Verwaltungsrecht, Europarecht und Völkerrecht, Tübingen
Isabel Taylor (BA history, Mount Allison, distinction; graduate diploma in law, Northumbria, distinction; Master of Archival Studies, UBC, Harold Naugler Memorial Prize) is pursuing an archival-law-focused LLM at Tübingen, and publishes on data protection and archives. She is an assistant in the Universitätsarchiv Tübingen and to Professor Dr. Martin Nettesheim, and also works on contract at the Hauptstaatsarchiv Stuttgart.
Entry: Principle of Pertinence

Tennis, Joseph T.

Associate Professor

University of Washington Information School

Joseph T. Tennis is an associate professor and director of faculty affairs at the University of Washington Information School University of Washington, and president of the International Society for Knowledge Organization. He is on the *Library Quarterly* (USA) and *Knowledge Organization* (Germany) editorial boards, and a member of the Dublin Core and InterPARES. He works in metadata versioning and authenticity.

Entry: Metadata Application Profiles

Theimer, Kate

Writer and Editor

Independent

Kate Theimer, the author of the ArchivesNext blog, is the editor of seven books on innovative practices in archives, and a frequent writer, speaker, and commentator on the ways in which social media and participatory practices are affecting the archival profession.

Entries: Digital Archives; Outreach; Participatory Archives

Thibodeau, Kenneth

Independent Consultant

A renowned expert in electronic records and digital preservation, Thibodeau directed the production of the world's first standard for records management software, the Department of Defense 5015.2-STD. He oversaw the development of the Electronic Records Archives systems for the U.S. National Archives and the George W. Bush Presidential Library, and sponsored several leading research projects on digital preservation.

Entries: Archival Management System(s); Digital Preservation

Thibodeau, Sharon

(Retired)

In 2011 Sharon Thibodeau retired from the National Archives and Records Administration (NARA), where she served in various capacities ranging from staff archivist to deputy assistant archivist for records services. She has participated in national and international working groups responsible for the development of standards applicable to archival description.

Entries: Archival Description; Archival Inventory; Archival Practice; Authority Control

Thomassen, Theo

Professor

University of Amsterdam

Theo Thomassen holds the chair in archival science in the Media and Information Section of the Department of Media Studies. He devotes his tenure to teaching and research in the area of archival theory and its development, archival theory related to personal records and cultural heritage, the history of records and archives management, and the archival profession and its development.

Entry: Archival Science

Trace, Ciaran B.

Assistant Professor, School of Information

The University of Texas at Austin

Ciaran B. Trace trained and worked as an archivist in Ireland before moving to the United States to pursue a doctoral degree in library and information science at UCLA. Ciaran currently works as an assistant professor in the School of Information at the University of Texas at Austin, where she teaches courses on archives and records management.

Entries: Archival Arrangement; Record Group

Tschan, Reto
Archivist
West Vancouver Archives
Reto Tschan has worked in archives in the UK and Canada for the last ten years, in both corporate banking and independent schools. He now works in a municipal archives. Reto has taught courses on the history of recordkeeping, the history of the Canadian juridical system, and an introductory archives course for library science students at the iSchool at UBC.
Entries: Archival Custody; Archivist

Turner, James M.
Professeur associé
École de bibliothéconomie et des sciences de l'information, Université de Montréal
James M. Turner holds a PhD in information science from the University of Toronto. His research areas include shot-level indexing of moving images, metadata for images, preserving digital audiovisual materials, and audio description and other access to images for users who are blind or have vision loss. More information is available at http://turner.ebsi.umontreal.ca.
Entry: Audio-Visual Records

Upward, Frank
(Retired)
Dr. Upward worked as an archivist, records manager, and information manager before accepting a position at Monash University, where he designed and taught in a wide range of courses. He is best known internationally for his records continuum model and is currently, with others, attempting to develop recordkeeping informatics as a disciplined base for the management of digital recordkeeping processes.
Entry: Records Continuum

Weber, Genevieve
Archivist
Government Records Service, Government of British Columbia
Genevieve Weber is an archivist with the BC government. She appraises government records and writes Operational Records Classification Systems (ORCS), integrated records retention, and classification schedules. Genevieve completed her MAS (First Nations concentration) at the University of British Columbia in 2008. Previously, she worked as an archivist with the Nisga'a Nation, the Mowachaht/Muchalaht First Nation, MOA, and the BC Archives.
Entry: Records Schedule

Willever-Farr, Heather
Instructor and Doctoral Student
College of Computing and Informatics, Drexel University
Ms. Willever-Farr studies amateur historians' research and production behaviors in virtual collaborative environments. Her dissertation research focuses on leveraging collaborative learning to encourage the production of high-quality user-contributed content on family history websites. Her research has implications for archival participatory practice and the design of systems that support archives users as consumers and producers of historical materials.
Entry: User Behavior

Williams, Caroline
Independent Archival Consultant
Caroline Williams is president of the Archives and Records Association and visiting professor at Liverpool John Moores University. Formerly head of research and collections development at UK National Archives

(2007–2009) and director of the Liverpool University Centre for Archive Studies (1996–2007), her research interests include the history and analysis of the record and the interface between theory and practice.

Entries: Collecting Archives; File

Wilson, Lara
Director, Special Collections, and University Archivist
University of Victoria

Lara Wilson holds an MA from the University of Victoria and an MAS from the University of British Columbia. She was appointed university archivist in 2007 and the director of special collections in 2013. She has twice served as president of the Archives Association of British Columbia (AABC) and currently chairs the Canadian Council of Archives.

Entry: Accountability

Wilsted, Thomas
Archival Facilities Consultant

Thomas Wilsted is a retired archivist and currently serves as an archival facilities consultant. He is the author of *Planning New and Remodeled Archival Facilities* (SAA, 2007) and coeditor of *Archival and Special Collections Facilities: Guidelines for Archivists, Librarians, Architects and Engineers* (SAA, 2009). He is currently the co-chair of the SAA's Archival Facilities Task Force.

Entry: Environmental Systems

Xie, Sherry L.
Professor
Renmin University of China, Beijing, China

Sherry L. Xie, BS, MLIS, MAS, and PhD, is a professor at the School of Information Resource Management, Renmin University of China; associate director of the Center for Electronic Records Management Research, Beijing, China; and adjunct professor at SLAIS, University of British Columbia. Her research focuses on archival science, digital records and information management, and digital preservation.

Entry: Functional Analysis

Yeo, Geoffrey
(Retired)

Geoffrey Yeo has worked as an educator, researcher, practitioner, and consultant in archives and records management. He is now an honorary senior research fellow at University College London, UK. His research interests include perceptions of the nature of records and recordkeeping; records classification, arrangement, and description; and relationships between records and the actions of individuals and organizations.

Entry: Record(s)

Zhang, Jane
Assistant Professor, Department of Library and Information Science
Catholic University of America

Jane Zhang is an assistant professor at the Department of Library and Information Science, Catholic University of America, Washington DC. She holds a PhD in library and information studies with an archival concentration from Simmons College, Boston, and a joint Master of Archival Studies (MAS) and Library and Information Studies (MLIS) from University of British Columbia, Canada.

Entry: Principle of *Respect des Fonds*

CPSIA information can be obtained at www.ICGtesting.com
Printed in the USA
BVOW09*1919100615

403788BV00002BA/3/P